Alastair
Sawday's

Special Places
to Stay

British
Bed & Breakfast

4 Contents

Alastair *Sawday's*

Special Places to Stay

Italy

Alastair *Sawday's*

Special Places to Stay

"Delightful, hand-picked accommodation."
Italia!

Edited by Fiammetta Oldfield

Pubs & Inns
of England & Wales

Alastair *Sawday's*

Special Places

"Sawday's has never once let us down – invaluable."
Simon Hoggart, The Guardian

Edited by David Hancock

British Hotels & Inns

Alastair *Sawday's*

Special Places to Stay

"Quirky, comfortable, independent places run by people who care."
The Daily Telegraph

Dog-friendly Breaks in Britain

Alastair *Sawday's*

Special Places to Stay

Foreword by Ben Fogle

Seventeenth edition
Copyright © 2012
Alastair Sawday Publishing Co. Ltd
Published in September 2012
ISBN-13: 978-1-906136-58-1

Alastair Sawday Publishing Co. Ltd,
The Old Farmyard, Yanley Lane,
Long Ashton, Bristol BS41 9LR, UK
Tel: +44 (0)1275 395430
Email: info@sawdays.co.uk
Web: www.sawdays.co.uk

The Globe Pequot Press,
P. O. Box 480, Guilford,
Connecticut 06437, USA
Tel: +1 203 458 4500
Email: info@globepequot.com
Web: www.globepequot.com

Series Editor Alastair Sawday
Editor Wendy Ogden
Editorial Assistance Lianka Varga
Editorial Director Annie Shillito
Senior Editor Jo Boissevain
Photo Processing Alec Studerus
Production Coordinator Alex Skinner
Writing Tom Bell, Jo Boissevain,
Nicola Crosse, Monica Guy,
Kate Mitchell, Wendy Ogden
Inspections Jan Adam, David Ashby,
Mandy Barnes, Tom Bell, Sue Birtwistle,
Neil Brown, Angie Collings, Peter Evans,
Maureen Flynn, David Hancock, Alison
Harper, Rebecca Harris, Kim Lawrence,
Vickie MacIver, John MacLean, Auriol
Marson, Margot Rawson, Aideen Reid,
Tristram Templer, Nicky Tennent, Jacqui
Vallis, Mandy Wragg
Thanks also to others who did an inspection or two.

Sales & Marketing & PR
01275 395433

We have made every effort to ensure the accuracy of the information in this book at the time of going to press. However, we cannot accept any responsibility for any loss, injury or inconvenience resulting from the use of information contained therein.

Maps: Maidenhead Cartographic Services
Printing: Butler Tanner & Dennis, Frome
UK distribution: The Travel Alliance, Bath
Production: PagebyPage

Cover photo credits. 1. Hill Farm House, entry 513 2. Jo Boissevain 3. Venton Vean, entry 52

5

The pace of change is leaving us all breathless: technology, social norms, language, style, ways of communicating – and the behaviours that change with each new piece of kit. What was rude a year ago, such as answering a mobile at the dinner table, seems less so now. Using 'Dear' to start an email seems like a waste of space. If we use a map we are fossils.

Assailed on all sides by bits of brilliant hardware and the conundrums they bring, it is no wonder that we still seek a bit of relief when travelling – the simplicity and solace of a damned good Bed and Breakfast! And where once the best were elusive, now they all shout at you from their internet pages. They all have stunning photos, seductive shots of coffee pots and lawn-size beds piled high with cushions. If there is a single bush in the

vicinity, it can serve as lush greenery in the background. It is hard to know quite which way to turn. This is where we at Sawday's are still as useful as ever.

Now that we can all look good with cosmetic tricks, we travellers need advice from someone who can say: "now THIS is special, and real; believe me". For almost 20 years we have been lavish with advice, sending inspectors to find places to stay where you will find real people, good manners, personality and wonderful food. The people we celebrate in this book are special – and so are their places. They are islands of sanity in a mad, mad world.

Those of you who have been with us for years will wonder what is new in this edition. Well, we have over 140 new places, which is exciting for us as it shows how fresh and vigorous the world of B&B is. There are some glorious gardens, too (not only in our Garden B&B book). People who were with us long ago are returning in new homes, with new ideas and ways of doing things. Another trend is the creation of independent B&B units – a room, for example, in the cottage in the garden. We are up to date and as authentic as ever.

If I have a tiny regret about the passing of B&B time, it is the dwindling in the number of real characters – eccentrics, even. We still celebrate them, but where are the young eccentrics? Come out and show yourselves!

Alastair Sawday

It's simple. There are no rules, no boxes to tick. We choose places that we like and are fiercely subjective in our choices. We also recognise that one person's idea of special is not necessarily someone else's so there is a huge variety of places, and prices, in the book. Those who are familiar with our Special Places series know that we look for comfort, originality, authenticity, and reject the insincere, the anonymous and the banal. The way guests are treated comes as high on our list as the setting, the architecture, the atmosphere and the food.

Inspections

We visit every place in the guide to get a feel for how both house and owner tick. We don't take a clipboard and we don't have a list of what is acceptable and what is not. Instead, we chat for an hour or so with the owner and look round. It's all very informal, but it gives us an excellent idea of who would enjoy staying there. If the visit happens to be the last of the day, we may stay the night. Once in the book properties are re-inspected every four years or so, to keep things fresh and accurate.

Feedback

In between inspections we rely on feedback from our army of readers, as well as from staff members who are encouraged to visit properties across the series. This feedback is invaluable to us and we always follow up on comments. So do tell us whether your stay has been

a joy or not, if the atmosphere was great or stuffy, the owners cheery or bored. The accuracy of the book depends on what you, and our inspectors, tell us. A lot of the new entries in each edition are recommended by our readers, so keep telling us about new places you've discovered too. Please visit our site, www.sawdays.co.uk/recommend to tell us about your discoveries.

However, please do not tell us if the bedside light was broken, or the shower head was scummy. Tell the owner, immediately, and get them to do something about it. Most owners are more than happy to correct problems and will bend over backwards to help. Far better than bottling it up and then writing to us a week later!

Photo: Prickwillows, entry 371

Subscriptions

Owners pay to appear in this guide. Their fee goes towards the high costs of inspecting, of producing an all-colour book and of developing our website. We only include places that we like and find special for one reason or another, so it is not possible for anyone to buy their way onto these pages. Nor is it possible for the owner to write their own description. We will say if the bedrooms are small, or if a main road is near. We do our best to avoid misleading people.

Disclaimer

We make no claims to pure objectivity in choosing these places. They are here simply because we like them. Our opinions and tastes are ours alone and this book is a statement of them; we hope you will share them. We have done our utmost to get our facts right but apologise unreservedly for any mistakes that may have crept in.

You should know that we don't check such things as fire regulations, swimming pool security or any other laws with which owners of properties receiving paying guests should comply. This is the responsibility of the owners.

Photo above: 22 Royal Circus, entry 663
Photo right: Park House, entry 608

Finding the right place for you

All these places are special in one way or another. All have been visited and then written about honestly so that you can take what you like and leave the rest. Those of you who swear by Sawday's books trust our write-ups precisely because we don't have a blanket standard; we include places simply because we like them. But we all have different priorities, so do read the descriptions carefully and pick out the places where you will be comfortable. If something is particularly important to you then do check when you book: a simple question or two can avoid misunderstandings.

Maps

Each property is flagged with its entry number on the maps at the front. These maps are a great starting point for planning your trip, but please don't use them as anything other than a general guide — use a decent road map for real navigation. Most places will send you detailed instructions once you have booked your stay.

Symbols

Below each entry you will see some symbols, which are explained at the very back of the book. They are based on the information given to us by the owners. However, things do change: bikes may be under repair or a new pool may have been put in. Please use the symbols as a guide rather than an absolute statement of fact and double-check anything that is

important to you — owners occasionally bend their own rules, so it's worth asking if you may take your child or dog even if they don't have the symbol.

Children – The 👶 symbol shows places which are happy to accept children of all ages. This does not mean that they will necessarily have cots, high chairs, etc. If an owner welcomes children but only those above a certain age, we have put these details at the end of their write-up. These houses do not have the child symbol, but even these folk may accept your younger child if you are the only guests. Many who say no to children do so not because they

don't like them but because they may have a steep stair, an unfenced pond or they find balancing the needs of mixed age groups too challenging.

Pets – Our  symbol shows places which are happy to accept pets. It means they can sleep in the bedroom with you, but not on the bed. Be realistic about your pet – if it is nervous or excitable or doesn't like the company of other dogs, people, chickens, children, then say so. Do let the owners know when booking that you intend to bring your pet – particularly if it is not the usual dog!

Owners' pets – The  symbol is given when the owners have their own pet on the premises. It may not be a cat! But it is there to warn you that you may be greeted by a dog, serenaded by a parrot, or indeed sat upon by a cat.

Quick reference indices

At the back of the book you'll find a number of quick-reference indices that will help you choose the place that is just right for you.

In this edition you'll find listings of properties where
• at least one bedroom or bathroom is accessible for wheelchair-users.
• owners have a single room, or they let a double bedroom to guests travelling alone for half the double occupancy or less.
• you can stay all day
• a double costs £70 or less

Photo above: The Glynhir Estate, entry 716
Photo right: Manor Farm, entry 407

Types of places

Some houses have rooms in annexes or stables, barns or garden 'wings', some of which feel part of the house, some of which don't. If you have a strong preference for being in the throng or for being apart, check those details. Consider your surroundings when you are packing: large, ancient country houses may be cooler than you are used to; city places and working farms may be noisy at times; and that peacock or cockerel we mention may disturb you. Light sleepers should pack ear plugs, and take a dressing gown if there's a separate bathroom (though these are sometimes provided).

Some owners give you a front door key so you may come and go as you please; others like to have the house empty between, say, 10am and 4pm. If you would prefer not to wander far during the day then look for the places that have the 'Stay all day' quick reference at the back of the book.

Rooms

Bedrooms – We tell you if a room is a double, twin/double (i.e. with zip and link beds), suite (with a sitting area), family or single. Most owners are flexible and can juggle beds or bedrooms; talk to them about what you need before you book. Staying in a B&B will not be like staying in a hotel; it is rare to be given your own room key and your bed will not necessarily be made during your stay, or your room

cleaned. Make sure you are clear about the room that you have booked, its views, bathroom and beds, etc.

Bathrooms – Most bedrooms in this book have an en suite bath or shower room; we only mention bathroom details when they do not. So, you may get a 'separate' bathroom (yours alone but not in your room) or a shared bathroom. Under certain entries we mention that two rooms share a bathroom and are 'let to same party only'. Please do not assume this means you must be a group of friends to apply; it simply means that if you book one of these rooms you will not be sharing a bathroom with strangers. If these things are important to you, please check when booking. Bath/shower means a bath with shower over; bath and shower means there is a separate shower unit.

Sitting rooms – Most B&B owners offer guests the family sitting room to share, or they provide a sitting room specially for guests. If neither option is available we

generally say so, but do check. And do not assume that every bedroom or sitting room has a TV.

Meals

Unless we say otherwise, a full cooked breakfast is included. Some owners – particularly in London – will give you a good continental breakfast instead. Often you will feast on local sausage and bacon, eggs from resident hens, homemade breads and jams. In some you may have organic yogurts and beautifully presented fruit compotes. Some owners are fairly unbending about breakfast times, others are happy to just wait until you want it, or even bring it to you in bed.

Apart from breakfast, no meals should be expected unless you have arranged them in advance. Although we don't say so on each entry – the repetition a few hundred times would be tedious – all owners who provide packed lunch, lunch or dinner

need ADVANCE NOTICE. And they want to get things right for you so, when booking, please discuss your diet and meal times. Meal prices are quoted per person, and dinner is often a social occasion shared with your hosts and other guests.

Do eat in if you can – this book is teeming with good cooks. And how much more relaxing after a day out to have to move no further than the dining room for an excellent dinner, and to eat and drink knowing there's only a flight of stairs between you and your bed. Very few of our houses are licensed, but most are happy for you to bring your own drink.

Prices and minimum stays

Each entry gives a price PER ROOM for two people. We also include prices for single rooms, and let you know if there is a supplement to pay should you choose to loll in a double bed on your own.

The price range for each B&B covers a one-night stay in the cheapest room in low season to the most expensive in high season. Some owners charge more at certain times (during regattas or festivals, for example) and some charge less for stays of more than one night. Some owners ask for a two-night minimum stay at weekends and we mention this where possible. Most of our houses could fill many times over on peak weekends and during the summer; book early, especially if you have specific needs.

Booking and cancellation

You may not receive a reply to your booking enquiry immediately; B&Bs are not hotels and the owners may be away. When you speak to the owner double-check the price you will pay for B&B and for any meals.

Requests for deposits vary; some are non-refundable, especially in our London homes, and some owners may charge you for the whole of the booked stay in advance. Some cancellation policies are more stringent than others. It is also worth noting that some owners will take the money directly from your credit/debit card without contacting you to discuss it. Ask them to explain their cancellation policy clearly before booking to avoid a nasty surprise.

Payment

All our owners take cash and UK cheques with a cheque card. Some take credit cards; if they do we have given them the appropriate symbol. Check that your particular credit card is acceptable.

Tipping

Owners do not expect tips. If you have been treated with extraordinary kindness, write to them, or leave a small gift. Please tell us, too – we love to hear, and we do note, all feedback.

Arrivals and departures

Say roughly what time you will arrive (normally after 4pm), as most hosts like to welcome you personally. Be on time if you have booked dinner; if, despite best efforts, you are delayed, phone to give warning.

Closed

When given in months this means the whole of the month stated.

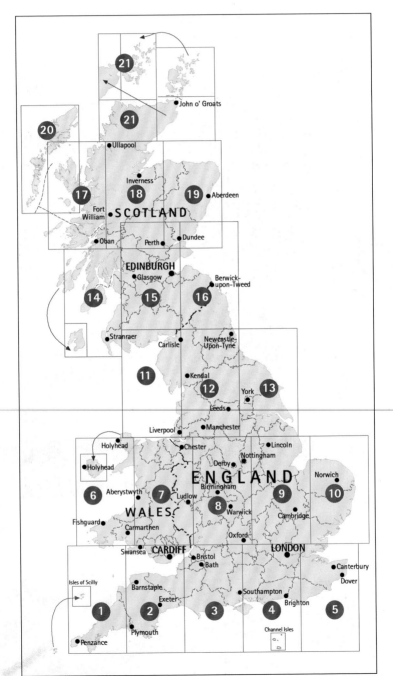

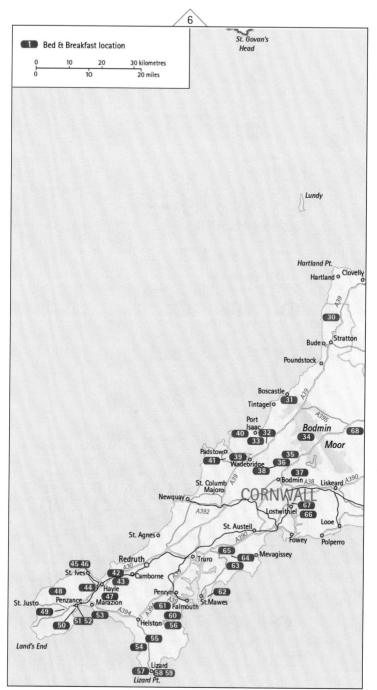

6

St. Govan's
Head

Bed & Breakfast location

0　　10　　20　　30 kilometres
0　　　　10　　　　　20 miles

Lundy

Hartland Pt.
Hartland ○　Clovelly

30

Bude ○　○ Stratton

Poundstock

Boscastle
31
Tintagel ○

Port
Isaac
40 ○ 32　　Bodmin　68
33　　34
Moor

Padstow ○
41　39
Wadebridge
38

35
36

37
St. Columb　○ Bodmin　A38　Liskeard　A390
Major
CORNWALL
Newquay ○
67
A392　Lostwithiel
66　　Looe

St. Austell
65　　Fowey　Polperro
St. Agnes ○
64　Mevagissey
Redruth　○ Truro　63
45 46
St. Ives ○　42
43
48　44　Hayle
47　Penryn ○　62
St. Just ○　Penzance　Marazion　61 Falmouth　St. Mawes
49　51 52　53　60
50　Helston　56

55

54

Lizard
57　58 59
Land's End　Lizard Pt.

©Maidenhead Cartographic, 2012

Map 2

17

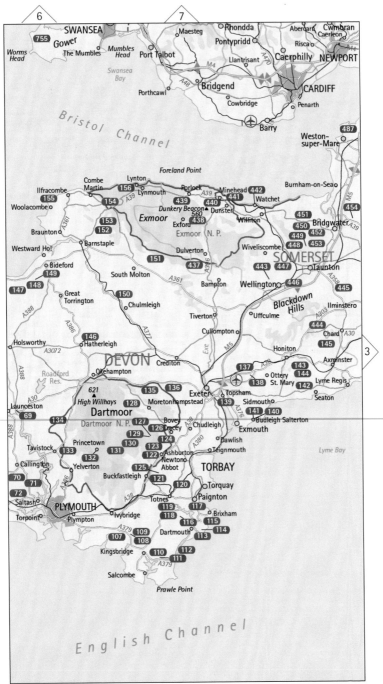

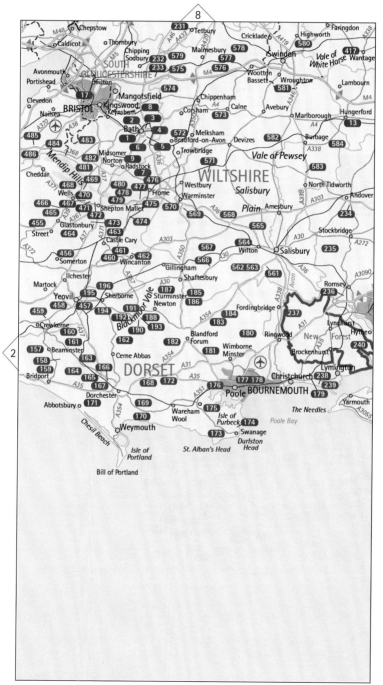

Map 4

19

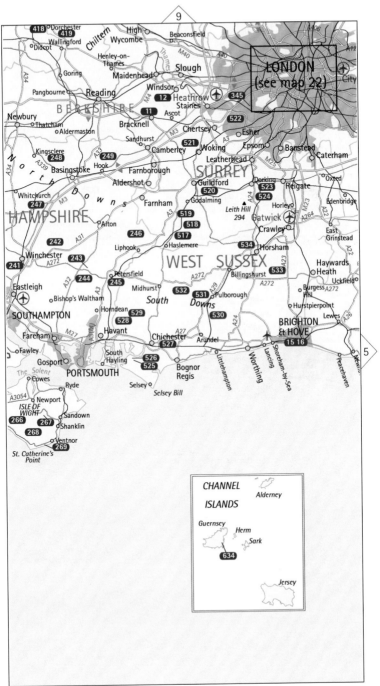

©Maidenhead Cartographic, 2012

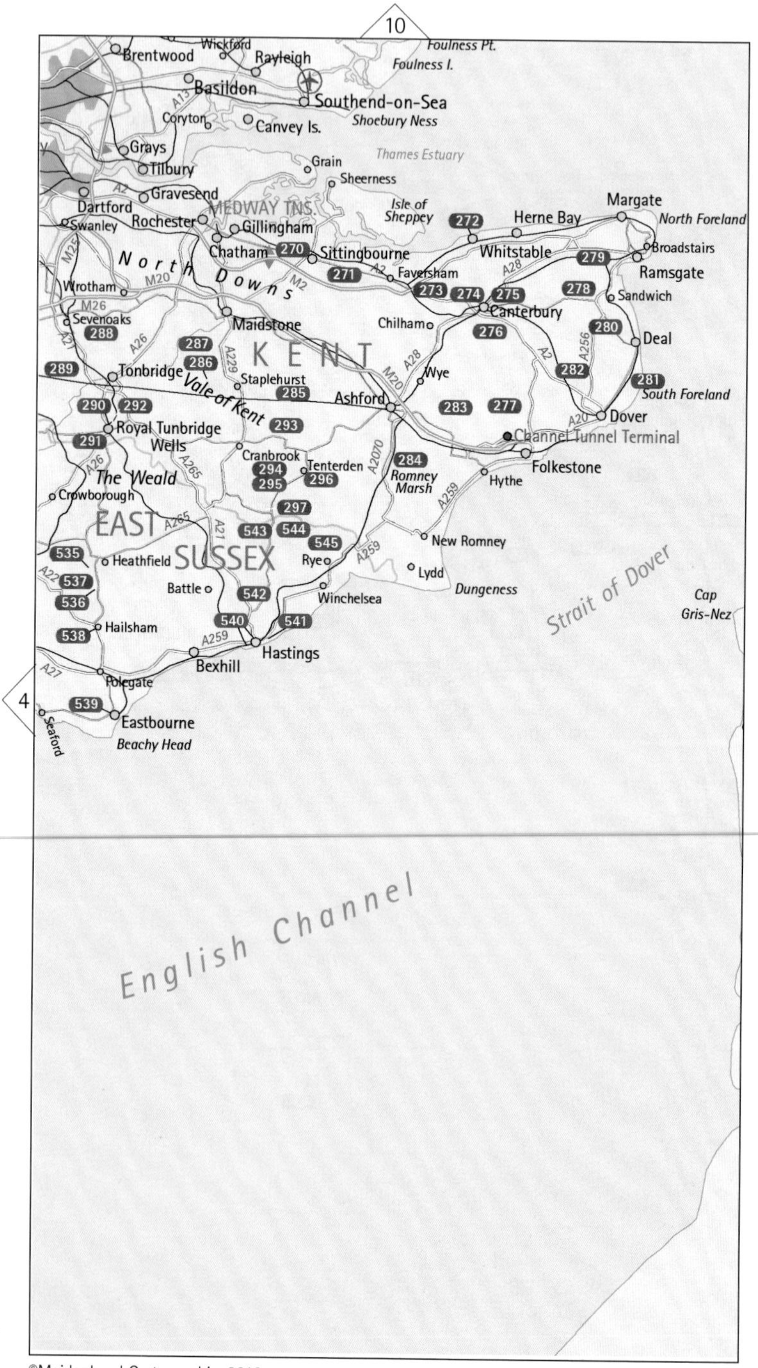

10

Wickford
Brentwood Rayleigh Foulness Pt.
Foulness I.
Basildon
Coryton Southend-on-Sea
Canvey Is. Shoebury Ness
Grays
Tilbury Grain
Gravesend Sheerness
Dartford Rochester MEDWAY TNS. Isle of Margate
Swanley Gillingham Sheppey 272 Herne Bay North Foreland
Chatham 270 Sittingbourne Whitstable 279 Broadstairs
Wrotham 271 Faversham 273 274 275 278 Ramsgate
Sevenoaks Maidstone Chilham 276 Canterbury 280 Sandwich
288 KENT Deal
287 Wye 282
Tonbridge 286 Staplehurst 281
289 Vale of Kent 285 Ashford South Foreland
290 292 283 277 Dover
Royal Tunbridge 293 A20 Channel Tunnel Terminal
291 Wells Folkestone
Cranbrook 284
The Weald 294 Tenterden 296 Romney Hythe
Crowborough 295 Marsh
297 New Romney
EAST 543 544 545
535 SUSSEX Rye Lydd Dungeness
537 Heathfield 542 Strait of Dover Cap
536 Battle 540 Winchelsea Gris-Nez
538 Hailsham 541
Polegate Hastings
Bexhill
539 Seaford
4 Eastbourne
Beachy Head

North Downs

The Weald

Thames Estuary

English Channel

Map 6

21

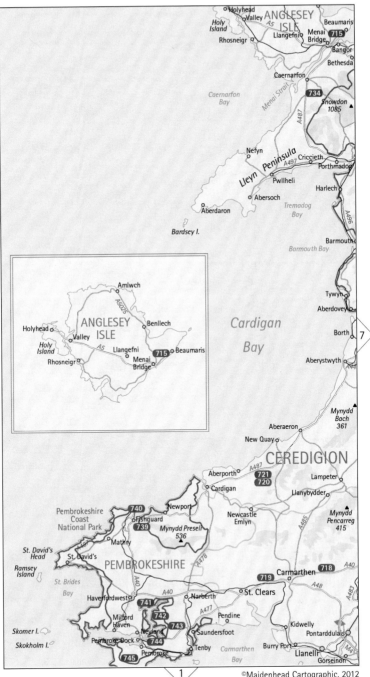

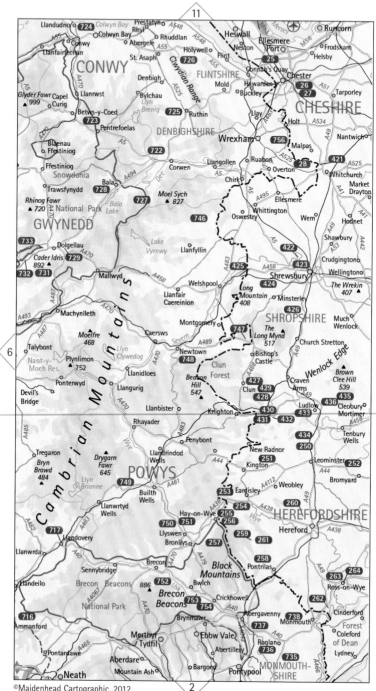

Map 8

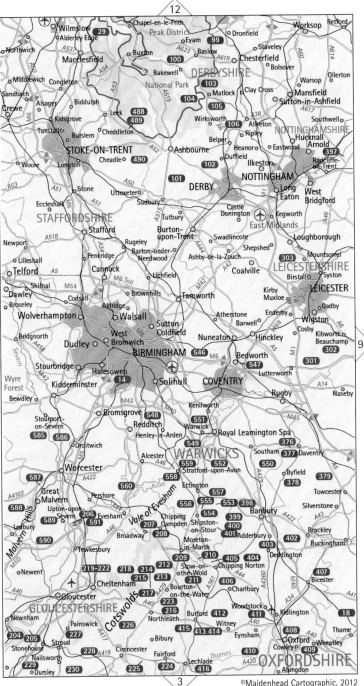

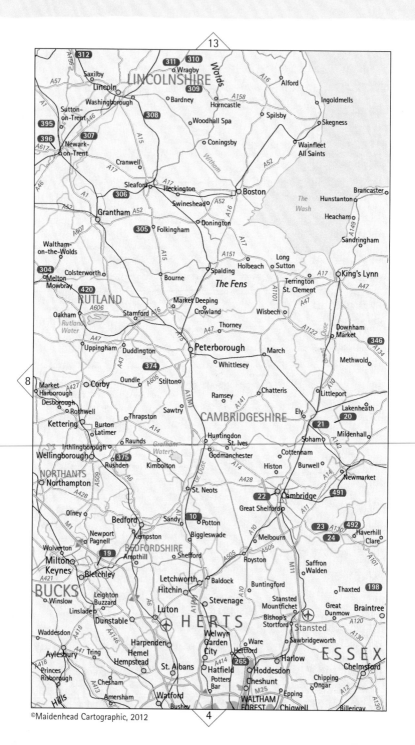

Map 10

25

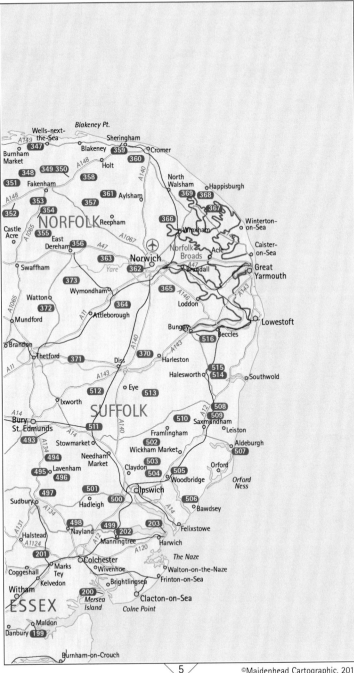

©Maidenhead Cartographic, 2012

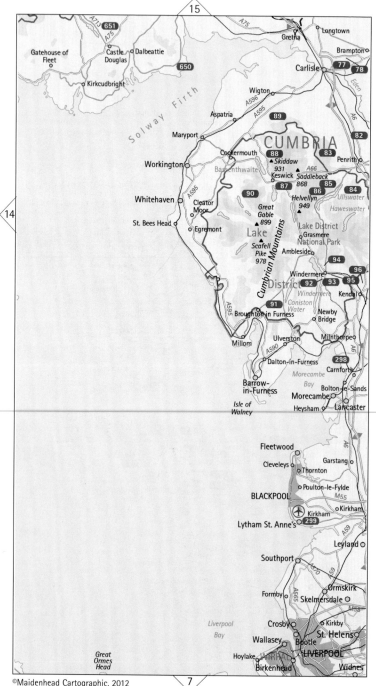

Map 12   27

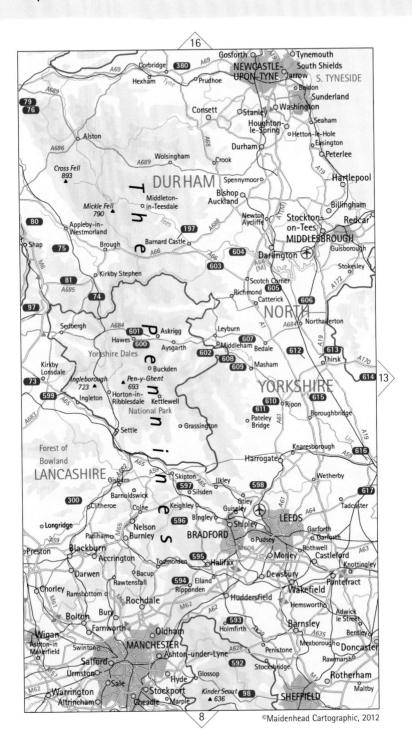

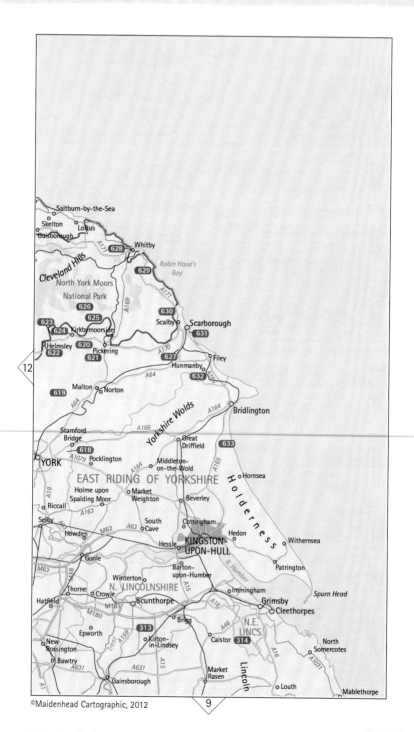

Saltburn-by-the-Sea
Skelton
Loftus
Guisborough
Whitby **628**
Cleveland Hills
629
Robin Hood's Bay
North York Moors National Park
A171
A169
626
625
623
624 Kirkbymoorside
630
Scalby
Scarborough
631
Helmsley **620** Pickering
622 **621**
A170
627
Filey
Hunmanby
619
A64
632
A165
Malton Norton
12
Yorkshire Wolds
A164
Bridlington
Stamford Bridge
A166
633
Great Driffield
618
A1079 Pocklington
YORK
A164
Middleton-on-the-Wold
A165
Hornsea
A19
EAST RIDING OF YORKSHIRE
Holme upon Spalding Moor
Market Weighton
Beverley
Riccall
A163
Holderness
Selby
South Cave
A63
Cottingham
Hedon
Howden
M62
Hessle
KINGSTON-UPON-HULL
Withernsea
Ouse
Goole
Barton-upon-Humber
R. Humber
Patrington
M62
Winterton
A15
Spurn Head
Thorne Crowle
N. LINCOLNSHIRE
Immingham
Hatfield
M180
M181
Scunthorpe
A18
Grimsby
Cleethorpes
Brigg
A46
N.E. LINCS.
Epworth
313
314
New Rossington
Kirton-in-Lindsey
A159
Caistor
North Somercotes
Bawtry
A631
A631
A15
Market Rasen
A16
A1031
Gainsborough
Lincoln
Louth
Mablethorpe

9

Map 14

29

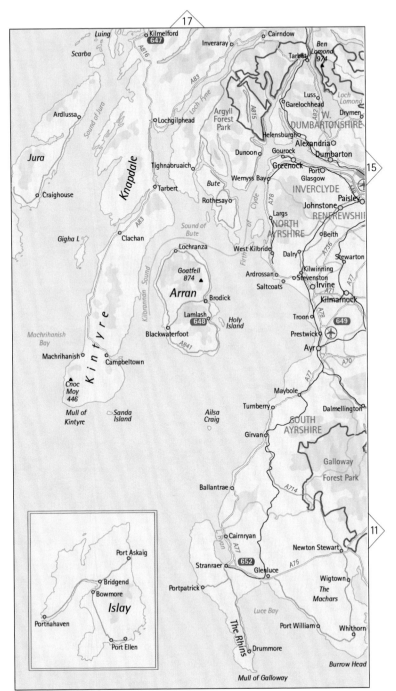

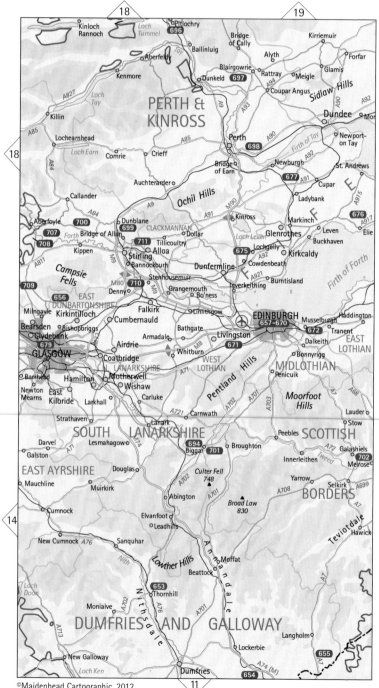

Map 16

31

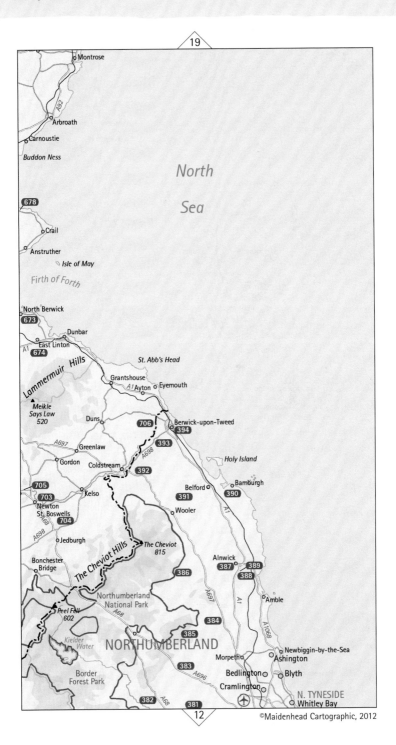

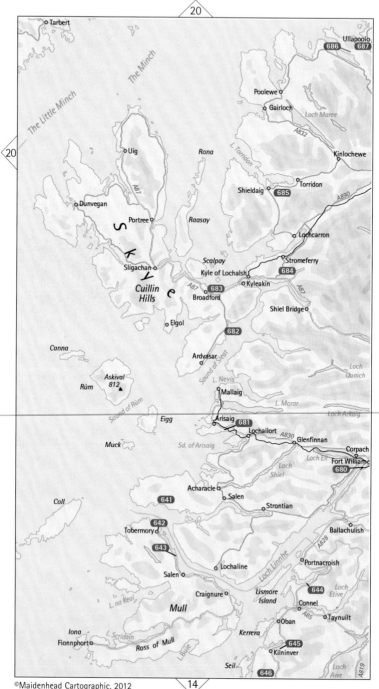

Map 18

33

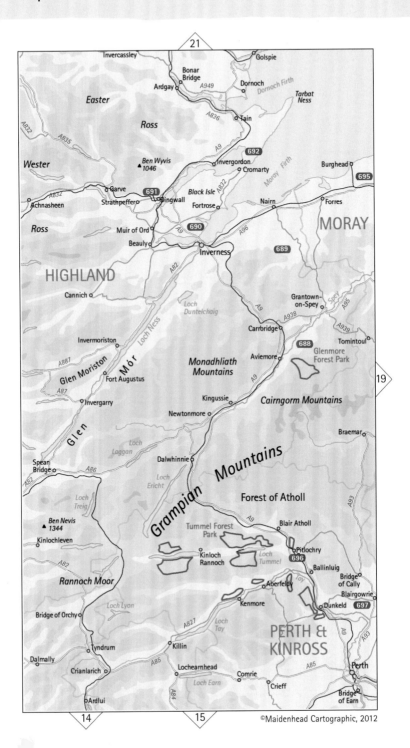

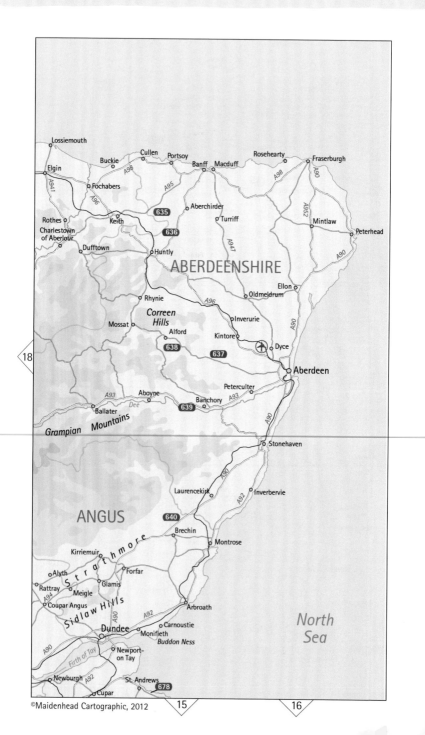

Map 20

35

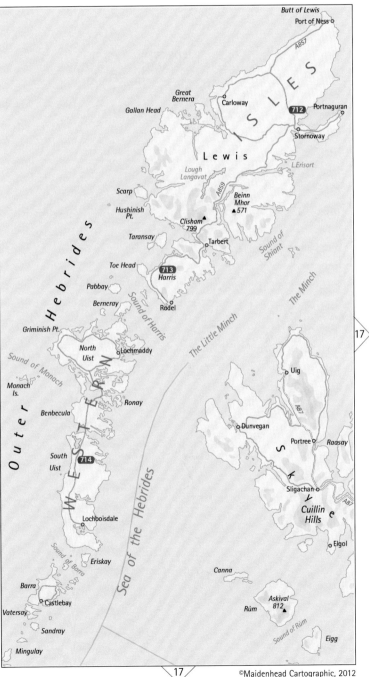

Butt of Lewis
Port of Ness ◦
A857
I S L E S
Great Bernera
Gallan Head
Carloway
712
Portnaguran
Stornoway ◦
L e w i s
Lough Langavat
L.Erisort
A859
Scarp
Hushinish Pt.
Beinn Mhor
▲571
Clisham 799 ▲
Tarbert
Sound of Shiant
Taransay
Toe Head
713
Harris
Pabbay
Berneray
Rodel
Sound of Harris
Griminish Pt.
The Minch
H e b r i d e s
North Uist
Lochmaddy
Sound of Monach
The Little Minch
17
Monach Is.
O u t e r
Ronay
Uig ◦
Benbecula
Dunvegan ◦
Portree ◦
Raasay
A87
W E S T E R N
South Uist
714
S k
Sligachan ◦
A87
Lochboisdale
Sea of the Hebrides
Cuilline Hills
Sound of Barra
Eriskay
Elgol ◦
Canna
Barra
Askival 812 ▲
Vatersay
Castlebay
Rùm
Sandray
Sound of Rùm
Eigg
Mingulay

©Maidenhead Cartographic, 2012

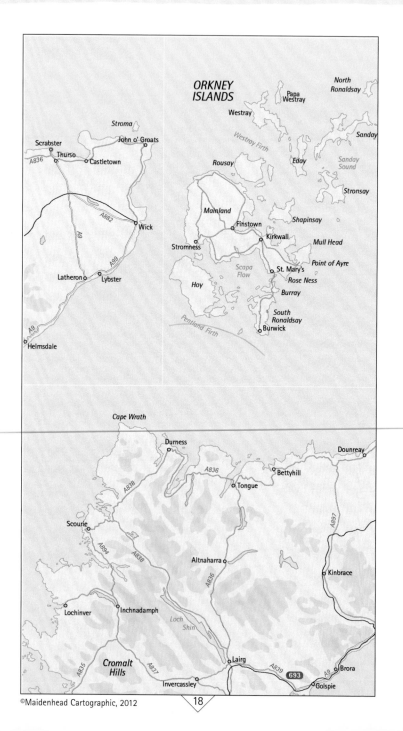

ORKNEY
ISLANDS

North
Ronaldsay

Papa
Westray

Westray

Sanday

Stroma

Scrabster
Thurso
Castletown

John o' Groats

A836

Rousay

Eday

Sanday
Sound

Stronsay

Mainland

Finstown

Shapinsay

A882

Wick

Kirkwall

Mull Head

A9

Stromness

Point of Ayre

St. Mary's

Scapa
Flow

Rose Ness

Latheron
Lybster

A99

Hoy

Burray

South
Ronaldsay

Pentland Firth

Burwick

A9

Helmsdale

Westray Firth

Cape Wrath

Durness

Dounreay

A836

Bettyhill

A838

Tongue

A897

Scourie

A894

A838

Altnaharra

A836

Kinbrace

Lochinver

Inchnadamph

Loch
Shin

Cromalt
Hills

A835

A837

Lairg

A839

693

A9

Brora

Invercassley

Golspie

18

Map 22

37

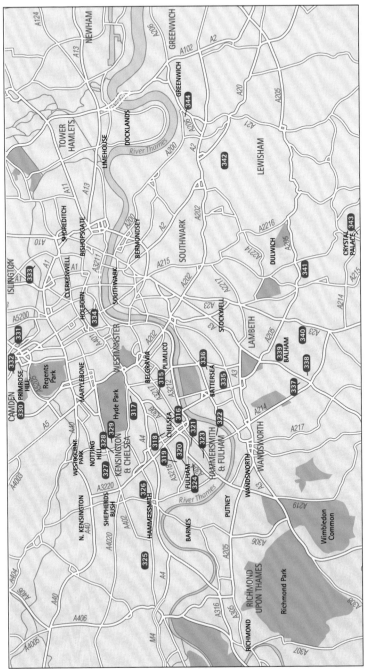

England

Pitt House

You couldn't be closer to the centre, nor on a calmer street. This Grade I-listed, seven-storey house, once home to William Pitt the Younger, is now inhabited by a warm, creative couple with a wry sense of humour. Inside: Georgian splendour matched by 21st-century eccentricity. Find sanded floorboards, walls of pure white, dazzling marble busts, a cow hide rug, a tumble of classical and oriental styles... collectors of antiques will keel over in a state of bliss. Bedrooms (up four flights of stairs) are only marginally less exotic, and share a fabulous bathroom and sitting room. Breakfast is the finest of continental. Outstanding.

Price	£75–£100.
Rooms	2 doubles sharing bath/shower.
Meals	Continental breakfast. Pubs/restaurants 2-minute walk.
Closed	Rarely.
Directions	Sent on booking. Parking by arrangement

David & Sarah Bridgwater
Pitt House,
15 Johnstone Street, Bath BA2 4DH
Tel   +44 (0)1225 471580
Mobile +44 (0)7710 124376
Email   david.j.bridgwater@btinternet.com

Entry 1   Map 3

77 Great Pulteney Street

Elegant stone steps lead down past exotic ferns to a spacious garden flat in this broad street of grand Grade I-listed houses. Inside all is pale wood, modern art, bergère chairs and palms. Downstairs is a large, smart bedroom and bathroom with loads of books and its own door to a delightful small sunny garden. On fine mornings you breakfast here, or choose the gorgeous upstairs dining room: fine local bacon and sausages and fruit from the allotment. Ian is a keen cook so dinner will also be special, but there are lots of good places to eat – and shop – nearby. Henry may play the Northumbrian pipes for you if you ask nicely...

Price	£80–£105. Singles from £55.
Rooms	1 double.
Meals	Dinner £25. Packed lunch from £5.
Closed	Rarely.
Directions	A4 into centre of Bath. Last house before Laura Place on south side of Great Pulteney St. Parking by arrangement; 7-minute walk from station.

Ian Critchley & Henry Ford
77 Great Pulteney Street,
Bath BA2 4DL
Tel   +44 (0)1225 466659
Email   critchford@77pulteneyst.co.uk
Web   www.77pulteneyst.co.uk

Entry 2   Map 3

Bath & N.E. Somerset

Sir Walter Elliot's House

The period, hand-printed wallpaper is just one of the remarkable features of this elegant Grade I-listed house: Julian is an expert. The house, in one of Bath's finest Regency terraces, has been so beautifully restored that the BBC used its rooms for Jane Austen's *Persuasion*. Bedrooms are flooded with light and views are stunning; one stylish bathroom has marquina marble, cherrywood and ebony. Have breakfast in the convivial family kitchen, or in the plant-filled conservatory; for the adventurous, Mechthild serves up an Austrian alternative of cold meats and cheeses, fresh rye breads and homemade cakes. Herrlich!

Price	£95-£145. Singles £85. Min. stay 2 nights at weekends.
Rooms	3 twins/doubles.
Meals	Pub/restaurant 300 yds.
Closed	Rarely.
Directions	A46 to Bath, then A4 for city centre. Left onto A36 over Cleveland Bridge; follow signs to Holburne Museum. Directly after museum, left. House on right.

Mechthild & Julian Self von Hippel
Sir Walter Elliot's House,
95 Sydney Place, Bath BA2 6NE
Tel   +44 (0)1225 469435
Mobile   +44 (0)7737 793772
Email   visitus@sirwalterelliotshouse.co.uk
Web   www.sirwalterelliotshouse.co.uk

Entry 3   Map 3

Bath & N.E. Somerset

The Georgian Stables

The perfect getaway minutes from Bath centre. Enjoy complete independence in these stylishly converted stables, with breakfast, delivered by Hilary's friendly housekeeper, at a time to suit you: homemade muesli, fruit salad or berries, free-range eggs, pains au chocolat. Snug with underfloor heating, all is white and airy inside with splashes of colour, original stone and a smart wet room. A cobbled terrace is all yours, and a canal runs past the bottom of lovely gardens with unbeatable views. Opposite: acres of National Trust land and the Skyline Circular Walk... take a picnic and watch the hot-air balloons rise over the city.

Price	£110-£150. Singles £100-£140. Minimum 2 nights at weekends.
Rooms	Stables: 1 double with sitting room & kitchenette.
Meals	Pubs/restaurants 8-minute walk.
Closed	Occasionally.
Directions	Sent on booking. Visitor parking permits can be arranged.

Hilary Cooper
The Georgian Stables,
41 Sydney Buildings,
Bath BA2 6DB
Tel   +44 (0)1225 465956
Mobile   +44 (0)7798 810286
Email   thegeorgianstables@gmail.com

Entry 4   Map 3

Bath & N.E. Somerset

55a North Road

Prepare yourself for a surprise. A short hop from Capability Brown-designed Prior Park, hidden down a narrow drive off one of Bath's less remarkable streets, is an architectural novelty – only the roof tiles give away the 1980s origins. Energetic owners Natalie and Guy offer you two completely private self-contained studios each with its own entrance, delightful small kitchen and elegant furniture. Find a charming mix of ultra-chic and traditional: oak floors, wool carpets, limestone tiles, old Irish bedheads and pure cotton linen. Natalie brings a very delicious breakfast to your room. *Ask about beauty & massage therapies.*

Price	From £120. Singles from £100. Min. 2 nights at weekends. (Room only: from £90; singles from £75. Min. 2 nights.)
Rooms	2 studios: 1 double, 1 twin, each with small kitchen.
Meals	Pubs/restaurants within 1 mile.
Closed	Rarely.
Directions	Turn off North Road in Combe Down between (and on same side as) Farrs Lane and Hadley Road into wide driveway. Keep left. 55a is behind number 55.

	Natalie & Guy Woods
	55a North Road,
	Combe Down, Bath BA2 5DF
Tel	+44 (0)1225 835593
Mobile	+44 (0)7977 904931
Email	info@55anorthroad.co.uk
Web	www.55anorthroad.co.uk

Entry 5   Map 3

Bath & N.E. Somerset

De Montalt Wood

Deep valley views, acres of gardens and woodland to roam, pretty places to sit and muse… all just a couple of miles from Bath. Charles and Ann's Victorian house is a smart family home with a comfortable country feel. Airy bedrooms have big beds with fine linen, a sofa, TV, and garden vistas; bathrooms are luxurious with rain showers and scented things. You breakfast in the elegant dining room: a full English, smoked salmon and scrambled eggs, fruits on the sideboard, lashings of coffee. There are lovely walks with good pubs on the way, bluebells fill the woods in spring and Bath brims with history, spa and good restaurants.

Price	£110–£120.
Rooms	2: 1 double; 1 double with separate bath.
Meals	Pubs/restaurants 5-minute drive.
Closed	Christmas & New Year.
Directions	Sent on booking.

	Charles & Ann Kent
	De Montalt Wood,
	Summer Lane, Combe Down,
	Bath BA2 7EU
Tel	+44 (0)1225 838001
Email	bookings@demontaltwood.co.uk
Web	www.demontaltwood.co.uk

Entry 6   Map 3

Bath & N.E. Somerset

Hollytree Cottage

Meandering lanes lead to this 16th-century cottage, with roses round the door, a grandfather clock in the hall and an air of genteel tranquillity. The cottage charm has been updated with Regency mahogany and sumptuous sofas. The bedrooms have views over undulating countryside; pretty bathrooms have oils and lotions. On sunny days breakfast is in the lovely garden room looking onto a colourful ornamental patio, sloping lawns, a pond, flowering shrubs and trees. A place to come for absolute peace, birdsong and walks; the joys of elegant Bath are 20 minutes away and Julia knows the area well; let her help plan your trips.

Price	£75-£90. Singles £45-£50.
Rooms	3: 1 double, 1 twin, 1 four-poster.
Meals	Pub/restaurant 0.5 miles.
Closed	Rarely.
Directions	From Bath, A36 to Wolverton. Just past Red Lion, turn for Laverton. 1 mile to x-roads; towards Faukland; downhill for 150 yds. On left, just above farm entrance on right.

Julia Naismith
Hollytree Cottage,
Laverton, Bath BA2 7QZ
Tel   +44 (0)1373 830786
Mobile   +44 (0)7564 196703
Email   jnaismith@toucansurf.com
Web   www.hollytreecottagebath.co.uk

Entry 7   Map 3

Bath & N.E. Somerset

The Power House

Think Grand Designs modernity with views to lift the soul – and spectacular sunsets. Rikki's vibrant house has been built into the hill and the walls of glass make the most of the setting. Inside, the big open-plan living space is friendly and fascinating with a communal table, rugs on oak floors, interesting art, Middle Eastern treasures, flowers and bold colours. Kick off your shoes, relax and feel part of the family. Big bedrooms have doors onto balconies; the private studio is snug with its own wood-burner, books and four-poster. Rikki is a great cook, and uses good local and home produce… and Bath is just down the road.

Price	£100-£120. Singles £70.
Rooms	3: 1 double, 1 single. Studio: 1 double. (2 smaller doubles available, sharing bathrooms.)
Meals	Dinner £25. Pubs/restaurants 3-minute drive.
Closed	Rarely.
Directions	Sent on booking.

Rikki Howard
The Power House,
Brockham End,
Lansdown,
Bath BA1 9BY
Tel   +44 (0)1225 446308
Email   rikkijacout@aol.com

Entry 8   Map 3

Bath & N.E. Somerset

Pitfour House

Georgian gentility in a village near Bath. This is where the rector would live in an Austen novel: it's handsome, respectable, and the feel extends inside, where convivial hosts Frances (a keen cook) and Martin (keen gardener) welcome you into their elegant home. The creamy guest sitting room gleams with period furniture, the dining room is panelled and parqueted, fresh flowers abound. The two bedrooms – one with en suite shower, one with a private bath – are compact but detailed with antiques. Take tea in the neat walled garden, admire the vegetable patch, then taste the spoils in one of Frances's fine suppers.

Bedfordshire

Warren Farm Lodge

Horses run to greet you at the field gate. Their owners, the delightful Deirdre and husband Robert, have transformed the old stables and cowsheds of this red-brick dairy farm into a beautiful home. The stunning 'long room' is the hub of the house: reclaimed beams over the Aga, a wood-burner for chilly evenings, worn leather sofas on terracotta tiles. The rest of the house is a joy to explore: the sun room, the lounge with its grand piano, the library on the mezzanine. Masses of space, light, and comfy corners at every turn; big bedrooms have views of the lovely gardens. Bring the kids, stay the weekend.

Price	£84-£94.	Price	£70-£115. Singles £70-£95. Family suite £135-£150.
Rooms	2: 1 twin/double; 1 twin/double with separate bath.	Rooms	3: 1 double, 1 suite, 1 family suite, each with separate bath.
Meals	Dinner £23-£28. Restaurant 1.5 miles.	Meals	Lunch £8-£9. Dinner £20. Pubs/restaurants within 3 miles.
Closed	Rarely.	Closed	Rarely.
Directions	Sent on booking.	Directions	From r'bout on A1M, take B1042 thro' Sandy dir. Potton. After approx. 2.8 miles right to Sutton into Carthagena Rd; approx. 50 yds on, then right at sign for Warren Farm.

	Frances Hardman		Deirdre Evans
	Pitfour House, High Street, Timsbury, Bath BA2 0HT		Warren Farm Lodge, Carthagena Road, Sutton, Sandy SG19 2NQ
Tel	+44 (0)1761 479554	Tel	+44 (0)1767 262927
Email	pitfourhouse@btinternet.com	Email	deirdre.evans@warrenfarmlodge.com
Web	www.pitfourhouse.co.uk	Web	www.warrenfarmlodge.com

Berkshire

Whitehouse Farm Cottage

Beyond the housing estates of Bracknell, an idyllic find: a 17th-century farmhouse with a gorgeous garden, and two charmingly converted buildings. Garden Cottage has a beamed drawing room downstairs and an immaculate gallery bedroom with an iron bed. The Forge – deliciously cosy – keeps the blacksmith's fireplace and overlooks an atmospheric courtyard garden with pebble mosaics. The single is in the house with its own cosy sitting room. Fabulous locally sourced breakfasts with freshly baked bread are served in the house by delightful Keir and Louise, film prop makers by profession. Just perfect!

Price	£80–£100. Singles £70–£90.
Rooms	3: 1 single & sitting room. The Forge: 1 double & summerhouse. Garden Cottage: 1 double & sitting room.
Meals	Pubs/restaurants within 1 mile.
Closed	Occasionally.
Directions	From A329, B3408 to Binfield. At 2nd traffic lights left into St Marks Rd. Then 2nd left Foxley Lane, 1st left Murrell Hill Lane. House immediately on right. Do not use postcode for satnav.

Keir & Louise Lusby
Whitehouse Farm Cottage,
Murrell Hill Lane, Binfield,
Bracknell RG42 4BY
Tel   +44 (0)1344 423688
Mobile +44 (0)7711 948889
Email   garden.cottages@ntlworld.com

Entry 11   Map 4

Berkshire

Gilbey's

Step up the stairs to your elegant top-floor studio; it's above a buzzy restaurant and in the heart of pretty Eton. Charming staff greet and look after you, and all is gleaming with rich autumn colours, cream carpets, immaculate linen, smart bathrooms and a rooftop view of Windsor Castle. Relax or work – there is a huge comfy sofa and flat-screen TV as well as useful desks. A generous continental breakfast is delivered to you: fresh bread and croissants, yogurts and fruit. There are interesting shops and galleries galore, you're a stroll from the college or river trips on the Thames, and Waterloo is 50 minutes by train.

Price	£175–£200.
Rooms	1 double.
Meals	Continental breakfast. Supper £18.50. Pubs/restaurants 300 yds.
Closed	Christmas.
Directions	Sent on booking. Paddington 20 minutes by train from Slough (2 miles from Gilbey's).

Caroline Gilbey
Gilbey's,
82-83 High Street,
Eton, Windsor SL4 6AF
Tel   +44 (0)1753 854921
Email caroline@gilbeygroup.com
Web   www.gilbeygroup.com/eton

Entry 12   Map 4

Berkshire

Wilton House

With its handsome Queen Anne frontage, "the most ambitious house in Hungerford" (Pevsner) conceals medieval origins – and the roofline is pure Dickens. A classic townhouse in a charming market town, its interior is a panelled, soft-painted delight. Light floods through sash windows onto paintings and prints, books, antiques and wide, inviting sofas; bedrooms are understatedly elegant and relaxing; bathrooms are a good size. So is your (almost all local or organic) breakfast in the 18th-century dining room: the Welfares, and their labradors, look after you perfectly. *Children over eight welcome.*

Price	From £78. Singles from £65.
Rooms	2: 1 double, 1 twin/double.
Meals	Packed lunch £5. Pub 100 yds.
Closed	Christmas & New Year.
Directions	M4 exit 14; A338 to A4; right for Marlborough, turning at Bear Hotel onto Salisbury road (A338). Over canal bridge into High St. House 200 yds past Town Hall on right.

Deborah & Jonathan Welfare
Wilton House,
33 High Street,
Hungerford RG17 0NF
Tel +44 (0)1488 684228
Email welfares@hotmail.com
Web www.wiltonhouse-hungerford.co.uk

Entry 13 Map 3

Birmingham

Woodbrooke Quaker Study Centre

A pleasure to find ten tranquil acres (woodlands, lawns, lake and walled garden) so close to the centre – run by such special people. This impressive Georgian mansion was donated by George Cadbury to the Quakers in 1903, as a place for study and contemplation. And so it remains. There are corridors aplenty and public rooms big and small: a library, a silent room, a lovely new garden lounge, and a dining hall where organic buffet meals feature fruit and veg from the grounds. Bedrooms, spread over several buildings, are carpeted, comfortable, light and airy, and most have en suite showers. Welcoming, nurturing, historic.

Price	£66. Singles from £42.50.
Rooms	70: 8 doubles, 9 twins, 53 singles (most rooms are en suite).
Meals	Lunch £10. Dinner £10. Pubs/restaurants 15-minute walk.
Closed	Christmas & Boxing Day.
Directions	Sent on booking.

Becky Thomas
Woodbrooke Quaker Study Centre,
1046 Bristol Road, Selly Oak,
Birmingham B29 6LJ
Tel +44 (0)121 472 5171
Email enquiries@woodbrooke.org.uk
Web www.woodbrooke.org.uk

Entry 14 Map 8

Brighton & Hove

4-5 Palmeira Square

Drift along Brighton seafront, and emerge into the Regency splendour of Palmeira Square. Susie with the twinkling eyes welcomes you into a fun, bohemian, ground-floor flat in Hove. Rooms are flooded with light, ceilings are high, furnishings have pizzazz – kilims on bamboo floors and funky chandeliers blend well with elegant antiques. Your bedroom is spacious, lilac and lovely, your newly done shower room has stylish toiletries. Susie has lived in Portugal, Brazil, Bordeaux, works from home and delivers a delicious breakfast to your door, or at a pretty seat in the window bay – turn your head and you'll catch the sea.

Price	£90–£110. Minimum stay 2 nights.
Rooms	1 double.
Meals	Continental breakfast. Pub/restaurant 500 yds.
Closed	Rarely.
Directions	Seafront towards Hove. Right onto Adelaide Crescent (white Regency buildings) then immediate right, following road up into Palmeira Square. No 5 is just after Crescent becomes Square.

Susie de Castilho
4-5 Palmeira Square,
Flat 1, Hove BN3 2JA

Tel	+44 (0)1273 719087
Mobile	+44 (0)7917 562771
Email	stay@2staybrighton.co.uk
Web	www.2staybrighton.co.uk

Entry 15   Map 4

Brighton & Hove

The Art House Hove

Peaceful, close to the sea and in the heart of popular Hove, this Victorian villa is a friendly town treat. Bedrooms on the top floor are furnished in an eclectic style, mixing antique finds with quirky light-fittings; art books, flowers and splashes of colour complete the picture. Dexter and Liz give you a vegetarian breakfast feast: muesli, fruit salad, patisseries fresh from the bakery that morning, eggs, smoked salmon, hash browns. Liz runs mosaic courses in the garden studio and her wonderful work decorates the house. Dozens of cafés and bistros are on the doorstep; Brighton is a 20-minute amble along the promenade.

Price	£85. Singles £65–£75.
Rooms	3: 2 doubles, 1 single, all sharing bathroom & 2 extra wcs.
Meals	Pubs/restaurants 0.5 miles.
Closed	Rarely.
Directions	Sent on booking. Parking meters: 11 hours £4.70. Free parking between 8pm & 9am.

Dexter Tiranti
The Art House Hove,
27 Wilbury Road,
Hove BN3 3PB

Tel	+44 (0)1273 775350
Email	enquiries@thearthousehove.co.uk
Web	www.thearthousehove.co.uk

Entry 16   Map 4

Bristol

9 Princes Buildings

A super city base with jolly comfortable beds, charming owners and, without a doubt, the best views in Clifton. You are a short hop from the elegant Suspension Bridge, good restaurants, shops and pubs of the village and a ferry to whisk you to town or the station; yet all is quiet, green and leafy. Walk in to a big square hall, a drawing room with a peaceful feel and a veranda for gazing in fine weather. Your bedroom is fresh, light and traditional, one downstairs overlooks the garden. Best of all, Simon and Joanna are easy-going and give you a breakfast cooked to order with homemade jams and marmalade.

Price	From £84. Singles from £58.
Rooms	4: 2 doubles, 1 twin/double; 1 twin/double with separate bath.
Meals	Pub/restaurant 100 yds.
Closed	Rarely.
Directions	In Bristol signs to Clifton and Clifton Suspension Bridge, just before bridge left down Sion Hill, past Avon Gorge hotel on right. House next to hotel with double red front doors.

Simon & Joanna Fuller
9 Princes Buildings,
Clifton,
Bristol BS8 4LB
Tel   +44 (0)117 973 4615
Email info@9pb.co.uk
Web   www.9princesbuildings.co.uk

Entry 17   Map 3

Buckinghamshire

Long Crendon Manor

Masses of history and oodles of character at this timbered listed house with high chimneys, dating from 1187... no wonder film companies are keen to get through the arched entrance and into the courtyard! The vast dining room is a dramatic setting for breakfast: sausages and black pudding from Sue's pigs, home-baked bread, plum and mulberry jam from the gardens. Windows on both sides bring light into the fire-warmed drawing room with leather sofas, gleaming furniture, family bits and bobs, pictures galore. Sleep soundly in comfortable, country-house style bedrooms (one with gorgeous yellow panelling). Peaceful.

Price	£100. Singles £80-£100.
Rooms	3: 2 doubles; 1 double with separate bath.
Meals	Supper £30. Pubs/restaurants 3-minute walk.
Closed	Occasionally.
Directions	M40 junc. 8a, A418 Aylesbury. On outskirts of Thame at services' roundabout take B4011 to Long Crendon; 1st left in village at square and continue straight down Frogmore Lane. Stone archway 50 yards on left.

Sue Soar
Long Crendon Manor,
Frogmore Lane, Long Crendon,
Aylesbury HP18 9DZ
Tel   +44 (0)1844 201647
Email sue.soar@longcrendonmanor.co.uk
Web   www.longcrendonmanor.co.uk

Entry 18   Map 8

Buckinghamshire

South Lodge

Handy for the M1, this interestingly developed single-storey building appears pleasant enough. But clever Julia has introduced modern English art, dramatic lighting and contemporary furniture. A dark slate corridor lit by fluorescent multicoloured ceiling sticks leads to big airy bedrooms (one is as large as a suite) with memory mattresses and hi-spec bathrooms; all generous, all different. Velux blinds are solar-powered, heating is underfoot, rainwater is harvested for loos. You have your own patio overlooking a colourful garden, you can walk to the Stables Theatre, and Woburn Abbey is nearby. Great for house parties.

Price	£130–£152. Singles £90–£102.
Rooms	4: 3 doubles, 1 suite/family room.
Meals	Supper, 2 courses, £18. Pubs/restaurants within 0.5 miles.
Closed	Occasionally.
Directions	See owner website.

Julia Cox
South Lodge, 33 Cross End,
Wavendon, Milton Keynes MK17 8AQ
Tel +44 (0)1908 582946
Mobile +44 (0)7989 541182
Email info@culturevultures.co.uk
Web www.culturevultures.co.uk

Entry 19   Map 9

Cambridgeshire

The Old Vicarage

Tug the bell pull and step inside a 19th-century parsonage with a labyrinth of rooms. Homemade flapjack and chocolates await, peaceful bedrooms are countrified and classy with stylish bathrooms – one a lovely en suite. Original artwork peppers every wall and is mostly for sale online. Take breakfast overlooking a big mature garden and brace yourself for a wonderful full English. Cats, dogs and chickens roam freely and if you're lucky you'll spot a proud peacock or muntjac deer within the trees. Explore Cambridge, walk Wicken Fen with its Konik ponies and birdlife, then stroll to one of the locals. *Ask about creative courses.*

Price	From £90. Singles from £45.
Rooms	2: 1 twin/double; 1 double with separate bath.
Meals	Pubs in village.
Closed	Christmas & New Year.
Directions	A14, junc. 37 A142 to Ely. At 3rd r'bout right onto B1102 for 0.8 miles, right onto River Lane, then Collins Hill and Isleham Rd. House opp. church next to social centre; iron gates.

Gill Pedersen
The Old Vicarage,
7 Church Street, Isleham,
Ely CB7 5RX
Tel +44 (0)1638 780095
Email gill@pedersen.co.uk
Web www.oldvicarageisleham.co.uk

Entry 20   Map 9

Cambridgeshire

The Old Hall

You'll feel spoilt in this stunning house, transformed phoenix-like by the charming Morbeys, who look after guests in style. Arrive to tea and homemade cake in the beamed sitting room with paintings, photographs, fresh flowers, soft places to unwind and a dreamy view of the cathedral. Sleep well in smart, large bedrooms (cleverly planted trees disguise any road noise) and wake to Ely sausages, hot waffles with maple syrup, or smoked salmon and scrambled eggs on ciabatta toast. Cambridge is a short train ride away but there is history galore here, a formal garden and 15 acres of parkland with lakeside walks. Excellent value.

Price	From £120. Singles from £100.
Rooms	3: 2 doubles, 1 twin.
Meals	Pub/restaurant 1 mile.
Closed	Christmas & New Year.
Directions	From Ely A142 towards Newmarket, under railway bridge. After 1 mile entrance gates on left, signed. Do not use satnav.

Anthony & Alison Morbey
The Old Hall,
Stuntney, Ely CB7 5TR
Tel +44 (0)1353 663275
Email stay@theoldhallely.co.uk
Web www.theoldhallely.co.uk

Entry 21   Map 9

Cambridgeshire

Cambridge University

Buses, bicycles and punting on the Cam: huge fun when you're in the heart of it all. Enter the Great Gate Tower of Christ's College – as did John Milton in 1625 – to be wooed by tranquil, beautiful quadrangle gardens, breakfasts beneath portraits of hallowed masters, and a serene chapel. At smaller Sidney Sussex – 1598-old with additions – you can play tennis in gorgeous gardens, picnic on perfect lawns and start the day with rare-breed sausages. More charm, and a candlelit chapel, at St Catharine's on King's Parade. Bedrooms and lounges are functional; well-informed porters are your first port of call. *14 colleges in total.*

Price	Doubles £80–£98. Twins £75–£128. Singles £41–£79. Apartments £85–£150.
Rooms	926: 36 doubles, 151 twins, 736 singles, 3 apartments for 2-3.
Meals	Breakfast included. Some colleges offer dinner from £7. See website for details.
Closed	Mid-Jan to mid-March; May/June; Oct/Nov; Christmas. A few rooms available throughout year.
Directions	Website booking. Limited parking at a few colleges.

University Rooms
Cambridge University,
Cambridge
Web www.cambridgerooms.co.uk

Entry 22   Map 9

Cambridgeshire

Springfield House

The former school house hugs the bend of a river, its French windows opening to delightful rambling gardens with scented roses, a yew garden, and a mulberry tree providing fruit for breakfast. Find interesting items from American history, maps and paintings; the conservatory, draped with a huge mimosa, is an exceptional spot for summer breakfasts. Large bedrooms have sink-into beds, interesting books, flowers and garden or river views; one is reached by narrow stairs and has steps to the garden too. This is an old-fashionedly elegant home and Judith is a thoughtful hostess. Good value and peaceful, yet close to Cambridge.

Price	£70–£80. Singles £45–£60.
Rooms	3: 2 doubles; 1 double with separate bath.
Meals	Pubs 150 yds.
Closed	Rarely.
Directions	A1307 from Cambridge, left into High St. 1st right after The Crown (on left) into Horn Lane. House on right next to chapel, before ford. Or bus no. 13 and 13A from Cambridge.

Judith Rossiter
Springfield House,
14-16 Horn Lane, Linton CB21 4HT
Tel +44 (0)1223 891383
Email springfieldhouselinton@gmail.com
Web www.springfieldhouse.org

Entry 23   Map 9

Cambridgeshire

Westoe Farm

Immerse yourself in miles of waving wheat and woodland. The house is a flint-knapped oasis of deep comfort with traditionally comfortable bedrooms, a large attractive hall and your own huge sitting room. Generous Tim and Henrietta are a capable pair and you are well looked after; they produce their own organic bacon, sausages, jams and honey, eggs are home-laid, breakfasts are award-winning and their home is self-sustaining in solar electricity. There's a fine, rose-filled garden, woods and fields – stroll around to your heart's content; visit Cambridge, Beth Chatto Gardens, antique shops… and Stansted is 25 minutes.

Price	£100–£110. Singles £65.
Rooms	2: 1 twin, 1 double.
Meals	Pub 1 mile.
Closed	Christmas & New Year.
Directions	A1307 to Linton, right at Bartlow crossroads through Bartlow, then 1 mile from village, house signed, 3rd farm track on right.

Henrietta Breitmeyer
Westoe Farm,
Bartlow CB21 4PR
Tel +44 (0)1223 892731
Mobile +44 (0)7776 258666
Email enquire@bartlow.u-net.com
Web www.westoefarm.co.uk

Entry 24   Map 9

Cheshire

Trustwood

Small and pretty and wrapped in beautiful country, Trustwood stands in peaceful gardens with National Trust woods at the end of the lane. Outside, sweetpeas flourish to the front, while lawns run down behind to a copse where bluebells thrive in spring. Inside, warm, fresh, contemporary interiors are just the ticket: super bedrooms, fabulous bathrooms, and a wood-burner and sofas in the sitting room. Free-range hens provide eggs for delicious breakfasts, Lin accounts for the lovely scones. As for the Wirral, much more beautiful than you probably imagine; coastal walks, botanic gardens and the spectacular Dee estuary all wait.

Price	£70. Singles £45.
Rooms	2 doubles.
Meals	Restaurants 2 miles.
Closed	Occasionally.
Directions	Sent on booking.

Lin & Peter Friend
Trustwood, Vicarage Lane,
Burton, Neston CH64 5TJ

Tel	+44 (0)151 336 7118
Mobile	+44 (0)7550 012462
Email	lin@trustwood.freeserve.co.uk
Web	www.trustwood.freeserve.co.uk

Entry 25 Map 7

Cheshire

Cotton Farm

Only a four-mile hop from Roman Chester and its 900-year-old cathedral is this sprawling, red-brick farmhouse. Elegant chickens peck in hedges, ponies graze, lambs frisk and cats doze. The farm, run by conservationists Nigel and Clare, is under the Countryside Stewardship Scheme – there are wildflower meadows, summer swallows and 250 acres to roam. Farmhouse bedrooms are large, stylish and cosy with lovely fabrics, robes, a decanter of sherry and huge bath towels, but best of all is the relaxed family atmosphere. Breakfasts, with homemade bread, are delicious and beautifully presented. *Stabling available. Over tens welcome.*

Price	£85. Singles £52.
Rooms	3: 2 doubles, 1 twin.
Meals	Pub 1.5 miles.
Closed	Rarely.
Directions	A51 Chester-Nantwich. 1.5 miles from outskirts, after golf course on left, right, down Cotton Lane, signed Cotton Edmunds; 1.5 miles, left on sharp right-hand bend; 2nd drive on right.

Clare & Nigel Hill
Cotton Farm,
Cotton Edmunds, Chester CH3 7PG

Tel	+44 (0)1244 336616
Mobile	+44 (0)7840 682042
Email	information@cottonfarm.co.uk
Web	www.cottonfarm.co.uk

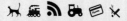

Entry 26 Map 7

Cheshire

Greenlooms Cottage

This pretty cottage was where the estate's chief hedger and ditcher lived. The smallholding has gone but the walnuts, quinces and garden pump remain – and the views still reach to the Peckforton Hills. Now it is a stylishly simple and fun place to stay, thanks to Deborah – traveller, ex-potter, fabulous cook – and Peter, furniture-maker and restorer. Follow your nose to the Aga-cosy kitchen where the best black pudding and bacon are waiting to fuel you for a day on the Cheshire cycle route. Return to two sweet bedrooms, one up one down: crisp white duvets, Floris soaps in simple walk-in showers, ethnic touches.

Price	£75. Singles from £50.
Rooms	2: 1 double, 1 twin.
Meals	Dinner, with wine, £25. Pub 3 miles.
Closed	Rarely.
Directions	A41 Chester-Whitchurch. After petrol station, 2nd left at antiques shop. On for 1.5 miles thro' village, right into Martins Lane; 1 mile on right.

Deborah Newman
Greenlooms Cottage, Martins Lane,
Hargrave, Chester CH3 7RX

Tel	+44 (0)1829 781475
Mobile	+44 (0)7791 014231
Email	dnewman@greenlooms.com
Web	www.greenlooms.com

Entry 27 Map 7

Cheshire

Mulsford Cottage

Delicious! Not just the food (Kate's a pro chef) but the sweet whitewashed cottage with its sunny conservatory and vintage interiors, and the green Cheshire countryside that bubble-wraps the place in rural peace. Chat – and laugh – the evening away over Kate's superb dinners, lounge by the sitting room fire, then sleep deeply in comfy bedrooms: cane beds, a bright red chair, a vintage desk. The double has a roll top bath, the twin a tiny shower-with-a-view. Step out to birdsong and the 34-mile Sandstone Trail to Shropshire. Wales starts just past the hammock, at the bottom of the large and lovely garden.

Price	£80. Singles £45.
Rooms	2: 1 twin, 1 double, each with separate bath/shower.
Meals	Dinner from £18. Pub 1.5 miles.
Closed	Rarely.
Directions	From Malpas B5069 to Worthenbury. After 5 miles left into Mulsford Lane. After 1 mile Mulsford Cottage on right.

Kate Dewhurst
Mulsford Cottage,
Mulsford, Sarn,
Malpas SY14 7LP

Tel	+44 (0)1948 770414
Email	katedewhurst@hotmail.com
Web	www.mulsfordcottage.co.uk

Entry 28 Map 7

Cheshire

Harrop Fold Farm

Artists, foodies and walkers adore this antique-filled farmhouse with soul-lifting views. On the edge of the Peak District, the oldest building on the farm dates from 1694 (Bonnie Prince Charlie visited here). The B&B part has a warm peaceful breakfast room, a stone-flagged sitting room, a spectacular studio. Fresh flowers, antique beds, fine fabrics, hot water bottles with chic covers, bathrooms with fluffy robes: you get the best. Gregarious Sue and daughter Leah hold art and cookery courses so the food too is outstanding. Bedrooms have stupendous views — and flat-screen TVs and DVDs just in case they pall.

Price	From £95. Singles from £60.
Rooms	2 doubles.
Meals	Cookery demo & dinner £60. Pub 1.9 miles.
Closed	Rarely.
Directions	B470 Macclesfield to Whaley Bridge. After 4 miles Highwayman pub; 0.25 miles further down track (rutted at top); on left, immed. before sharp right bend.

Sue Stevenson
Harrop Fold Farm,
Rainow, Macclesfield SK10 5UU
Tel +44 (0)1625 560085
Email stay@harropfoldfarm.co.uk
Web www.harropfoldfarm.co.uk

Entry 29 Map 8

Cornwall

The Old Vicarage

The first sight of quirky chimneys — the spires of former owner Reverend Hawker's parish churches — sets the scene for a huge house packed with interest and steeped in Victoriana. Jill and Richard, both delightful, know the local history — and the cliff-top walks, which are glorious. Rooms are casually grand, dotted with *objets* — brass gramophone, magic lantern, eccentric Hawker memorabilia. Browse books in the study, play the grand piano, sip brandy over billiards. Bedrooms with wide floorboards are country-house pretty, bathrooms smart, lawns well tended and views are to the sea. Supper at a good pub is a stroll.

Price	From £80. Singles from £40.
Rooms	3: 1 double, 1 twin, 1 single.
Meals	Pub/tea rooms 5-10 minute walk.
Closed	December/January.
Directions	From A39 at Morwenstow, follow signs towards church. Small turning on right, just before church, marked 'public footpath'. Drive down to house.

Jill & Richard Wellby
The Old Vicarage,
Morwenstow EX23 9SR
Tel +44 (0)1288 331369
Email jillwellby@hotmail.com
Web www.rshawker.co.uk

Entry 30 Map 1

Cornwall

The Old Parsonage

A spellbinding coastline, secret coves, spectacular walks. All this and a supremely comfortable Georgian rectory with pretty gardens. Morag and Margaret are relaxed and welcoming hosts. Superb pitch pine floors and original woodwork add warmth and a fresh glow, the big engaging bedrooms (one on the ground floor) have a quirky, upbeat mix of furniture and furnishings, and the bathrooms are pampering. Breakfasts are wonderful: savoury mushrooms, Cornish oak-roasted mackerel, French toast with bacon... In front of the house the land slopes away to the Atlantic, just a five-minute walk across a SSSI. A peaceful retreat.

Cornwall

Tremoren

Views stretch sleepily over the Cornish countryside. You might feel inclined to do nothing more than wander the lovely garden or snooze by the pool, but the surfing beaches, the Camel Trail and the Eden Project are so close. The stone and slate former farmhouse has been smartly updated and your airy ground-floor bedroom comes with soft colours, pretty china, crisp linen, a comfortable bathroom. And its own cosy sitting room, full of books and interesting maps, leading to a flower-filled terrace — perfect for a pre-dinner drink. Lanie, bubbly and engaging, runs her own catering company; your dinner will be delicious!

Price	From £90. Singles from £70.
Rooms	5 twins/doubles.
Meals	Packed lunch £5.95. Pub/restaurant 600 yds.
Closed	November-January.
Directions	In Boscastle head towards Tintagel on B3263. 500 yds after garage on left turn right into Green Lane. After bend, house 3rd on right.

Price	£90-£100.
Rooms	1 double & sitting room.
Meals	Dinner, 4 courses, £26. Inns 0.5 miles.
Closed	Rarely.
Directions	A39 to St Kew Highway through village; left at Red Lion. Down lane, 1st left round sharp right-hand bend. 2nd drive on right; signed.

	Morag Reeve & Margaret Pickering
	The Old Parsonage,
	Forrabury, Boscastle PL35 0DJ
Tel	+44 (0)1840 250339
Mobile	+44 (0)7890 531677
Email	morag@old-parsonage.com
Web	www.old-parsonage.com

	Philip & Lanie Calvert
	Tremoren,
	St Kew,
	Bodmin PL30 3HA
Tel	+44 (0)1208 841790
Email	la.calvert@btopenworld.com

Entry 31   Map 1

Entry 32   Map 1

Cornwall

The Corn Mill

This restored mill in a quiet Cornish valley is a relaxed and friendly home. Step inside and find a country cottage medley of flowers and family furniture, antique rugs and interesting market finds. Artist Suzie has her studio in a folly in the pretty garden; ducks and chicks wander in the orchard. Cosy bedrooms have flowery fabrics, antique eiderdowns, warm blankets and good cotton; bathrooms are simple and fresh with fluffy towels. Breakfast well in the farmhouse kitchen on locally sourced food and bread fresh from the Rayburn. Exceptional coastal walking, music festivals, great beaches and Port Isaac are all nearby.

Price	£75.
Rooms	2: 1 double, 1 family room.
Meals	Pub/restaurant 2 miles.
Closed	Christmas & New Year.
Directions	A39 Wadebridge dir. Camelford. Left at St Kew Highway dir. Trelill. Left at crossroads for Pendoggett, then 300 yds down hill. House on right.

Susan Bishop
The Corn Mill,
Port Isaac Road,
Trelill,
Bodmin PL30 3HZ
Tel   +44 (0)1208 851079

Entry 33   Map 1

Cornwall

The Barn at The Old Stables

The closer you inch down the lane to The Barn, the greener the fields become, the louder the spring-time bleating lambs. But that's all the noise here: this converted hay barn is a hubbub–free hideaway. Find a lavish double bedroom with fine touches: vast bathroom, sublime 'sink in' mattress and contemporary furniture made by Judith's son. Judith lives opposite and is most at home by her Aga, whipping up a delicious breakfast with local bacon or preparing extraordinary three–course suppers: after a day's walking or cycling the Camel Trail and Cornish coast, you can eat in the candlelit dining room, the valley unfolding beyond.

Price	£80–£95.
Rooms	Barn: 1 double.
Meals	Dinner, 3 courses, £25. Pub/restaurant 5 miles.
Closed	Christmas & New Year.
Directions	From A30 follow road to Helland. Over crossroads; after 0.5 miles right by large grass verge with sign Coldrenick Farm Offices. Follow signs to The Old Stables.

Judith Argent
The Barn at The Old Stables,
Helland, Bodmin PL30 4QE
Tel   +44 (0)1208 75543
Email   juargent@hotmail.com
Web   www.thebarnincornwall.co.uk

Entry 34   Map 1

Cornwall

Higher Lank Farm

Families rejoice: you can only come if you have a child under five! Celtic crosses in the garden and original panelling hint at the house's 500-year history; bedrooms, newly decorated, have pocket sprung mattresses and large TVs. Nursery teas begin at 5pm, grown-up suppers are later and energetic Lucy will cheerfully babysit while the rest of you slink off to the pub. Farm-themed playgrounds are covered in safety matting and grass, there are piglets and chicks, eggs to collect, pony and trap rides, a sand barn for little ones and cream teas in the garden. Oh, and real nappies are provided!

Price	From £100. Singles by arrangement.
Rooms	3 family rooms.
Meals	Supper £23. Nursery tea £7. Pub 1.5 miles.
Closed	November-Easter.
Directions	A30 past Launceston. Right to St Breward 4 miles. Across moor through Bradford, then first right. Humpback bridge and crossroads, turn left (no sign & not straight on to St Breward). Follow road to bottom of hill; house signed opposite.

Lucy Finnemore
Higher Lank Farm,
St Breward, Bodmin PL30 4NB
Tel   +44 (0)1208 850716
Email   lucyfin@higherlankfarm.co.uk
Web   www.higherlankfarm.co.uk

Entry 35   Map 1

Cornwall

Lavethan

A glorious house in the most glorious of settings: views sail down to the valley. It rambles on many levels and is part 15th-century: walls are stone, floors are flagged, stairs are oak. The sunny bedroom in the house is best, with its panelled walls and smart bathroom; bedrooms across the courtyard are very private with their own entrances and have pretty quilted bedspreads. Catherine, a warm hostess, has decorated in country style; the guest sitting room is hugely welcoming with books, flowers and piano. All this and acres of ancient woods, Celtic crosses and a heated pool in the old walled garden. *Children over ten welcome.*

Price	£90. Singles £50.
Rooms	3: 2 twins/doubles, 1 double.
Meals	Pub 0.25 miles.
Closed	Rarely.
Directions	From A30, turn for Blisland. There, past church on left & pub on right. Take lane at bottom left of village green. 0.25 miles on, drive on left (granite pillars & cattle grid).

Christopher & Catherine Hartley
Lavethan,
Blisland, Bodmin PL30 4QG
Tel   +44 (0)1208 850487
Email   chrishartley@btconnect.com
Web   www.lavethan.com

Entry 36   Map 1

Cornwall

Cabilla Manor

There's a treasure round every corner and an opera house in one of the barns. Instant seduction as you enter the old manor house out on the moor, brimful of interest and colour. Rich exotic rugs and cushions, artefacts from around the world, Louella's sumptuous hand-stencilled quilts, huge beds, coir carpets, garden flowers. There's a dining room crammed floor to ceiling with books, many of them Robin's (a writer and explorer) and a lofty conservatory for friendly meals overlooking a semi-wild garden – with tennis and elegant lawns. The views are heavenly, the generous hosts wonderful and the final mile thrillingly wild.

Price	£90. Singles £45.
Rooms	4: 1 double; 1 double with separate bath; 1 double, 1 twin, sharing bath (let to same party only).
Meals	Dinner, 3 courses with wine, £35. Pub 4 miles. Restaurant 8-10 miles.
Closed	Christmas.
Directions	6 miles after Jamaica Inn on A30, left for Cardinham. Through Millpool & straight on, ignoring further signs to Cardinham. After 2.5 miles, left to Manor 0.75 miles; on right down drive.

	Robin & Louella Hanbury-Tenison
	Cabilla Manor,
	Mount, Bodmin PL30 4DW
Tel	+44 (0)1208 821224
Mobile	+44 (0)7770 664218
Email	louella@cabilla.co.uk
Web	www.cabilla.co.uk

Entry 37   Map 1

Cornwall

Menkee

From this handsome Georgian farmhouse there are long views towards the sea; you're 20 minutes away from the coastal path and wild surf but you may not want to budge. Gage and Liz are deliciously unstuffy and look after you well: newspapers and a weather forecast appear with a scrumptious breakfast, your gorgeously comfortable bed is turned down in the evening and walkers can be dropped off and collected. The elegant house is filled with beautiful things, gleaming furniture, fresh flowers, roaring fires and pretty fabrics – all you have to do is slacken your pace and wind down. *Minimum stay two nights in high season.*

Price	£80-£90. Singles from £40.
Rooms	2: 1 double, 1 twin.
Meals	Pub/restaurant 3 miles.
Closed	Rarely.
Directions	A389 Bodmin-Wadebridge; 2.5 miles, then fork right on B3266; on for 2 miles for Camelford; 600 yds after St Mabyn turn-off, left down drive.

	Gage & Liz Williams
	Menkee,
	St Mabyn, Wadebridge PL30 3DD
Tel	+44 (0)1208 841378
Mobile	+44 (0)7999 549935
Email	gagewillms@aol.com
Web	www.cornwall-online.co.uk/menkee

Entry 38   Map 1

Cornwall

Roskear

Drive down the fields to this 17th-century working farmhouse, a blissfully peaceful escape. A snug sitting room with a log fire, a warm and smiling hostess, happy dogs, comfy bedrooms and simple bathrooms, a cheerful Aga, fabulous estuary views – country life at its most old-fashioned and charming. Delicious breakfasts are served on blue china, doors open to the sunny garden and there are acres of woodland and grassland all around. Good restaurants include Rick Stein's in Padstow, the ferry takes you to Rock, surfing is a short drive and the Camel cycle trail is nearby (hire bikes locally). Uncomplicated, good value B&B.

Price	From £70. Singles £35.
Rooms	2: 1 double with separate bath; 1 twin/double sharing bath (let to same party only).
Meals	Pubs/restaurants 0.5-6 miles.
Closed	Rarely.
Directions	Bypass Wadebridge on A39 for Redruth. Over bridge, pass garage on left, straight over roundabout, filter 1st right to Edmonton. By modern houses turn immed. right to Roskear over cattle grid.

Rosina Messer-Bennetts
Roskear,
St Breock, Wadebridge PL27 7HU

Tel	+44 (0)1208 812805
Mobile	+44 (0)7748 432013
Email	rosina@roskear.com
Web	www.roskear.com

Entry 39 Map 1

Cornwall

Porteath Barn

A converted 'upside-down' barn in an exquisite valley setting, elegantly uncluttered inside. Downstairs bedrooms – not vast – have fresh flowers, quilted bedspreads and beautiful bathrooms, and French windows that open onto a large and lovely garden. From here a path leads down to Epphaven Cove and the beach – fabulous. Continue further for wonderful walks on the coastal path if you're feeling hearty, return to a sitting room with seagrass flooring and a wood-burner. Jo and Michael are gracious and delightful and their breakfasts (kedgeree, kippers, pancakes, homemade jams) are superb. *Over 12s by arrangement.*

Price	From £90. Singles by arrangement.
Rooms	3: 2 twins/doubles, each with separate bath or shower; 1 double sharing bath (let to same party only).
Meals	Pub 1.5 miles.
Closed	Rarely.
Directions	A39 to Wadebridge. At r'bout signed for Polzeath, then to Porteath Bee Centre. Through Bee Centre shop car park, down farm track; house signed on right after 150 yds.

Jo & Michael Bloor
Porteath Barn,
St Minver,
Wadebridge PL27 6RA

Tel	+44 (0)1208 863605
Email	m.bloor17@btinternet.com

Entry 40 Map 1

Cornwall

Molesworth Manor

It's a splendid old place, big enough to swallow hoards of people, peppered with art and interesting antiques. There are palms and a play area in the garden, two charming drawing rooms with an honesty bar and open fires for cosy nights, a carved staircase leading to bedrooms that vary in style and size – His Lordship's at the front, the Maid's in the eaves – and bathrooms that are lovely and pampering. The whiff of homemade muffins and a delicious breakfast lures you downstairs in the morning, Padstow and its food delights will keep you happy when you venture out. A superb bolthole run by Geoff and Jessica, youthful and fun.

Price	£80–£120. Singles from £75.
Rooms	9: 7 doubles, 1 twin/double; 1 twin with separate shower.
Meals	Pubs/restaurants 2 miles.
Closed	November–January. Open off-season by arrangement for larger parties.
Directions	Off A389 between Wadebridge & Padstow. Entrance clearly signed; 300 yds from bridge in Little Petherick.

Geoff French & Jessica Clarke
Molesworth Manor,
Little Petherick,
Padstow PL27 7QT
Tel   +44 (0)1841 540292
Email   molesworthmanor@aol.com
Web   www.molesworthmanor.co.uk

Entry 41   Map 1

Cornwall

Calize Country House

Beneath wheeling gulls and close to blond beaches, the big square 1870 guest house has amazing views of skies and sea. Virginia Woolf's lighthouse is in the bay and winter seals cavort at the colony nearby. A fresh, uncomplicated décor brings the tang of the sea to every room. Artworks recall a world of surf; deckchair stripes clothe the dining table and dress the window; traditional sofas call for quiet times with a book. Upstairs, patterned or pale walls, practical bath or shower rooms, perhaps a sea view. Jilly and Nigel are testament to the benefits of sea air and look after you beautifully.

Price	£80–£90. Singles £60.
Rooms	4: 2 doubles, 1 twin, 1 single.
Meals	Packed lunch £5. Pub 350 yds.
Closed	Rarely.
Directions	Exit A30 at Camborne (west) A3047. Left, then right at r'bout. Right on entering Connor Downs, then on for 2 miles. House on right after sign for Gwithian.

Jilly Whitaker
Calize Country House,
Gwithian,
Hayle TR27 5BW
Tel   +44 (0)1736 753268
Email   jilly@calize.co.uk
Web   www.calize.co.uk

Entry 42   Map 1

Cornwall

House at Gwinear

An island of calm, this grand old rambling house sits in bird-filled acres but is only a short drive from St Ives. The Halls are devoted to the encouragement of the arts and crafts which is reflected in their lifestyle. Find shabby chic with loads of character and no stuffiness – fresh flowers on the breakfast table, a piano in the corner, rugs on polished floors, masses of books. In a separate wing is your cosy bedroom and sitting room, with a fine view of the church from the bath. The large lawned gardens are there for bare-footed solace, and you can have breakfast in the Italianate courtyard on sunny days.

Price	From £80.
Rooms	1 twin/double with separate bath & sitting room.
Meals	Supper, 2 courses with wine, £25. Pub 1.5 miles.
Closed	Rarely.
Directions	From A30 exit Hayle (Loggans Moor r'bout); 100 yds left at mini r'bout; 400 yds left for Gwinear; 1.5 miles, top of hill, driveway on right, just before 30mph Gwinear sign.

Charles & Diana Hall
House at Gwinear,
Gwinear,
St Ives TR27 5JZ

Tel +44 (0)1736 850444
Email charleshall@btinternet.com

Entry 43   Map 1

Cornwall

Penquite

A doll's house of a B&B in a constellation of Cornwall's best attractions, set in a quiet village overlooking the Hayle estuary and bird reserve. A doctor's house from 1908, it oozes Arts and Crafts with chunky stone walls, sloping roof, winding stairs and polished oak enhanced by Stephanie's ceramics. All yours: a snug, bay-windowed sitting room; a private suite of cute bedrooms in the eaves; a mature garden of lofty pines, palms and summer house; a generous continental spread on the terrace or light-filled dining room. Stroll to pubs and deli, or past a golf course to the coastal path and St Ives Bay views.

Price	£85-£110.
Rooms	2: 1 family room for 3; 1 single with extra z-bed (let to same party only).
Meals	Continental breakfast. Restaurant 2-minute walk.
Closed	Rarely.
Directions	Sent on booking.

Stephanie Pace
Penquite,
Vicarage Lane, Lelant,
St Ives TR26 3EA

Tel +44 (0)1736 755002
Email stephaniepace@hotmail.com
Web www.penquite-seasidesuite-cornwall.com

Entry 44   Map 1

Cornwall

11 Sea View Terrace

In a smart row of Edwardian villas, with stunning harbour and sea views, is a delectable retreat. Sleek, softy coloured interiors are light and gentle on the eye – an Italian circular glass table here, a painted seascape there. Bedrooms are perfect with crisp linen and vistas of whirling gulls from private terraces; bathrooms are state of the art. Rejoice in softly boiled eggs with anchovy and chive-butter soldiers for breakfast – or continental in bed if you prefer. Grahame looks after you impeccably and design aficionados will be happy. *Free admission to Tate Gallery & Barbara Hepworth Museum. Over 12s welcome.*

Cornwall

Organic Panda B&B & Gallery

A five-minute walk from St Ives, with a panoramic view of the bay, boutique B&B in perfect harmony with this artistic spot: enjoy vibrant modern art, and dine at a ten-seater rustic table. Spacious contemporary bedrooms have a laid-back style with organic linen, bamboo towels, chunky beds, white walls and raw-silk cushions. Shower rooms are small but perfectly formed. Andrea is an artist and theatre designer, Peter a photographer and organic chef; the food is delicious and bread home-baked. The most beautiful coastal road in all England leads to St Just. *House available to rent Christmas, New Year, Easter & school holidays.*

Price	£100–£135. Singles from £75.
Rooms	3 suites.
Meals	Dinner, with wine, from £25 (groups only). Packed lunch from £15. Pubs/restaurants 5-minute walk.
Closed	Rarely.
Directions	At Porthminster Hotel, signs for Tate; down Albert Rd, right just before Longships Hotel. Limited parking.

Price	£80–£150.
Rooms	3: 2 doubles, 1 twin.
Meals	Packed lunch £10. Restaurants nearby.
Closed	Rarely.
Directions	A3074 to St Ives. Follow leisure centre sign; house on corner of Talland Rd and Albert Rd. Train station 5-minute walk.

Grahame Wheelband
11 Sea View Terrace,
St Ives TR26 2DH
Tel   +44 (0)1736 798440
Mobile   +44 (0)7973 953616
Email   info@11stives.co.uk
Web   www.11stives.co.uk

Peter Williams & Andrea Carr
Organic Panda B&B & Gallery,
1 Pednolver Terrace, St Ives TR26 2EL
Tel   +44 (0)1736 793890
Mobile   +44 (0)7787 854380
Email   info@organicpanda.co.uk
Web   www.organicpanda.co.uk

Entry 45   Map 1

Entry 46   Map 1

Cornwall

Ennys

Prepare to be spoiled. A fire smoulders in the sumptuous sitting room, tea is laid out in the Aga-warm kitchen, bedrooms are luxurious (a king-size bed, an elegant modern four-poster, a powerful shower) and breakfasts are served at separate tables. The stylishness continues into the suites and everywhere there are fascinating artefacts from Gill's travels, designer fabrics and original art. The road ends at Ennys, so it is utterly peaceful; walk down to the river and along the old towpath to St Ives Bay. Or stay put: play tennis (on grass!) and swim in the heated pool sunk deep into the tropical gardens.

Price	£95-£175. Singles from £75.
Rooms	5: 3 doubles; 2 suites (twins/doubles) each with kitchenette.
Meals	Pub 3 miles.
Closed	25 October-1 April.
Directions	2 miles east of Marazion on B3280, look for sign & turn left leading down Trewhella Lane between St Hilary & Relubbus. On to Ennys.

Gill Charlton
Ennys,
St Hilary,
Penzance TR20 9BZ

Tel   +44 (0)1736 740262
Email   ennys@ennys.co.uk
Web   www.ennys.co.uk

Entry 47   Map 1

Cornwall

Keigwin Farmhouse

Off the glorious coast road to St Ives, in two walled acres overlooking the sea, is a very old farmhouse lived in by Gilly. Walk to the beach at Portheras Cove, dine well at Gurnard's Head, return to little whitewash-and-pine bedrooms with views that make you want to get out your paints, and a big shared bathroom with a massive old bath, fresh with organic cotton towels. A treat: Gilly's scones on arrival, eggs from the neighbour's farm, stacks of books above the stairs and an arty feel – wide floorboards, creamy colours, family pieces, sculptures, ceramics, glass. A relaxed, delightful – and musical instrument-friendly – B&B.

Price	From £70. Singles from £35.
Rooms	3: 2 doubles, 1 single, sharing 2 bathrooms (let to same party only).
Meals	Pubs/restaurants 3 miles.
Closed	Rarely.
Directions	Coast road from St Ives, B3306, dir. St Just. Keigwin between Morvah & Bojewyan. Turn off road at Yew Tree Gallery sign. Farmhouse next to the Gallery.

Gilly Wyatt-Smith
Keigwin Farmhouse,
Keigwin, Morvah,
Penzance TR19 7TS

Tel   +44 (0)1736 786425
Email   sleep@keigwinfarmhouse.co.uk
Web   www.keigwinfarmhouse.co.uk

Entry 48   Map 1

Cornwall

Trereife House

Sweep past ponies to a country house of high culture. Find period antiques, comfortable sofas and open fires, beautifully bound books, roll top baths, lavish rooms in powder-blues or greens, and sprawling grounds where summer fairs are held. A serene and special setting for a wedding or celebration, or a break from the daily grind – the delights of Penzance and the coast are an amble away. At breakfast, choose between the full English or kedgeree, or croissants and fig compote, served at the antique dining table. The family have lived on the estate for generations; an authentic, rich and marvellous place.

Cornwall

Marine Lodge

Come for independence in this 1970s hillside house with wide views of Mount's Bay. Your suite is decorated in natural tones with attractive lamps and splashes of colour from Richard's art. The sitting room opens to a terrace and subtropical garden below. Your hosts are charming; they leave your laissez-faire continental breakfast for you, so wake when you want to homemade muesli and jams, dried fruit marinated in Earl Grey, toast and coffee, and relish the privacy of it all. Newlyn is still an art and fishing hub; watch the sun rise over St Michael's Mount, the dolphins in the bay and the fishing boats returning home.

Price	£80–£120.
Rooms	5: 4 doubles; 1 double sharing bath (let to same party only).
Meals	Restaurant 2 miles.
Closed	Rarely.
Directions	Sent on booking.

Price	£130. Singles £100.
Rooms	1 suite.
Meals	Continental breakfast. Pubs/restaurants in village.
Closed	Rarely.
Directions	Sent on booking.

Peter Le Grice
Trereife House,
Penzance TR20 8TJ
Tel +44 (0)1736 362750
Email trereifepark@btconnect.com
Web www.trereifepark.co.uk

John Charlick
Marine Lodge,
Old Paul Hill, Newlyn,
Penzance TR18 5BX
Tel +44 (0)1736 362462
Email johncharlick@hotmail.co.uk
Web www.marinelodgenewlyn.co.uk

Cornwall

Sophia's

Lovely Lynn welcomes you in her chef's whites – with a cappuccino and a truffle if you're lucky! Inspired by her father and his organic garden, she's opened this small sweet restaurant with rooms; word is spreading for the deliciousness of her food, especially the ocean-fresh fish. Upstairs are two light airy bedrooms, with white floorboards and window seats facing the sea; cross the road and you're on the prom. Mattresses are deep, bathrooms luxurious and breakfasts a delight: homemade breads and marmalade from organic oranges. Walk to Mousehole or St Michael's Mount, get high on sea breezes, unwind.

Price	£90–£100.
Rooms	2 doubles.
Meals	Dinner £12.90–£17.50. Restaurant downstairs.
Closed	End October to March.
Directions	Sent on booking.

Lynn Ryder
Sophia's,
Promenade, Penzance TR18 4HH

Tel	+44 (0)1736 333363
Mobile	+44 (0)7811 025417
Email	info@sophiaspenzance.co.uk
Web	www.sophiaspenzance.co.uk

Entry 51   Map 1

Cornwall

Venton Vean

You can tell this place opened recently – everything is tip-top. Immensely helpful owners Philippa and David moved from London with their family and have transformed a dilapidated Victorian house into a supremely cool and elegant B&B. Moody colours, mid-century design classics and interesting reclamation finds make for a stunning and eclectic interior. Food is a passion – expect freshly ground coffee in your room and some of the most tantalising breakfasts around: Mexican, Spanish, even a good old full English will have you dashing down in the morning. Arty Penzance is a joy as is the craggy-coved beauty all around.

Price	£80–£105. Singles from £60.
Rooms	3 doubles.
Meals	Dinner, 3 courses, from £20. Packed lunch from £5. Cream tea £4.
Closed	Rarely (see availability calendar on website).
Directions	Sent on booking.

Philippa McKnight
Venton Vean,
Trewithen Road,
Penzance TR18 4LS

Tel	+44 (0)1736 351294
Email	info@ventonvean.co.uk
Web	www.ventonvean.co.uk

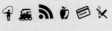

Entry 52   Map 1

Cornwall

Ednovean Farm

There's a terrace for each fabulous bedroom (one truly private) with views to the wild blue yonder and St Michael's Mount Bay, an enchanting outlook that changes with the passage of the day. Come for peace, space and the best of eclectic fabrics and colours, pretty lamps, Christine's sculptures, fluffy bathrobes and handmade soaps. The beamed open-plan sitting/dining area is an absorbing mix of exotic, rustic and elegant; have full breakfast here (last orders nine o'clock) or continental in your room. A footpath through the field leads to the village; walk to glorious Prussia Cove and Cudden Point, or head west to Marazion.

Price	£95–£115.
Rooms	3: 2 doubles, 1 four-poster.
Meals	Pub 5-minute walk.
Closed	Christmas & rarely.
Directions	From A30 after Crowlas r'bout, A394 to Helston. 0.25 miles after next r'bout, 1st right for Perranuthnoe. Farm drive on left, signed.

Christine & Charles Taylor
Ednovean Farm,
Perranuthnoe,
Penzance TR20 9LZ
Tel   +44 (0)1736 711883
Email   info@ednoveanfarm.co.uk
Web   www.ednoveanfarm.co.uk

Entry 53   Map 1

Cornwall

Halftides

Hugely enjoyable and special, surrounded by three acres with dazzling views down the coast and out to sea. Fresh funky bedrooms, not huge but filled with light, have gorgeous fabrics, crisp bedding, dreamy views; bathrooms (one a small pod-shower in the room) are sleek in glass and chrome. Susie is great fun, an artist and chef and gives you a delicious organic breakfast in the pretty, airy dining room. Take the coastal path north or south, visit the working harbour in the village, head for a swim down the private path to the beach below. A perfect place to relax and unwind. *Minimum stay two nights. Over threes welcome.*

Price	£95–£120. Singles £60–£75.
Rooms	3: 1 double; 1 double, 1 single sharing separate bath.
Meals	Dinner, 2-3 courses with wine, £30–£35. Pub within walking distance.
Closed	February.
Directions	A3083 to Lizard, right to Cury, 5 miles; past Poldhu beach & into Mullion. Right into Laflouder Lane, past 'No Through Road' sign. Ignore side road on right. House 1st on right.

Charles & Susie Holdsworth Hunt
Halftides,
Laflouder Lane, Mullion,
Helston TR12 7HU
Tel   +44 (0)1326 241935
Email   halftides@btinternet.com
Web   www.halftides.co.uk

Entry 54   Map 1

Cornwall

Halzephron House

The coastal path runs through the grounds and the view is to die for – you can see St Michael's Mount on a clear day. Be greeted by homemade biscotti and organic coffee roasted in Cornwall: lovely Lucy and Roger – foodies, designers – have a café and shop in the cottage next door. Bedrooms, contemporary, quirky and full of charm, are super-private; 'Tower' is in the house, with a velvet sofa and a French bed. Elsewhere: recycled wooden floors, art on white walls, bowls of wild flowers. You can walk to three amazing beaches, a 13th-century church, a golf course and a gastropub. Heaven. *Dogs welcome in Observatory & Cabin.*

Price	£80–£130.
Rooms	3: 1 suite. Cabin: 1 suite. Observatory: 1 double.
Meals	Pub 0.25 miles.
Closed	Rarely.
Directions	From Helston head towards the Lizard. After 2 miles, right signed Gunwalloe. In village lane towards Church Cove passing Halzephron Inn on left. House at top of hill overlooking the sea.

Lucy & Roger Thorp
Halzephron House,
Gunwalloe,
Helston TR12 7QD
Tel   +44 (0)1326 241719
Email   info@halzephronhouse.co.uk
Web   www.halzephronhouse.co.uk

Entry 55   Map 1

Cornwall

The Hen House

Greenies will be delighted: Sandy and Gary, truly welcoming, are passionately committed to sustainability and happy to advise on the best places to eat, visit and walk; there are OS maps on loan too. Enlightened souls will adore the spacious colourful rooms, the bright fabrics, the wildflower meadow with inviting sun loungers, the pond, the tai chi, the fairy-lit courtyard at night, the scrumptious locally sourced breakfasts, the birdsong. There's even a sanctuary room for reiki and reflexology set deep into the earth in this generous, peaceful retreat. *Over 12s welcome. Self-catering in Barn available.*

Price	From £80. Singles £70. Min. two nights.
Rooms	3 doubles in 3 barns.
Meals	Pub/restaurant 1 mile.
Closed	Rarely.
Directions	A3083 from Helston, then B3293 to St Keverne; left to Newtown-in-St Martin. After 2 miles, right at T-junc. Follow road for 2.3 miles then left fork. Round 7 bends then right at triangulation stone for Tregarne.

Sandy & Gary Pulfrey
The Hen House, Tregarne,
Manaccan, Helston TR12 6EW
Tel   +44 (0)1326 280236
Mobile   +44 (0)7809 229958
Email   henhouseuk@aol.com
Web   www.thehenhouse-cornwall.co.uk

Entry 56   Map 1

Cornwall

Carmelin

The setting of this bungalow is sensational, gazing straight out to sea from the Lizard, England's most southerly point. Your peaceful bedroom shares the views, and leads into a sun room just for you: a sofa, a log-effect fire, a private entrance, more beautiful views. Breakfast – a spread of breads and pastries, fruits, freshly made yogurt and homemade jams – fights for your attention against the breaking waves and sparkling sea. John and Jane are gentle dog-loving people, seasoned B&B providers who enjoy their guests. Walk the coastal path, stroll to the pub for a meal. *French & German spoken.*

Price	From £90. Singles by arrangement.
Rooms	1 double with separate bath/shower & sitting room.
Meals	Pub/restaurant within walking distance.
Closed	Rarely.
Directions	From Helston to the Lizard; at Lizard Green, right, opp. Regent Café (head for Smugglers Fish & Chips); immed. right, pass wc on left. Road unmade; on for 500 yds; double bend; 2nd on right.

Jane & John Grierson
Carmelin,
Pentreath Lane, The Lizard,
Helston TR12 7NY
Tel   +44 (0)1326 290677
Email   pjcarmelin@gmail.com
Web   www.bedandbreakfastcornwall.co.uk

Entry 57   Map 1

Cornwall

Landewednack House

The pug dogs will greet you enthusiastically and Susan will give you tea and biscuits in the drawing room of this immaculate house with a boutique hotel feel. Antony the chef keeps the wheels oiled and the food coming – treat yourself to green crab soup or succulent lobster; the wine cellar holds over 2,000 bottles so there's plenty of choice. Upstairs to bedrooms that are not huge and not all with sea views, but everything you could possibly need is there, from robes to brandy. The pool area is stunning, the garden is filled with interest and it's a three-minute walk to the sea. *Minimum two nights July/August.*

Price	From £110. Singles £85.
Rooms	5: 4 doubles, 1 twin.
Meals	Dinner, 3 courses, £38.
Closed	Rarely.
Directions	From Helston, A3083 south. Just before Lizard, left to Church Cove. Follow signs for about 0.75 miles. House on left behind French blue gates.

Susan Thorbek
Landewednack House,
Church Cove, The Lizard,
Helston TR12 7PQ
Tel   +44 (0)1326 290877
Email   luxurybandb@landewednackhouse.com
Web   www.landewednackhouse.com

Entry 58   Map 1

Cornwall

Bay House

Perched on the edge of the map, high on rugged, seapink-tufted cliffs, Bay House is as close to the sea as you can get. Rooms are spacious (one with a bay window), the dining room defers to stunning sunsets and the attention to detail is immaculate. Expect fine original artwork and antiques, Ralph Lauren dressing gowns, designer linen, Molton Brown lotions, iPod docks and DVD players. Scramble down to secluded beaches, stroll to the famous Lizard Lighthouse or relax to the sound of the surf in the beautiful garden under rustling palms and hovering kestrels. Breakfast is outstanding – with John's homemade bread and jams.

Price	£120-£150.
Rooms	2 twins/doubles.
Meals	Pubs/restaurants 5-minute walk.
Closed	Christmas.
Directions	Left in Lizard village, then past playing fields. Take 1st right and at end of road right into Bay House.

Carla Caslin
Bay House,
Housel Bay, The Lizard TR12 7PG
Tel +44 (0)1326 290235
Mobile +44 (0)7740 168805
Email carla.caslin@btinternet.com
Web www.mostsoutherlypoint.co.uk

Cornwall

Trerose Manor

Follow winding lanes through glorious countryside to find the prettiest, listed manor house, a warm family atmosphere and welcoming tea in the beamed kitchen. Large, light bedrooms, one with floor-to-ceiling windows, sit peacefully in your own wing and have views over the stunning garden. All are dressed in pretty colours, have comfy seats for gazing and smartly tiled bathrooms. A sumptuous breakfast can be taken outside in summer, there are lovely walks over fields to river or beach, stacks of interesting places to visit and lots to read in the library for the lazy. Lovely. *French, German & Italian spoken.*

Price	£110-£125. Singles £75.
Rooms	3 doubles.
Meals	Pubs/restaurants within walking distance.
Closed	Rarely.
Directions	Left at Red Lion in Mawnan Smith. After 0.5 miles right down Old Church Road. After 0.5 miles house on right through white gate immediately after Trerose Farm.

Tessa Phipps
Trerose Manor,
Mawnan Smith,
Falmouth TR11 5HX
Tel +44 (0)1326 250784
Email info@trerosemanor.co.uk
Web www.trerosemanor.co.uk

Cornwall

Bosvathick

A huge old Cornish house that's been in Kate's family since 1760 – along with Indian rugs, heavy furniture, ornate plasterwork, pianos, portraits, pets... even a harp. Historians will be in their element: pass three Celtic crosses dating from the 7th century before the long drive finds the imposing house (all granite gate posts and lions) and a rambling garden with grotto, lake, pasture and woodland. Bedrooms are simple and traditional, full of books and antiques; bathrooms are spick and span, one plain and functional, one new. Come to experience a 'time warp' and charming Kate's good breakfasts. Close to Falmouth University, too.

Price	From £80. Singles £40-£60.
Rooms	4: 1 twin/double, 1 twin, 2 singles; 2 bathrooms. Each party has sole use of a bathroom.
Meals	Supper, with wine, from £30. Packed lunch £5-£10. Pubs 2 miles.
Closed	Rarely.
Directions	From Constantine, signs to Falmouth. 2 miles, pass Bosvathick Riding Stables, next entrance on left. Drive thro' gateposts & green gate. A map can be sent to visitors.

Kate & Stephen Tyrrell
Bosvathick,
Constantine,
Falmouth TR11 5RD
Tel   +44 (0)1326 340103
Email   kate@bosvathickhouse.co.uk
Web   www.bosvathickhouse.co.uk

Entry 61   Map 1

Cornwall

Nearwater

St Mawes is gorgeous, a tiny town on the Roseland peninsula that paddles in the sea. In summer sailing boats flutter on the water, dodging the ferry as it nips across to Falmouth. Nearwater matches the mood perfectly, its airy interiors filled with seaside chic. White walls soak up the light, a driftwood mirror hangs above the fire, there are maps for walkers, a sofa to sink into, games and books aplenty. Uncluttered bedrooms have blond wood furniture, blue and white blankets, crisp linen, fantastic bathrooms. Delicious breakfasts set you up for the day, so pull on your walking boots or hire a kayak in town.

Price	£95-£105. Singles from £85.
Rooms	3: 2 doubles, 1 twin/double.
Meals	Pubs/restaurants in village.
Closed	24-27 December.
Directions	A3078 south into St Mawes. Keep left and house signed on left in village.

Tim & Amelia Whitaker
Nearwater,
Polvarth Road, St Mawes,
Truro TR2 5AY
Tel   +44 (0)1326 279278
Email   bookings@nearwaterstmawes.co.uk
Web   www.nearwaterstmawes.co.uk

Entry 62   Map 1

Cornwall

Hay Barton

Giant windows overlook many acres of farmland, and Jill and Blair look after you so well! Breakfasts are special with the best local produce, homemade granola, yogurt and more. Arrive for tea and lovely home-baked cake, laid out in a comfortable guest sitting room with a log fire and plenty of books and maps. Bedrooms are fresh and pretty with garden flowers, soft white linen on big beds and floral green walls. Gloriously large panelled bathrooms have long roll top baths and are painted in earthy colours. You can knock a few balls around the tennis court, and you're near to good gardens and heaps of places to eat.

Price	£80. Singles £60.
	Min. stay 2 nights in summer.
Rooms	3 twins/doubles.
Meals	Pubs 1-2 miles.
Closed	Rarely.
Directions	A3078 from Tregony village
	towards St Mawes. After 1 mile,
	house on left, 100 yds down lane.

Jill & Blair Jobson
Hay Barton,
Tregony, Truro TR2 5TF
Tel   +44 (0)1872 530288
Mobile   +44 (0)7813 643028
Email   jill@haybarton.com
Web   www.haybarton.com

Entry 63   Map 1

Cornwall

Ashby Villa

Lesley is wonderfully friendly and outgoing and invites you for a cream tea in her kitchen. The village is lively but the Dog House, just for guests, is tucked into the courtyard behind, overlooking gardens and fields. Comfy bedrooms have a roll top tub or power shower, cosy rugs on tiled floors, local art, French country furniture and doors opening to a shared terrace. Zip over to the communal conservatory of this Edwardian home for a tasty breakfast and John's homemade bread. The Roseland Peninsula has secret coves and Truro is close; return with fresh fish for your own barbecue! Then relax in the candlelit conservatory.

Price	£80-£85. Studio £105.
	Singles on request.
Rooms	Dog House: 2 doubles; 1 studio
	with extra sofabed & kitchenette.
Meals	Light meals available. Pub in
	village. Barbecue available.
Closed	Rarely.
Directions	Sent on booking.

Lesley Black
Ashby Villa,
Fore Street,
Tregony, Truro TR2 5RW
Tel   +44 (0)1872 530189
Email   blacklesley5@aol.com
Web   www.cornwallvillagebedandbreakfast.co.uk

Entry 64   Map 1

Cornwall

Creed House

A beautiful Georgian rectory surrounded by a truly lovely Cornish garden. Light pours into every elegant corner and your gracious hosts give you fresh, traditional bedrooms in a peaceful wing where sheets are crisp, colours are gentle, flowers are from the garden and you have your own cosy sitting room. Local breads and jams, fruit salads and a full English await you at breakfast – enjoyed in the handsome dining room warmed by a log fire. Perfect for exploring Cornwall's wonderful gardens and coast – excellent restaurants are nearby. *NGS garden.*

Price	£90.
Rooms	2: 1 double, 1 twin.
Meals	Pub/restaurant 1 mile.
Closed	Christmas & New Year.
Directions	From St Austell, A390 to Grampound. Just beyond clock tower, left into Creed Lane. After 1 mile, left at grass triangle opp. church. House behind 2nd white gates on left.

Jonathon & Annabel Croggon
Creed House,
Creed,
Grampound, Truro TR2 4SL
Tel   +44 (0)1872 530372
Email   jrcroggon@btinternet.com
Web   www.creedhouse.co.uk

Entry 65   Map 1

Cornwall

Collon Barton

Come for the lofty position on a grassy hillside, the heartlifting views over unspoiled countryside and the pretty creekside village of Lerryn. This 18th-century house is a working sheep farm and an artistic household (sculptures galore). Interesting and generous Anne and Iain give you eggs from their free-range chickens, traditional airy bedrooms in pink or blue and an elegant drawing room. Anne sells huge dried hydrangeas and, on sunny days, welcomes you with tea in the summer house. Wonderful riverside and coastal walks and good gardens; the Eden Project is 20 minutes away. *Children & pets by arrangement.*

Price	£80. Singles £40.
Rooms	2: 1 twin/double, 1 twin/double with dressing room & extra beds.
Meals	Pub 10-minute walk.
Closed	Rarely.
Directions	A390 to Lostwithiel. After Lostwithiel sign 1st left, signed Lerryn. 200 yds, left at 1st x-roads for Lerryn. After 2 miles, at top of hill, hard left signed Bodmin & Liskeard. Immed. right by 5-bar gate, stone farm lane.

Anne & Iain Mackie
Collon Barton,
Lerryn,
Lostwithiel PL22 0NX
Tel   +44 (0)1208 872908
Mobile   +44 (0)7721 090186
Email   annemackie@btconnect.com

Entry 66   Map 1

Cornwall

Polgassick Farmhouse

Trundle down the lovely leafy track to emerge into the remains of a former farm. The B&B is in the main farmhouse, 300 years old, where Sue, Becky and their family live. Passionate about local produce they are generous to a fault, and their meals are delicious and convivial. Off the dining room, cosy with Cornish art and gas-fired burner, a staircase leads to good bedrooms above, one with a super-king bed, the other, high-raftered, opening to outside stone steps with pretty garden below. Stay all day if you like – it's bliss for families (and pets!). Or be ferried into charming Fowey and Lostwithiel. Great value.

Price	£75–£90. Singles £60. Family room from £100
Rooms	3: 2 doubles; 1 family room for 2-4 by arrangement.
Meals	Dinner, 2 courses, from £25. Pub 1.5 miles.
Closed	Rarely.
Directions	Sent on booking.

	Sue Tarry
	Polgassick Farmhouse,
	Nomansland, Lostwithiel PL22 0HY
Tel	+44 (0)1208 873503
Mobile	+44 (0)7900 577700
Email	polgassick@aol.com
Web	www.lostwithielbandb.co.uk

Entry 67   Map 1

Cornwall

Hornacott

The garden, in its lovely valley setting, has seats in little corners poised to catch the evening sun – perfect for a pre-dinner drink. The peaceful house is named after the hill and you have a private entrance to your airy suite: a room with a large bed plus a lofty sitting room with a balcony and windows that look down onto the wooded valley. With CD player, music, chocolates and magazines you are truly self-contained. Jos, a kitchen designer, and Mary-Anne love having guests and living the slow life – busily! – and give you top-notch local produce and free-range eggs for breakfast.

Price	From £95. Singles £50.
Rooms	2: 1 suite; 1 twin with separate shower.
Meals	Dinner, 3 courses, £20. BYO. Pubs/restaurants 4.5 miles.
Closed	Christmas.
Directions	B3254 Launceston-Liskeard. Through South Petherwin, down steep hill, last left before little bridge. House 1st on left.

	Jos & Mary-Anne Otway-Ruthven
	Hornacott,
	South Petherwin,
	Launceston PL15 7LH
Tel	+44 (0)1566 782461
Email	otwayruthven@btinternet.com
Web	www.hornacott.co.uk

Entry 68   Map 1

Cornwall

St Leonards House

Enjoy gardens, history, riding, fishing? John runs tailormade tours for groups and individuals, and knows Cornwall like the back of his hand; Jane is an embroiderer whose curtains add colour to the rooms. The twin, downstairs, overlooks the garden; the doubles are up; expect good mattresses, anti-allergic duvets, bath oils and waffle robes. Breakfast is served in a low-ceilinged dining room whose beams attest to the house's age and whose tiled floor is elegantly rugged. You are on the edge of Launceston, quaint capital of Cornwall, and close to the great beaches of Widemouth Bay, Crackington Haven and Bude.

Price	£80. Singles £50.
Rooms	3: 2 doubles, 1 twin.
Meals	Pub/restaurant 2 miles.
Closed	Christmas & New Year.
Directions	From Launceston A30 towards Polson. Opposite rugby club take road to St Leonards. After 150 yds house is next to the Equitation Centre.

John & Jane Marshall
St Leonards House,
Polson, Launceston PL15 9QR
Tel   +44 (0)1566 779195
Email   enquiries@stleonardshouse.co.uk
Web   www.stleonardshouse.co.uk

Entry 69   Map 2

Cornwall

Cadson Manor

This lovely old manor, with spectacular views across the Lynher valley, has been in the Crago family for generations. Chatty and friendly Brenda looks after you well; expect flowers, log fires, homemade cakes and delicious breakfasts with eggs from the hens. Everything shines, from the slate hall floor and antique furniture to the pretty china and talkative parrot. Fish in the lake, picnic in the grounds or walk Cadson Bury among Highland cattle. Bedrooms and bathrooms have hotel comfort, rich drapes and thoughtful extras. Historic houses, gardens, the Eden Project, golf and the coast are all close, and the walks are sublime.

Price	£96. Singles £65.
Rooms	4: 2 doubles; 1 double, 1 twin sharing bath (let to same party only).
Meals	Pub/restaurant 3 miles.
Closed	Occasionally.
Directions	From Callington, A390 Liskeard road. House signed on left just after going over the river Lynher.

Brenda Crago
Cadson Manor,
Callington PL17 7HW
Tel   +44 (0)1579 383969
Email   brenda.crago@btclick.com
Web   www.cadsonmanor.co.uk

Entry 70   Map 2

Cornwall

Pentillie Castle

So many temptations: woodland gardens that tumble down to the Tamar, a walled Victorian kitchen garden still being restored, a magnificent Victorian bathing hut… and Pentillie beef cattle, uniquely theirs, grazing either side of the great drive up to the handsome house. Bedrooms are smart, spacious and deeply comfortable, bathrooms pamper. Ted and Sarah, with daughter Sammie, have mastered that delicate balancing act between luxury and stuffiness, bringing out one and banishing the other. It's the sort of place where you gasp at the perfection of it all and then throw your shoes off before diving into the sofa.

Price	£125–£200.
Rooms	9: 8 twins/doubles, 1 four-poster suite.
Meals	Dinner, 3 courses, £30. Pubs/restaurants 15-minute drive.
Closed	Rarely.
Directions	Cross Tamar River into Cornwall on A38. Right onto A388. 3.1 miles, then right at Paynters Cross. Entrance within 100 yds.

Sammie Coryton
Pentillie Castle,
St Mellion, Saltash PL12 6QD
Tel +44 (0)1579 350044
Email contact@pentillie.co.uk
Web www.pentillie.co.uk

Entry 71   Map 2

Cornwall

Lantallack Farm

You will be inspired here, in generous Nicky's heart-warming old Georgian farmhouse. Find a straw-yellow sitting room with a log fire, books to read and a grand piano; views are breathtaking across countryside, streams and wooded valley. Bedrooms have deliciously comfy beds; Polly's Bower, a romantic hideaway in the old cider barn, is a charming open-plan space with whitewash and old beams, wood-burner and freestanding tub. Breakfast in the walled garden on fine days: apple juice from the orchard and bacon and sausages from down the road. There are 40 acres to explore, a leat-side trail and a heated outdoor pool; marvellous.

Price	From £95. Polly's Bower £120. Min. stay 2 nights.
Rooms	2: 1 double. Polly's Bower: 1 double with sitting area & kitchen.
Meals	Pubs/restaurants 1 mile.
Closed	Rarely.
Directions	A38 thro' Saltash, continue 3 miles. At Landrake 2nd right at West Lane. After 1 mile, left at white cottage for Tideford. House 150 yds on, on right.

Nicky Walker
Lantallack Farm,
Landrake, Saltash PL12 5AE
Tel +44 (0)1752 851281
Email enquiries@lantallack.co.uk
Web www.lantallackgetaways.co.uk

Entry 72   Map 2

Cumbria

Lavender House

An 1850s house – the local vet's for many years – a comfortable stroll from the centre of the bustling little market town with its interesting shops and pubs; John can collect you if you come by train. Tea and homemade cake are served in the sitting room – admire Diana's lovely paintings on the walls – with comfy chairs and a fire on chilly days. Bedrooms are bright, with vibrant cushions and antique furniture; bathrooms have big mirrors, thick towels and plenty of soaps and bubbles. On sunny mornings try a Manx kipper on the roof terrace with its 'Mary Poppins' views and smart potted plants. *Minimum two nights at weekends.*

Price	£75–£85. Singles from £40.
Rooms	2: 1 double; 1 twin/double with separate bath.
Meals	Packed lunch £6. Pub/restaurant 150 yds.
Closed	Rarely.
Directions	M6 junc. 36; A65 Kirkby Lonsdale. After 6.5 miles, left at r'bout. Pass Booth's supermarket. Right at junc. House 50 yds on left; park in drive.

John & Diana Craven
Lavender House, 17 New Road,
Kirkby Lonsdale LA6 2AB
Tel   +44 (0)1524 272086
Mobile   +44 (0)7775 564157
Email   info@lavenderhousebnb.co.uk
Web   www.lavenderhousebnb.co.uk

Entry 73   Map 12

Cumbria

A Corner of Eden

In this Georgian farmhouse, set in a glorious valley with infinite sky and distant Cumbrian hills, tradition and comfort luxuriously combine. The sitting room has a cosy log fire and delicious candlelit breakfasts are served in the beamed dining room. Bedrooms glow with original fireplaces, polished wooden floors and rich fabrics. Engaging Richard and Debbie live in the byre and show a passion for detail: robes and slippers for shared bathrooms, sloe gin in the rooms, barbours by the door, an honesty bar and home-bakes in the dairy. Offset any indulgence by a walk to the pub across the fields. *Self-catering available.*

Price	£120.
Rooms	4: 2 doubles, 1 four-poster, 1 twin, all sharing 2 bathrooms. Max 3 rooms let at any one time (unless whole house let).
Meals	Dinner, 3 courses, £34 (only for house parties). Pub 1 mile.
Closed	Christmas.
Directions	M6 junc. 38, Brough A685. Right into Ravenstonedale; through village until The Fat Lamb, then right. After 0.5 miles left to Stennerskeugh, keep bearing left.

Debbie Temple & Richard Greaves
A Corner of Eden, Low Stennerskeugh,
Ravenstonedale, Kirkby Stephen CA17 4LL
Tel   +44 (0)1539 623370
Mobile   +44 (0)7759 469059
Email   enquiries@acornerofeden.co.uk
Web   www.acornerofeden.co.uk

Entry 74   Map 12

Cumbria

Drybeck Hall

Looking south to fields, woodland and beck this Grade II* listed, 1679 farmhouse has blue painted mullion windows and exposed beams. Expect a deeply traditional home with good furniture, an open fire and pictures of Anthony's predecessors looking down on you benignly; the family has been in the area for 800 years. Comfortable bedrooms have pretty floral fabrics and oak doors; bathrooms are simple but sparkling. Lulie is relaxed and charming and a good cook: enjoy a full English with free-range eggs in the sunny dining room, and home-grown vegetables and often game for dinner. A genuine slice of history.

Cumbria

Sirelands

Sirelands, once a gardener's cottage, stands among rhododendrons and spreading trees on a sunny slope, a stream trickling by: a stunning spot. The Carrs have lived here for years and the house has a relaxed and homely feel. Enjoy home-grown produce at dinner on a polished table, then retire to the sitting room, delightful with log basket, honesty bar, flowers and books. Sash windows overlook the wooded garden, visited by roe deer and a wide variety of birds. Bedrooms and bathrooms are pleasant, peaceful and spotless; one loo has an amazing view! Friendly Angela loves cooking and treats you to tea and homemade cake.

Price	£90. Singles £45.		Price	£90.
Rooms	2: 1 double, 1 twin.		Rooms	2: 1 twin; 1 double with separate bath/shower.
Meals	Dinner, 3 courses, £25. Pub/restaurant 4 miles.		Meals	Dinner, 2-3 courses, £22-£27.50. Pubs within 5 miles.
Closed	Rarely.		Closed	Christmas & New Year.
Directions	From A66 south on B6260. After Hoff take 2nd left signed Drybeck, left at bottom of hill, then left at fork. House on left.		Directions	M6 to junc. 43; A69 Newcastle; 3 miles to traffic lights. Right, on to Heads Nook; house 2 miles after village.

Lulie & Anthony Hothfield
Drybeck Hall,
Appleby-in-Westmorland CA16 6TF

Tel	+44 (0)1768 351487
Email	lulieant@aol.com
Web	www.drybeckhall.co.uk

David & Angela Carr
Sirelands,
Heads Nook, Brampton,
Carlisle CA8 9BT

Tel	+44 (0)1228 670389
Mobile	+44 (0)7748 101513
Email	carr_sirelands@btconnect.com

Cumbria

Warwick Hall

The position here is magnificent, a slice of English heaven. The house stands resplendently in 260 acres on the banks of the river Eden, one of the best salmon beats in the country; a two-mile stroll hugs the water. Inside, everything is gorgeous: vast windows that flood the place with light; a wonderful drawing room with sofas in front of the fire; a dining room with views of hill and river. Delightful country-house bedrooms have high ceilings, beautiful fabrics, super bathrooms; one has its own fire. Bonnie Prince Charlie once stayed, though not in the comfort you can expect. Delicious food and a great atmosphere, too.

Price	£120. Suites £180. Catered house party rates available.
Rooms	8: 6 twins/doubles; 2 suites with kitchenettes.
Meals	Dinner, 3 courses, £30. Restaurant 1 mile.
Closed	Rarely.
Directions	M6, junc. 43, then A69 east. After 2 miles, pass town sign and on left down hill before bridge.

Val Marriner
Warwick Hall,
Warwick-on-Eden, Carlisle CA4 8PG
Tel +44 (0)1228 561546
Mobile +44 (0)7818 448756
Email info@warwickhall.org
Web www.warwickhall.org

Entry 77 Map 11

Cumbria

Chapelburn House

Yomp in the most dramatic scenery close to the best bits of Hadrian's Wall, then head for Chapelburn House. Matt and Katie are young, charming, unflappable, food is reared happily then cooked with more flavour than fuss. Honey is from their bees, bread is home-baked. You have a sitting room with an open fire, lots of books and squishy sofas, *and* a south-facing garden room for summer dreaming. Bedrooms are deeply comfortable and bathrooms (one definitely not for fatties!) brand spanking new. Children are more than welcome to join in. This would delight exhausted refugees from London, too.

Price	£70-£90. Singles £55.
Rooms	2 doubles.
Meals	Dinner, 3 courses, £25. Packed lunch £5-£7.50. Restaurant 5 miles.
Closed	Christmas & New Year.
Directions	From Newcastle, A69 west for 40 miles. Right to RAF Spadeadam; next left to Low Row. Chapelburn House 1 mile on left.

Matthew & Katie McClure
Chapelburn House,
Low Row,
Brampton CA8 2LY
Tel +44 (0)1697 746595
Email stay@chapelburn.com
Web www.chapelburn.com

Entry 78 Map 11

Cumbria

Black Dub

History, country and culture in a Victorian farmhouse with views to the North Lakes and Pennines: a wonderful, secluded location near Hadrian's Wall and the Scots border. Sweep through antique-filled drawing and dining rooms where deep blues, pinks and golds set off watercolours and modern oils; sash windows filter afternoon sun, views sail over paddocks, ornamental lake and bird-rich gardens. Your big comfortable bedroom with small pretty bathroom faces west. Ask Liz and Patrick (born and bred Cumbrians) about their horsewoman daughter and Richard Hoare's art, Everest, their spaniels and the best pubs, abbeys, castles...

Price	£90. Singles £55.
Rooms	1 double with separate bath & sitting room (extra bed available).
Meals	Pub 2 miles.
Closed	Christmas & New Year.
Directions	Sent on booking.

	Liz & Patrick Osborne
	Black Dub,
	Heads Nook, Brampton CA8 9BX
Tel	+44 (0)1768 896258
Mobile	+44 (0)7713 643315
Email	osborne.blackdub@gmail.com
Web	www.blackdubcumbria.co.uk

Entry 79   Map 12

Cumbria

Morland House

Off the village 'square' and down the drive is Morland House – with a four-acre garden so special it opens to the public. Your friendly hosts welcome you in to an eccentrically historic and rambling home, early Victorian but with older parts, full of dark panelling and oak boarded floors, family antiques and big old oils... rugs, china, glass, swords and medals. After a convivial supper, sink into the sofa by the wood-burner or retire to a cosy carpeted bedroom upstairs, one with pretty views to Morland's church (with rare Saxon tower). Wake to a full Cumbrian breakfast; book a steamer to cross Ullswater – it's only 12 miles!

Price	£98-£120. Singles £64-£75.
Rooms	3: 1 double, 1 twin; 1 double with separate bath/shower.
Meals	Supper, 2 courses with glass of wine, £20. Café/restaurant in village (Fri/Sat).
Closed	Most of November to March.
Directions	See owner website.

	Suzanna Balfour
	Morland House,
	Morland,
	Penrith CA10 3AZ
Tel	+44 (0)1931 714989
Email	enquiries@morlandhouse.net
Web	www.morlandhouse.net

Entry 80   Map 12

Cumbria

Kelleth Old Hall

Glorious unimpeded views of fields, cows and the Howgill Fells from this fun and characterful B&B. Charlotte – chutney enthusiast, writer of three novels – has moved into an ancient manor (the fourth owner in 400 years); now it glows with paintings, antiques and books. Short steep stairs lead from 17th-century flagstones to a big canopied brass bed and yellow silk curtains at mullion windows. All is warm, charming, inviting, and that includes the roll top bath beneath a vaulted ceiling. Fuel up on a Cumbrian breakfast, return to a delicious supper of exotic flavours. Near the A685 but peaceful at night.

Price	£84. Singles £67.
Rooms	1 double (with extra single bed).
Meals	Dinner, 2-3 courses, £18-£22.
	Pub/restaurant 5 miles.
Closed	Rarely.
Directions	Sent on booking.

Charlotte Fairbairn
Kelleth Old Hall,
Kelleth, Penrith CA10 3UG
Tel   +44 (0)1539 623344
Mobile +44 (0)7754 163941
Email   charlottefairbairn@hotmail.co.uk
Web   www.kelletholdhall.co.uk

Entry 81   Map 12

Cumbria

Lazonby Hall

The pinky sandstone façade rises, château-like, from bright flowers, box hedges, crunchy gravel: enchanting. Views, from sash windows and garden folly, yawn over the Eden valley to the Pennines. Step past pillars to panelled, antique-filled rooms of heavy curtains, marble fires, mahogany and oils. Formal, yet not daunting – the Quines and their daschunds bring life, flexibility, and delicious Cumbrian breakfasts. Wake to birdsong and garden views. This sweet area of winding lanes and dry stone walls is near the north Lakes, Penrith, Carlisle, Scotland, ripe for exploration by foot, bike, canoe or train.

Price	£80-£120. Singles £50-£80.
Rooms	3: 1 double;
	1 twin, 1 double sharing bath.
Meals	Supper, 3 courses, £20-£40.
	Cold platters from £10.
	Pub/restaurant 2 miles.
Closed	Rarely.
Directions	Sent on booking.

Mr & Mrs Quine
Lazonby Hall,
Lazonby,
Penrith CA10 1BA
Tel   +44 (0)1768 870800
Email info@lazonbyhall.co.uk
Web   www.lazonbyhall.co.uk

Entry 82   Map 11

Cumbria

Johnby Hall

You are ensconced in the quieter part of the Lakes and have independence in this Elizabethan manor house – once a fortified Pele tower, now a family home. Two suites (one in the studio, next to the main house) are fresh and light: each has its own sitting room with lots of books and pictures, squashy sofas, pretty fabrics and whitewashed walls. Beds have patchwork quilts, windows have stone mullions and there is absolute quiet. Henry gives you sturdy breakfasts, and good home-grown suppers by a roaring fire in the great hall; he and Anna can join you or leave you in peace. Walks from the door are sublime.

Price	£110-£125. Singles £80-£90.
Rooms	2: 1 family suite. Studio: 1 family suite.
Meals	Supper, 2 courses, £20. Pub 1 mile.
Closed	Rarely.
Directions	M6 Penrith junc. 40. A66 west approx. 2 miles; right-hand exit signed Greystoke. At T-junction left to Greystoke. At Greystoke follow signs right then left to Johnby. Hall on left after 1 mile.

Henry & Anna Howard
Johnby Hall,
Johnby,
Penrith CA11 0UU
Tel +44 (0)17684 83257
Email bookings@johnbyhall.co.uk
Web www.johnbyhall.co.uk

Entry 83 Map 11

Cumbria

Whitbysteads

Swing into the yard of a gentleman's farmhouse at the end of a drive lined with gorse, stone walls and sheep. It's a working farm, so lots going on with four-wheel drives, dogs, busy hens and relaxed bustle. Victoria does styles and periods well: warm rugs, flowery sofas with plain linen armchairs, modern family paintings. The main bedroom is sumptuous and stylish, the smaller rooms simpler; bathrooms are wonderfully vintage, eclectic and big. Great hosts who make you feel instantly at home here; enjoy the breathtaking views over the fells – easy for the M6 too. Dress up in the evening for dinner at Sharrow Bay.

Price	£90-£110. Singles £45.
Rooms	3: 1 double; 1 double, 1 twin sharing bath (let to same party only).
Meals	Dinner from £20. Children's tea £5. Pub 0.5 miles.
Closed	Rarely.
Directions	From the South, exit 39 M6. From the North, exit 40 M6. North of Askham. See owner website for full directions.

Victoria Lowther
Whitbysteads,
Askham, Penrith CA10 2PG
Tel +44 (0)1931 712284
Mobile +44 (0)7976 276961
Email victoria@whitbysteads.org
Web www.whitbysteads.org

Entry 84 Map 11

Cumbria

Greenah

Tucked into the hillside off a narrow lane, this 1750s smallholding is surrounded by fells, so is perfect for walkers. Absolute privacy for four friends or family with your own entrance to a beamed and stone-flagged sitting room with wood-burning stove, creamy walls and cheery floral curtains. Warm bedrooms have original paintings, good beds, hot water bottles, bathrobes and a sparkling bathroom with a loo with a remarkable view. Malcolm is a climber; Marjorie is totally committed to organic food so you get a fabulous breakfast, and good advice about the local area. Fell walking is not compulsory! *Over eights welcome.*

Price	£90–£95. Singles £60–£65.
Rooms	2: 1 double; 1 twin sharing shower (let to same party only).
Meals	Pubs/restaurants 3 miles.
Closed	December/January.
Directions	M6 junc. 40 follow A66 west. Left for Matterdale; after 1.5 miles, left signed Dacre. Up the hill, right fork to Lowthwaite, house 100 yds on right.

Marjorie & Malcolm Emery
Greenah,
Matterdale, Penrith CA11 0SA
Tel   +44 (0)1768 483387
Mobile   +44 (0)7767 213667
Email   info@greenah.co.uk
Web   www.greenah.co.uk

Entry 85   Map 11

Cumbria

Lowthwaite

Leave your worries behind as you head up the lanes to the farmhouse tucked into the fell. Jim, ex-hiking guide, and Danish Tine moved back from Tanzania with their daughters in 2007 and give you four peaceful bedrooms in the view-filled barn wing. Handsomely chunky twin beds are of recycled dhow wood, crisp light bathrooms sport organic soaps and you wake to the smell of homemade bread; breakfasts are fine Scandinavian and English inspired spreads. In a garden full of bird feeders and pheasants a stream trickles through one of the guest terraces, and there are endless fells to explore. A treat for peace-seekers and families.

Price	£60–£90. Singles £40–£70.
Rooms	4: 2 twins/doubles, 2 family rooms.
Meals	Packed lunch £6. Dinner £18–£27. Pubs 2.5 miles.
Closed	Christmas.
Directions	Penrith M6 junc. 40, A66 towards Keswick. Left opposite B5288 onto Matterdale road. After 1.25 miles, left after Walloway Farm. Up hill, then right signed 'Lowthwaite 1'.

Tine & Jim Boving Foster
Lowthwaite,
Matterdale,
Penrith CA11 0LE
Tel   +44 (0)1768 482343
Email   info@lowthwaiteullswater.com
Web   www.lowthwaiteullswater.com

Entry 86   Map 11

Cumbria

Howe Keld

Dismiss all thoughts of the chintzy Keswick guest house: David and Val have swept through with carpets made of Herdwick sheep wool, bedroom furniture made by a local craftsman, gorgeous fabrics, striking wallpaper and smart bathrooms with green slate. It's luxurious but not flashy, and there's a cosy sitting room in primary colours crammed with local info; theatre, shops and restaurants are all strolling distance (choose rooms at the front if you need total quiet). Fill up at breakfast on home-baked bread, freshly made smoothies or a jolly good fry-up. *Minimum stay two nights at weekends, three on bank holidays.*

Price	£80–£130. Singles £45–£60.
Rooms	14: 13 doubles, 1 single.
Meals	Pub/restaurant 300 yds.
Closed	Part of December including Christmas. Most of January excluding New Year.
Directions	Penrith M6, junc. 40; W A66. 18 miles; r'bout with A591. Left towards Keswick; 800 yds, left at junc. On to mini r'bout in high street, then right. After 600 yds right into The Heads.

David Fisher
Howe Keld,
5/7 The Heads,
Keswick CA12 5ES

Tel	+44 (0)1768 772417
Email	david@howekeld.co.uk
Web	www.howekeld.co.uk

Entry 87   Map 11

Cumbria

Willow Cottage

Gaze across rooftops through tiny windows towards the towering mass of Skiddaw, the Lakes' third highest mountain. Here is a miniature cottage garden with sweet peas, herbs and vegetables... all suitably rambling; admire it from the cosy garden room. Roy and Chris have kept most of the old barn's features: wooden floorboards, wonderful beams. Dried flowers, pretty china, antique linen, glowing lamps and patchwork quilts, a collection of christening gowns... dear little bedrooms have panelled bathrooms (one small) and old pine furniture. TV is delightfully absent, classical music plays and you are in the heart of a farming village.

Price	£65–£70. Singles £50.
Rooms	Barn: 1 double, 1 twin.
Meals	Packed lunch £5. Pub 300 yds.
Closed	December/January.
Directions	From Keswick A591 towards Carlisle (6.5 miles) right for Bassenthwaite village (0.5 miles). Straight on at village green, house on right.

Roy & Chris Beaty
Willow Cottage,
Bassenthwaite,
Keswick CA12 4QP

Tel	+44 (0)1768 776440
Email	chriswillowbarn@googlemail.com
Web	www.willowbarncottage.co.uk

Entry 88   Map 11

Cumbria

Boltongate Old Rectory

The setting of this lovely old rectory could hardly be more pastoral; many of its rooms face south and have superb fells views. Furniture is a beautiful mix of antique and contemporary – handmade Harris mattresses, big chunky sofas – in a house whose roots go back to 1360. The treats continue at table: Gill is passionate about sourcing organic and local ingredients for her kitchen, David knows his wines and you eat by candlelight in a 16th-century room. They're relaxed and charming and, when the place is full, create a fabulous house-party feel. Outside: red squirrels and well-fed rabbits, a croquet lawn and stunning Skiddaw.

Price	From £120. Singles from £95.
Rooms	3: 1 double, 1 twin/double; 1 double with separate bath.
Meals	Dinner, 3 courses, £33. Pub 10-minute drive.
Closed	Sundays & Mondays. December/January.
Directions	B5305 to Wigton; at A595, left. After 5 miles, left to Boltongate. Left at T-junc.; in village, signs for Ireby; down hill, last driveway on left.

Gill & David Taylor
Boltongate Old Rectory,
Boltongate, Ireby, Wigton CA7 1DA

Tel +44 (0)1697 371647
Mobile +44 (0)7763 242969
Email boltongate@talk21.com
Web www.boltongateoldrectory.com

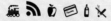

Entry 89   Map 11

Cumbria

New House Farm

The large comfy beds, the extravagant baths, the linen, the fabrics, the pillows – comfort par excellence! The renovation is impressive, too; the plasterwork stops here and there to reveal old beam, slate or stone. A trio of the bedrooms are named after the mountain each faces; Swinside brings the 1650s house its own spring water. The breakfast room has a wood-burner, hunting prints and polished tables for Hazel's breakfasts to fuel your adventures, the sitting room sports fireplaces and brocade sofas, and walkers will fall gratefully into the hot spring spa. Luxurious, and huge fun. *Children over six welcome.*

Price	£140-£180. Singles £70-£120.
Rooms	5: 2 doubles, 1 twin/double. Stables: 2 four-posters.
Meals	Lunch from £6 (April-November). Dinner, 3-5 courses, £30-£37. Packed lunch £8. Afternoon tea £3. Pubs 2.5 miles.
Closed	Rarely.
Directions	A66 to Cockermouth, then B5289 for Buttermere. Signed left 2.5 miles south of Lorton.

Hazel Thompson
New House Farm,
Lorton,
Cockermouth CA13 9UU

Mobile +44 (0)7841 159818
Email hazel@newhouse-farm.co.uk
Web www.newhouse-farm.com

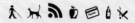

Entry 90   Map 11

Cumbria

Cockenskell Farm

The house and hill farm garden with its wild rhododendrons and damson orchard sits at the southern end of Lake Coniston and the views are glorious. Inside find beamed rooms, art and antique pine; bedrooms have pretty patchwork covers and lovely wallpapers. Relax with a book in the conservatory, stroll through the magical, bird-filled garden or tackle a bit of the Cumbrian Way which meanders through the fields to the back. On sunny days Sara will give you breakfast in the conservatory. History seeps from every pore, the place glows with loving care and to stay here is a treat. *Children over 12 welcome.*

Price	£90. Singles from £45.
Rooms	2: 1 twin; 1 twin with separate bath.
Meals	Packed lunch £7.50. Pubs 2-4 miles.
Closed	November-February.
Directions	In Blawith, opp. church up a narrow lane, through farmyard. Right after cattle grid, over fell, right at fork through gates & up drive.

Sara Keegan
Cockenskell Farm,
Blawith, Ulverston LA12 8EL

Tel	+44 (0)1229 885217
Mobile	+44 (0)7909 885086
Email	keegan@cockenskell.fsnet.co.uk
Web	www.cockenskell.co.uk

Entry 91   Map 11

Cumbria

Low Fell

Steve and Louise are great fun, their warmth is infectious and their well-orchestrated house is packed with maps, lists, books and guides. Bedrooms are bright, sunny, pretty, with elegant patterned or checked fabrics, heavenly big beds, plump pillows, warm towels; the suite up in the loft is a super hideaway and you overlook trees animated with birds. Tuck into warm homemade bread, croissants and bacon butties at breakfast, warm your toes by the fire in winter, relax in the lovely secluded garden with a glass of wine in summer. The house is a five-minute stroll from the lake, good bistros and bustling Bowness. *Over tens welcome.*

Price	£70. Half price for children.
Rooms	2: 1 double, 1 family suite (1 double, 1 twin).
Meals	Continental breakfast. Full breakfast menu available at owners' hotel, £8, 0.75 miles. Pubs/restaurants 200 yds.
Closed	Christmas.
Directions	Sent on booking.

Louise & Stephen Broughton
Low Fell, Ferney Green, Bowness-on-Windermere, Windermere LA23 3EW

Tel	+44 (0)1539 445612
Mobile	+44 (0)7921 057552
Email	louisebroughton@btinternet.com
Web	www.low-fell.co.uk

Entry 92   Map 11

Cumbria

Gilpin Mill

Come to be seriously spoiled. Down leafy lanes is a pretty white house by a mill pond, framed by pastures and trees. Steve took a year off to build new Gilpin Mill, and Jo looks after hens, labs and guests – beautifully. In the country farmhouse sitting room oak beams span the ceiling and a slate faux-lintel sits above the log fire. Bedrooms are equally inviting: beds are topped with duck down, luscious bathrooms are warm underfoot. Alongside is a lovely old barn where timber was made into bobbins; in the mill pond is a trout ladder and dam, soon to provide power for the grid. And just six cars pass a day!

Price	£85-£105. Singles £60-£70.
Rooms	3 twins/doubles.
Meals	Pub 2.5 miles.
Closed	Christmas.
Directions	Kendal to Windermere, 1st roundabout B5284 to Crook. Left at Crook church, follow signs to Winster; house is on the river.

Jo & Steve Ainsworth
Gilpin Mill,
Crook,
Windermere LA8 8LN
Tel   +44 (0)1539 568405
Email   info@gilpinmill.co.uk
Web   www.gilpinmill.co.uk

Entry 93   Map 11

Cumbria

Fellside Studios

Off the beaten tourist track, a piece of paradise in the Troutbeck valley: seclusion, stylishness and breathtaking views. Prepare your own candlelit dinners, rise when the mood takes you, come and go as you please. The flower beds spill with heathers, hens cluck, and there's a decked terrace for continental breakfast in the sun – freshly prepared by your gently hospitable hosts who live in the attached house. In your studio apartment you get oak floors, slate shower rooms, immaculate kitchenettes with designer touches, DVD players, comfy chairs, luxurious towels. Wonderful. *Minimum stay two nights.*

Price	£70-£90. Singles from £45.
Rooms	2 studios: 1 double, 1 twin/double & kitchenette each.
Meals	Pub/restaurant 0.5 miles.
Closed	Rarely.
Directions	From Windermere, A592 north for 3 miles; after bridge, immed. before church, left signed Troutbeck; 300 yds, 1st house on right.

Monica & Brian Liddell
Fellside Studios,
Troutbeck,
Windermere LA23 1PE
Tel   +44 (0)1539 434000
Email   brian@fellsidestudios.co.uk
Web   www.fellsidestudios.co.uk

Entry 94   Map 11

Cumbria

Gillthwaite Rigg

All is calm and ordered in this airy and tranquil Arts and Crafts house. Come for nature and to be surrounded by Beatrix Potter countryside – you may spot a badger or deer. Find panelled window seats, gleaming oak floors, leaded windows, wooden latched doors and motifs moulded into white plaster. Bedrooms with original fireplaces and large comfy beds have an uncluttered simplicity and lake and fell views. Banks of books, wood-burners, proper Cumbrian breakfasts and kind, affable hosts add cheer. Rhoda and Tony are passionate about conservation and wildlife in their 14 acres of garden and woodland. *Babies & children over six welcome.*

Price	£70–£85. Singles £55.
Rooms	2: 1 double, 1 twin/double.
Meals	Pubs/restaurants 1 mile.
Closed	Christmas & New Year.
Directions	M6 junc. 36; A590 & A591 to r'bout; B5284 (signed 'Hawkshead via ferry') for 6 miles. After golf club, right for Heathwaite. Bear right up hill past nursery. Next drive on right; central part of manor.

Rhoda M & Tony Graham
Gillthwaite Rigg, Heathwaite Manor,
Lickbarrow Rd, Windermere LA23 2NQ
Tel   +44 (0)1539 446212
Mobile   +44 (0)7765 415934
Email   tony_rhodagraham@hotmail.com
Web   www.gillthwaiterigg.co.uk

Entry 95   Map 11

Cumbria

Summerhow House

In four acres of fine landscaping and fun topiary is a large and inviting home of flamboyant wallpapers and shades of aqua, lemon and rose. Stylish but laid-back, grand but unintimidating, both house and hosts are a treat. Bedrooms have gilt frames and marble fireplaces, Molton Brown goodies and garden views, there are two sitting rooms to retreat to and breakfasts to delight you – fruits from the orchard, eggs from Sizergh Castle (John's family home). Two miles from Kendal: hop on the train to the Lakes. Walkers, sailors, skiers, food-lovers, dog-lovers will be charmed... aspiring actors too (talk to Janey!).

Price	£80–£120. Singles £50–£69.
Rooms	2: 1 double, 1 twin.
Meals	Pub/restaurant 1.5 miles.
Closed	Occasionally.
Directions	M6, junc. 36 for Kendal. Then follow signs for A6 Shap & on outskirts of Kendal, as 40mph zone ends, immediate next right at white gates. House signed on wall next to gate.

Janey & John Hornyold-Strickland
Summerhow House,
Shap Road,
Kendal LA9 6NY
Tel   +44 (0)1539 720763
Email   stay@summerhowbedandbreakfast.co.uk
Web   www.summerhowbedandbreakfast.co.uk

Entry 96   Map 11

Cumbria

Lapwings Barn

In the back of most-beautiful-beyond, down narrow lanes, this converted barn is a gorgeous retreat for two – or four. Delightful generous Gillian and Rick give you privacy and an upstairs sitting room with log stove, sofa and a balcony with views. Bedrooms (separate entrances) are elegantly rustic with sweeping beams and modern, stone-tiled bathrooms. Breakfast is delivered: sausages and bacon from their Saddlebacks, eggs from their hens, superb homemade bread and marmalade. Stroll along lowland tracks, watch curlews and lapwings, puff to the top of Whinfell. Ambleside and Beatrix Potter's house are near. One of the best.

Price	£60–£90. Singles from £35.
Rooms	Barn: 2 twins/doubles & sitting room.
Meals	Packed lunch £5. Pub/restaurant 3.5 miles.
Closed	Rarely.
Directions	A685 Kendal-Appleby. After 500 yds, left signed Mealbank; over hill after Mealbank, after 2nd bridge at Patton, middle road of 3. After Borrans Farm, left fork; 0.25 miles on left.

Rick & Gillian Rodriguez
Lapwings Barn,
Whinfell, Kendal LA8 9EQ

Tel	+44 (0)1539 824373
Mobile	+44 (0)7901 732379
Email	stay@lapwingsbarn.co.uk
Web	www.lapwingsbarn.co.uk

Entry 97   Map 12

Derbyshire

Underleigh House

A Derbyshire longhouse in Brontë country built by a man called George Eyre. The position is unbeatable – field, river, hill, sky – but the stars of the show are Philip and Vivienne, dab hands at spoiling guests rotten. There's a big sitting room with maps for walkers, a dining room hall for hearty breakfasts, and tables and chairs scattered about the garden. Back inside, bedrooms vary in size, but all have super beds, goose down duvets and good views; a couple have doors onto the garden, the suites have proper sitting rooms. Fantastic walks start from the front door, Castleton Caves are on the doorstep, Chatsworth is close.

Price	£85–£105. Singles from £65.
Rooms	5: 3 doubles, 2 suites.
Meals	Packed lunches £5. Pubs/restaurants 0.5 miles.
Closed	Christmas & January.
Directions	A6187 west into Hope. Right for Edale opposite church. Left onto Lose Hill Lane after 0.6 miles, then house on right in 0.25 miles.

Philip & Vivienne Taylor
Underleigh House,
Lose Hill Lane, Hope,
Hope Valley S33 6AF

Tel	+44 (0)1433 621372
Email	info@underleighhouse.co.uk
Web	www.underleighhouse.co.uk

Entry 98   Map 12

Derbyshire

Horsleygate Hall

Hens and guinea fowl animate the charming old stable yard, and the gardens are vibrant and fascinating, with stone terraces and streams, hidden patios, modern sculptures and seats in every corner... the Fords, attentive and kind, encourage you to explore. Inside the 1783 house, Margaret has created yet more charm. There is a warm, timeless, harmonious feel, with worn kilims on pine boards, striped and floral wallpapers, deep sofas and pools of light. Breakfast is served round a big table in the old schoolroom – homemade jams and oatcakes, garden fruit, eggs from the hens. Special. *Children over five welcome.*

Price	£70–£85. Singles £45–£55.
Rooms	3: 1 double; 1 family room, 1 twin sharing bath.
Meals	Pubs/restaurant 1 mile.
Closed	23 December–4 January.
Directions	M1 exit 29; A617 Chesterfield. 4th exit, 1st r'bout A61, dual c'way; 2nd exit at 3rd r'bout B6050. 2 miles then right at T-junc., B6051 to Barlow & Millthorpe; 1 mile to Horsleygate Lane on right. House at bottom of lane.

Robert & Margaret Ford
Horsleygate Hall,
Horsleygate Lane,
Holmesfield S18 7WD

Tel +44 (0)1142 890333

Entry 99 Map 8

Derbyshire

River Cottage

Well-travelled Gilly and John have restored their large house – built in the 1740s – and given it a fresh modern twist. Interiors are light and airy, with mirrors, antiques and immaculate fabrics giving each room a charm of its own. Attention to detail includes Gilly's legendary breakfasts – and five types of tea! Outside: a lovely tiered garden with the river Wye running through; easy to ignore the busy A6 when settled here with a glass of wine. Ashford-in-the-Water is one of the prettiest villages in the Peaks, fishing can be arranged and you are ten minutes from Chatsworth – there's a bus stop right outside the door.

Price	£90–£125. Singles from £75. Min. 2 nights at weekends Easter–October.
Rooms	4: 3 doubles; 1 double with separate bath.
Meals	Pubs 600 yds.
Closed	Rarely.
Directions	On northern edge of Ashford village, 1.5 miles N of Bakewell on A6. Buses from Nottingham, Matlock, Manchester & Buxton stop outside the door.

Gilly & John Deacon
River Cottage, Buxton Road,
Ashford-in-the-Water,
Bakewell DE45 1QP

Tel +44 (0)1629 813327
Email info@rivercottageashford.co.uk
Web www.rivercottageashford.co.uk

Entry 100 Map 8

Derbyshire

Hungry Bentley Barn

Off a lane in the tranquil Dales, a beautiful, light-filled, modern interpretation of a barn conversion, renovated by Jane and Brian. Genial and relaxed, she breeds dressage horses and walls are hung with equine prints and oils; his passion is vintage cars... a spin in the Bentley may be offered. Find pale chintzy sofas by a huge fireplace, and a grand piano on a toasty warm floor. Up handcrafted oak stairs is a small library of books and maps: a lovely spot to read. Uncluttered cream bedrooms have high ceilings, oak timbers and sandstone floors; bathrooms are fabulous. Wake to rare-breed sausages and homemade preserves.

Derbyshire

Park View Farm

An extravagant refuge after a long journey, run by hospitable hosts. Daringly decadent, every inch of this Victorian farmhouse brims with flowers, sparkling trinkets, polished brass, plump cushions and swathes of chintz. The rooms dance in swirls of colour, frills, gleaming wood, lustrous glass, buttons and bows; eggs from the hens, fresh fruits, homemade breads and their own rare-breed sausages accompany the grand performance. Have afternoon tea on the vine-covered terrace, roam the 370 organic acres. Kedleston Hall Park provides a stunning backdrop. *Children over eight welcome.*

Price	From £78.
Rooms	3: 1 double, 2 four-posters.
Meals	Pubs/restaurants 1.5 miles.
Closed	Christmas, New Year & January.
Directions	From A50 take A515 to Ashbourne. After 4 miles right at crossroads. House 1 mile on right, next to Bentley Hall.

Price	£85-£90. Singles £60.
Rooms	3: 2 four-posters; 1 four-poster with separate bath.
Meals	Pub/restaurant 1 mile.
Closed	Christmas.
Directions	From A52 & A38 r'bout west of Derby, A38 north, 1st left for Kedleston Hall. House 1.5 miles past park on x-roads in Weston Underwood.

Jane Boothroyd
Hungry Bentley Barn, Derby Lane,
Alkmonton, Ashbourne DE6 3DJ

Tel +44 (0)1335 330296
Mobile +44 (0)7931 564985
Email bandb@hungrybentleybarn.co.uk
Web www.hungrybentleybarnbandb.co.uk

Linda Adams
Park View Farm, Weston Underwood,
Ashbourne DE6 4PA

Tel +44 (0)1335 360352
Mobile +44 (0)7771 573057
Email enquiries@parkviewfarm.co.uk
Web www.parkviewfarm.co.uk

Entry 101   Map 8

Entry 102   Map 8

Derbyshire

Tinkersley Cottage

Sarah has painstakingly reassembled two run-down cottages at the very top of a hill, with the giddiest views over the Peak District's loveliest parts. You can tell she's a stylist: find pretty stripes and florals, painted wood panelling, chandeliers and shabby chic. Your comfortable small bedroom, restful with antique linen, painted French bed, Farrow & Ball colours – is delightfully private with its own sitting area, terrace for the views and entrance up steps from the colourful garden. Sarah is bright and bubbly and loves having guests; breakfast is sourced locally – Chatsworth farm shop and Bakewell farmers' market are nearby.

Price	£85.
Rooms	Garden Room: 1 suite.
Meals	Pubs/restaurants within 1 mile.
Closed	Rarely.
Directions	A6 Bakewell to Matlock. Through Rowsley, East Lodge Hotel on left, after 0.5 miles Barn Lane on left. House at top of hill.

Sarah Copley
Tinkersley Cottage,
Tinkersley, Rowsley,
Matlock DE4 2NJ
Tel +44 (0)7802 494814
Email sarahcopley16@hotmail.co.uk
Web www.tinkersleycottage.co.uk

Entry 103　Map 8

Derbyshire

Old Shoulder of Mutton

The lively village of Winster is mega-pretty; the Old Shoulder of Mutton, once a pub, sits in its middle. Steven and Julie are friendly and their home is as cosy as can be. Find a charming contemporary and traditional mix, framed clay pipes (found during renovations), a little drawing room, luxurious bedrooms and snazzy bathrooms. Breakfast is by the wood-burner: feast on eggs Benedict, homemade jam, local bacon and the famous Derbyshire oatcakes. There's a lovely and unexpected garden at the back; Bakewell, with its legendary Monday market and Chatsworth House, is a short drive, and the walking is dreamy. *Over 12s welcome.*

Price	From £90.
Rooms	3: 2 doubles, 1 twin/double.
Meals	Pubs in village.
Closed	Rarely.
Directions	Sent on booking.

Steven White
Old Shoulder of Mutton,
West Bank, Winster,
Matlock DE4 2DQ
Tel +44 (0)1629 650005
Email steven@theoldshoulderofmutton.co.uk
Web www.oldshoulderofmutton.co.uk

Entry 104　Map 8

Derbyshire

Manor Farm

Between two small dales, close to great houses (Chatsworth, Hardwick Hall, Haddon Hall), lies this cluster of ancient farms and church; welcome to the 16th century! Simon and Gilly, warm, delightful and fascinated by the history, have restored the east wing to create big, beamy rooms in the old hayloft and a pretty garden room on the ground floor; a cosy and quaint bedroom overlooks the church. Wake to a scrumptious organic breakfast in the atmospheric Elizabethan kitchen. There's a 'book exchange' in the old milking parlour and a lovely garden with sweeping views across the valley and distant hills. *Children over six welcome.*

Price	£80–£90. Singles £55–£70.
Rooms	4: 1 double, 3 twins/doubles.
Meals	Pubs within 10-minute drive.
Closed	Rarely.
Directions	M1 exit 28. A38, then A615 dir. Matlock. Thro' Wessington, after 1 mile, past Plough pub on right. Take 3rd turning on left after Plough (Dethick Lane). Down lane for 1 mile to Dethick.

Simon & Gilly Groom
Manor Farm,
Dethick, Matlock DE4 5GG
Tel   +44 (0)1629 534302
Mobile   +44 (0)7944 660814
Email   gilly.groom@w3z.co.uk
Web   www.manorfarmdethick.co.uk

Entry 105   Map 8

Derbyshire

Mount Tabor House

On a steep hillside between the Peaks and the Dales, a chapel with a peaceful aura and great views. Enter a hall where light streams through stained-glass windows – this is a relaxed, easy place to stay with a distinctive and original interior and a log-burner to keep you toasty; Fay is charming and generous. Breakfast, served in a dining room with open stone walls, is delicious, mainly from the village shops and as organic as possible; you can eat on the balcony in summer. Walk to the pub for dinner, then retire to your inviting, big comfortable bed. *Usually minimum stay two nights at weekends.*

Price	£85. Singles £60.
Rooms	1 twin/double.
Meals	Occasional dinner £25. Pub 100 yds.
Closed	Rarely.
Directions	M1 exit 26; A610 towards Ripley. At Sawmills, right under r'way bridge, signed Crich. Right at marketplace onto Bowns Hill. Chapel 200 yds on right. Can collect from local stations.

Fay Whitehead
Mount Tabor House,
Bowns Hill, Crich,
Matlock DE4 5DG
Tel   +44 (0)1773 857008
Mobile   +44 (0)7813 007478
Email   mountabor@msn.com

Entry 106   Map 8

Devon

Orchard Cottage

Tucked into a quiet village corner, this is the last cottage in a row of three. Walk through the pretty garden, past seats that bask in the English sun and around to your own entrance and terrace... you may come and go as you please. Your bedroom is L-shaped and large, with a comfortable brass bed and a super en suite shower; it is both rustic and spotless. The Ewens are friendly and fun – their spaniel equally so. Modbury has an eclectic mix of shops and you're brilliantly positioned for Dartmoor, Plymouth and sandy beaches. Breakfasts in the beamy light-filled dining room are generous and delicious. This is excellent value B&B.

Price	From £60. Singles £45.
Rooms	1 double.
Meals	Pubs 300 yds.
Closed	Christmas.
Directions	A379 from Plymouth for Modbury. On reaching Church St at top of hill, before Modbury, fork left at Palm Cross, then immed. 1st right into Back St. Cottage 3rd on left, past village hall.

Maureen Ewen
Orchard Cottage,
Back Street, Palm Cross Green,
Modbury PL21 0RF
Tel +44 (0)1548 830633
Mobile +44 (0)7979 558568
Email moewen@talktalk.net

Entry 107   Map 2

Devon

Annapurna

Rural bliss: the garden of this pretty, cream-painted longhouse surrounded by fields of cows looks down the folded valley to the steeple of Modbury Church. Inside, Carol and Peter spoil you with blueberry pancakes, organic home-baked bread and eggs from their happy hens for breakfast. Charming bedrooms with a fresh country feel have garden flowers, sparkling bathrooms and wonderfully comfortable beds. The views over the church and valley stretch for miles, fabulous walking starts from the door and you are close to the watery delights of Salcombe and Dartmouth. Guests love this place: "Carol and Peter are perfect hosts!"

Price	£70–£80. Singles £35–£40.
Rooms	2: 1 twin/double; 1 single (double bed) with separate bath.
Meals	Pubs/restaurants 1 mile.
Closed	Rarely.
Directions	A38 Modbury & Ermington. After 1.5 miles approx. Kittaford Cross straight on, thro' California Cross. After 2.4 miles left down unmarked lane. House 300 yds on right.

Carol Farrand & Peter Foster
Annapurna,
Mary Cross, Modbury PL21 0SA
Tel +44 (0)1548 831299
Mobile +44 (0)7977 200324
Email carolfarrand@tiscali.co.uk
Web www.annapurna-devon.co.uk

Entry 108   Map 2

Devon

High Barn

A quiet spot among rolling hills with artist Nick, cook Jill, two pointers, an inquisitive cat and roaming chickens. This is a warm, generous household with an easy-going atmosphere: large sofas round a wood-burner, big art and a snooker table. Comfy bedrooms with colourful quilts are downstairs, one opens onto the sunken courtyard. At breakfast you get freshly squeezed juice, homemade preserves, local bacon and just-laid eggs; suppers can be simple or elaborate, or a barbecue in the garden. Explore Dartmoor, walk the coastal paths or head for the beaches; there's plenty of space for your dingy, boards and sandy wetsuits.

Devon

Washbrook Barn

Hard not to feel happy here – even the blue-painted windows on rosy stone walls make you want to smile. Inside is equally sunny. Penny's renovated barn rests in a quiet valley, a short bridleway walk from town. She has transformed it into a series of big light-filled rooms with polished wooden floors, pale beams and richly coloured walls lined with fabulous watercolours; the effect is one of gaiety and panache. No sitting room as such, but armchairs in impeccable bedrooms with pretty rural views. The beds are divinely comfortable and the fresh bathrooms sparkle; wake refreshed to a delicious breakfast served at 8.30.

Price	£60–£70. Singles £40–£45.
Rooms	3: 1 twin/double; 2 family rooms (extra bed/cots available).
Meals	Dinner, 2 courses, from £15. Pubs within 2 miles.
Closed	Rarely.
Directions	A379 west from Kingsbridge to Aveton Gifford. Thro' village, then right past church. Continue 2 miles to Chillaton Cross, then left (after Lixton turning). House 1st on left.

Price	From £80. Singles £60.
Rooms	3 doubles.
Meals	Dinner occasionally available. Pubs/restaurants 10-minute walk.
Closed	Christmas & New Year.
Directions	From Kingsbridge quay to top of Fore St; right into Duncombe St; on to T-junc.; left to Church St. Right into Belle Cross Rd; 150 yds, right into Washabrook Lane; 250 yds left; at bottom on right.

Nick & Jill Bremer
High Barn,
Chillaton, Loddiswell,
Kingsbridge TQ7 4EG

Tel	+44 (0)1548 550838
Email	stay@highbarndevon.co.uk
Web	www.highbarndevon.co.uk

Penny Cadogan
Washbrook Barn, Washabrook Lane,
Kingsbridge TQ7 1NN

Tel	+44 (0)1548 856901
Mobile	+44 (0)7989 502194
Email	penny.cadogan@gmail.com
Web	www.washbrookbarn.co.uk

Entry 109   Map 2

Entry 110   Map 2

Devon

Keynedon Mill

An ancient stone mill with chic refurbished rooms in the old miller's house. Step into a welcoming kitchen with old stone floors and a cheerful red Aga. There's a beamed dining room with a long polished table, a guest sitting room with a wood-burner and a pretty garden with a stream running through; picnic, read and enjoy a glass of wine in secluded spots. Fresh elegant bedrooms are charming too: tip top bedding, antique linen curtains, robes, slippers, garden views and morning tea trays. You eat well on locally sourced produce; Jennifer's coffee is excellent. Walk the coastal path; explore a myriad of tiny coves.

Price	£85–£120. Singles £65.
Rooms	4: 1 double, 1 family room for 3; 2 twins/doubles, each with separate bath/shower.
Meals	Lunch from £10. Picnics from £5. Dinner, 2 courses, from £15. Pub 0.5 miles.
Closed	Rarely.
Directions	Sent on booking.

	Stuart & Jennifer Jebb
	Keynedon Mill,
	Sherford, Kingsbridge TQ7 2AS
Tel	+44 (0)1548 531485
Mobile	+44 (0)7775 501409
Email	bookings@keynedonmill.co.uk
Web	www.keynedonmill.co.uk

Entry 111   Map 2

Devon

Strete Barton House

Contemporary, friendly, exotic and exquisite: French sleigh beds and Asian art, white basins and black chandeliers, and a garden with sofas for the views. So much to love – and best of all, the coastal path outside the door. Your caring hosts live the dream, running immaculate B&B by the sea, in an old manor house at the top of the village. Breakfasts are exuberantly local (village eggs, sausages from Dartmouth, honey from the bay), there's a wood-burner in the sitting room, warm toasty floors and Kevin and Stuart know exactly which beach, walk or pub is the one for you. Heavenly.
Pets in cottage only.

Price	£105–£160. Minimum 2 nights in summer.
Rooms	6: 3 doubles, 1 twin/double; 1 twin/double with separate shower. Cottage: 1 suite & sitting room.
Meals	Pub/restaurant within 50 yds.
Closed	Rarely.
Directions	From Dartmouth, A379 to Kingsbridge. At mini r'bout, left onto A379 signed Stoke Fleming. A379 to Strete, then right into Totnes Rd. House 20 yds up hill on right.

	Stuart Litster & Kevin Hooper
	Strete Barton House,
	Totnes Road, Strete,
	Dartmouth TQ6 0RU
Tel	+44 (0)1803 770364
Email	info@stretebarton.co.uk
Web	www.stretebarton.co.uk

Entry 112   Map 2

Devon

Nonsuch House

The photo says it all! You are in your own crow's nest, perched above the flotillas of yachts zipping in and out of the estuary mouth: stunning. Kit and Penny are great fun and look after you well; ex-hotelier Kit smokes his own fish fresh from the quay and produces brilliant dinners. Further pleasures lie across the water... and a five-minute walk brings you to the ferry that transports you, and your car, to the other side. Breakfasts in the conservatory are a delight, bedrooms are big and comfortable, and fresh bathrooms sparkle. *Over tens welcome. Disabled ramps available.*

Devon

Brightwater House

Hearts will soar: you're right up in the crow's nest here and feeling smugly private, with breathtaking views over the yacht-spotted river to Dartmouth and the Naval College. Painter Susie's 1930s house is splashed with sunlight from three sides in the tiled conservatory with Lloyd Loom chairs, fresh flowers, shelves of books; you breakfast heartily here while boat-watching. The bedroom has its own entrance from the garden terrace (down steep steps), and is small and pretty with white painted furniture, pale silk curtains and Susie's paintings; the bathroom is modern, new and fresh with cream stone tiles. Beguiling.

Price	£110-£150. Singles £85-£125. Min. 2 nights at weekends.
Rooms	4: 3 twins/doubles, 1 double.
Meals	Dinner, 3 courses, £37.50. (Not Tues/Wed/Sat.) Pub/restaurant 5-minute walk & short boat trip.
Closed	Rarely.
Directions	2 miles before Brixham on A3022, A379. Right at r'bout, 100yds on fork left (B3205) downhill, through woods, left up Higher Contour Rd, down Ridley Hill. At hairpin bend. Parking nearby.

Price	£110-£115. Singles £95-£105.
Rooms	1 twin.
Meals	Pubs/restaurants 5-minute walk.
Closed	Rarely.
Directions	Sent on booking.

	Kit & Penny Noble
	Nonsuch House,
	Church Hill, Kingswear,
	Dartmouth TQ6 0BX
Tel	+44 (0)1803 752829
Email	enquiries@nonsuch-house.co.uk
Web	www.nonsuch-house.co.uk

	Susie Bennett
	Brightwater House,
	Higher Contour Road, Kingswear,
	Dartmouth TQ6 0DE
Tel	+44 (0)1803 752898
Email	sben2121@yahoo.co.uk
Web	www.brightwaterhouse.co.uk

Entry 113   Map 2

Entry 114   Map 2

Devon

Kaywana Hall

With glossy modern lines and sparkling glass in its own wooded valley, this is a 'Grand Designs' project in the making. All is smart and contemporary from the great oil paintings and slate and wooden floors to the ultra-crisp bed linen and immaculate bathrooms. The bedrooms are separate from the main house and up steps; one has views over the pool, and its own terrace. The feel is spacious and uncluttered but warm and cosy, too. Friendly Tony gives you delicious locally sourced choices at breakfast, you can hop on the ferry for Dartmouth and close by are regattas, gardens to visit, beaches and steam train and river trips.

Price	£135–£150. Singles £135.
Rooms	3: 2 doubles, 1 twin/double.
Meals	Pub/restaurant 0.5 miles.
Closed	February.
Directions	Torquay towards Brixham; 1 mile from Brixham, turn towards Kingswear. Pass cemetery on left. House next on left.

Anthony Pithers & Gordon Craig
Kaywana Hall,
Higher Contour Road, Kingswear,
Dartmouth TQ6 0AY
Tel +44 (0)1803 752200
Email res@kaywanahall.co.uk
Web www.kaywanahall.co.uk

Entry 115   Map 2

Devon

Kerswell Farmhouse

Close to Totnes yet out in the wilds, this house and barn sit on a ridge with glorious views to Dartmoor. Twelve years ago the Devon longhouse was in poor repair: you'd never know now! All has been transformed by oak – seasoned and new – while the front sports a gorgeous conservatory. Graham sells British art (on fabulous display), Nichola is an interior designer, together they run truly welcoming B&B. Bedrooms are super-comfortable with electronic slatted blinds, bathrooms are state of the art, and the suite comes with its own slice of garden. Books and DVDs are on tap, food and wines are a serious treat. *Over 12s welcome.*

Price	£90–£110. Suite £120–£130. Singles £50–£85. Supplement during Regatta; discount for 6 nights stay.
Rooms	5: 2 doubles; 1 single with separate bath. Barn: 1 twin/double, 1 suite.
Meals	Supper £20. Dinner £30. Restaurants 2 miles.
Closed	24 December–3 January.
Directions	Sent on booking.

Graham & Nichola Hawkins
Kerswell Farmhouse, Kerswell,
Cornworthy, Totnes TQ9 7HH
Tel +44 (0)1803 732013
Mobile +44 (0)7503 335507
Email gjnhawkins@rocketmail.com
Web www.kerswellfarmhouse.co.uk

Entry 116   Map 2

Devon

Stoke Gabriel Lodgings

Deep in dreamy Devon countryside – but up, up high, free, above the river Dart – a deliciously simple, shiny new house where balconies gulp in long light views and large rooms are shot with rich raspberry, deep turquoise, and purple hues. David and Helen's enthusiasm is infectious, both for their home (white walls, oak floors, silk and swish fittings) and village (millpond, jetty, pubs, café and ancient yew). So let them spoil you: cream tea on arrival, smoked salmon for breakfast, an open fire in the family sitting room, a crossword in the conservatory. With these hosts, with this view – you won't want to go home.

Devon

Riverside House

The loveliest 18th-century house with the tidal river estuary bobbing past with boats and birds; dip your toes in the water while sitting in the garden. Felicity, an artist, and Roger, a passionate sailor, give you pretty bedrooms with paintings, poetry, little balconies, wide French windows and binoculars; spot swans at high tide, herons (perhaps a kingfisher) when the river goes down. Stroll to the pub for quayside barbecues and jazz in summer; catch the ferry from Dittisham to Agatha Christie's house; discover delightful Dartmouth. Kayaks and inflatables are welcome by arrangement. *Minimum two nights at weekends.*

Price	£90. Singles £60.
Rooms	3: 2 doubles, 1 twin/double.
Meals	Pubs/restaurants within walking distance.
Closed	Rarely.
Directions	Sent on booking.

Price	From £80. Singles from £65.
Rooms	2: 1 double; 1 double with separate shower.
Meals	Pubs 100 yds.
Closed	Rarely.
Directions	In Tuckenhay, pass Maltsters Arms on left to 2nd thatched house on left, at right angle to road. Drive past, turn at bridge and return to slip lane.

Helen & David Littlefair
Stoke Gabriel Lodgings,
Badger's Retreat, 2 Orchard Close,
Stoke Gabriel, Totnes TQ9 6SX
Tel   +44 (0)1803 782003
Mobile   +44 (0)7785 710225
Email   info@stokegabriellodgings.com

Felicity & Roger Jobson
Riverside House,
Tuckenhay, Totnes TQ9 7EQ
Tel   +44 (0)1803 732837
Mobile   +44 (0)7710 510007
Email   felicity.riverside@hotmail.co.uk
Web   www.riverside-house.co.uk

Entry 117   Map 2

Entry 118   Map 2

Devon

Avenue Cottage

The tree-lined approach is steep and spectacular; the cottage sits in 11 wondrous acres of rhododendron, magnolia and wild flowers with a lily-strewn pond, grassy paths and lovely views over the river. Find a quiet spot in which to read or simply sit and absorb the tranquillity. Richard is a gifted gardener, and the archetypal gardener's modesty and calm have penetrated the house itself – it is uncluttered, comfortable and warmed by a log fire. The old-fashioned twin room has a big, faded bathroom with a faux-marble basin and a balcony with sweeping valley views; the pretty village and pub are a short walk away.

Price	£60–£80. Singles £40–£50.
Rooms	2: 1 twin/double; 1 double sharing shower with owner.
Meals	Pub 0.25 miles.
Closed	Rarely.
Directions	A381 Totnes to Kingsbridge for 1 mile; left for Ashprington; into village, then left by pub ('Dead End' sign). House 0.25 miles on right.

Richard Pitts
Avenue Cottage,
Ashprington, Totnes TQ9 7UT

Tel	+44 (0)1803 732769
Mobile	+44 (0)7719 147475
Email	richard.pitts@btinternet.com
Web	www.avenuecottage.com

Entry 119   Map 2

Devon

Manor Farm

Sarah is a happy gardener, keeping bees and hens too so you can have honey and eggs for breakfast, served in a super red dining room. Michael produces vegetables that will find their way into your (excellent) dinner, and raspberries for your muesli. The farmhouse, facing a communal courtyard, twists and turns around unexpected corners thanks to ancient origins, and its good traditional bedrooms in bright farmhouse colours are reached via two separate stairs – nicely private. Sarah and Michael's labradors are charming and the village is pure Devon: surrounded by apple orchards and with two good pubs for eating out.

Price	From £70. Singles £55–£65.
Rooms	2: 1 double; 1 twin with separate bath/shower.
Meals	Dinner £20–£25. Packed lunch £7.50. Pubs 500 yds.
Closed	Rarely.
Directions	From Newton Abbot, A381 for Totnes. After approx. 2.5 miles, right for Broadhempston. Past village sign, down hill & 2nd left. Pass pub on right & left after high stone wall into courtyard.

Sarah Clapp
Manor Farm,
Broadhempston,
Totnes TQ9 6BD

Tel	+44 (0)1803 813260
Email	mandsclapp@btinternet.com

Entry 120   Map 2

Devon

Kilbury Manor

You can stroll down to the Dart from the garden and onto their little island, when the river's not in spate! Back at the Manor — a listed longhouse from the 1700s — are four super-comfortable bedrooms, the most private in the stone barn. Your genuinely welcoming hosts (with dogs Dillon and Buster) moved to Devon to renovate a big handsome house and open it to guests. Julia does everything beautifully so there's organic smoked salmon and delicious French toast for breakfast, baskets of toiletries by the bath, the best linen on the best beds and a drying room for wet gear — handy if you've come to walk the Moor. Spot-on B&B.

Devon

Agaric Rooms at Tudor House

A merchant's townhouse now happily given over to rooms for the Agaric Restaurant. Sophie and Nick are young, fun and very clever: in these mostly large, individually styled rooms, fabrics are plush, colours rich and bathrooms have roll tops, robes and smart towels; the ground floor double has a striking wet room. A breakfast room is cool with leather and palms; full English or anything else you want is served here. Don't come without booking into the restaurant for fabulous modern British cooking — then stagger two steps down the street to your well-earned bed. Ashburton bustles with good food shops, antiques and books.

Price	£75–£90. Singles from £65.
Rooms	4: 1 double; 1 double with separate bath. Barn: 2 doubles.
Meals	Pubs/restaurants 1.5–4 miles.
Closed	Rarely.
Directions	Leaving A38, left for Totnes. After 0.5 miles, right over river on narrow bridge; follow lane over railway bridge then imm. left into Colston Rd. House 0.25 miles on left.

Price	£110–£130. Singles £50.
Rooms	4: 2 doubles, 1 family room, 1 single.
Meals	Owners' restaurant next door. Packed lunch from £10 for 2.
Closed	Rarely.
Directions	From A38 follow signs to Ashburton. North Street is the main street, house is on right after Town Hall.

Julia & Martin Blundell
Kilbury Manor,
Colston Road,
Buckfastleigh TQ11 0LN
Tel   +44 (0)1364 644079
Email   info@kilburymanor.co.uk
Web   www.kilburymanor.co.uk

Entry 121   Map 2

Sophie & Nick Coiley
Agaric Rooms at Tudor House,
36 North Street,
Ashburton TQ13 7QD
Tel   +44 (0)1364 654478
Email   eat@agaricrestaurant.co.uk
Web   www.agaricrestaurant.co.uk

Entry 122   Map 2

Devon

Penpark

Clough Williams-Ellis of Portmeirion fame did more than design an elegant house; he made sure it communed with nature. High on a hill overlooking the valley, light pours in to this lovely house from every window, and the views stretch across rolling farmland to Dartmoor and Hay Tor. The big double has a comfy sofa and its own balcony; the spacious private suite has arched French windows to gardens and pretty woodland beyond, and an extra room for young children. All is traditional and comforting: antiques, heirlooms, African carvings, silk and fresh flowers, richly coloured rugs. Your charming, generous hosts look after you well.

Price	From £76. Singles by arrangement.
Rooms	3: 1 family suite; 2 twins/doubles, each with separate bath/shower.
Meals	Pubs/restaurants 1-2 miles.
Closed	Rarely.
Directions	A38 west to Plymouth; A382 turn off; 3rd turning off r'bout, signed Bickington. There, right at junc. (to Plymouth), right again (to Sigford & Widecombe). Over top of A38 & up hill; 1st entrance on right.

Madeleine & Michael Gregson
Penpark,
Bickington,
Ashburton TQ12 6LH

Tel	+44 (0)1626 821314
Email	maddy@penpark.co.uk
Web	www.penpark.co.uk

🏵 🐈 🐕 📶 🎑 ✕

Entry 123   Map 2

Devon

Hooks Cottage

At the end of a long bumpy track, the hideaway mine captain's house may have few original features but the woodland setting is gorgeous. Mary and Dick have a finely judged sense of humour; labradors Archie and Cobble will charm you. It is simple, rural, close to the Moors, with woodland birds and a gentle river to unwind stressed souls. Carpeted bedrooms have a faded floral charm and pretty stream views; bathrooms are plain. Enjoy local sausages and Mary's marmalade for breakfast, a lovely garden and amazing bluebells in spring; walks from the house are sublime. Great value, and dogs are welcome too!

Price	From £65. Singles from £40.
Rooms	2: 1 double en suite (wc across landing); 1 twin with separate bath.
Meals	Pub/restaurant 2 miles.
Closed	Rarely.
Directions	From A38, A382 at Drumbridges for Newton Abbot; 3rd left at r'bout for Bickington. 2.7 miles on, down hill, right for Haytor. Under bridge, 1st left & down long, bumpy track, past thatched cottage to house.

Mary & Dick Lloyd-Williams
Hooks Cottage,
Bickington,
Ashburton TQ12 6JS

Tel	+44 (0)1626 821312
Email	hookscottage@yahoo.com
Web	www.hookscottage.co.uk

🏵 🐈 🐕 🚂 📶 🐾 ✕

Entry 124   Map 2

Devon

Longacre

Full of healing energy, a beautiful refuge deep in Devon. Alex, once in the wine trade, now sells his own organic herbs and honey, gets his vegetables from Riverford down the road, seeks out young painters and displays their work, and is passionate about being off-grid. He is also kind, gentle and charming. Bedrooms, zen-like, funky and chic, smell deliciously of wood – the double is womb-like and cosy, with smooth chalky walls and quirky touches, the vaulted suite, flooded with light, has its own little patio. Walk to Dartmoor (four miles), return to comfy sofas, a big log-burner, delicious meals, ancient peace.

Price	£75-£85.
Rooms	2 doubles. Extra single available.
Meals	Supper, 3 courses, £25 (including 2 glasses of wine). Pub/restaurant 300 yds.
Closed	Rarely.
Directions	Sent on booking.

Alex Sampson
Longacre,
Landscove, Ashburton,
Newton Abbot TQ13 7LZ
Tel   +44 (0)1803 762364
Email alex@longacre-bb.co.uk
Web   www.longacre-bb.co.uk

Entry 125   Map 2

Devon

Highfield House

Come for complete peace in the Dartmoor National Park and be bowled over by the glorious garden. Helen is charming and her smart contemporary house gleams; light floods in through huge windows and the south-facing terrace runs the length of the house. Large bedrooms with armchairs are sumptuous, one has its own roof terrace with views of the moor; bathrooms are sparkling and modern. The birds sing, the pale oak floors are heated from underneath and the locally sourced breakfast is generous. Wonderful walks start at the end of the garden and the pretty village has a friendly pub serving good food.

Price	£80-£90. Singles £75-£85.
Rooms	3: 1 double, 2 twins/doubles.
Meals	Pub 300 yds. Restaurants within 5 miles.
Closed	December/January.
Directions	A382 past Bovey Tracey, then left to Lustleigh. Over railway bridge, into village; 3 bungalows & steep hill on right. Up hill & house 7th on left.

Helen Waterworth
Highfield House,
Mapstone Hill, Lustleigh,
Newton Abbot TQ13 9SE
Tel   +44 (0)1647 277577
Email helen@highfieldhousedevon.co.uk
Web   www.highfieldhousedevon.co.uk

Entry 126   Map 2

Devon

Little Shotts at The Shotts

Your own cosy lodge is set in peaceful Dartmoor and edged by beech trees and pines. Inside are huge carved beams (from an Indonesian temple) around the wood-burner, a wonderful collection of amazing doors and a rustic-chic mix of interesting furnishings and vibrant colour. Bedrooms have soft lambswool duvets and good linen – on a Vietnamese four-poster in one; there's a freestanding tub in the pretty bathroom and a small but shiny shower room. Gemma is charming and leaves breakfast for you to cook, so you can rise with the birds or laze until later. Paddle in the brook; walk through the woods for a pub supper.

Price	£85-£139. Minimum stay 3 nights.
Rooms	Lodge: 1 double, 1 four-poster.
Meals	Pubs/restaurants 5-minute walk.
Closed	Rarely.
Directions	Sent on booking.

Gemma Roberts
Little Shotts at The Shotts,
Haytor,
Newton Abbot TQ13 9XX
Tel   +44 (0)1364 661536
Email   gemmasophiaroberts@yahoo.co.uk

Entry 127   Map 2

Devon

Cyprian's Cot

A charming 16th-century terraced cottage filled with beams and burnished wood. The old stone fireplace is huge, the grandfather clock ticks, the views are stunning and Shelagh is warm and welcoming. Guests have their own sitting room with a crackling fire; up the narrow stairs and into cosy bedrooms – a small double and a tiny twin. Tasty breakfasts, served in the dining room, include free-range eggs, sausages and bacon from the local farm and garden fruits. Discover the lovely town with its pubs, fine restaurant and interesting shops. With the Dartmoor Way and the Two Moors Way on the doorstep, the walking is wonderful too.

Price	From £60. Singles from £30.
Rooms	2: 1 twin; 1 double with separate bath.
Meals	Pubs/restaurants 4-minute walk.
Closed	Rarely.
Directions	In Chagford pass church on left; 1st right beyond Globe Inn opposite. House 150 yds on right.

Shelagh Weeden
Cyprian's Cot,
47 New Street, Chagford,
Newton Abbot TQ13 8BB
Tel   +44 (0)1647 432256
Email   shelaghweeden@btinternet.com
Web   www.cyprianscot.co.uk

Entry 128   Map 2

Devon

Bagtor House

What a setting! A ten-minute walk and you're on top of the moor. Enfolded by garden, fields and sheep, the 15th-century listed house with the Georgian façade is the last remaining manor in the parish. Find ancient beauty in granite flagstones, oak-panelled walls, great fireplaces glowing with logs, country dressers brimming with china. Sue looks after hens, geese, labs, guests, grows everything and makes her own muesli. She gives you a large and elegant double room with an antique brass bed, and an oak-panelled family room with a four-poster and adjoining twin. Warm, homely, spacious, civilised, and close to beautiful Hay Tor.

Price	From £80. Singles by arrangement.
Rooms	2: 1 double; 1 family room with separate bath/shower.
Meals	Restaurants/pubs 1.5 miles.
Closed	Christmas.
Directions	From A38 to Plymouth, A382 turn off at r'bout, 3rd exit to Ilsington; up through village, 2nd left after hotel (to Bickington), 1st crossroads right to Bagtor, 0.5 miles, on right next to farm.

Sue & Nigel Cookson
Bagtor House,
Ilsington, Newton Abbot TQ13 9RT
Tel +44 (0)1364 661538
Email sawreysue@hotmail.com
Web www.bagtormanor.co.uk

Entry 129 Map 2

Devon

Corndonford Farm

An ancient Devon longhouse and an engagingly chaotic haven run by warm and friendly Ann and Will, along with their Shire horses and Dartmoor ponies. Steep, stone circular stairs lead to bedrooms: bright colours, a four-poster with lacy curtains, gorgeous views over the cottage garden and a bathroom with a beam to duck. A place for those who want to get into the spirit of it all – maybe help catch an escaped foal, chatter to the farm workers around the table; not for fussy types or Mr and Mrs Tickety Boo! Delicious Aga breakfasts and good for walkers too – the Two Moors Way is on the doorstep. *Over tens by arrangement.*

Price	£70. Singles £35.
Rooms	2: 1 four-poster; 1 twin with separate bathroom.
Meals	Pub 2 miles.
Closed	Rarely.
Directions	From A38 2nd Ashburton turn for Dartmeet & Princetown. In Poundsgate pass pub on left; 3rd right on bad bend signed Corndon. Straight over x-roads, 0.5 miles, farm on left.

Ann & Will Williams
Corndonford Farm,
Poundsgate,
Newton Abbot TQ13 7PP
Tel +44 (0)1364 631595
Email corndonford@btinternet.com

Entry 130 Map 2

Devon

Heron Cottage

Folded into a valley in an idyllic corner of Dartmoor is a freshly renovated riverside B&B – one of two adjoining 18th-century cottages. You have complete privacy in your own Swedish style wooden house down by the water – a light, airy, roomy space with cosy triple-glazing and sparkling shower room. Your hosts – outgoing, musical, hospitable and well-travelled – bring you delicious breakfasts (local eggs and sausages, homemade bread and jams) at flexible times; in summer it's served beside the tumbling river with buzzards soaring above. The Two Moors Way runs right by the door and this magical haven is loved by all who stay.

Price	£85. Singles £55.
Rooms	Garden house: 1 double.
Meals	Pub 2 miles.
Closed	Rarely.
Directions	Bovey Tracy to Widecombe, then Ponsworthy road for 1.2 miles, then 1st right and 1st left to Jordan. Left again, down to bottom of hill. Cottage on bend.

Sue Bottomley
Heron Cottage, Jordan,
Widecombe-in-the-Moor,
Newton Abbot TQ13 7PN
Tel   +44 (0)1364 631596
Email sue@patrickgarvey.demon.co.uk
Web   www.heroncottagedartmoor.co.uk

Entry 131   Map 2

Devon

Tor Royal Farm

A Georgian farmhouse with a regal history, and sweeping views over the rolling moor; a peace-seeker's dream. Behind the listed façade find an enclosed courtyard and bell tower, a big light-filled open-sitting room, plush beds (one downstairs, the rest up), soft carpets and soothing colours. Farmer's wife Justine serves a full English breakfast (almost all their own produce, from apple juice to bacon) at antique drop-leaf tables, loves meeting guests and will happily tell you of the history. Spot foxes, badgers, plovers in the garden, gallop off on a horse, stroll to the village pubs – and return to a lovely warm wood-burner.

Price	£100. Singles from £50.
Rooms	5: 2 doubles, 2 twins/doubles, 1 single.
Meals	Dinner from £30. Packed lunch available. Pubs/restaurants 1 mile.
Closed	Rarely.
Directions	Sent on booking.

Justine Colton
Tor Royal Farm, Tor Royal Road,
Princetown, Yelverton PL20 6SL
Tel   +44 (0)1822 890189
Mobile +44 (0)7892 910666
Email   torroyal@gmail.com
Web   www.torroyal.co.uk

Entry 132   Map 2

Devon

Mount Tavy Cottage

Between Dartmoor and Tavistock, this 250-year-old former gardener's bothy has been made into a warm and welcoming home by Jo and Graham. Pretty bedrooms in the house have stripped floorboards, a four-poster or half-tester bed and freestanding baths. Two simpler bedrooms, each with a big shower, are across the courtyard in the garden studios; here you can be completely independent, or trot over to the house for a delicious breakfast. Lots to enjoy outside too: a cider orchard with beehives, a walled garden, rare-breed pigs in the wood and a lake with a thatched dining spot. *Arrivals after 5pm, unless previously arranged.*

Price	From £70. Singles from £35.
Rooms	4: 1 double, 1 four-poster, both with separate bath. 2 studios: 1 twin/double & kitchenette each.
Meals	Dinner, 3 courses, £25. Pub 2 miles.
Closed	Rarely.
Directions	From Tavistock B3357 towards Princetown; 0.25 miles on, after Mount House School, left. Drive past lake to house.

	G H Moule Mount Tavy Cottage, Tavistock PL19 9JL
Tel	+44 (0)1822 614253
Mobile	+44 (0)7776 181576
Email	mounttavy@btinternet.com
Web	www.mounttavy.co.uk

Entry 133   Map 2

Devon

Burnville House

Granite gateposts, Georgian house, rhododendrons, beechwoods and rolling fields of sheep: that's the setting. But there's more. Beautifully proportioned rooms reveal subtle colours, elegant antiques, squishy sofas and bucolic views, stylish bathrooms are sprinkled with candles, there are sumptuous dinners and pancakes at breakfast. Your hosts left busy jobs in London to settle here, and their place breathes life – space, smiles, energy. Swim, play tennis, walk to Dartmoor from the door, take a trip to Eden or the sea. Or… just gaze at the moors and the church on the Tor and listen to the silence, and the sheep.

Price	From £80. Singles £55.
Rooms	3 doubles.
Meals	Dinner from £19. Pub 2 miles.
Closed	Rarely.
Directions	A30 Exeter-Okehampton; A386 dir. Tavistock. Right for Lydford opp. Dartmoor Inn; after 4 miles (thro' Lydford), Burnville Farm on left (convex traffic mirror on right).

	Victoria Cunningham Burnville House, Brentor, Tavistock PL19 0NE
Tel	+44 (0)1822 820443
Mobile	+44 (0)7881 583471
Email	burnvillef@aol.com
Web	www.burnville.co.uk

Entry 134   Map 2

Devon

Higher Eggbeer Farm

Over 900 years old and still humming with life. A farming menagerie share the rambling gardens, and children can't believe their luck: ponies to shampoo, kittens to play with, piglets to feed. Sally Anne and sons, Alistair and Robin, are wonderful hosts: friendly, artistic, fun and slightly wacky. It's an adventure to stay so keep an open mind as the house is a historic gem and undeniably rustic. Huge fireplaces, interesting art, books, piano, wellies, muddle and lived-in charm; the family are happy to babysit too. Be wrapped in peace in one of two wings, immersed in a panorama of forest, hills and fields of waving wheat.

Price	£85. Singles £65.
Rooms	East wing: 1 double, 1 twin sharing bath & shower (same party only). West wing: 2 doubles, 1 twin, 1 single, all sharing bath & 2nd wc. Self-catering option.
Meals	Restaurants 5-minute walk.
Closed	Rarely.
Directions	A30 to Okehampton. 10 miles, left exit into Cheriton Bishop; 1st left after Old Thatch pub, signed Woodbrooke. Down & up hill; road turns sharp left but you don't. Right down private lane.

Sally Anne Selwyn & Alistair Scott Lawson
Higher Eggbeer Farm,
Cheriton Bishop, Exeter EX6 6JQ
Tel +44 (0)1647 24427
Mobile +44 (0)7850 136131
Email ascottlawson@gmail.com

Entry 135 Map 2

Devon

Brook Farmhouse

Tuck yourself up in the peace and quiet of Paul and Penny's whitewashed, thatched cottage, surrounded by glorious countryside. Inside find your own charming sitting room with a huge inglenook, good antiques, fresh flowers, and comfy sofa and chairs; breakfast here on homemade apple juice, eggs from the owners' hens and delicious local bacon and sausages. Up the ancient spiral stone stairs is your warm, beamed bedroom with smooth linen, chintzy curtains, lots of cushions. You are near Dartmoor and can reach the Devon beaches and the north Cornish coast; perfect for hearty walkers, birdwatchers, surfers and picnic-lovers.

Price	£80. Singles £50.
Rooms	1 double with separate bathroom.
Meals	Pub 2 miles.
Closed	Christmas & New Year.
Directions	In Tedburn village turn into North Park Rd opp. garage, then right at T-junc. after bridge. House on right after 1.4 miles at bottom of steep hill.

Paul & Penny Steadman
Brook Farmhouse,
Tedburn St Mary,
Exeter EX6 6DS
Tel +44 (0)1647 270042
Email penny.steadman@btconnect.com
Web www.brook-farmhouse.co.uk

Entry 136 Map 2

Devon

Larkbeare Grange

Expectations rise as you follow the tree-lined drive to the immaculate Georgian house… and are met, the second you enter. The upkeep is perfect, the feel is chic and the whole place exudes well-being. Sparkling sash windows fill big rooms with light, floors shine and the grandfather clock ticks away the hours. Expect the best: good lighting, goose down duvets, contemporary luxury in fabric and fitting, a fabulous suite perfect for a small family, flexible breakfasts and lovely views from the bedrooms at the front. Charlie, Savoy-trained, and Julia are charming and fun: you are in perfect hands.

Price	£102–£185. Singles £85–£115.
Rooms	4: 2 doubles, 1 twin/double, 1 suite.
Meals	Pub 1.5 miles.
Closed	Rarely.
Directions	From A30 Exmouth & Ottery St Mary junc. At r'bouts follow Whimple signs. 0.25 miles, right; 0.5 miles, left signed Larkbeare. Grange 1 mile on left.

Charlie & Julia Hutchings
Larkbeare Grange,
Larkbeare,
Talaton, Exeter EX5 2RY
Tel +44 (0)1404 822069
Email stay@larkbeare.net
Web www.larkbeare.net

Entry 137   Map 2

Devon

Lower Allercombe Farm

Horses in the paddock and no-frills bedrooms at this down-to-earth, very friendly B&B. Don't expect twinsets and pearls; Susie, ex-eventer, may greet you in two-tone jodhpurs instead. She and Lizzie (her terrier) live at one end of the listed longhouse, guests at the other. There's a sitting room with horsey pictures and wood-burner, and bedrooms upstairs that reflect the fair price. You'll feast on home eggs and tomatoes in the morning, and rashers from award-winning pigs. Very handy for Exeter, the south coast and Dartmoor; the airport is ten minutes away, the A30 is one mile. *Stabling available.*

Price	£60–£70. Singles £40–£50.
Rooms	3: 1 double, 1 twin; 1 double with separate bath.
Meals	Pub/restaurant 2 miles.
Closed	Rarely.
Directions	From Exeter junc. 29, M5. A30 towards Honiton. At Daisymount exit to Ottery St Mary, B3180 off r'bout. 200 yds, then right to Allercombe. 1 mile until x-roads, then right. House 50 yds on right.

Susie Holroyd
Lower Allercombe Farm,
Rockbeare, Exeter EX5 2HD
Tel +44 (0)1404 822519
Mobile +44 (0)7980 255107
Email holroyd.s@gmail.com
Web www.lowerallercombefarm.co.uk

Entry 138   Map 2

Devon

Beach House

Lapping at the riverside garden is the Exe estuary, wide and serene. Birds and boats, the soft hills beyond, a gorgeous Georgian house on the river and interesting hosts who have been here for years. The garden is pretty with quirky rooster-shaped topiary and old apple trees; you may have a locally sourced breakfast in the conservatory or dining room, and there are raspberries and blackberries from the garden when in season. Relax on comfortable chairs in bedrooms with lovely estuary views; charmingly old-fashioned bathrooms are sparkling. Cycle into Exeter for culture and cathedral; an RSPB reserve is five minutes away.

Price	From £90. Singles £60.
Rooms	2: 1 twin, 1 double.
Meals	Pubs/restaurants 8-minute walk.
Closed	December–March.
Directions	M5 exit 30; signs to Exmouth. After approx. 2 miles right at pub. After 1 mile, immed. left after level crossing. At mini r'bout, left down The Strand. House last on left by beach.

Trevor & Jane Coleman
Beach House,
45 The Strand,
Topsham,
Exeter EX3 0BB
Tel +44 (0)1392 876456
Email janecoleman45@hotmail.com

Entry 139   Map 2

Devon

Pebbles

Once owned by the Duchess of Westminster, this neat 1920s house has spectacular views of sea, surf and seagulls. Gentle, friendly Humfrey and Rosemary have mixed old with new, fun art with recycled pieces. Bedrooms, with big comfy beds, face the sea; spotless bathrooms sport robes and good lotions. The Sail Loft has two plantation chairs and a sweet extra room with twin beds; two rooms have their own little conservatories. Breakfast is a spread: compotes, homemade muesli, good bacon. Stride the coast path, visit castles, spot dolphins from the conservatory, soak up those huge views.
Minimum two nights April-Sept.

Price	From £99. Singles from £89.
Rooms	3: 1 twin/double; 2 twins/doubles each with separate bath.
Meals	Pubs/restaurants within 100 yds.
Closed	Rarely.
Directions	From Exeter A30 or M5 to junc. 30. A365 signed Exmouth. Left on B3179 signed Budleigh Salterton. Into town, thro' high street. House on right next to tourist information centre.

Humfrey & Rosemary Temple
Pebbles,
16 Fore Street,
Budleigh Salterton EX9 6NG
Tel +44 (0)1395 442417
Email stay@bedandbreakfastbythebeach.com
Web www.bedandbreakfastbythebeach.com

Entry 140   Map 2

Devon

Rosehill

A stunning original veranda runs along this fine listed Victorian house, and busy Budleigh is a five-minute walk. Sharon and Willi, natural, warm and friendly, run a cookery school here with exciting courses that you can book. Upbeat bedrooms have seaside names, garden views and sofas; bathrooms with slate style floors gleam. Nip downstairs for a delicious breakfast of porridge with honey and cream, muffins, croissants, a full English, and a choice of seven mueslis! The rose-filled cottage garden has sunny seats. Exeter and Sidmouth are close, the coastal path and the beach are a mere saunter.

Price	£90–£110.
Rooms	4: 3 doubles; 1 double with separate bath/shower.
Meals	Pubs/restaurant 5-minute walk.
Closed	Rarely.
Directions	Sent on booking.

Willi & Sharon Rehbock
Rosehill,
30 West Hill,
Budleigh Salterton EX9 6BU
Tel   +44 (0)1395 444031
Email   info@rosehillroomsandcookery.co.uk
Web   www.rosehillroomsandcookery.co.uk

Entry 141   Map 2

Devon

Glebe House

Set on a hillside with fabulous views over the Coly valley, this late-Georgian vicarage is now a heart-warming B&B. The views will entice you, the hosts will delight you and the house is filled with interesting things. Chuck and Emma spent many years at sea – he a Master Mariner, she a chef – and have filled these big light rooms with cushions, kilims and treasured family pieces. There's a sitting room for guests, a lovely conservatory with a vintage vine, peaceful bedrooms with blissful views and bathrooms that sparkle. All this, two sweet pygmy goats, wildlife beyond the ha-ha and the fabulous coast a hike away.

Price	From £80. Singles £50.
Rooms	3: 1 double, 1 twin/double, 1 family room.
Meals	Dinner, 3 courses £25. Pubs/restaurants 2.5 miles.
Closed	Christmas & New Year.
Directions	A375 from Honiton; left opposite Hare & Hounds on B3174 to Seaton. 2nd left to Southleigh, 1.5 miles. In village 1st left to Northleigh; 600 yds, drive on left.

Emma & Chuck Guest
Glebe House,
Southleigh, Colyton EX24 6SD
Tel   +44 (0)1404 871276
Mobile   +44 (0)7867 568569
Email   emma_guest@talktalk.net
Web   www.guestsatglebe.com

Entry 142   Map 2

Devon

West Colwell Farm

Devon lanes, pheasants, bluebell walks *and* sparkling B&B. The Hayes clearly love what they do; ex-TV producers, they have converted this 18th-century farmhouse and barns into a cosy, warm and stylish place to stay. Be charmed by original beams and pine doors, heritage colours and clean lines. Bedrooms feel self-contained, two have terraces overlooking the wooded valley and the most cosy is tucked under the roof. Linen is luxurious, showers are huge and breakfasts (Frank's pancakes, lovely bacon, eggs from next door) are totally flexible. A pretty garden in front, beaches nearby, peace all around. Bliss.

Price	From £85. Singles £70.
Rooms	3 doubles.
Meals	Restaurants 3 miles.
Closed	December/January.
Directions	3 miles from Honiton; Offwell signed off A35 Honiton–Axminster road. In centre of village, at church, down hill. Farm 0.5 miles on.

Frank & Carol Hayes
West Colwell Farm,
Offwell,
Honiton EX14 9SL
Tel +44 (0)1404 831130
Email stay@westcolwell.co.uk
Web www.westcolwell.co.uk

Entry 143   Map 2

Devon

Haye Farm

At the end of winding lanes bursting with flowers is a big stone farmhouse with sweeping views. Seven minutes from River Cottage HQ, this rare-breed farm is run by the warm, humorous Rumsbys whose passion for good husbandry is infectious; slow-grown beef and pork is their speciality. Find inside a chic, fabulous, eclectic décor: polished flagstone floors, vibrant textiles, Italian painted furniture, French antiques, and a huge bed to dive into… your pink polka-dot mini fridge in the hall says it all! Chickens dot the yard, birds chirrup, buzzards soar and the Aga breakfasts (their own farm produce) are generous and delicious.

Price	From £85.
Rooms	1 double with separate bath & shower.
Meals	Pub 3 miles.
Closed	Rarely.
Directions	Sent on booking.

Susan Rumsby
Haye Farm,
Musbury,
Axminster EX13 8ST
Tel +44 (0)1297 551504
Email susanrumsby@aol.com
Web www.hayefarm.net

Entry 144   Map 2

Devon

Applebarn Cottage

A tree-lined drive leads to a long white wall, and a gate opening to an explosion of colour – the garden. Come for a deliciously restful place and the nicest, most easy-going hosts; the wisteria-covered 17th-century cottage is full of books, paintings and fresh flowers. Bedrooms – one in an extension that blends in beautifully – are large, traditional, wonderfully comfortable, and the views down the valley are sublime. Patricia trained as a chef and dinners at Applebarn are delicious and great fun. Breakfast, served in a lovely oak-floored dining room, includes a neighbour's homemade honey. *Minimum stay two nights.*

Devon

Raymont House

Delightful to be in the heart of a historic little town with a Tuesday market and good pubs yet close to the wilds of Dartmoor. This is civilised B&B: your charming hosts give you one bedroom (or, if you're a party, three), peaceful, pretty and serene, and a wow of a bathroom that mixes period features with beautiful modern fittings. No guest sitting room but TVs, homemade biscuits, delicious breakfasts with lots of choices, dressing gowns, radios and fresh flowers. The breakfast room is warmed by a wood-burner, there's a drying room for wet gear, you're on the Tarka Trail and near to RHS Rosemoor. Great value.

Price	£76–£80. Half-board option (dinner & aperitif) £60–£65 p.p.
Rooms	2 suites.
Meals	Pub/restaurant 3 miles.
Closed	November to mid-March.
Directions	A30 Chard to Honiton. Left at top of hill, Wambrook & Stockland. Straight on at next x-roads (Membury); 0.75 miles, left, Cotley & Ridge. Past Hartshill Boarding Kennels; signed 2nd right.

Price	From £75. Singles £45–£55.
Rooms	3: 2 doubles, 1 single all sharing bath (let to same party only).
Meals	Pub/restaurant 50 yds.
Closed	Christmas & New Year.
Directions	From Okehampton, signs to Hatherleigh for 6 miles. At r'bout, right thro' Hatherleigh to top of Market Street. House on left.

Patricia & Robert Spencer
Applebarn Cottage,
Bewley Down,
Axminster EX13 7JX

Tel   +44 (0)1460 220873
Email paspenceruk@yahoo.co.uk
Web   www.applebarn.wordpress.com

Entry 145   Map 2

Jan & Alan Toogood
Raymont House,
49 Market Street, Hatherleigh,
Okehampton EX20 3JP

Tel   +44 (0)1837 810850
Email info@raymonthouse.co.uk
Web   www.raymonthouse.co.uk

Entry 146   Map 2

Devon

Leworthy Barton

Biscuits, scones, sweet vases of hedgerow flowers. Breakfasts are left for you to cook and come courtesy of Rupert's Tamworth pigs and happy hens; bread and jams are homemade, wellies and waxed jackets are on tap. Rupert is a busy farmer and designer who chooses to give guests what he would most like himself. So… you have the whole of the stables, tranquil, beautifully restored and with field and sky views. Downstairs is open-plan, with kitchen and log-burner; up are sloping ceilings, wooden floors, big bed, soft towels. It's cosy yet spacious, stylish yet homely, and the Atlantic coast is the shortest drive.

Price	£80–£100. Singles £60.
Rooms	Barn: 1 double, sitting room & kitchen.
Meals	Pub 3 miles.
Closed	Rarely.
Directions	A39 to Woolfardisworthy. At T-junc. in village, left. 0.5 miles left to Stibb Cross. Over bridge bear right, then left. Uphill, right towards Leworthy & Mill; 0.5 miles; on left.

	Rupert Ashmore
	Leworthy Barton,
	Woolsery,
	Bideford EX39 5PY
Tel	+44 (0)1237 431140

Entry 147   Map 2

Devon

Beara Farmhouse

The moment you arrive at the whitewashed farmhouse you feel the affection your hosts have for their home and gardens. Richard is a lover of wood and a fine craftsman – every room echoes his talent; he also created the pond that's home to mallards and geese. Ann has laid brick paths, stencilled, stitched and painted, all with an eye for colour; bedrooms and guest sitting room are delectable and snug. Open farmland all around, sheep, pigs and hens in the yard, the Tarka Trail on your doorstep and hosts happy to give you 6.30am breakfast should you plan a day on Lundy Island. Guests love this place.

Price	£75. Singles by arrangement. Min. 2 nights weekends, bank holidays & June-Sept.
Rooms	2: 1 double, 1 twin.
Meals	Pub 1.5 miles.
Closed	20 December-5 January.
Directions	From A39, left into Bideford, round quay, past old bridge on left. Signs to Torrington; 1.5 miles, right for Buckland Brewer; 2.5 miles, left; 0.5 miles, right over cattle grid & down track.

	Ann & Richard Dorsett
	Beara Farmhouse,
	Buckland Brewer,
	Bideford EX39 5EH
Tel	+44 (0)1237 451666
Web	www.bearafarmhouse.co.uk

Entry 148   Map 2

Devon

South Yeo

In Devon – down windy lanes with tall grassy banks and the smell of the sea – is a lovely Georgian country house with two walled gardens and barns at the back. You'll fall for this place the moment you arrive, and its owners: Jo runs an interiors business, Mike keeps the cattle and sheep that graze all around. You have an inviting bedroom overlooking the valley, a small pretty sitting room (adjoining) with TV, an elegant drawing room with a real fire... find a cream French bed, a pretty quilted cover, a claw foot bath. Delicious breakfasts with home eggs and homemade jams are brought to a snug room that catches the morning sun.

Price	From £80.
Rooms	1 double & sitting room.
Meals	Pub 1.5 miles.
Closed	Rarely.
Directions	Sent on booking.

Joanne Wade
South Yeo,
Yeo Vale, Bideford EX39 5ES

Tel	+44 (0)1237 451218
Mobile	+44 (0)7766 201191
Email	stay@southyeo.com
Web	www.southyeo.com

Entry 149   Map 2

Devon

Hillbrow House

This lovely 'house on the hill' has a deep veranda and glorious views over the Taw valley, Exmoor (and, on a clear day, to distant Dartmoor). The light, uncluttered rooms are neat as a pin with coordinated colours, thick fabrics, antiques and your own upstairs studio sitting room; bedrooms have feather pillows, proper blankets and luxurious bathrooms. Golfers and walkers will be in paradise, Highbullen Golf Club is a short walk, surfers can reach Croyde easily and many gentler beaches lie in the other direction. RHS Rosemoor is also within striking distance; stoke up on Clarissa's delicious homemade granola for breakfast.

Price	From £90. Singles £50.
Rooms	2: 1 double; 1 double with separate bath.
Meals	Dinner, 3 courses, £30. Pubs/restaurants within walking distance.
Closed	Christmas.
Directions	B3226 from South Molton for 5 miles. Turn right for Chittlehamholt, left at T-junc., then through village. House is last on right.

Clarissa Roe
Hillbrow House, Chittlehamholt,
Umberleigh EX37 9NS

Tel	+44 (0)1769 540214
Mobile	+44 (0)7774 784601
Email	clarissaroe@btinternet.com
Web	www.hillbrowhouse.com

Entry 150   Map 2

Devon

Sannacott

On the southern fringes of Exmoor you're in peaceful rolling hills and hidden valleys. The Trickeys produce point-to-point and national hunt horses from their Georgian style farmhouse; find roaring log fires, antiques, pretty fabrics and a friendly relaxed feel. Bedrooms are traditional and comfortable, some have lovely views over the garden and countryside. Generous breakfasts include homemade bread and jams and organic or local goodies. There's a pretty bird-filled garden to wander, walkers can enjoy the North Devon coastal path nearby, birdwatchers and riders will be happy and there are well-known gardens to visit too.

Price	From £80. Singles £45.
Rooms	3: 1 double, 1 twin/double sharing bath/shower (let to same party only). Annexe: 1 twin & kitchenette.
Meals	Occasional dinner, 3 courses, £25. Pub 2.5 miles.
Closed	Rarely.
Directions	M5 junc. 27; A361 Barnstaple, past Tiverton, 15.5 miles; right next r'bout (Whitechapel). 1.5 miles to junc., right Twitchen & N. Molton; 1.5 miles to 3rd on left, black gates.

Clare Trickey
Sannacott,
North Molton EX36 3JS
Tel   +44 (0)1598 740203
Email   mctrickey@hotmail.com
Web   www.sannacott.co.uk

Entry 151   Map 2

Devon

Rosehill Barn

Up and down the rolling hills of Devon, along the long grassy track, to the oldest house in the hamlet and Rob and Rosie full of warmth and smiles. Your very private barn is surrounded by cottage garden loveliness, in a garden you may share. The old stone barn, fabulously stocked with books, is warm and cheerful: pale blue armchairs on a wooden floor, white walls, fresh flowers, a decanter of sherry, lashings of hot water and a gorgeously comfortable bed. Breakfasts, served in the lofty 16th-century Open Hall, are a feast of homemade deliciousness straight from the Aga. Walks from the door abound.

Price	From £85. Singles from £60.
Rooms	Barn: 1 double & sitting room.
Meals	Pub 2 miles.
Closed	Rarely.
Directions	Sent on booking.

Robert Ingram
Rosehill Barn,
Hill, Loxhore, Barnstaple EX31 4SU
Tel   +44 (0)1271 850415
Email   rob@hill-loxhore.co.uk
Web   www.rosehillbarn.co.uk

Entry 152   Map 2

Devon

Bratton Mill

Absolute privacy down the long lane to a wooded and beautifully secluded valley: watch for dragonflies, red deer, buzzards and the flash of the kingfisher. Breakfast, locally sourced and superb, may be served in summer by the Exmoor trout stream – to deafening birdsong! To the backdrop of the rushing stream is the house, painted white and filled with treasure – including Marilyn, who spoils you with elegant china, garden flowers, a warm bathroom, embroidered bed linen and a decanter of port; your peaceful bedroom overlooks the river. There are strolls and hikes straight from the door. Wonderful.

Devon

Beachborough Country House

Welcome to this gracious 18th-century rectory with stone-flagged floors, lofty windows, wooden shutters and charming gardens. Viviane is vivacious and spoils you with dinners and breakfasts straight from the Aga; dine in the elegant dining room before a twinkling fire. Hens cluck, horses whinny but otherwise the peace is deep. Ease any walker's pains away in a steaming roll top tub; big airy bedrooms have Turkish rugs and great views: admire them from your window seat. There's a games room for kids in the outbuildings and Combe Martin is a short hop for a grand beach day. Huge fun.

Price	From £95. Singles £65.
Rooms	1 twin/double. Extra single available..
Meals	Occasional supper from £15. Pub within walking distance.
Closed	Rarely.
Directions	From Bratton Fleming High Street turn right into Mill Lane. Down road for 0.5 miles through railway cutting; turn right.

Price	From £75. Singles from £50. Dogs £5.
Rooms	3: 1 twin/double (extra single available), 2 doubles.
Meals	Dinner, 2-3 courses, from £19. Catering for house parties. Pub 3 miles.
Closed	Rarely.
Directions	From A361 take A399 for 12 miles. At Blackmoor Gate, left onto A39. House 1.5 miles on right.

	Marilyn Jacobs Holloway Bratton Mill, Bratton Fleming, Barnstaple EX31 4RU
Tel	+44 (0)1598 710026
Email	contact@brattonmill.co.uk
Web	www.brattonmill.co.uk

	Viviane Clout Beachborough Country House, Kentisbury, Barnstaple EX31 4NH
Tel	+44 (0)1271 882487
Mobile	+44 (0)7732 947755
Email	viviane@beachborough.freeserve.co.uk
Web	www.beachboroughcountryhouse.co.uk

Entry 153   Map 2

Entry 154   Map 2

Devon

Victoria House

Beachcombers, surfers and walkers will be in their element in this Edwardian seaside villa where each bedroom has a magnificent view. Choose between the two in the main house (with sofas) and the beach-hut annexe with a big romantic deck facing the sea. Heather is lively and fun, she and David are ex-RAF and go out of their way to give you the best; bathrooms are state of the art, breakfasts are a tour de force – fruits, yogurts, waffles, eggs Benedict or the full Monty. No garden but you are on the coastal road to Woolacombe (of surf and kite surfing fame) and the beach is a ten-minute walk. A top spot.

Price	£90–£140.
Rooms	3: 1 double, 1 twin/double. Annexe: 1 double.
Meals	Pubs/restaurants 200 yds.
Closed	Rarely.
Directions	From B3343, right for Mortehoe. Through village & past the old chapel. Down steep hill, with the bay ahead; house 3rd on left.

Heather & David Burke
Victoria House,
Chapel Hill, Mortehoe,
Woolacombe EX34 7DZ
Tel   +44 (0)1271 871302
Email   heatherburke59@fsmail.net
Web   www.victoriahousebandb.co.uk

Entry 155   Map 2

Devon

North Walk House

Sea views, brass bedsteads and big rooms at this calm retreat, perfectly positioned on a cliff-top path – super for walkers and foodies. Ian and Sarah welcome you with homemade cake in a cosy guest lounge, and give you light bedrooms with sparkling bathrooms and seductive beds. Enjoy the coastal and Exmoor walks, or genteel Lynton and Lynmouth; return to log fire and armchairs. Take your tea on a sea-view terrace, or be tempted by Sarah's four-course supper, seasonal and mostly organic. Everything here is thoughtful, from the welcome to the décor and the refreshments: arrive, unpack, unwind…

Price	£80–£150. Singles £50–£100.
Rooms	5: 4 doubles, 1 twin.
Meals	Dinner, 4 courses, from £26. Pub/restaurant 0.25 miles.
Closed	Rarely.
Directions	A39 from Barnstaple to Lynton Town Hall. From there, left turn at the church down North Walk. Third hotel on left.

Ian & Sarah Downing
North Walk House,
North Walk,
Lynton EX35 6HJ
Tel   +44 (0)1598 753372
Email   walk@northwalkhouse.co.uk
Web   www.northwalkhouse.co.uk

Entry 156   Map 2

Dorset

Crosskeys House

In previous lives a pub, a cobbler's shop and a smithy, this listed stone house, right on the village crossroads, is well settled into its B&B role. Robin and Liz offer you a fabulous breakfast, in the conservatory or dining room, and will happily advise on the glories of west Dorset (walks, pubs, stately homes): nothing is too much trouble. Their sitting room is softly traditional – plump sofas, family portraits and antiques, flowers, glossy magazines – while lovely cosy bedrooms have king-size beds and interesting books. The house is near the road but there's a pretty flower-filled garden and water fresh from the well.

Price	From £90. Singles from £70.
Rooms	3: 1 double, 2 twins/doubles.
Meals	Pub 200 yds.
Closed	Rarely.
Directions	A35 to Bridport then A3066 to Beaminster. B3163 to Broadwindsor. House is at end of one-way system, the last on the right (just before crossroads).

Robin & Liz Adeney
Crosskeys House,
High Street, Broadwindsor,
Beaminster DT8 3QP
Tel   +44 (0)1308 868063
Email   robin.adeney@care4free.net
Web   www.crosskeyshouse.com

Entry 157   Map 3

Dorset

Pear Tree Farm

Just four miles from bustling Bridport, this traditional pretty Dorset farmhouse is reached down secret narrow lanes and surrounded by deep valleys. A keen traveller and garden designer, Emma has created a vibrant home brimming with interesting art, good antique furniture, rugs, comfy old armchairs and books galore; there is an extraordinary collection of glass walking sticks. The garden is a delight and blissful views from flowery bedrooms will charm you. Wake to a breakfast of local bacon and home-laid eggs in the sunny kitchen. Close to River Cottage, Bridport Literary Festival and the coast; a walker's paradise.

Price	£75. Singles £50.
Rooms	2: 1 twin/double; 1 twin sharing bath (2nd room let to same party only).
Meals	Pubs/restaurants within 4 miles.
Closed	Christmas & Easter.
Directions	Bridport A3066 towards Beaminster. At Melplash right towards Loscombe; 0.25 miles right to Loscombe. 1 mile to bottom of hill; left at T-junc. House 2nd on left.

Emma Poë
Pear Tree Farm,
Loscombe,
Bridport DT6 3TL
Tel   +44 (0)1308 488223
Email   poe@gotadsl.co.uk
Web   www.peartreefarmbedandbreakfast.co.uk

Entry 158   Map 3

Dorset

No 27

In Bridport — all seafood restaurants, market stalls and pretty façades — is a rambling 1780 artisan's house with steep stairs and an irresistible charm. Juliet has opened up walls then painted them chalky hues, revealed flagstones, laid floorboards and added kilims… and books, paintings, antiques and flowers. Find an orchard with hens at the end of the garden, a spacious drawing room, airy bedrooms and a modern and elegant bathroom or luxury wet room; the Shaker room has views to the hills. All is uncluttered and calm. Juliet's passions are cooking, gardening and wild water swimming — you'll love her! *Ask about parking.*

Price	£75–£120.
Rooms	2: 1 double; 1 double with separate bath.
Meals	Supper from £15. Pubs/restaurants in town.
Closed	Rarely.
Directions	At Bridport r'bout on to A3066. Then 1st left into St Andrews Road and forward into Barrack Street. No 27 is the tall house with a brick façade on right.

Juliet Lewis
No 27,
27 Barrack Street,
Bridport DT6 3LX
Tel +44 (0)1308 426378
Email julietalewis@gmail.com
Web www.no27bridport.co.uk

Entry 159   Map 3

Dorset

Wooden Cabbage House

Leafy lanes and a private drive lead you to Martyn and Susie's beautifully restored keeper's cottage, hidden in rolling West Dorset. Leave the hubbub behind, savour the valley views, relax in this spacious stylish home amongst flowers, fine antiques and paintings. Cosy bedrooms have country-house charm. A delicious breakfast is served in the gorgeous garden room — home-grown fruits, local eggs and sausages — and French windows open to a productive potager and terraced gardens. Local walks are good and the Jurassic coast is half-an-hour away; return to comfy sofas by the log fire. Fabulous hosts — nothing is too much trouble.

Price	From £110. Singles from £75.
Rooms	3: 2 doubles, 1 twin.
Meals	Dinner, 3 courses with wine, £40. Supper, 2 courses with wine, £30. Pubs/restaurants 3 miles.
Closed	Rarely.
Directions	3 miles S of Yeovil on A37, turn west to Closworth. Continue on this road, past turn to Halstock; 200 yds on right, over cattle grid. House down drive on left.

Martyn & Susie Lee
Wooden Cabbage House, East Chelborough, Dorchester DT2 0QA
Tel +44 (0)1935 83362
Mobile +44 (0)7805 378583
Email relax@woodencabbage.co.uk
Web www.woodencabbage.co.uk

Entry 160   Map 3

Dorset

Old Forge

Snug in a stream-tickled hamlet, deep in Hardy country, this B&B is as pretty as a painting – and just as peaceful. That is, until owner Judy starts to giggle: she is full of smiles and laughter. This is a happy place, a real country home, a no-rules B&B. The one guest double, sharing the former forge with a self-catering pad for two, is neat, warm and cosy with yellow hues, thick carpets and trinkets from travels. The 17th-century farmhouse opposite is where you breakfast: Prue Leith-trained Judy serves a neighbour s eggs, a friend's sausages, in an eclectically furnished room with bucolic views to garden, meadows and hills.

Price	£70-£90. Extra person £15.
Rooms	Old Forge: 1 double.
Meals	Restaurant 1.5 miles.
Closed	Rarely.
Directions	Sent on booking.

Judy Thompson
Old Forge,
Lower Wraxall Farmhouse,
Lower Wraxall, Dorchester DT2 0HL
Tel   +44 (0)1935 83218
Email   judyjthompson@hotmail.co.uk
Web   www.lowerwraxall.co.uk

Entry 161   Map 3

Dorset

Holyleas House

This is a fabulous house, comfortable and easy; Tia and her two friendly dogs are genuinely welcoming. You breakfast by a log fire in the elegant dining room in winter: free-range eggs, bacon and sausages from the farmers' market, homemade jams and marmalade. Sleep in light, softly-coloured bedrooms with lovely views across the well-tended gardens, and spotless bathrooms. Walkers and explorers will be happy: return to a roaring fire and a good book in the drawing room. It's a short hop to the pub for supper and Tia is happy to babysit too. *Min. two nights in high season & at weekends.*

Price	£80-£90. Singles £40.
Rooms	3: 1 double, 1 family room; 1 single with separate bath.
Meals	Pub a short walk.
Closed	Christmas & New Year.
Directions	From Dorchester, B3143 into Buckland Newton over x-roads; Holyleas on right opp. village cricket pitch.

Tia Bunkall
Holyleas House, Buckland Newton,
Dorchester DT2 7DP
Tel   +44 (0)1300 345214
Mobile   +44 (0)7968 341887
Email   tiabunkall@holyleas.fsnet.co.uk
Web   www.holyleashouse.co.uk

Entry 162   Map 3

Dorset

Fullers Earth

Such an English feel: the village with pub, post office and stores, the rose-filled walled garden with fruit trees beyond, the tranquil church view. This listed house – its late-Georgian frontage added in 1820 – is a treat: flowers and white linen, a lovely sitting room where you settle with tea and cake by the fire, roomy bedrooms with comfortable beds, books and views. At breakfast enjoy perfect compotes and jams from the garden, Fullers Earth muesli and local produce. Friendly Ian and Wendy will plan great walks with you in this AONB, the Jurassic coast is 20 minutes away and you walk to the pub through the garden.

Price	£90–£100. Singles from £60.
Rooms	2 doubles.
Meals	Pub 500 yds.
Closed	Christmas.
Directions	From A37 take Cattistock turning downhill to T-junc. Left through village. Pub on left. After 90 degree right-hand bend, 5th house on right.

Wendy Gregory
Fullers Earth,
Cattistock, Dorchester DT2 0JL

Tel	+44 (0)1300 320190
Mobile	+44 (0)7792 654543
Email	stay@fullersearth.co.uk
Web	www.fullersearth.co.uk

Entry 163   Map 3

Dorset

West Compton Manor

Pheasants stroll along grassy lanes, red kites fly overhead and this stunning stone manor house is a delight. Easy-going Oonagh gives guests their own wing, and a courtyard garden with seats by the koi ponds and Orangery. Bedrooms come in comfortable country style; the Rose suite with antique linen and pretty wallpaper is charming. The dining room gleams with antiques, silver and flowers; feast on a breakfast of home-laid eggs, homemade jams and local sausages. Lurchers and collie add to the relaxed family feel, you can climb Eggardon Hill and the Jurassic coast is just 10 minutes' drive. *Coarse fishing available on estate lake.*

Price	From £75.
Rooms	3: 1 suite; 1 double, 1 twin each with separate bath/shower.
Meals	Dinner, 2-3 courses, £20-£25 (Mon-Fri only). Packed lunch available. Pub/restaurant 1.5 miles.
Closed	Rarely.
Directions	Sent on booking.

Oonagh Stewart
West Compton Manor,
West Compton, Dorchester DT2 0EY

Tel	+44 (0)1300 320400
Mobile	+44 (0)7958 968798
Email	info@westcomptonmanor.co.uk
Web	www.westcomptonmanor.co.uk

Entry 164   Map 3

Dorset

Manor Farm

You are high up on the chalk hills that fall to the Jurassic Coast. Tessa's family have lived in the flint and stone house since 1860 and it is crammed with history: solid antiques, books galore, pictures, maps and photographs. From all the windows views soar to sheep-dotted hills. You can settle by the wood-burner in the snug, and your Aga-cooked breakfast or supper is served in the handsome dining room, or the garden in summer; cooking is one of Tessa's passions. Bedrooms are without frills but clean and comfortable; the bathroom is large and sparkling. Outdoor heaven is yours; find a pet pig called Pork!

Dorset

Wrackleford House

The lawns of this quintessentially English Georgian manor house sweep down to the river Frome; sound the bell pull and you'll be greeted by Katie and Oliver, relaxed and charming hosts. Their gem of a house is gloriously unstuffy with a friendly feel: deep sash windows, wide archways, huge bedrooms with flowers and antiques, paintings, porcelain and old family treasures. An Aga-cooked breakfast is taken in the conservatory overlooking beautiful estate gardens: eggs from the farm, fruit from the garden and homemade jams. Fishing and shooting weekends are organised and you can happily stroll gardens, meadows and riverbank.

Price	From £70.
Rooms	2: 1 double, 1 twin sharing bath (let to same party only).
Meals	Dinner, 2-3 courses, from £15. Pub/restaurant 4 miles.
Closed	Rarely.
Directions	A35 direction: down hill, stone wall and gate on right. A37 direction: down hill, 3rd turning on left. Satnav does not always work.

Price	£120. Singles £95.
Rooms	4: 2 doubles, 1 twin/double, 1 twin.
Meals	Pub 1 mile.
Closed	Rarely.
Directions	Sent on booking.

Tessa Russell
Manor Farm, Compton Valence,
Dorchester DT2 9ES
Tel   +44 (0)1308 482227
Mobile   +44 (0)7818 037184 (signal unreliable)
Email   tessa.nrussell@btinternet.com
Web   www.manor-farm.uk.com

Oliver & Katie Pope
Wrackleford House,
Wrackleford,
Dorchester DT2 9SN
Tel   +44 (0)1305 264141
Email   katie@wrackleford.co.uk
Web   www.wrackleford.co.uk

Entry 165   Map 3

Entry 166   Map 3

Dorset

Whitfield Farm Cottage

Jackie and David are warm and helpful hosts, and their pretty thatched 18th-century cottage is full of character and charm. A delicious breakfast is served in their large beamed kitchen, or in the walled courtyard on sunny days – the garden brims with roses, lavender and sweet peas in summer. Your bedroom (with its own shower) is immaculate in blue and white and leads out to the garden; the sitting room is cosy and comfy with inglenook fireplace and window seats. A mile from the town centre, but with a peaceful rural feel; the Frome – beloved by local fishermen – is 150 yards away and day tickets are sometimes available.

Price	£80-£85. Singles £50.
Rooms	1 twin/double. Extra room available. Minimum stay two nights at weekends.
Meals	Pubs/restaurants 1.25 miles.
Closed	Christmas & Easter.
Directions	From r'bout at top of Dorchester, west on B3150 for 100 yds. Right onto Poundbury Rd (before museum); 1 mile; over another road; 2nd track on right by house sign. Cottage set back from road.

	Jackie & David Charles Whitfield Farm Cottage, Poundbury Road, Dorchester DT2 9SL
Tel	+44 (0)1305 260233
Email	dcharles@gotadsl.co.uk
Web	www.whitfieldfarmcottage.co.uk

Entry 167   Map 3

Dorset

The White Cottage

Strolling distance from lovely old Athelhampton House and its gardens is this thatched cottage where Lindsay and Mark are slowly becoming self-sufficient. You will be well fed: home-grown vegetables, bacon from the pigs, eggs from Clarissa the chicken. It's a lively young-family household with gorgeous bedrooms, super linen, fresh flowers, plump pillows, chocolates; generous bathrooms have thick towels and eco-friendly lotions. The suite has its own entrance and a big comfortable sitting room. Help feed the animals and enjoy the river Piddle running through the garden – fish for brown trout but please put them back!

Price	£75-£120. Singles from £55.
Rooms	3: 1 double, 1 suite for 2-4 (with sofabed); 1 twin with separate bath.
Meals	Pubs 1 mile.
Closed	Rarely.
Directions	A35 exit Puddletown & Athelhampton; signs for Athelhampton House. Left at lights in Puddletown; house 200 yds on right, after Athelhampton House.

	Lindsay & Mark Piper The White Cottage, Athelhampton, Dorchester DT2 7LG
Tel	+44 (0)1305 848622
Mobile	+44 (0)7788 166322
Email	bookings@white-cottage-bandb.co.uk
Web	www.white-cottage-bandb.co.uk

Entry 168   Map 3

Dorset

Yoah Cottage

Rosemary makes delicate, sometimes humorous, pieces, Furse creates bold works in clay; their thatched, cob-walled, rambling house is a jaw-dropping gallery of modern art, ceramics, tapestries. The cottage garden's colours complete the vibrant picture. A private guest wing holds a country-pretty double and a twin under the eaves, sharing a bathroom (with friends or family). Breakfast is next to the couple's studio; Rosemary will also whip up a Swedish-style supper on a tray if you can't bear to budge from the sitting room fire. Such enthusiastic, artistic owners — and you're deep in Hardy country. *Minimum stay two nights.*

Price	£65–£85. Singles £40–£50.
Rooms	2: 1 double, 1 twin sharing bath (let to same party only).
Meals	Supper on a tray £15. Pub next door.
Closed	Christmas & Easter.
Directions	A352 out of Dorchester towards Wareham. Thro' Whitcombe, then next turning left to West Knighton. Left again, to New Inn. House next to pub.

Furse & Rosemary Swann
Yoah Cottage,
West Knighton,
Dorchester DT2 8PE
Tel +44 (0)1305 852087
Email roseswann@tiscali.co.uk
Web www.yoahcottage.co.uk

Entry 169   Map 3

Dorset

Marren

On the Dorset coastal path, with spectacular views of Portland, a blissfully tranquil, bird-rich spot. The owners have transformed this 1920s house, set in six acres of terraced and wooded garden, and their style reflects their penchant for natural materials and country life. Bedrooms are elegant and comfortable; one has a door onto the garden; from the other you can marvel at the sun setting over the sea. Enjoy superb Slow Food spreads of farm produce and homemade bread, then head off to the secluded beach below and a turquoise sea swim. Leave the low-slung Morgan at home: the track is adventurously steep!

Price	£95–£135.
Rooms	2 doubles.
Meals	Pub 1 mile.
Closed	Rarely.
Directions	Sent on booking.

Peter Cartwright
Marren,
Holworth, Dorchester DT2 8NJ
Tel +44 (0)1305 851503
Mobile +44 (0)7957 886399
Email marren@lineone.net
Web www.marren.info

Entry 170   Map 3

Dorset

Waddon House

Don't be daunted when this magnificent Dorset manor house swings into view: it's grand yet gracious and Suzie is lovely. The house breathes 500 years of history and at every turn you'll discover a fine artefact or period feature, from white hounds at the courtyard entrance to silver tureens in a handsome dining room. Bedrooms are in the east wing, one a vision of fine yellow silk and antiques, the other a raftered art deco dream with stained glass windows and furniture from the Queen Mary Liner. Formal gardens envelop the house, a maze of balustrades, finials, statues and steps, with stunning views to the Jurassic coast. Unique.

Price	£110–£150. Singles £90–£100.
Rooms	2: 1 twin/double; 1 four-poster with separate bath.
Meals	Dinner, 4 courses, £28. Pub/restaurant 2 miles.
Closed	Occasionally.
Directions	A30 from Dorchester; at Winterbourne Abbas take left towards Portesham. In Portesham take the left turning to Upwey. House 1 mile on left.

Suzie Chaffyn-Grove
Waddon House, Waddon,
Portesham, Weymouth DT3 4ER

Tel	+44 (0)1305 871241
Mobile	+44 (0)7966 436420
Email	suzie@waddonhouse.co.uk
Web	www.waddonhouse.co.uk

Entry 171   Map 3

Dorset

Honeycombe Cottage

As dreamy as its name, the 16th-century cottage in the village, with deep walls, open fireplaces and flagged floors houses one dog, one cat and gentle, generous Heather. Now her children have flown the nest, she gives you a garden that blooms as wonderfully as the house and, up under the eaves, soft curtains, soothing colours, aromatic oils and delicious beds. Have breakfast (pancakes with maple syrup, bacon from up the road) in the homely kitchen, or outside on fine days, where lawns and borders drift effortlessly into orchard, fields and hills. An all-year-round delight. *Children over five welcome.*

Price	From £80.
Rooms	2: 1 twin/double; 1 double with separate shower.
Meals	Pubs/restaurants 0.33 miles.
Closed	Rarely.
Directions	From A31 to Bere Regis on West Street. At end of village, left down 'No Through Road', over bridge. Thatched wall on left, cottage at end.

Heather Loxton
Honeycombe Cottage,
Shitterton, Bere Regis BH20 7HU

Tel	+44 (0)1929 471660
Mobile	+44 (0)7717 783839
Email	info@honeycombecottage.com
Web	www.honeycombecottage.com

Entry 172   Map 3

Dorset

Lower Lynch House

On the glorious Isle of Purbeck, between the old stone village of Corfe Castle and Kingston atop a hill, this wisteria-strewn house sits at the end of a long woodland track. Aga-cooked breakfast is served at tables overlooking courtyard and garden; cosy, traditional bedrooms with pale colours and florals are as peaceful as can be. No sitting room, but a small sofa in the double. You are a five-minute drive from the coastal path: a great spot for walkers and peace-seekers. Bron and Nick are warm and friendly, their home a relaxing retreat with a mature garden to wander and wild deer roaming.

Price	£80. Minimum 2 nights.
Rooms	2: 1 twin; 1 double with separate bath.
Meals	Inn 0.75 miles.
Closed	Christmas & New Year.
Directions	A351 from Wareham to Corfe Castle. At end of village fork right on B3069 for Kingston. Left 0.5 miles down track (sign on roadside).

Bron & Nick Burt
Lower Lynch House,
Kingston Hill,
Corfe Castle BH20 5LG
Tel   +44 (0)1929 480089
Email bronburt@btinternet.com

Entry 173   Map 3

Dorset

The Old Post Office

The stunning coastal path comes past the front door of this restored bungalow on a private cliff-top estate. Clamber down to a hidden beach and a short walk will take you to Swanage. The house glows with warm colour and a friendly, informal feel. Comfortable sunny bedrooms have painted furniture and French windows onto an inviting veranda, set with rocking chairs and candles. Toasty bathrooms sparkle. Artist Rowena and rare-book dealer David look after you very well; Rowena loves to cook and chat and breakfast is local and delicious, with mushrooms, herby potatoes and eggs from Arabella the hen. To stay is a treat!

Price	From £75. Singles £55.
Rooms	2: 1 twin; 1 double with separate bath.
Meals	Pub/restaurant 0.3 miles.
Closed	Rarely.
Directions	A351 to Swanage seafront, then left. Up hill, round one-way. Left into Ballard Way (corner shop on left). Through private estate barrier. House 2nd on right.

Rowena Bishop
The Old Post Office, 4 Ballard Estate,
Swanage BH19 1QZ
Tel   +44 (0)1929 422041
Mobile +44 (0)7976 356013
Email   rowena@outwardbound.plus.com
Web   www.oldpostofficeswanage.co.uk

Entry 174   Map 3

Dorset

Gold Court House

Anthea and Michael have created a mood of restrained luxury and uncluttered, often beautiful, good taste in their Georgian townhouse. Restful bedrooms have antiques, beams, linen armchairs, radios and TVs. There's an eye-catching collection of aqua marine glass, interesting art, and a large drawing room and pretty walled garden in which to relax after a day out. Views are soft and lush yet you are in the small square of this attractive town with cafés and galleries a short walk. Your hosts are delightful – "they do everything to perfection," says a guest; both house and garden are a refuge. *Over tens welcome.*

Price	£85. Singles £60.
Rooms	3: 1 double; 1 twin/double, 1 twin/double each with separate bathroom.
Meals	Restaurants 50 yds.
Closed	Rarely.
Directions	From A35, A351 to Wareham. Follow signs to town centre. In North St, over lights into South St. 1st left into St John's Hill; house on far right corner of square.

Anthea & Michael Hipwell
Gold Court House,
St John's Hill,
Wareham BH20 4LZ
Tel +44 (0)1929 553320
Email info@goldcourthouse.co.uk
Web www.goldcourthouse.co.uk

Entry 175 Map 3

Dorset

Bering House

Fabulous in every way. Renate's attention to detail reveals a love of running B&B: the fluffy dressing gowns and bathroom treats, the biscuits, fruit and sherry... she and John are welcoming and delightful. Expect pretty sofas, golden bath taps, a gleaming breakfast table, and a big sumptuous suite with views across sparkling Poole harbour to Brownsea Island and Purbeck Hills. Breakfasts are served on blue and white Spode china: exotic fruits with Parma ham, smoked salmon with poached eggs and muffins, kedgeree, smoked haddock gratin, warm figs with Greek yogurt and honey: the choice is superb. An immaculate harbourside retreat.

Price	£80–£95. Singles £70–£85.
Rooms	2: 1 twin/double; 1 suite (twin/double) & kitchenette.
Meals	Pub 400 yds. Restaurant 500 yds.
Closed	Rarely.
Directions	From A35 & A350 at Upton, B3068 south to Hamworthy & Rockley Park. 1.5 miles on at pub on left, right into Lake Rd; under bridge; 2nd left down Branksea Ave. House last on left.

Renate & John Wadham
Bering House,
53 Branksea Avenue,
Hamworthy,
Poole BH15 4DP
Tel +44 (0)1202 673419
Email johnandrenate1@tiscali.co.uk

Entry 176 Map 3

Dorset

7 Smithfield Place

Valerie adores large mirrors – which she paints and distresses herself – rich fabrics, real wood, dainty antiques. She also delights in looking after guests, so no detail is missed in her elegant home, from the gorgeous bathroom to a 'full works' breakfast – taken in the spanking new breakfast room or on a sunny patio. Built in 1880 as a worker's cottage, the house sits on a quiet cul-de-sac off Winton's thriving high street, two miles from Bournemouth town centre with easy public transport. The garden is lit up in spring by blooming camellias and cherry blossom, and the whole house sparkles – as does your charming hostess.

Price	£80. Singles £55.
Rooms	1 double.
Meals	Packed lunch £15. Pub/restaurant 100 yds.
Closed	Christmas.
Directions	M27 to New Forest, on to A31, then exit A338 Bournemouth. Exit to A3049, up to r'bout, 3rd exit still on A3049. 1.5 miles, right into Wimborne Rd, then left into Smithfield Place.

Valerie Johns
7 Smithfield Place,
Winton, Bournemouth BH9 2QJ

Tel	+44 (0)1202 520722
Mobile	+44 (0)7743 481671
Email	valeriejohns@btinternet.com
Web	www.smithfieldplace.co.uk

Entry 177   Map 3

Dorset

The Park 24

All is lush and leafy on this quiet street, a mere stroll from the centre. The garden teems with lavender and agapanthus; tea on the terrace is glorious. Chris and Fiona's Edwardian home is full of grace and style and the sitting room elegant with deep bay windows, high ceilings, beautiful antiques, flowers. Cosy chic ground-floor bedrooms with cream carpets have ultra sleek shower rooms. Chat away at the refectory table while Fiona cooks breakfast, tuck into porridge with cinnamon and cream. Work it off on the beach, then back for a summerhouse nap – and a possible sighting of a sweet spaniel nosing through the undergrowth!

Price	From £85. Singles from £65.
Rooms	2: 1 double, 1 twin/double.
Meals	Pub/restaurant 1 mile.
Closed	Rarely.
Directions	Sent on booking.

Chris & Fiona Dixon-Box
The Park 24, 24 Meyrick Park Crescent,
Talbot Woods, Bournemouth BH3 7AQ

Tel	+44 (0)1202 296473
Mobile	+44 (0)7740 425623
Email	info@thepark24.co.uk
Web	www.thepark24.co.uk

Entry 178   Map 3

Dorset

Sondela

All is leafy and sedate, with tall pines and rhododendrons hiding large houses: a short drive sweeps you to the front of this colonial style bungalow smothered in roses. Glynda and Selwyn, warm and intelligent, have filled their lovely light home with interesting antiques, textiles and artefacts from their years in South Africa; guests have their own sitting room in soft blues with a stone fireplace and fresh flowers. Bedrooms are quiet (the double is bigger and more contemporary) with pure white cotton sheets and splashes of colour from bedspreads or cushions; on sunny days you breakfast in the glorious garden.

Price	£75–£85. Singles £60.
Rooms	2: 1 double, 1 twin.
Meals	Restaurant 5-minute walk.
Closed	Rarely.
Directions	After Lyndhurst follow A35 to Christchurch for 9 miles. Past East Close Hotel on left, 1 mile to junction, left to Walkford. Thro' Walkford, left Chewton Farm Road; 500 yards on left.

	Glynda & Selwyn Morrison
	Sondela, 20 Chewton Farm Road,
	Highcliffe, Christchurch BH23 5QN
Tel	+44 (0)1425 270978
Mobile	+44 (0)7734 991034
Email	morglyn@hotmail.com
Web	www.chewtonbedandbreakfast.com

Entry 179   Map 3

Dorset

Thornhill

This pretty thatched house has peaceful views from every window... of fields, woods and superb gardens. Sara and John are charming hosts and love having people to stay; they have lots of local knowledge too. Downstairs are pastel walls, polished antiques, beautiful cedar floors and interesting art. All is neat, tidy, spacious and spotless, and Sara pays great attention to detail: fruit, chocolates and a choice of teas in comforting bedrooms with an old-fashioned feel. You can spot deer on the lawn, stride out straight from the door, visit the Minster, drive to beaches. Come on a Thursday if you like to play bridge!

Price	From £64. Singles from £32.
Rooms	3: 1 double, 1 twin, 1 single, all sharing 2 baths. Possible use of separate bath.
Meals	Pub/restaurant 400 yds.
Closed	Rarely.
Directions	From Wimborne B3078 towards Cranborne. Right to Holt. After 2 miles Thornhill on right, 200 yds beyond Old Inn. Up straight drive, do not turn into Thornhill Cottage driveway.

	John & Sara Turnbull
	Thornhill,
	Holt,
	Wimborne BH21 7DJ
Tel	+44 (0)1202 889434
Email	scturnbull@lineone.net

Entry 180   Map 3

Dorset

Crawford House

Below, the river Stour winds through the valley and under the medieval, nine-arched bridge. Above, an Iron Age hill fort; between is Crawford House. It's an elegant Georgian house in an acre of walled garden, soft and pretty inside with an easy, relaxed atmosphere. Carpeted bedrooms are homely and warm, with long curtains; one room has four-poster twin beds with chintz drapes. The sun streams through the floor-to-ceiling windows of the downstairs rooms, and charming 18th- and 19th-century oil paintings hang in the dining room. Andrea is fun, and a great host, with lots of local knowledge. *Broadband available.*

Price	From £65. Singles £35.
Rooms	3: 1 twin/double; 1 twin with separate bath; 1 twin with separate shower.
Meals	Pub in village.
Closed	Mid-October to mid-April.
Directions	North on A350; after entering Spetisbury, 1st gateway immediately on left after crossroads (B3075).

Andrea Lea
Crawford House,
Spetisbury,
Blandford Forum DT11 9DP
Tel   +44 (0)1258 857338
Email   andrea@lea8.wanadoo.co.uk

Entry 181   Map 3

Dorset

Stickland Farmhouse

Charming Dorset... welcome to a soft, delightful thatched cottage in an enviably rural setting. Sandy and Paul have poured love into this listed farmhouse and garden, the latter bursting with lupins, poppies, foxgloves, clematis, delphiniums. Sandy gives you delicious breakfasts with homemade muesli, eggs from the hens and soda bread from the Aga. Pretty, cottagey bedrooms have crisp white dressing gowns and lots of books and pictures – one room opens onto your own seating area in the garden. The village has a good pub, and Cranbourne Chase, rich in barrows and hill forts, is close by. *Over tens welcome.*

Price	£70–£75. Singles £55. Min. 2 nights at weekends in summer.
Rooms	3: 2 doubles, 1 twin.
Meals	Pub 3-minute walk.
Closed	Rarely.
Directions	Leave Blandford for SW, cross river Stour. Hard right after Bryanston school for W. Stickland. Down North St, right signed W. Houghton. House 150 yds on left with 5-bar gate.

Sandy & Paul Crofton-Atkins
Stickland Farmhouse, Winterborne
Stickland, Blandford Forum DT11 0NT
Tel   +44 (0)1258 880119
Mobile +44 (0)7932 897774
Email   sandysticklandfarm@tiscali.co.uk
Web   www.sticklandfarmhouse.co.uk

Entry 182   Map 3

Dorset

Launceston Farm

Farmhouse chic in the most glorious of surroundings. The bedrooms, all named after the fields, are an exquisite blend of contemporary and traditional; two have roll tops in the room itself. Take tea by the open fire or find a secluded spot in the ornamental, walled gardens. Breakfast and candlelit dinner are farm-sourced and deliciously rustic. Sarah, who was born in this listed house, provides a truly relaxing stay; son Jimi's organic farm tours are a must and there are footpaths through the surrounding AONB from the door. You will leave this country retreat feeling completely rejuvenated. *Over 12s welcome.*

Price	From £80. Singles from £55.
Rooms	6: 4 doubles, 2 twins.
Meals	Dinner, 2 courses, £22.50 (Mon & Fri only). Pub 1 mile.
Closed	Rarely.
Directions	From Salisbury, A354 to Blandford Forum. Left at Tarrant Hinton. First village is Tarrant Launceston; house is on right.

Sarah Worrall
Launceston Farm,
Tarrant Launceston,
Blandford Forum DT11 8BY
Tel +44 (0)1258 830528
Email info@launcestonfarm.co.uk
Web www.launcestonfarm.co.uk

Entry 183   Map 3

Dorset

Sarunds Cottage

Steep lanes tumble down to wooded Farnham and the famous Museum Inn. A little further, up a gravelled driveway, are Josephine's interior design studio and elegant Georgian house. Through a gate, privately in its own lane, is a cottage housing your suite – spacious, luxurious, on the first floor and bliss for independent souls. Light-filled and beamy, with a rococo-esque bed and toile de Jouy curtains, it's a vision of cream, grey and soft ochre; the chandelier'd bathroom is stunning too. Breakfast in a basket is a cook-your-own affair. Deer bound in the forests of Cranbourne Chase, Salisbury is 20 minutes away.

Price	£120. Singles £80–£100.
Rooms	Cottage: 1 suite with sitting room & kitchenette.
Meals	Pub/restaurant 200 yds.
Closed	Rarely.
Directions	A354 Blandford to Salisbury road. After 6 miles left to Farnham, 1.5 miles into village and past The Museum Inn. House 200 yds on left.

Josephine Browning
Sarunds Cottage,
Farnham,
Blandford Forum DT11 8DE
Tel +44 (0)1725 552555
Email jb@countryhouse-interiordesign.co.uk
Web www.sarundscottage.co.uk

Entry 184   Map 3

Dorset

Glebe Farm

You're in Dorset's highest village – views from the house sprawl for miles. Ian farms 1,000 acres, Tessa looks after horses, ponies and chickens. Their home, newly built, comes with green oak, soaring ceilings and walls of glass that frame spectacular views ("Emmerdale meets Grand Designs" to quote a happy guest). Aga-cooked breakfasts include local bacon and home-laid eggs, while bedrooms, one up, one down, have warm colours, big beds, beautiful views, super bathrooms. The Wessex Ridgeway starts in the village, so follow it over to magnificent Hambledon Hill, an Iron Age hill fort. Dine on the terrace in summer. *Over 14s welcome.*

Price	£100–£120. Singles from £60.
Rooms	2 twins/doubles.
Meals	Dinner, 2 courses, £25 (Mon-Thurs only). Pubs 2 miles.
Closed	Christmas & New Year.
Directions	A350 south to Fontwell Magna, then left at Fontmell Inn for Ashmore. Straight ahead, over x-roads, up hill to village. On left at pond.

Tessa & Ian Millard
Glebe Farm, High Street,
Ashmore, Salisbury SP5 5AE

Tel	+44 (0)1747 811974
Mobile	+44 (0)7799 858961
Email	stay@glebefarmbandb.co.uk
Web	www.glebefarmbandb.co.uk

Entry 185   Map 3

Dorset

The Old Forge, Fanners Yard

Step back in time in this beautifully restored forge: retro signs, museum pieces, ponies in the paddock and a simpler, slower way of life… Tim and Lucy's smallholding gives you a taste of harmonious living with the seasons, and they recycle everything. This includes Tim's classic cars, a cosy gypsy caravan and a vintage shepherd's hut. The attic bedrooms are snug – Lucy's quilts, country antiques, sparkling bathrooms, flowers – and their breakfasts are renowned: eggs from their hens, organic bacon and sausages, home-grown jams, apple juice straight from the orchard. A happy place, a tonic to stay. *Self-catering in the Smithy.*

Price	£75–£95.
Rooms	4: 1 double, 1 family. Gypsy caravan & shepherd's hut: 1 double each (each with shower/wc close by).
Meals	Pub/restaurant within 1 mile.
Closed	Rarely.
Directions	From Shaftesbury, A350 to Compton Abbas. House 1st on left before Compton Abbas sign. Left; entrance on left.

Tim & Lucy Kerridge
The Old Forge, Fanners Yard,
Compton Abbas,
Shaftesbury SP7 0NQ

Tel	+44 (0)1747 811881
Email	theoldforge@hotmail.com
Web	www.theoldforgedorset.co.uk

Entry 186   Map 3

Dorset

Lawn Cottage

In a quiet village in the Blackmore Vale, the path to this spacious cottage is lined with tulips and vegetables. Easy-going June is a collector of pretty things; fine sketches and watercolours, antiques and china blend charmingly with soft colours and zingy kilims. The sunny bedroom is downstairs, full of books and flowers and delightful in toile de Jouy; it has its own entrance and you can come and go as you please. Breakfast is served in the lovely big kitchen or out in the cottage garden; the tiny sitting room is a perfect snug. Visit Sherborne for its abbey, castle and smart shops; walk from the gate to Duncliffe Woods.

Dorset

Gorse Farm House

Wendy is a generous soul and throws open her lovely house; you are free to wander the garden, grab a book and laze in the sunny conservatory or settle into the snug and watch TV. Upstairs find light-filled, peaceful bedrooms with dreamy views over fields, a bowl of sweets, dainty china and more books; bathrooms are sparkling. Lee is a sculptor and his work peeps out from clever planting around the garden: find a pretty spot there or a seat on the veranda and listen to the birds. Breakfast on local sausages, bacon and free-range farm eggs then tackle some fabulous walks and cycles straight from the door.

Price	From £70. Singles £40.
Rooms	1 twin/double.
Meals	Pub/restaurant 1 mile.
Closed	Rarely.
Directions	See owner website and sent on booking.

Price	From £65. Singles £45.
Rooms	2: 1 twin/double; 1 twin/double with separate bath.
Meals	Pub/restaurant 2 miles.
Closed	Christmas.
Directions	West of Sturminster Newton, south off A357 signed Hazlebury Bryan. 0.5 miles Rivers Corner, left signed Fifehead St Quintin. 0.5 miles bear right at sign for Fifeheads. House 0.25 miles on left.

June Watkins
Lawn Cottage,
Stour Row, Shaftesbury SP7 0QF
Tel   +44 (0)1747 838719
Mobile   +44 (0)7809 696218
Email   enquiries@lawncottagedorset.co.uk
Web   www.lawncottagedorset.co.uk

Wendy Dickenson
Gorse Farm House, Fifehead St Quintin,
Sturminster Newton DT10 2AW
Tel   +44 (0)1258 475343
Mobile   +44 (0)7725 238344
Email   contactus@gorsefarmhousebb.co.uk
Web   www.gorsefarmhousebb.co.uk

Entry 187   Map 3

Entry 188   Map 3

Dorset

Blackrow Farm

Blackrow Farm is tucked up a lane in Hardy's 'Valley of the Dairies'. You stay in the barn annexe – beautifully converted and steeped in character. The airy bedroom in the Dutch Barn comes with its own balcony and wonderful views over Blackmore Vale. The Dairy Cottage has high ceilings and old beams; its ground floor bedroom, cleverly created out of the old milking parlour, has wheelchair access and a big wet room. A delicious locally sourced breakfast is served in the farmhouse, in a historic room with listed panelling and huge inglenook (old bread oven and smokery intact), and the views spread over orchards and fields.

Price	From £80. Singles from £50.
Rooms	Barn annexe: 2 twins/doubles.
Meals	Pub 1 mile.
Closed	Rarely.
Directions	From Sturminster Newton A357 to Stalbridge. After Lydlinch left onto A3030. Just after the deer park left onto B3143. Farm approx. 350 yds on left.

Annie Coultas
Blackrow Farm,
Kings Stag,
Sturminster Newton DT10 2BE
Tel   +44 (0)1963 23156
Email   anniecoultas@gmail.com
Web   www.blackrowfarm.co.uk

Entry 189   Map 3

Dorset

Old Causeway Bakery

In an unpretentious village, a quirky gem. Inside, abundant flower arrangements and bold colours – deep green and cerise – glow alongside oils, prints and antiques dotted around; bookcases bow with the weight of walking guides. In the self-contained bakery wing is a theatrical boudoir (think gold drapes and chaise longue). The main house bedrooms are more serene though still eclectic, with art and a tapestry-upholstered headboard or brass bed; bathrooms are super throughout. Full English breakfasts are all locally sourced, and can be had whenever you like. Come prepared to cuddle Henry and Bertie – the friendly resident dogs.

Price	£85–£95. Bakery Wing £100–£120. Doubles when shared £150. Singles £75–£85.
Rooms	4: 1 double; 2 doubles with shared bath (let to same party only). Bakery Wing: 1 double.
Meals	Pub 30 yds.
Closed	Rarely.
Directions	From Sturminster Newton B3092 Blandford; right at lights, then left signed Hazelbury Bryan. 4 miles into village centre, right after pub. House immed. on left.

Sandra Williams & Simon Boggon
Old Causeway Bakery, Hazelbury Bryan,
Sturminster Newton DT10 2BH
Tel   +44 (0)1258 817228
Mobile +44 (0)7825 815796
Email   sandrasimonbw@btinternet.com
Web   www.oldcausewaybakery.co.uk

Entry 190   Map 3

Dorset

Golden Hill Cottage

Deep in the countryside lies Stourton Caundle and this charming thatched cottage. You have the peace and privacy of your own sitting room, traditionally furnished with antiques, paintings and open fire; up a private stair is your carpeted twin room with a small shower. Anna, courteous and kind, brings you splendid platefuls of local bacon and sausage, homemade jams and Dorset honey for breakfast; nothing is too much trouble for these hosts. There are glorious walks from the village, a good pub that serves food and real ales, and Sherborne, Montacute and Stourhead for landscape, culture and history. *Babes in arms welcome.*

Price	£80–£90. Singles £50.
Rooms	1 twin & sitting room.
Meals	Pubs/restaurants within 3 miles.
Closed	Rarely.
Directions	From Sherborne, A352 to Dorchester; after 1 mile, left onto A3030; on to far end of Bishops Caundle, left to Stourton Caundle; after sharp left into village street, house 200 yds on right.

Anna & Andrew Oliver
Golden Hill Cottage,
Stourton Caundle,
Sturminster Newton DT10 2JW
Tel   +44 (0)1963 362109
Email   anna@goldenhillcottage.co.uk
Web   www.goldenhillcottage.co.uk

Entry 191   Map 3

Dorset

Glebe House

Clematis and wisteria cover much of the mellow brickwork of this spacious and uncluttered 1950s house, down a quiet lane in a tiny hamlet in the heart of stunning Blackmore Vale. From the hall look right through to the mature pretty garden; it's open house and David and Barbara love having guests to stay. Enjoy tea and scones in the garden room, neat-as-a-pin bedrooms and bathrooms, and wide views from every window. Tuck into all sorts of tasty choices at breakfast, by the fire in the dining room. Magnificent castle and abbey are close, and walks from the door are outstanding – you could stay a week and never do the same one!

Price	£70–£80. Singles £50.
Rooms	2: 1 double, 1 twin/double.
Meals	Pub/restaurant within 1 mile.
Closed	Rarely.
Directions	A352 from Sherborne, then left to A3030 (dir. Sturminster Newton). After 1.5 miles at Alweston right to Folke. Glebe House 800 yds on left.

David & Barbara Fifield
Glebe House,
Folke, Sherborne DT9 5HP
Tel   +44 (0)1963 210337
Mobile   +44 (0)7980 864033
Email   glebe.house@hotmail.com
Web   www.glebehouse-dorset.co.uk

Entry 192   Map 3

Dorset

Munden House

This is a super B&B – a couple of farm cottages and assorted outbuildings beautifully stitched together. It's run with great warmth by Colin and Annie, who buy and sell colourful rugs and have travelled the world to do it. Outside, long views shoot off over open country; inside, airy interiors, pretty bedrooms and lots of colour. The garden studios are bigger and more private; one has a galleried bedroom above a lovely sitting room. Annie cooks fantastic food – local meat, fish from Brixham – but her vegetarian dishes will seduce die-hard carnivores. You eat at smartly dressed tables; breakfast is on the terrace in good weather.

Dorset

Holt Cottage

The house stands on high ground and views are fabulous. Richard and Annabel give you a big welcome and two super suites in the cottage a step away. One upstairs, one down, each has its own sitting room, and private entrance so you can come and go as you please. All is sparkling and inviting, with elegant prints on the walls. Bedrooms have wonderful mattresses, good linen and flowers; find fluffy towels and lots of potions in immaculate bathrooms. Delicious breakfast by the Aga in the large beamed kitchen: fruit salad, local bacon and sausages, home-laid eggs; Annabel brings a continental breakfast to your suite if you prefer.

Price	£80-£120. Singles from £70.
Rooms	7: 2 doubles, 1 twin/double, 1 four-poster, 3 garden studios.
Meals	Dinner, 3 courses, £25. Pub 0.5 miles.
Closed	Christmas.
Directions	A352 south from Sherborne, then A3030, east to Alweston. In village, pass post office on right, then left into Mundens Lane before bakery.

Price	From £85. Singles £65.
Rooms	Cottage: 1 double & sitting room, 1 twin/double & sitting room.
Meals	Pub/restaurant 1 mile.
Closed	Rarely.
Directions	From Sherborne, A352 south. After 1 mile, left onto A3030 Blandford road. In Bishops Caundle, left at Murco garage. House 1 mile on left.

	Annie & Colin Fletcher
	Munden House,
	Mundens Lane, Alweston,
	Sherborne DT9 5HU
Tel	+44 (0)1963 23150
Email	stay@mundenhouse.co.uk
Web	www.mundenhouse.co.uk

	Richard & Annabel Buxton
	Holt Cottage,
	Alweston, Sherborne DT9 5JF
Tel	+44 (0)1963 23014
Mobile	+44 (0)7766 583344
Email	annabelbuxton@hotmail.com
Web	www.holtcottagedorset.com

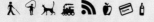

Entry 193 Map 3

Entry 194 Map 3

Dorset

Avalon Townhouse

You'll feel lucky to end up at Paul and Nicky's smart Edwardian townhouse just a few minutes' walk from the station. A large, high-ceilinged sitting room has a cosy fire, sash windows, paintings and prints, and a baby grand piano if you fancy showing off. Bedrooms nod to the contemporary and are as neat as a pin, with beech furniture and satin throws and cushions; bathrooms are spanking new and filled with pleasant things in bottles. Wander down in the morning to a menu bursting with local food and a bit of 'interactive time' with Paul and his Aga. Antiques, medieval buildings and music in the Abbey await. Perfect town B&B.

Price	£80–£90. Singles £70–£80.
Rooms	3 doubles.
Meals	Pub/restaurant 300 yds.
Closed	Rarely.
Directions	A30 to Sherborne. Come off A30 heading south for train station. House 300 yds from station.

Paul & Nicky Aleman
Avalon Townhouse,
South Street,
Sherborne DT9 3LZ
Tel   +44 (0)1935 814748
Email enquiries@avalontownhouse.co.uk
Web   www.avalontownhouse.co.uk

Entry 195   Map 3

Dorset

Windrush Farm

Fun to eat in the light farmhouse kitchen with its Aga, polished oak table, and rag-rolled dresser full of colourful plates. Upstairs, too, is delightful – creaky floors, sloping ceilings and a maze of corridors brightened by new Zoffany wallpapers. Pretty bedrooms are in soft colours; everywhere there are paintings, prints and photos. On colder evenings, your charming hosts will light a fire for you in the guest sitting room – lived-in and snug with artwork and piles of books – while for summer there's a scented rambler-strewn garden and a terrace with the loveliest views. Bustling Sherborne is a ten-minute drive.

Price	From £80. Singles from £55.
Rooms	2: 1 double with separate bath; 1 twin sharing bath (2nd room let to same party only).
Meals	Dinner £25. Pub/restaurant 1 mile.
Closed	Christmas.
Directions	A357 Wincanton-Templecombe. Right at 2nd turn Stowell, opp. entrance to Horsington House. On for approx. 1 mile, then steep hill; pass church on left. House on left after 0.5 miles.

Richard & Jenny Gold
Windrush Farm,
Stowell,
Sherborne DT9 4PD
Tel   +44 (0)1963 370799
Email jennygold@hotmail.co.uk
Web   www.windrushfarmbedandbreakfast.com

Entry 196   Map 3

Durham

Cooper House Farm

Lucy's clever and original use of vibrant colours, combined with antique and vintage pieces, produces astonishing results! And there are lots of wonderful pictures of cows. Hearty breakfasts are served at one large table in the kitchen with orange Aga, juke box and jolly sofas. Stoke up on homemade bread and jams, eggs from their hens – walk it off furiously in the glorious Dales or amble along the river; perhaps visit Barnard Castle. Return to hugely comfortable colourful bedrooms with pastoral views, warm shining bathrooms, a guests' sitting room with a roaring fire and three gentle dogs. *Over sevens welcome.*

Price	£90–£95.
Rooms	2: 1 twin/double; 1 twin/double with separate bath.
Meals	Pubs/restaurants 1–3 miles.
Closed	Rarely.
Directions	Sent on booking.

Lucy Blackmore
Cooper House Farm,
Cotherstone,
Barnard Castle DL12 9QR

Tel	+44 (0)1833 650187
Email	contact@cooperhouse.org.uk
Web	www.cooperhouse.org.uk

Essex

Brook Farm

Large low Georgian windows fill the house with light, unpretentious family pieces warm the bedrooms, and the stunning carved crossbeam in the interconnecting family rooms is late-medieval. Anne, a country lover, has farmed here for over 30 years; outbuildings dot the yard, sheep and horses roam the acres. In Anne's sitting room logs fill the copper and hunting prints line the walls – no TV, but magazines and books aplenty – and you breakfast (deliciously) at a long table with fine antique benches. The handsome pink farmhouse oozes history and a faded country charm, there are some good pubs nearby and Stansted is 30 minutes.

Price	£70–£80. Singles £35–£45.
Rooms	3: 1 twin with en suite shower room; 1 double, 1 family room, each with separate bath.
Meals	Packed lunch £3–£5. Pubs within 2 miles.
Closed	Rarely.
Directions	House on B1053, 500 yds south of Wethersfield.

Anne Butler
Brook Farm,
Wethersfield, Braintree CM7 4BX

Tel	+44 (0)1371 850284
Mobile	+44 (0)7770 881966
Email	abutlerbrookfarm@aol.com
Web	www.brookfarmwethersfield.co.uk

Essex

32 The Hythe

The Thames barge in all her glory: the Gibbs' garden runs almost into the river Blackwater where these majestic old craft are moored and the mudflats are a birdwatcher's dream. Summer breakfast on the deck – local smoked kippers and free-range eggs – watching the barges sail up the river is a rare treat. Beneath wide limpid skies this sensitively extended fisherman's cottage looks out to 12th-century St Mary's at the back where Kim and Gerry ring the Sunday bells. It's immaculate and comfortable inside, an inspired mix of modern and antique lit by myriad candles, among other romantic touches. *Over 14s welcome.*

Price	£90. Singles £70.
Rooms	2: 1 double;
	1 double with separate bath.
Meals	Pub 100 yds.
Closed	Christmas & Boxing Day.
Directions	From A12 to Maldon. House on The Hythe by river, signed for river. Past St Mary's church then right at bottom. House at end of road on right.

Kim & Gerry Gibbs
32 The Hythe,
Maldon CM9 5HN
Tel   +44 (0)1621 859435
Mobile   +44 (0)7753 135108
Email   gibbsie@live.co.uk
Web   www.thehythemaldon.co.uk

Entry 199   Map 10

Essex

Bromans Farm

The island of Mersea is surprisingly secluded, and Bromans Farm is in a most tranquil corner; the sea murmurs across the Saltings where Brent geese wheel and Constable skies stretch. The house began in 1343 – nearly as old as the exquisite village church; the Georgians added their bit, but the venerable beams shine through. Ruth and Martin are charming and give you a very pretty bedroom in yellow and blue, a superb bathroom off the landing, log fires in the snug sitting room, homemade breakfast jams at a beautiful antique table, and tea from Grandmother's blue and white china. Wild walks beckon and the garden is much-loved.

Price	£70-£80. Singles £40-£50.
Rooms	1 twin/double with separate bath.
Meals	Pub 0.5 miles.
Closed	Rarely.
Directions	From Colchester B1025, over causeway, bear left. After 3 miles, pass Dog & Pheasant pub; 3rd right into Bromans Lane. House 1st on left.

Ruth Dence
Bromans Farm,
East Mersea CO5 8UE
Tel   +44 (0)1206 383235
Email   ruth.dence@btconnect.com
Web   www.bromansfarm.co.uk

Entry 200   Map 10

Essex

Caterpillar Cottage

Traditional brick and clapboard, dormer windows, tall chimney – this looks like the real thing. But the 'converted farm building' in the grounds of Patricia's former grand house is only seven years old. Filled with fine furniture, family photographs and *objets* from far-flung travels, it invites relaxation. The double-height, vaulted sitting room brims with sofas and books, logs crackle on chilly nights and bedrooms are simple and comfortable with decent-sized bathrooms. Patricia, a lively grandmother, adores children while her big garden promises home-grown fruit and tranquillity.

Price	From £65. Singles from £35.
Rooms	2: 1 triple; 1 double with separate bath/shower.
Meals	Packed lunch available. Pubs 50 yds.
Closed	Rarely.
Directions	A12 to A1124. In Fordstreet, cottage through gateway shared with Old House, opposite Old Queens Head pub. 88 bus stops at the gate.

	Patricia Mitchell
	Caterpillar Cottage, Fordstreet, Aldham, Colchester CO6 3PH
Tel	+44 (0)1206 240456
Mobile	+44 (0)7776 202713
Email	bandbcaterpillar@tiscali.co.uk
Web	www.caterpillarcottage.co.uk

Entry 201   Map 10

Essex

Emsworth House

Unexpectedly tranquil is this 1937 vicarage, with wide views over the Stour and some wonderful light for painting. Penny, an artist, is a flexible and generous host and you can laze or picnic in her two-acre garden. This is Constable country – great for walking; you are near to Frinton beach and golf, sailing and riding. Return to comfy sofas and chairs, open fires and good books, and redecorated bedrooms with a country feel and the odd African throw or splash of colour. There's heaps of lovely art and a garden full of birds. Penny has camp beds and high chairs and a can-do attitude. Great fun.

Price	From £60. Singles from £50.
Rooms	3: 1 double, 1 twin; 1 double with separate bath.
Meals	Pub/restaurant 0.5 miles.
Closed	Rarely.
Directions	A12-A120 (to Harwich) & left to B1035; right at TV mast to Bradfield, 2 miles; house on right. Manningtree Station 5 miles. A14-A137-B1352, house on left.

	Penny Linton
	Emsworth House, Ship Hill, Station Rd, Bradfield, Manningtree CO11 2UP
Tel	+44 (0)1255 870860
Mobile	+44 (0)7767 477771
Email	emsworthhouse@hotmail.com
Web	www.emsworthhouse.co.uk

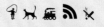

Entry 202   Map 10

Gloucestershire

Trinity House

Meet Zelie: generous, charming, and passionate about the Cotswolds. Off a lane in dreamy Upper Oddington is a smart modern house with a crisp gravel drive and newly planted borders. Inside, a country elegance prevails. Antique furniture shines with care and polish, walls are covered with 20th-century art and splendid sofas front the fire. Bedrooms and bathrooms ooze comfort and joy: one with its own terrace, all with village views. But don't snuggle under the goose down for too long: breakfast verges on the sinful and is locally sourced and delicious. Prepare to be thoroughly spoiled!

Price	From £100. Singles from £60.
Rooms	3 twins/doubles.
Meals	Pubs within walking distance.
Closed	Rarely.
Directions	From Stow-on-the-Wold A436. Fork right dir. Bledington & Kingham, 0.75 miles left Upper Oddington. Drive imm. after phone box on right.

Zelie Mason
Trinity House, Upper Oddington,
Moreton-in-Marsh GL56 0XH

Tel	+44 (0)1451 831284
Mobile	+44 (0)7809 429365
Email	info@trinityhousebandb.co.uk
Web	www.trinityhousebandb.co.uk

Entry 211   Map 8

Gloucestershire

Windy Ridge House

Everyone loves Windy Ridge. It's comfortable, it's cosy, it's run by cheerful staff and it's well positioned for touring the Cotswolds. Nick's father was in construction and built this in traditional style using the finest timbers and stone; refurbishment sees brand new carpets for bedrooms, stairs and landings. There's a green marble bathroom with mirrored walls, a proper four-man lift, a pine-panelled drawing room and polished things at every turn. Take a book to a velveteen sofa and help yourself from the honesty bar; visit the arboretum, the prize-winning gardens and the summer heated pool.

Price	From £100. Singles from £80.
Rooms	4: 2 doubles; 1 double, 1 twin/double each with separate bath.
Meals	Pub 100 yds.
Closed	Rarely.
Directions	From Stow, north for Broadway on A424 for 2 miles to Coach & Horses pub. Opp., right by postbox & 30mph signs down single-track lane. Entrance 100 yds down on left, bear left up drive.

Nick & Jennifer Williams
Windy Ridge House,
Longborough,
Moreton-in-Marsh GL56 0QY

Tel	+44 (0)1451 830465
Email	nick@windy-ridge.co.uk
Web	www.windy-ridge.co.uk

Entry 212   Map 8

Gloucestershire

Rectory Farmhouse

Once a monastery, now a farmhouse with style. Passing a development of converted farm buildings to reach the Rectory's warm Cotswold stones makes the discovery doubly exciting. More glory within: Sybil, a talented designer, has created something immaculate, fresh and uplifting. A wood-burner glows in the sitting room, bed linen is white, walls cream; beds are superb, bathrooms sport cast-iron slipper baths and power showers and views are to the church. Your hosts are naturally friendly; Sybil used to own a restaurant and her breakfasts – by the Aga or in the conservatory under a rampant vine – are a further treat.

Price	From £96. Singles £70.
Rooms	2 doubles.
Meals	Pubs/restaurants 1 mile.
Closed	Christmas & New Year.
Directions	B4068 from Stow to Lower Swell, left just before Golden Ball Inn. Far end of gravel drive on right.

Sybil Gisby
Rectory Farmhouse,
Lower Swell, Stow-on-the-Wold,
Cheltenham GL54 1LH
Tel   +44 (0)1451 832351
Email   rectoryfarmhouse@yahoo.com
Web   www.rectoryfarmhouse.yolasite.com

Entry 213   Map 8

Gloucestershire

Aylworth Manor

Set in a peaceful Cotswolds valley and surrounded by attractive gardens, John and Joanna's gorgeous manor is immaculate. Sit beside the wood-burner in the comfy snug or play the piano in a grand drawing room, rich with art and family photos: your hosts have that happy knack of making you feel instantly at home. Large sunny bedrooms come with garden and valley views, perfect linen on seriously cushy beds, antiques and lavish bathrooms. Wake refreshed for breakfast in the dining room: homemade bread, eggs from the ducks and hens, coffee in a silver pot. The Windrush Way passes the gate at the end of the drive. What a treat!

Price	£90–£100. Singles £55.
Rooms	2: 1 double; 1 twin/double with separate bath.
Meals	Pub 2.5 miles.
Closed	Rarely.
Directions	Sent on booking.

John & Joanna Ireland
Aylworth Manor,
Naunton,
Cheltenham GL54 3AH
Tel   +44 (0)1451 850850
Email   enquiries@aylworthmanor.co.uk
Web   www.aylworthmanor.co.uk

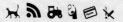

Entry 214   Map 8

Gloucestershire

North Farmcote

Step back 50 years, to a solid 19th-century farmhouse high on the escarpment, and views falling away to the west; on a clear day you can see Hay Bluff. A brilliant spot for North Cotswolds' exploration, it is run by charming and gently self-deprecating David – farmer of cereals and sheep, keen walker, good shot. The exploits of his family decorate the walls (racing at Brooklands, hunting in Africa), there's a floral three-piece to sink into, a terrace with outstanding views, and a great pub you can stride to across fields. Bedrooms and bathrooms are old-fashioned, spacious, comfortable and spotless.

Price	£75-£95. Singles from £50.
Rooms	3: 1 double, 1 twin; 1 twin with separate bath.
Meals	Pub 2 miles.
Closed	January/February.
Directions	B4077 from Stow-on-the-Wold. After Ford, left to Farmcote (signed). After 1.5 miles right. House at end on left.

David Eayrs
North Farmcote,
Winchcombe,
Cheltenham GL54 5AU
Tel   +44 (0)1242 602304
Email   davideayrs@yahoo.co.uk
Web   www.northfarmcote.co.uk

Entry 215   Map 8

Gloucestershire

Sherborne Forge

You are in a quiet Cotswolds corner, in your own restored cottage across the garden from the owner's 17th-century house, and overlooking Sherborne Brook. Walk in to a large living space with a high beamed ceiling, comfy sofas, bright rugs, antiques, flowers, books and a dining table and chairs. You have your own small kitchen for toast and tea; Karen brings over a delicious organic breakfast, served on a private terrace on sunny mornings. Your bedroom has pretty fabrics and fine linen; the bathroom has a big tub for long soaks. Fish for trout in the brook, head off for glorious walks and bike rides... this is a sanctuary.

Price	From £98. Singles £75.
Rooms	Cottage: 1 twin/double, sitting room & kitchenette.
Meals	Pub/restaurant 2.5 miles.
Closed	Rarely.
Directions	A429 at Northleach; A40 towards Oxford. 3 miles, left signed Clapton & Sherborne. After 1 mile, left signed Farmington & Turkdean. 400 yds past houses, right before 30mph exit sign. 100 yds down small lane to house.

Karen Kelly
Sherborne Forge, Number 1
Sherborne, Cheltenham GL54 3DW
Tel   +44 (0)1451 844286
Mobile +44 (0)7796 146130
Email   karen.j.kelly@btinternet.com
Web   www.sherborneforge.co.uk

Entry 216   Map 8

Gloucestershire

Fieldways

High in the Wolds, close to a sleepy village green, are a secluded house and garden where life ticks over beautifully inside and out. Rosewood mahogany, heaps of flowers, a pretty gazebo and a staircase lined with art – all this is the creation of Scottish-Canadian Alan, generous to a fault, a perfectionist in all he does. Marble bathrooms have heated floors while classic country bedrooms are full of deep-carpeted comfort. An immaculate, traditional drawing room and conservatory are yours to share. Wake to the prospect of a fine cooked breakfast, homemade jams, teas from all over the world. Marvellous.

Price	£85–£110. Singles £65–£75. Dogs £10.
Rooms	3: 1 double, 2 twins.
Meals	Lunch £15–£20. Dinner from £40. Pub 50 yds.
Closed	Rarely.
Directions	From M40, exit at junc. 15 onto A429. At Bourton-on-the-Water take A436, then left at sign for Cold Aston. Ask for Fieldways or phone mobile.

	Alan Graham
	Fieldways, 12 Chapel Lane,
	Cold Aston, Cheltenham GL54 3BJ
Tel	+44 (0)1451 810659
Mobile	+44 (0)7790 024532
Email	cascadegroup@aol.com
Web	www.fieldways.com

Entry 217   Map 8

Gloucestershire

Westward

Susie and Jim are highly organised and efficient, juggling farm, horses and B&B. She's also a great cook (Leith trained). The grand, but cosy, house sits above Sudeley Castle surrounded by its own 600 acres; all bedrooms look west to long views. Colours, fabrics and furniture are in perfect harmony, beds and linen are inviting, and the easy mix of elegant living and family bustle is delightful. There's tea on the terrace in summer and by a log fire in winter... your hosts delight in sharing this very English home. Wonderful walks, Cheltenham, Cotswold villages, fabulous restaurants and pubs are near.

Price	From £90. Singles from £60.
Rooms	3: 1 double, 2 twins/doubles.
Meals	Pubs/restaurants 1 mile.
Closed	December/January.
Directions	From Abbey Sq., Winchcombe, go north; after 50 yds, right into Castle St. Follow for 1 mile; after farm buildings, right for Sudeley Lodge; follow for 600 yds. House on right; first oak door.

	Susie & Jim Wilson
	Westward,
	Sudeley Lodge, Winchcombe,
	Cheltenham GL54 5JB
Tel	+44 (0)1242 604372
Email	westward@haldon.co.uk
Web	www.westward-sudeley.co.uk

Entry 218   Map 8

Gloucestershire

Detmore House

Down a private drive, surrounded by seven acres, this smart shiny house has been the home of poets, artists and writers. Gill carries on the creativity with her cooking, interior design, jewellery, gardening and chickens; she and Hugh are easy natural hosts. Supremely comfortable bedrooms have a smart hotel feel, bathrooms are immaculate and you and your dinner party guests will be spoiled with organic produce from the garden. There are wide lawns and mature trees and you can lap up the views across Charlton Hills from lots of lovely sitting spots. Cheltenham and the Cotswold Way are on the doorstep.

Price	From £85. Singles from £65.
Rooms	4: 2 twins/doubles, 1 family room for 3, 1 twin.
Meals	Dinner from £28.50 (for groups of 6+). Packed lunch £6. Pub 1 mile.
Closed	Christmas & New Year.
Directions	A40 from Cheltenham dir. Oxford, thro' Charlton Kings. After 1 mile BP garage on right, next left into Detmore Close. Driveway immed. on right (signed).

Gill Kilminster
Detmore House,
London Road, Charlton Kings,
Cheltenham GL52 6UT
Tel   +44 (0)1242 582868
Email   gillkilminster@btconnect.com
Web   www.detmorehouse.com

Entry 219   Map 8

Gloucestershire

The Courtyard Studio

This smart first-floor studio, attractive in reclaimed red brick, is reached via its own wrought-iron staircase; you are beautifully private. The friendly owners live next door, and will cook you a delicious breakfast in the house, or leave you a continental one in your own fridge. Find a clever, compact, contemporary space with a light and uncluttered living area, a mini window seat opposite two very comfortable boutiquey beds, fine linen, wicker armchair, and a patio area for balmy days. A 20-minute walk brings you to the centre of Cheltenham and you're a two-minute canter from the races. *Minimum stay two nights.*

Price	£80.
Rooms	Studio: 1 twin.
Meals	Restaurants/pubs within 1 mile.
Closed	Rarely.
Directions	Racecourse r'bout, A435 dir. town centre, right Cleevelands Drive. 300 yards on left, thro' pillared gateway in front of mansion. Keep left, enter courtyard. No 1 in left corner.

John & Annette Gill
The Courtyard Studio, 1 The
Cleevelands Courtyard, Cleevelands
Drive, Cheltenham GL50 4QF
Tel   +44 (0)1242 573125
Mobile   +44 (0)7901 978917
Email   courtyardstudio@aol.com

Entry 220   Map 8

Gloucestershire

5 Ewlyn Road

In a bustling suburb of Cheltenham, Barbara's red-brick villa remains firmly unmodernised. The whiff of beeswax fills the air and Barbara looks after you with old-fashioned ease; the front room has an open fire where you can read a book or chat. Your bedroom is peaceful, the bed is firm, and the white cotton sheets robustly pressed; the clean and purposeful bathroom is shared but not noticeably. In the warm parlour Barbara gives you freshly squeezed orange juice, best Gloucester Old Spot bacon, sausages and free-range eggs – have it outside the sunny back door in summer. Authentic, great value B&B.

Price	£60. Singles £30.
Rooms	1 twin sharing bath (& separate shower) with owner.
Meals	Pubs/restaurants 5-minute walk.
Closed	Rarely.
Directions	From A40, signs to Stroud. Up Bath Road past shops; at mini r'bout bear left, then left signed Emmanuel Church. House 2nd on right; front door to side.

Barbara Jameson
5 Ewlyn Road,
Cheltenham GL53 7PB
Tel   +44 (0)1242 261243

Entry 221   Map 8

Gloucestershire

Hanover House

The former home of Elgar's wife, in a Victorian terrace in Cheltenham's heart, is warm, elegant, inviting and surprisingly peaceful. There are big trees all around and the river Chelt laps at the foot of the garden. Inside, find a graceful period décor enlivened by exuberant splashes of colour; the delectable drawing room, with pale walls and a trio of arched windows, is the perfect foil for great art, books and rugs. Bedrooms are beautiful in vibrant red and amber; bathrooms are simply stylish. Breakfast is superb and served in the dining room window. Best of all are Veronica and James: musical, well-travelled, irresistible.

Price	£100. Singles £70.
Rooms	3: 1 double, 1 twin; 1 double with separate bath.
Meals	Pubs/restaurants 200 yds.
Closed	Rarely.
Directions	In Cheltenham town centre, 200 yds from bus & coach station; 800 yds from railway station. Parking available.

Veronica & James Ritchie
Hanover House,
65 St George's Road,
Cheltenham GL50 3DU
Tel   +44 (0)1242 541297
Email   info@hanoverhouse.org
Web   www.hanoverhouse.org

Entry 222   Map 8

Gloucestershire

Clapton Manor

Karin and James's 16th-century manor is as all homes should be: loved and lived-in. And, with three-foot-thick walls, rich Persian rugs on flagstoned floors, sit-in fireplaces and stone-mullioned windows, it's gorgeous. The garden, enclosed by old stone walls, is full of birdsong and roses. One bedroom has a secret door leading to a fuchsia-pink bathroom; the other room, smaller, has a revealed Tudor stone fireplace and wonderful garden views. Wellies, dogs, barbours, a comfy guest sitting room with lots of books… and breakfast by a vast fireplace: homemade bread and jams and eggs from the hens. A happy, charming family home.

Price	From £100. Singles £90.
Rooms	2: 1 double, 1 twin/double.
Meals	Pub/restaurants within 15-minute drive.
Closed	Rarely.
Directions	A429 Cirencester-Stow. Right signed Sherborne & Clapton. In village, pass grassy area to left, postbox in one corner; house straight ahead on left on corner, facing down hill.

Karin & James Bolton
Clapton Manor,
Clapton-on-the-Hill GL54 2LG
Tel   +44 (0)1451 810202
Mobile   +44 (0)7967 144416
Email   bandb@claptonmanor.co.uk
Web   www.claptonmanor.co.uk

Entry 223   Map 8

Gloucestershire

Kempsford Manor

On the edge of the Cotswolds, this 17th-century village manor house is surrounded by mature trees. Crunch up the gravelled drive to find floor-to-ceiling windows, dark floors and patterned rugs, wooden panelling, a piano, a library. Spacious bedrooms have garden views; one comes with a Chinese theme, a mix of rugs, blankets and a pretty quilt. Bathrooms are functional and old-fashioned. Beautifully tended gardens (snowdrops are special here) lead to an orchard and canal walk; stoke up on Zehra's homemade muesli and bread and return for dinner — vegetables are home-grown. *NGS garden. Art exhibitions held. Painting weekends.*

Price	£65-£75. Singles from £45.
Rooms	3: 2 doubles, 1 single all sharing 2 bathrooms.
Meals	Dinner from £17.50. Pub 200 yds.
Closed	Rarely.
Directions	A419 Cirencester-Swindon; Kempsford is signed with Fairford. Right into village, past small village green; on right, through stone columns. Glass front door, by a fountain.

Zehra I Williamson
Kempsford Manor, High Street,
Kempsford, Fairford GL7 4EQ
Tel   +44 (0)1285 810131
Mobile   +44 (0)7980 543882
Email   info@kempsfordmanor.com
Web   www.kempsfordmanor.com

Entry 224   Map 8

Gloucestershire

The Old Rectory

English to the core — and to the bottom of its lovely garden, with a woodland walk and plenty of quiet places to sit. You sweep into the circular driveway to a yellow labrador welcome. This beautiful 17th-century high gabled house is comfortably lived-in with an understated décor, antiques, creaky floorboards and a real sense of history. The bedrooms, one with a garden view, have very good beds, a chaise longue or an easy chair; bathrooms are vintage but large. Caroline is calm and competent and serves breakfasts with organic eggs and local bacon at the long polished table in the rich red dining room. A special place.

Price	£80–£95. Singles from £50.
Rooms	2: 1 double, 1 twin/double.
Meals	Pub 200 yds.
Closed	December/January.
Directions	South through village from A417. Right after Masons Arms. House 200 yds on left, through stone pillars.

Roger & Caroline Carne
The Old Rectory,
Meysey Hampton,
Cirencester GL7 5JX
Tel +44 (0)1285 851200
Email carolinecarne@cotswoldwireless.co.uk
Web www.meyseyoldrectory.co.uk

Entry 225   Map 8

Gloucestershire

The Guest House

You get your own new timber-framed house with masses of light and space, a terrace, and spectacular valley and woodland views. The living room has wooden floors, lovely old oak furniture and French windows onto the rose-filled garden. Sue brims with enthusiasm and is a flexible host: breakfast can be over in her kitchen or continental in yours. Look forward to the papers, eggs from the hens, delicious dinners with produce from the veg patch. The bedroom is a charming up-in-the-eaves room with oriental rugs, colourful linen and a big comfy bed; your fresh, simple wet room is downstairs. A peaceful, secluded place.

Price	From £120.
Rooms	Cottage: 1 double, sitting room & kitchenette.
Meals	Dinner, 2 courses, from £15; 3 courses, from £20. Pub 1 mile.
Closed	Rarely.
Directions	From Circencester, A435 dir. Cheltenham. Left after golf course; over x-roads; 1st left. Left in Bagendon after phone box, immed. left up steep hill signed 'No through Road'.

Sue Bathurst
The Guest House,
Manor Cottage, Bagendon,
Cirencester GL7 7DU
Tel +44 (0)1285 831417
Email heritage.venues@virgin.net
Web www.cotswoldguesthouse.co.uk

Entry 226   Map 8

Gloucestershire

St Annes

Step straight off the narrow pavement into a sunny hall and a warm and welcoming family home. Iris and Greg have made their pretty 17th-century house, in the heart of this lovely bustling village, as eco-friendly as possible. Comfy bedrooms are charming; the four-poster room has a tiny en suite shower room. Farmers' market breakfasts are a feast, bantams wander into the kitchen and Rollo the dog loves children. Painswick is known as 'the Queen of the Cotswolds': enjoy superb walks through orchid meadows and beech woods carpeted with bluebells; visit good pubs on the way. Great value. *Min. two nights at weekends April-Sept.*

Price	£70. Singles £45.
Rooms	3: 1 double, 1 twin, 1 four-poster.
Meals	Packed lunch £5. Restaurants/pubs in village.
Closed	Rarely.
Directions	A46 Stroud to Painswick; in Painswick, left after lights; house 3rd door on right. Bus: from Cheltenham & Stroud. Parking within 100 yds.

	Iris McCormick
	St Annes,
	Gloucester Street,
	Painswick GL6 6QN
Tel	+44 (0)1452 812879
Email	greg.iris@btinternet.com
Web	www.st-annes-painswick.co.uk

Entry 227   Map 8

Gloucestershire

Well Farm

Perhaps it's the gentle, unstuffy attitude of Kate and Edward. Or the great position of the house with its glorious views across the valley. Whichever, you'll feel comforted and invigorated by your stay. It's a real family home and you get both a fresh, pretty bedroom that feels very private and the use of a comfortable, book-filled sitting room opening to a flowery courtyard: Kate is an inspired gardener. Sleep soundly on the softest of pillows, wake to the deep peace of the countryside and the delicious prospect of eggs from their own hens, local sausages and good bacon. The area teems with great walks – lovely pubs too.

Price	From £85.
Rooms	1 twin/double & sitting room.
Meals	Dinner from £20. Pubs nearby.
Closed	Rarely.
Directions	See owner website and sent on booking.

	Kate & Edward Gordon Lennox
	Well Farm,
	Frampton Mansell,
	Stroud GL6 8JB
Tel	+44 (0)1285 760651
Email	kategl@btinternet.com
Web	www.well-farm.co.uk

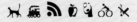

Entry 228   Map 8

Gloucestershire

Drakestone House

A treat by anyone's reckoning. Utterly delightful people with wide-ranging interests (ex-British Council and college lecturing; arts, travel, gardening) in a manor-type house full of beautiful furniture. The house was born of the Arts and Craft movement: wooden panels painted green, a log-fired drawing room for guests, handsome old furniture, comfortable proportions, good beds with proper blankets. The garden's massive clipped hedges, Monterey pines and smooth, great lawn are impressive, as is the whole place – and the views stretch to the Severn Estuary and Wales.

Price	£88. Singles £55.
Rooms	3: 1 twin/double, 1 double, 1 twin, each with separate bath/shower.
Meals	Dinner £35. BYO. Pub/restaurant under 1 mile.
Closed	Christmas & New Year.
Directions	B4060 from Stinchcombe to Wotton-under-Edge. 0.25 miles out of Stinchcombe village. Driveway on left marked, before long bend.

Hugh & Crystal Mildmay
Drakestone House,
Stinchcombe,
Dursley GL11 6AS
Tel   +44 (0)1453 542140

Entry 229   Map 8

Gloucestershire

Lodge Farm

A plum Cotswolds position, a striking garden, a rolling programme of improvements, exceptional linen – there are plenty of reasons to stay. Then there are your flexible hosts, who can help wedding groups, give you supper en famille next to the Aga or something smart and candlelit round the dining room table: perfect for a house party. Sometimes there is home-produced lamb for dinner, always excellent coffee at breakfast, homemade bread and their own free-range eggs; the sitting room has flowers, family photographs and lots of magazines. Peace and quiet lovers will delight, yet you are a short walk from Tetbury.

Price	£70-£80. Singles from £60. Family suite £95.
Rooms	4: 2 twins/doubles; 1 family suite, 1 twin/double sharing bath.
Meals	Dinner, 2-3 courses, £15-£25. Pub/bistro 2.5 miles.
Closed	Rarely.
Directions	From Cirencester A433 to Tetbury, right B4014 to Avening. After 250 yds, left onto Chavenage Lane. Lodge Farm 1.3 miles on right; left of barn on drive.

Robin & Nicky Salmon
Lodge Farm,
Chavenage, Tetbury GL8 8XW
Tel   +44 (0)1666 505339
Mobile   +44 (0)7836 221457
Email   nsalmon.lodgefarm@btinternet.com
Web   www.lodgefarm.co.uk

Entry 230   Map 8

Gloucestershire

York House

In bustling Tetbury, a Georgian townhouse that cuts a dash. Brock left London to chase his dream of opening a B&B; his listed home is smart, unstuffy and he's an enthusiastic host. Hallways are filled with quirky artwork, photos, the odd stuffed animal; the upbeat sitting room comes with splendid fireplace and comfy sofas. Superior beds ensure blissful sleep, bathrooms are replete with Penhaligon's treats. Enjoy breakfast – full English or other choices – at an antique table in the dining room. Wander out to laze by the pond on the sunny terrace or admire the stone folly and wells; the garden is a jewel in the heart of town.

Price	£80–£120. Singles £70–£110.
Rooms	4: 3 doubles, 1 twin.
Meals	Pubs/restaurants 150 yds.
Closed	Rarely.
Directions	Sent on booking. See owner website.

	Brock Bergius
	York House,
	8 Silver Street, Tetbury GL8 8DH
Tel	+44 (0)1666 504508
Mobile	+44 (0)7774 796210
Email	brock@yorkhousetetbury.com
Web	www.yorkhousetetbury.com

Entry 231   Map 3

Gloucestershire

The Moda House

A fine house and a big B&B, but one that retains a deeply homely feel; Duncan and Jo are hugely well-travelled and have filled it with pictures and artefacts from all over the world. Bedrooms differ (three are in a neat annexe) but all are cosy and well decorated with lovely colours, good fabrics, pocket sprung mattresses and bright bathrooms with thick towels. Breakfast is a truly local feast and will set you up for fabulous walks (you are a mile from the Cotswold Way), there's a basement sitting room with comfy armchairs and lots of books, and you have the bustling town to explore with its shops and restaurants.

Price	From £82. Singles from £62.
Rooms	11: 8 doubles, 3 singles.
Meals	Pubs/restaurants within 0.25 miles.
Closed	Rarely.
Directions	Exit M4 at junction 18. Follow A46 northbound. Turn left and follow A432 into town centre. House is at top of High Street.

	Duncan & Jo MacArthur
	The Moda House,
	1 High Street,
	Chipping Sodbury BS37 6BA
Tel	+44 (0)1454 312135
Email	enquiries@modahouse.co.uk
Web	www.modahouse.co.uk

Entry 232   Map 3

Gloucestershire

Little Smithy

Minutes from the M4, the farming village is fairly quiet and your little cottage with mullioned windows completely private. Your front door opens into a hallway which runs the length of the building: at one end, the creamy twin with bright red bedspreads and sparkling bathroom next door, at the other, your L-shaped sitting room with an electric wood-burner. Upstairs is the comfy double and another smart bathroom; all is as neat as a pin. Joanna gives you breakfast in the main house, or on warm days in the garden: eggs from next door's hens, homemade bread and marmalade. Right on the Cotswold Way so perfect for walkers.

Price	£75. Singles £60.
Rooms	2: 1 double, 1 twin/double.
Meals	Pub/restaurant 1 mile.
Closed	Christmas & Easter.
Directions	Bath A46 north. Cross M4 signed Stroud, then almost immed. 1st turning on right. After Compass Inn, 2nd turning on right into village. Past church; house 1st on right after left-hand bend.

Joanna Bowman
Little Smithy,
Smithy House, Tormarton,
Badminton GL9 1HU

Tel +44 (0)1454 218412
Email richardbowman@uk2.net
Web www.littlesmithy.com

Entry 233   Map 3

Hampshire

Meadow Lodge

A summerhouse treat, tucked away beside the handsome Lodge, overlooking a pool and pretty landscaped gardens. French windows open to a terrace of tumbling wisteria, shrubs and pots. The huge bedroom is elegant and light, the bathroom luxurious; beds are well-dressed, there are books to read, rattan sofa and chairs, wide-screen TV, CDs and a lovely mix of family pieces, antiques and Liza's art. A traditional English with home-laid eggs is brought over; help yourself to cereals, patisserie, toast, coffee... and your fridge is stocked with nibbles and drinks. Amble over the trout-filled river Anton and meadows for a pub supper.

Price	£100 (£140 for 3; £180 for 4). Singles £85.
Rooms	Summerhouse: 1 double (with extra beds).
Meals	Pubs 5-minute walk.
Closed	Rarely.
Directions	Sent on booking.

Elizabeth Butterworth
Meadow Lodge, Green Meadow Lane,
Goodworth Clatford, Andover SP11 7HH

Tel +44 (0)1264 352965
Mobile +44 (0)7930 532822
Email liza.butterworth@googlemail.com
Web www.greenmeadowlodge.co.uk

Entry 234   Map 3

Hampshire

Hampshire

Yew Tree House

Philip and Janet's house is artistic and tranquil. The views, the house and the villagers are said to have inspired Dickens, who escaped London for the peace of the valley. The exquisite red brick was there 200 years before him; the rare dovecote in the next door churchyard, to which you may have the key, 300 years before that. Thoughtful hosts, interesting to talk to, have created a home of understated elegance: a yellow-ochre bedroom with top quality bed linen, cashmere/silk curtains designed by their son, enchanting garden views, flowers in every room, a welcoming log fire. Breakfast with good coffee is delicious too.

Lee Manor

Cross the river Test, amble down a quiet country lane, arrive at Deb and Phil's family home. Their pretty manor is elegant yet friendly and the sitting room is inviting: books, games, sofas and open fire. Lovely bedrooms have feather toppers on good beds, beautiful fabrics, a decanter of port and homemade biscuits. Expect huge breakfasts: Phil's home-roasted coffee, black pudding, waffles, kippers, eggs from the hens... delicious! There are historic houses to visit (admire the roses at Montisfont Abbey), trout fishing can be arranged and the Southampton Boat Show and New Forest are a hop. *Painting & chicken-keeping courses.*

Price	£85. Singles by arrangement.
Rooms	2: 1 twin; 1 double with separate bath.
Meals	Pub in village.
Closed	Rarely.
Directions	From A30 west of Stockbridge for 1.5 miles, left at minor x-roads. After 2 miles left at T-junc. House on left at next junc. opposite Greyhound.

Price	£75-£130. Singles from £35.
Rooms	3: 2 doubles, 1 twin/double. Extra single room available.
Meals	Dinner, 3 courses, £25 (for parties). Pubs/restaurants 2.5 miles.
Closed	Rarely.
Directions	Sent on booking.

Philip & Janet Mutton
Yew Tree House,
Broughton,
Stockbridge SO20 8AA
Tel   +44 (0)1794 301227
Email   pandjmutton@onetel.com

Deb Newman
Lee Manor,
Lee Lane, Lee, Romsey SO51 9LH
Tel   +44 (0)2380 730123
Email   leemanorbandb@gmail.com
Web   www.leemanor.co.uk

Entry 235   Map 3

Entry 236   Map 3

Hampshire

Sandy Corner

Stride straight onto open moorland from this smallholding on the edge of the New Forest – a good place for anyone who enjoys walking, cycling, riding, wildlife and the great outdoors. And there's plenty of room for wet clothes and muddy boots. You may hear the call of a nightjar in June, Dartford warblers nest nearby, hens cluck around the yard. Sue also keeps a horse, two cats, a few sheep. You have a little guest sitting room, fresh sunny bedrooms, your own spot in the garden and a marvellous, away-from-it-all feel. You can walk to one pub; others are nearby.

Hampshire

Vinegar Hill Pottery

A sylvan setting, stylish pottery, a young and talented family. The cobalt blues and rich browns of David's ceramics fill the old stables of a Victorian manor house. Take pottery courses (one hour to a long weekend) or just enjoy the creative Mexican-inspired décor. A narrow staircase spirals up to a modern loft: crisp whites, cathedral ceiling with sunny windows, brilliant shower. The ground-floor garden suite has a patio (with a gorgeous Showman's wagon!), sitting room, painted bed and optional children's beds. Lucy brings breakfast to your room. Stroll to the beach: stretch out and you almost touch the Isle of Wight.

Price	From £78. Singles from £50.
Rooms	2 doubles.
Meals	Packed lunch £8. Pub within walking distance.
Closed	Rarely.
Directions	On A338, 1 mile S of Fordingbridge, at small x-roads, turn for Hyde & Hungerford. Up hill & right at school for Ogdens; left at next x-roads for Ogdens North; on right at bottom of hill.

Price	From £75. Singles from £60. Min. stay 2 nights at weekends April-October; 3 on bank holidays.
Rooms	2: 1 double, 1 suite for 2-4. Showman's wagon for 2 (with separate wet room) is an optional extra for the suite (occasionally let independently, so enquire).
Meals	Pub/restaurant 0.25 miles.
Closed	Rarely.
Directions	A339 towards Christchurch. Left onto B3058. Next right into Manor Road, round bend into Barnes Lane. After Baptist church, Vinegar Hill is 3rd on right.

Sue Browne
Sandy Corner,
Ogdens North,
Fordingbridge SP6 2QD
Tel   +44 (0)1425 657295

Lucy Rogers
Vinegar Hill Pottery,
Vinegar Hill,
Milford on Sea SO41 0RZ
Tel   +44 (0)1590 642979
Email info@davidrogerspottery.co.uk
Web   www.davidrogerspottery.co.uk

Entry 237   Map 3

Entry 238   Map 3

Hampshire

Bay Trees

The Isle of Wight and the Needles loom large as you approach Milford on Sea: the beach is shingle, the views are amazing. Mark and Sarah, excited about their new B&B venture, welcome you in to a sun-filled conservatory with Ercol elm and beech tables and chairs; the home-bakes and award-winning breakfasts are delicious. Comfortable bedrooms, with good linen, are spotless and warm; bathrooms ooze white towels. One room opens to the lush garden, all towering bamboos, magnolias and pond: choose an arbour for tea! With Mark's background in hospitality and Sarah's passion for cooking the service here is second to none.

Price	£90-£130. Singles £80. Min. 2 nights at weekends.
Rooms	3: 1 double, 1 four-poster, 1 family room.
Meals	Restaurants 100 yds.
Closed	Rarely.
Directions	Sent on booking.

Mark & Sarah Clayson
Bay Trees,
8 High Street, Milford on Sea,
Lymington SO41 0QD

Tel	+44 (0)1590 642186
Email	mark.clayson@btinternet.com
Web	www.baytreebedandbreakfast.co.uk

Entry 239   Map 3

Hampshire

Home Close

The setting is gorgeous, surrounded by the New Forest – walks start from the gate. The house, once a farm belonging to the Beaulieu estate, is now home to friendly Sally and Bob. You sleep in a sunshine-yellow bedroom overlooking the lovely garden, there are Lloyd Loom chairs for reading or TV, bottled water, proper milk, homemade shortbread. A generous breakfast, sometimes with home-baked bread, is taken in the pretty blue dining room at a solid oak table, from where you can watch the comings and goings of interesting birds beneath the arbour. Perfect for exploring the New Forest or a day trip to the Isle of Wight.

Price	From £80.
Rooms	1 double.
Meals	Packed lunch £7. Pubs/restaurants within 7 miles.
Closed	Christmas, New Year & occasionally.
Directions	M27 junc. 2. A326, then B3054 signed Beaulieu 1.1 miles from New Forest cattle grid, down gravel track signed Home Close & Vanguard. Left past cottage to gate.

Sally Brearley
Home Close,
Hill Top,
Beaulieu SO42 7YR

Tel	+44 (0)1590 612287
Email	homeclose@talktalk.net
Web	www.homeclosebedandbreakfast.co.uk

Entry 240   Map 3

Hampshire

Brymer House

Complete privacy in a B&B is rare. Here you have it, a 12-minute walk from town, cathedral and water meadows. Relax in your own half of a Victorian townhouse immaculately furnished and decorated and with a garden to match – all roses and lilac in the spring. Fizzy serves sumptuous breakfasts, there's a log fire in the guests' sitting room and fresh flowers abound – guests have been delighted. You are also left with an 'honesty box' so you may help yourselves to drinks. Bedrooms are small and elegant, with antique mirrors, furniture and bedspreads; bathrooms are warm and spotless. *Children over seven welcome.*

Price	£75-£85. Singles £54-£60.
Rooms	2: 1 double, 1 twin.
Meals	Pubs/restaurants nearby.
Closed	Rarely.
Directions	M3 junc. 9; A272 Winchester exit, then signs for Winchester Park & Ride. Under m'way, straight on at r'bout signed St Cross. Left at T-junc.

Guy & Fizzy Warren
Brymer House,
29-30 St Faith's Road, St Cross,
Winchester SO23 9QD
Tel   +44 (0)1962 867428
Email   brymerhouse@aol.com
Web   www.brymerhouse.co.uk

Entry 241   Map 4

Hampshire

Mulberry House

Deep into Jane Austen country, among ancient apple trees and rose bushes, is Mulberry House – the red-brick stable block of Old Alresford House. Peter and Sue are charming, and so is their home, filled with interesting pictures, fresh flowers and family photos. Private, quietly elegant guest rooms share a sitting room and kitchenette; the one in the eaves overlooks a pretty courtyard where a fountain plays. The dining room is elegant, but in fine weather you breakfast beneath the wisteria and vine-hung pergola on home-laid eggs and homemade jams. Comfortably English with a lovely garden.

Price	£90. Singles £65.
Rooms	2: 1 double, 1 twin/double.
Meals	Pubs/restaurants within 15-minute walk.
Closed	Rarely.
Directions	M3 exit 9, signs to Alresford. In town centre, left onto B3046 to church on right. Then right into Colden Lane. House is 3rd on right through field gate.

Sue & Peter Paice
Mulberry House, Colden Lane,
Old Alresford, Alresford SO24 9DY
Tel   +44 (0)1962 735518
Mobile   +44 (0)7801 931905
Email   suepaice@btinternet.com
Web   www.mulberryhousebnb.com

Entry 242   Map 4

Hampshire

The Threshing Barn

You are on the edge of the rolling Meon valley in South Downs National Park, the approach through hedge-lined lanes is bucolic and the beautifully restored barn sits on a conservation award-winning farm run by John. Choose between a colourful and homely double in the main house or independence in the glorious bothy – a beamed and light space with a big walk-in shower. Find flowers, good mattresses and feather and down pillows. Guests are greeted with tea, breakfast is a local or home-grown extravaganza (check out Emma's borage honey) and views are to one of the tallest village church spires in Hampshire. *Minimum stay two nights.*

Price	£95. Singles £85.
Rooms	2: 1 double with separate bath. Bothy: 1 twin/double.
Meals	Packed lunch £7-£8. Pub 2 miles.
Closed	Rarely.
Directions	A272 Winchester to Petersfield. After A32 & A272 crossing, continue 0.8 miles towards Petersfield. Then left up Stocks Lane, 0.5 miles to the house.

	Emma Bird
	The Threshing Barn,
	Stocks Lane, Privett GU34 3NZ
Tel	+44 (0)1730 828382
Mobile	+44 (0)7980 841154
Email	emmacbird@stocksfarmprivett.co.uk
Web	www.thethreshingbarn.co.uk

Entry 243   Map 4

Hampshire

Shafts Farm

The 1960s farmhouse has many weapons in its armoury: a tremendous South Downs thatched-village setting, owners who know every path and trail, comfortable, generous bedrooms and a stunning rose garden designed by David Austin Roses (parterres, obelisks, meandering paths). The two bedrooms are fresh in cream, florals and plaids, each with a shower room with heated floors to keep toes toasty. Homemade granola, garden fruit and the full English make a fine start to the day; the airy, cane-furnished conservatory is the place for afternoon tea and a read. Your hosts are both geographers and have an intriguing display of maps.

Price	£80. Singles £45.
Rooms	2 twins.
Meals	Dinner, 3 courses, £17. Pubs/restaurants 500 yds.
Closed	Rarely.
Directions	Sent on booking.

	Rosemary Morrish
	Shafts Farm,
	West Meon,
	Petersfield GU32 1LU
Tel	+44 (0)1730 829266
Email	info@shaftsfarm.co.uk
Web	www.shaftsfarm.co.uk

Entry 244   Map 4

Hampshire

Mizzards Farm

The central hall is three storeys high, its vaulted roof open to the rafters. This is the oldest part of this lovely, wisteria-clad, mostly 16th-century farmhouse: kilims and fine antiques look splendid with old flagstones and wooden floors. There's a drawing room for musical evenings and an upstairs conservatory from which you can see the garden with its lake, outdoor chess and Harriet's sculptures. The four-poster is luxuriously kitsch with electric curtains, the other bedrooms are traditional and fresh. Come in the summer for occasional mini Glyndebournes on the lawn. *Children over eight welcome. Min. two nights.*

Price	£80–£90. Singles by arrangement.
Rooms	3: 1 double, 1 twin, 1 four-poster.
Meals	Pubs 0.5 miles.
Closed	Christmas & New Year.
Directions	From A272 at Rogate, turn for Harting & Nyewood. Cross humpback bridge; drive signed to right after 300 yds.

Harriet & Julian Francis
Mizzards Farm,
Rogate,
Petersfield GU31 5HS
Tel   +44 (0)1730 821656
Email francis@mizzards.co.uk

Entry 245   Map 4

Hampshire

Land of Nod

A 1939 house of character with hosts to match and a magnificent garden: seven tended acres within 100 acres of woodland. There are azaleas and camellias, specimen trees, croquet, tennis, masses of bluebells, grapevines and a wisteria 40 years old: Jeremy will give a guided tour. The chinoiserie dining room has a charming allegorical tableau and the needlework on the walls dates from 1901. No sitting room, but bedrooms are big with soft sink-into beds and garden views; original baths have vast taps. Flexible breakfasts are tasty with seasonal fruit from the garden, homemade jams and local sausages. *Over tens welcome.*

Price	From £80. Singles from £50.
Rooms	2: 1 twin; 1 twin with separate bath.
Meals	Restaurants 5-minute drive.
Closed	Rarely.
Directions	South on A3, London to Hindhead tunnel. At exit, signs for Hindhead, Grayshott. Over bridge, left signed Bramshott Chase. After 0.2 miles, right Grayshott. Left at church, signed Headley. Entrance (signed) 2.1 miles on; on right in a wood.

Jeremy & Philippa Whitaker
Land of Nod,
Headley,
Bordon GU35 8SJ
Tel   +44 (0)1428 713609
Email pwhitaker100@hotmail.com

Entry 246   Map 4

Hampshire

Weston Farm

Country life at its loveliest: a beautifully restored Georgian house and farm; fresh-laid eggs; a donkey and pony in the paddock, and generous, helpful hosts who will fetch you off the London train. Horse and hound wallpaper gallops over the hall, the sitting room has wood panelling, sash windows and a giant marble fireplace; comfortable bedrooms have writing desks, pretty curtains and white linen. A footpath traces the 800-acre arable farm so roam free over water meadows. Stroll to the typical Hampshire village of Micheldever (thatched cottages, handsome church) for dinner – or it's eight miles to historic Winchester.

Price	£80. Singles £50.
Rooms	2: 1 twin/double, 1 four-poster.
Meals	Pub 1.5 miles.
Closed	Christmas.
Directions	M3 junc. 11 then A33 northbound. Left to Micheldever, then left at T-junc., 2nd left to Weston Colley. At bottom of hill Weston Farm on left.

Laura Stevens
Weston Farm, Weston Down Lane,
Weston Colley, Winchester SO21 3AG

Tel	+44 (0)1962 774791
Mobile	+44 (0)7999 816417
Email	westonfarmbandb@googlemail.com
Web	www.westonfarmaccommodation.co.uk

Entry 247   Map 4

Hampshire

Browninghill Farm

Complete independence here: your own prettily converted threshing barn down an oak-lined lane. Hattie lives in the farm next door and looks after you well; breakfasts and dinners are rustled up for you in your little kitchen – eggs from the hens, homemade bread and jams and local produce. The attractive dining/sitting space has a soaring ceiling, beams, a duck egg blue dresser holding cheerful crockery and a picture window with views across the fields. Bedrooms (one up, one down) are cosy with comfy feather pillows and white linen; bathrooms are small yet perfect with robes and big towels. Snug and romantic.

Price	£110. Singles £50-£75. Minimum 2 nights.
Rooms	Barn: 1 double, 1 single.
Meals	Supper, 2 courses, £25. Pubs/restaurants 0.5 miles.
Closed	Rarely.
Directions	Sent on booking.

Hattie Pigot
Browninghill Farm, Browninghill
Green, Baughurst, Tadley RG26 5JZ

Tel	+44 (0)1189 815537
Mobile	+44 (0)7789 431220
Email	hattie@browninghillfarm.com
Web	www.browninghillfarm.com

Entry 248   Map 4

Hampshire

Little Cottage

Just 45 minutes from Heathrow but the peace is deep, the views are long and the wildlife thrives – watch fox and deer, listen out for the rare nightjar. Chris and Therese grow summer salads and soft fruits and give you superb home cooking; eat in a big conservatory filled with greenery. Guests have a lovely sitting room with an eclectic mix of modern and antique furniture, and a pretty terrace overlooks the garden; bedrooms, likewise, are on the ground-floor, fresh and light, the double with distant views. Perfect for walkers and those who seek solace from urban life but don't want to stray too far. *Over 12s welcome.*

Price	£80–£95. Singles £55. Min. 2 nights at weekends.
Rooms	3: 1 twin/double, 1 double, 1 single.
Meals	Dinner from £20. Pub 1.5 miles.
Closed	Christmas, New Year & occasionally.
Directions	B3011 from A30 in Hartley Wintney for 1.5 miles. Cottage on left, down a small track then fork left.

Chris & Therese Abbott
Little Cottage, Hazeley Heath,
Hartley Wintney, Hook RG27 8LY
Tel   +44 (0)1252 845050
Mobile   +44 (0)7721 462214
Email   info@little-cottage.co.uk
Web   www.little-cottage.co.uk

Entry 249   Map 4

Herefordshire

Bunns Croft

The timbers of the medieval house are probably 1,000 years old. Little of the structure has ever been altered and it is an absolute delight: stone floors, rich colours, a piano, dogs, books and cosy chairs – all give a homely, warm feel. Cruck-beamed bedrooms are snugly small, the stairs are steep – this was a yeoman's house – and the twin's bathroom has its own sweet fireplace. The countryside is 'pure', too, with 1,500 acres of National Trust land five miles away. Anita is charming, loves to look after her guests, grows her own fruit and vegetables and makes fabulous dinners. Just mind your head.

Price	£80–£85. Singles from £40.
Rooms	4: 1 twin; 1 double, 2 singles, sharing bath (let to same party only).
Meals	Dinner, 3 courses, £25. Pub 7 miles.
Closed	Rarely.
Directions	From Leominster, A49 towards Ludlow; 4 miles to village of Ashton, then left. House on right behind postbox after 1 mile.

Anita Syers-Gibson
Bunns Croft,
Moreton Eye,
Leominster HR6 0DP
Tel   +44 (0)1568 615836

Entry 250   Map 7

Herefordshire

Staunton House

This handsome Georgian rectory with light, colourful and well-proportioned rooms brims with beautiful furnishings. The original oak staircase leads to peaceful bedrooms with comfortable beds; the blue room looks onto garden and pond. It's a house that matches its owners – quiet, traditional and country-loving. Wander through the lovely garden, drive to Hay or Ludlow, stride some ravishing countryside, play golf near Offa's Dyke; return to Rosie and Richard's lovely home to relax in their drawing room before enjoying a delicious dinner in the elegant dining room. You will be well tended here.

Herefordshire

Grendon Manor

The best of traditional meets modern country living: this 16th-century manor house is a super mix of the very old and very new. A working sheep and cattle farm is wrapped around it and you can walk over fields and down to a pretty Norman church. Jane is easy company and looks after you well. Guests in their own wing will rejoice in bedrooms with old beams, crisply comfortable linen and new bathrooms, while the guest sitting room downstairs has marvellous dark oak panelling, rich colours and glowing lamps. A farmhouse-tasty breakfast sets you up for beautiful Herefordshire walks, and Ludlow is close.

Price	From £80. Singles from £50.
Rooms	2: 1 double, 1 twin/double.
Meals	Dinner, 2-3 courses, £22-£25. Pub/restaurant 2.5 miles.
Closed	Rarely.
Directions	A44 Leominster-Pembridge; right to Shobdon. After 0.5 miles, left to Staunton-on-Arrow; at x-roads, over into village. House opp. church, with black wrought-iron gates.

Price	From £90. Singles £50.
Rooms	3: 2 doubles, 1 twin.
Meals	Dinner £25 (groups only). Pub/restaurant 2 miles.
Closed	Rarely.
Directions	A44 through Bromyard. House 4 miles in village of Bredenbury. Past Bredenbury Arms pub, 2nd drive on the left 200 yds on.

	Rosie & Richard Bowen	
	Staunton House, Staunton-on-Arrow, Pembridge, Leominster HR6 9HR	
Tel	+44 (0)1544 388313	
Mobile	+44 (0)7780 961994	
Email	rosbown@aol.com	
Web	www.stauntonhouse.co.uk	

	Jane Piggott	
	Grendon Manor, Bredenbury, Bromyard HR7 4TH	
Tel	+44 (0)1885 482226	
Mobile	+44 (0)7977 493083	
Email	jane.piggott@btconnect.com	
Web	www.grendonmanor.com	

Entry 251   Map 7

Entry 252   Map 7

Herefordshire

Hall's Mill House

Quiet lanes bring you to this most idyllic spot – a stone cottage in a light and open valley. The sitting room is snug with wood-burner and sofas but the kitchen is the hub of the place – delicious breakfasts and dinners are cooked on the Aga. Grace, chatty and easy-going, obviously enjoys living in her modernised mill house. Rooms are small, fresh, with exposed beams and slate sills; only the old mill interrupts the far-reaching, all-green views. Drift off to sleep to the sound of the Arrow burbling by – a blissful tonic for walkers and nature lovers. Great value, too. *Children over four welcome.*

Price	£55–£60. Singles £27.50–£30.
Rooms	3: 1 double; 1 double, 1 twin, sharing bath.
Meals	Dinner from £15. Pub/restaurant 3 miles.
Closed	Christmas.
Directions	A438 from Hereford. After Winforton, Whitney-on-Wye & toll bridge, sharp right for Brilley. Left fork to Huntington, over x-roads & next right to Huntington. Next right into 'No Through Road', then 1st right.

Grace Watson
Hall's Mill House,
Huntington,
Kington HR5 3QA
Tel +44 (0)1497 831409

Entry 253   Map 7

Herefordshire

Winforton Court

Dating from 1500, the Court is dignified in old age: undulating floors, oak beams, thick walls, a long gallery for family parties. It is a dramatic, colourful home with exceptional timber-framed bedrooms; one room has an Indian-style bathroom and roll top bath, the sumptuous suite has a sitting area with sofas. Choose a book from the small library and relax by a warming log fire in the elegant guest sitting room; all is immaculate. Your hosts are delightful and generous: decanters of sherry, bedside chocolates, delicious breakfasts. Visit Hay, walk down to the Wye, relax in the splendid bird-filled garden. *Fishing can be arranged.*

Price	£90–£115. Singles from £75.
Rooms	3: 1 double, 1 four-poster, 1 four-poster suite.
Meals	Pub/restaurant 2-minute walk.
Closed	20–30 December.
Directions	From Hereford, A438 into village. Past Sun Inn, house on left with a green sign & iron gates.

Jackie Kingdon
Winforton Court,
Winforton HR3 6EA
Tel +44 (0)1544 328498
Email jackie@winfortoncourt.co.uk
Web www.winfortoncourt.co.uk

Entry 254   Map 7

Herefordshire

Tinto House

Bang in the centre of Hay-on-Wye, opposite the clock tower, amid a sea of bookshops, this beautiful Georgian townhouse brims with period features and original art. John and Karen have decorated their home with love: in the dining room, John's eye-catching paintings set off oak antiques, bookshelves, a fireplace; bedrooms bear mementos of France; one room holds art exhibitions. The garden, on the Wye's banks, is resplendent with roses and sculptures. Breakfast on local sausages and compotes from home-grown fruit before hitting the Black Mountains or Hay's independent shops. Perfect for lovers of outdoor and armchair pursuits.

Price	£85-£95. Singles £60-£80.
Rooms	4: 2 doubles, 1 twin; 1 double with separate bath.
Meals	Packed lunch £5. Pub/restaurant 100 yds.
Closed	Christmas & New Year.
Directions	From Hereford A438 towards Brecon. After 19 miles left at Clyro to Hay (1 mile). Cross river; right at T-junc. House 100 yds on right facing clock tower.

Karen Clare
Tinto House, 13 Broad Street, Hay-on-Wye HR3 5DB

Tel	+44 (0)1497 821556
Mobile	+44 (0)7985 559355
Email	tintohouse@tiscali.co.uk
Web	www.tinto-house.co.uk

Entry 255   Map 7

Herefordshire

Lower House

A luxuriant garden in a magical valley; strike out for the Black Mountains from the door. The house, itself a forest of old timber, is almost lost within the garden. It is old, but restored with affection. Stairs twist and creak, the unexpected awaits you. Irresistible bedrooms are panelled or timber-clad; bathrooms are new. There's a handsome room downstairs where you eat breakfast (plentiful, delicious), play the piano or read by the fire. Nicky and Pete are kind and generous, steeped in good taste and this exquisite project, next to Offa's Dyke path and on the Welsh border. One of the best!

Price	From £90. Minimum 2 nights.
Rooms	2: 1 double; 1 double with separate bath/shower.
Meals	Pubs/restaurants in Hay-on-Wye, 1 mile.
Closed	Rarely.
Directions	East through Hay on B4348 for Bredwardine. On the edge of Hay, right into Cusop Dingle; 0.75 miles, old mill house on left; drive on right, across stone bridge over stream.

Nicky & Peter Daw
Lower House, Cusop Dingle, Hay-on-Wye HR3 5RQ

Tel	+44 (0)1497 820773
Mobile	+44 (0)7779 480783
Email	nicky.daw@btinternet.com
Web	www.lowerhousegardenhay.co.uk

Entry 256   Map 7

Herefordshire

Ty-Mynydd

Six miles over open heathland from Hay-on-Wye, it is a remote approach up the mountainside to Ty-Mynydd, and this renovated, stone-flagged farmhouse is absolutely gorgeous. Sheep graze the hillside, the views are simply the best and the garden is colourful, informal, delightful. Turn on the taps and taste water straight from your hosts' own mountain stream; awake to delicious rare-breed sausages and eggs produced in the fields around you (this is a working organic farm). The lovely young family give you two sweetly restful rooms on the ground floor, one with 'that view', and a simple country bathroom. The sunsets are magical.

Herefordshire

Rock Cottage

Birds, books and beautiful Black Mountain views highlighted by morning sun, turning to an inky black line at dusk; the cottage glows. There's an instant feeling of warmth and friendliness as you step into the snug hall; find rich autumnal colours, old rugs, a big wood-burner and comfy sitting rooms. Local art and photos line the walls, bedrooms have sumptuous beds, perfect linen and garden posies. You eat (very well) at the communal oak table, or out on the pretty terrace. Thoughtful Chris and Sue will take you to hear the dawn chorus and there are food and literary festivals, bookshops and walks galore. *Dogs by arrangement.*

Price	From £85. Singles £60.
Rooms	2 doubles sharing bath (let to same party only).
Meals	Pubs 6-8 miles.
Closed	Christmas & New Year.
Directions	From Hay on A438, 1st left after Swan Hotel; 6 miles uphill to open heath under Hay Bluff; 2nd right signed Capel Y Ffin; 1 mile, signed.

Price	£70-£90. Singles from £45.
Rooms	2 doubles.
Meals	Packed lunch £6. Dinner, 3 courses, £20. Pub/restaurant 4 miles.
Closed	Christmas & New Year.
Directions	Hereford A465. After approx. 4.5 miles right onto B4348 to Vowchurch; left then 1st left signed 'St Margaret's & Church'. Pass church, down hill. Cottage 2nd on left. Park in space on right.

N Spenceley
Ty-Mynydd,
Llanigon, Hay-on-Wye HR3 5RJ
Tel   +44 (0)1497 821593
Mobile +44 (0)7896 020459
Email   nikibarber@tiscali.co.uk
Web   www.tymynydd.co.uk

Entry 257   Map 7

Chris & Sue Robinson
Rock Cottage,
Newton St Margarets,
Hereford HR2 0QW
Tel   +44 (0)1981 510360
Email   robinsrockcottage@googlemail.com
Web   www.rockcottagebandb.co.uk

Entry 258   Map 7

Herefordshire

Yew Tree House

Sue and John's gorgeous 19th-century home is surrounded by gardens bejewelled with roses and fruit trees – plus stunning views across the Golden Valley to Hay Bluff. Meet these delightful people over tea and homemade cake in a tastefully decorated guest sitting room with comfy sofas, an open fire and shelves groaning with books. Generous bedrooms in pretty pastels are supremely comfortable, bathrooms have plenty of fluffy towels. Wake to the smell of baking bread, hasten to the dining room for a delicious breakfast of local produce. Dore Abbey's down the road, and Hay-on-Wye a half-hour jaunt. The countryside is glorious.

Price	£80–£95.
Rooms	3: 1 double, 1 twin, 1 suite for 3.
Meals	Dinner, 3 courses, £25. Pub/restaurant 3.5 miles.
Closed	Rarely.
Directions	Sent on booking.

John & Susan Richardson
Yew Tree House,
Batcho Hill, Vowchurch,
Hereford HR2 9PF
Tel +44 (0)1981 251195
Email enquiries@yewtreehouse-hereford.co.uk
Web www.yewtreehouse-hereford.co.uk

Entry 259   Map 7

Herefordshire

Burghill Grange

A big, happy, friendly family house. Harriet and John are marvellous hosts and their home – all waxed elm floors, beams and fine 18th-century ceilings – is a delight. Your cosy bright sitting room has a fire, bold fabrics and interesting books; enjoy home-laid eggs, fresh bread, delicious coffee and sausages from Ludlow, as you gaze over the peaceful garden and pond. A first-floor double is calm and uncluttered, the others beamed and large with great views to church tower and orchards; smart bathrooms have chunky roll tops, big towels, oodles of hot water and organic bubbles. Handy for Hay, golf, antiques and the Brecons.

Price	From £90. Singles from £50.
Rooms	3: 1 double; 1 twin/double with separate shower; 1 twin with separate bath.
Meals	Occasional dinner £20. Pubs/restaurants 1–4 miles.
Closed	Rarely.
Directions	A4103 north of Hereford, then A4110 north to Cannon Pyon. After 2 miles, after Portway sign, left to Burghill. After Burghill sign, house 1st on left.

Harriet Gordon
Burghill Grange,
Burghill, Hereford HR4 7SE
Tel +44 (0)1432 761016
Mobile +44 (0)7525 215414
Email enquiries@burghillgrange.com
Web www.burghillgrange.com

Entry 260   Map 7

Herefordshire

Ladywell House

Wrapped by ancient oaks and a deep peacefulness, a wonderful place to relax in the Golden Valley. Charles and Sarah are generous hosts; their Edwardian dower house is welcoming and informal and glows with colour, family paintings and antiques. Luxurious bedrooms have handsome fabrics, garden views, flat-screen TVs and smart immaculate bathrooms. A superb, local or organic breakfast with homemade bread is served in the conservatory; enjoy afternoon tea and cakes, or drinks, in the garden's Breeze House on summer days, or by the open fire in winter. Walk from the door, explore the Black Mountains, browse in bustling Hay-on-Wye.

Price	From £70. Singles from £55.
Rooms	2: 1 four-poster; 1 twin with separate bath.
Meals	Bistro 5-minute drive. Pub 12-minute drive.
Closed	Occasionally.
Directions	From A465 Hereford to Abergavenny, B4348 to Hay-on-Wye. Go 6.5 miles then left to Michaelchurch Escley & Vowchurch. After approx. 1 mile house opposite tall fir tree.

Charles & Sarah Drury
Ladywell House,
Turnastone, Vowchurch HR2 0RE
Tel +44 (0)1981 550235
Mobile +44 (0)7970 510110
Email sarah@ladywellhouse.com
Web www.ladywellhouse.com

Entry 261   Map 7

Herefordshire

Granton House

Climbing roses, the hum of bees, frogs splashing in the pond… the walled garden of Liz and John's 17th-century village home is as bountiful as it is beautiful. Liz picks fruit for muesli and preserves which combine with John's home-baked bread, Gloucester Old Spot sausages and local honey for breakfast. Rooms are soothingly elegant with beams, fireplaces and stained-glass windows; the garden bedroom is a sun-filled joy with dazzling views of Coppet Hill. Venture forth to local glories like Symonds Yat, the Forest of Dean and the Brecons; return to relax in the garden or by an open fire in chilly months.

Price	£90–£100. Singles £70.
Rooms	3: 2 doubles, 1 triple.
Meals	Pubs/restaurants within 1 mile.
Closed	Christmas & New Year.
Directions	Sent on booking.

Liz & John Bloxham
Granton House,
Goodrich,
Ross-on-Wye HR9 6JE
Tel +44 (0)1600 890277
Email granton@stayonwye.com
Web www.stayonwye.com

Entry 262   Map 7

Herefordshire

Caradoc Court

Down the long drive, past the grand pillars and the Wellingtonia pines, to a lovely Jacobean manor, former seat of the Viscounts Scudamore. In 2009 the Handbys arrived, created four uncluttered, soft-carpeted bedrooms for guests and are mindfully making their mark on the place. Be wowed by impressive fireplaces and mullioned windows, massive oak roof trusses and polished sleigh beds, billiard room, ballroom and 12 wooded, landscaped acres, high on a bluff overlooking the Wye. The vistas are superb, the peace is restorative, the breakfasts are exemplary and there's a civilised pub at the end of the drive.

Price	From £95. Singles £75-£90.
Rooms	4: 3 doubles, 1 twin.
Meals	Pub 500 yds.
Closed	November-February.
Directions	From Ross-on-Wye, A49 to Hereford. After 0.5 miles, right to Sellack. Follow lane for 2 miles to Lough Pool pub. Entrance gates to drive just past pub, on right.

John Handby
Caradoc Court,
Sellack,
Ross-on-Wye HR9 6LS
Tel   +44 (0)1989 730257
Email   kathy@caradoccourt.co.uk
Web   www.caradoccourt.co.uk

Entry 263   Map 7

Herefordshire

The Coach House

Pots of flowers by the front door and Farne the friendly terrier greet you. Iola and Michael are warm and chatty too and give you a continental breakfast of homemade breads and preserves, eggs from Michael's hens, croissants from the local bakery. Their house is airy and pleasing with comfy sofas and an open fire in the sitting room, a huge dining room overlooking farmland and an inviting bedroom with painted beams, good linen and a bookcase full of novels. Sit in the garden and admire the glorious views to the south; head off for Ross-on-Wye, Ledbury, the music festival in Malvern, Cheltenham races and Wye valley walks.

Price	£80. Singles £50.
Rooms	1 double.
Meals	Continental breakfast. Pubs/restaurants 5 miles.
Closed	Rarely.
Directions	Sent on booking.

Iola & Michael Fass
The Coach House,
Old Gore,
Ross-on-Wye HR9 7QT
Tel   +44 (0)1989 780339
Email   iolafass@btinternet.com
Web   www.thecoachhousebandb.com

Entry 264   Map 7

Hertfordshire

Number One

It's worth hopping out of bed for Annie's breakfast: luxury continental with raspberry brioche or the full delicious Monty. Her house is a sparkling Aladdin's cave of mirrors, bunches of white twigs with birds atop, candles, cherubs, painted wooden floors, big open fires and generous bunches of roses. Bedrooms are lavishly done; nifty bathrooms have Italian tiles – and more roses! Close to the centre, this good-looking Georgian terrace house featured in Pevsner's guide to Hertfordshire, and the market town is busy with theatre, shops and galleries. Return for a gourmet dinner; Annie, and Violet who helps, are great fun.

Isle of Wight

Northcourt

A Jacobean manor with matchless grounds: 15 acres of terraced gardens, exotica and subtropical flowers – nature's paradise. The house is magnificent too, huge but a lived-in home, its big comfortable guest bedrooms in two wings. The formal dining room has separate tables; breakfast is served here and includes homemade bread and jams, garden fruit and honey and local produce. There's a snooker table in the library, a chamber organ in the hall and a grand piano in the vast music room. Groups are welcome and John offers garden tours. The peaceful village is in lovely downland, and you can walk from the garden to the Needles.

Price	£90–£110. Singles £85–£100.
Rooms	3: 2 twins/doubles; 1 double with separate bath/shower.
Meals	Dinner £25. BYO. Pubs/restaurants 5-minute walk.
Closed	Rarely.
Directions	Sent on booking. Limited spaces to park on road; paying car park close by.

Price	£70–£105. Singles £47.50–£67.50.
Rooms	6 twins/doubles.
Meals	Pub 3-minute walk through gardens.
Closed	Rarely.
Directions	From Newport, into Shorwell; down steep hill, under rustic bridge & right opp. thatched cottage. Signed. From Brighstone left on bend after Crown Inn & village shop.

Annie Rowley
Number One,
1 Port Hill, Hertford SG14 1PJ
Tel   +44 (0)1992 587350
Mobile   +44 (0)7770 914070
Email   annie@numberoneporthill.co.uk
Web   www.numberoneporthill.co.uk

John & Christine Harrison
Northcourt,
Shorwell PO30 3JG
Tel   +44 (0)1983 740415
Mobile   +44 (0)7955 174699
Email   christine@northcourt.info
Web   www.northcourt.info

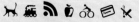

Entry 265   Map 9

Entry 266   Map 4

Isle of Wight

Redway Farm

Immerse yourself in the rolling landscape of the sunny Arreton Valley... up a winding lane find a handsome, south-facing Georgian farmhouse and friendly Linda. Bedrooms are quiet, large, light and sumptuous with thick mattresses, gorgeous linen and lovely views over the gardens; warm bathrooms sparkle. Downstairs is delightful with antiques, roaring fires and fresh flowers. You breakfast on fresh croissants from the Aga – or the full works with eggs from the hens, in the sun-filled morning room or the dining room with wood-burner. Explore acres of garden with birdsong, cycle to sandy beaches. Bliss.

Price	£89-£99. Singles £69-£79.
Rooms	2 doubles, each with separate bath.
Meals	Pub 3 miles.
Closed	Rarely.
Directions	Sent on booking.

	Linda James
	Redway Farm, Budbridge Lane,
	Merstone, Newport PO30 3DJ
Tel	+44 (0)1983 865228
Mobile	+44 (0)7775 480830
Email	lindajames2@tiscali.co.uk
Web	www.bedbreakfast.redwayfarm.co.uk

Entry 267   Map 4

Isle of Wight

Gotten Manor

Miles from the beaten track and bordered by old stone barns, the guest wing of this Saxon house is charmingly simple. Up steep stone steps (you must be nimble!) and through a low doorway find big bedrooms in laid-back rustic, funky French style: beams, limewashed stone, wooden floors, Persian rugs and a sweet window. Sleep on a rosewood bed and bathe by candlelight – in a roll top tub in your room. Friendly, informal Caroline serves breakfast in the old creamery: homemade yogurts, compotes and organic produce. There's a walled garden and a guest living room with cosy wood-burner. *Over 12s welcome.*

Price	£80-£100. Singles by arrangement. Min. 2 nights at weekends.
Rooms	2 doubles.
Meals	Pub 1.5 miles.
Closed	Rarely.
Directions	0.5 miles south of Chale Green on B3399. After village, left at Gotten Lane. House at end of lane.

	Caroline Gurney-Champion
	Gotten Manor,
	Gotten Lane, Chale PO38 2HQ
Tel	+44 (0)1983 551368
Mobile	+44 (0)7746 453398
Email	as@gottenmanor.co.uk
Web	www.gottenmanor.co.uk

Entry 268   Map 4

Isle of Wight

Lisle Combe

How many gardens sport tall palms, miniature donkeys and lawns that slope down to woods, fields and beach – with Botanic Gardens next door? The grounds are huge, the position is uplifting and upper rooms have views of the sea. Author Alfred Noyes lived here in the 1930s and the feel is timeless; today grandson Robert, wife Ruth and their young family, run gentle, charming, traditional B&B. After a day exploring Ventnor and all the coves and beaches, return to carpeted corridors, faded satin sofas, delightful gilt-framed oils and old-fashioned tranquility. Bedrooms are homely, lofty, with candlewick bedspreads and florals.

Kent

Hartlip Place

The house resonates with a faded, funky grandeur. Be greeted by family portraits and antiques, sash windows with sweeping views, happy dogs and hens, a garden intricate and special. After a candlelit dinner, up the circular stair to an Indian bedroom (or delightful four-poster) with garden views, decanter of sherry, old-fashioned bathroom and – big treat – real winter fire. John is a touch mischievous, Gillian cooks, daughter Sophie greets – you'll like the whole family. A friendly home in a peaceful spot with lots to do on the doorstep: Sissinghurst Gardens, Canterbury Cathedral and more. *Over 12s welcome. Wedding licence.*

Price	£70–£100. Child £25.
Rooms	3: 1 double; 1 double, 1 triple, both with separate bath/shower.
Meals	Pubs/restaurants 2 miles.
Closed	November–March.
Directions	Sent on booking.

Price	From £90. Singles £50.
Rooms	2: 1 four-poster; 1 twin/double with separate bath.
Meals	Dinner £25. Pub 1 mile.
Closed	Christmas & New Year.
Directions	From Dover, M2 to Medway Services. Into station, on past pumps. Ignore no exit signs. Left at T-junc., 1st left & on for 2 miles. Left at next T-junc. House 3rd on left.

Robert & Ruth Noyes
Lisle Combe,
Undercliff Drive, St Lawrence,
Ventnor PO38 1UW

Tel +44 (0)1983 852582
Email lislecombe@yahoo.com
Web www.lislecombe.co.uk

Entry 269 Map 4

Sophie & Richard Ratcliffe
Hartlip Place,
Place Lane, Sittingbourne ME9 7TR

Tel +44 (0)1795 842323
Mobile +44 (0)7990 971614
Email hartlipplace@btinternet.com
Web www.hartlipplace.co.uk

Entry 270 Map 5

Kent

Dadmans

Once the dower house to Lynsted Park, Dadmans sits in parkland with nearby orchards and grazing cattle and sheep. Your breakfast eggs are laid by rare-breed hens and Amanda sources fantastic local produce for dinner, served in the dining room on gleaming mahogany or in the Aga-warmed kitchen. There's an elegant drawing room to enjoy, and lovely bedrooms have indulgent beds, flowers, views and good bathrooms. Pretty outside too with ancient trees, walled areas, a nuttery and box-edged herb garden, and plenty of castles and cathedrals to visit nearby. A special retreat where you feel part of the family. *Over fours welcome.*

Price	£90. Singles by arrangement.
	Min. 2 nights at weekends April–Sept.
Rooms	2: 1 twin;
	1 double with separate bath.
Meals	Dinner, 4 courses, £35.
	Supper from £15.
	Pubs/restaurants nearby.
Closed	Rarely.
Directions	M20 junc. 8, then east on A20; left in Lenham towards Doddington. At The Chequers in Doddington, left; house 1.7 miles on left before Lynsted.

Amanda Strevens
Dadmans,
Lynsted, Sittingbourne ME9 0JJ

Tel	+44 (0)1795 521293
Mobile	+44 (0)7931 153253
Email	amanda.strevens@btopenworld.com
Web	www.dadmans.co.uk

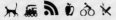

Entry 271   Map 5

Kent

The Apartment

The entire top floor of Mark and Frances's elegant Edwardian house is yours: perfect for those who prefer independence. Find a super open-plan Art Deco lounge with bright rugs, comfy leather retro chairs, piles of books and views over Whitstable Castle grounds to the sea and the Isle of Sheppey. Both bedrooms have antique beds, original eiderdowns and wooden shutters; the bathroom has a black and white checked floor, roll top tub and big fluffy towels. A fabulous continental breakfast is delivered, Frances offers treatments in her beauty therapy room downstairs and the harbour with its seafood restaurants is a short hop.

Price	£130–£200.
Rooms	2: 1 double, 1 twin/double sharing bath (let to same party only).
Meals	Continental breakfast.
	Pubs/restaurants 5-minute walk.
Closed	Rarely.
Directions	Sent on booking.

Mark Arden
The Apartment, 3 Tankerton Road,
Whitstable CT5 2AB

Tel	+44 (0)1227 280151
Mobile	+44 (0)7973 392615
Email	francesprescott@mac.com
Web	www.theapartmentwhitstable.com

Entry 272   Map 5

Kent

The Linen Shed

A weatherboard house with a winding footpath to the front door and a pot-covered veranda out the back: sit here and nibble something delicious and homemade while you contemplate the pretty garden with its gypsy caravan. Vickie, wreathed in smiles, has created a 'vintage' interior: find wooden flooring, reclaimed architectural pieces, big old roll tops, a mahogany loo seat. Bedrooms (two up, one down) are painted in the softest colours, firm mattresses are covered in fine linen, cotton or linen dressing gowns wait patiently in the smart bathrooms. Food is seriously good here, and adventurous – try a seaside picnic hamper!

Price	From £80. Singles from £75.
Rooms	3: 2 doubles with separate bath/shower; 1 double with separate bath (occasionally sharing with family).
Meals	Picnic hamper from £20. Pub/restaurant 300 yds.
Closed	Rarely.
Directions	M2, junc. 7; A2 for Canterbury. 1st immediate turnoff (100 yds) for Boughton, after 1 mile at T-junc. left. After 1 mile, left at phone box. House further along.

Vickie Hassan
The Linen Shed, 104 The Street, Boughton-under-Blean, Faversham ME13 9AP

Tel	+44 (0)1227 752271
Mobile	+44 (0)7714 646469
Email	bookings@thelinenshed.com
Web	www.thelinenshed.com

Entry 273 Map 5

Kent

7 Longport

A delightful, unexpected hideaway bang opposite the site of St Augustine's Abbey and a five-minute walk to the Cathedral. You pass through Ursula and Christopher's elegant Georgian house to emerge in a pretty courtyard, with fig tree and rambling rose, to find your self-contained cottage. Downstairs is a cosy sitting room with pale walls, tiled floors and plenty of books, and a clever, compact wet room with mosaic tiles. Then up steep stairs to a swish bedroom with crisp cotton sheets on a handmade bed and views of magnolia and ancient wisteria. You breakfast in the main house or in the courtyard on sunny days. Perfect.

Price	£90. Singles £70.
Rooms	Cottage: 1 double & sitting room.
Meals	Restaurants 5-minute walk.
Closed	Rarely.
Directions	Follow ring road around Canterbury. Signs for Sandwich A257, at St George's r'bout turn for Dover. After 300 yds left for Sandwich. At mini r'bout, left; house on left just before corner. No parking; paying public car park nearby.

Ursula & Christopher Wacher
7 Longport,
Canterbury CT1 1PE

Tel	+44 (0)1227 455367
Email	info@7longport.co.uk
Web	www.7longport.co.uk

Entry 274 Map 5

Kent

14 Westgate Grove

Slap bang in the city, overlooking the river Stour and within strolling distance of the cathedral… step inside to find a surprising, cool contemporary feel. Pippa is an interior designer, her husband an architect, and fresh bedrooms have good lighting, smart fabrics and pretty flowers. Bathrooms come with the fluffiest towels; the one for the cosy smaller double has a rain shower and Brazilian black slate. On warm days you breakfast in the walled garden with ancient vines, olives, lemons, mimosa; for cooler evenings there is an outdoor fireplace. Pippa is welcoming and friendly; a great place to stay for exploring Canterbury.

Price	£80–£100.
Rooms	2: 1 double;
	1 double with separate bath.
Meals	Pub/restaurant 50 yds.
Closed	Rarely.
Directions	Centre of Canterbury, on river by the Westgate Towers.

Pippa Clague
14 Westgate Grove,
Canterbury CT2 8AA
Tel +44 (0)1227 769624
Mobile +44 (0)7815 107032
Email pippaclague@me.com

Kent

North Court

Feel at home in this large, friendly, 17th-century country house. Suzie and Mark are cheerful and kind, breakfast is from the farm shop and your bedroom is quiet and comfortable. You're only three miles from bustling Canterbury, a short hop to Whitstable and the north Kent coast, or Dover with its smart castle, but it's peaceful and green here, with Jacob sheep and Alpacas lining the drive. Sleep soundly in your own private wing: find an iron bed with delicious white cotton, soft cream carpets, pale lemon walls and garden views. The bathroom is large and warm with good-sized towels and a wicker chair for chatterers. Relaxed.

Price	£85.
Rooms	1 double.
Meals	Pubs 1 mile.
Closed	Rarely.
Directions	Sent on booking.

Suzie Baker White
North Court,
School Lane, Lower Hardres,
Canterbury CT4 5NS
Tel +44 (0)1227 700216
Mobile +44(0)7802 618677
Email sbw@farming.co.uk

Kent

Park Gate

Peter and Mary are a generous team and their conversation is informed and easy. Behind the wisteria-clad façade are two sitting rooms with inglenook fireplaces, ancient beams and polished wood. Fresh comfortable bedrooms have TVs, gorgeous views over the garden to the fields beyond and gleaming bathrooms. Meals are delicious! More magic outside: croquet, tennis and thatched pavilions, wildlife and roses and a sprinkling of sheep to mow the paddock. The house dates back to 1460 and has a noble history: Sir Anthony Eden lived here and Churchill visited during the war. Great value, and convenient for Channel Tunnel and ferries.

Price	£85. Singles £45.
Rooms	3: 2 twins/doubles; 1 single with separate shower.
Meals	Occasional dinner, 3 courses, £30. Simple supper £17.50. Pubs/restaurants 1 mile.
Closed	Christmas, New Year & January.
Directions	A2 Canterbury to Dover road; Barham exit. Through Barham to Elham. After Elham sign 1st right signed Park Gate 0.75 miles. Over brow of hill; house on left.

Peter & Mary Morgan
Park Gate,
Elham,
Canterbury CT4 6NE
Tel   +44 (0)1303 840304
Email   marylmorgan@hotmail.co.uk

Entry 277   Map 5

Kent

Great Weddington

The listed house of perfect proportions was built by a Sandwich brewer of ginger beer. The décor is classic country house, the bedrooms desirable and cosy, the bathrooms snug and spotless, and Katie fills the rooms with flowers; she also arranges the flowers for Canterbury Cathedral. The drawing room glows with rich fabrics, shelves of books, fine watercolours and much-loved antiques. Outside, stunning hedges and lawns and a terrace for tea in the summer. An enchanting home in a farmland setting; you're close to the north Kent coast and the area hums with history. *Min. two nights at weekends April-Sept. Pets by arrangement.*

Price	£110-£130. Singles £95-£130.
Rooms	2 twins/doubles.
Meals	Supper £25. Dinner £40. Both occasional and not on Sundays.
Closed	Christmas & New Year.
Directions	From Canterbury, A257 for Sandwich. On approach to Ash, stay on A257 (do not enter village), then 3rd left at sign to Weddington. House 200 yds down on left.

Katie & Neil Gunn
Great Weddington,
Ash, Canterbury CT3 2AR
Tel   +44 (0)1304 813407
Email   greatweddington@hotmail.com
Web   www.greatweddington.co.uk

Entry 278   Map 5

Kent

Hoo Farmhouse

Jane and Nicolas are keen shrimpers – let them take you to Minnis Bay and cook your catch for supper! They are generous hosts and their striking Georgian farmhouse has a warm, relaxed atmosphere; Jane welcomes you with home-baked cake or scones. Big, sunny bedrooms have huge sash windows, books and incredibly comfortable beds. Wake refreshed for breakfast in the charming dining room, or out in the walled garden: homemade jams, fruit and local produce. Lots to explore in the area with Canterbury Cathedral, Whitstable, castles and sandy beaches all nearby. Return to a perfect drawing room with deep sofas, garden views and log fire.

Price	£90. Singles £65.
Rooms	2 twins/doubles.
Meals	Pub 1 mile.
Closed	Rarely.
Directions	A28 from Canterbury to Sarre, then A253 to Ramsgate. 4th exit at Monkton r'bout onto Willets Hill. Left at mini r'bout. House 0.75 miles on left.

Jane Irwin
Hoo Farmhouse,
Monkton Road, Minster,
Ramsgate CT12 4JB
Tel   +44 (0)1843 821322
Email   stay@hoofarmhouse.com
Web   www.hoofarmhouse.com

Entry 279   Map 5

Kent

Orchard Barn

Alison knows how to spoil (big beds, bread from the mill, home-grown soft fruit, homemade jams), David knows the wildlife, and they both love doing B&B. The big beautiful barn has been sympathetically restored, its middle section left open to create a stunning covered courtyard: find soaring beams, a comfortable leather sofa, fresh flowers. You get two snug, carpeted bedrooms up in the eaves – pale beams, bright colours, and a sweet bath (or shower) room. A delightful village, the ancient port of Sandwich nearby and egrets, kingfishers, swallows and squirrels a walk away. Superb. *Children over seven welcome.*

Price	£75-£90. Singles from £50.
Rooms	2: 1 double, 1 twin/double.
Meals	Pubs/restaurants within 1.5 miles.
Closed	Christmas & January.
Directions	A258 Sandwich to Deal. 1st right after Worth sign into Felderland Lane; 0.5 miles concealed entrance on left, opp. black barn.

David & Alison Ross
Orchard Barn,
Felderland Lane, Worth CT14 0BT
Tel   +44 (0)1304 615045
Mobile   +44 (0)7950 599304
Email   orchardbarnworth@gmail.com
Web   www.orchardbarn-worth.co.uk

Entry 280   Map 5

Kent

Kingsdown Place

Wow. A huge white villa set in stunning terraced gardens running down to the sea; on clear days you can see France! Tan has renovated both house and garden with panache: works of modern art festoon the walls, statues lurk and all is contemporary inside. Upstairs are neat bedrooms: one four-poster with long views, and, up a spiral staircase in the loft, a fabulous, very private bedroom with a sitting room and terrace. All have Conran mattresses and white linen. Breakfast on scrambled eggs and smoked salmon or the full works; take it out on the terrace in good weather. Seaside chic and a mere hop from Deal, Dover and Sandwich.

Price	£95–£120. Singles from £75.
Rooms	3: 1 double & sitting room; 1 double, 1 four-poster each with separate bath & sitting room.
Meals	Packed lunch £10. Dinner £25. Restaurant 500 yds. Pub 0.5 miles.
Closed	Christmas & New Year.
Directions	Through Kingsdown village towards sea; at high flint wall on right, turn right, through gateway, then 3rd gateway on left.

Tan Harrington
Kingsdown Place,
Upper Street,
Kingsdown CT14 8EU
Tel   +44 (0)1304 380510
Email tan@tanharrington.com

Entry 281   Map 5

Kent

Farthingales

Deep in rural Kent (yet 15 minutes from Canterbury and Dover) is a village hall-house of great character with a Victorian draper's shop addition. Welcome to a warm, cosy and inviting B&B, with the private guest quarters, overlooking Nonington Church and fields beyond, in the 'shop' wing. Find comfy beds and fluffy towels upstairs (even headphones for the TV), and a spacious sitting room down, delightful with Knole sofa and wood-burner. Ex-radio presenter Peter brings a fine English breakfast to your table as you gaze on beautiful orchard, pond, treehouse and lawns; you can breakfast outside on balmy days.

Price	£75–£85. Singles £65.
Rooms	2: 1 double, 1 twin.
Meals	Pubs 1 mile.
Closed	Rarely.
Directions	Sent on booking.

Peter Deeley
Farthingales,
Old Court Hill, Nonington,
Dover CT15 4LQ
Tel   +44 (0)1304 840174
Email farthingalesbandb@yahoo.co.uk
Web   www.farthingales.co.uk

Entry 282   Map 5

Kent

Stowting Hill House

A classic manor house in an idyllic setting, close to Canterbury and the North Downs Way. This warm, civilised home mixes Tudor beams with Georgian proportions, there's a huge conservatory full of greenery, a guest sitting room with sofas and log fire, and breakfasts fresh from the Aga. Traditional bedrooms are carpeted and cosily furnished. Your charming, country-loving hosts welcome you with tea and flowers from the garden – a perfect summer spot with its lawns, tree-lined avenue and stone obelisk. You are ten minutes from the Chunnel but this is worth more than one night. *Children over ten welcome.*

Price	£95–£100. Singles £70.
Rooms	2: 1 twin/double, 1 twin.
Meals	Dinner from £30. Pub 1 mile.
Closed	Christmas & New Year.
Directions	M20 junc. 11, B2068 north. After 4.6 miles, sharp left opposite Jet garage. House at bottom of hill on left, after 1.7 miles. Left into drive.

	Richard & Virginia Latham Stowting Hill House, Stowting, Ashford TN25 6BE
Tel	+44 (0)1303 862881
Email	vjlatham@hotmail.com
Web	www.stowtinghillhouse.co.uk

Entry 283   Map 5

Kent

The Old Rectory

On a really good day (about once every five years) you can see France. But you'll be more than happy to settle for the superb views over Romney Marsh, the Channel in the distance. The big, friendly house, built in 1850, has impeccable, elegant bedrooms and good bathrooms; the large, many-windowed sitting room is full of books, pictures and flowers from the south-facing garden. Marion and David are both charming and can organise transport to Ashford International for you. It's remarkably peaceful – perfect for walking (right on the Saxon Shore path), cycling and birdwatching. *Children over ten welcome.*

Price	£70–£80. Singles £50.
Rooms	2: 1 twin; 1 twin with separate bath/shower.
Meals	Pubs within 4 miles.
Closed	Christmas & New Year.
Directions	M20, exit 10 for Brenzett & Hastings on A2070. After 6 miles, right for Hamstreet; immed. left; in Hamstreet, left B2067. After 1.5 miles, left (Ash Hill); 700 yds on right.

	Marion & David Hanbury The Old Rectory, Ruckinge, Ashford TN26 2PE
Tel	+44 (0)1233 732328
Email	oldrectory@hotmail.com
Web	www.oldrectoryruckinge.co.uk

Entry 284   Map 5

Kent

Hereford Oast

Jack the Jack Russell will meet you, swiftly followed by Suzy – and tea and cake in the garden: sheer heaven in summer. The 1876 oast house, set back from a country road and gazing on lush fields, has become the loveliest B&B. Downstairs is the dining room, as unique as it is round. Upstairs is the guest room, sunny, fresh and bright, with a blue and white theme and a rural view. As for the village – white-clapboard cottages, pubs, fine church – it's the prettiest in Kent. Sausages from Pluckley and homemade soda bread set you up for cultured jaunts: Leeds Castle, Sissinghurst, Great Dixter... all marvellously close.

Price	£75-£85. Singles £50-£55.
Rooms	1 twin/double.
Meals	Pubs 1 mile.
Closed	Rarely.
Directions	Sent on booking.

	Suzy Hill Hereford Oast, Smarden Bell Road, Smarden, Ashford TN27 8PA
Tel	+44 (0)1233 770541
Email	suzy@herefordoast.fsnet.co.uk
Web	www.herefordoast.co.uk

Entry 285   Map 5

Kent

Merzie Meadows

You get your own suite in this lovely ranch-style house with huge windows, pergolas groaning with climbers, and a Mediterranean-style swimming pool in the twittering garden. Pamela is just as light and bright: she keeps horses and hens and gives you locally sourced breakfasts. Your bedroom has a contemporary, uncluttered feel and is beautifully dressed in pale colours with pretty fabrics and a super bed, your own sitting room looks onto the garden and the bathroom is sleek with Italian marble and plump towels. All is peaceful; garden and nature lovers will adore it here. *Minimum two nights at weekends April-Sept.*

Price	£98-£110.
Rooms	1 suite for 2-3.
Meals	Pub 2.5 miles.
Closed	Mid-December to February.
Directions	A229 Maidstone to Hastings road, then B2079 for Marden. 1st right into Underlyn Lane, 2.5 miles, large Chainhurst sign, right onto drive.

	Pamela Mumford Merzie Meadows, Hunton Road, Marden, Maidstone TN12 9SL
Tel	+44 (0)1622 820500
Mobile	+44 (0)7762 713077
Email	merziemeadows@me.com
Web	www.merziemeadows.co.uk

Entry 286   Map 5

Kent

Reason Hill

Brian and Antonia's 200-acre fruit farm is perched on the edge of the Weald of Kent, with stunning views over orchards and oast houses. The farmhouse has 17th-century origins (low ceilings, wonky floors, stone flags) and a conservatory for sunny breakfasts; colours are soft, antiques gleam, the mood is relaxed. The roomy twin has a bay window and armchairs, the pretty double looks over the garden. Come in spring for the blossom, summer for the fresh fruit and veg from the garden and anytime for a break. The Greensand Way runs along the bottom of the farm, you are close to Sissinghurst Castle and 45 minutes from the Channel Tunnel.

Price	From £80.
Rooms	3: 1 twin; 1 double with separate shower, 1 single sharing shower (let to same party only).
Meals	Pubs within 1 mile.
Closed	Christmas & New Year.
Directions	From Maidstone A229 for Hastings. After 4.5 miles, right at lights on B2163. In Coxheath, left up Westerhill Rd, 0.2 miles then right into private road; through fruit trees to Reason Hill.

	Brian & Antonia Allfrey
	Reason Hill,
	Linton, Maidstone ME17 4BT
Tel	+44 (0)1622 743679
Mobile	+44 (0)7775 745580
Email	antonia@allfrey.net
Web	www.reasonhill.co.uk

Entry 287   Map 5

Kent

Ightham

Lord it through electric oak gates to find B&B in your own modern barn. Gardening enthusiast Caroline's house is close but not hugely visible: you're wonderfully independent. Bedrooms on the ground floor are eclectic and appealing, with pine floors, dazzling white walls and slatted wooden blinds for a moody light; the bathroom is big and contemporary with a walk-in shower. Upstairs: an enormous family space for sitting, eating, playing, and glass doors on to a terrace for outdoor fun. Breakfast is delivered: eggs from the hens, pancakes, French toast. Great walks start from the door; return for supper – Caroline loves to cook.

Price	£95. Singles from £50.
Rooms	Barn: 1 double, 1 twin (let to same party only).
Meals	Dinner, 3 courses, £25. Pub/restaurant 5-minute walk.
Closed	Rarely.
Directions	Sent on booking.

	Caroline Standish
	Ightham,
	Hope Farm, Sandy Lane,
	Ightham, Sevenoaks TN15 9BA
Tel	+44 (0)1732 884359
Email	clstandish@gmail.com
Web	www.ighthambedandbreakfast.co.uk

Entry 288   Map 5

Kent

Charcott Farmhouse

The 1750 tile-hung brick farmhouse is very much a family home; if you don't come expecting an immaculate environment you will enjoy it here. There's a pretty sitting room in the old bakehouse with original beams and bread oven, and cats and a dog to keep you company. Bedrooms are unfussy, with oriental rugs, antiques, pretty country fabrics and simple bathrooms. Ginny is charming and loves books while Nicholas – a tad eccentric for some – is knowledgeable about the area and a brilliant chef. Breakfast is an unrushed, happy affair with heaps of homemade bread and marmalade and eggs from the chickens. Come and go as you please.

Price	From £65. Singles from £50.
Rooms	3: 2 twins; 1 twin with separate bath.
Meals	Pub 5-minute walk.
Closed	Rarely.
Directions	B2027 0.5 miles north of Chiddingstone Causeway. Equidistant between Tonbridge & Edenbridge. Look for signs to Greyhound pub.

Nicholas & Ginny Morris
Charcott Farmhouse, Charcott,
Leigh, Tonbridge TN11 8LG

Tel	+44 (0)1892 870024
Mobile	+44 (0)7508 683985
Email	charcottfarmhouse@btinternet.com
Web	www.charcottfarmhouse.com

Entry 289   Map 5

Kent

Swan Cottage

A delightful Georgian townhouse in Tunbridge Wells, just near the Pantiles with its covered walkways between shops, coffee houses and spas. Your genial host is an artist, his studio can be seen through the glass wall in the open-plan dining room and his engaging pen and ink drawings dot every wall. Comfortable and contemporary bedrooms have plenty of space, big sash windows and fresh flowers; bathrooms are roomy, light and white, one with rooftop views. In summer there's a little patio for a tasty breakfast (local sausages and eggs) at a pink table under the magnolia tree. And the High Street is at the bottom of the road.

Price	£95. Singles £50.
Rooms	2: 1 twin/double; 1 single with separate bath.
Meals	Pubs/restaurants 200 yds.
Closed	Rarely.
Directions	From railway station follow High Street for 300 yds, left up Little Mt Sion. House faces you at top of hill. Parking in garage at back of house on request.

David Gurdon
Swan Cottage, 17 Warwick Road,
Tunbridge Wells TN1 1YL

Tel	+44 (0)1892 525910
Mobile	+44 (0)7775 897427
Email	swancot@btinternet.com
Web	www.swancottage.co.uk

Entry 290   Map 5

Kent

40 York Road

A smart Regency townhouse, slap bang in the centre of Royal Tunbridge Wells and a five-minute walk from the beautiful Pantiles. Patricia will enjoy cooking for you; in another life she served up delights for hungry skiers coming off the French mountains. A delightful host, she leaves you to come and go as you please; guests have a comfy sitting room, bright spotless bedrooms that are quieter than you may think and thoughtful extras. In the summer you will breakfast deliciously in the pretty courtyard garden — try the lemon pancakes! Wander into town for great little shops and restaurants. Truly excellent. *Over 12s welcome.*

Price	From £80. Singles from £50.
Rooms	2 twins/doubles.
Meals	Supper £13. Dinner, 4 courses with wine, £25. Picnic available. Pub/restaurant nearby.
Closed	23 December–2 January.
Directions	From M25 junc. 5 onto A21, then A26 through Southborough to Tunbridge Wells. Sign for Lewes, then 4th road left. Halfway along, on left. Car parks nearby, from £3.50 per 24 hours.

	Patricia Lobo
	40 York Road,
	Tunbridge Wells TN1 1JY
Tel	+44 (0)1892 531342
Email	yorkrd@uwclub.net
Web	www.yorkroad.co.uk

Entry 291 Map 5

Kent

22 Lansdowne Road

Built in 1861, the house in leafy Tunbridge Wells "has never been as Victorian as it is now". So says Harold, whose devotion to Victoriana knows no bounds. Deep colours, rich velvets, marble tables, authentic wallpapers, tasselled lamps, portraits of Queen Victoria, tea and scones by the fire… be prepared to take a serious step back in time. Bedrooms are simple in comparison: ruched chintz in the ground-floor double, damask in the twin below — and a door to the conservatory. Bathrooms have large mirrors and brand new fittings, breakfast is a locally sourced spread. Those in search of heritage will marvel. *Off-road parking.*

Price	£80–£120. Singles £80.
Rooms	3: 1 double, 1 twin/double; 1 studio with shower & kitchenette.
Meals	Dinner, 2 courses, £30. Pubs/restaurants within 5-minute walk.
Closed	January.
Directions	From A21 to Tonbridge A26 to T. Wells centre. Grosvenor Rd one-way system left onto Victoria Rd. Onto Garden Rd, right onto Lansdowne Rd.

	Harold Brown
	22 Lansdowne Road,
	Tunbridge Wells TN1 2NJ
Tel	+44 (0)1892 533633
Mobile	+44 (0)7714 264489
Email	haroldmbrown@hotmail.com
Web	www.thevictorianbandb.com

Entry 292 Map 5

Kent

Barclay Farmhouse

Lynn's breakfasts are fabulous: fresh fruit, warm croissants, home-baked breads and a daily changing twist on the traditional English. The weatherboarded guest barn may be in perfect trim but has a been-here-forever feel; you have a country-cosy dining room for breakfast or playing cards, a patio for summer, a big peaceful garden, a bird-happy pond. Gleaming bedrooms have handmade oak bedheads, chocolates, slippers, flat-screen TVs and radios; shower rooms are in perfect order. Couples, honeymooners, garden lovers – many would love it here (but no children: the pond is deep). Warm-hearted B&B, and glorious Sissinghurst nearby.

Price	£90. Singles from £65. Min. 2 nights at weekends in high season.
Rooms	Barn: 3 doubles.
Meals	Pubs/restaurants 1 mile.
Closed	Rarely.
Directions	From Biddenden centre, south on A262: Tenterden road. 0.7 miles, bear right (signed Par3 Golf, Vineyard & Benenden). Immed. on right.

	Lynn Ruse
	Barclay Farmhouse,
	Woolpack Corner,
	Biddenden TN27 8BQ
Tel	+44 (0)1580 292626
Email	info@barclayfarmhouse.co.uk
Web	www.barclayfarmhouse.co.uk

Entry 293   Map 5

Kent

Ramsden Farm

A truly interesting and comfortable house, with south-facing views across the Wealds; charming Sally has renovated these former farm buildings with flair. Unhurried breakfasts are eaten in the huge kitchen with a lemon-coloured Aga and floor to ceiling glass doors opening on to a wooden deck; spill outside on warm days. After a hearty walk you can doze in front of a tree-devouring inglenook; find lovely sunny bedrooms too, with more of that view from each, tip-top mattresses and the crispest white linen. Sparkling bathrooms have travertine marble and underfloor heating. Spoiling. *Self-catering in cottage.*

Price	From £80.
Rooms	3: 1 double, 1 twin; 1 double with separate bath.
Meals	Pub 1 mile.
Closed	Rarely.
Directions	From Benenden on B2086 towards Rolvenden, Dingleden Lane on right after 1 mile. House is 3rd on left.

	Sally Harrington
	Ramsden Farm,
	Dingleden Lane,
	Benenden TN17 4JT
Tel	+44 (0)1580 240203
Email	sally@ramsdenfarmcottage.co.uk
Web	www.ramsdenfarmcottage.co.uk

Entry 294   Map 5

Kent

Pullington Barn

Up a private drive and straight in to a vast, beamed expanse of bright light, warm colours, beautiful art and a cheery welcome from Gavin and Anne in their converted barn. There are endless books to choose: settle in the comfy drawing room with its grand piano. Or sit in the pretty south-facing garden on a fine day; on the other side, views from the orchard spread over oast houses and church spires. Big bedrooms (one on the ground floor) have good mattresses, coordinated bed linen and feather pillows. You breakfast well on local and homemade produce, served at the travertine table in the dining hall. Lovely walks from the door.

Price	From £75. Singles £55.
Rooms	2: 1 double, 1 twin.
Meals	Pub/restaurant 0.5 miles.
Closed	Christmas.
Directions	A228 out of Tunbridge Wells. A21 to The Weald Garden of England r'bout. A262 to Sissinghurst. Right to Benenden. Final directions on booking.

Gavin & Anne Wetton
Pullington Barn,
Benenden TN17 4EH
Tel +44 (0)1580 240246
Mobile +44 (0)7849 759929
Email anne@wetton.info
Web www.wetton.info/bandb

Entry 295 Map 5

Kent

The Tower House

Peacefully back from the road, a stroll from the antique shops of Tenterden, is a delightful Georgian house with a turreted tower, an Edwardian folly. The box-lined path to the door sets the tone: this is a very well-cared for and hospitable home. Pippa collects vintage china, Mike is the gardener, both delight in meeting people and ensure your stay is happy. Deeply comfortable bedrooms, the biggest at the back, have antique iron beds and romantic white furnishings, flowers and delicious linen. A sofa'd guest sitting room, a gazebo in the garden, homemade blackcurrant jelly at breakfast, Sissinghurst a short drive. Perfect!

Price	From £80. Singles £60.
Rooms	2: 1 double; 1 double with separate shower.
Meals	Pubs/restaurants 200 yds.
Closed	Christmas.
Directions	Junc. 8 on M20 to Sutton Valence, then Tenterden. Tower House on right (tower very visible).

Pippa Carter
The Tower House,
27 Ashford Road,
Tenterden TN30 6LL
Tel +44 (0)1580 761920
Email pippa@towerhouse.biz
Web www.towerhouse.biz

Entry 296 Map 5

Kent

Lamberden Cottage

Down a farm track find two 1780 cottages knocked into one, with flagstone floors, a cheery wood-burner in the guest sitting room and welcoming Beverley and Branton. There's a traditional country-cottage feel with pale walls, thick oak beams, soft carpeting and very comfortable bedrooms (the twin has a child's bedroom adjoining); views from all are across the Weald of Kent. Wander the lovely gardens to find your own private spot, sip a sundowner on the terrace, eat well in the family dining room on home-grown vegetables and fruit. Near to Sissinghurst, Great Dixter and many historic places.

Price	From £75. Singles from £55.
Rooms	2: 1 double, 1 twin with adjoining room for children.
Meals	Pub 1 mile.
Closed	Christmas & New Year.
Directions	From Tenterden A28 to Hastings. 2.5 miles Rolvenden. 2.5 miles to junc. A268 right to Sandhurst. 300 yds Sandhurst sign on left. 20 yds right down farm track. House 80 yds on left.

Beverley & Branton Screeton
Lamberden Cottage, Rye Road,
Sandhurst, Cranbrook TN18 5PH
Tel   +44 (0)1580 850743
Mobile   +44 (0)7768 462070
Email   thewalledgarden@lamberdencottage.co.uk
Web   www.lamberdencottage.co.uk

Entry 297   Map 5

Lancashire

Challan Hall

The wind in the trees, the boom of a bittern and birdsong. That's as noisy as it gets. On the edge of the village, delightful Charlotte's former farmhouse overlooks woods and Lake Haweswater; deer, squirrels and Leighton Moss Nature Reserve are your neighbours. The Cassons are well-travelled and the house, filled with a colourful mish-mash of mementos, is happily and comfortably traditional. Expect a sofa-strewn sitting room, a smart red and polished-wood dining room and two freshly floral bedrooms. Morecambe Bay and the Lakes are on the doorstep – come home to lovely views and stunning sunsets.

Price	£75. Singles from £45.
Rooms	2: 1 twin/double; 1 twin/double with separate bath.
Meals	Packed lunch available. Pubs 1 mile.
Closed	Rarely.
Directions	M6 exit 35 to Carnforth, past railway station to Warton. Turn left signed Silverdale. After 2.5 miles T-junc., turn right, past golf club on left. Further 1 mile, house on right.

Charlotte Casson
Challan Hall,
Silverdale LA5 0UH
Tel   +44 (0)1524 701054
Mobile   +44 (0)7790 360776
Email   cassons@btopenworld.com
Web   www.challanhall.co.uk

Entry 298   Map 11

Lancashire

Northwood

A super stretch of golden beach with sand dunes is just across the road and delightful Lytham is a couple of miles away. The Victorian façade conceals light, lofty rooms mixing vintage and modern: bold wallpaper on odd walls, huge displays of flowers, original artwork. Your hosts happily find babysitters, advise on restaurants (then drive you there) and offer you maple syrup pancakes at breakfast, along with other treats. Bedrooms are generous: find coir carpets, baskets of plump blankets and towels, lovely colours and DVDs to watch on wet days. The whole place has an informal, warm and happy family vibe.

Price	£80. Family £90. Singles from £75.
Rooms	2: 1 double, 1 double/family room.
Meals	Restaurants 5-minute walk.
Closed	Christmas & New Year.
Directions	M6 exit 32 then M55 to Blackpool. Follow signs for Lytham St Annes then St Annes. Head for the promenade.

Shannon Kuspira
Northwood,
24 North Promenade,
St Annes on Sea FY8 2NQ
Tel   +44 (0)1253 782356
Email   skuspira@hotmail.com
Web   www.24northwood.co.uk

Entry 299   Map 11

Lancashire

Peter Barn Country House

Wild deer roam and the views are fabulous – this is the Ribble Valley, an AONB that feels like a time-locked land. In the former 18th-century tithe barn, where old church rafters support a big yet cosy guest sitting room, find plump sofas, log fire and flat-screen TV. Bedrooms, too, are on the top floor – nicely private. The Smiths couldn't be more helpful and breakfast is a feast: jams and muesli are homemade, stewed fruits are from the gardens. Step outside: Jean has transformed a field into a riot of colour and scent, there are pretty corners, a meandering stream and water lilies bask in still pools. *Minimum two nights.*

Price	£68-£74. Singles £40.
Rooms	3: 1 double, 1 twin/double; 1 double with separate bath.
Meals	Restaurants/pubs 1.5 miles.
Closed	Christmas & New Year.
Directions	M6 junc. 31, A59 to Clitheroe. Through Clitheroe to Waddington. Through village 0.5 miles, left on Cross Lane for 0.75 miles, past Colthurst Hall, house on left.

Jean & Gordon Smith
Peter Barn Country House,
Cross Lane/Rabbit Lane, Waddington,
Clitheroe BB7 3JH
Tel   +44 (0)1200 428585
Email   jean@peterbarn.co.uk
Web   www.peterbarn.co.uk

Entry 300   Map 12

Leicestershire

The Grange

Behind the mellow brick exterior (Queen Anne in front, Georgian at the back) is a warm family home. Log fires brighten chilly days and you are greeted with kindness and generosity by Mary and Shaun and their sweet dog. Big, beautifully quiet bedrooms, one an atmospheric beamed room in the attic, are hung with strikingly unusual wallpapers and furnished with excellent beds and pretty antiques; bathrooms are simple yet impeccable. Wake to breakfast in the big, flagstoned hall: homemade bread, local bacon and award-winning sausages. The newly designed garden has a treehouse and is large enough to roam. *NGS garden.*

Price	£80. Singles £50.
Rooms	2: 1 twin, 1 double.
Meals	Pubs/restaurants 0.5-1.5 miles.
Closed	Christmas & New Year.
Directions	M1 exit 20; A4304 towards Market Harborough. 1st left after Walcote marked 'Gt Central Cycle Ride'; 2 miles, then right into Kimcote, pass church on left. On right after Poultney Lane.

Shaun & Mary Mackaness
The Grange,
Kimcote LE17 5RU
Tel   +44 (0)1455 203155
Mobile   +44 (0)7808 242530
Email   shaunandmarymac@hotmail.com
Web   www.thegrangekimcote.co.uk

Entry 301   Map 8

Leicestershire

Kicklewell House

The last house in the village overlooks miles of fields and the garden includes paddocks and stables. Fiona, easy, hospitable, great fun, loves horses, dogs and fine art: her cream walls glow with artwork, much of which she frames and sells. The house is warm, inviting and a visual delight: big deep sofas, bright ethnic rugs, a trusty Aga, heaps of books. After a scrumptious local breakfast, stride off to the lovely Foxton Canal, or visit one of the big local houses and gardens like Cottesbrooke Hall and Holdenby. Bedrooms are as peaceful and as charming as can be; good dogs are welcomed with open arms.

Price	£90. Singles £50.
Rooms	2: 1 twin, 1 double.
Meals	Dinner, 3 courses, £25. Packed lunch £7.50. Pubs 2 miles.
Closed	Christmas & Easter.
Directions	Sent on booking.

Fiona Shann
Kicklewell House,
Laughton,
Lutterworth LE17 6QF
Tel   +44 (0)1162 404173
Email   fonishann@hotmail.co.uk

Entry 302   Map 8

Leicestershire

Curtain Cottage

A pretty village setting for this cottage on the main street, next door to Sarah's interior design shop. You have your own entrance by the side and through a large garden, which backs onto fields with horses and the National Forest beyond. A conservatory is your sitting room: wicker armchairs, wooden floors, a contemporary take on the country look. Bedrooms are light and fresh, linen from The White Company on sumptuous beds, slate-tiled bathrooms, stunning fabrics. Breakfast is full English with eggs from the hens or fresh fruit and croissants from the local shop — all is delivered to you. Perfect privacy.

Price	£85. Singles £60.
Rooms	2: 1 double, 1 twin.
Meals	Pubs/restaurants 150 yds.
Closed	Rarely.
Directions	Gravel driveway to left of Barkers Interiors Design Showroom on Main Street. From car park, access to cottage thro' gate into garden at rear of showroom.

	Sarah Barker
	Curtain Cottage, 92-94 Main Street, Woodhouse Eaves LE12 8RZ
Tel	+44 (0)1509 891361
Mobile	+44 (0)7906 830088
Email	sarah@curtaincottage.co.uk
Web	www.curtaincottage.co.uk

Entry 303   Map 8

Leicestershire

The Gorse House

Passing cars are less frequent than passing horses — this is a peaceful spot in a pretty village. Lyn and Richard's 17th-century cottage has a feeling of lightness and space; there's a fine collection of paintings and furniture, and oak doors lead from dining room to guest sitting room. Country style bedrooms have green views and are simply done. The garden layout was designed by Bunny Guinness, the stables accommodate up to six horses and it's a stroll to a good pub dinner. The house is filled with laughter, breakfasts with home-grown fruits are tasty and the Cowdells are terrific hosts who love having guests to stay.

Price	From £60. Singles £35.
Rooms	3: 1 double, 1 family room for 3. Stable: 1 triple & kitchenette.
Meals	Packed lunch £5. Pub 75 yds (closed on Sun eves).
Closed	Rarely.
Directions	From A46 Newark-Leicester; B676 for Melton. At x-roads, straight for 1 mile; right to Grimston. There, up hill, past church. House on left, just after right-hand bend at top.

	Lyn & Richard Cowdell
	The Gorse House, 33 Main Street, Grimston, Melton Mowbray LE14 3BZ
Tel	+44 (0)1664 813537
Mobile	+44 (0)7780 600792
Email	cowdell@gorsehouse.co.uk
Web	www.gorsehouse.co.uk

Entry 304   Map 9

Lincolnshire

The Barn

Simon and Jane – the nicest people – have farmed for 30 years and love having guests to stay. Breakfasts and suppers are entirely local or home-grown, and delicious; there are endless extras and nothing is too much trouble. In this light-filled barn conversion find old beams, new walls and good antiques; a brick-flanked fireplace glows and heated floors keep toes warm. Above the high-raftered main living/dining room is a comfy, good-sized double; in the adjoining stables, two further rooms, a crisp feel, sparkling showers, restful privacy. Views are to sheep-dotted fields and the village is on a 25-mile cycle trail.

Price	£70. Singles £50.
Rooms	3: 1 twin/double. Stables: 1 double (extra single available); 1 single with separate bath/shower.
Meals	Supper, 2 courses, £17.50. Dinner, 3 courses, £25. BYO. Pubs in village & 2 miles.
Closed	Rarely.
Directions	Midway between Lincoln & Peterborough. From A15, in Folkingham, turn west into Spring Lane next to village hall; 200 yds on right.

	Simon & Jane Wright
	The Barn, Spring Lane,
	Folkingham, Sleaford NG34 0SJ
Tel	+44 (0)1529 497199
Mobile	+44 (0)7876 363292
Email	sjwright@farming.co.uk
Web	www.thebarnspringlane.co.uk

Entry 305   Map 9

Lincolnshire

Churchfield House

The little house was built in the sixties; inside glows with character and charm. Bridget is an interior decorator whose eye for detail and sense of fun will delight you. A snug bedroom sports fresh checks in creams and greens, firm mattress, down pillows, interesting art, even a gilt-trimmed copy of a Louis XIV chair; the bathroom is small but spotless. There's a conservatory mood to the warm red, stone-tiled dining room, where glass doors open to a suntrap patio and a large garden filled with clematis and pretty pots. You're close to a good golf course, Bridget cooks and chats with warmth and humour and it's great value too.

Price	From £64. Singles £40.
Rooms	1 twin with separate bath.
Meals	Dinner, 2 courses, from £18. Pubs/restaurants 3 miles.
Closed	Rarely.
Directions	A607 Grantham to Lincoln road. On reaching Carlton Scroop, 1st left for Hough Lane. Last house on left.

	Bridget Hankinson
	Churchfield House,
	Carlton Scroop,
	Grantham NG32 3BA
Tel	+44 (0)1400 250387
Email	info@churchfield-house.co.uk
Web	www.churchfield-house.co.uk

Entry 306   Map 9

Lincolnshire

Brills Farm

There aren't many hills in Lincolnshire, but Sophie and Charlie's early Georgian farmhouse is at the top of one of them. Built of warm brick, near a Roman settlement site, it shines with country elegance and charm, subtle colours and antique furniture. The drawing and dining rooms, filled with fresh flowers, overlook the valley, the beautiful airy bedrooms have goose down duvets and lovely linen. The Whites are a delightful young couple with a flourishing family (Sophie is a professional cook and event rider). Enthusiastic and hospitable, they offer guests innovative dinners, and bacon from their pigs. *Children over 12 welcome.*

Price	£90–£100. Singles £55–£60.
Rooms	3: 2 doubles, 1 twin/double.
Meals	Supper £20. Dinner £30. Packed lunch £10. Pubs 5-minute drive.
Closed	Christmas & New Year.
Directions	A46 Newark-Lincoln. Exit Brough, Norton Disney & Stapleford. Right at T-junc.; 0.5 miles; 1st left onto lane; 0.75 miles; wide gravel entrance, on right before hill (unsigned).

	Charles & Sophie White
	Brills Farm, Brills Hill,
	Norton Disney, Lincoln LN6 9JN
Tel	+44 (0)1636 892311
Mobile	+44 (0)7947 136228
Email	admin@brillsfarm-bedandbreakfast.co.uk
Web	www.brillsfarm-bedandbreakfast.co.uk

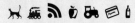

Entry 307   Map 9

Lincolnshire

Ryelands House

Farmer Mike and charming Caroline built this large red-brick and slate house on their land and are much committed to the Countryside Stewardship programme; hang out of your bedroom window to watch waders, even deer, round the nearby pond. Inside is warm with underfloor heating, and spacious. Your bedroom has a boutique hotel feel in shades of cream and brown, while two beautifully-lit sitting rooms are smoothly uncluttered and have comfortable armchairs. Pedal along those lovely flat lanes after breakfast, head to Lincoln and its cathedral or Horncastle for antiques; walk to the local pub for excellent bar food.

Price	From £75. Singles from £50.
Rooms	1 twin/double & sitting room.
Meals	Supper from £10 (Monday only). Packed lunch from £5. Restaurant 0.5 miles.
Closed	Christmas & New Year.
Directions	A15 Lincoln, Sleaford turn. Left at Mere onto B1178 for 3 miles; over staggered x-roads into Potterhanworth. At T-junc. right for 100 yds; left onto Barff Road, 0.5 miles, driveway on left.

	Michael & Caroline Norcross
	Ryelands House, Barff Road,
	Potterhanworth, Lincoln LN4 2DU
Tel	+44 (0)1522 793563
Mobile	+44 (0)7977 590375
Email	norcross@ukfarming.co.uk
Web	www.ryelands-house.co.uk

Entry 308   Map 9

Lincolnshire

Baumber Park

Lincoln red cows and Longwool sheep surround this attractive rosy-brick farmhouse – once a stud that bred a Derby winner. The old watering pond is now a haven for frogs, newts and toads; birds sing lustily. Maran hens conjure delicious eggs and charming Clare, a botanist, is hugely knowledgeable about the area. Bedrooms are light and traditional with mahogany furniture; two have heart-stopping views. Guests have their own wisteria-covered entrance, sitting room with a log-burner, dining room with local books and the lovely garden to roam. This is good walking, riding and cycling country; seals and rare birds on the coast.

Price	From £66. Singles from £45.
Rooms	3: 2 doubles; 1 twin with separate bath.
Meals	Pubs 1.5 miles.
Closed	Christmas & New Year.
Directions	From A158 in Baumber take road towards Wispington & Bardney. House 300 yds down on right.

Clare Harrison
Baumber Park,
Baumber, Horncastle LN9 5NE
Tel +44 (0)1507 578235
Mobile +44 (0)7977 722776
Email mail@baumberpark.com
Web www.baumberpark.com

Entry 309 Map 9

Lincolnshire

The Grange

Wide open farmland and an award-winning farm on the edge of the Lincolnshire Wolds. This immaculately kept farm has been in the family for generations; Sarah and Jonathan are delightful and make you feel instantly at home. Find acres of farmland and a two mile farm trail to explore, a trout lake to picnic by and an open fire to warm you in an elegant drawing room with Georgian windows. Sarah gives you delicious homemade cake on arrival and huge Aga breakfasts with home-laid eggs and local produce. Comfortable bedrooms have TVs, tea trays and gleaming bathrooms. Fabulous views stretch to Lincoln Cathedral and the walks are superb.

Price	From £68. Singles from £45.
Rooms	2 doubles.
Meals	Supper from £18. Dinner, 2 courses, from £25. BYO. (No meals during harvest.) Pub/restaurant 1 mile.
Closed	Christmas & New Year.
Directions	Exit A157 in East Barkwith at War Memorial, into Torrington Lane. House 0.75 miles on right after sharp right-hand bend.

Sarah & Jonathan Stamp
The Grange, Torrington Lane,
East Barkwith LN8 5RY
Tel +44 (0)1673 858670
Mobile +44 (0)7951 079474
Email sarahstamp@farmersweekly.net
Web www.thegrange-lincolnshire.co.uk

Entry 310 Map 9

Lincolnshire

The Manor House

One guest's summing up reads: "Absolutely perfect – hostess, house, garden and marmalade." Delightful Ann – interested in horses, food, photography, people – makes you feel immediately at home. You have the run of downstairs: all family antiques, fresh flowers and space. Chintzy, carpeted bedrooms have dreamy views of the lovely sweeping gardens and duck-dabbled lake; dinners are delicious: game casserole, sticky toffee pudding with homemade ice cream… Perfect stillness at the base of the Wolds and a pretty one-mile walk along the route of the old railway that starts from the front door. Very special, and great value.

Price	From £70. Singles £50.
Rooms	2: 1 double, 1 twin.
Meals	Dinner from £20. BYO. Pub/restaurant 2 miles.
Closed	Christmas.
Directions	From Wragby A157 for Louth. After approx. 2 miles, at horse road sign, right. Red postbox & bus shelter at drive entrance, before graveyard.

Ann Hobbins
The Manor House,
West Barkwith LN8 5LF
Tel +44 (0)1673 858253
Mobile +44 (0)7751 891274

Entry 311   Map 9

Lincolnshire

Knaith Hall

This intriguing place, medieval church at its gate, dates from the 16th century. Lawns slope down to the river Trent; daffodils, lambs, a passing barge and waterfowl pattern the serenity. And the skyscapes are terrific; at night, a distant power station shines, enhancing that 'great rurality of taste' referred to in Pevsner. Indoors, diamond-paned windows, a domed dining room and fine furniture are softened by an easy décor and a log fire twinkles in the drawing room. Bedrooms are large with comfortable beds; wake to breakfast with award-winning sausages. An appealing family house, with friendly hosts and a relaxed atmosphere.

Price	From £70. Singles from £40.
Rooms	2: 1 double with separate shower; 1 twin with separate bath.
Meals	Dinner, 3 courses with wine, £20. Pub 4 miles.
Closed	Rarely.
Directions	Knaith 3 miles south of Gainsborough on A156 Lincoln to Gainsborough road. After Knaith signs, look for white gateposts on west side with sign for St Mary's Church.

John & Rosie Burke
Knaith Hall,
Knaith, Gainsborough DN21 5PE
Tel +44 (0)1427 613005
Mobile +44 (0)7796 881328
Email rosemary@knaith.com

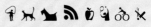

Entry 312   Map 9

Lincolnshire

The Manor House

At the end of a neatly raked gravel drive, a new manor house with wide views and stunning sunsets over the peaceful Trent valley. The Days have farmed in the village since 1898 and look after you with rich warm comfort and friendly ease. Rooms have opulent curtains with chintzy roses, period furniture and rural art. Beautiful gardens are awash with summer roses, ducks on the pond, horses in the paddock, sunny patios — one in front of the annexe is for guests' exclusive use. You can fish for carp in the lake, shooting can be arranged and there are music and art festivals, antique fairs and walks in abundance.

Price	£70. Singles £45.
Rooms	2: 1 double. Annexe: 1 twin/double with kitchenette.
Meals	Supper from £15. Pub/restaurant 3.5 miles.
Closed	Christmas & New Year.
Directions	A15 from Lincoln for 17.1 miles. Left on to Gainsthorpe Rd, right on to B1398 to Scunthorpe, then left for Manton. Down hill, right at bottom. 50 yds before end of road, gravel driveway on left.

Judy Day
The Manor House, Manton,
Kirton Lindsey, Gainsborough DN21 4JT

Tel	+44 (0)1652 649508
Mobile	+44 (0)7712 766347
Email	enquiries@manorhousebedandbreakfast.co.uk
Web	www.manorhousebedandbreakfast.co.uk

Entry 313   Map 13

Lincolnshire

The Old Farm House

Hidden in the Lincolnshire Wolds, an 18th-century, ivy-covered house — and Nicola's father still farms the fields beyond the ha-ha. The stone-flagged, terracotta-washed hall gives a hint of warm colours to come; creamy walls show off tawny fabrics, prints and antiques; the beamed sitting/breakfast room has a big, rosy brick inglenook fireplace and tranquil views. Such a welcoming, tucked-away place, hopping with pheasant but just an easy drive from shops, golf and racing in the nearby towns. Excellent value, good plentiful food, and perfect if you fancy privacy and space. *Children over eight welcome.*

Price	£80. Singles £55.
Rooms	3: 2 doubles, 1 triple.
Meals	Pub 2 miles.
Closed	Christmas, New Year & occasionally.
Directions	M180 exit 5 from north; A18 signed Louth. Past airport; 2.5 miles after junc. of A46 right signed Hatcliffe. House third on right, before village.

Nicola Clarke
The Old Farm House, Low Road,
Hatcliffe, Grimsby DN37 0SH

Tel	+44 (0)1472 824455
Mobile	+44 (0)7818 272523
Email	clarky.hatcliffe@btinternet.com
Web	www.oldfarmhousebandbgrimsby.com

Entry 314   Map 13

London

20 Bywater Street

In a quiet, pretty cul-de-sac off the fashionable King's Road, a delightful pastel-coloured house and a welcoming B&B. Caroline and Richard give you a light, quiet bedroom downstairs, with a deep green carpet and a wicker chair, fresh flowers, lots of magazines and books and a digital radio. The private shower room is next door with fluffy towels and good toiletries. Breakfast on freshly squeezed juice, fruit, muesli, croissants, muffins and more across the hall in the kitchen/conservatory, a cheery room that swims in morning sun, with doors opening onto a flower filled Yorkstone patio garden. The best of London laps at the door.

Price	From £115.
Rooms	1 double with adjacent private shower.
Meals	Continental breakfast. Pubs/restaurants/cafés nearby.
Closed	Occasionally.
Directions	Tube: Sloane Square 6-minute walk (down King's Road, 6th street on right). Parking available locally.

Caroline & Richard Heaton-Watson
20 Bywater Street,
Chelsea,
London SW3 4XD
Email   caheatonw@aol.com
Web   www.20bywaterstreet.com

Entry 315   Map 22

London

90 Old Church Street

In a quiet street facing the Chelsea Arts Club is an enticing, contemporary haven. Softly spoken Nina is passionate about the arts, knows Chelsea inside out and takes real pleasure in looking after her guests. Antique shop spoils stand alongside more modern delights, the attention to detail is amazing and there are plentiful bunches of flowers. A lush carpet takes you up to the second floor and your super-private, surprisingly peaceful and deliciously designed bedroom and bathroom. Breakfast – fruit platters, yogurt and croissants – is shared with Nina in the kitchen. We love No. 90 – and the little black poodles!

Price	From £115. Singles from £100.
Rooms	1 double.
Meals	Continental breakfast £10. Restaurants nearby.
Closed	Occasionally.
Directions	Tube: South Kensington.

Nina Holland
90 Old Church Street,
Chelsea, London SW3 6EP
Tel   +44 (0)20 7352 4758
Mobile   +44 (0)7831 689167
Email   ninastcharles@gmail.com
Web   www.chelseabedbreakfast.com

Entry 316   Map 22

London

37 Trevor Square

A three-minute walk from Hyde Park or Harrods – a fabulous find. The square is peaceful, private, exquisite, so find a pretty corner and enjoy. Margaret runs an interior design company – rather successfully, by the look of things – and serves a superb full English breakfast in the kitchen/diner; there's also a small conservatory you are welcome to use. Bedrooms (one downstairs has an enormous bed and a little patio) have goose down pillows, cashmere duvets, electric blankets and a mini fridge; slip on your robe, listen to some music or watch a DVD – it's all here. Blissful luxury in the middle of Knightsbridge.

Price	From £185. Singles £120.
Rooms	3: 1 twin/double; 1 double, 1 twin sharing shower (let to same party only).
Meals	Restaurants 200 yds.
Closed	Occasionally.
Directions	Tube: Knightsbridge. Nearest car park £25 for 24 hrs (closed overnight).

Margaret & Holly Palmer
37 Trevor Square,
Knightsbridge,
London SW7 1DY
Tel   +44 (0)20 7823 8186
Email   margaret@37trevorsquare.co.uk
Web   www.37trevorsquare.co.uk

Entry 317   Map 22

London

6 Oakfield Street

This district dates from the mid-1660s and local historian Simon has maps to prove it; their road is the second smallest in London. Hospitable Margaret and Simon, language, art and Egypt lovers, live in a stylish 1860s house with a beautiful roof mural (hers), a marble-topped table in the dining room and a collection of Egyptian prints. There's an open-plan feel to the kitchen, and a roof terrace where you can sit in summer. Bedrooms are at the top of the house: the twin is little but, being at the back, is silent at night; the double has a big wooden bed and an antique armoire. Stroll to restaurants on Hollywood Road.

Price	£90. Singles £70.
Rooms	2: 1 double, 1 twin.
Meals	Restaurants nearby.
Closed	Occasionally.
Directions	Tube: Earl's Court 12-minute walk. South Kensington 20-minute walk or 5-minute bus ride on 14 or 414. Nearest car park £25 for 24 hrs.

Margaret & Simon de Maré
6 Oakfield Street,
Little Chelsea, London SW10 9JB
Tel   +44 (0)20 7352 2970
Mobile   +44 (0)7990 844008
Email   margaretdemare@googlemail.com
Web   www.athomeinnchelsea.com

Entry 318   Map 22

London

15 Delaford Street

A pretty Victorian, terraced Fulham home, inside all charming and spacious. In a tiny, sun-trapping courtyard you can have continental breakfast in good weather – tropical fruits are a favourite and the coffee is very good; a second miniature garden bursts with life at the back. The bedroom, up a spiral staircase, looks down on it all. Expect perfectly ironed sheets on a comfy bed, a quilted throw, books in the alcove, a sunny bathroom and fluffy white towels. The tennis at Queen's is in June and on your doorstep. Tim and Margot – she's from Melbourne – are fun, charming and happy to pick you up from the nearest tube.

Price	From £90. Singles £70.
Rooms	1 double.
Meals	Restaurants nearby.
Closed	Occasionally.
Directions	Tube: West Brompton. Parking free eves & weekends; otherwise pay & display. 74 bus to West End nearby.

Margot & Tim Woods
15 Delaford Street,
Fulham,
London SW6 7LT
Tel   +44 (0)20 7385 9671
Email woodsmargot@hotmail.co.uk

Entry 319   Map 22

London

35 Burnthwaite Road

Near Queen's Club and Wimbledon for tennis and Fulham Broadway's tube, a sweet terraced house on the sunny side of the street. A fresh aqua carpet ushers you up to a bright bedroom on the second floor, and a spotless white bathroom squeezed under the eaves. It's as peaceful as can be. No sitting room but a rather smart dining table for breakfast – croissants, cereals, fresh fruit salad. A traditional and civilised feel prevails, thanks to lovely family pieces, fine china, touches of chintz – and friendly Diana who helps you plan your day. Buses to Piccadilly and Westminster, a stroll to the Thames, all of London at your feet.

Price	From £90. Singles from £75.
Rooms	1 twin/double.
Meals	Pubs/restaurants within walking distance.
Closed	Rarely.
Directions	Tube: Fulham Broadway 6-minute walk. Parking pay & display. Bus: 211, 414, 14.

Diana FitzGeorge-Balfour
35 Burnthwaite Road,
Fulham, London SW6 5BQ
Tel   +44 (0)20 7385 8081
Mobile +44 (0)7831 571449
Email diana@dianabalfour.co.uk
Web   www.dianabalfour.co.uk

Entry 320   Map 22

London

21 Barclay Road

The grand piano is a magnet for conductors and music professors from around the world. Delightful Charlotte and Adrian host lively social music evenings; Charlotte, who does something unspeakably high-powered by day, happily advises the best outings. All is swish here: polished oak floors, a sunny roof terrace, beautifully done bedrooms with decanters of sherry and luxuriously dressed beds (one a splendid king), and smart sparkling bathrooms. Help yourself to good espresso and a light breakfast tray in your room before setting off to tour London. Bring your instrument... a great city find. *Use of grand piano by arrangement.*

Price	From £100.
Rooms	2 doubles.
Meals	Food & music evenings occasionally. Restaurants 2-minute walk.
Closed	Occasionally.
Directions	Tube: Fulham Broadway 2-minute walk. Parking free 8pm-9am & all Sunday. 9am-8pm pay & display.

Charlotte Dexter
21 Barclay Road,
Fulham, London SW6 1EJ
Tel +44 (0)20 7384 3390
Email info@barclayhouselondon.com
Web www.barclayhouselondon.com

Entry 321   Map 22

London

123 Hazlebury Road

Step straight into Fiona's sitting room – she's an interior designer and there's an elegant feel with seagrass floors, pretty armchairs, a huge Italian oil painting and a bookcase full of books. Your bedroom, sunny and cheerful in the eaves, has cosy robes, a bright bathroom and stunning London skyline views. In the morning, tuck into a continental breakfast with very good coffee. For supper, find a great choice of restaurants in Parsons Green or walk to the local brasserie or pub. Fiona is a relaxed host and her garden is a sanctuary, with pots of flowers and decked seating. A perfect place to stay for the Chelsea Flower Show.

Price	£90-£110.
Rooms	1 double.
Meals	Continental breakfast. Pubs/restaurants 5-minute walk.
Closed	Rarely.
Directions	Sent on booking. Parking £15 per day, 9.30-5.30 Mon-Sat, Sunday free.

Fiona Andrews
123 Hazlebury Road,
Fulham,
London SW6 2LX
Tel +44 (0)20 7610 9119
Email fi@fandrewsdesign.com

Entry 322   Map 22

London

8 Parthenia Road

Caroline, an interior designer, mixes the sophistication of the city with the feel of the countryside and her handsome big kitchen is the engine-room of the house. It leads through to a light breakfast room with doors onto a pretty brick garden with chairs and table – hope for fine days. The house is long and thin, Fulham style, and reaches up to a big sloping-ceilinged bedroom in the eaves, cosy, sunny and bright. A remarkably quiet place to stay in an accessible part of town, near the King's Road with all its antique and designer shops, and Chelsea Football ground.

Price	From £110. Singles from £85.
Rooms	1 twin/double.
Meals	Continental breakfast. Restaurants nearby.
Closed	Rarely.
Directions	Tube: Parsons Green 4-minute walk. Parking £17.60 per day in street (9am-5pm), free on Sunday. Bus: 22, 2-minute walk.

Caroline & George Docker
8 Parthenia Road,
Fulham,
London SW6 4BD
Tel +44 (0)20 7384 1165
Email dockercaroline@gmail.com

Entry 323   Map 22

London

22 Marville Road

Smart railings help a pink rose climb, orange lilies add a touch of colour, and breakfast is in the pretty back garden on sunny days. Ben, the spaniel, and Christine – music lover, traveller, rower – make you feel at home. Your spacious bedroom in the eaves comes in elegant French grey and has crisp linen on comfortable beds, pretty lamps, a smart bathroom and a chaise longue for lounging and reading. The house is friendly with treasures from Christine's travels and gentle music at breakfast; there's a baby grand to play too. Restaurants and shops are a stroll away – and the Boat Race down the river.

Price	From £95. Singles from £80.
Rooms	1 twin/double.
Meals	Continental breakfast. Pubs/restaurants nearby.
Closed	Rarely.
Directions	At Fulham Rd junc. with Parson's Green Lane, down Kelvedon Rd. Cross Bishop Rd into Homestead Rd; 1st left into Marville Rd. Nearest tube: Parsons Green.

Christine Drake
22 Marville Road,
Fulham, London SW6 7BD
Tel +44 (0)20 7381 3205
Email christine.drake@btinternet.com
Web www.londonguestsathome.com

Entry 324   Map 43

London

Chiswick B&B

In a suburb of London long favoured by artists is a neat brick Victorian house framed by a beautiful maple; inside is a stylish and contemporary home. Warm gentle Ragini – life coach and English teacher – welcomes you in. Find cream marble floors, a fabulous kitchen, Indian art on the walls and the scent of fresh lilies. All feels spacious, generous and calm, and there's a sweet garden behind. Bedrooms are upstairs: fresh, snug, with waffle robes and goose down; breakfast is vegetarian and delicious. Chiswick House, Kew and the river are wonderfully close, and the 94 bus whisks you straight to Piccadilly!

Price	£80-£120.
Rooms	3: 1 double; 2 doubles with shared bath.
Meals	Dinner £30. Pubs/restaurants 5-minute walk.
Closed	Rarely.
Directions	5-minute walk from Turnham Green underground station; across park, right on street with red postbox.

	Ragini Annan
	Chiswick B&B,
	Chiswick,
	London W4 1JG
Mobile	+44 (0)7973 327662
Email	raginiannan@yahoo.co.uk
Web	www.chiswickbandb.com

Entry 325   Map 22

London

31 Rowan Road

Terrific value for money in Brook Green. Two private studios: one under the eaves (a big comfy bed, a window seat, a deep cast-iron bath from which you can gaze at the birds), the other larger and more contemporary in style, on the lower ground floor, with its own wisteria-clad entrance. Continental breakfast is popped into your fridge the night before. Or do proper B&B and join in with family life in a pink bedroom with books and hats (there's a spacious teenager's bedroom, too), then take breakfast in the pretty conservatory with Vicky and Edmund. There's a garden full of blossom and super restaurants close by.

Price	£80-£120. Singles £65-£100. Extra person £15.
Rooms	4: 2 doubles sharing bath/shower; 2 studios, each with twin/double, bath/shower & kitchenette. Extra bed available.
Meals	Continental breakfast. Pubs/restaurants 2 minutes.
Closed	Occasionally.
Directions	Tube: Hammersmith. Off-street parking £20 a day.

	Vicky & Edmund Sixsmith
	31 Rowan Road, Brook Green,
	Hammersmith, London W6 7DT
Tel	+44 (0)20 8748 0930
Mobile	+44 (0)7966 829359
Email	vickysixsmith@btconnect.com
Web	www.abetterwaytostay.co.uk

Entry 326   Map 22

London

26 Hillgate Place

This is bohemian, bustling Notting Hill: a movie at the Coronet, a pint at the Windsor Castle, the best Thai at the Churchill and the chic-est shops. Roll back to Hilary and Maryo's informal, lived-in home for a bit of eastern spice: Indian textiles, old teak dressers, the odd wooden elephant, wildly colourful art (Hilary paints). Downstairs, both bedrooms have an Indo-Caribbean influence, bathrobes and small fridge; the bigger double shares a bathroom up a flight of stairs, the smaller is smarter with a sofa and claw-foot bath. Outside is a patio garden and roof terrace; Muna and Hummer the dachshunds will keep you company.

Price	£90–£112. Singles £75–£90.
Rooms	2: 1 double; 1 double sharing family bath.
Meals	Pubs/restaurants nearby.
Closed	Occasionally.
Directions	Tube: Notting Hill Gate 5-minute walk.

Hilary Dunne & Maryo Josef
26 Hillgate Place,
Notting Hill Gate,
London W8 7ST
Tel   +44 (0)20 7727 7717
Email   hilary.dunne@virgin.net
Web   www.26hillgateplace.co.uk

Entry 327   Map 22

London

1 Peel Street

Pretty, gabled and surprisingly quiet with central London on your doorstep. Fascinating old maps, photos from Susie and Trevor's world travels and objets d'art all create an unusual and elegant feel. The top floor is all yours: the bedroom is full of character, framed by the slanting angles of the roof and soothingly decorated in neutral shades; the shelf above the snug-looking bed is crammed with interesting reads. Hop up a spiral stair to the roof terrace. Breakfast is at a table overlooking the patio: organic bread, pastries, fruit and excellent coffee. Just a stroll to good tapas, wine bars, Hyde Park and Notting Hill.

Price	£115. Singles £80.
Rooms	1 double with separate bath/shower.
Meals	Continental breakfast. Pubs/restaurants 2-minute walk.
Closed	Occasionally.
Directions	Sent on booking.

Susan & Trevor Laws
1 Peel Street,
Kensington,
London W8 7PA
Tel   +44 (0)20 7792 8361
Mobile   +44 (0)7776 140060
Email   susan@susielaws.co.uk

Entry 328   Map 22

London

101 Abbotsbury Road

The area is one of London's most desirable and Sunny's family home is opposite the borough's loveliest park, with open-air opera in summer. The whole top floor is generally given over to visitors. Warm, homely bedrooms are in gentle yellows and greens, with pale carpets, white duvets, pelmeted windows and a pretty dressing table for the double. The bathroom, marble-tiled and sky-lit, shines. You are well placed for Kensington High Street, Olympia, Notting Hill, Portobello Market, Kensington Gardens, the Albert Hall, Knightsbridge and Piccadilly! Relax, unwind, feel free to come and go. *Children over six welcome.*

Price	From £110. Singles from £55.
Rooms	2: 1 double, 1 single, sharing bath.
Meals	Continental breakfast. Pubs/restaurants 5-minute walk.
Closed	Occasionally.
Directions	Tube Central line: Holland Park 7-minute walk. Off-street parking sometimes available.

Sunny Murray
101 Abbotsbury Road,
Holland Park,
London W14 8EP
Tel   +44 (0)20 7602 0179
Mobile +44 (0)7768 362562
Email   sunny.murray@googlemail.com

Entry 329   Map 22

London

The Black and White House

Your own smart penthouse in a characterful turn-of-the-century house, on a peaceful street near Belsize Park tube. Expect to be pampered by friendly Carol-anne: a continental breakfast can be brought to you, in your sleek, sweet kitchen. The open-plan apartment spans the whole house; large sash windows let the light flood in to a modern chaise longue, a glass table, stacks of interesting books, a blue Union Jack rug. On the garden side of the room the double bed with its rich pink bedhead is deep and plump, and the walk-in shower gleams. Walk to bustling Camden market, pose in the cool cafés of Primrose Hill.

Price	From £125. Minimum 2 nights.
Rooms	1 suite (& extra sofabed) & kitchen.
Meals	Continental breakfast £5 for 2. Pubs/restaurants 5-minute walk.
Closed	Rarely.
Directions	Sent on booking.

Carol-anne Turner
The Black and White House,
Camden Town, London NW3 4LJ
Tel   +44 (0)20 7722 2781
Mobile +44 (0)7855 494974
Email   bwhouselondon@gmail.com
Web   www.theblackandwhitehouse.com

Entry 330   Map 22

London

66 Camden Square

A modern, architect designed house made of African teak, brick and glass. Climb wooden stairs under a glazed pyramid to light-filled, Japanese-style bedrooms with low platform beds, modern chairs and private sitting room/study. Sue and Rodger have travelled widely so there are pictures, photographs and ethnic pieces everywhere – and a burst of colour from Peckam the parrot. Share their lovely open-plan dining space overlooking a verdant bird-filled courtyard at breakfast – a delicious start to the day. Cool Camden's bustling market is close, along with theatres, restaurants, bars and zoo. *Children by arrangement.*

Price	£100. Singles £60. Min. 2 nights at weekends.
Rooms	2: 1 double; 1 single sharing bath (2nd room let to same party only).
Meals	Pubs/restaurants nearby.
Closed	Occasionally.
Directions	Tube: Camden Town or Kentish Town. Parking free at weekends; meters during week. 10 minutes by taxi or 20-minute walk from St Pancras Eurostar Terminal.

	Sue & Rodger Davis
	66 Camden Square,
	Camden Town,
	London NW1 9XD
Tel	+44 (0)20 7485 4622
Email	rodgerdavis@btopenworld.com

Entry 331   Map 22

London

30 King Henry's Road

Shops, restaurants and sublime views of Primrose Hill are a five-minute stroll from this interesting 1860s house; walls are covered in a lifetime collection of watercolours, drawings and maps. Your room on the top floor has a comfortable brass bed, a sisal floor, fine pieces of furniture, a wall of books, digital TV and a smart new bathroom. Breakfast on homemade bread and jams, bagels, croissants, yogurts and fresh fruit salad in the large kitchen/dining room with a big open fire and garden views. There's open-air theatre in Regent's Park in summer; Carole and Ted know London well and will happily advise.

Price	£120. Singles £90.
Rooms	1 double.
Meals	Pubs/restaurants 2-minute walk.
Closed	Occasionally.
Directions	Tube: Chalk Farm 5-minute walk. Free parking weekends, ticket parking nearby.

	Carole & Ted Cox
	30 King Henry's Road,
	Primrose Hill, London NW3 3RP
Tel	+44 (0)20 7483 2871
Mobile	+44 (0)7976 389350
Email	carole.l.cox@gmail.com

Entry 332   Map 22

London

Arlington Avenue

This 1848 townhouse is a real find – from here you can follow the canal up to Islington. Inside you find a world of books and art; immaculate bedrooms (the double very spacious) are colourful and filled with pictures, etchings and pretty furniture, with views over several gardens to the back. The grey marble shared guest bathroom is two flights down, but if you don't mind that, you've struck gold. Shop locally, eat picnic suppers in the red and gold dining room, chill drinks in the fridge. You help yourself to breakfast in a lemon coloured country style kitchen; this is laissez-faire B&B and fantastic value.

Price	£55–£70. Singles £45–£65.
Rooms	2: 1 double, 1 single sharing bath.
Meals	Pubs/restaurants 100 yds.
Closed	Rarely.
Directions	Equal distance from Angel and Old Street tubes (15-minute walk). 2 minutes for bus stop to City, St Pauls, Tate Modern (City 5 mins). 7 minutes to bus stop for West End (West End 20 minutes). Limited parking (by arrangement).

Thomas Blaikie
Arlington Avenue,
Islington,
London N1 7AX
Mobile   +44 (0)7711 265183
Email   thomas@arlingtonavenue.co.uk
Web   www.arlingtonavenue.co.uk

Entry 333   Map 22

London

Fleet River Bakery Rooms

Meet real Londoners, not tides of tourists, in the narrow streets of this vibrant, interesting part of town. Your handsome, city-sharp studio is above the bustling bakery/café: nip downstairs for delicious complimentary breakfast and coffee. You have a kitchen cum living area with sweeping wooden floor, sofa, and seriously comfortable bed. All warm and good-looking in a refreshingly frill-free way – and surprisingly quiet. People-watch through the long sash windows, cook up some local market produce or head out for a bundle of good restaurants – Covent Garden, Bloomsbury and the West End are all an easy walk.

Price	£115. Singles £84.
Rooms	4 studios: 1 double & kitchenette each.
Meals	Lunch in café downstairs, from £6.50. Packed lunch £7.50.
Closed	Rarely.
Directions	From Holborn tube: left from the main exit, down Kingsway, 2nd lane on left (Twyford Place). House on right at the end (corner of Twyford Place & Gate St).

Lucy Clapp
Fleet River Bakery Rooms, 71 Lincoln's Inn Fields, Holborn, London WC2A 3JF
Tel   +44 (0)20 7691 1457
Mobile   +44 (0)7966 267401
Email   rooms@fleetriverbakery.com
Web   www.fleetriverbakery.com

Entry 334   Map 22

London

26 Montefiore Street

Step off a quiet street into a hall of rich golds and a charming, elegant and comfortable bolthole. There's a little bird-filled garden where you can breakfast in summer: an organic spread with homemade jams and bread. This house is brimful of books – your bedroom too. Find white linen on a good handmade mattress, dressing gowns and, down steps, a fresh chic bathroom with fluffy towels and bath oils. No sitting room but there are wicker chairs in a corner of the library/dining room facing the pretty garden. Walk to Battersea Arts Centre and Battersea Park with its festivals and art fairs; not far from Chelsea Flower Show too.

Price	From £110. Singles from £80.
Rooms	1 double with separate bath/shower (1 single in attached study, suitable for child).
Meals	Restaurants 300 yds.
Closed	Occasionally.
Directions	Bus: 452 & 137, 9 minutes to Sloane Sq., 77 to South Bank, 87 to Westminster & Covent Garden. Tube: Clapham Common. Train: Queenstown Rd & Battersea Park, 2 & 4 min Victoria & Waterloo. Parking: day pass £5 (free 5.30pm-9.30am Mon-Fri, all day Sat, Sun).

	D Porter
	26 Montefiore Street,
	Battersea,
	London SW8 3TL
Tel	+44 (0)20 7720 0939
Email	bedandbreakfast.london.sw8@gmail.com

Entry 335   Map 22

London

20 St Philip Street

Come to retreat from the frenzy of city life. In the 1890 Victorian cottage all is peaceful and calm and Barbara looks after you beautifully. The dining room, with the odd oriental piece from past travels, is where you have your full English breakfast – unusual for London – and across the hall is the elegant sitting room, with gilt-framed mirrors, sumptuous curtains, and a piano. Upstairs is a bright and restful bedroom with pretty linen and a cloud of goose down. The large, sparkling bathroom next door is all yours – fabulous. Nothing has been overlooked and the tiny courtyard garden is a summer oasis.

Price	From £110. Singles from £80.
Rooms	1 double with separate bath & shower.
Meals	Pubs/restaurants 200 yds.
Closed	Occasionally.
Directions	Railway stations (6-min Waterloo, 3-min Victoria). Or 137 & 452 bus (Sloane Sq) & 156 (Vauxhall); tubes 10 mins. Parking max 4 hrs (£2 per hr) or £10 day, 9.30-5.30 (free all day Sat/Sun).

	Barbara Graham
	20 St Philip Street,
	Battersea,
	London SW8 3SL
Tel	+44 (0)20 7498 9967
Email	stay@bed-breakfast-battersea.co.uk
Web	www.bed-breakfast-battersea.co.uk

Entry 336   Map 22

London

The Coach House

A rare privacy: you have your own coach house, separated from the Notts' home by a stylish terracotta-potted courtyard with Indian sandstone paving and various fruit trees (peach, pear, nectarine). Breakfast in your own sunny kitchen, or let Meena treat you to a full English in hers (she makes great porridge, too). The lovely big attic bedroom has beams, cream curtains, rugs on polished wood floors; the brick-walled ground-floor twin is pleasant and airy; both look over the peaceful garden. Urban but bucolic – just perfect as a romantic retreat, or a family getaway.

Price	£110. £190 for whole coach house. Min. 3 nights; 2 nights Jan/Feb.
Rooms	Coach House: 1 family room for 2-3; 1 twin with separate shower. Same-party bookings only.
Meals	Pub/restaurant 200 yds.
Closed	Occasionally.
Directions	From r'bout on south side of Wandsworth Bridge, south down Trinity Rd on A214. At 3rd set of lights, 1.7 miles on, left into Upper Tooting Park. 4th left into Marius Rd, then 3rd left.

Meena & Harley Nott
The Coach House,
2 Tunley Road, Balham,
London SW17 7QJ
Tel   +44 (0)20 8772 1939
Email   coachhouse@chslondon.com
Web   www.coachhouse.chslondon.com

Entry 337   Map 22

London

108 Streathbourne Road

It's a handsome house in a conservation area that manages to be both elegant and cosy. The cream-coloured double bedroom has an armchair, a writing desk, pretty curtains and a big comfy walnut bed; the twin is light and airy. The dining room overlooks a secluded terrace and garden and there are newspapers at breakfast. You can eat in – David, who works in the wine trade, always puts a bottle on the table – or out, at one of the trendy new restaurants in Balham. A friendly city base on a quiet, tree-lined street – maximum comfort, delicious food and good value for London. Delightful. *Minimum stay two nights.*

Price	£95-£100. Singles £80-£85.
Rooms	2: 1 double with separate bath; 1 twin sharing bath (let to same party only).
Meals	Dinner £35. Restaurants 5-minute walk.
Closed	Occasionally.
Directions	Tube: Tooting Bec 7-minute walk. 319 bus from Sloane Square. Free parking weekends, otherwise meters or £5.50 daily permit.

Mary & David Hodges
108 Streathbourne Road,
Balham,
London SW17 8QY
Tel   +44 (0)20 8767 6931
Email   davidandmaryhodges@gmail.com

Entry 338   Map 22

London

28 Old Devonshire Road

Gardeners will love it here, in this surprisingly quiet part of Balham, a brisk stroll from the leafy common. Georgina's award-winning plot is brimming with colour and scent; enjoy breakfast under the pear tree on sunny days, or repair to the long wooden table in the dining room, distinguished by its marble fireplace and a friend's watercolours. Your bedroom is big, sunny, cosy and peaceful, with flowers from the garden, lots of books, a flat-screen TV; the bathroom is spacious, the shower is drenching and you get lovely waffle robes to pad about in. Heaps of interesting restaurants beckon. *French & Italian spoken.*

Price	£95. Singles £75. Minimum 2 nights.
Rooms	1 double.
Meals	Pubs/restaurants 500 yds.
Closed	Rarely.
Directions	Old Devonshire Road is a turning off Balham High Road, which is part of A24 London to Dorking road. 8-minute walk from Balham mainline and tube stations. Visitors' parking permits available £5.50 per day.

Georgina Ivor
28 Old Devonshire Road,
Balham, London SW12 9RB

Tel	+44 (0)20 8673 7179
Mobile	+44 (0)7941 960199
Email	georgina@balhambandb.co.uk
Web	www.balhambandb.co.uk

London

38 Killieser Avenue

On a quiet leafy street, the Haworths have brought country-house chic to South London. Philip and Winkle have filled their elegant Victorian townhouse with stunning fabrics, warm sunny colours and treasures from far-flung travels. The house glows, the garden is ravishing, breakfasts are delicious (so are the scones!) and bedrooms are spacious: fine linen, lambswool throws, waffle robes, the scent of roses. Few people do things with as much natural good humour as Winkle, whose passions are cooking, gardening and garden history. Transport is close and you can be in Victoria in 15 minutes. *Garden tours & cream tea courses.*

Price	From £100. Singles from £75.
Rooms	2: 1 twin; 1 single with separate bath.
Meals	Dinner £30–£35.
Closed	Occasionally.
Directions	5-minute walk from Streatham Hill station (15 minutes to Victoria); 15-minute walk from Balham tube.

Winkle Haworth
38 Killieser Avenue,
Streatham Hill,
London SW2 4NT

Tel	+44 (0)20 8671 4196
Email	winklehaworth@hotmail.com
Web	www.thegardenbedandbreakfast.com

London

The Lilac Door

You're conveniently close to London, without being in the smoke. Lovely Jane invites you in, to a bright, warm, peaceful house with a friendly feel, and a garden you can sit out in on sunny days. Breakfast is a generous, continental spread, served at the convivial pine table; bedrooms are light and uncluttered, those in the loft (new conversions) with sparkling bathrooms and laminate wood floors. All have brilliant extras: room fans, hot water bottles, waffle robes, chocolates, the best white linen. The parking is easy, the train to Victoria takes ten minutes, and Dulwich's restaurants are a tempting stroll. *Over 12s welcome.*

London

113 Pepys Road

This Victorian terraced house overlooks the first landscaped park of its kind in south-east London; the pretty garden, designed by David's father, is graced with majestic magnolias. Find a quirky mix of classic British furniture and oriental antiques. Picking up from his Chinese mother Anne, David has now taken on the B&B (helped by his housekeeper) and breakfast can be English or oriental. It's a convivial, lived-in home full of family portraits, batiks and books; the Chinese 'Peony' room downstairs has a huge bed, bamboo blinds, kimonos for the bathroom. A short walk to buses and tubes… and blissfully quiet for London.

Price	£90–£105. Singles £70–£90.
Rooms	3: 2 doubles; 1 double with separate bath/shower.
Meals	Continental breakfast. Pubs/restaurants 2-minute walk.
Closed	Rarely.
Directions	Sent on booking.

Price	£110. Singles £85.
Rooms	3: 1 double, 1 twin/double; 1 twin with separate bath.
Meals	Restaurant 0.5 miles.
Closed	Rarely.
Directions	Sent on booking.

Jane Waldegrave
The Lilac Door,
140 Rosendale Road, Dulwich,
London SE21 8LG

Tel   +44 (0)20 8766 6267
Email   jane.waldegrave@virgin.net
Web   www.lilacdoor.co.uk

Entry 341   Map 22

David Marten
113 Pepys Road,
New Cross,
London SE14 5SE

Tel   +44 (0)20 7639 1060
Email   davidmarten@pepysroad.com
Web   www.pepysroad.com

Entry 342   Map 22

London

London

24 Fox Hill

This part of London is full of sky, trees and wildlife; Pissarro captured on canvas the view up the hill in 1870 (the painting is in the National Gallery). There's good stuff everywhere – things hang off walls and peep over the tops of dressers; bedrooms are stunning, with antiques, textiles, paintings and big, firm beds. Sue, a graduate from Chelsea Art College, employs humour and intelligence to put guests at ease and has created a special garden too. Tim often helps with breakfasts: eggs from the hens, good coffee. Owls hoot at night, woodpeckers wake you in the morning, in this lofty, peaceful retreat. *Cookery courses.*

16 St Alfege Passage

The peaceful approach is along the passage between the Hawksmoor church and its graveyard, away from Greenwich hubbub. At the end of the lane is a 'cottage' set about with greenery, lamp posts and benches; inside, a cup of tea and flapjack await you in the eccentrically furnished (stuffed cat on dentist chair, huge parasol) sitting room. Bedrooms are cosy and colourful, with double beds (not huge) that positively encourage intimacy. Breakfast – delicious – is in the basement, another engagingly furnished room awash with character. Robert, an actor, is easy, funny, chatty – and has created an unusual and attractive place.

Price	£90-£120. Singles £50.		Price	£90-£125. Singles from £80.
Rooms	3: 1 twin/double; 1 double, 1 twin sharing shower.		Rooms	3: 1 four-poster, 1 double, 1 single.
Meals	Dinner £35. Pubs/restaurants 5-minute walk.		Meals	Pubs/restaurants 2-minute walk.
Closed	Rarely.		Closed	Rarely.
Directions	Train: Crystal Palace (7-minute walk). Underground: East London line. Collection possible. Good buses to West End & Westminster. Victoria 20 minutes by train.		Directions	3-minute walk from Greenwich train & Docklands Light Railway station or Cutty Sark DLR station. Parking free from 5pm (6pm Sundays) to 9am.

Sue & Tim Haigh
24 Fox Hill,
Crystal Palace,
London SE19 2XE
Tel   +44 (0)20 8768 0059
Email   suehaigh@hotmail.co.uk
Web   www.foxhill-bandb.co.uk

Nicholas Mesure & Robert Gray
16 St Alfege Passage,
Greenwich,
London SE10 9JS
Tel   +44 (0)20 8853 4337
Email   info@st-alfeges.co.uk
Web   www.st-alfeges.co.uk

Entry 343   Map 22

Entry 344   Map 22

Middlesex

Middle Cottage

What a find! A terrific spot right next to the Thames: Jonathan and Sarah have an eye for detail and do things well; you have your own, very private space in one half of their early Victorian cottages. Your light, upstairs sitting room has a dazzling collection of art and sculpture, chunky glass shelves full of design magazines and a soft grey sofa for reading. Your bedroom (not huge) is crisp and uncluttered with excellent lighting and blindingly white sheets; the funky bathroom is toasty with underfloor heating. Browse the newspapers over a robust breakfast; you can stroll to great shops and restaurants.

Price	From £110. Singles from £95.
Rooms	1 double. (Sofabed in sitting room.)
Meals	Pub/restaurant 20 yds.
Closed	Rarely.
Directions	Follow Teddington High Street towards the river. Middle Cottage sits within a terrace of 3, beside the footbridge near Teddington Lock.

Jonathan & Sarah Barker
Middle Cottage, 12 Ferry Road,
Teddington TW11 9NN

Tel	+44 (0)20 8973 0777
Mobile	+44 (0)7775 803664
Email	sarah@middlecottage.org
Web	www.middlecottage.org

Entry 345 Map 4

Norfolk

The Old Rectory

A stately place indeed: a venerable English rectory replete with period furniture, art, history, well-bred hosts (he shoots, she rides) and, in the expansive grounds, a ruined chapel, lake, croquet lawn and pool. Breakfast is served on the terrace in summer. You dine by candlelight on local game and the kitchen garden's offerings, then settle in the Georgian drawing room by the rocking horse. Sleep in the Coach House where plush beds have beautiful linen, warm throws and beaded cushions; dogs can stay in the stables. A rare chance to experience the best of British country life. *Riding & shooting can be arranged.*

Price	£85-£105. Singles £65-£85.
Rooms	Coach House: 1 double, 1 twin/double, 1 twin.
Meals	Dinner, 2 courses, £25; 3 courses, £35. Pub 1 mile. Restaurant 5 miles.
Closed	Rarely.
Directions	From Stone Ferry bypass, take road to Oxborough. 0.5 miles before Oxborough Hall, right down Ferry Road. House is 0.5 miles on left.

Veronica de Lotbiniere
The Old Rectory, Ferry Road,
King's Lynn, Oxborough PE33 9PT

Tel	+44 (0)1366 328962
Mobile	+44 (0)7769 687599
Email	onky.del@btinternet.com
Web	www.oldrectoryoxboroughbandb.co.uk

Entry 346 Map 9

Norfolk

The Merchants House

The oak four-poster – a beauty – came with the house. Part of the building (1400) is the oldest in Wells; in those days, the merchant could bring his boats up to the door. Liz and Dennis know the history, and happily share it. Inside is friendly and inviting: the mahogany shines, bathrooms sparkle, there are books to borrow and pretty sash windows overlook salt marshes. Breakfasts are a treat: homemade bread and jams, local produce and flowers on the table. As for Wells, it's on the famous Coastal Path, has a quay bustling with boats and 16 miles of sands. Birdwatch by day, dine out at night – easy when you're in the centre.

Price	£80. Singles £60.
Rooms	2: 1 double; 1 four-poster with separate bath/shower.
Meals	Pubs/restaurants 300 yds.
Closed	Rarely.
Directions	B1105 from Fakenham to Wells-next-the-Sea, then follow signs to beach & quay. House is 150 yds west of the quay.

Elizabeth & Dennis Woods
The Merchants House, 47 Freeman St,
Wells-next-the-Sea NR23 1BQ
Tel   +44 (0)1328 711877
Mobile   +44 (0)7816 632742
Email   denniswoods@talktalk.net
Web   www.the-merchants-house.co.uk

Entry 347   Map 10

Norfolk

1 Leicester Meadows

Up among 13 acres of wild meadow and woodland – not another building in sight. It's all so relaxed and unhurried: barn owls roosting in the outhouse, hens strutting, geese pottering up from the pond. The 19th-century cottages have been imaginatively restored; Bob was an architect, Sara an art teacher, and both are immensely friendly and helpful. Polished wood and old brick are topped with bright rugs; paintings and ceramics engage the eye; bedrooms have flowers and colourful covers. Hop downstairs for a superb breakfast at the big convivial table: rare-breed bacon, homemade jams and bread, fruits from the kitchen garden.

Price	From £70. Singles from £60.
Rooms	2: 1 twin/double, 1 double with sitting room.
Meals	Supper from £20. Pub 1 mile.
Closed	Rarely.
Directions	Off A148 near Fakenham; B1355 dir. Burnham Market. In S. Creake, left by flint bus shelter, right into Avondale Rd; 1 mile, taking left fork. At bottom of hill, house set back 100 yds on left.

Bob & Sara Freakley
1 Leicester Meadows,
South Creake,
Fakenham NR21 9NZ
Tel   +44 (0)1328 823533
Email   rf@freakley.com
Web   www.leicestermeadows.com

Entry 348   Map 10

Norfolk

Green Farm House

Sun streams in through the French windows of your own chic garden room – make yourself at home amid books, DVDs, rugs on slate floors, photos and watercolours, pots of flowers and a comfy sofa by the wood-burner; if you're peckish there are tea and biscuits. Sleep peacefully in the well-dressed bed and soak in the large shower. Lucy's house is next door and she's friendly and helpful; breakfast is across the garden in her conservatory: local sausages and bacon, homemade marmalade and muesli, smoked salmon and scrambled egg. Lucy can arrange sailing... heaven too for walkers, cyclists, birdwatchers.

Price	£87.50.
Rooms	Garden Room: 1 double.
Meals	Pub within 2 miles.
Closed	Rarely.
Directions	Sent on booking.

Lucy Jupe
Green Farm House, Balls Lane,
Thursford, Fakenham NR21 0BX
Tel   +44 (0)1328 878507
Mobile   +44 (0)7768 542645
Email   ljupe@enviroden.co.uk
Web   www.nnv.org.uk

Entry 349   Map 10

Norfolk

Holly Lodge

The whole place radiates a lavish attention to detail, from the spoilingly comfortable beds to the complimentary bottle of wine. It's perfect for those who love their privacy: these three snug guest 'cottages' have their own entrances as well as smart iron bedsteads and rugs on stone tiles, neat little shower rooms and tapestry-seat chairs, and books, music and TVs. Enjoy the Mediterranean garden with pond and decking in summer, the handsome conservatory and the utter peace. Your hosts are delightful: ex-restaurateur Jeremy who cooks enthusiastically, ethically and with panache, and Canadian-raised Gill.

Price	£90–£120. Singles £70–£100.
Rooms	3 cottages for 2.
Meals	Dinner, 3 courses with wine, £19.50. Pubs/restaurants 1 mile.
Closed	Rarely.
Directions	From Fakenham A148, Fakenham-Cromer road; 6 miles; left at Crawfish pub. Signs to Thursford Collection, past village green; 2nd drive on left.

Jeremy Bolam
Holly Lodge,
Thursford Green NR21 0AS
Tel   +44 (0)1328 878465
Email   info@hollylodgeguesthouse.co.uk
Web   www.hollylodgeguesthouse.co.uk

Entry 350   Map 10

Norfolk

Norfolk

Church Farmhouse

This attractive period farmhouse is part of the Sandringham Estate. Bedrooms have a cottage feel with flowers, cotton sheets, blankets or duvets, and an embroidered cover. Nigel, sociable and chatty, is a keen gardener keeping a neat veg patch; Marie is the cook and often makes her own sausages (and bread). Dinner may include their organically grown produce, Brancaster mussels and local asparagus – or nip over the road for supper at the pub. Indian Runners swim on the pond, walks start from the door and you're minutes from Burnham Market and Brancaster Beach. Hunstanton and Brancaster golf courses are a short drive.

Meadow House

Handmade oak banisters, period furniture: this new-build is beautifully traditional. Breakfast is served in the lovely large drawing room, where you find a warm, sociable atmosphere with squashy sofas and comfy chairs for anytime use. One bedroom is cosy and chintzy, one is larger and more neutral; brand-new bathrooms gleam. Amanda knows B&B, does it well, and plans to grow vegetables once her land is tamed. There are footpaths from the door and plenty to see, starting with Walpole's Houghton Hall, a short walk. A bucolic setting for a profoundly comfortable stay, perfect for country enthusiasts.

Price	£85-£95. Singles £60-£75.
Rooms	2: 1 double; 1 double with separate bath.
Meals	Dinner, 2-3 courses with wine, £25-£35.
Closed	Rarely.
Directions	Sent on booking.

Price	From £70. Singles £40.
Rooms	2 twins/doubles.
Meals	Packed lunch £5-£7. Pub 9-minute walk.
Closed	Rarely.
Directions	From King's Lynn, A148 for Cromer. 3 miles after Hillington, 2nd of 2 turnings right to Harpley (no signpost) opp. Houghton Hall sign. 200 yds on; over x-roads, house 400 yds on left.

	Marie Viney
	Church Farmhouse,
	Lynn Road, Great Bircham,
	King's Lynn PE31 6RJ
Tel	+44 (0)1485 576087
Email	enquiry@church-farmhouse.com
Web	www.church-farmhouse.com

	Amanda Case
	Meadow House,
	Harpley, King's Lynn PE31 6TU
Tel	+44 (0)1485 520240
Mobile	+44 (0)7890 037134
Email	amandacase@amandacase.plus.com
Web	www.meadowhousebandb.co.uk

Entry 351   Map 10

Entry 352   Map 10

Norfolk

The Close

A large, creeper-clad, Victorian house in the middle of the village, with a smooth lawn, mature trees, curved herbaceous border and a stream (source of the river Wensum). Bedrooms, one with a garden view, are large, light and airy, with a mix of antique and contemporary furniture, flowers, comfortable sofas with floral cushions; shower rooms are spotlessly tiled. You breakfast on home-baked bread and the local butcher's finest at a huge mahogany table in the dining room. Val and Rory know their patch well, so do ask: this is wonderful walking countryside and you are near the coast; Sandringham and Houghton, too.

Price	From £85. Singles £70.
Rooms	2 doubles.
Meals	Pub/restaurant 200 yds.
Closed	Rarely.
Directions	King's Lynn A148 to Fakenham. After 12 miles, through East Rudham. Right immed. after village opp. church. House 100 yds on right. Map provided on booking.

Valerie McGouran
The Close,
Station Road, East Rudham,
King's Lynn PE31 8SU

Tel   +44 (0)1485 528925
Email   rorymcgouran@hotmail.com
Web   www.closenorfolk.com

Entry 353   Map 10

Norfolk

Manor House Farm

In the private stable wing and next door cottage of this traditional Norfolk farmhouse, surrounded by four acres of lovingly tended gardens, are beautiful fresh rooms with wildly comfortable beds and their own sitting room opening onto the garden. Expect antiques, colourful rugs and flowers. Breakfast, served in the elegant dining room of the main house, is home-grown and delicious: fruit, eggs from the hens, bacon and sausages from their happy pigs. Libby and Robin have won conservation awards for the farm; Sandringham is close and Holkham Hall and the North Norfolk coast are 20 minutes. *Garden open for NGS. Over tens welcome.*

Price	£90–£100. Singles £60–£75.
Rooms	2: 1 double, 1 twin/double.
Meals	Restaurant 1.5 miles.
Closed	Rarely.
Directions	A1065 Swaffham-Fakenham road. 6 miles on, through Weasenham. After 1 mile, right for Wellingham. House on left, next to church.

Elisabeth Ellis
Manor House Farm,
Wellingham, Fakenham,
King's Lynn PE32 2TH

Tel   +44 (0)1328 838227
Email   libby.ellis@btconnect.com
Web   www.manor-house-farm.co.uk

Entry 354   Map 10

Norfolk

Litcham Hall

For the whole of the 19th century this was Litcham's doctor's house; the Hall is still at the centre of the community. The big-windowed guest bedrooms look onto stunning gardens with yew hedges, a lily pond and herbaceous borders. This is a thoroughly English home with elegant proportions – the hall, drawing room and dining room are gracious and beautifully furnished, and there's a large sitting room for guests. The garden fills the breakfast table with soft fruit in season and John and Hermione are friendly and most helpful. Close to Fakenham, Burnham Market and the coast. *Children & pets by arrangement.*

Price	£70-£90. Singles by arrangement.
Rooms	3: 2 doubles; 1 twin with separate bath.
Meals	Pub/restaurant 3 miles.
Closed	Christmas.
Directions	From Swaffham, A1065 north for 5 miles, then right to Litcham on B1145. House on left on entering village. Georgian red-brick with stone balls on gatepost.

John & Hermione Birkbeck
Litcham Hall,
Litcham,
King's Lynn PE32 2QQ
Tel +44 (0)1328 701389
Email hermionebirkbeck@hotmail.com
Web www.litchamhall.co.uk

Entry 355   Map 10

Norfolk

Carrick's at Castle Farm

This warm-bricked farmhouse is up a long drive and surrounded by 720 acres; John's family have lived here since the 1920s. He and Jean are passionate about conservation and the protection of wildlife, and here you have absolute quiet – for birdwatching, fishing or walking. Return to the drawing room with its open fire, books, and decanter of sherry. Your friendly hosts give you coffee and cake, or wine, when you arrive, and bedrooms are light and luxurious with pretty fabrics and homemade biscuits. Breakfasts and candlelit dinners are delicious, and the garden leads to a footpath alongside the river.

Price	£95. Singles £65.
Rooms	4: 1 double, 2 twins/doubles; 1 double with separate bath.
Meals	Dinner, 3 courses, £30. BYO. Pub 0.5 miles.
Closed	Rarely.
Directions	Norwich A47 to Dereham (don't go into Dereham). B1147 to Swanton Morley. In village, take Elsing Road at Darby's pub; farm drive 0.5 miles on left.

Jean Wright
Carrick's at Castle Farm,
Castle Farm, Swanton Morley,
Dereham NR20 4JT
Tel +44 (0)1362 638302
Email jean@castlefarm-swanton.co.uk
Web www.carricksatcastlefarm.co.uk

Entry 356   Map 10

Norfolk

Norfolk Courtyard

Walk straight in through French windows to your own, underfloor-heated room in the courtyard; privacy from the main house where young and friendly Simon and Catherine live. The rooms are decorated in soft colours, mattresses are perfect, cotton sheets are smooth and your handsome bathroom has limestone tiles – all rather luxurious. There's a welcome tea tray, a fridge to cool a bottle, continental breakfast in the old, beamed barn next door with French iron chairs, croissants, crumpets, homemade jams and muesli. Very civilised! Stunning walks await on the coast. *Minimum stay two nights (peak season weekends).*

Price	£80–£90. Singles from £60.
Rooms	4: 3 doubles, 1 twin.
Meals	Pub/restaurant 0.5 miles.
Closed	Rarely.
Directions	From Fakenham take Norwich road for 10 minutes. Take Foulsham turning at the large water tower. House is first on left.

Simon & Catherine Davis
Norfolk Courtyard, Westfield Farm,
Foxley Rd, Foulsham, Dereham NR20 5RH

Tel	+44 (0)1362 683333
Mobile	+44 (0)7969 611510
Email	info@norfolkcourtyard.co.uk
Web	www.norfolkcourtyard.co.uk

Entry 357   Map 10

Norfolk

Burgh Parva Hall

Sunlight bathes the Norfolk longhouse on sunny afternoons; the welcome from the Heals is as warm. The listed house is all that remains of the old village of Burgh Parva, deserted after the Great Plague. It's an inviting, handsome home... old furniture, rugs, books, pictures and Magnet the terrier-daschund. Large guest bedrooms face the sunsets and the garden flat makes a delightful hideaway, especially in summer. Breakfast eggs come from the garden hens, vegetables and fruits are home-grown, fresh fish is locally-sourced and the game may have been shot by William: settle down by the fire and tuck in!

Price	£70–£90. Singles £45–£55.
Rooms	3: 1 double; 1 twin with separate bath. Garden Flat: 1 twin.
Meals	Dinner £24. BYO. Pub/restaurant 4 miles.
Closed	Rarely.
Directions	Fakenham A148 for Cromer. At Thursford B1354 for Aylsham. Just before Melton, speed bumps, left immed. before bus shelter, signed St Mary's church. 1st house on right after farmyard.

Judy & William Heal
Burgh Parva Hall,
Melton Constable NR24 2PU

Tel	+44 (0)1263 862569
Email	judyheal@dsl.pipex.com

Entry 358   Map 10

Norfolk

Cleat House

A fantastic welcome in a peaceful street, a short walk from town and beach. This attractive late-Victorian seaside villa, built for a London merchant, has been sumptuously renovated inside. Bedrooms have original fireplaces and sash windows, upbeat fabrics and original art, and a warm inviting mix of antique and traditional. The guest sitting room comes with an honesty bar, games, books, DVDs and guides — set off for Holkham or Sandringham! Rob and Linda greet you with homemade treats and serve a tasty breakfast at separate tables — try Linda's hot dish of the day. You're beautifully cared for here. *Min. two nights at weekends.*

Price	£85-£130. Singles £70-£100.
Rooms	3: 2 suites; 1 suite with separate bath.
Meals	Pubs/restaurants within 0.5 miles.
Closed	Occasionally.
Directions	Off A148 onto A1082, at r'bout left, then right into Church St. 1st left into The Boulevard, 2nd left into North St. Montague Rd at the end of North St.

Rob & Linda Ownsworth
Cleat House, 7 Montague Road,
Sheringham NR26 8LN
Tel +44 (0)1263 822765
Mobile +44 (0)7557 356952
Email roblinda@cleathouse.co.uk
Web www.cleathouse.co.uk

Entry 359   Map 10

Norfolk

Plumstead Hall Farmhouse

Percy and Emma's large farmhouse has a gently bustling family feel, and you are made to feel at home as soon as you step onto the lovely old Norfolk pamments in the hall. The bedrooms, up higgledy-piggledy stairs, have feather duvets and pretty covers, green views and a huge bathroom; the second room with a sloping ceiling is simpler. Breakfast is a relaxed, do-it-yourself affair on the mini stove: eggs, bacon, cereals, breads and jams, all locally sourced and eaten in the guest dining room. The north Norfolk beaches are close and there are historic homes to visit. Birdwatchers, walkers and cyclists will be happy as Larry.

Price	£80. Singles £60.
Rooms	2 doubles sharing bath (2nd room let to same party only).
Meals	Dinner, 2 courses, £15. Pub/restaurant 5 miles.
Closed	Rarely.
Directions	Sent on booking.

Percy & Emma Stilwell
Plumstead Hall Farmhouse,
Northfield Lane, Plumstead,
Norwich NR11 7PT
Tel +44 (0)1263 577660
Email plumsteadhall@gmail.com
Web plumsteadhallfarmhouse.co.uk

Entry 360   Map 10

Norfolk

Stable Cottage

Sarah's home is set in the grounds of Heydon, one of Norfolk's finest Elizabethan houses. In the Dutch-gabled stable block, fronted by Cromwell's Oak, is her cottage – fresh, sunny and enchanting. Each room is touched by her warm personality and love of beautiful things: seagrass floors, crisp linen and pretty china; the cosy sitting room is set with tea and biscuits for your arrival. Bedrooms are cottagey and immaculate; bathrooms have baskets of treats. Sarah serves a delicious breakfast with golden eggs from her hens, homemade marmalade and garden fruit. Thursford is close and you're 20 minutes from the coast.

Price	£90. Singles from £45. Min. 2 nights at weekends.
Rooms	2 twins/doubles.
Meals	Pub 1 mile.
Closed	Christmas.
Directions	From Norwich, B1149 for 10 miles. 2nd left after bridge, for Heydon. 1.5 miles, right into village, over cattle grid, into park. Pass Hall on left, cottage in front of you; left over cattle grid and into stable yard.

Sarah Bulwer-Long
Stable Cottage,
Heydon Hall, Heydon,
Norwich NR11 6RE

Tel	+44 (0)1263 587343
Mobile	+44 (0)7780 998742
Web	www.heydon-bb.co.uk

Entry 361   Map 10

Norfolk

The Grove

A 15-minute stroll to the centre, but tucked down a tree-lined drive, this grand 1840s building once housed staff from the Colman's mustard factory. Tony and Sue are passionate about good food and delight in welcoming guests to their perfectly restored home. A staggering choice of goodies at breakfast includes lemon pancakes, locally smoked bacon, award-winning sausages and homemade bread. Walls are covered in interesting art, views through large sash windows are garden green, and each warm boutique-hotel style bedroom (all on the first floor) has an immaculate bathroom with a roll top bath. Spoiling.

Price	£85-£95. Singles £70-£80.
Rooms	3 doubles.
Meals	Pubs/restaurants within walking distance.
Closed	Rarely.
Directions	Sent on booking.

Tony Hamm
The Grove,
59 Bracondale, Norwich NR1 2AT

Tel	+44 (0)1603 622053
Mobile	+44 (0)7811 064705
Email	thegrovenorwich@live.co.uk
Web	thegrovenorwich.co.uk

Entry 362   Map 10

Norfolk

The Buttery

Down a farm track, a treasure: your own thatch-and-flint octagonal dairy house perfectly restored by local craftsmen and as neat as a new pin. You get a jacuzzi bath, a little kitchen and a fridge stocked with delicious bacon and ground coffee so you can breakfast when you want; take it to the sun terrace in good weather. The sitting room is terracotta-tiled and has a music system, a warming fire and a sofabed for those who don't want to tackle the steep wooden stair to the snug bedroom on the mezzanine. You can play a game of tennis, and walk from the door into peaceful parkland and woods. Lovely!

Norfolk

Sallowfield Cottage

In a beautifully remote part of Norfolk is a hospitable house crammed with treasures: gorgeous prints and paintings, polished family pieces, leather fender seats by the drawing room fire. One bedroom, not huge but handsome, has a Regency-style canopied bed and decoration to suit the house (1850); another room is on the ground floor. Drift into the garden to find hedged rooms and a jungly pond with a jetty on which you breakfast (deliciously): magical in spring and summer. Caroline gives you the best, her lovely lurchers add to the charm, and if you have friends locally she can do lunch for up to ten. *Over nines welcome.*

Price	£80–£100.
Rooms	Cottage: 1 double, sitting room & small kitchen.
Meals	Pub 10-minute walk.
Closed	Rarely.
Directions	From A47 Barnham Broom & Weston Longville x-roads, south towards Barnham Broom. After 150 yds, 1st farm track on right. Left at T-junc., left again, house on left.

Price	£75. Singles £50.
Rooms	3: 1 double, 1 twin; 1 double with separate bath.
Meals	Lunch £15. Dinner from £25. Pub 2.5 miles.
Closed	Christmas & New Year.
Directions	A11 Attleborough-Wymondham, Spooner Row sign. Over x-roads beside Three Boars pub. 1 mile; left at T-junc. to Wymondham for 1 mile. Rusty barrel on left, turn into farm track.

	Deborah Meynell
	The Buttery, Berry Hall, Honingham, Norwich NR9 5AX
Tel	+44 (0)1603 880541
Email	thebuttery@paston.co.uk
Web	www.thebuttery.biz

	Caroline Musker
	Sallowfield Cottage, Wattlefield, Wymondham, Norwich NR18 9NX
Tel	+44 (0)1953 605086
Mobile	+44 (0)7778 316616
Email	caroline.musker@tesco.net
Web	www.sallowfieldcottage.co.uk

Entry 363   Map 10

Entry 364   Map 10

Norfolk

Washingford House

Tall octagonal chimney stacks and a Georgian façade give the house a stately air. In fact, it's the friendliest of places to stay and Paris gives you a delicious, locally sourced breakfast including plenty of fresh fruit. The house, originally Tudor, is a delightful mix of old and new. Large light-filled bedrooms have loads of good books and views over the four-acre garden, a favourite haunt for local birds. Bergh Apton is a conservation village seven miles from Norwich and you are in the heart of it; perfect for cycling, boat trips on the Norfolk Broads and the twelve Wherryman's Way circular walks.

Price	£65-£80. Singles £35-£50.
Rooms	2: 1 twin/double; 1 single with separate bath.
Meals	Pubs/restaurants 4-6 miles.
Closed	Christmas.
Directions	A146 from Norwich to Lowestoft for 4 miles. Right after Gull Pub, signed Slade Lane. First left, then left at T-junc. for 1 mile. Straight over x-roads; house on left past post office.

	Paris & Nigel Back Washingford House, Cookes Road, Bergh Apton, Norwich NR15 1AA
Tel	+44 (0)1508 550924
Mobile	+44 (0)7900 683617
Email	parisb@waitrose.com
Web	www.washingford.com

Entry 365   Map 10

Norfolk

Sloley Hall

A grand and gracious yellow-brick Georgian house with formal gardens, tree-studded parkland and glorious views from every window. It has also been beautifully renovated, with flagstoned floors, Persian rugs, gleaming circular tables and vases of garden-grown flowers. Your hosts are delightful – Barbara and Simon were married here and are charmingly easy-going and helpful. A huge light-flooded dining room is perfect for breakfast; the drawing room is comfy and uncluttered with a marble fireplace and long views. Bedrooms are large and elegant with sumptuous bed linen, and generous bathrooms glow with warmth.

Price	£70-£90. Singles from £50.
Rooms	3: 1 suite; 1 double with separate shower; 1 twin with separate bath. Child bed available.
Meals	Pubs/restaurants 2-4 miles.
Closed	January/February.
Directions	From Norwich ring road, B1150 through Coltishall & Scottow. Right after Three Horseshoes pub (byway to Sloley); across staggered junc., 1st drive on right.

	Barbara Gorton Sloley Hall, Sloley, Norwich NR12 8HA
Tel	+44 (0)1692 538582
Mobile	+44 (0)7748 152079
Email	babsgorton@hotmail.com
Web	www.sloleyhall.com

Entry 366   Map 10

Norfolk

Sutton Hall

Sweep up a gravel drive to a red-brick Victorian country house, in quiet parkland near the Norfolk Broads and coast. Sue serves eggs freshly laid by running hens, tomatoes from the kitchen garden, and knobbly apples from an orchard where deer and ducks roam free... breakfast on the terrace, or in a chandelier'd dining room with bay windows to the morning sun. Rooms are in keeping with the home's comfortable elegance – tall sash windows, a four-poster, fireplace, power showers, an extra bed for children; a Chinese screen adorns the high-ceilinged sitting room. Spend the day on the Broads with the binoculars.

Price	From £90. Singles from £70.
Rooms	2 doubles. Extra child bed and cot.
Meals	Packed lunch from £6. Pubs/restaurant 1.5 miles.
Closed	Rarely.
Directions	A47 E of Norwich, A1064 at Acle, then B1152 to A149. Left dir. North Walsham, Stalham, 1st right into Sutton, then 1st right, 1st left and 2nd right into Hall Rd.

Sue Berry
Sutton Hall, Hall Road, Sutton, Norwich NR12 9RX

Tel	+44 (0)1692 584888
Mobile	+44 (0)7977 575788
Email	enquiries@suttonhallnorfolk.co.uk
Web	www.suttonhallnorfolk.co.uk

Entry 367   Map 10

Norfolk

Manor Farmhouse

A family buzz and candlelight in the farmhouse where you eat, peace in the 17th-century barn where you stay. All rooms lead off its charming, stylish, vaulted sitting room with cosy winter fire. You have a modern four-poster and a tiny shower on the ground floor, then two narrow staircases to two beautifully dressed bedrooms upstairs – small, quirky, fun, with a tucked-up-in-the-roof feel. Come for a sunny courtyard, billiards in the old stable, fresh flowers, lovely hosts, gorgeous food – and you may come and go as you please. Great value, a perfect rural retreat. *Children over seven welcome.*

Price	From £50. Singles from £40.
Rooms	3: 1 double, 1 twin/double, 1 four-poster.
Meals	Dinner, 3 courses, £17.50. BYO. Pubs 1 mile.
Closed	Christmas & New Year.
Directions	From Norwich, A1151 & A149 almost to Stalham. Left Walcott. At T-junc. left; 1 mile on, right H'burgh. Next T-junc., right. Next T-junc., left. Road bends right, sign by wall.

David & Rosie Eldridge
Manor Farmhouse,
Happisburgh NR12 0SA

Tel	+44 (0)1692 651262
Email	manorathappisburgh@hotmail.com
Web	www.northnorfolk.co.uk/manorbarn

Entry 368   Map 10

Norfolk

The Old Rectory

Conservation farmland all around; acres of wild heathland busy with woodpeckers and owls; the coast two miles away. Relax in the spacious drawing room of this handsome 17th-century rectory and friendly family home, set in four acres of grounds. Fiona loves to cook and bakes her bread daily, food is delicious, seasonal and locally sourced, jams are homemade. Comfortable bedrooms have *objets* from diplomatic postings and the spacious suite comes with mahogany furniture and armchairs so you can settle in with a book. Super views, friendly dogs, tennis in the garden and masses of space.

Price	From £60. Singles £40.
Rooms	2: 1 suite; 1 double with separate bath & shower.
Meals	Dinner from £20. Pubs 2 miles.
Closed	Rarely.
Directions	From Norwich A1151 for Stalham. Just before Stalham, left to Happisburgh. Left at T-junc.; 3 miles; 2nd left after E. Ruston church, signed byway to Foxhill. Right at x-roads; 1 mile on right.

Peter & Fiona Black
The Old Rectory,
Ridlington NR28 9NZ
Tel +44 (0)1692 650247
Mobile +44 (0)7774 599911
Email blacks7@email.com
Web www.oldrectorynorthnorfolk.co.uk

Entry 369 Map 10

Norfolk

Rushall House

Plenty of treats to be had in this light, bright Victorian rectory: blue-shelled eggs for breakfast, homemade cake for tea, and radios, books and sofas in each double bedroom. The woodburner-cosy guest drawing room is classically decorated with a contemporary touch, airy bedrooms have pale walls, rich fabrics and a grand mix of colours and textiles; Jane's vintage furniture and fabrics are for sale in her courtyard studio. Walk or cycle after breakfast – it's good flat countryside and there are many restorative pubs. Jane and Martin are relaxed hosts; children will love collecting the hens' eggs. *One day sewing courses.*

Price	From £70. Singles from £45.
Rooms	3: 1 double; 1 double, 1 twin sharing bath/shower.
Meals	Dinner £23. BYO. Pubs/restaurants 0.5-3 miles.
Closed	Rarely.
Directions	Turn off A140 at r'bout to Dickleburgh; right at village store. After two miles pass Lakes Rd & Vaunces Lane, on right. Shortly after z-bend sign, house on right. White button on post opens gate.

Martin Hubner & Jane Gardiner
Rushall House,
Dickleburgh Road, Rushall,
Diss IP21 4RX
Tel +44 (0)1379 741557
Email janegardineruk@aol.com
Web www.rushallhouse.co.uk

Entry 370 Map 10

Norfolk

Prickwillows

Up a winding track through woodland to tea and cake, smiling Anita and the perfect antidote to life's usual rush. Set in over an acre of garden, you have your own entrance and a sitting room with wooden floors and colourful kilims. The pretty bathroom is downstairs; hop up fairly steep steps to a lovely, airy south-facing bedroom with roses peeping in and a padded window seat for dreaming. Sleep deeply in the quiet and wake to a scrummy continental or cooked breakfast on jolly, spotted china; enjoy it in the beamed dining room or the bird-filled garden on sunny days. Great walks from the door, and Norwich is a short drive away.

Price	From £70.
Rooms	1 suite with dining & sitting room.
Meals	Pubs 4 miles.
Closed	Rarely.
Directions	Sent on booking.

	Anita Eldridge
	Prickwillows,
	Garboldisham,
	Diss IP22 2RN
Tel	+44 (0)1953 681494
Email	anitaeldridge1@gmail.com
Web	www.prickwillows.co.uk

Entry 371   Map 10

Norfolk

College Farm

Katharine is a natural at making guests feel like friends. Her beautiful farmhouse tucks itself away on the edge of the village and the big friendly kitchen is filled with delicious smells of home baking. Meals are served by the large wood-burner in the grand Jacobean dining room, filled with lovely antiques, period furnishings and cosy places to sit; food is home-grown, seasonal and local. Sleep well in charming bedrooms with garden views, smooth linen and pretty furniture; bathrooms are small and simple. A fascinating area teeming with pingos, wildlife, old churches and glorious antique shops.

Price	From £70. Singles £35.
Rooms	3: 2 twins/doubles; 1 double with separate bath.
Meals	Dinner from £15. Pub 1 mile.
Closed	Rarely.
Directions	Sent on booking.

	Katharine Wolstenholme
	College Farm,
	Thompson,
	Thetford IP24 1QG
Tel	+44 (0)1953 483318
Email	rwolstenholme@aol.com
Web	www.collegefarmnorfolk.co.uk

Entry 372   Map 10

Norfolk

Home Farmhouse

A big yellow Jacobean farmhouse that stands in a couple of deeply rural acres. John and Anne rebuilt the house, removing the front wall to refit seasoned oak. Outside, birdsong fills the air; inside, the drawing-room fire crackles with gusto, and you can pick up the daily papers and sink into a sofa. John, a military historian, cooks breakfast (eggs from the resident hens, apple juice from local orchards), while Anne whisks up delicious dinners. Smart bedrooms are wonderfully comfortable with crisp linen, fresh flowers and interesting books. There are stables for horses and secure bike storage, too.

Price	£100. Singles £50.
Rooms	2: 1 double, 1 twin/double.
Meals	Dinner, 3 courses with cheese, £28. Family supper, adults £15, children £10.
Closed	Rarely.
Directions	A11 for Norwich, then A1075 to Shipdham. In village 1st right, signed Cranworth. 2nd left; house 1st on left.

Anne & John Smales
Home Farmhouse,
Letton, Thetford IP25 7PS

Tel	+44 (0)1362 820502
Mobile	+44 (0)7730 398744
Email	anne@homefarmhouseletton.co.uk
Web	www.homefarmhouseletton.co.uk

Entry 373   Map 10

Northamptonshire

Bridge Cottage

A truly peaceful place, yet only a few miles from Peterborough. Sip a glass of wine on the decking down by the Willowbrook; beautiful countryside envelops you, the cattle doze, kingfishers flash by and you may see a red kite (borrow some binoculars). Inside find pretty bedrooms with sloping ceilings, the purest cotton sheets and proper blankets; bathrooms are thickly towelled and full of lovely lotions and bubbles. Breakfast is local and scrumptious and served in the friendliest kitchen facing that heavenly view, there's a tranquil conservatory for a quiet read, and Judy and Rod are brilliant hosts. A hidden gem.

Price	From £85. Singles £50-£60.
Rooms	3: 1 double, 1 twin; 1 double with separate bath.
Meals	Pub/restaurant 500 yds.
Closed	Christmas.
Directions	From south A1 to Peterborough junc. A605 signed Oundle & Northampton for 4 miles. At 1st r'bout right thro' Fotheringhay, then Woodnewton. House 1st on left on bridge.

Judy Colebrook
Bridge Cottage, Oundle Road,
Woodnewton, Peterborough PE8 5EG

Tel	+44 (0)1780 470860
Mobile	+44 (0)7979 644864
Email	enquiries@bridgecottage.net
Web	www.bridgecottage.net

Entry 374   Map 9

Northamptonshire

The Old House

Northamptonshire is the county of spires and squires. And here, on the through-road of this fascinating medieval town, is a listed squire's house – once home to a merchant who traded in the marketplace opposite. Enter the heavy oak door and step back 400 years. William, courteous, hospitable and renovating with aplomb, is full of plans. Facing the courtyard at the back (furnished for summery breakfasts and aperitifs) are the quietest rooms; all have sumptuous fabrics and wallpapers, dramatic touches and divine beds. Bathrooms are a work in progress – but will, no doubt, be as special as all the rest.

Northamptonshire

Staverton Hall

Through impressive iron gates to a grand house in a spectacular setting with masses of room, and friendly owners Rupert and Serena who have young children of their own; they love having families to stay. Relaxed breakfasts (and dinner) at flexible times are served at one table; all is local and delicious. Large, light bedrooms and super-modern shared bathrooms are upstairs, have good views and feel private. Relax in the huge, creamy-yellow guest sitting room with sash windows, log fire, board games and comfy sofas; there's also a heated pool, a play area, acres of garden, and the pub a walk away. Family heaven.

Price	£60-£65. Singles £45-£50.
Rooms	3: 2 doubles, 1 twin/double.
Meals	Pubs/restaurants 150 yds.
Closed	Rarely.
Directions	Sent on booking.

Price	£90. Singles £50. (One party sharing 3 rooms: £200.)
Rooms	4: 3 doubles, 1 single, all sharing 2 bathrooms.
Meals	Dinner, 3 courses, £30 (min. 4 people). Pub 3-minute walk.
Closed	Rarely.
Directions	Sent on booking.

William Evans
The Old House,
5 Market Square, Higham Ferrers,
Rushden NN10 8BP
Tel   +44 (0)1933 314006
Email   theoldhousehighamferrers@gmail.com
Web   www.theoldhousehighamferrers.co.uk

Rupert Frost
Staverton Hall,
Manor Road, Staverton NN11 6JD
Tel   +44 (0)1327 878296
Email   serena@stavertonhall.co.uk
Web   www.stavertonhall.co.uk

Entry 375   Map 9

Entry 376   Map 8

Northamptonshire

Colledges House

Huge attention to comfort here, and a house full of laughter. Liz clearly derives pleasure from sharing her 300-year-old stone thatched cottage, immaculate garden, conservatory and converted barn with guests. Sumptuous bedrooms have deep mattresses with fine linen, sparkling bathrooms are a good size. The house is full of interesting things: a Jacobean trunk, a Bechstein piano, mirrors and pictures, pretty china, bright fabrics, a beautiful bureau. Cordon Bleu dinners are elegant affairs – and great fun. Stroll around the conservation village of Staverton – delightful. *Children over eight & babes in arms welcome.*

Price	£95–£99. Singles £67.50–£69.50.
Rooms	4: 1 single; 1 double with separate bath. Cottage: 1 double, 1 twin.
Meals	Dinner, 3 courses, £35. Pub 4-minute walk.
Closed	Rarely.
Directions	From Daventry, A425 to Leamington Spa. 100 yds past Staverton Park Conference Centre, right into village, then 1st right. Keep left, & at 'Give Way' sign, sharp left. House immed. on right.

Liz Jarrett
Colledges House, Oakham Lane,
Staverton, Daventry NN11 6JQ
Tel   +44 (0)1327 702737
Mobile   +44 (0)7710 794112
Email   liz@colledgeshouse.co.uk
Web   www.colledgeshouse.co.uk

Entry 377   Map 8

Northamptonshire

The Vyne

Weighed down by wisteria, this 16th-century cottage rests in a honey-hued conservation village on the cusp of Oxfordshire. Beams and wonky lines abound; rooms are filled with good antiques and eclectic art. The spacious twin is enchanting, tucked under the rafters, its beds decorated in willow-pattern chintz, its walls glinting with gilded frames; the double has a Georgian four-poster and a sampler-decorated bathroom that's a quick flit next door. Warm and charming, Imogen not only works in publishing but is a dedicated gardener and Cordon Bleu cook – enjoy supper in her sunny secluded garden. *Babies welcome.*

Price	£75. Singles from £45.
Rooms	2: 1 twin; 1 four-poster with separate bath.
Meals	Supper £20. Dinner £30. BYO. Pub 2-minute walk.
Closed	Christmas & New Year.
Directions	M40 exit 11. A422 to Northampton, left onto B4525. 2 miles, left to Thorpe Mandeville. 3 miles, left to Culworth. After Culworth, right to Eydon.

Imogen Butler
The Vyne,
High Street, Eydon,
Daventry NN11 3PP
Tel   +44 (0)1327 264886
Mobile   +44 (0)7974 801475
Email   imogen@ibutler2.wanadoo.co.uk

Entry 378   Map 8

Northamptonshire

The Coach House

Sunlight and flower-scent fill this sprawling, rosy-brick home. Originally a coach house and stables, it's now a series of elegant light-filled rooms wrapped round a central courtyard; you can breakfast out on sunny days. Sarah's eye for colour shows in the design of her large gardens, and her clever mix of modern and traditional furnishings. Bedrooms ooze country-house luxury with fine cotton, fluffy towels and glossy magazines; the first-floor family room has a magnificent shower room, the ground floor twin opens onto a private terrace. Play tennis, have a day out at Silverstone, visit historical landmarks.

Price	£80–£90. (£120 during Grand Prix & Classic weekends.) Singles £55.
Rooms	3: 1 double, 1 twin, 1 family room.
Meals	Packed lunch on request. Pub/restaurant within 5 miles.
Closed	Rarely.
Directions	From A43 dual carriageway, A5 north for Hinckley. After 1.1 miles sharp left to Duncote. First house on left, 300 yds, 2nd gate.

Sarah Baker Baker
The Coach House,
Duncote, Towcester NN12 8AQ

Tel	+44 (0)1327 352855
Mobile	+44 (0)7875 215705
Email	sarahbb54@gmail.com
Web	www.thecoachhouseduncote.co.uk

Entry 379   Map 8

Northumberland

Matfen High House

Bring the wellies – and jumpers! You are 25 miles from the border and the walking is a joy. Struan and Jenny are amusing company, love sporting pursuits and will drive you to Matfen Hall for dinner. The sturdy stone house of 1735 is a lived-in, pretty place to stay: the en suite bedrooms have fine fabrics and good pictures, immaculate bathrooms are stocked with fluffy towels and the drawing room promises books and choice pieces. Enjoy local bacon and sausages at breakfast, with Struan's marmalade and bread warm from the oven. The countryside is stunning, Hadrian's Wall and the great castles (Alnwick, Bamburgh) beckon.

Price	£70–£75. Singles £40.
Rooms	4: 1 double, 1 twin; 1 double, 1 twin sharing bath.
Meals	Packed lunch £4.50. Restaurant 2 miles.
Closed	Rarely.
Directions	A69 at Heddon on the Wall, onto B6318; 500 yds, right to Moorhouse; right at next junc. signed Brewery & visitor centre; past Hadrian Pet Hotel; 300 yds, right, opp. cottages.

Struan & Jenny Wilson
Matfen High House,
Matfen,
Corbridge NE20 0RG

Tel	+44 (0)1661 886592
Email	struan@struan.enterprise-plc.com
Web	www.matfenhighhouse.co.uk

Entry 380   Map 12

Northumberland

Bog House

Blissfully quiet here and the views are fabulous, yet it's only a 30-minute drive to Newcastle. Rosemary is charming and her home a stunning barn conversion with attractive, comfortable ground floor bedrooms and pretty antiques. You have your own entrance in a separate wing, and can come and go as you please. Rosemary produces excellent meals: local sausages and bacon, home-baked bread, home-grown fruits and veg; she will happily serve breakfast as late as 11am at the weekend. The garden is full of daffodils in spring, Hadrian's Wall is a hop and this is an indulgent, wonderful retreat. *Over 12s welcome. Broadband available.*

Price	£90. Singles £50.
Rooms	2: 1 twin, 1 double.
Meals	Dinner £25.
	Pubs/restaurants 15-minute drive.
Closed	Rarely.
Directions	A68; 3 miles north of Corbridge, right onto B6318. After 3.5 miles, left signed Moorhouse. On for 1 mile, right; left to Bog House after 1 mile. Last farm on left.

Rosemary Stobart
Bog House,
Matfen NE20 0RF
Tel +44 (0)1661 886776
Mobile +44 (0)7850 375535
Email rosemary.stobart@btinternet.com
Web www.boghouse-matfen.co.uk

Entry 381 Map 16

Northumberland

The Hermitage

A magical setting, three miles from Hadrian's wall, in a house full of friendship and comfort. Through ancient woodland, up the drive, over the burn and there it is: big, beautiful and Georgian. Interiors are comfortable country-house, full of warmth and charm; bedrooms, carpeted, spacious and delightful, are furnished with antiques, paintings and superb beds; bathrooms have roll top baths. Outside are lovely lawns, a walled garden, wildlife, and breakfasts on the terrace in summer. Katie – who was born in this house – looks after you brilliantly. *Guests back by 11pm please. Over sevens & babes in arms welcome.*

Price	From £85. Singles from £50.
Rooms	3: 1 double, 1 twin;
	1 twin with separate bath.
Meals	Pub 2 miles.
Closed	October-February.
Directions	7 miles north of Corbridge on A68. Left on A6079 for 1 mile, then right through lodge gates with arch. House 0.5 miles down drive.

Simon & Katie Stewart
The Hermitage,
Swinburne,
Hexham NE48 4DG
Tel +44 (0)1434 681248
Mobile +44 (0)7708 016297
Email katie.stewart@themeet.co.uk

Entry 382 Map 16

Northumberland

Shieldhall

The guest rooms are in the charming 18th-century farm buildings, each with its own entrance. Stephen and his sons make and restore furniture and rooms are named after the wood used within: Elm, Oak, Mahogany, Pine. Bathrooms are spacious, there's a beautiful sitting room/library full of books, and you pop across the courtyard for meals in the main house – once home to the family of Capability Brown. Celia, and daughter Sarah, are friendly and attentive and love cooking; ingredients are often organic or locally sourced. There's also a secret bar and a small but interesting wine list. Peaceful, hospitable B&B – with fine views.

Price	£80. Singles £60.
Rooms	3: 1 double, 1 twin, 1 four-poster.
Meals	Dinner, 4 courses, £28. Pub 7 miles.
Closed	Rarely.
Directions	From Newcastle A696 for Jedburgh. 5 miles north of Belsay, right onto B6342. On left after 500 yds (turn into front courtyard).

	Celia & Stephen Robinson-Gay Shieldhall, Wallington, Morpeth NE61 4AQ
Tel	+44 (0)1830 540387
Email	stay@shieldhallguesthouse.co.uk
Web	www.shieldhallguesthouse.co.uk

Entry 383   Map 16

Northumberland

Thistleyhaugh

The family thrives on hard work and humour, and if Enid's not the perfect B&B hostess, she's a close contender. Her passions are pictures, cooking and people, and certainly you eat well – local farm eggs at breakfast and their beef at dinner. Choose any of the five large, lovely bedrooms and stay the week; they are awash with old paintings, silk fabrics and crisp linen. Wake refreshed and nip downstairs, past the log fire, to a laden and sociable table, head off afterwards to find 720 acres of organic farmland and a few million more of the Cheviots beyond. Wonderful hosts, a glorious region, a happy house.

Price	£90. Singles £60-£85.
Rooms	5: 3 doubles, 1 twin, 1 single.
Meals	Dinner, 3 courses, £25. Pub/restaurant 2 miles.
Closed	Christmas, New Year & January.
Directions	Leave A1 for A697 for Coldstream & Longhorsley; 2 miles past Longhorsley, left at Todburn sign; 1 mile to x-roads, then right; on 1 mile over white bridge; 1st right, right again, over cattle grid.

	Henry & Enid Nelless Thistleyhaugh, Longhorsley, Morpeth NE65 8RG
Tel	+44 (0)1665 570629
Email	thistleyhaugh@hotmail.com
Web	www.thistleyhaugh.co.uk

Entry 384   Map 16

Northumberland

East Hepple Farmhouse

In the farmhouse sitting room, a wood-burner blazes away in winter. The double, too, has a sitting room, with an original cast-iron range and shelves groaning with books – bibliophile heaven. The peace is so deep in the Coquet valley that you may sleep until the whiff of sizzling local bacon hits your nostrils. Beds are firm, old pine pieces pretty, pillows feathery soft and views over the river to the Simonside hills abundant. Joan and Brian are expert at looking after you, will drive you to dinner and guide you the next day to beaches, Cragside, Alnwick Castle and fabulous walks. To stay is a treat. *Fishing can be arranged.*

Price	£70–£75. Singles from £50.
Rooms	2: 1 double & sitting room, 1 twin (usually let to same party only).
Meals	Packed lunch £5. Pubs/restaurants 2.5 miles.
Closed	Rarely.
Directions	West from Rothbury on B6341. Thro' Thropton to Hepple, pass church on left; next right, then immediate hard right into driveway.

Joan & Brian Storey
East Hepple Farmhouse,
Hepple,
Rothbury NE65 7LH
Tel   +44 (0)1669 640221
Email   joanstorey@coquetdale.net
Web   www.eastheppletarm.co.uk

Entry 385   Map 16

Northumberland

Alnham Farm

Delve deep into the glorious sheep-dotted hills and valleys of the Northumberland National Park to find Jenny's handsome Georgian farmhouse and a dollop of urban chic in bedrooms and bathrooms. Walkers will be in heaven: set off with a tummy full of farmhouse porridge, home-reared sausages and bacon or a smashing Craster kipper. Spot whirling buzzards, the elusive red squirrel, otters if you are lucky; return to the crispest linen, gleaming mahogany, fresh flowers, and a power shower or a soak in a freestanding tub (bubbles and lotions provided). Castles, deep dunes and long white beaches are an easy drive.

Price	£80. Singles £50.
Rooms	2: 1 double; 1 twin/double with separate bathroom.
Meals	Pub/restaurant 7 miles.
Closed	December–February.
Directions	From Whittingham, over bridge left to Netherton; 3miles right to Little Ryle & left passing Unthank Farm. Left at T-junc. & down front drive before 1st cottage on left.

Jenny Sordy
Alnham Farm,
Alnwick NE66 4TJ
Tel   +44 (0)1669 630210
Email   jenny@alnhamfarm.co.uk
Web   www.alnhamfarm.co.uk

Entry 386   Map 16

Courtyard Garden

In the county town of Northumberland, with its grand castle and innovative gardens, step directly off the pavement and enter a courtyard surrounded by shrubs and pretty pots; sit out here on sunny days and sip a glass of something cool. Bedrooms (one overlooking the church, the other the garden) are traditional and immaculate; bathrooms, one with a roll top bath, have original wooden floors, thick towels. Friendly Maureen gives you breakfast in the comfortable sitting room at a round Georgian table underneath the window. Explore the town on foot, stride along white beaches, discover more castles; history is all around you.

Bilton Barns

A solidly good farmhouse B&B whose lifeblood is still farming. The Jacksons know every inch of the countryside and coast that surrounds their 1715 home; it's a pretty spot. They farm 400 acres of mixed arable land that sweeps down to the coast yet always have time for guests. Dorothy creates an easy and sociable atmosphere with welcoming pots of tea and convivial breakfasts – all delicious and locally sourced. Comfortable, smartly done bedrooms are traditional with a contemporary feel, the conservatory is huge and filled with sofas and chairs and there's an airy guests' sitting room with an open fire and views to the sea.

Price	From £80. Singles from £60.
Rooms	2: 1 double, 1 twin/double.
Meals	Pub/restaurant within 300 yds.
Closed	Rarely.
Directions	A1, Alnwick turn off A1068. Over roundabout; left at next roundabout B6346. Prudhoe Street 1st left. Pass police station; house opposite St Paul's church.

Price	£78-£85. Singles £38-£65.
Rooms	3: 1 double, 1 twin, 1 four-poster.
Meals	Packed lunch £4-£6. Pub/restaurant 2 miles.
Closed	Christmas & New Year.
Directions	From Alnwick, A1068 to Alnmouth. At Hipsburn r'bout follow signs to station & cross bridge. 1st lane to left, 0.3 miles down drive.

	Maureen Mason
	Courtyard Garden,
	10 Prudhoe Street,
	Alnwick NE66 1UW
Tel	+44 (0)1665 603393
Email	maureenpeter10@btinternet.com
Web	www.courtyardgarden-alnwick.com

	Brian & Dorothy Jackson
	Bilton Barns,
	Alnmouth, Alnwick NE66 2TB
Tel	+44 (0)1665 830427
Mobile	+44 (0)7939 262028
Email	dorothy@biltonbarns.com
Web	www.biltonbarns.com

Entry 387   Map 16

Entry 388   Map 16

Northumberland

Redfoot Lea

Prepare to be thoroughly spoiled. This fine renovation of an old farmsteading lies just off the A1 up a quiet lane – perfect for touring the county or a great stopover. Amiable Philippa gives you a super south-facing sitting room and ground-floor bedrooms with comfortable beds, crisp linen, fluffy bathrobes and heated floors; bathrooms are smart and spotless. You breakfast at a large table in the magnificent open-plan hall, scented with glorious flower arrangements; enjoy freshly squeezed orange juice, homemade compotes, local produce, excellent coffee. A short hop from Alnwick Castle and gardens, and stunning beaches.

Northumberland

Broome

A totally surprising one-storey house, full of beautiful things. It is an Aladdin's cave and sits in the middle of a coastal village with access to miles of sandy beaches. The garden/breakfast room is its hub and has a country cottage feel; enjoy locally smoked kippers here, award-winning 'Bamburgh Bangers' and home-cured bacon from the village butcher. There's also a sun-trapping courtyard full of colourful pots for breakfasts in the sun. Guests have a cheerful sitting/dining room and bedrooms with fresh flowers and good books. Mary is welcoming and amusing and has stacks of local knowledge.

Price	From £85. Singles £55.
Rooms	2: 1 double, 1 twin.
Meals	Pubs/restaurants 1.5 miles.
Closed	Rarely.
Directions	Sent on booking.

Price	£100–£110. Singles £70.
Rooms	2: 1 double, 1 twin sharing bath/shower (2nd room let to same party only).
Meals	Pubs/restaurants 2-minute walk.
Closed	1 November–1 April.
Directions	From Newcastle north on A1; right for Bamburgh on B1341. To village, pass 30mph sign & hotel; 1st right at Victoria Hotel. House 400 yds on right.

	Philippa Bell
	Redfoot Lea, Greensfield Moor Farm,
	Alnwick NE66 2HH
Tel	+44 (0)1665 603891
Mobile	+44 (0)7870 586214
Email	info@redfootlea.co.uk
Web	www.redfootlea.co.uk

	Mary Dixon
	Broome,
	22 Ingram Road,
	Bamburgh NE69 7BT
Tel	+44 (0)1668 214287
Mobile	+44 (0)7956 013409
Email	mdixon4394@aol.com

Entry 389   Map 16

Entry 390   Map 16

Northumberland

Laundry Cottage

History lovers, peace seekers and observers of nature will mellow further in this glorious spot overlooking the Cheviot hills. On arrival enjoy cake and tea with the evening sun – in the sun room, or in the garden on warm days. Douse yourself in one of Ginia's hiker's breakfasts, stride through iron age forts and the remains of Saxon palaces or visit long white beaches; return to Welsh slate floors, wood-burners, good home cooking, feather and down on deep comfy mattresses and fluffy towels. The feel is light and airy, Peter and Ginia are amiable hosts and the super garden is filled with roses in summer.

Price	£70. Singles £45.
Rooms	2: 1 double, 1 twin.
Meals	Dinner £17–£21.
	Pub/restaurant 5 miles.
Closed	December to mid-March.
Directions	Out of Wooler on the Chatton road (B6348). A few miles on, turn left over narrow bridge to East Horton.

Peter & Ginia Gadsdon
Laundry Cottage,
East Horton,
Wooler NE71 6EZ
Tel +44 (0)1668 215383
Email peter@gadsdon.me.uk
Web www.laundry-cottage-bnb.co.uk

Entry 391 Map 16

Northumberland

Crookham Eastfield Farmhouse

Delicious Northumberland; perfect B&B. Be looked after in the heart of nowhere by lovely Mhairi, who cooks you the freshest local fish and game in season. Two gorgeous bedrooms with adjacent bathrooms are each down their own private, separate corridors; both bask in the palest colours with perfect antiques, and warm bathrooms are immaculate. Stoke up with a Craster kipper, or home-laid eggs at breakfast, stride the Cheviots, discover history in castles and battlefields, fish or simply watch the bird life; return to an elegant, cosy drawing room. Bring your horse, take off in a cool camper van with bell tent, all is possible…

Price	From £95. Singles £65.
Rooms	2: 1 double, 1 twin, each with separate bath/shower.
Meals	Dinner, 2-3 courses, £20–£28. Pub 15-minute walk.
Closed	Christmas & New Year.
Directions	Sent on booking.

Mhairi Seymour
Crookham Eastfield Farmhouse,
Cornhill-on-Tweed TD12 4SQ
Tel +44 (0)1890 820568
Mobile +44 (0)7831 121416
Email thefarmhouse@crookhameastfield.co.uk
Web www.crookhameastfield.co.uk

Entry 392 Map 16

Northumberland

Chain Bridge House

Overlooking an idyllic stretch of the River Tweed is the last house in England – Scotland is 100 yards away across Captain Samuel Brown's magnificent Union suspension bridge. In the sitting room find books and a log fire; in the bedrooms goose down duvets and a fresh, airy feel. Livvy, a professional cook, is an active supporter of the Slow Food movement and local food producers. Visit the neighbouring honey farm or glorious Bamburgh, Holy Island and the Farnes, and the unspoilt borders beyond: return to a revolving summerhouse in the garden for tea. Children and dogs get a generous welcome too in this charming family home.

Price	£90–£95. Singles £60–£65.
Rooms	2: 1 double, 1 twin.
Meals	Dinner £30. Supper £15. Packed lunch from £7.50. Pubs/restaurants 5-7 miles.
Closed	Rarely.
Directions	A698; exit from A1 at East Ord, west of Berwick. After 1 mile, right for Horncliffe; follow signs for Honey Farm; past farm 200 yds; house on right.

Livvy Cawthorn
Chain Bridge House,
Horncliffe,
Berwick-upon-Tweed TD15 2XT
Tel +44 (0)1289 382541
Email info@chainbridgehouse.co.uk
Web www.chainbridgehouse.co.uk

Entry 393   Map 16

Northumberland

West Coates

Slip through the gates of this Victorian townhouse and you're in the country. Two acres of leafy gardens, with pretty spots to relax, belie the closeness of Berwick's centre. From the lofty ceilings and sash windows to the soft colours, paintings and gleaming furniture, the house has a calm, ordered elegance. Bedrooms have antiques and garden views; one has a roll top bath; fruit, homemade cakes, flowers welcome you. Warm, friendly Karen is a stunning cook, inventively using local produce and spoiling you; she runs a cookery school here too. The coastline is stunning and there are castles and country houses galore to visit.

Price	£90–£100. Singles from £60.
Rooms	2 twins/doubles.
Meals	Dinner £35. Pub/restaurant 15-minute walk.
Closed	December/January.
Directions	From A1 take A6105 into Berwick. House 300 yds on left. Stone pillars at end of drive. Train station 10-minute walk.

Karen Brown
West Coates, 30 Castle Terrace,
Berwick-upon-Tweed TD15 1NZ
Tel +44 (0)1289 309666
Mobile +44 (0)7814 281973
Email westcoatesbandb@gmail.com
Web www.westcoates.co.uk

Entry 394   Map 16

Nottinghamshire

Willoughby House

Past the village pub, through a gate, this three-storey brick farmhouse reflects its owners' skilful interior design. The house brims with tokens of its 18th century past, like meat hooks in the scullery-turned-sitting room, but feels ever so smart. Bedrooms are large and comfortable: climb up to Harry's room with its brass bed and toy soldiers over the fireplace; Edward's and George's share raftered loft space and a swish bathroom. Sarah rustles up delicious meals in a dining room embraced by poppy red walls and shutters. Get out on hikes or bikes; round the little village, or Southwell and Newark are close.

Price	£85–£105. Singles £65–£75.
Rooms	5: 2 twins/doubles (both en suite); 1 double, 1 twin/double sharing bath (let to same party only); 1 double with separate bath/shower.
Meals	Dinner for special occasions. Packed lunch £7.50. Pub 3-minute walk.
Closed	Rarely.
Directions	1.5 miles off A1, Cromwell & Norwell exit. At Cromwell left Norwell, 1.5 miles. House opp. school lane on corner of Willoughby Court.

Andrew & Sarah Nesbitt
Willoughby House, Main Street,
Norwell, Newark NG23 6JN
Tel   +44 (0)1636 636266
Mobile +44 (0)7789 965352
Email   willoughbybandb@aol.com
Web   www.willoughbyhousebandb.co.uk

Entry 395   Map 9

Nottinghamshire

Compton House

Two minutes from Newark's antique shops and old market, seek out this terraced Georgian townhouse where the mayor once lived. Naturally elegant, and overlooking Fountain Gardens, the sunny drawing room has a marble fireplace; Lisa and Mark have filled the place with lovely personal touches. Rooms are named after friends, from plush red-gold Judy's room to Harry's bijou single; the best is Cooper's, with a four-poster bed, a roll top bath through a draped archway and a wall hand-painted by a local artist. Pad down to the sunny basement for Mark's feast of a breakfast. Hotel comforts but a truly homely feel. *Dogs by arrangement.*

Price	£90. Singles from £65.
Rooms	7: 2 doubles, 1 twin/double, 2 twins, 1 four-poster; 1 single with separate shower.
Meals	Packed lunch £6. Buffet lunch £15. Dinner, 2 courses, from £25. Pub/restaurant 0.5 miles.
Closed	Occasionally Christmas.
Directions	Nottingham, A52; join A46 N to Newark. At r'about, 2nd exit. Right at lights, left at next lights then 1st right. House on left.

Mark & Lisa Holloway
Compton House, 117 Baldertongate,
Newark NG24 1RY
Tel   +44 (0)1636 708670
Mobile +44 (0)7817 446485
Email   info@comptonhousenewark.com
Web   www.comptonhousenewark.com

Entry 396   Map 9

Nottinghamshire

East Bridgford Hill

Sweep up the drive on the village edge to a fine Georgian house with beautiful views. One side of Alfred and Patricia's home is for guests, with quiet countrified bedrooms and bucolic garden views; there are seven acres to roam. Stunning, spoiling communal rooms have high ceilings, period pieces, candlesticks entwined with flowers, greenery, mirrors, paintings... Breakfast is served in the orangery, with local jams and eggs from the hens. Walk the Fosse Way, stroll to the pub, enjoy croquet and tennis. The family is delightful, the ducks are rare-breed, the dear labrador is called Fred. *Parties a speciality.*

Price	£120. Singles £75. Suite from £140.
Rooms	4: 2 doubles, 1 suite for 3; 1 twin with separate bath/shower.
Meals	Dinner, 3 courses, from £35 (Fri & Sat only). Pub 5-minute walk.
Closed	Rarely.
Directions	Sent on booking.

	Emma Robens
	East Bridgford Hill, Kirk Hill, East Bridgford, Nottingham NG13 8PE
Tel	+44 (0)1949 20232
Mobile	+44 (0)7950 569773
Email	eastbridgfordhill@gmail.com
Web	www.eastbridgfordhill.com

Entry 397   Map 8

Oxfordshire

Uplands House

Come to be spoiled at this 'farmhouse' built in 1875 for the Earl of Jersey's farm manager. Renovated by a talented couple, it's elegant and sumptuously furnished; expect large light bedrooms, crisp linen, thick towels and long bucolic views from the Orangery where you have tea and cake. Relax here with a book as the sounds and scents of the pretty garden waft by, or chat to charming Poppy while she creates delicious dinner — a convivial occasion enjoyed with your hosts. Breakfast is Graham's domain — try smoked salmon with scrambled eggs and red caviar. You're well placed for exploring but you'll find it hard to leave.

Price	£100-£180. Singles £65-£100.
Rooms	3: 1 double; 1 twin/double, 1 four-poster, each with separate bath.
Meals	Dinner, 2-4 courses, £20-£30. Pub 1.25 miles.
Closed	Rarely.
Directions	M40 junc. 11; thro' Banbury, A422 towards Stratford. Thro' Wroxton; just after 'Upton House' National Trust sign, right single lane drive marked 'Uplands Farm'. 1st house on right up drive.

	Poppy Cooksey & Graham Paul
	Uplands House, Upton, Banbury OX15 6HJ
Tel	+44 (0)1295 678663
Mobile	+44 (0)7836 535538
Email	poppy@cotswolds-uplands.co.uk
Web	www.cotswolds-uplands.co.uk

Entry 398   Map 8

Oxfordshire

Gower's Close

All the nooks, crannies and beams you'd expect from an ancient thatched cottage in a Cotswold village... and more besides: good food, lively conversation and lots of inside information about gardens to visit. Judith is a keen gardener who writes books on the subject (her passion for plants is evident from her own glorious garden) and her style and intelligence are reflected in her home. Pretty, south-facing and full of sunlight, the sitting room opens onto the garden and terrace. Bedrooms are light, charming and cottagey; the twin is at garden level. A thoroughly relaxing place to stay.

Price	£75-£80. Singles £50.
Rooms	2: 1 double, 1 twin.
Meals	Dinner, 4 courses, £28 (min. 4 people). Pub/restaurant 100 yds.
Closed	Christmas & New Year.
Directions	In Sibford Gower, 0.5 miles south off B4035 between Banbury & Chipping Campden. House on Main Street, same side as church & school.

Judith Hitching & John Marshall
Gower's Close,
Sibford Gower, Banbury OX15 5RW
Tel   +44 (0)1295 780348
Mobile   +44 (0)7776 231588
Email   judith@gowersclose.co.uk
Web   www.gowersclose.co.uk

Entry 399   Map 8

Oxfordshire

Buttslade House

Choose between a gorgeous ground-floor retreat across the courtyard, or a very pretty twin in the 17th-century farmhouse with barns and stables. The guest sitting room is a clever melody of ancient and contemporary styles: Spanish art, antique sofas, velvet cushions. Beds have seriously good mattresses, feather and down pillows and crisp white linen; bathrooms are smart and sparkling – one with a Victorian roll top. Diana is lovely and will pamper you or leave you, there's a blissful garden to stroll through, breakfast is a feast of fruits and homemade bread and it's a hop to the village pub. A fun and stylish treat.

Price	£80. Singles £50.
Rooms	2: 1 double; 1 twin with separate bath.
Meals	Dinner, 3 courses, £25. Lunch £7. Pub 100 yds.
Closed	Rarely.
Directions	From B4035 look for signs to Wykham Arms. Buttslade is 2nd house beyond pub, going down hill.

Diana Thompson
Buttslade House,
Temple Mill Road,
Sibford Gower, Banbury OX15 5RX
Tel   +44 (0)1295 788818
Email   diana@buttsladehouse.co.uk
Web   www.buttsladehouse.co.uk

Entry 400   Map 8

Oxfordshire

Minehill House

Wind your way up the farm track to the top of a beautiful hill and you arrive at a gorgeous family farmhouse with views for miles and young, energetic Hester to care for you. Children will adore the ping-pong table and the trampoline; their parents will enjoy the gleaming old flagstones, vibrant contemporary oils, wood-burning stove and seriously sophisticated food. Rest well in the big double room with its gloriously comfortable bed, verdant leafy wallpaper and stunning views, and a cubby-hole door to extra twin beds; bathrooms are sparklingly clean and spacious. Bracing walks start straight from the door.

Price	£95. Singles from £50. Family £135.
Rooms	1 double/family.
Meals	Dinner, 3 courses, £35. Supper £20. BYO. Packed lunch available. Pubs 1-5 miles.
Closed	Christmas & New Year.
Directions	From Banbury B4035 to Brailes; after 10 miles take road left signed Hook Norton; 0.5 miles, right onto unmarked uphill farm track to house.

Hester & Ed Sale
Minehill House,
Lower Brailes, Banbury OX15 5BJ
Tel   +44 (0)1608 685594
Mobile   +44 (0)7890 266441
Email   hester@minehillhouse.co.uk
Web   www.minehillhouse.co.uk

Entry 401   Map 8

Oxfordshire

Home Farmhouse

This 400-year-old house is charming, with low ceilings, inglenook fireplaces and winding stairs. All rooms are faded and brimming with character: the drawing room is elegant and beamed and pretty bedrooms are decorated with antiques and old-fashioned chintz. Comfortable beds have good mattresses and traditional blankets; bathrooms are small and a little dated. Enjoy independence in the simple barn room with its mixture of time-worn furniture and own entrance up old stone steps. The family's travels are evident all over and it's all so laid-back you'll find it hard to leave. The dogs are delightful too – Samson and Goliath.

Price	£88. Singles £56.
Rooms	3: 1 double, 1 twin/double. Barn: 1 twin/double.
Meals	Dinner £28. Supper £20 (min. 4 people). Pub 100 yds.
Closed	Christmas.
Directions	M40 junc. 10, A43 for Northampton. After 5 miles, left to Charlton. There, left & house on left, 100 yds past Rose & Crown.

Rosemary & Nigel Grove-White
Home Farmhouse,
Charlton, Banbury OX17 3DR
Tel   +44 (0)1295 811683
Mobile   +44 (0)7795 207000
Email   grovewhite@lineone.net
Web   www.homefarmhouse.co.uk

Entry 402   Map 8

Oxfordshire

The Old Post House

Great natural charm in the 17th-century Old Post House, where shiny flagstones, rich dark wood and mullion windows combine with warm fabrics, deep sofas and handsome furniture. Bedrooms are big, with antique wardrobes, oak headboards and a comforting old-fashioned feel. The walled gardens are lovely – rich with espaliered fruit trees, and with a pool for sunny evenings. Christine, a well-travelled ex-pat, has an innate sense of hospitality; her breakfasts are delicious. There's village traffic but your sleep should be sound. Deddington is delightful – and you will love Harry the friendly terrier too! *Children over 12 welcome.*

Price	£90. Singles £60.
Rooms	3: 1 twin/double; 1 double with separate bath; 1 four-poster with separate shower.
Meals	Occasional dinner. Pubs/restaurants in village.
Closed	Rarely.
Directions	A4260 Oxford to Banbury. In Deddington, on right next to cream Georgian house. Park opposite.

Christine Blenntoft
The Old Post House,
New Street, Deddington OX15 0SP
Tel   +44 (0)1869 338978
Mobile   +44 (0)7713 631092
Email   kblenntoft@aol.com
Web   www.oldposthouse.co.uk

Entry 403   Map 8

Oxfordshire

Hawk Hill House

Generous parkland and gardens lead to tailored fields, happy dogs and the odd grazing horse. Sensible, hospitable, relaxed Alison gives guests floral traditional bedrooms in a big extended house full of corridors and separate stairs – a refuge for busy lives. Expect china, chintz, feathery pillows and hand-held showers, privacy, tranquillity and a livery for visiting steeds, and an inviting family kitchen for fruit crumbles and shepherd pies; there's a more formal dining room if you prefer. It's a 20-minute walk over the fields to a brilliant pub in Great Tew – and heaps more beyond.

Price	£95. Singles from £55.
Rooms	3: 2 doubles, 1 twin.
Meals	Supper, 2-3 courses, £20-£25. Pubs/restaurants 2-3 miles.
Closed	Rarely.
Directions	Oxford & Banbury to Deddington, then B4031 towards Chipping Norton. Through Hempton, and down steep hill, then left to Nether Worton. Only house in village on right hand side.

James & Alison Kerr-Muir
Hawk Hill House, Nether Worton,
Chipping Norton OX7 7AP
Tel   +44 (0)1608 683355
Mobile   +44 (0)7710 353224
Email   hawkhillhouse@gmail.com
Web   www.hawkhill-house.co.uk

Entry 404   Map 8

Oxfordshire

Rectory Farm

A general sense of peaceful order pervades at this solid, big house set in a manicured lawn. Inside find large, light bedrooms, floral and feminine, with bold chintz bed covers, draped kidney-shaped dressing tables, thick mattresses; some have garden views, others face the farm buildings. Sink into comfy sofas flanking a huge fireplace in the drawing room, breakfast on local bacon and sausage with free-range eggs, stroll the pretty garden, or grab a rod and try your luck on one of the trout lakes. Elizabeth knows her patch well; walkers can borrow maps, and she can point the way to lovely shops for the dedicated.

Oxfordshire

Upper Court Farm

In a peaceful, gently hilly spot in the Cotswolds, the super smart Edwardian farmhouse comes with groomed gardens and 30 acres for Chloë's horses – bring yours! A dressage rider, she and Tim are interesting hosts and their home is laden with good quality fabrics, country art and family pieces. Charming bedrooms (two on the top floor) have madly comfortable beds, pretty covers, TVs, smart bathrooms and drenching showers. Tim is a foodie and breakfast is generous and local; people come for miles for Slatters, an organic shop in the village. Relax in the rose garden with a drink – two sweet dogs will join you.

Price	£90-£100. Singles £65-£75.
Rooms	3: 1 double, 1 twin/double; 1 twin/double with separate bath.
Meals	Pub/restaurant 1.5 miles.
Closed	December/January.
Directions	A44 out of Chipping Norton towards Moreton-in-the-Marsh. After 1.5 miles right into Salford. Right at pub, then immediate left uphill past green on right. Left into drive for Rectory Farm, continue 200 yds then left.

Price	£80-£100. Singles £70-£100. £10 supplement for one-night stay at weekends.
Rooms	3: 2 doubles; 1 twin/double with separate bath (all share a sitting room.)
Meals	Pub 200 yds, café 5-minute walk.
Closed	Christmas & Boxing Day.
Directions	From Chipping Norton A361 south, after approx. 3 miles 2nd left to Chadlington. After 0.5 miles, 1st drive on the left.

Elizabeth Colston
Rectory Farm,
Salford, Chipping Norton OX7 5YY
Tel   +44 (0)1608 643209
Mobile   +44 (0)7866 834208
Email   enquiries@rectoryfarm.info
Web   www.rectoryfarm.info

Chloë Robson
Upper Court Farm,
Mill End, Chadlington,
Chipping Norton OX7 3NY
Tel   +44 (0)1608 676296
Mobile   +44 (0)7717 571792
Email   chloe.uppercourt@gmail.com

Oxfordshire

Manor Farm

An attractive old farmhouse dating from the 17th century with a warm friendly atmosphere. Jeannette and Andrew are generous hosts; Andrew built his own heating system, which runs on pallets and linseed straw – now he's starting on a four-seater plane! Elegant, light bedrooms with garden views have pretty lamps and fabrics, sofas and comfortable beds. Wake for a full English served around a big table in an immaculate kitchen: homemade bread, eggs from the hens. There's a wood-burner in the snug sitting room, the garden has a pond and lots of birds, the little village is peaceful and Oxford is a half hour drive.

Price	£80-£85. Singles £40-£50.
Rooms	3: 2 doubles, 1 twin.
Meals	Pubs/restaurants 3 miles.
Closed	Rarely.
Directions	Sent on booking.

Jeannette Collett
Manor Farm,
Main Street, Poundon,
Bicester OX27 9BB
Tel   +44 (0)1869 277212
Email   ajcollett@live.co.uk
Web   www.manorfarmpoundon.co.uk

Entry 407   Map 8

Oxfordshire

Oxford University

Oxford at your fingertips – at a fair price. In the city's ancient heart are Wadham and Keble; in leafy North Oxford is small friendly St Hugh's. Keble's sleeping quarters, functional though a good size, stand in stark contrast to the neo-gothic grandeur of its dining hall – pure Hogwarts! Wadham's hall, medieval, soaring, is yet more glorious – with top breakfasts. Its student-simple bedrooms are reached via crenellated cloisters and lovely walled gardens; ask for a room facing the beautiful quad. At St Hugh's: three residences (one historic), a student bar, romantic gardens and a 15-minute walk into town. *23 colleges in total.*

Price	Doubles £88-£110. Twins £60-£120. Singles £30-£75. Family rooms £85-£150.
Rooms	1,237: 52 doubles, 121 twins, 1,052 singles, 12 family rooms for 3-4.
Meals	Breakfast included. Keble: occasional supper £10.20. Restaurants 2-15 minutes' walk.
Closed	Mid-Jan to mid-March; May/June; Oct/Nov; Christmas. A few rooms available throughout year.
Directions	Website booking. On-request parking at St Hugh's & Lady Margaret Hall.

University Rooms
Oxford University,
Oxford
Web   www.oxfordrooms.co.uk

Entry 408   Map 8

Oxfordshire

Willow Cottage

You are a short step from a village with an excellent pub (return across fields with a torch). Or treat yourself to dinner at Le Manoir aux Quat'Saisons. Katrina's delicious thatched cottage sits down a quiet lane. Through your own entrance find a guest dining room with armchairs by the old range, interesting prints and paintings, an eclectic mix of antiques and contemporary furniture. Bedrooms are warm, comfortable and stylish with views over the garden; shower rooms (not huge) are brand new and deeply smart. Breakfast, unhurried and bristling with local produce, sets walkers up for the Chiltern Way and the Ridgeway.

Price	£80. Singles £55.
Rooms	2 doubles.
Meals	Packed lunch £7. Pubs/restaurants 0.5 miles.
Closed	Rarely.
Directions	M40 junc. 7, left off slip road. 5.5 miles to pub on right, after 0.5 miles right to Denton. On for 2 miles, pass right turn to Cuddesdon, take next right, 'Brookside only'. House 200 yds on right.

	Katrina Sheldon
	Willow Cottage,
	Denton,
	Oxford OX44 9JG
Tel	+44 (0)1865 874728
Email	katrinasheldon@aol.com
Web	www.willowcottage.info

Entry 409   Map 8

Oxfordshire

Rectory Farm

Come for the happy relaxed vibe, and Mary Anne's welcome with tea and homemade shortbread. There's a wood-burner in the guest sitting room, and bedrooms have beautiful arched mullion windows. The huge twin with ornate plasterwork overlooks the garden and church, the pretty double is cosier and both have good showers and big fluffy towels. Wake for an excellent Aga breakfast with eggs from the hens, garden and hedgerow compotes, home or locally produced bacon and homemade jams. A herd of Red Ruby Devon cattle are Robert's pride and joy; the family have farmed for generations and you can buy the beef. It's a treat to stay.

Price	£86. Singles £64. Min. two nights at weekends & high season.
Rooms	2: 1 double, 1 twin.
Meals	Pub 2-minute walk.
Closed	Mid-December to mid-January.
Directions	From Oxford, A420 for Swindon for 8 miles & right at r'bout, for Witney. Over 2 bridges, immed. right by pub car park. After 1 mile right at T-junc.; drive on right, past church.

	Mary Anne Florey
	Rectory Farm,
	Northmoor, Witney OX29 5SX
Tel	+44 (0)1865 300207
Mobile	+44 (0)7974 102198
Email	pj.florey@farmline.com
Web	www.oxtowns.co.uk/rectoryfarm

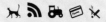

Entry 410   Map 8

Oxfordshire

Manor Farmhouse

Helen and John radiate pleasure and good humour in this old Cotswold stone farmhouse, once part of the Blenheim estate (a short walk down the lane). Find comfortable, traditional living with good prints and paintings, venerable furniture and nothing cluttered or overdone. Shallow, curvy, 18th-century stairs lead up to the two pretty doubles in a completely private wing of the house. Breakfast is by the stone fireplace and ancient dresser. On warm days have tea in a sheltered corner by the fig tree and pots, and wander in the lovely garden. The pretty Cotswolds surround you, and the village is quiet yet close to Oxford.

Price	£80-£85. Singles from £70.
Rooms	2 doubles sharing shower (let to same party only).
Meals	Pub within walking distance.
Closed	Christmas.
Directions	A44 north from Oxford's ring road. At r'bout, 1 mile before Woodstock, left onto A4095 into Bladon. Last left in village; house on right, on 2nd bend in road, with iron railings.

Helen Stevenson
Manor Farmhouse, Manor Road,
Bladon, Woodstock OX20 1RU
Tel   +44 (0)1993 812168
Email   helstevenson@hotmail.com
Web   www.oxtowns.co.uk/woodstock/
          manor-farmhouse/

Entry 411   Map 8

Oxfordshire

Lowbarrow

Swoop through wooden electric gates to find newly planted young trees, a soft, creamy Cotswold stone house and horses in the paddock. Walk straight in to travertine tiles in an enormous hall, a real fire in the book-filled drawing room with squishy sofas and gorgeous fabrics, bedrooms that will lull, state of the art bathrooms. Nothing is mean, all is generous and big; views soar through sash windows. Philippa gives you proper sausages, bread and eggs from the community shop, pretty china, delicious suppers. Wander the gardens, play tennis, swim in the pool, explore the Cotswolds on foot or for retail therapy. Live the dream.

Price	£90-£110. Singles £60. Horse stabling available at £15 a night. Well-behaved dogs can stay in boot room.
Rooms	3: 2 doubles, 1 twin.
Meals	Dinner, 2-3 courses, £20-£30. Pubs 1 mile.
Closed	Rarely.
Directions	Sent on booking.

Philippa Grace
Lowbarrow, The Ridings, Leafield,
Witney OX29 9NH
Tel   +44 (0)1993 878825
Mobile   +44 (0)7712 880738
Email   philippa@lowbarrow.com
Web   www.lowbarrow.com

Entry 412   Map 8

Oxfordshire

Star Cottage

Classic Cotswolds – from the cottagey stone walls to the flower-bright garden – and swathes of open countryside for cyclists and walkers. Step inside to hand-sewn fabrics, cute lampshades, country furniture, fresh flowers and calm, pretty bedrooms: Sally delights in details. She and Peter, a plant biologist, love their winding stone-walled garden with its herbs, climbers and medlar tree; its jelly appears at breakfast, alongside smoked haddock and local sausage. The pub (yards away) offers dinner, Burford market town is a ten-minute walk, Cheltenham and Oxford a half-hour drive. Or kind Peter will fetch from the station.

Oxfordshire

Box Tree Cottage

Down a winding road in an idyllic, well-heeled, tumbling hamlet, this classic L-shaped cottage has immense charm; outside are topiary, bursting borders and birdsong. The comfortable, book-filled sitting room with log-burner, the restful, charming, immaculate bedrooms with velvety carpets and laundered linen, and the splendid Bayliss & Harding-scented bathrooms make for considered perfection. Your hosts Richard and Caroline (ex-hoteliers) are entertaining and experienced. Look forward to an excellent breakfast at the French refectory table, then set off with your guests' maps for wonderful Cotswold walks.

Price	£75-£110. Singles £65-£75.
Rooms	3: 1 double, 1 family room. Barn: 1 family room & kitchen.
Meals	Pubs/restaurants within walking distance.
Closed	Rarely.
Directions	Sent on booking.

Price	From £85.
Rooms	2 doubles.
Meals	Pubs/restaurants 1 mile.
Closed	Rarely.
Directions	Sent on booking.

Peter & Sally Wyatt
Star Cottage,
Meadow Lane, Fulbrook,
Burford OX18 4BW
Tel   +44 (0)1993 822032
Email   wyattpeter@btconnect.com
Web   www.burfordbedandbreakfast.co.uk

Caroline & Richard de Wolf
Box Tree Cottage,
36 Taynton,
Burford OX18 4UH
Tel   +44 (0)1993 824821
Email   info@boxtreecottage.com
Web   www.boxtreecottage.com

Entry 413   Map 8

Entry 414   Map 8

Oxfordshire

Fox House

In idyllic stonewalled little Holwell is a big stylish house on a corner – the old village school. Welcoming Susan, who is in the antiques business, gives you two super sitting rooms (one with a friendly wood-burner, the other with a barn window and a heated flagstone floor), and three immaculately cosy bedrooms (one double downstairs) and serves delectable breakfasts on pretty blue china and jams and juices from the orchard. The garden is open and leads to pasture and horses, the countryside is delicious in every season and footpaths radiate from the door. The Cotswolds at its finest!

Price	£80–£125. Singles from £65.
Rooms	3: 1 double; 1 twin, 1 double sharing bath (let to same party only).
Meals	Packed lunch £6. Dinner, 3 courses, £25. Pubs/restaurants 2 miles.
Closed	Rarely.
Directions	A361 south from Burford over A40. Right at sign for Cotswold wildlife park, then right signed Holwell. First house left on corner.

	Susan Blacker
	Fox House,
	Holwell,
	Burford OX18 4JS
Tel	+44 (0)1993 823409
Email	foxhouse-rooms@btconnect.com
Web	www.foxhouse-rooms.co.uk

Entry 415   Map 8

Oxfordshire

Buscot Manor

Fringing National Trust land, the hamlet is startlingly beautiful, minutes from Lechlade's market square and a tree-lined Thames with thundering weir. Just as surprising is the 1690s Queen Anne manor at its heart, all flags, oak and open fires – plus rich fabrics, four-posters, roll top baths, sumptuous wall hangings and silk flowers. Peep through mullioned windows at fruit trees, horses, a walled garden with lavender path; explore the countryside by foot, bike, horse or canoe. Easy-going Romney juggles B&B and family with energy: expect heaped Aga-cooked breakfasts and a warm welcome for dogs, horses and children.

Price	£85–£90. Singles £65.
Rooms	3: 2 doubles, 1 twin, sharing 2 bathrooms.
Meals	Pub/restaurant 2 miles.
Closed	Rarely.
Directions	Sent on booking.

	Romney Pargeter
	Buscot Manor,
	Buscot, Faringdon SN7 8DA
Tel	+44 (0)1367 252225
Mobile	+44 (0)7973 831690
Email	romneypargeter@hotmail.co.uk
Web	www.buscotmanor.co.uk

Entry 416   Map 8

Oxfordshire

Brook Barn

Up a sweeping drive to find smart barn buildings, fluffy-legged hens and a beautiful brook – not your average country B&B! Inside: light oak, soaring rafters, an honesty bar with optics, bedrooms that leave nothing to chance. The attention to detail is remarkable: slippers, chocolates, complimentary afternoon tea. Breakfast at a time to suit you, and book in for dinner: it's a fabulous treat. The Hayloft suite, airy and light, has a dreamy bathroom, the Stable is full of country charm, the Garden Room comes with a Mediterranean patio. Grab a book, stroll round the garden, find a sofa to flop into. Lovely owners, too.

Price	£100-£225. Singles £80-£135.
Rooms	5: 1 suite, 3 doubles; 1 twin/double with separate bath/shower.
Meals	Dinner, 3 courses, from £30. Packed lunch £10.50-£19.50. Pub/restaurant 2 miles.
Closed	Christmas.
Directions	Ashbury road out of Wantage. Left to Letcombe Regis, round right-hand bend, 400 yds after cream house, drive on left.

Sarah-Jane & Mark Ashman
Brook Barn,
Letcombe Regis,
Wantage OX12 9JD
Tel   +44 (0)1235 766502
Email   info@brookbarn.com
Web   www.brookbarn.com

🐕 🔊 🚲 📖 🍷 ✕

Entry 417   Map 3

Oxfordshire

Crown Cottage

In a history-rich village, a welcoming home with a remarkable feel. Deirdre, gentle, artistic, well-travelled, treats you to summer tea in the garden up the alley, and breakfast with fresh fruit compotes and Wallingford sausages in the Aga-warm kitchen. Sleep like a log in lovely peaceful bedrooms, one with an ancient oak casement window overlooking the courtyard of the (former) Crown Inn. Charm lies in sloping floors, sash windows and wide stairs; art, books and an open fire; and a big traditional bathroom to share. Step outside to find narrow winding streets, a very special abbey, and a bus to the dreaming spires.

Price	£70. Singles £45-£50.
Rooms	2 doubles sharing bathroom.
Meals	Pubs within walking distance.
Closed	October-February.
Directions	Sent on booking.

Deirdre Wollaston
Crown Cottage,
52 High Street,
Dorchester-on-Thames,
Wallingford OX10 7HN
Tel   +44 (0)1865 341584
Web   www.crowncottage.net

🏄 🐕 🔊

Entry 418   Map 4

Oxfordshire

Fyfield Manor

A fabulous house in Oxfordshire (once owned by Simon de Montfort) with vast water gardens and a water wheel for eco underfloor heating. The Browns have added solar panels too. From the grand wood-panelled hall enter a beamed dining room with high-backed chairs, brass rubbings, wood-burner and pretty 12th-century arch; breakfast on eggs from the hens, garden fruit, organic bacon. Charming bedrooms have views, slippers and comfy sofas. Oxford Park & Ride is nearby, there's walking from the door and delightful Christine has wangled you a free glass of wine in the local pub if you walk or cycle to get there! Superb. *Over tens welcome.*

Price	£75-£85. Singles £55-£65.
Rooms	2: 1 twin/double; 1 family room with sofabed & separate bath.
Meals	Pubs within 1 mile.
Closed	Rarely.
Directions	Exit 6 from M40, then B4009 to Benson. Left to Benson village. Thro' village for 0.5 mile dir. Ewelme. 8 foot wall immed. after cream house on right. Thro' gates at end of wall to main house.

Christine Brown
Fyfield Manor,
Benson,
Wallingford OX10 6HA
Tel   +44 (0)1491 835184
Email   chris_fyfield@hotmail.co.uk
Web   www.fyfieldmanor.co.uk

Entry 419   Map 4

Rutland

Old Rectory

Jane Austen fans will swoon. This elegant 1740s village house was used as Mr Collins's 'humble abode' by the BBC: you breakfast in the beautiful dining room that was 'Mr Collins's hall', and you can sleep in 'Miss Bennett's bedroom'. Victoria is wonderful – feisty, fun and gregarious – and looks after you beautifully with White Company linen in chintzy old-fashioned bedrooms, a log fire in the drawing room, fruit from the lovely garden, homemade jams and Aga-cooked local bacon and eggs. Guests love it here. You are near to some pleasant market towns and good walking and riding country. Don't forget the smelling salts!

Price	£85. Singles £45.
Rooms	2: 1 double, 1 twin.
Meals	Pubs within 3 miles.
Closed	Rarely.
Directions	5 miles NE of Oakham, through Ashwell. Or 7 miles west of A1 from Stretton.

Victoria Owen
Old Rectory,
Teigh, Oakham LE15 7RT
Tel   +44 (0)1572 787681
Mobile +44 (0)7717 223678
Email   torowen@btinternet.com
Web   www.teighbedandbreakfast.co.uk

Entry 420   Map 9

Shropshire

Tybroughton Hall

Off a winding country lane, surrounded by 40 acres of grassland, find a pretty white listed farmhouse and a wonderful welcome from Daisy, her family and two dear dogs. Step into the hallway with its polished antique table and bright garden flowers and you know you've made the right choice: this is a house to unwind in. After a day's hiking or biking, bliss to return to bedrooms cosy and comfortable – the traditional double with its country view or the large lovely twin. Breakfasts are worth getting up for: Tim makes the preserves, bees make the honey, hens lay the eggs and the pigs (five beauties!) provide the bacon.

Shropshire

The Isle

History buffs and nature lovers will delight: these 800 acres are almost enfolded by the River Severn; drive through lion-topped stone pillars to the house, built in about 1682 and extended later. Charming Ros and Edward are truly hands-on: all wood for fires is grown on the estate which also provides eggs, bacon, ham and vegetables – so you eat well! Flop in front of a huge fire in the drawing room with Chinese rug, family antiques and sublime views. Peaceful bedrooms are large and light with pocket-sprung memory mattresses and snazzy, upmarket bathrooms. Super walks, rides and fishing on the estate.

Price	£80–£85. Singles £50-£55.
Rooms	2: 1 double; 1 twin with separate bath.
Meals	Dinner £20-£25. Pub 4 miles.
Closed	Rarely.
Directions	From Whitchurch A525 (Wrexham). After 3.6 miles right at crossroads at top of hill (Malpas, Tybroughton). Continue for 1.1 miles, then left. After 0.3 miles 1st house on right.

Price	£75–£90. Singles £50-£60.
Rooms	3: 2 doubles; 1 twin with separate bath.
Meals	Packed lunch £5. Dinner £20. Pub/restaurant 4.3 miles.
Closed	Rarely.
Directions	From Shrewsbury signs for Oswestry & Bicton (B4380). At Four Crosses pub right into Isle Lane. After 0.5 mile drive thro' pillars with lions. Follow B&B signs.

Daisy Woodhead
Tybroughton Hall, Tybroughton,
Whitchurch SY13 3BB

Tel   +44 (0)1948 780726
Mobile +44 (0)7850 395885
Email   daisy.woodhead@btinternet.com
Web   www.tybroughtonhall-bedandbreakfast.co.uk

Entry 421   Map 7

Ros & Edward Tate
The Isle,
Bicton, Shrewsbury SY3 8EE

Tel   +44 (0)1743 851218
Mobile +44 (0)7776 257286
Email   ros@isleestate.co.uk
Web   www.the-isle-estate.co.uk

Entry 422   Map 7

Shropshire

Hardwick House

On a quiet street in the heart of Shrewsbury, this fine Georgian house has been in Lucy's family for generations. The dining room (oak panelling, a huge fireplace) is a lovely space to breakfast on locally sourced produce and homemade bread; vases of garden flowers are dotted all around this cheerful family home. Bedrooms are traditional and comfortable with pretty china tea cups; bathrooms are old-fashioned. The walled garden is fabulous; take tea in an 18th-century summerhouse. Birthplace of Darwin, this is a fascinating historic town; walk to the abbey, castle, theatre, festivals and great shops. Lucy is delightful.

Price	£75-£95. Singles £55-£65.
Rooms	2 twins/doubles.
Meals	Pubs/restaurants 150 yds.
Closed	Christmas & New Year.
Directions	Follow signs to town centre. House near St Chad's church. Train: left out of station & up the hill. Staight down Pride Hill, then up into St John's Hill.

Lucy Whitaker
Hardwick House,
12 St John's Hill,
Shrewsbury SY1 1JJ
Tel +44 (0)1743 350165
Email gilesandlucy@btinternet.com
Web www.hardwickhouseshrewsbury.co.uk

Entry 423   Map 7

Shropshire

Whitton Hall

Down a long private drive with fields on either side is a lovely 18th-century farmhouse, elegant but not intimidating, with a sense of timelessness. A large open hallway with a warming fire is a comfortable, peaceful space for relaxing with a book. You breakfast in the dining room, on local muesli, bread, marmalades and jams, milk from their Jersey cows, soft fruit from their garden, sausages and bacon from down the road. Up a stunning staircase are peaceful, light and large bedrooms, with graceful, country house furniture and long views to glorious gardens. Unwind in the peace. *Over 12s welcome.*

Price	From £80. Singles from £50.
Rooms	2: 1 double with separate bathroom, 1 twin/double with separate shower.
Meals	Supper £20. Packed lunch available. Restaurant 1.5 miles.
Closed	Christmas & New Year.
Directions	From Shrewsbury bypass (A5), B4386 to Westbury. Rght at x-roads opposite Lion pub, Immediate left, 50 yds on, left for Vennington. After 0.75 miles, drive on left; house at end, on right.

Christopher & Gill Halliday
& Kate Boscawen
Whitton Hall, Westbury,
Shrewsbury SY5 9RD
Tel +44 (0)1743 884270
Email accommodation@whittonhall.com
Web www.whittonhall.co.uk

Entry 424   Map 7

Shropshire

Brimford House

Beautifully tucked under the Breidden Hills, farm and Georgian farmhouse have been in the Dawson family for four generations. Views stretch all the way to the Severn; the simple garden does not try to compete. Bedrooms are spotless and fresh: a half-tester with rope-twist columns and Sanderson fabrics, a twin with Victorian wrought-iron bedsteads, a double with a brass bed, a big bathroom with a roll top bath. Liz serves you farm eggs and homemade preserves at breakfast, and there's a food pub just down the road. Sheep and cattle outdoors, a lovely black lab in, and wildlife walks from the door. Good value.

Price	£60–£75. Singles £40–£60.
Rooms	3: 2 doubles, 1 twin.
Meals	Packed lunch £4.50. Pub 3-minute walk.
Closed	Rarely.
Directions	From Shrewsbury A458 Welshpool road. After Ford, right onto B4393. Just after Crew Green, left for Criggion. House 1st on left after Admiral Rodney pub.

	Liz Dawson
	Brimford House,
	Criggion, Shrewsbury SY5 9AU
Tel	+44 (0)1938 570235
Mobile	+44 (0)7801 100848
Email	info@brimford.co.uk
Web	www.brimford.co.uk

Entry 425   Map 7

Shropshire

Lawley House

A lovely calm sense of the continuity of history and family life emanates from this large, comfortable Victorian home. Jackie and Jim are delightful hosts and great fun. Bedrooms welcome you with flowers, books, duck down pillows – and stupendous views of the Stretton Hills, even from bed. Tuck into a generous breakfast in the dining room, elegant with family portraits and a grand piano you are welcome to play. Enjoy long hilltop views from the spectacular conservatory or the garden – lush with lupins, sweet peas, delphiniums and 50 types of rose that bloom in profusion. A charming and friendly place. *Over 12s welcome.*

Price	£60–£80. Singles £40–£55.
Rooms	2: 1 double, 1 twin/double.
Meals	Pub/restaurant 1.5 miles.
Closed	Christmas & New Year.
Directions	From Shrewsbury, south on A49. Ignore turn in Dorrington, keep on for 3 miles. 0.5 miles before Leebotwood, right to Smethcott. Follow signs uphill for 2 miles; drive on left just before Smethcott.

	Jackie & Jim Scarratt
	Lawley House,
	Smethcott, Church Stretton SY6 6NX
Tel	+44 (0)1694 751236
Mobile	+44 (0)7980 331792
Email	jscarratt@onetel.com
Web	www.lawleyhouse.co.uk

Entry 426   Map 7

Shropshire

Clun Farm House

These young relaxed owners make a great team. Susan gives you homemade marmalade at breakfast and seasonal produce at dinner; Anthony helps you discover the secrets of the village and the heavenly hills. Both are enthusiastic collectors of country artefacts and have filled their listed 15th-century farmhouse with eye-catching things; the cowboy's saddle by the old range echoes Susan's roots. Bedrooms have aged and oiled floorboards, fun florals and bold walls; bathrooms are small and simple. Walk Offa's Dyke and the Shropshire Way; return to a cosy wood-burner, a warm smile and a delicious dinner. Good value.

Price	From £75. Singles by arrangement.
Rooms	2: 1 double (with extra bunk bed room); 1 twin/double with separate shower.
Meals	Dinner from £25. Packed lunch £4. Pubs/restaurants nearby.
Closed	Occasionally.
Directions	A49 from Ludlow & onto B4368 at Craven Arms, for Clun. In High St on left 0.5 miles from Clun sign.

Anthony & Susan Whitfield
Clun Farm House, High Street,
Clun, Craven Arms SY7 8JB
Tel   +44 (0)1588 640432
Mobile   +44 (0)7885 261391
Email   susanwhitfield@talk21.com
Web   www.clunfarmhouse.co.uk

Shropshire

Hopton House

Karen looks after her guests wonderfully and even runs courses on how to do B&B! Unwind in this fresh and uplifting converted granary with old beams, high ceilings and a sun-filled dining/sitting room overlooking the hills. The bedroom above has its own balcony; those in the barn, one up, one down, each with its own entrance, are as enticing: beautifully dressed beds, silent fridges, good lighting, homemade cakes. Bathrooms have deep baths (and showers) – from one you can lie back and gaze at the stars. Karen's breakfasts promise Ludlow sausages, home-laid eggs, fine jams and homemade marmalade.

Price	From £105.
Rooms	3: 1 double. Barn: 2 doubles.
Meals	Restaurant 3 miles.
Closed	19-27 December.
Directions	A49 Craven Arms exit, B4368 west. After 1 mile, left signed Hopton Heath. At Hopton Heath x-roads, right over bridge, follow road right. House 2nd on left.

Karen Thorne
Hopton House,
Hopton Heath,
Craven Arms SY7 0QD
Tel   +44 (0)1547 530885
Email   info@shropshirebreakfast.co.uk
Web   www.shropshirebreakfast.co.uk

Shropshire

The Birches Mill

Just as a mill should be, tucked in the nook of a postcard valley. It ended Gill and Andrew's search for a refuge from the city, and it's a treat to share its seclusion and beauty; all you hear is the river. Fresh breezy bedrooms in the 17th-century part have elegant brass beds, goose down duvets and fine linen – one keeps the original long roll top bath – while the new stone and oak extension blends beautifully and has become a big attractive twin. Happy hens provide the breakfast eggs. Gill and Andrew are affable hosts in a stunning valley of meadowland and woods. *Children over 12 welcome.*

Price	£82–£92. Singles by arrangement.
Rooms	3: 1 double, 1 twin; 1 double with separate bath.
Meals	Packed lunch £6. Pub 3 miles.
Closed	November–March.
Directions	From Clun A488 for Bishops Castle. 1st left, for Bicton. 2nd left for Mainstone, then narrow winding lane for 1.5 miles. Up bank to farm, then 1st right for Burlow. House at bottom of hill on left by river.

Gill Della Casa & Andrew Farmer
The Birches Mill,
Clun SY7 8NL
Tel   +44 (0)1588 640409
Email birchesmill@btinternet.com
Web   www.birchesmill.co.uk

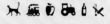

Entry 429   Map 7

Shropshire

Upper Buckton

You can't help being bowled over by the beautiful setting and the grandeur of the place. In lush gardens that slope peacefully down to millstream, meadows and river, this Georgian house, complete with heronry and point-to-point course, stands on a motte and bailey site. Convivial dinners, preceded by drinks in the drawing room, are delicious: Yvonne's cooking using local produce is upmarket and creative, Hayden's wine list is a treat. Retire to large bedrooms with huge beds made to perfection (proper blankets, lovely linen). Marvellous for walkers returning from a day in the glorious Welsh Borders. *Children by arrangement.*

Price	£96–£110. Singles £63–£70.
Rooms	3: 1 double, 1 twin/double; 1 twin/double with separate bath.
Meals	Dinner, 4 courses, £30. Pub/restaurant 2 miles.
Closed	Rarely.
Directions	From Ludlow, A49 to Shrewsbury. At Bromfield, A4113. Right in Walford for Buckton, on to 2nd farm on left. Large sign on building.

Hayden & Yvonne Lloyd
Upper Buckton, Leintwardine,
Craven Arms, Ludlow SY7 0JU
Tel   +44 (0)1547 540634
Email ghlloydco@btconnect.com
Web   www.upperbuckton.co.uk

Entry 430   Map 7

Shropshire

Lower Buckton Country House

You are spoiled here in house-party style; Carolyn – passionate about Slow Food – and Henry, are born entertainers. Kick off with homemade cake in the drawing room with its oil paintings, antique furniture and old rugs; return for delicious nibbles when the lamps and wood-burner are flickering. Dine well at a huge oak table (home-reared pork, local cheeses, dreamy puddings), then nestle into the best linen and the softest pillows; bedrooms feel wonderfully restful. This is laid-back B&B: paddle in the stream, admire the stunning views, find a quiet spot with a good book. Great fun! *Cookery courses. Stabling for horses.*

Walford Court

Come for a break from clock-watching and a spot of fresh air. Large bedrooms delight with the comfiest mattresses on king-size beds, scented candles, antiques, books, games and double-end roll top baths – one under a west facing window. Aga-cooked breakfasts include eggs from 'the ladies of the orchard'; candlelit dinners may be served outside on fine evenings. Wander through apple, plum and pear trees, find a motte and bailey, strike out for a long hike. Craig and Debbie are thoughtful and hugely keen on wildlife (you get binoculars) and this is the perfect place to bring a special person – and a bottle of champagne.

Price	£90.
Rooms	3: 2 doubles; 1 twin/double with separate bath. Self-catering in Millstream Camp (shepherd's hut) available.
Meals	Dinner, 4 courses, £35. Pub/restaurant 4 miles.
Closed	Rarely.
Directions	South through Leintwardine; after 0.25 miles right A4113. At Walford right at x-roads down narrow lane for Buckton. Over river, 2nd house on left, entrance by village green; white gate with postbox in wall.

Price	£90–£95. Singles £80–£85.
Rooms	3: 1 double; 2 doubles each with sitting room.
Meals	Dinner, 2-3 courses, £22.50–£28. Cold platters. Packed lunch available. Pubs/restaurants 1-3 miles.
Closed	Christmas & Boxing Day.
Directions	A49 N of Ludlow; A4113 Knighton. Thro' Leintwardine; right Walford. There, left for Presteigne, then immed. left. Signs to Walford Court Tea Room.

Henry & Carolyn Chesshire
Lower Buckton Country House,
Buckton, Leintwardine SY7 0JU
Tel   +44 (0)1547 540532
Mobile   +44 (0)7960 273865
Email   carolyn@lowerbuckton.co.uk
Web   www.lowerbuckton.co.uk

Debbie & Craig Fraser
Walford Court,
Walford, Leintwardine,
Ludlow SY7 0JT
Tel   +44 (0)1547 540570
Email   info@romanticbreak.com
Web   www.romanticbreak.com

Shropshire

35 Lower Broad Street

You're almost at the bottom of the town, near the river and the bridge. Elaine's terraced Georgian cottage is spotless and cosy; her office doubles as a sitting area for guests with leather armchairs and desk space for workaholics. Upstairs are two good-sized doubles with a country crisp feel, king-size beds and a pretty blue and white bathroom. Walkers, shoppers, antique- and book-hunters can fill up on a superb breakfast of homemade potato scones, black pudding, organic eggs and good coffee before striding out to explore. This is excellent value, comfortable B&B and can be enjoyed without a car. Perfect for two couples.

Shropshire

Rosecroft

A pretty, quiet, traditional house with charming owners, well-proportioned rooms, an elegant sitting room and not a trace of pomposity. Breakfasts are huge enough to set you up for the day: Pimhill organic muesli, smoked or unsmoked local bacon, black pudding, delicious jams. The garden is a delight to stroll through – in summer you can picnic here – while serious walkers are close to the Welsh borders. Bedrooms and bathrooms are polished to perfection; there are fresh flowers, plenty of interesting books, home-baked cakes when you arrive. The village has a super pub and Ludlow is close by. *Children over 12 welcome.*

Price	£70. Singles £45.
Rooms	2: 1 double & sitting room; 1 double sharing bath (let to same party only).
Meals	Pubs/restaurants 100 yds.
Closed	Rarely.
Directions	Right out of railway station, 200 yds to lights. Left onto Corve St, then up to top of hill. At lights, right & follow to Broad St; thro' arch into Lower Broad St. On right towards bottom.

Price	£75-£80. Singles £55-£60.
Rooms	2: 1 double; 1 double with separate bath.
Meals	Packed lunch £4. Pub 200 yds.
Closed	Rarely.
Directions	Between Ludlow & Leominster on A49, turn onto B4362 at Woofferton. After 1.5 miles, left into Orleton. Past school & small green, house on right, opp. vicarage.

	Elaine Downs
	35 Lower Broad Street,
	Ludlow SY8 1PH
Tel	+44 (0)1584 876912
Mobile	+44 (0)7980 037576
Email	a.downs@tesco.net
Web	www.ludlowbedandbreakfast.blogspot.com

	Gail Benson
	Rosecroft,
	Orleton,
	Ludlow SY8 4HN
Tel	+44 (0)1568 780565
Email	gailanddavid@rosecroftorleton.co.uk
Web	www.rosecroftbedandbreakfast.co.uk

Entry 433   Map 7

Entry 434   Map 7

Shropshire

Timberstone Bed & Breakfast

The house is young and engaging – as are Tracey and Alex, new generation B&Bers. Come for charming bedrooms – two snug under the eaves, two in the smart oak-floored extension – roll top baths, pretty fabrics, thick white cotton, beams galore… and reflexology, massage or a sauna in the garden studios; Tracey, once in catering, is a reflexologist. In the warm guest sitting/dining room find art, books, comfortable sofas and glass doors onto the terrace. Breakfasts are special with croissants and local eggs and bacon; suppers are delicious too, or you can head off to Ludlow and its clutch of Michelin stars.

Price	£90–£100. Singles £50–£90.
Rooms	5: 2 doubles, 1 double with sofabed, 1 family. Summerhouse: 1 double (summer only).
Meals	Dinner, 3 courses, £25. Pubs/restaurants 5 miles.
Closed	Rarely.
Directions	B4364 Ludlow-Bridgnorth. After 3 miles, right to Clee Stanton; on for 1.5 miles; left at signpost to Clee Stanton; 1st house on left.

Tracey Baylis & Alex Read
Timberstone Bed & Breakfast,
Clee Stanton, Ludlow SY8 3EL

Tel	+44 (0)1584 823519
Mobile	+44 (0)7905 967263
Email	timberstone1@hotmail.com
Web	www.timberstoneludlow.co.uk

Entry 435   Map 7

Shropshire

The Old Rectory

With its own spring water, horses, dogs and slow pace this Georgian rectory is comfortable country living at its best. Izzy and Andy are charming and interesting and give you scones and tea by the fire in a drawing room full of family photos, plump sofas and books. Elegant bedrooms have fluffy hot water bottles; smart bathrooms have scented lotions in pretty bottles, robes and slippers. Candlelit dinner will often be fish or game with garden vegetables; breakfast is local and leisurely with homemade granola and jams. There's a bootroom for muddy feet and paws, stabling and seven acres to roam. *Pets sleep in bootroom.*

Price	From £80. Singles from £65.
Rooms	2: 1 double, 1 twin/double.
Meals	Dinner, 3 courses, £29.50. Packed lunch £10. Pubs 1.25–4 miles.
Closed	Rarely.
Directions	From Ludlow B4117 dir. Cleobury Mortimer. After 0.5 miles left onto B4364. After 6 miles right at 3 Horse Shoes pub. Straight on for 1.25 miles. Drive on right by red letter box.

Isabel Barnard
The Old Rectory,
Wheathill,
Bridgnorth WV16 6QT

Tel	+44 (0)1746 787209
Email	enquiries@theoldrectorywheathill.com
Web	www.theoldrectorywheathill.com

Entry 436   Map 7

Somerset

West Liscombe

Down deep Devon lanes, then up, up, up to the remote farmhouse encircled by footpaths and bridle paths, breezes and green views. Heaven! Inside is comfy, cheery, chintzy and English to the core. Deborah, true country lady and Cordon Bleu cook, was born to do B&B; she runs the Pony Club and welcomes all. The grandfather clock tick-tocks in the sitting room, the silver shines, the log-burner glows, and the guest bedrooms, with books, great beds and posies of flowers, are well-groomed and inviting. Sheep roam the drive, the garden stretches down the valley, Exmoor is 600 yards, the sea is 11 miles.

Price	From £75. Singles £45.
Rooms	2: 1 double; 1 twin with separate bath.
Meals	Lunch £7.50. Dinner £20. Pub 5 miles.
Closed	Rarely.
Directions	In East Anstey village pass school on left; continue 1 mile to Waddicombe, up hill for 50 yds. Postbox in wall, turn right; house 500 yds.

Robert & Deborah Connell
West Liscombe,
Waddicombe,
Dulverton TA22 9RX
Tel +44 (0)1398 341282
Email deborahconnell@btinternet.com

Entry 437 Map 2

Somerset

North Wheddon Farm

Pootle through the vibrant green patchwork of Exmoor National Park and bowl down a pitted track to land in Blyton-esque bliss – a classic Somerset farmyard, crackling with geese and hens, round which is the gentleman farmer's house. Bedrooms are airy and comfortable with grand views, books, fresh flowers and small, but neat-as-a-pin bathrooms. Bring children and they will be in heaven, with eggs to collect and pigs to pat, or come just for yourself and a bit of indulgence. Food is 'River Cottage' style and much is home-reared, the walking is fabulous for miles and kind Rachael sends you off with a thermos of tea.

Price	£75-£80. Singles £38.50.
Rooms	3: 1 double, 1 twin/double; 1 single with separate bath.
Meals	Dinner from £24. Cold/hot packed lunch £7.50-£9.75. Pub 0.25 miles.
Closed	Rarely.
Directions	From Minehead A396 to Wheddon Cross. Pass pub on right & Moorland Hall on left. North Wheddon is next driveway on right. Satnav not reliable.

Rachael Abraham
North Wheddon Farm,
Wheddon Cross TA24 7EX
Tel +44 (0)1643 841791
Email rachael@go-exmoor.co.uk
Web www.northwheddonfarm.co.uk

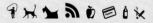

Entry 438 Map 2

Somerset

Glen Lodge

Come for the food and Meryl and David's comfy open house vibe. Their sheltered, secluded Victorian home is spacious, comfortable and surrounded by high banks of woodland. Enjoy delicious meals with an American slant using local venison, lamb, honey, cheeses and fish; they grow fruit and veg, make jams and serve tea and cakes every day – perfect brownies! Polished oak floors are dotted with oriental rugs and log fires burn. Wander the 21 acres, play croquet, sip a sunset drink on the terrace overlooking the wide bay. Exmoor and popular Porlock are on the doorstep; sandy beaches, harbours and boat trips will keep you happy too.

Price	£90-£95. Singles £60.
Rooms	5: 3 doubles; 1 double, 1 twin each with separate bath.
Meals	Dinner, 3 courses, £30. Supper £20. Packed lunch £8. Pub/restaurant 0.5 miles.
Closed	Rarely.
Directions	From Minehead, A39 to Porlock; on entering town, left at church into Parsons Street 0.5 miles up. Left over bridge. Gate to house in front.

	Meryl Salter Glen Lodge, Hawkcombe, Porlock TA24 8LN
Tel	+44 (0)1643 863371
Mobile	+44 (0)7786 118933
Email	glenlodge@gmail.com
Web	www.glenlodge.net

Entry 439   Map 2

Somerset

Higher Orchard

A little lane tumbles down to the centre of lovely old Dunster. The village is a two minute-walk yet here you have open views of fields, sheep and sea. Exmoor footpaths start behind the house and Janet encourages explorers, by bike or on foot; ever helpful and kind, she is a local who knows the patch well. The 1860s house keeps its Victorian features, bedrooms are quiet and simple and the double has a view to Blue Anchor Bay and Dunster castle and church. All is homely, with stripped pine, cream curtains, fresh flowers, garden fruit and home-laid eggs for breakfast. *Children & pets by arrangement.*

Price	£70. Singles from £35.
Rooms	3: 1 double, 2 twins/doubles.
Meals	Packed lunch from £3.50. Restaurants 2-minute walk.
Closed	Christmas.
Directions	From Williton, A39 for Minehead for 8 miles. Left to Dunster. There, right fork into 'The Ball'. At T-junc. at end of road, right. House 75 yds on right.

	Janet Lamacraft Higher Orchard, 30 St George's St, Dunster TA24 6RS
Tel	+44 (0)1643 821915
Mobile	+44 (0)7896 464420
Email	lamacraft@higherorchard.fsnet.co.uk
Web	www.higherorchard-dunster.co.uk

Entry 440   Map 2

Somerset

The Old Priory

The 12th-century priory leans against its church, with a rustic gate, an enchanting garden, a tumble of flowers. Both house and hostess are dignified, unpretentious and friendly. Here are old oak tables, flagstones, wood panelling, higgledy-piggledy corridors and large bedrooms filled with family antiques. But an ancient English house in a sweet Somerset village needs a touch of pepper and cosmopolitan Jane adds her own special flair with artistic and eccentric touches here and there, and books and Horace the dog for company. Peaceful spots and scents in the garden, Dunster Castle above on the hill and walks from the door.

Price	£90. Singles by arrangement.
Rooms	3: 1 twin, 1 four-poster; 1 double with separate shower.
Meals	Pubs/restaurants 5-minute walk.
Closed	Christmas.
Directions	From A39 into Dunster, right at blue sign 'Unsuitable for Goods Vehicles'. Follow until church; house adjoined.

Jane Forshaw
The Old Priory,
Priory Green,
Dunster TA24 6RY
Tel   +44 (0)1643 821540
Web   www.theoldpriory-dunster.co.uk

Entry 441   Map 2

Somerset

Wyndham House

A charming Georgian house tucked away in the unspoilt town of Watchet, with its interesting little shops. Susan and Roger will greet you with homemade cake and biscuits, either in their pretty dining room – or in the unexpectedly large and beautiful garden, which overlooks the harbour and small marina. Bedrooms are comfortable and traditional, one overlooking the pretty courtyard and the other with views to Wales. Delicious breakfasts are relaxed affairs accompanied by newspapers; walk it all off in the delightful Quantocks or Exmoor National Park – you are near to both. *Children & dogs by arrangement.*

Price	From £80. Singles from £40.
Rooms	2: 1 twin/double; 1 double with separate shower/bath.
Meals	Pubs/restaurants a short walk.
Closed	Christmas.
Directions	From railway station & footbridge in Watchet, up South Rd (for Doniford). After 50 yds, left into Beverley Drive. House 50 yds on left with gravel parking area.

Susan & Roger Vincent
Wyndham House,
4 Sea View Terrace,
Watchet TA23 0DF
Tel   +44 (0)1984 631881
Email   info@wyndhamhousebb.co.uk
Web   www.wyndhamhousebb.co.uk

Entry 442   Map 2

Somerset

Cider Barn

Set back from the lane is a newly converted and refurbished barn. Elm boards have been removed for heated floors, fine old proportions remain, Louise's stunning living quarters spread under the beams and the bedrooms lie privately below on the ground floor. Happy to share her elevated space, delightful Louise, Cordon Bleu trained, serves breakfasts at the long table. You can walk through fields to the river or the hills, book an Indian head massage, get snug upstairs by the wood-burner, stroll to the pub for supper. Bedrooms, one opening to the courtyard, are fresh, airy and peaceful with modern fabrics and cream walls. Lovely.

Price	£70-£75. Singles £35-£37.50.
Rooms	2: 1 double, 1 twin/double.
Meals	Pub 0.5 miles.
Closed	Rarely.
Directions	Sent on booking.

Louise Bancroft
Cider Barn,
Runnington,
Wellington TA21 0QW
Tel   +44 (0)1823 665533
Email   louisegaddon@btinternet.com
Web   www.runningtonciderbarn.co.uk

Entry 443   Map 2

Somerset

Pyle House

Swoop down onto a buttermilk yellow lodge with landscaped gardens hugged by Somerset's rolling green fields: it's so well renovated you'd never guess it was an 1800s hunting lodge for Whitestaunton Estate. Past the flagstoned hallway, discover a house of pristine paintwork, valley views, swish bathrooms and immaculate bedrooms. Madeleine loves to cook so expect a breakfast worthy of the fine china it comes on; Michael's pride and joy are his fossil finds – proof of the area's antiquity. It's perfect for walkers: kick boots into the drying room, browse through maps, stroll to the pub for a meal. *Children over ten welcome.*

Price	From £70. Singles £45.
Rooms	3: 1 double, 1 twin/double (with sofabed);1 double with separate shower room.
Meals	Pub/restaurant 0.5 miles.
Closed	Christmas & New Year.
Directions	From Chard A30 for Honiton. After 4 miles, right for Howley. Take 2nd right through stone pillars, signed Pyle, to cream house at end of drive.

Madeleine Berry
Pyle House,
Whitestaunton,
Chard TA20 3DZ
Tel   +44 (0)1460 239268
Email   info@pylehouse.co.uk
Web   www.pylehouse.co.uk

Entry 444   Map 2

Somerset

Frog Street Farmhouse

Through a pastoral landscape, past green paddocks and fine thoroughbreds, to a beautiful longhouse set in pretty secluded gardens surrounded by 130 acres. Its heart dates back to 1436 and its renovation is remarkable, highlighting beamed ceilings, Jacobean panelling and open fireplaces. Louise and David, brimful of enthusiasm for both house and guests, give you four exquisite bedrooms in French country style, one with its own sitting room – very romantic. Louise happily does evening meals and hosts small house parties with ease. After a day out, return to great leather sofas and a wood-burning stove. What value!

Price	From £90. Singles from £70. Suite from £140.
Rooms	4: 3 doubles, 1 family suite for 4.
Meals	Dinner, 3 courses, £27.50. Pubs within 2.5 miles.
Closed	Rarely.
Directions	A358 to Illminster. 1st exit to Hatch Beauchamp. At Hatch Inn left into Station Rd. Left after 0.5 miles; over humpback bridge, Frog St Farm in front.

	Louise & David Farrance
	Frog Street Farmhouse,
	Hatch Beauchamp, Taunton TA3 6AF
Tel	+44 (0)1823 481883
Mobile	+44 (0)7811 700789
Email	frogstreet@hotmail.com
Web	www.frogstreet.co.uk

Entry 445   Map 2

Somerset

Causeway Cottage

Robert and Lesley are ex-restaurateurs, so guests heap praise on their food, most of which is sourced from a local butcher and fishmonger; charming Lesley is an author, runs cookery courses and once taught at Prue Leith's. This is the perfect, pretty Somerset cottage, with an apple orchard and views to the church across a cottage garden and a field. The bedrooms are light, restful and have a country-style simplicity with their green check bedspreads, white walls and antique pine furniture; guests have their own comfortable sitting room. Easy access to the M5 yet with a rural feel. Very special. *Children over ten welcome.*

Price	From £80. Singles by arrangement.
Rooms	3: 1 double, 2 twins.
Meals	Supper from £25. Pub/restaurant 0.75 miles.
Closed	Christmas.
Directions	From M5 junc. 26, West Buckland road for 0.75 miles. 1st left just before stone building. Bear right; 3rd house at end of lane, below church.

	Lesley & Robert Orr
	Causeway Cottage,
	West Buckland,
	Taunton TA21 9JZ
Tel	+44 (0)1823 663458
Email	causewaybb@talktalk.net
Web	www.causewaycottage.co.uk

Entry 446   Map 2

Somerset

Rock House

Tucked away in an AONB, near the Quantocks and Exmoor, this elegant Georgian house hides behind a tall hedge in a sleepy village. Deborah greets her guests with impeccable manners and scrumptious biscuits; take tea in the drawing room where flowers are beautifully arranged and there are books to read. Big bedrooms are richly decorated, comfortable and full of thoughtful touches like fresh milk and a torch; bathrooms have generous towels and Molton Brown lotions. The Rock House fry-up will set you up for miles of walking, or a quick stroll to the top of the pretty garden with its croquet lawn. *Children & pets by arrangement.*

Price	From £80. Singles from £50.
Rooms	2: 1 twin/double; 1 double (extra single bed) with separate bath.
Meals	Pub 100 yds.
Closed	Christmas.
Directions	M5 exit 25, signs to A358 Minehead. Left to Halse. House in middle of village, near pub.

Christopher & Deborah Wolverson
Rock House,
Halse, Taunton TA4 3AF
Tel   +44 (0)1823 432956
Mobile   +44 (0)7849 330487
Email   dwolverson@rockhousesomerset.co.uk
Web   www.rockhousesomerset.co.uk

Entry 447   Map 2

Somerset

Bashfords Farmhouse

A feeling of warmth and happiness pervades this exquisite 17th-century farmhouse in the Quantock hills. The Ritchies love doing B&B – after 20 years! – and interiors have a homely feel with well-framed prints, natural fabrics, comfortable sofas, and a sitting room with inglenook, sofas and books. Bedrooms are pretty, fresh and large and look over the cobbled courtyard or open fields. Charles and Jane couldn't be nicer, know about local walks (the Macmillan Way runs by) and love to cook: local meat and game, tarte tatin, homemade bread and jams. A delightful garden rambles up the hill; the pub is just a minute away.

Price	£75. Singles £45.
Rooms	3: 1 twin/double; 1 twin/double with separate shower; 1 twin with separate bath.
Meals	Dinner £27.50. Supper £22.50. Pub 75 yds.
Closed	Rarely.
Directions	M5 junc. 25. A358 for Minehead. Leave A358 at West Bagborough turning. Through village for 1.5 miles. Farmhouse 3rd on left past pub.

Charles & Jane Ritchie
Bashfords Farmhouse,
West Bagborough,
Taunton TA4 3EF
Tel   +44 (0)1823 432015
Email   info@bashfordsfarmhouse.co.uk
Web   www.bashfordsfarmhouse.co.uk

Entry 448   Map 2

Somerset

Cothelstone Manor

A gloriously grand manor quite without stuffiness, on the edge of Exmoor, gazing up to the Quantock Hills. Nigel and Finny, naturally friendly, invite you into their family home. Inside, find elegant rooms, logs burning in the galleried hall, family photos, art and beautiful antiques; all gleams. Bedrooms have pretty views through mullion-leaded windows, immaculate linen and comfortable bathrooms with fluffy towels and flowers. Wake to Sunday church bells and breakfasts of local bacon and sausages, homemade jams and eggs from hens who roam the walled gardens. The Coleridge Way is on the doorstep.

Somerset

Parsonage Farm

The Quantock Hills are wonderful for walking and cycling, with the Coleridge Way starting down the lane. In this 17th-century farmhouse relaxed hosts give you easy comfort with quarry floors, books, a cosy log-fired sitting room and spacious bedrooms with tranquil country views. Suki, from Vermont, has turned a stable into a studio – her pots and paintings add charm to the décor. Breakfast by the fire is a feast: homemade bread and jam, eggs from the hens, juice from the orchard, porridge and pancakes with maple syrup. Relax in the beautiful walled kitchen garden; there's an outdoor wood-fired pizza oven too! *Over twos welcome.*

Price	£98.
Rooms	2 doubles (extra bed available).
Meals	Picnic hamper £10. Pub within 2 miles.
Closed	Rarely.
Directions	M5 junc.25. A358 towards Minehead. At turning to Bishops Lydeard, up through village for approx. 1.5 miles. House signed.

Price	£60-£80. Singles £45-£65.
Rooms	3: 1 double (extra sofabed), 1 twin/double (extra sofabed); 1 double sharing bath & shower.
Meals	Supper £10. Dinner, 2-3 courses, £20-£25. Pub/restaurant 1 mile.
Closed	Christmas.
Directions	A39 Bridgwater-Minehead. 7 miles on, left at Cottage Inn for Over Stowey; 1.8 miles; house on right after church. Signed car park.

Nigel & Finny Muers-Raby
Cothelstone Manor,
Cothelstone, Taunton TA4 3DS
Tel   +44 (0)1823 433480
Mobile   +44 (0)7709 434411
Email   finny@cothelstonemanor.co.uk
Web   www.cothelstonemanor.co.uk

Susan Lilienthal
Parsonage Farm,
Over Stowey, Nether Stowey TA5 1HA
Tel   +44 (0)1278 733237
Mobile   +44 (0)7928 368836
Email   suki@parsonfarm.co.uk
Web   www.parsonfarm.co.uk

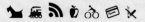

Entry 449   Map 2

Entry 450   Map 2

Somerset

Westleigh Farm

The stone farmhouse rises grandly from tree-lined fields and paddocks; the only sound is birdsong. A fine West Country base for walks, cycles, rides in all directions, the Quantocks, Taunton market… A pleasure to return to tea by the log-burner, a home-cooked dinner, a game of snooker. Fairly new to B&B, Kerstin treats guests with bedside fruit and biscuits and just-laid eggs. Little luxuries sweeten quirky furnishings: mother's quilts, hunt trophies, a rocking horse, piano, a Japanese cabinet in the deep red dining hall. Join the Jack Russells in a lush garden which melts to Somerset countryside. *Over tens welcome.*

Price	£85. Singles £50.
Rooms	3 doubles.
Meals	Dinner, 2-3 courses, £25-£30. Pubs/restaurants 3 miles.
Closed	Rarely.
Directions	Sent on booking.

Kerstin Sharpe
Westleigh Farm,
Broomfield,
Bridgwater TA5 2EH
Tel   +44 (0)1823 452100
Email bookings@westleighfarm.com
Web   www.westleighfarm.com

Entry 451   Map 2

Somerset

Blackmore Farm

Come for atmosphere and architecture: the Grade I-listed manor-farmhouse is remarkable. Medieval stone, soaring beams, ecclesiastical windows, giant logs blazing in the Great Hall. Ann and Ian look after guests and busy dairy farm with equal enthusiasm. Furnishings are comfortable, decor is rich, bedrooms are cavernous and the oak-panelled suite (with secret stairway) takes up an entire floor. The rooms in the stables are simpler with green oak and wide doorways. Breakfast is generous and organic and eaten at the 20-foot polished table in baronial splendour; visit the calves in the dairy and don't miss the excellent farm shop.

Price	£100. Singles £50.
Rooms	5: 1 double, 1 four-poster, 1 suite. Courtyard stables: 1 double, 1 twin.
Meals	Occasional dinner for parties. Pubs/restaurants 5-minute walk.
Closed	Rarely.
Directions	From Bridgwater, A39 west around Cannington. After 2nd r'bout, follow signs to Minehead; 1st left after Yeo Valley creamery; 1st house on right.

Ann Dyer
Blackmore Farm,
Cannington,
Bridgwater TA5 2NE
Tel   +44 (0)1278 653442
Email dyerfarm@aol.com
Web   www.dyerfarm.co.uk

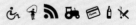

Entry 452   Map 2

Somerset

Huntstile Organic Farm

Catapult yourself into country life in the foothills of the Quantocks; make that connection between the rolling green hills, the idyllic munching animals and the delicious, organic food on your plate; here it is understood. Lizzie and John buzz with energy in this gorgeous old house with Jacobean panelling and huge walk-in fireplaces, two sitting rooms, sweet and cosy rustic bedrooms, a café, and a restaurant serving their own meat, eggs and vegetables. House parties, weddings, team building, a stone circle for hand-fasting ceremonies – all come under Lizzie's happy and efficient umbrella. And there are woodlands to roam.

Price	From £85. Singles from £60.
Rooms	8: 5 doubles, 1 family room. Apartment: 1 double, 1 twin with sitting room.
Meals	Dinner, 3 courses, £22.50–£27. Packed lunch from £6.50. Pub/restaurant 3 miles.
Closed	22 December–7 January.
Directions	M5 junc. 24, North Petherton. Before village right to Goathurst and Broomfield. Take 2nd right to Goathurst. House 1 mile on right.

Lizzie Myers
Huntstile Organic Farm,
Goathurst,
Bridgwater TA5 2DQ
Tel   +44 (0)1278 662358
Email   huntstile@live.co.uk
Web   www.huntstileorganicfarm.co.uk

Entry 453   Map 2

Somerset

Edington House

Step back in time into this rambling, ancient English country house, where twists and turns link panelled rooms replete with silk curtains, portraits, fireplaces, chandeliers, objets d'art. Families will love exploring the countless sitting and dining rooms and large sweeping gardens: discover a pool, tennis court, Georgian summerhouse, kitchen garden, orchard and ponies. Your easy-going, well-travelled hosts (she Austrian, he English) want guests to enjoy it all. Bedrooms are just as grandiose, with draped floral fabrics, antiques and patterned wallpapers. Inge is a serious cook and suppers are a highlight.

Price	£136. Singles £100.
Rooms	3: 1 four-poster, 1 double, 1 family suite for 3–4.
Meals	Supper, 3 courses, £25. Dinner, 4 courses, £35. Pub/restaurant 1 mile.
Closed	Christmas.
Directions	Leave M5 junc. 23, A30 dir. Glastonbury. After 4 miles left signed Edington. Left at crossroads in village; house immediately on left behind high wall.

Inge Sprawson
Edington House,
Edington,
Bridgwater TA7 9JS
Tel   +44 (0)1278 722238
Email   inge@edingtonhouse.co.uk
Web   www.edingtonhouse.co.uk

Entry 454   Map 2

Somerset

Church Cottage

Partly clothed in English garden and with views to the church, this 400-year-old cottage has wooden beams, low ceilings and wonky walls. Ignore the modern house on the other side of the road and restore your senses with neutral colours, soft cushions, a flash of Thompson gazelle skin, the whiff of woodsmoke and floppy roses on a scrubbed table. Caroline rustles up a fine breakfast in her calm kitchen; relax in the charming walled garden or sitting room. Bedrooms are simple and comfy – pine furniture, good linen; the Potting Shed is a private, sweet nest for two. Miles of walking straight from the door.

Price	£75–£90. Singles £65–£80.
Rooms	2: 1 double. Potting Shed: 1 double.
Meals	Pubs 1 mile.
Closed	Rarely.
Directions	M5 exit 23 to A39. 7 miles; left to Shapwick. Cottage on left next to church.

Caroline Hanbury Bateman
Church Cottage, Station Road,
Shapwick, Bridgwater TA7 9NH
Tel   +44 (0)1458 210904
Mobile   +44 (0)7875 598155
Email   c.hanbury.bateman@btinternet.com
Web   www.churchcottageshapwick.co.uk

Entry 455   Map 3

Somerset

The Lynch Country House

Peace and privacy at this immaculate Regency house in a Somerset valley. First-floor bedrooms are traditionally grand, attic rooms are small but pretty; those in the coach house have a more modern feel. Rich colours prevail, fabrics are flowery and linen best Irish. You'll feel as warm as toast and beautifully looked after. A stone staircase goes right to the top where the observatory lets in cascading light; the flagged hall, high ceilings, long windows and private tables at breakfast create a country-house hotel feel. The lovely garden has black swans on a lake, hundreds of trees and a terrace from which to drink it all in.

Price	£80–£115. Singles £65–£80.
Rooms	9: 2 doubles, 1 twin/double, 1 double (extra single bed); 1 double with separate bath (extra single bed). Coach house: 2 doubles, 2 twins/doubles.
Meals	Restaurants 5-minute walk.
Closed	Rarely.
Directions	From London, M3 junc. 8, A303. At Podimore r'bout A372 to Somerton. At junc. of North St & Behind Berry.

Mike McKenzie
The Lynch Country House,
4 Behind Berry,
Somerton TA11 7PD
Tel   +44 (0)1458 272316
Email   enquiries@thelynchcountryhouse.co.uk
Web   www.thelynchcountryhouse.co.uk

Entry 456   Map 3

Somerset

Barwick Farm House

A 17th-century farmhouse sitting in ten acres of organically managed land dotted with hens, horses and Dorset sheep. Charming Angela and Robin have limewashed the walls in vibrant colours, restored ancient elm boards and exposed sandstone fireplace lintels, in a house full of open fires, books and flowers. Roomy bedrooms have good cotton sheets, comfortable beds and a mishmash of styles; one bathroom, painted bubble-gum pink, has a freestanding bath and views over fields. Wake to birdsong and the sizzle of good local bacon; excellent walking and cycling start from the door and there are gardens to visit.

Price	£60-£75. Singles from £35.
Rooms	2: 1 double, 1 family suite for 4.
Meals	'Early Bird' packed breakfasts also available. Restaurant 100 yds.
Closed	Rarely.
Directions	A37 to Dorchester; 0.25 miles outside Yeovil, 1st exit off r'bout (opp. Red House pub) following signs to Little Barwick House restaurant. House in fork of road.

Angela Nicoll
Barwick Farm House,
Barwick, Yeovil BA22 9TD
Tel +44 (0)1935 410779
Mobile +44 (0)7967 385307
Email info@barwickfarmhouse.co.uk
Web www.barwickfarmhouse.co.uk

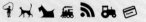

Entry 457 Map 3

Somerset

The Fat Pigeon

The Fat Pigeon is a wing of Brympton House – a fortified manor and "the most beautiful house in England". A treat for gardeners and historians, it was used as a backdrop in *Chocolat*; just three families have lived here in 700 years, and the glorious gardens are listed. Your bedrooms are simple, light and fresh and have laundered linen and TVs; some have garden or lake views. Large bathrooms have claw foot baths or showers. The Bridal Suite has a very special feel and the rooms in the ancient Tower are fun for a group. Breakfast is by a 1350s fireplace in the snug; enjoy eggs from the hens and the housekeeper's preserves.

Price	£70-£140.
Rooms	15: 9 doubles, 5 family rooms, 1 family suite.
Meals	Pub 2 miles.
Closed	Occasionally.
Directions	Sent on booking.

Sara-Jane Glossop
The Fat Pigeon,
Odcombe,
Yeovil BA22 8TD
Tel +44 (0)1935 863404
Email info@thefatpigeon.co.uk
Web www.thefatpigeon.co.uk

Entry 458 Map 3

Lower Severalls Farmhouse

This is one for garden lovers, with a number of gardens in the area and three acres here: lovely lawns and curving borders, bulbs, wildflowers and hidden hostas, a 'dogwood basket', a nursery on site. The guest suites are in the stable block behind the beautiful old farmhouse – two up, one down, refurbished to a very high standard with bathrooms shiny and new. Breakfast is served beneath dark aged beams in the mullioned house: Mike enjoys the cooking, Mary is passionate about the garden, and the pigs and the chickens roam free. For dinner: a mill hotel across the road and a super pub in Hinton St George.

Price	£70. Singles £55.
Rooms	Stables: 3 suites (2 with kitchenettes).
Meals	Restaurant within walking distance.
Closed	Rarely.
Directions	Sent on booking.

Mary Pring & Mike Wycherley
Lower Severalls Farmhouse,
Lower Severalls,
Crewkerne TA18 7NX
Tel   +44 (0)1460 73234
Email   mary@lowerseveralls.co.uk
Web   www.lowerseveralls.co.uk

Entry 459   Map 3

Yarlington House

A mellow Georgian manor surrounded by impressive parkland, romantic rose gardens, apple tree pergola and laburnum walk. Your hosts are friendly and flexible, artists with an eye for quirky detail; Carolyn's embroideries are everywhere. Something to astound at every turn: fine copies of 18th-century wallpapers, elegant antiques, statues with hats atop and tremendous art. Traditional bedrooms with glorious garden views and proper 50s bathrooms have a faded charm. Enjoy a full English breakfast, grape juice from the glasshouse vines, log fires and lovely local walks. Surprising, unique. *Children by arrangement. Heated pool in summer.*

Price	£120. Singles £60.
Rooms	2: 1 double, 1 twin.
Meals	Pubs/restaurants within 0.5 miles.
Closed	25 July-23 August.
Directions	From Wincanton take A371 to Castle Cary. After Holbrook House take 2nd left, then 3rd right (both signed Yarlington). First stone gateposts on left.

Charles & Carolyn de Salis
Yarlington House,
Yarlington,
Wincanton BA9 8DY
Tel   +44 (0)1963 440344
Email   carolyn.desalis@yarlingtonhouse.com

Entry 460   Map 3

Somerset

Bratton Farmhouse

A gorgeous old 1600 house around which strut hens and happy Jacob sheep. Intelligent and generous Suellen has created warm contemporary interiors and the bedrooms are a joy. One, in the main house, has oak-panelled walls, bucolic views and a vast bed with vintage French embroidered linen. Another, in a converted studio across the courtyard, gives you independence; you have your own book-filled sitting room made cosy with a wood-burner, while lovers can laze till late in a huge nest of feather and down. Good books and art surround you, breakfasts are delicious and imaginative, walks start from the door.

Price	From £80. Studio £110. Singles from £70.
Rooms	3: 2 doubles, each with separate bath/shower. Studio: 1 twin/double & sitting room.
Meals	Lunch £10. Dinner, 3 courses, £28. Packed lunch £5. Pub 2 miles.
Closed	Rarely.
Directions	A303 then A371 signed Wincanton & Castle Cary. Follow signs to Castle Cary. After approx. 2.5 miles, right to Bratton Seymour. House 0.4 miles on right.

	Suellen Dainty
	Bratton Farmhouse, Bratton Seymour, Wincanton BA9 8BY
Tel	+44 (0)1963 32458
Mobile	+44 (0)7780 848567
Email	sdainty52@googlemail.com
Web	www.brattonfarmhouse.co.uk

Entry 461   Map 3

Somerset

Rectory Farm House

Lavinia has showered love and attention on her early Georgian house and garden in a landscape that has changed little since the 18th century. Beams, sash windows, wood fires and high ceilings are the backdrop for polished family furniture and delightfully arranged flowers. Good-sized bedrooms in restful colours have starched linen on gloriously comfortable beds, fluffy robes and binoculars for watching the wildlife; the beautiful, peaceful garden draws deer, badgers, foxes, hares. Breakfast is so local it could walk to the table — and includes homemade marmalade and jams. A lovely summery place — and only a mile off the A303!

Price	From £100. Singles from £70.
Rooms	3: 1 double; 1 twin/double, 1 double sharing bath (let to same party only).
Meals	Dinner £32.50. Pub 0.5 miles.
Closed	Christmas & New Year.
Directions	From the east, exit A303 on to B3081 for Bruton. After 1 mile, left into Rectory Lane. House 0.25 miles on right.

	Michael & Lavinia Dewar
	Rectory Farm House, Charlton Musgrove, Wincanton BA9 8ET
Tel	+44 (0)1963 34599
Mobile	+44 (0)7775 651868
Email	l.dewar@btconnect.com
Web	www.rectoryfarmhouse.com

Entry 462   Map 3

Somerset

The Cottage

An old farmworker's house, modernised and freshly spruced, stands proud in verdant countryside. Long views from the clipped garden drift into the distance; warm Sue (plus cute Jack Russells) greets you. You sleep in the extension to the front of the house; one bedroom has valley views, one has check curtains. Both have comfy beds, books, homely touches and peacefulness. Breakfast is a leisurely affair of local bacon and eggs. Tramp off on an inspiring walk — Leland trail, MacMillan Way — you're spoilt for choice — and return to the friendly living room. Escape London by train (95 minutes) and be collected from the station.

Price	£70. Singles from £45.
Rooms	2: 1 twin/double; 1 twin/double with separate bath.
Meals	Dinner £25. Packed lunch £5. Pub/restaurant 1 mile.
Closed	Christmas & rarely.
Directions	Maggs Lane east off the A371, halfway between Wincanton and Shepton Mallet.

Susan Begg
The Cottage,
Ansford Park Farm,
Ansford Park, Maggs Lane,
Castle Cary BA7 7JJ
Tel +44 (0)1963 351066
Email beggsusan@tiscali.co.uk

Entry 463   Map 3

Somerset

Westbrook House

David is an interior designer; Keith does gardens — hence this blend of good taste and style in a revamped 1870s house with generous, well-tended grounds. Wander through a young orchard, spot unusual plants, sit on stone benches or a sunny patio; a wildlife meadow contrasts with clipped lawns. Inside, every object has a story (your hosts are full of smiles and stories too): tapestries from India, a mirrored cabinet from an officer's mess, ornate brass lanterns. Light floods into the dining room as you breakfast on local treats — all the while absorbing the peace of this tranquil hamlet, where cows amble calmly down the lane.

Price	From £100. Singles £65-£80.
Rooms	3: 1 double, 1 twin; 1 double with separate bath.
Meals	Dinner £30. Pub/restaurant 4 miles.
Closed	Rarely.
Directions	From Glastonbury A361 to Shepton Mallet. After 2 miles, right for W. Bradley. Signed for W. Bradley; at fork in road, right for Baltonsborough. House on left.

Keith Anderson & David Mendel
Westbrook House,
West Bradley,
Glastonbury BA6 8LS
Tel +44 (0)1458 850604
Email mail@westbrook-bed-breakfast.co.uk
Web www.westbrook-bed-breakfast.co.uk

Entry 464   Map 3

Somerset

Chindit House

Inside this light and elegant Arts and Crafts mansion you will find fine architectural features, charming furniture, fresh flowers, vibrant paintings and compelling sculptures. There are long views over garden and town from the spacious living and dining rooms; bedrooms have spoilingly serious mattresses, good art, thick curtains and sleek, contemporary bathrooms. Felicity, an art consultant, is easy-going and fun and gives you an enormous breakfast: organic and locally sourced with speciality breads. You are a short hop from the town with its lively mix of exotic independent shops and cafés.

Price	£100–£125. Singles £70–£85.
Rooms	4: 2 doubles; 2 singles with shared bath (let to same party only).
Meals	Pubs/restaurants 5-minute walk.
Closed	Rarely.
Directions	In the centre of Glastonbury. Left at top of High Street on to Wells Road. House is about 200 yds along on left - just before corner with St Edmunds Road.

Felicity Wright
Chindit House, 23 Wells Road,
Glastonbury BA6 9DN
Tel   +44 (0)1458 830404
Mobile +44 (0)7812 077175
Email   enquiries@chindit-house.co.uk
Web   www.chindit-house.co.uk

Entry 465   Map 3

Somerset

Upper Crannel Farm Barn

Your views, across sheep and the lush flat Levels, reach to both Glastonbury and Wells; birds wing across a vast, silent sky. Phoebe has created a magical place: up you climb to the first floor of the barn, into a huge sitting room with a vast medieval painted fireplace. Each room is a work of art, with stacks of it on the walls – the kitchen is handsome and seductive, the bedroom is generous and richly clad. Breakfast will be left for you to cook when you want, you can walk across fields to climb Glastonbury Tor and Wells is just five miles. This house is a treat, and Phoebe is too. *Minimum stay two nights.*

Price	£120.
Rooms	1 double with sitting room & kitchen (extra bedrooms available).
Meals	Pubs/restaurants 2.5 miles.
Closed	Rarely.
Directions	A39 north of Glastonbury towards Wells. From r'bout by hospital go approx. 0.3 miles. At lollipops sharp left; follow single track. After one mile small bridge straight ahead and entrance to long tree-lined drive.

Phoebe Judah
Upper Cranel Farm Barn,
Glastonbury BA6 9AD
Tel   +44 (0)1458 831758
Email   phoebe.judah@btinternet.com

Entry 466   Map 3

Somerset

The Coach House

Take a glass of wine to your private courtyard and absorb the peace; or picnic in the gardens. In the hamlet of Dulcote, a mile from Wells, is your own two-storey coach house flooded with light, full of character and the latest mod cons. Downstairs, a black and white zebra theme plays; upstairs, white walls, crisp linen, high beams, and views that reach to the Mendips. And then there's Karen, full of ideas for your stay, who leaves eggs from her hens and other goodies in your fridge so you can breakfast in your jim-jams. For nature lovers and dog-walkers – meet Chumbawumba! – this is B&B at its most independent. Delightful.

Price	£95.
Rooms	Coach House: 1 double, 1 twin & sitting/dining room, sofabeds, kitchen, shower (let to same party only).
Meals	Pubs within 2 miles.
Closed	Rarely.
Directions	See owner website.

Karen Smallwood
The Coach House, Little Fountains,
Dulcote, Wells BA5 3NU
Tel   +44 (0)1749 678777
Mobile   +44 (0)7789 778880
Email   stay@littlefountains.co.uk
Web   www.littlefountains.co.uk

Entry 467   Map 3

Somerset

Stoberry House

Super swish B&B in this old coach house surrounded by 26 acres of parkland, but within walking distance of Wells; Frances has thought of everything and has oodles of local knowledge. Bedrooms are sumptuous and differently styled; two are in the main house, and there's one little love nest in a richly clad studio. Bathrooms are vamped up and spacious. There is a huge choice at breakfast: fresh fruit, porridge, boiled eggs with soldiers, prunes and berries, ham and salami, pancakes with grilled bacon, whatever you desire. Work it off with a stroll around the gorgeous gardens: the scents, sculptures and views are fantastic.

Price	£75-£155. Singles £65-£135.
Rooms	3: 1 double, 1 twin/double. Studio: 1 double & sitting room.
Meals	Supplement for cooked breakfast. Pubs/restaurants 0.5 miles.
Closed	Rarely.
Directions	A39 from Bristol, enter Wells, left into College Rd. Immediately left into Stoberry Park, follow track to Stoberry House at top of park.

Frances Young
Stoberry House,
Stoberry Park,
Wells BA5 3LD
Tel   +44 (0)1749 672906
Email   stay@stoberry-park.co.uk
Web   www.stoberry-park.co.uk

Entry 468   Map 3

Somerset

Beryl

A lofty, mullioned, low-windowed home – yet bright and devoid of Victorian gloom. Every bedroom has a talking point – an extravagantly draped four-poster, an original bath clad in mahogany reached by a tiny private stair... The flowery rooms in the attic have a 'gothic revival' feel, thanks to arched doorways. Holly and her gentle staff serve delicious breakfasts in the sunny dining room, and drinks in the richly elegant drawing room. The antiques are remarkable; visit the jewellery boutique in the Coach House. The old walled garden is full of roses, ancient figs and espaliered apples; the wonders of Wells lie just below.

Price	£90–£150.
Rooms	11: 3 doubles, 1 twin, 2 twins/doubles, 1 four-poster, 3 family rooms (2 with four-poster); 1 double with separate shower. Kitchenette; stairlift to first floor.
Meals	Pubs/restaurants within 1 mile.
Closed	Christmas.
Directions	Wells B3139 to Radstock. Signs to Horringtons; opp. BP garage, left into Hawkers Lane, by bus pull in. At top of lane, past Beryl sign; 500 yds to main gate.

Holly Nowell
Beryl,
Hawkers Lane,
Wells BA5 3JP

Tel	+44 (0)1749 678738
Email	stay@beryl-wells.co.uk
Web	www.beryl-wells.co.uk

Entry 469   Map 3

Somerset

numbertwelve

Simple pleasures: after a day exploring England's smallest city or the Mendip Hills, return to tea on the balcony and sunlight glinting on Wells Cathedral. Cathy's family house is spacious, secluded, fantastically located, with a private guest wing. Settle on huge sofas around the sitting room fire; snuggle in new king beds; awaken to Cathedral bells, a south-facing view over the lovely walled garden and kedgeree or corned beef hash. Cathy's art studio is next door and she'll help connect you to the local community: tiny Wells – a five-minute walk – bustles with markets, music, art and life.

Price	£80–£95. Singles £60–£80.
Rooms	2 doubles.
Meals	Pub 0.25 miles. Restaurant 0.5 miles.
Closed	Rarely.
Directions	From Bristol A39, 1st left into College Rd. Round into North Rd, house 150 yds on right. Train station 20-minute drive, bus station 15-minute walk.

Cathy Charles
numbertwelve,
12 North Road, Wells BA5 2TJ

Tel	+44 (0)1749 679406
Mobile	+44 (0)7980 881861
Email	ccharles@btinternet.com
Web	www.numbertwelve.info

Entry 470   Map 3

Somerset

Manor Farm

Hens, ducks and geese stroll around the pond and the peace is supreme. And there's a magical view of the cathedral: you can walk to Wells across the fields. Ros, a geologist and keen walker, looks after guests with immense kindness and is happy for folk to linger. The ancient beamed house is much loved and packed with books, pictures and a comfy mishmash of furniture. A log fire warms the garden suite in winter and French windows open to a walled garden, illuminated at night. Water comes from the spring, breakfast can be a different treat each day — in the lovely conservatory in summer. Bliss. *Pets welcome in garden suite.*

Price	£75-£95. Singles from £45.
Rooms	4: 1 suite & sitting room, 2 doubles; 1 twin/double with separate bath/shower.
Meals	Packed lunch & light meals from £6. Pubs/restaurants 1 mile.
Closed	Rarely.
Directions	From Wells, A371 for Shepton Mallet for 1 mile; left onto B3139. In Dulcote, left at stone fountain. House on right after Manor Barn.

	Rosalind Bufton
	Manor Farm, Dulcote, Wells BA5 3PZ
Tel	+44 (0)1749 672125
Mobile	+44 (0)7597 021708
Email	rosalind.bufton@talktalk.net
Web	www.wells-accommodation.co.uk

Entry 471   Map 3

Somerset

Hillview Cottage

Catherine is a wonderful host: warm-spirited, cultured and humorous. She knows the area well, and is happy to show you around Wells Cathedral — she's an official guide. This is a comfy tea-and-cakes family home with rugs on wooden floors and antique quilts. Bedrooms have a French feel, the bathroom an armchair for chatting and there's a friendly sitting room with an open fire. The stunning vaulted breakfast room has huge beams, an old Welsh dresser with hand painted mugs, a cheerful red Aga, a wood-burner to sit by and glorious views; breakfasts are superb. Guests love it here; excellent value too. *Self-catering in Garden Studio.*

Price	From £70. Singles from £35.
Rooms	2: 1 twin/double, 1 twin sharing bath (2nd room let to same party only).
Meals	Pubs 5-minute walk.
Closed	Rarely.
Directions	From Wells A371 to middle of Croscombe. Right at red phone box & then immed. right into lane. House up on left after 0.25 miles. Straight ahead into signed drive.

	Michael & Catherine Hay
	Hillview Cottage, Paradise Lane, Croscombe, Wells BA5 3RN
Tel	+44 (0)1749 343526
Mobile	+44 (0)7801 666146
Email	cathyhay@yahoo.co.uk
Web	www.hillviewcottage.me.uk

Entry 472   Map 3

Somerset

Pennard House

Splendid Pennard has been in Susie's family since the 1600s – a comfortably lived-in home with bedrooms as big as any we've seen. Discover a library and billiard room, a drawing room and dining room, and, upstairs, old-fashioned bedrooms with a mix of furniture, fine linen and beautiful views. The gardens are stunning with terraces leading on to sweeping lawns, roses, mature trees, a grass tennis court and a Victorian spring-fed swimming pool (swim with the newts!). The Georgian Coach House has been converted into a venue for weddings and conferences, and you're free to roam 60 tranquil acres of orchards, meadows and woods.

Price	£100. Singles from £50.
Rooms	3: 1 double, 1 twin; 1 twin/double with separate bath/shower.
Meals	Pub 2 miles.
Closed	Rarely.
Directions	From Shepton Mallet south on A37, through Pylle, over hill & next right to East Pennard. After 500 yds, right & follow lane past church to T-junc. at very top. House on left.

Martin & Susie Dearden
Pennard House, East Pennard,
Shepton Mallet BA4 6TP
Tel +44 (0)1749 860266
Mobile +44 (0)7767 487554
Email susie@pennardhouse.com
Web www.pennardhouse.com

Entry 473 Map 3

Somerset

Glyde Cottages

Smell Victoria's freshly baked bread as you enter this charmingly restored merchant's house – all 16th-century stone walls and aged oak beams. Relax in the peaceful guests' sitting room with its massive inglenook or stroll to the pub; wind your way up a spiral staircase to a beautifully rustic room with a hand-crafted bed and stripped floors. Children may venture up to the attic twin where a rocking horse waits; breakfasts are a home-cooked delight at the long wooden table. Strike out to Alfred's Tower – or opt for a plump slice of cake and croquet on the lawn. Just watch out for errant chickens!

Price	£95. Child £25.
Rooms	2: 1 double, 1 twin sharing bath (let to same party only).
Meals	Dinner, 2 courses, £13. Pub in village.
Closed	Rarely.
Directions	Sent on booking.

Victoria Savage
Glyde Cottages,
Upton Noble,
Shepton Mallet BA4 6BA
Tel +44 (0)1749 850230
Email v.savage@live.com
Web www.glydecottages.co.uk

Entry 474 Map 3

Somerset

Broadgrove House

Head down the long, private lane and arrive at Sarah's peaceful 17th-century stone house with its pretty walled cottage garden and views to Alfred's Tower and Longleat. Inside is just as special. Beams, flagstones and inglenook fireplaces have been sensitively restored; rugs, pictures, comfy sofas and polished antiques add warmth and serenity. The twin, at the end of the house, has its own sitting room. Breakfast on homemade and farmers' market produce before exploring Stourhead, Wells, Glastonbury. Sarah, engaging, well-travelled and a great cook, looks after you warmly. *Shooting available. Children by arrangement.*

Price	From £80. Twin £90. Singles £60.
Rooms	2: 1 twin & sitting room; 1 double with separate bath.
Meals	Pub/restaurant 1 mile.
Closed	Christmas.
Directions	Sent on booking.

Sarah Voller
Broadgrove House,
Leighton, Frome BA11 4PP

Tel	+44 (0)1373 836296
Mobile	+44 (0)7775 918388
Email	broadgrove836@tiscali.co.uk
Web	www.broadgrovehouse.co.uk

Entry 475   Map 3

Somerset

The Cyder Barn

Somerset cider was once pressed in this cute stone barn – now hugged by honeysuckle. Its beamed cathedral ceiling and new windows enclose a bijou studio for two. Pure pizzazz: spot-lit stone walls, dashing pinks, browns and terracottas on a king-size bed overhung by striped kilims, a swish wet room, and a gravel terrace and table in mature gardens alive with birds and bright colours. Step over to the main farmhouse for breakfast among art and antiques (for dinner, a good restaurant is opposite). Roger will relate the area's history and Jackie can show you her jewellery studio; both are happy, humorous and relaxed.

Price	£80.
Rooms	Barn: 1 twin/double.
Meals	Restaurant opposite.
Closed	Rarely.
Directions	Cottage & barn on Frome-Whatley road: 2nd house on right, past Whatley Village sign.

Jackie Truman
The Cyder Barn, Park Farm Cottage,
Whatley, Frome BA11 3JU

Tel	+44 (0)1373 836703
Mobile	+44 (0)7721 579814
Email	rwtrumanstamps.jtruman@virgin.net
Web	www.thecyderbarn.co.uk

Entry 476   Map 3

Somerset

Penny's Mill

The old part of Nunney village, with its small pretty streets, has a shop, a café and Rosie's gorgeous old stone millhouse down in the river valley. You are greeted warmly with tea and biscuits at a large wooden table in the kitchen, or in the drawing room upstairs with family photos, paintings and a big window looking over the millpond. Bedrooms are light and bright, painted in gentle blues and greens with a mix of antique and modern furniture; bathrooms have Bayliss & Harding soaps and white fluffy towels. Rosie's fine breakfast sets you up for a short walk to Nunney Castle, or a yomp further afield. *Cookery courses.*

Somerset

Claveys Farm

For the artistic seeker of inspiration, not those who thrill to standardised luxury. Fleur is a talented artist, Francis works for English Heritage, both have a passion for art, gardening and lively conversation. Rugs are time-worn, panelling and walls are distempered with natural pigment, bedrooms are better than simple, bathrooms old. From the Aga-warm kitchen of this lived-in, historic farmhouse come eggs from the hens, honey from the bees, oak-smoked bacon from Fleur's rare-breed pigs and homemade bread and jams. Fields, footpaths and woodland for walks, and a garden for children to adore. Bring your woolly jumpers!

Price	£80-£85.		Price	£70. Singles £50.
Rooms	3: 1 double; 1 twin/double, 1 double sharing bath (let to same party only).		Rooms	2: 1 double/family; 1 twin with separate bath (shared with owner sometimes).
Meals	Dinner £25. Pub 300 yds.		Meals	Dinner, 3 courses, £25. BYO. Packed lunch £7. Pub in village.
Closed	Rarely.		Closed	Rarely.
Directions	Sent on booking.		Directions	At Mells Green on Leigh-on-Mendip road SW from Mells (NGR ST718452). Past red phone box; house last on right before speed de-restriction signs. If lost, Mells PO, by village pond, has map outside.

Rosie Davies
Penny's Mill,
Horn Street, Nunney,
Frome BA11 4NP
Tel   +44 (0)1373 836210
Email   stay@pennysmill.com
Web   www.stayatpennysmill.com

Fleur & Francis Kelly
Claveys Farm,
Mells,
Frome BA11 3QP
Tel   +44 (0)1373 814651
Mobile   +44 (0)7968 055398
Email   bandb@fleurkelly.com

Entry 477   Map 3

Entry 478   Map 3

Somerset

The Old Vicarage

The vicarage sits at the foot of Jack and Jill's hill in a sleepy Mendip village. Your room has its own courtyard entrance and comfy sitting room, goose down on an antique French bed, beautiful carpets designed by Lizzy and a limestone wet room. Your hosts are informal and friendly and their home exudes charm: a medieval stone floor in the hall, old flagstones, flowers, wood-burners and a pretty kitchen. Hens potter in the garden, carp laze in the canal pond; breakfast when you want on a full English, garden compotes and delicious coffee. National Trust gems and splendid walking on the Colliers Way will keep you busy.

Price	£95.
Rooms	1 double & sitting room.
Meals	Pub 100 yds.
Closed	Christmas; two weeks in August & occasionally.
Directions	The Old Vicarage is at the centre of Kilmersdon opposite the church. The village is on the B3139 off the A362 Radstock to Frome road.

Elizabeth Ashard
The Old Vicarage,
Church Street, Kilmersdon,
Radstock BA3 5TA
Tel   +44 (0)1761 436926
Email   lizzyashard@btinternet.com
Web   www.theoldvicaragesomerset.co.uk

Somerset

Flint House

Off a village lane, up a sweeping drive, is an elegant 18th-century home with a private chapel. Smart yet relaxed, it's a perfect mix: a sophisticated sitting room with low valley views, a roaring fire in the snug. Be seduced by the Mendips in your modern-classic bedroom with roll top bath; and a cosy twin for a larger party. Breakfast treats await on the summer veranda, from pancakes to poached plums. Take to the tennis court or sit under wisteria, cake in hand, and gaze on the noble garden — Jacquie is loving its restoration. Pop to a local or arrange dinner with your relaxed hosts. Walks galore — and Bath irresistibly near.

Price	From £85. Singles £60.
Rooms	2: 1 double; 1 twin sharing shower (let to same party only).
Meals	Dinner, 3 courses, £20-£25. Picnic lunch £8. Afternoon tea £4. Pubs 10-minute walk.
Closed	Rarely.
Directions	Radstock A367 to Shepton Mallet. At r'bout B3139 to Frome, take right signed Holcombe. At village shop left into Common Lane. House after chapel on left through green gates.

Jacquie Hamshaw Thomas
Flint House, Common Lane,
Holcombe, Radstock BA3 5DS
Tel   +44 (0)1761 232419
Mobile   +44 (0)7723 031378
Email   stay@flinthousebandb.co.uk
Web   www.flinthousebandb.co.uk

Somerset

The Post House

Four centuries old, this was Chewton Mendip's post office; now it's a delightful home with a sunny feel. Smiling, stylish Karen loves meeting new people – make the most of her and John's knowledge of Bath, Bristol and Wells. After a day's exploring, return to fresh, lovely bedrooms and bathrooms; the suite, limewashed, pretty and private, has oak floors and a fridge. Huge flagstones cover the oldest part downstairs, there's a big stone fireplace in the Old Bakery Cottage and the odd low beam; pale walls display charming sketches from an artist friend, much of the furniture is French country, and a Gallic-rustic mood prevails.

Price	£80–£120.
Rooms	3: 1 double, 1 suite. Old Bakery Cottage: 1 double.
Meals	Pub 0.5 miles.
Closed	Rarely.
Directions	Situated 0.5 miles south of Chewton Mendip centre. The Post House can be found on left hand side heading south on A39. Private parking and entrance are found at rear of property.

Karen Price
The Post House,
Bath Way, Chewton Mendip,
Wells BA3 4NS
Tel   +44 (0)1761 241704
Email   info@theposthousebandb.co.uk
Web   www.theposthousebandb.co.uk

Entry 481   Map 3

Somerset

Harptree Court

A gorgeous Georgian house that has been in Charles' family for generations. Inside all is elegant and grand, but this is very much a family home; there's a welcoming log fire in the hall and Charles and Linda are charming and relaxed. The interior gleams with flowers, art and polished wood, and the dining room looks onto the beautiful garden; warm, sunny bedrooms have delicate fabrics, china pieces and antiques, and bathrooms sparkle. An excellent breakfast of garden fruits, local honey and sausages sets you up for a walk in the grounds: acres of parkland with ponds, an ancient bridge, carpets of spring flowers. A peaceful delight.

Price	£120.
Rooms	4: 3 doubles, 1 twin/double.
Meals	Pub 300 yds.
Closed	Rarely.
Directions	Turn off A368 onto B3114 towards Chewton Mendip. After approx. 0.5 miles, right into drive entrance, straight after 1st x-roads. Left at top of drive.

Linda Hill
Harptree Court,
East Harptree, Bristol BS40 6AA
Tel   +44 (0)1761 221729
Mobile   +44 (0)7970 165576
Email   bandb@harptreecourt.co.uk
Web   www.harptreecourt.co.uk

Entry 482   Map 3

Somerset

The Tithe Barn

You are in a quiet, well-kept village surrounded by softly rolling hills, but the joys of Bath and Bristol are a short drive. Down a narrow lane with lawns and orchard on either side, find Stephen and Pauline's pinky-red stone 15th-century tithe barn. Step up the spiral staircase leading to a gallery to the roomy, simple bedrooms; there are views from both rooms over the lovely garden and bathrooms have fine toiletries. You breakfast well in the conservatory: smoked salmon, local sausages and bacon, home-laid eggs, delicious homemade jams, honey from the garden. There are smart new stables for your horse, too.

Price	£70-£100. Singles £70-£90.
Rooms	2 doubles.
Meals	Pubs/restaurants 2 miles.
Closed	Rarely.
Directions	From Chew Magna on B3130, right after about 2 miles at little white cottage in middle of road. Right in village to Sandy Lane. House 200 yds on right.

Stephen & Pauline Croucher
The Tithe Barn,
Sandy Lane, Stanton Drew,
Bristol BS39 4EL
Tel   +44 (0)1275 331887
Email   stephen.jcroucher@btinternet.com
Web   www.thetithebarnsomerset.co.uk

Entry 483   Map 3

Somerset

Burrington Farm

High in the Mendips, Ros and Barry's 15th-century longhouse is blissfully rural, yet Bristol, Bath and Wells are close. Their wonderful house glows: rugs and flagstones, books, burnished beams, paintings and fine old furniture. Guests have a cosy sitting room and bedrooms are charming; you'll need to be nimble to negotiate ancient steps and stairs. For those who prefer a bit more privacy there's a lovely family room in a separate green oak barn — stunningly converted and with views over the enchanting garden. Wake for a locally sourced breakfast round a big table. A friendly, relaxed and special place. *Airport pick-up offered.*

Price	£80-£120.
Rooms	4: 1 double; 1 double, 1 twin sharing bath (let to same party only). Garden Room: 1 family room.
Meals	Pub 10-minute walk.
Closed	Christmas.
Directions	A368 Bath to Weston-super-Mare, between Blagdon and Churchill. Take Burrington village sign, on to square with school on right. House 4th on left after Parish Rooms, immed. after Stable Cottage.

Barry & Ros Smith
Burrington Farm,
Burrington BS40 7AD
Tel   +44 (0)1761 462127
Mobile +44 (0)7825 237144
Email   unwind@burringtonfarm.co.uk
Web   www.unwindatburringtonfarm.co.uk

Entry 484   Map 3

Somerset

Stonebridge

A country house with scrumptious food, a friendly black labrador and croquet on the lawn. When their daughters flew the nest, Liz and Richard opened an independent wing of their listed house: perfect for families and couples. You have two pretty bedrooms (one up, one down) with country furniture and super bathrooms. In winter, a wood-burner keeps your little sitting room cosy; in summer, laze in a sea of flowers. You feast on local eggs, homemade bread and delicious dinners with garden veg. Just off the village road, it's close to Bristol airport, the M5, Wells… early days, but with hosts this friendly you can't go wrong.

Price	£75.
Rooms	2: 1 double, 1 twin/double.
Meals	Dinner £17–£20. Pub 2 miles.
Closed	Christmas.
Directions	Sent on booking.

Richard & Liz Annesley
Stonebridge,
Wolvershill Road,
Banwell BS29 6DR
Tel +44 (0)1934 823518
Email liz.annesley@talktalk.net
Web www.stonebridgebandb.co.uk

Entry 485   Map 3

Somerset

Barton Drove Cottage

Come for the views – on a clear day you can see the Black Mountains. The pretty cottage extension is tucked into the hill so the first-floor drawing room opens directly to the terrace. All is polished and spotless inside: pretty bedrooms have patterned rugs on soft carpets, goose down and crisp linen, fresh flowers, gleaming bathrooms and a loo with a view. Charming, child-friendly, Sarah gives you bacon and sausages from Mendip piggies, eggs from her hens, soft fruit from the garden and maybe pheasant casserole for supper. Roe deer in the field, primroses in the woods, wonderful walking on Wavering Down.

Price	£70. Singles £35.
Rooms	2: 1 double; 1 twin with separate bath.
Meals	Dinner from £17.50. Packed lunch £5. Pub 1 mile.
Closed	Rarely.
Directions	From A38 0.5 miles up Winscombe Hill. When road begins to descend, left between houses onto unmade track. Cottage 100 yds on the left.

Sarah Gunn
Barton Drove Cottage,
Winscombe Hill, Winscombe BS25 1DJ
Tel +44 (0)1934 842373
Mobile +44 (0)7736 417363
Email sarahgunn2000@hotmail.com
Web www.bartondrovecottage.com

Entry 486   Map 3

Somerset

Church House

Feel happy in this warm Georgian rectory with sweeping views over gardens, seaside homes and the dramatic Bristol channel. Tony and Jane are great fun, enormously generous and love what they do. Bedrooms are large, pristine and indulgent with goose down duvets as soft as a cloud, swish modern bathrooms, huge towels and thoughtful extras like fluffy hot water bottles and scrumptious biscuits. Breakfasts are a grand feast of eggs from their hens, organic sausages and homemade preserves, all served on delightful china at a long mahogany table. Take the whole house and be cosseted – great for large gatherings.

Staffordshire

Stoop House Farm

Step through a rosy arch from this enchanting 18th-century farmhouse: the view across garden, fields and valley will bowl you over. Inside, oak beams, heated flagged floors, a cast-iron range, a bedroom shot through with olive and gold. In this thriving conservation village (with lovely pub), the farm draws on the latest in green design, while two Andalusian horses share the grounds with sheep, pigs and poultry – expect superb eggs at breakfast! Your warm, lovely hosts, she a midwife, he a climber, share their passion for the outdoors with their guests – and the Peak District National Park lies at your feet.

Price	£85. Singles £65.		Price	From £90. Singles £75.
Rooms	5: 4 doubles, 1 twin.		Rooms	1 suite & sitting room.
Meals	Pubs 400 yds.		Meals	Pub 1-minute walk.
Closed	Rarely.		Closed	Rarely.
Directions	M5 junc. 21, follow signs for Kewstoke. After Old Manor Inn on right, left up Anson Rd. At T-junc. right into Kewstoke Rd. On for 1 mile; church on right; drive between church & church hall.		Directions	From Leek A523 towards Ashbourne. At crossroads left B5053. Thro' Onecote, up hill then 2nd right signed Butterton. Thro' village past shop on right, 200 yds, then right fork. House 2nd on right.

	Jane & Tony Chapman		Andrea Evans
	Church House,		Stoop House Farm,
	27 Kewstoke Road, Kewstoke,		Butterton, Leek ST13 7SY
	Weston-super-Mare BS22 9YD	Tel	+44 (0)1538 304486
Tel	+44 (0)1934 633185	Mobile	+44 (0)7966 135979
Email	churchhouse@kewstoke.net	Email	bnfrench@yahoo.co.uk
Web	www.churchhousekewstoke.co.uk	Web	www.stoophousefarm.co.uk

Staffordshire

Martinslow Farm

High up in the Peaks, lost to the world with the most amazing, uninterrupted views, this listed 300-year-old farmhouse once sheltered donkeys... the accommodation has since stepped up a gear. The sitting room is warm and inviting with beams, log-burner and muted chintz. Peaceful, comfortable bedrooms in the stable block have a country, cosy feel; the Tack Room has mahogany beds and the rooms can interconnect for families. Diana and Richard love country pursuits, dogs and good company. Perfect tranquillity, a sheltered patio for those great views, and delicious locally sourced food. *Children over nine welcome.*

Price	From £95. Singles £60.
Rooms	Stables: 1 double, 1 twin.
Meals	Dinner, 3 courses, £27.50. Supper £20. Pub 15-minute walk.
Closed	Rarely.
Directions	A523 Leek-Ashbourne. At Winkhill, signs to Grindon. Over x-roads, left at T-junc.; 300 yds; house on right below lane.

Richard & Diana Bloor
Martinslow Farm,
Winkhill,
Leek ST13 7PZ
Tel   +44 (0)1538 304500
Email   richard.bloor@btclick.com
Web   www.martinslowfarm.co.uk

Entry 489   Map 8

Staffordshire

Manor House Farm

A working rare-breed farm in an area of great beauty, a Jacobean farmhouse with oodles of history. Behind mullioned windows is a glorious interior crammed with curios and family pieces, panelled walls and wonky floors... hurl a log on the fire and watch it roar. Three rooms have four-posters; one bathroom flaunts rich red antique fabrics. Chris and Margaret are passionate hosts who serve perfect breakfasts (eggs from their own hens, sausages and bacon from their pigs and home-grown tomatoes) and give you the run of a garden resplendent with plants, vistas, tennis, croquet, two springer spaniels and one purring cat. Heaven.

Price	£62-£75. Singles £40-£50.
Rooms	4: 1 double, 2 four-posters, 1 four poster family room for 4.
Meals	Pub/restaurant 1.5 miles.
Closed	Christmas.
Directions	From Uttoxeter, B5030 for Rocester. Beyond JCB factory, left onto B5031. At T-junc. after church, right onto B5032. 1st left for Prestwood. Farm 0.75 miles on right over crest of hill, through arch.

Chris & Margaret Ball
Manor House Farm, Prestwood,
Denstone, Uttoxeter ST14 5DD
Tel   +44 (0)1889 590415
Mobile +44 (0)7976 767629
Email   cm_ball@yahoo.co.uk
Web   www.towersabovetherest.com

Entry 490   Map 8

Suffolk

Pavilion House

A conservation village surrounded by chalk grassland – famous for its flora, fauna and butterflies; marked walks are straight from this 16-year-old red-brick house. Friendly Gretta teaches cooking and you are in for a treat: homemade cake, enormous breakfasts with her own bread and jams, proper dinners or simple suppers. Sleep peacefully in traditional, comfortable bedrooms (one up, two down) with crisp linen and TVs. There's a guest sitting room too: English comfort with an oriental feel, parquet floors, antiques, original drawings, a cosy log-burner. Wander the superb garden. Newmarket and Cambridge are close.

Suffolk

The Old Vicarage

Up the avenue of fine horse chestnut trees to find just what you'd expect from an old vicarage: a Pembroke table in the flagstoned hall, a refectory table sporting copies of *The Field*, a piano, silver pheasants, a log fire that warms the sitting room and homemade cake on arrival. The house is magnificent, with huge rooms and passageways. Comfy mattresses are dressed in old-fashioned counterpanes, and the double has hill views. Weave your way through the branches of the huge copper beech to the garden that Jane loves; she grows her own vegetables, keeps hens and cooks a fine breakfast. *Children over seven welcome.*

Price	£75. Singles £45.	Price	£80. Singles £50.
Rooms	3: 1 double, 1 twin/double, 1 single each with separate bath/shower.	Rooms	2: 1 double; 1 twin with separate bath. Single room available with either room (let to same party only).
Meals	Lunch from £10. Dinner from £25. Supper from £15. BYO. Pub 1.5 miles.	Meals	Dinner £20. BYO. Packed lunch £6. Pub 1 mile.
Closed	Christmas.	Closed	Christmas.
Directions	4 miles south of Newmarket. A1304, over r'bout with horse statue, further 1.5 miles, then left to Dullingham. Pavilion House 1st on right after 1 mile. Train station 400 yds.	Directions	Cambridge, A1307 Haverhill. Left Withersfield; T-junc., left. Almost 3 miles on, high yew hedge; 'Concealed Entrance' sign on left, sharp turn into drive.

Gretta & David Bredin
Pavilion House, 133 Station Road,
Dullingham, Newmarket CB8 9UT
Tel +44 (0)1638 508005
Mobile +44 (0)7776 197709
Email gretta@thereliablesauce.co.uk
Web www.pavilionhousebandb.co.uk

Entry 491   Map 9

Jane Sheppard
The Old Vicarage, Great Thurlow,
Newmarket CB9 7LE
Tel +44 (0)1440 783209
Mobile +44 (0)7887 717429
Email s.j.sheppard@hotmail.co.uk
Web www.thurlowvicarage.co.uk

Entry 492   Map 9

Suffolk

The Lucy Redman Garden

Off a country lane, through an estate village, hides this immaculate, thatched, 1930s house – a gem. Lucy and Dominic are full of life and fun. Lucy is an artistic garden designer so all glows with texture and colour, and the garden is a stunner. Family antiques blend with multi-cultural pieces, there are books, paintings, pets, piano, a drawing room fire, and, at the furthest end, a bedroom for you: an ethnic hanging on the wall, organic chocolates on the bed. Wake to eggs from the hens, bacon from the pigs, plum jams from the trees. Views swoop over garden, grazing horses and miles of Suffolk countryside. A happy place!

Price	£70. Singles £65.
Rooms	1 double.
Meals	Pubs/restaurants 2 miles.
Closed	Rarely.
Directions	See owner website.

Lucy Redman & Dominic Watts
The Lucy Redman Garden,
6 The Village, Rushbrooke,
Bury St Edmunds IP30 0ER
Tel   +44 (0)1284 386250
Email   lucyredman7@gmail.com
Web   www.lucyredman.co.uk

Entry 493   Map 10

Suffolk

The Old Manse Barn

A large, lush loft apartment in sleepy Suffolk; this living/eating/sleeping space of blond wood, white walls and big windows has an urban feel yet overlooks glorious countryside. Secluded from the main house, in a timber-clad barn, the style is thrillingly modern: leather sofas, glass dining table, stainless steel kitchenette. Floor lights dance off the walls, CD surround-sound creates mood and you can watch the stars from your bed. Homemade granola, local bread and ham in the fridge – breakfast when you like. There's peace for romance, solitude for work, a garden to sit in and friendly Sue to suggest the best pubs.

Price	From £70.
Rooms	Apartment: 1 double & kitchenette.
Meals	Pubs within walking distance.
Closed	Rarely.
Directions	A134 towards Bury St Edmunds & Sudbury; A1141 Lavenham, left after 1.4 miles towards Cockfield & Stowmarket; house 1.2 miles on right.

Sue & Ian Jones
The Old Manse Barn, Chapel Road,
Cockfield, Bury St Edmunds IP30 0HE
Tel   +44 (0)1284 828120
Mobile +44 (0)7931 753996
Email   bookings@theoldmansebarn.co.uk
Web   www.theoldmansebarn.co.uk

Entry 494   Map 10

Suffolk

16 Bolton Street

The house is 15th century and rests on a quiet street in lovely, bustling Lavenham: part medieval, part Tudor, this is one of England's showpiece towns. Heavy beams, low doorways, books, magazines, fresh flowers and gentle hosts create a warm happy feel; steep oak stairs lead to fresh, cosy bedrooms where patchwork quilts, colourful cushions and handmade curtains abound. Gillian likes nothing better than to spoil her guests with breakfasts of local sausages and bacon, potato cakes, very special mushrooms and fresh fruit. A delightful, relaxed, generous place to stay. *Minimum stay two nights at weekends.*

Price	£80–£90.
Rooms	2: 1 twin/double, 1 double.
Meals	Pubs/restaurants within walking distance.
Closed	Rarely.
Directions	From the market square in Lavenham, pass The Great House Restaurant, then left into Bolton Street. Long pink house at bottom on right. Park outside to unload; Gillian will help with parking.

Gillian de Lucy
16 Bolton Street,
Lavenham CO10 9RG
Tel +44 (0)1787 249046
Mobile +44 (0)7747 621096
Email gdelucy@aol.com
Web www.guineahouse.co.uk

Entry 495 Map 10

Suffolk

Milden Hall

Generations of Hawkins have lived in this seemingly grand 16th-century hall farmhouse with its enormous sash windows and vast fireplaces. Bedrooms ranging from big to huge are elegantly old-fashioned and filled with fascinating wall hangings, maps, prints, etchings and lovely furniture. Juliet is a passionate conservationist, full of ideas for making the most of the surrounding countryside, on foot or by bike. Expect delicious home-grown bacon, sausages, bantam eggs and compotes for breakfast in the sunny living room, warmed by a wood-burner in the winter. Great fun, with a friendly, family feel. *Self-catering barn for groups.*

Price	£65–£90. Singles from £45.
Rooms	3: 2 twins, 1 double/family room, with separate shared bath & 2nd wc.
Meals	Occasional supper from £20. BYO. Pubs/restaurants 2–3 miles.
Closed	Rarely.
Directions	Lavenham, A1141 for Monks Eleigh. After 2 miles, right to Milden. At x-roads, right, Sudbury B1115. Hall's long drive 0.25 miles on left. Train to Sudbury 7 miles.

Christopher & Juliet Hawkins
Milden Hall,
Milden,
Lavenham CO10 9NY
Tel +44 (0)1787 247235
Email hawkins@thehall-milden.co.uk
Web www.thehall-milden.co.uk

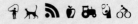

Entry 496 Map 10

Suffolk

The Old Rectory Country House

In a hamlet of thatched cottages by the Church of St Lawrence sits a handsome rectory, quietly steeped in ancient history. Find elegant proportions, family antiques and owner Frank who asks only that you feel at home. The drawing room has an honesty bar and walking maps, the garden is a delight and you can use the pool. Feel spoiled in big smart bedrooms with pretty fabrics, smooth linen and lovely views; the Stables are charming with books, a garden suite and comfy sofas. Be lazy and have continental breakfast in your room, or rouse yourself for local sausages and bacon by a log fire in the magnificent dining room. A treat.

Price	£105–£130. Singles £85 (Sun–Thurs only).
Rooms	6: 2 doubles, 1 twin/double. The Old Stables: 3 doubles with sitting/dining room & kitchen (self-catering available).
Meals	Simple supper & lunch from £25. Pub 1 mile.
Closed	Rarely.
Directions	Sent on booking.

Frank Lawrenson
The Old Rectory Country House,
Rectory Road, Great Waldingfield,
Sudbury CO10 0TL
Tel   +44 (0)1787 372428
Email   info@theoldrectorycountryhouse.co.uk
Web   www.theoldrectorycountryhouse.co.uk

Entry 497   Map 10

Suffolk

Hill House

Nayland is a charming village and this apricot-coloured, listed house sits on a quiet lane. Enter an unusual tunnel hall with flagstones, rugs and fresh flowers, to find a beamed drawing room and an elegant dining room. There are well-polished antiques, good art, and creamy colours dotted with bright chintz; smart, fresh bedrooms have good views over the pretty garden and you get a choice of pillows. Pauline happily shares her home with you and provides generous Aga breakfasts — with homemade bread and preserves. Good walks abound in Constable country; Beth Chatto gardens nearby. *Min. two nights at weekends in summer.*

Price	From £78. Singles from £45.
Rooms	2: 1 twin/double; 1 double with separate bath.
Meals	Pub/restaurant a short walk.
Closed	Christmas & New Year.
Directions	Enter village from A134 into Bear St. Past T-junction into Birch St. 100 yds turn left, house 70 yds uphill on right.

Pauline & David Heigham
Hill House,
Gravel Hill,
Nayland CO6 4JB
Tel   +44 (0)1206 262782
Email   heighamhillhouse@hotmail.com
Web   www.heighamhillhouse.co.uk

Entry 498   Map 10

Suffolk

West Lodge

This beautifully mellowed brick 1600s coach house has the original huge front door and stunning views from the garden over Dedham Vale. There's a comfortable snug for guests with pinky, terracotta walls and a red sofa; go up your own staircase to simple, light and airy bedrooms and old-fashioned, compact bathrooms. Friendly Penny, and ex-chef Paul, will give you local bacon and sausages and very good dinners in a colourful dining room stuffed full of gleaming antiques and silver – or on balmy evenings in the summer house, maybe with a cocktail up in the trees first. *Babes in arms & over eights welcome. French & Spanish spoken.*

Price	£70–£75. Singles £50–£60.
Rooms	3: 2 doubles, 1 family suite.
Meals	Dinner, 3 courses, £22.50. Pub/restaurant 140 yds.
Closed	Rarely.
Directions	From A12 exit for B1070, at junc. left towards East Bergholt. At Carriers Arms pub (0.8 miles) right. At post office (0.4 miles), right into Cemetery Lane. Entrance to house 80 yds on left.

Paul & Penny Lewis
West Lodge, The Street,
East Bergholt, Colchester CO7 6TF

Tel	+44 (0)1206 299808
Mobile	+44 (0)7886 075369
Email	westlodgebandb@talktalk.net
Web	www.westlodge.uk.com

Entry 499   Map 10

Suffolk

Poplar Farm House

Only a few miles from Ipswich but down a green lane, this rambling farmhouse has a pretty, whitewashed porch and higgledy-piggledy roof. All light, elegant and spacious with wonderful flowers, art, sumptuous soft furnishings (made by Sally) and quirky sculptures; expect comfy beds, laundered linen and smart bathrooms. Sally is relaxed and friendly and will give you eggs from her handsome hens, homemade bread, veg from the garden on an artistically laid table. Play tennis, swim, steam in the sauna or book one of Sally's arts and crafts courses, then wander in the woods beyond with beautiful dogs Shale and Rune. Great value.

Price	£65. Singles £45.
Rooms	3: 2 doubles, 1 twin sharing 2 bath/shower rooms. Yurt: 1 double.
Meals	Dinner, 3 courses, £15–£25. Packed lunch £7. Pub 1 mile.
Closed	Rarely.
Directions	From Ipswich A1214 signed Colchester. After 2 miles at Holiday Inn turn right (at lights) onto A1071, signed Hadleigh. Poplar Lane is immediately on left. House first on right.

Sally Sparrow
Poplar Farm House, Poplar Lane,
Sproughton, Ipswich IP8 3HL

Tel	+44 (0)1473 601211
Mobile	+44 (0)7950 767226
Email	sparrowsally@aol.com
Web	www.poplarfarmhousesuffolkbb.eu

Entry 500   Map 10

Suffolk

Aldham Mill

Roses dance over the red-brick mill, a river tinkles past, Suffolk history abounds. The Burton family saved the listed mill from dereliction, and the inside teems with family treasures: open fires, fine china, lace-edged towels, tip-top wool and horsehair mattresses. Children love the granary games room with ping-pong – worthy of an Enid Blyton novel. Breakfast on homemade bread and marmalade, local eggs and bacon, then stroll among the snowdrops; Lady Burton opens her gardens for charity in summer. A whisper of a bygone age, and a wonderful, traditional launch pad for Constable country. *Stair lift to single room.*

Suffolk

The Cottage at The Old Wheelwrights

Your own romantic cottage, detached from the owners' house, has been renovated well: soft colours, terracotta tiles, painted wood. Cosy with underfloor heating and wood-burner, the TV-free sitting room has a breakfast area, books, maps, striped blinds and a basket full of logs. The warm wet-room is downstairs; up the seagrass stairs is a comfy brass bed and curtains made out of pretty scarves. A piping hot breakfast of hash browns, local eggs and the full Monty is delivered by friendly Bel; by the door, with a clambering vine, is a flowery patio and a bench for enjoying the evening sun. Stroll to the pub for a good supper.

Price	From £70. Singles £40.
Rooms	2: 1 twin; 1 single with separate bath.
Meals	Pub/restaurant 0.5 miles.
Closed	Christmas & rarely.
Directions	A1071 to Hadleigh. Down High St to end, then right signed Aldham & Elmsett. After 0.5 miles road crosses Hadleigh bypass. Mill immed. on left (don't go to Aldham village). Trains to Ipswich, 10 miles; Colchester 8 miles.

Price	£80. Singles £65.
Rooms	Cottage: 1 double.
Meals	Packed lunch available. Pub 5-minute walk.
Closed	Rarely.
Directions	Sent on booking.

	Priscilla Burton
	Aldham Mill,
	Aldham Mill Hill,
	Hadleigh,
	Ipswich IP7 6LE
Tel	+44 (0)1473 822486
Email	priscillaburton@btinternet.com

	Stewart & Bel Goldie-Morrison
	The Cottage at The Old Wheelwrights,
	Low St, Brandeston, Woodbridge IP13 7AN
Tel	+44 (0)1728 684862
Mobile	+44 (0)7798 525212
Email	bgm@countrytrust.org.uk
Web	www.oldwheelwrightscottage.co.uk

Suffolk

Church House

A short hop from riverside Woodbridge and musical Snape Maltings, between a conservation churchyard and a history-rich field, is something different and unusual: a customised house of gentle colours and textures, home to an architect and a designer. From the hand-carved, wood-reclaimed porch to the lovely wildlife garden, there's a feeling of warmth and delight. Under the eaves: two jewel-bright bedrooms full of books and fresh flowers. In the kitchen: a big farmhouse table laid for beautiful breakfasts. And, a short walk away, "one of the best gastropubs in East Anglia". Brilliant! *Children over eight welcome.*

Price	£70–£80. Singles £60–£70.
Rooms	2: 1 twin/double; 1 twin with separate bath/shower.
Meals	Pub 1 mile.
Closed	Rarely.
Directions	From A12 at Woodbridge take B1079 dir. Grundisburgh. After approx. 4 miles double bend round Burgh church. House opp. the Clopton parish sign.

Sally Pirkis
Church House,
Clopton,
Woodbridge IP13 6QB
Tel +44 (0)1473 735350
Email sallypirkis@gmail.com
Web www.churchhousebandbsuffolk.co.uk

Entry 503   Map 10

Suffolk

Bealings House

A picture postcard of a setting and a large, beautifully proportioned, Georgian house sitting high in mature parkland. Charming Selina and Jonathan give the whole thing an unpretentious feel and you are encouraged to make yourself at home – among family memorabilia, grand marble fireplaces, Irish linen, well-trodden floorboards, fading Persian rugs, first-class antiques, gilt-framed landscape paintings and bursts of dried flowers. Bedrooms and bathrooms are fearfully old-fashioned and you may need to bring an extra jumper if you are a pampered city-dweller. Quirky, with wonderful grounds.

Price	From £70. Singles from £50.
Rooms	3: 1 double, 1 twin each with separate bath/shower. Apartment: 1 double, sitting room, kitchen & separate bath.
Meals	Pub/restaurant 1 mile.
Closed	Rarely.
Directions	From Ipswich A12 N. At Woodbridge r'bout, N on A12; after 150 yds left at Seckford Hall Hotel sign. After 1 mile left at T-junc. at bottom of hill; then 1st right. Entrance immed. on right.

Selina & Jonathan Peto
Bealings House,
Great Bealings,
Woodbridge IP13 6NP
Tel +44 (0)1394 382631
Email jonathanpeto@btinternet.com
Web www.bealingshouse.co.uk

Entry 504   Map 10

Suffolk

Melton Hall

There's more than a touch of theatre to this beautiful listed house. The dining room is opulent red; the drawing room, with its delicately carved mantelpiece and comfortable sofas, has French windows to the terrace. There's a four-poster in one bedroom, an antique French bed in another and masses of fresh flowers and books. The garden includes an orchid and wildflower meadow: a designated County Wildlife Site. River walks, the coast and the Saxon burial site Sutton Hoo are close. Generous Cindy, her delightful children, little dog Poppy and cats Bea and Bubbles, all give a great welcome.

Price	£105-£130. Singles from £60.
Rooms	3: 1 double; 1 double, 1 single sharing bath.
Meals	Dinner, 1-3 courses, £19-£38. BYO. Pubs/restaurants nearby.
Closed	Rarely.
Directions	From A12 Woodbridge bypass, exit at r'bout for Melton. Follow for 1 mile to lights; there, right. Immediately on right.

	Lucinda de la Rue
	Melton Hall,
	Woodbridge IP12 1PF
Tel	+44 (0)1394 388138
Mobile	+44 (0)7775 797075
Email	cindy@meltonhall.co.uk
Web	www.meltonhall.co.uk

Entry 505   Map 10

Suffolk

The Old Rectory

Through the front door to a generously proportioned and flagstoned hall and a smiling welcome from Christopher. Archways lead down the corridor to the library (cosy with maps, books and open fire) and a tall elegant staircase leads to spacious bedrooms, one with delightful bow windows and a view of the sea. There are sash windows and shutters, pelmets and antiques, heaps of good books. Outside: 20 acres of woodlands, meadows, paddocks, croquet lawn and vegetable garden (walled and wonderful). Walks galore on the Deben Peninsula, music at Snape Maltings; it's Suffolk at its best and peace reigns supreme.

Price	From £75. Singles from £50.
Rooms	3: 2 doubles, 1 twin. Extra bed available.
Meals	Dinner, 3 courses, £30. Supper, 2 courses, £20. Pub 5-minute walk.
Closed	Occasionally.
Directions	From A12 Woodbridge bypass A1152. After railway line at r'bout, B1083 for 7 miles to Alderton. Driveway on left after 30mph & Alderton signs.

	Christopher Langley
	The Old Rectory,
	Alderton,
	Woodbridge IP12 3DE
Tel	+44 (0)1394 410003
Email	clangley@keme.co.uk
Web	www.oldrectoryaldertonbandb.co.uk

Entry 506   Map 10

Suffolk

Dunan House

Relish new-laid eggs, homemade bread and marmalade for breakfast – wild mushrooms too sometimes. This is a relaxed and lovely place to stay, with entertaining hosts and a lively décor: Ann is a potter, Simon an illustrator, and their artistry is abundant. Bedrooms are upbeat and attractive, with rugs, silk blinds and imaginative and decorative touches, while the delightful family room in the eaves has its own little sitting/sleeping room and garden views. Wonderfully close to the sea with long views across the marshes to the river Alde and beyond. *See website for availability.*

Price	From £75. Singles from £65. Min. 2 nights at weekends; 3 on bank holidays.
Rooms	3: 1 twin/double, 1 double, 1 family room.
Meals	Pubs/restaurants 7-minute walk.
Closed	Christmas.
Directions	From A1094 drive towards town from r'bout. First right towards hospital, through 'Private Road' gate. House 100 yds on left, opp. tennis courts.

Simon Farr & Ann Lee
Dunan House,
41 Park Road,
Aldeburgh IP15 5EN

Tel	+44 (0)1728 452486
Email	dunanhouse@btinternet.com
Web	www.dunanhouse.co.uk

Entry 507   Map 10

Suffolk

The Old Methodist Chapel

Welcome to a converted, listed, Victorian chapel full of atmosphere, warm colours and beautiful stained-glass windows. Your bedroom has its own entrance, vaulted ceiling, oak floor with rugs and French windows to a private courtyard; there are potions and lotions by your bath, DVDs and music in your room. Breakfast is a feast of bacon and sausages from Peasenhall, local eggs and honey, homemade jams and organic bread. The chapel is comfortably, cosily cluttered, with books and flowers in every corner; your hostess, a cookery writer, is easy-going and interesting. Yoxford is lively with antique shops, art galleries and pubs.

Price	£100. Singles £75. Min. stay 2 nights. Small charge for dogs.
Rooms	1 double.
Meals	Restaurant directly opposite. Pubs/restaurants within walking distance.
Closed	Occasionally.
Directions	From A12 in Yoxford, A1120 signed Peasenhall & Stowmarket. Chapel 200 yds on right.

Jackum Brown
The Old Methodist Chapel,
High Street,
Yoxford IP17 3EU

Tel	+44 (0)1728 668333
Email	browns@chapelsuffolk.co.uk
Web	www.chapelsuffolk.co.uk

Entry 508   Map 10

Suffolk

Willow Tree Cottage

Seductively near RSPB Minsmere, medieval castles, fabulous walks and the glorious coast; and Edwardian Southwold with its pier and sandy beach. The evening sun pours into the back of this contemporary cottage with butter yellow walls; you are on the edge of the village but all is quiet with an orchard behind and a bird-filled garden for tea. No sitting room, but easy chairs in your bedroom face views, your bed is carefully dressed and the bathroom sparkles. Caroline is a good cook and breakfast is large (try her kedgeree). Snape Maltings, for music lovers, is just four miles away. *Minimum two nights at weekends.*

Price	£65-£70. Singles £50-£60.
Rooms	1 double.
Meals	Pub/restaurant 1.5 miles.
Closed	Rarely.
Directions	1.5 miles north of Saxmundham on B1121 & 100 yds north off turning to Kelsale. Belvedere Close on left immediately after Cloutings Close, behind White Gables.

	Caroline Youngson
	Willow Tree Cottage, 3 Belvedere Close,
	Kelsale, Saxmundham IP17 2RS
Tel	+44 (0)1728 602161
Mobile	+44 (0)7747 624139
Email	cy@willowtreecottage.me.uk
Web	www.willowtreecottage.me.uk

Entry 509   Map 10

Suffolk

Sandpit Farm

Idyllic views of the wide Alde valley stretch from this deeply comfortable, listed farmhouse. The river borders 20 acres of beautiful meadows, orchard, gardens, tennis court, ponds and the remains of a brick-lined moat; be charmed by Susie's hens and guinea fowl too. Step inside to family antiques and portraits, easy colour schemes, beams and open fires; pretty bedrooms have every cossetting thing. Susie and her Aga will make a scrumptious breakfast of homemade and local produce and home-grown tomatoes, plus fresh fruits and juices. You're near the coast, Snape for concerts, great birdwatching, walks and cycling... bliss!

Price	£65-£90. Singles from £50.
Rooms	2: 1 double, 1 twin.
Meals	Pub/restaurant 1.5 miles.
Closed	Rarely.
Directions	From A14, take A1120 Stowmarket to Yoxford; east of Dennington take B1120 Framlingham Road. First left; house 1.5 miles on left.

	Susie Marshall
	Sandpit Farm,
	Bruisyard,
	Saxmundham IP17 2EB
Tel	+44 (0)1728 663445
Email	smarshall@aldevalleybreaks.co.uk
Web	www.aldevalleybreaks.co.uk

Entry 510   Map 10

Suffolk

Haughley House

A timber-framed medieval manor in three acres of garden overlooking farmland. The attractive village is in a conservation area, and your hosts, the Lord of the Manor and his wife, are accomplished cooks and passionate about organic food; they produce their own beef, game, eggs, vegetables and soft fruits. Breakfast is an Aga-cooked feast of homemade bread, Suffolk cured bacon and black pudding, fresh juices and compote; delicious dinners are served in an elegant, silk-lined dining room. You'll find genuine country-house style here with tea and homemade cake on arrival, pretty wallpapers, flowers and a welcoming fire in the hall.

Price	£90–£100. Singles £60–£65.
Rooms	3: 2 doubles, 1 twin.
Meals	Dinner, 3 courses, £28. Restaurants 12 miles.
Closed	Rarely.
Directions	From A14 exit 49, follow signs to Haughley. Fork left at village green, house 100 yds on left.

Jeffrey & Caroline Bowden
Haughley House,
Haughley IP14 3NS
Tel +44 (0)1449 673398
Email bowden@keme.co.uk
Web www.haughleyhouse.co.uk

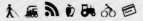

Entry 511 Map 10

Suffolk

Oak House

A wonderful, higgledy-piggledy Suffolk pink farmhouse – and owners who love good food and adventure. Inside creaks with medieval character: lead windows, crooked stairs, low carved ceilings, inglenook fireplaces, a roll top bath, a bread oven (Tom plans pizzas). With Kathy's 60s Royal Doulton and dazzling colours you're in for some fun. Outside: fruit trees, trampoline, an unfenced pond (wild swimming?) and a pheasant that breakfasts with Kathy's chickens. Over a candlelit dinner in the 15th-century kitchen (a sitting room in progress), ask what treats hide in these quiet surroundings, from walks and castles to camels.

Price	£110. Child £20. Dogs £10.
Rooms	1 suite.
Meals	Dinner from £21. BYO. Packed lunch £8. Pub 2 miles.
Closed	Rarely.
Directions	A14 at Stowmarket take B1113 dir. Finningham and Botesdale for 6 miles; 1 mile beyond Finningham, right into Mill St for Gislingham. House 1 mile on left.

Kathy Brooke
Oak House,
Mill Street, Gislingham IP23 8JT
Tel +44 (0)1379 788959
Email kathy@oakhousesuffolk.co.uk
Web www.oakhousesuffolk.co.uk

Entry 512 Map 10

Suffolk

Hill Farm House

Close to the village yet surrounded by fields is a listed farmhouse steeped in character, with sloping floors and 400-year-old beams. Ex-restaurateur John, generous and great fun, makes scrumptious breads for breakfast and an array of jams, from hedgerow to strawberry to damson; relish it all in the delightful dining room. Stylish bedrooms, real value, are upstairs. The Oak room is huge, with a mahogany sleigh bed and a view to wildflower paddock, ducks and long pond; the Poppy room has a bathroom and its own sitting room off the landing. Utterly peaceful, perfect for unwinding – and Framlingham's fortress is close!

Price	£60-£75. Singles £45-£60.
Rooms	2: 1 double; 1 double with separate bath/shower.
Meals	Restaurant 3.5 miles.
Closed	December/January.
Directions	Sent on booking.

John Brown
Hill Farm House,
Redlingfield Road, Horham,
Eye IP21 5ED

Tel   +44 (0)1379 388832
Email   jr@hillfarmbb.plus.com
Web   www.hillfarmbb.moonfruit.com

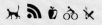

Entry 513   Map 10

Suffolk

Church Farmhouse

This Elizabethan farmhouse is by the ancient thatched church in a little hamlet close to Southwold. Minsmere RSPB bird sanctuary, Snape Maltings and the coast are nearby for lovely days out. Sarah, characterful, well-travelled and entertaining, is also an excellent cook, so breakfast will be a treat with bowls of fruit, Suffolk bacon and free-range eggs; occasional candle-lit dinners are worth staying in for, too. Bedrooms have supremely comfy beds well-dressed in pure cotton. Although there is no sitting room, you can enjoy tea and cake and linger in the garden, there are flowers in every room and books galore. *Over 12s welcome.*

Price	From £85. Singles from £50. Min. 2 nights at weekends.
Rooms	3: 1 double, 1 twin/double; 1 double with separate bath.
Meals	Dinner from £28. Pubs/restaurants within 4 miles.
Closed	Christmas.
Directions	A12 for Wangford; left signed Uggeshall; house 1 mile on left before church.

Sarah Lentaigne
Church Farmhouse,
Uggeshall, Southwold NR34 8BD

Tel   +44 (0)1502 578532
Mobile +44 (0)7748 801418
Email   uggeshalljupp@btinternet.com
Web   www.uggeshall.fsnet.co.uk

Entry 514   Map 10

Suffolk

Valley Farm

Soaps and sweeties in baskets, walking and cycle route maps on tap, DVDs for your TVs: some of the personal touches you'll find at this delightfully unpretentious B&B. The soft brick farmhouse in a lovely corner of Suffolk sits in two acres of new landscaped garden, with a play area for children, a field for kite flying and a wonderful indoor solar-heated pool, shared with the self-catering guests. You get jams from their fruits for breakfast – Jackie and Andrew have a passion for real food – and two friendly and comfortable carpeted bedrooms, each with a spotless new shower. *Minimum stay two nights at weekends.*

Price	£75-£95. Singles £75-£95.
Rooms	2: 1 double, 1 family room for 3-4.
Meals	Pub 0.4 miles.
Closed	Rarely.
Directions	From A144 at Halesworth, B1123 signed Holton & Southwold. Fork left at Holton, on to school, then left. Valley Farm 0.25 miles on left.

Jackie Circus
Valley Farm,
Bungay Road, Holton,
Halesworth IP19 8LY
Tel   +44 (0)1986 874521
Email mail@valleyfarmholton.co.uk
Web   www.valleyfarmholton.co.uk

Entry 515   Map 10

Suffolk

Carlton House Farm

At the end of the long drive sits a soft red-brick farmhouse in over 1,000 acres from which walks and bridleways splay: bring your horses! Lovely Becky grew up here, not so long ago; now she does B&B. All is immaculate, from the small beamed sitting room with window seat, board games and books to the creamy carpeted bedrooms upstairs. Each is pretty – Blue and Rose smallish, Hummingbird spacious – with good mattresses and a spotless bathroom that is shared; it's great for a family. Breakfast on eggs from hens down the road and fruits from the garden, in a cheery yellow room with a convivial table. *Children over four welcome.*

Price	£70. Singles £45. Child £25. Minimum two nights at weekends.
Rooms	3: 1 double, 2 twins sharing bath (2nd room let to same party only).
Meals	Restaurant 2 miles.
Closed	Rarely.
Directions	Sent on booking.

Becky Servaes
Carlton House Farm,
Mettingham, Bungay NR35 1TF
Tel   +44 (0)1986 892231
Mobile +44 (0)7771 717571
Email becksservaes@hotmail.com
Web   www.carltonhousefarm.com

Entry 516   Map 10

Surrey

The Dovecote at Greenaway

An enchanting cottage in an idyllic corner of Chiddingfold. People return time and again – for the house (1545), the garden with dovecote, vegetables, flowers and hens, the glowing interiors, and Sheila and John. The sitting room is inviting with rich colours and textures, and the turning oak staircase leads to bedrooms that are cosy and sumptuous at the same time. Bathrooms are bliss, with deep roll top tubs. Come for gorgeous countryside and walks on the Greensand Way… who would guess London and the airports were so close? Delightful B&B; guests are full of praise.

Surrey

Hambledon House

Through an old ornate iron gate, up a sweeping drive in rolling parkland and… enter another world. With an Elizabethan core and Victorian additions, Vanessa's house is a unique celebration of the Arts and Crafts movement. It's been in her family for generations and the restoration, with a marvellous Italian slant, is well underway. Find rooms of pure opulence with regal beds and bags of character, fabulous bathrooms, art, antiques, vast fireplaces, stunning stained glass, an orangery for breakfasts and a wonderful garden with a long reflecting pond. Vanessa is great fun and you're free to wander everywhere. Magical.

Price	From £95. Singles from £65.
Rooms	3: 1 double; 1 double, 1 twin sharing bath.
Meals	Inns 300 yds.
Closed	Rarely.
Directions	A3 to Milford, then A283 for Petworth. At Chiddingfold, Pickhurst Road off green. House 3rd on left, with black dovecote in front.

Price	£95. Singles £75.
Rooms	3 doubles.
Meals	Pubs/restaurants 10-minute walk.
Closed	Rarely.
Directions	Sent on booking.

	Sheila & John Marsh
	The Dovecote at Greenaway,
	Pickhurst Road,
	Chiddingfold GU8 4TS
Tel	+44 (0)1428 682920
Mobile	+44 (0)7879 665533
Email	jfmarsh@btinternet.com

	Vanessa Rhode
	Hambledon House,
	Vann Lane, Hambledon,
	Godalming GU8 4HW
Tel	+44 (0)1428 683815
Mobile	+44 (0)7768 645500
Email	vanessaswarbreck@yahoo.co.uk

Entry 517   Map 4

Entry 518   Map 4

Surrey

Lower Easing Farmhouse

A homely place with a lovely walled garden and super hosts; Gillian, who speaks French, German and Spanish, welcomes people from all over the world. The house, 16th to 19th century, has exposed timbers, books and bold colours. The dining room is red; the guest sitting room – with open fire and fascinating artefacts from around the world – is big enough for a small company meeting, or a wedding group. Your hosts, who are great fun, run an efficient and caring ship. In the walled garden, sipping tea, the distant rumble of the A3 reminds you how well placed you are for Gatwick and Heathrow.

Price	From £80. Singles from £50.
Rooms	4: 1 twin/double; 1 twin/double with separate bath/shower; 2 singles sharing shower.
Meals	Pub 300 yds.
Closed	Occasionally.
Directions	A3 south. 5 miles after Guildford, Eashing signed left at service station. Third house on left behind white fence.

David & Gillian Swinburn
Lower Eashing Farmhouse,
Lower Eashing,
Godalming GU7 2QF
Tel   +44 (0)1483 421436
Email   davidswinburn@hotmail.com

Entry 519   Map 4

Surrey

Old Great Halfpenny

It feels as rural as Devon, yet you are perfectly placed for airports and London, with Guildford a few minutes away. This 16th-century farmhouse sits on a country lane beneath the Pilgrim's Way; there are stunning views from every room and glorious walks from the door. You have your own entrance up fairly steep steps to bedrooms which Alison (an interior designer) has made beautiful with fine fabrics and antique French beds. Wake to the smell of freshly baked bread; in summer, you breakfast on a terrace with the lavender scented garden and wildflower meadow beyond. Michael and Alison are wonderfully relaxed hosts. Special.

Price	£85-£95. Singles from £65.
Rooms	2 doubles, each with separate bath.
Meals	Pub 0.5 miles.
Closed	Rarely.
Directions	From London, exit A3 before Guildford, signed Burpham. From here 2 miles to house. Ring for detailed directions.

Michael & Alison Bennett
Old Great Halfpenny,
Halfpenny Lane, St Martha,
Guildford GU4 8PY
Tel   +44 (0)1483 567835
Mobile +44 (0)7768 745765
Email   bennettbird@gmail.com

Entry 520   Map 4

Surrey

Swallow Barn

A squash court, coach house and stables, once belonging to next-door's manor, have become a home of old-fashioned charm. Full of family memories and run very well by Joan, the B&B is excellently placed for Windsor, Wisley and golf courses; close to both airports, too. Lovely trees in the garden, fields and woods beyond, a paddock and a summer pool… total tranquillity, and you can walk to the pub. None of the bedrooms is huge but the beds are firm, the garden views are pretty and the downstairs double has its own sitting room. Breakfasts are both generous and scrumptious. *Children over eight welcome.*

Price	From £80. Singles from £45.
Rooms	3: 1 double & sitting room; 1 twin with separate shower. Apple Store: 1 twin.
Meals	Pub/restaurant 0.75 miles.
Closed	Rarely.
Directions	From M25, exit 11, A319 into Chobham. Left at T-junc.; left at mini r'bout onto A3046. After 0.7 miles, right between street light & postbox. House 2nd on left.

Joan Carey
Swallow Barn, Milford Green, Chobham, Woking GU24 8AU

Tel	+44 (0)1276 856030
Mobile	+44 (0)7768 972904
Email	swallowbarn@web-hq.com
Web	www.swallow-barn.co.uk

Entry 521   Map 4

Surrey

Willows on the Mole

Have breakfast in the amazing Victorian conservatory at the large table, surrounded by lush ferns and colourful umbrellas. Penelope is friendly and lively and cooks you a full English, with fresh fruit and good coffee in a big pot. The house is in a central leafy crescent; the deep-raspberry living room has a library corner and warming fire. Eclectic art, goose down comfort in large bedrooms, sparkling bathrooms and green views add to the cheerful feel. Flowers and shrubs surround the pool, a garden runs to the river Mole, Pushkin the cat and Calamity the Jack Russell keep you company. *Over 12s welcome. Dogs can stay by Aga.*

Price	£80–£130.
Rooms	3: 1 double with separate bath/shower; 1 double, 1 twin/double sharing bath (let to same party only).
Meals	Pubs/restaurants 500 yds.
Closed	Rarely.
Directions	Sent on booking.

Penelope Lee
Willows on the Mole, 27 Matham Road, East Molesey KT8 0SX

Tel	+44 (0)20 8979 5466
Mobile	+44 (0)7968 541349
Email	penelopelee@mac.com

Entry 522   Map 4

Surrey

South Lodge

The beautiful Surrey Hills surround this smart home overlooking the village green. Paul and Joanna's house gets the sun all day and has a chintzy, country chic feel. They look after you well, and give you tea and cake on arrival, three cosy, pretty bedrooms in the eaves and locally sourced and homemade treats at breakfast. Joanna's catering business is run from the house so there are always people coming and going – this is a fun place to stay with a lovely friendly feel. Hop next door for a tasty supper at The Grumpy Mole (popular so you need to book). Handy for Gatwick, too – it's a 15-minute drive.

Price	£85. Singles £80.
Rooms	3: 2 doubles; 1 twin with separate bath.
Meals	Pub next door.
Closed	Christmas.
Directions	Sent on booking.

Joanna Rowlands
South Lodge,
Brockham Green, Brockham,
Betchworth RH3 7JS
Tel   +44 (0)1737 843883
Email   bookings@brockhambandb.com
Web   www.brockhambandb.com

Entry 523   Map 4

Surrey

Blackbrook House

A large Victorian house sitting in lawns and garden and with a wide gravel drive; this has a rural feel but you are less than two miles from the centre of Dorking. Emma and Rae, both easy-going, give you a super little sitting room with a hidden TV and space to make a cup of tea; both bedrooms are spacious, smart and feminine with floral fabrics, deep pocket sprung mattresses and good linen, bathrooms are tip-top. Breakfast is beautifully presented with cereals and fruit or the full Monty. Walk it off over lawns, shrubs and woods – or strike out further over National Trust land.

Price	£90–£95. Singles from £60.
Rooms	2 doubles.
Meals	Pub 0.5 miles.
Closed	Christmas & New Year.
Directions	R'bout outside Dorking A24 intersects A25. A24 0.5 miles. Left into Blackbrook, signed. 1 mile until Plough pub. Turn into pub & up track. House 3rd on left.

Emma & Rae Burdon
Blackbrook House,
Blackbrook, Dorking RH5 4DS
Tel   +44 (0)1306 888898
Mobile   +44 (0)7880 723512
Email   blackbrookbb@btinternet.com
Web   www.blackbrookhouse.org.uk

Entry 524   Map 4

Sussex

Church Gate

Janie has added a conservatory and huge, sunny, Aga kitchen to her 1930s house; she greets with afternoon tea, and rustles up a tasty continental breakfast with cereals, fruits, organic yogurt and sometimes home-baked bread and muffins, served on the terrace in summer. The house is adorned with Nigerian musical instruments and Janie's photographs; bedrooms in the separate cottage are fresh with low windows looking onto the garden, lovely soaps in the bath and shower rooms, driftwood lamps in the airy flagstoned sitting room. Set off for nearby Chichester with its theatre and shops, pretty Itchenor or West Wittering beach.

Sussex

Itchenor Park House

The Duke of Richmond reportedly built Itchenor Park for his French mistress in 1783; it's a listed Georgian house in beautiful formal gardens on a 700-acre farmed estate. It is remote and utterly peaceful, and a path across the fields brings you to Chichester harbour for boat trips and sailing bustle. There are great walks to the beach, too, and around the village. You stay in a cosy self-contained apartment in the wing with your own sitting room, kitchenette and wood-burner. And you may enjoy the lovely little walled garden, sheltered from the winds. Susie leaves you breakfast to have at your leisure.

Price	From £90. Singles from £70.
Rooms	Cottage: 1 double, 1 twin & sitting room.
Meals	Continental breakfast. Pub within 0.5 miles.
Closed	Often in the winter months.
Directions	From A27 at Chichester A286 Witterings; 5 miles; at r'bout bear right onto B2179. 0.5 miles right to Itchenor. 1 mile, house opp. church.

Price	From £100. Singles from £80.
Rooms	Apartment: 1 twin/double & sitting room with sofabed & kitchenette.
Meals	Breakfast in fridge. Pub 5-minute walk.
Closed	Rarely.
Directions	A27 at Chichester onto A286 towards the Witterings. At Birdham, right at garage onto B2179; 500 yds, right to Itchenor. Driveway on left past church, signed.

	Janie Impey
	Church Gate,
	Itchenor, Chichester PO20 7DL
Tel	+44 (0)1243 514700
Email	janie.allen@btinternet.com
Web	www.chichesterbandb.co.uk

	Susie Green
	Itchenor Park House,
	Itchenor, Chichester PO20 7DN
Tel	+44 (0)1243 512221
Mobile	+44 (0)7718 902768
Email	susie.green@lineone.net

Entry 525   Map 4

Entry 526   Map 4

Sussex

The Old Manor House

Wild flowers in jugs, old wooden floors and beams, pretty cottagey curtains: Judy's manor house near Chichester has bags of character and she is friendly and kind. Originally constructed round a big central fireplace, the rooms are all refreshingly simple allowing features to shine. Sweet bedrooms up steep stairs have seagrass floors, limed furniture, gentle colours and warm bathrooms. Enjoy delicious breakfasts by the wood-burner in the dining room: fresh fruit smoothies and an organic full English. Great for horse racing, castle visiting, sailing, theatre and festivals; fantastic walks on the south downs, too. Lovely.

Price	From £90.
Rooms	3: 2 doubles; 1 double sharing shower room with owner.
Meals	Pub/restaurant 500 yds.
Closed	Christmas.
Directions	From Arundel, A27 west to Fontwell r'bout.Then A29 towards Bognor Regis, along Westergate Street. House on left with large forecourt.

Judy Wolstenholme
The Old Manor House,
Westergate Street, Westergate,
Chichester PO20 3QZ
Tel +44 (0)1243 544489
Email judy@veryoldmanorhouse.com
Web www.veryoldmanorhouse.com

Entry 527   Map 4

Sussex

Lordington House

Croquet on the lawn in summer, big log fires and woolly jumpers in winter, brilliant food all year round. On a sunny slope of the Ems valley, life ticks by peacefully as it has always done… The house is vast and impressive, a lime avenue links the much-loved garden with the AONB beyond and friendly guard dog Shep looks on. The 17th-century staircase is a glory, the décor is engagingly old-fashioned: Edwardian beds with firm mattresses and floral covers, carpeted Sixties-style bathrooms, toile wallpaper on wardrobe doors. A privilege to stay in a house of this age and character!
Over fives welcome. Dogs by arrangement.

Price	From £110. Singles from £50.
Rooms	4: 1 double; 1 twin/double with separate bath/shower; 1 double, 1 single sharing bath/shower.
Meals	Dinner from £25. Packed lunch from £6. Pub 1 mile.
Closed	Rarely.
Directions	Off B2146 south of Walderton. After 0.5 miles, turn right on bend thro' white railings. Fork right up long drive to house.

Mr & Mrs Hamilton
Lordington House,
Lordington,
Chichester PO18 9DX
Tel +44 (0)1243 375862
Email hamiltonjanda@btinternet.com

Entry 528   Map 4

Sussex

West Marden Farmhouse

Bowl down a gentle valley in the South Downs to this 16th-century farmhouse with beautiful Sussex granaries and barn; the Edney family has farmed the land for generations. Your delightful, helpful hosts, committed to the environment, give guests a sitting/dining room with a huge old fireplace, comfortable sofas, flowers, oak floor and French windows to the garden. Find beamed bedrooms with a luxurious feel and thoughtful touches; fabulous bathrooms (freestanding baths, swish showers) burst with aromatic soaps and oils. Breakfasts are delicious, the walking is great and Goodwood is a 20-minute drive.

Price	From £115. Min. stay 2 nights at weekends and April to end October.
Rooms	2 doubles.
Meals	Pub 75 yds.
Closed	Occasionally.
Directions	West Marden Farmhouse is in centre of village opposite Noredown Way.

Carole Edney
West Marden Farmhouse,
West Marden,
Chichester PO18 9ES
Tel   +44 (0)2392 631761
Email   info@westmardenfarm.com
Web   www.westmardenfarmhousebandb.co.uk

Entry 529   Map 4

Sussex

Stream Cottage

One of Sussex's prettiest villages, an endearing 1587 thatched cottage, the cheeriest hosts and a breakfast menu including blueberry pancakes, smoked salmon, homemade plum compote and, for the very hungry, 'The Famous Amberley Monty'! Through a private door and up a narrow staircase find your own sweet sitting room with comfy sofa and chair, plenty of books and a charming bedroom with plenty of space and dual aspect low windows overlooking the garden. Your sparkling bathroom is downstairs (robes are provided) with big bottles of Cowshed potions and a sleek bath for resting weary limbs. Arundel and the South Downs await.

Price	£90. Singles £70.
Rooms	1 double with separate bath & sitting room.
Meals	Pubs in village.
Closed	Christmas & occasionally.
Directions	Sent on booking.

Mike & Janet Wright
Stream Cottage,
The Square, Amberley,
Arundel BN18 9SR
Tel   +44 (0)1798 831266
Email   janet@streamcottage.co.uk
Web   www.streamcottage.co.uk

Entry 530   Map 4

Riverhill Lodge

Views, views and more views over gorgeous National Park, from this handsome red-brick house with early Georgian origins. A sunny, airy sitting room with open fire and elegant cream and pink sofas, looks onto the well-planted garden; you breakfast copiously in a cosy terracotta-coloured dining room – cheerful Chris and Jenny serve up homemade bread, eggs from local hens and smoked bacon. Bedrooms are newly prettified in pale, neutral colours, with fresh fabrics and deep mattresses; bathrooms are sleekly up-to-date and toasty warm, with the thickest towels. Walk from the house for miles; the peace and quiet is palpable.

Fitzlea Farmhouse

A wooded track leads to the beautiful, mellow, 17th-century farmhouse with tall chimneys and a cluster of overgrown outbuildings – a sensational house in a breathtaking setting. Wood-panelled walls and ancient oak beams, a vast open fireplace, mullioned windows and deep sofas create a mood of relaxed country charm. Maggie gives you a delicious locally sourced breakfast in her Aga-warm kitchen; in spring, the scent of bluebells wafts through open doors. A winding staircase leads to comfortable timbered bedrooms which overlook fields, rolling lawns and woodland where you can stroll in peace. *Children by arrangement.*

Price	£85–£125.
Rooms	2: 1 double, 1 twin/double.
Meals	Pub 0.75 miles.
Closed	Christmas & occasionally Easter.
Directions	From Petworth go east, past Welldiggers pub on right. 0.5 miles, then left. As road ceases to be a green 'tunnel' (before house on left) take right. Beech hedge on right.

Price	£65–£90. Singles by arrangement.
Rooms	3: 1 family room; 1 double, 1 twin, sharing bath.
Meals	Packed lunch available. Pubs/restaurants 2 miles.
Closed	Rarely.
Directions	Sent on booking.

Christopher & Jenny Leaver
Riverhill Lodge,
Riverhill, Fittleworth,
Pulborough RH20 1JY
Tel   +44 (0)1798 343872
Email bookings@riverhilllodge.co.uk
Web   www.riverhilllodge.co.uk

Maggie Paterson
Fitzlea Farmhouse,
Selham,
Petworth GU28 0PS
Tel   +44 (0)1798 861429

Entry 531   Map 4

Entry 532   Map 4

Sussex

The Hyde Granary

A 1,000-acre estate, where roe deer roam and the odd buzzard circles above. The granary stands at the end of a one-mile drive, alongside a coach house and clock tower, in the shadow of the big house. Airy interiors are just the ticket: timber frames, exposed walls, beams in the dining room and a drying room for walkers. Bedrooms are uncluttered and have a country feel: one has a claw-foot bath, the other is in the eaves. Margot, a homeopath, can realign your back after a long journey, and does super breakfasts. There's a small garden for sundowners in summer, you can walk to the village and Gatwick is close.

Price	£80. Singles £60.
Rooms	2: 1 double; 1 double with separate bath/shower.
Meals	Pub 1.7 miles.
Closed	Christmas & New Year.
Directions	Leave village for Crawley on B2114. Pass through 30mph zone, then 1st left up drive onto Hyde Estate. Follow drive for 1 mile. Keep left at houses; house on right.

	Margot Barton
	The Hyde Granary, The Hyde, London Road, Handcross, Haywards Heath RH17 6EZ
Tel	+44 (0)1444 401930
Email	margot@thehydegranary.com
Web	www.thehydegranary.com

Entry 533   Map 4

Sussex

Mayes Park Lodge

It's nicely private here, up a bird-filled lane, and you stay in a stunning converted dairy near to the Lodge where charming owners James and Hannah live. Two super bedrooms are filled with cleverly sourced furniture – if you fall in love with anything you can buy it and take it home! Beds are deeply comfy, linen is crisp, fabrics are luxurious and the bathroom is immaculate with underfloor heating and Moroccan tiles. It's all on one floor with a lovely shared sitting/dining room; an organic breakfast is brought to you at a time you choose so you can snooze for longer. Good pubs and restaurants are near; perfect for friends.

Price	£105-£120. Singles £90-£105.
Rooms	The Old Dairy: 2 doubles sharing bathroom & sitting room.
Meals	Supper £15-£25. Pub 1 mile.
Closed	Rarely.
Directions	Sent on booking. See owner website.

	Hannah Clapshaw
	Mayes Park Lodge, Mayes Lane, Warnham, Horsham RH12 3SG
Tel	+44 (0)1403 218879
Mobile	+44 (0)7976 846810
Email	enquiries@mayespark.com
Web	www.mayespark.com

Entry 534   Map 4

Sussex

Thimbles

Enter the characterful hallway of this higgledy-piggledy house and fall under the spell of its charm. Imagine family antiques, pictures, plates, just-picked flowers and duvets as soft as a cloud: a timeless elegance, a fresh country style. Feast your eyes on the garden, six gentle acres that rise to fantastic views… a hammock, 89 varieties of roses, humming honey bees, a lake with an island (for barbecues!), a long lazy swing. Breakfasts and suppers are a dream: eggs from the hens, bacon from the pigs, jams from a jewel of a kitchen garden. Vicki, her family and Lottie the Irish terrier are the icing on the cake.

Price	£90. Singles £55-£75.
Rooms	2: 1 suite; 1 single sharing bathroom (let to same party only).
Meals	Dinner, 1-3 courses, £12.50-£21.50. Lunch £12.50. Pub 1 mile.
Closed	Rarely.
Directions	Sent on booking.

Vicki Wood
Thimbles, New Pond Hill,
Cross in Hand, Heathfield TN21 0NB
Tel   +44 (0)1435 860745
Mobile   +44 (0)7960 588447
Email   vicki.simonwood@btinternet.com
Web   www.thimblesbedandbreakfast.co.uk

Entry 535   Map 5

Sussex

Walnut Cottage

Christine's cottage – one of two tucked down a pretty lane – has a beautiful country-house feel. Bedrooms tempt with chocolates, flowers and comfy beds. Rise for a delicious breakfast: homemade yogurt and granola, coddled eggs with cream and nutmeg, or sausages from a nearby farm. Christine uses local seasonal produce; autumn dinners can feature game or venison. On arrival enjoy tea and homemade biscuits in an elegant sitting room; the garden, with views towards the South Downs, has a lovely terrace for al fresco meals. Days out include the Cuckoo Trail, Glyndebourne and Rudyard Kipling's house. *Over 12s welcome.*

Price	£70-£80. Singles £55-£65.
Rooms	2: 1 double; 1 double with separate bath.
Meals	Dinner £30. BYO. Pub 3 miles.
Closed	Rarely.
Directions	Sent on booking.

Christine Jermyn
Walnut Cottage,
Hanging Birch Lane,
Horam, Heathfield TN21 0PE
Tel   +44 (0)1435 812781
Email   info@walnutcottagesussex.com
Web   www.walnutcottagesussex.com

Entry 536   Map 5

Sussex

Old Whyly

Breakfast in a light-filled, chinoiserie dining room — there's an effortless elegance to this manor house, once home to one of King Charles's Cavaliers. Bedrooms are atmospheric, one in French style. The treats continue outside with a beautiful flower garden annually replenished with 5,000 tulips, a lake and orchard, a swimming pool and a tennis court — fabulous. Dine under the pergola in summer: food is a passion and Sarah's menus are adventurous with a modern slant. Glyndebourne is close so make a party of it and take a divine 'pink' hamper, with blankets or a table and chairs included. Sheer bliss.

Price	£95–£135. Singles by arrangement.
Rooms	3: 2 twins/doubles; 1 twin/double with separate bath.
Meals	Dinner, 3 courses, £32.50. Hampers £35. Pub/restaurant 0.5 miles.
Closed	Rarely.
Directions	0.5 miles past Halland on A22, south from Uckfield; 1st left off Shaw r'bout towards E. Hoathly; on for 0.5 miles. Drive on left with postbox; central gravel drive.

Sarah Burgoyne
Old Whyly,
London Road,
East Hoathly BN8 6EL
Tel   +44 (0)1825 840216
Email   stay@oldwhyly.co.uk
Web   www.oldwhyly.co.uk

Entry 537   Map 5

Sussex

Hailsham Grange

Come for elegance and ease. Noel looks after you very well in his lovely Queen 'Mary Anne' home. No standing on ceremony here, despite the décor: classic English touched with chinoiserie in perfect keeping with the house; all is luxurious and special. Busts on pillars, delicious fabrics, books galore and bedrooms a treat: a sunny double, a romantic four-poster, smart suites. Summery breakfasts are served on the flagged terrace, marmalades and jams on a silver salver. The town garden, with its box parterre and gothic summerhouse, is an equal joy. Close by are gardens to visit, Glyndebourne, the sea and South Downs National Park.

Price	£110–£140. Singles from £70. Min. 2 nights bank holidays.
Rooms	4: 1 double, 1 four-poster. Coach house: 2 suites.
Meals	Pub/restaurant 300 yds.
Closed	Rarely.
Directions	From Hailsham High St, left into Vicarage Rd. House 200 yds on left. Park in adjacent coach yard.

Noel Thompson
Hailsham Grange,
Hailsham BN27 1BL
Tel   +44 (0)1323 844248
Email   noel@hgrange.co.uk
Web   www.hailshamgrange.co.uk

Entry 538   Map 5

Sussex

Ocklynge Manor

On top of a peaceful hill, a short stroll from Eastbourne, find tip-top B&B in an 18th-century house with an interesting history – ask Wendy! Now it is her home, and you will be treated to home-baked bread, delicious tea time cakes and scrummy jams – on fine days you can take it outside. Creamy carpeted, bright and sunny bedrooms, all with views over the lovely walled garden, create a mood of relaxed indulgence and are full of thoughtful touches: dressing gowns, DVDs, your own fridge. Breakfasts are superb and there's a chintzy, comfortable sitting room: this is a very spoiling, nurturing place.

Sussex

St Benedict

The grand seaside villa, in a conservation area, has been meticulously restored by Stephen using the original 1880 floor plan. Lovers of Victoriana will swoon: find hand-printed wallpapers, gleaming mahogany, Persian rugs, Dutch marquetry furniture, coal fires in winter, decorative objects and artwork galore. Bedrooms are all extremely comfy with brass beds, eiderdowns and Victorian linen; wake to a full English, kedgeree or local kippers, served in the family dining room from a working dumb waiter. Relax in a sumptuous drawing room or borrow a book from the lovely library and head for a summerhouse tea in the walled garden.

Price	From £90. Singles from £50.
Rooms	3: 1 twin, 1 suite for 3; 1 double with separate shower.
Meals	Pub 5-minute walk.
Closed	Rarely.
Directions	From Eastbourne General Hospital, over r'bout on A2021. 1st right to Kings Avenue; up hill to T-junc. Cream house faces you on right.

Price	£90. Singles £60.
Rooms	3 doubles each with separate bath.
Meals	Dinner £30. Packed lunch £10. Pub/restaurant 0.5 miles.
Closed	Rarely.
Directions	From Hastings, west A27 Marine Parade until London Rd, St L. on Sea. Right (signed London) away from sea. Take 5th on left, just before disused church. At top of hill, over junc. beside St John's Church, house 100 yds, on left.

Wendy Dugdill
Ocklynge Manor,
Mill Road, Eastbourne BN21 2PG
Tel   +44 (0)1323 734121
Mobile   +44 (0)7979 627172
Email   ocklyngemanor@hotmail.com
Web   www.ocklyngemanor.co.uk

Stephen Groves
St Benedict,
81 Pevensey Road,
St Leonards on Sea TN38 0LR
Tel   +44 (0)1424 434973
Email   stephen.groves@zen.co.uk
Web   www.victorian-bed-and-breakfast.com

Entry 539   Map 5

Entry 540   Map 5

Sussex

Swan House

Effortless style drifts through the beamed rooms of this boutiquey B&B in a 1490s bakery, from a roaring inglenook fireplace to an honesty bar in a mock bookcase – all run by relaxed creative hosts Brendan and Lionel. Bedrooms hold surprises: Elizabethan frescoes, an old pulley for bags of flour, a window seat, seashell mosaics and handmade soaps. Step out into lively Old Hastings, wander down to see fishing boats tucked in for the night or find an antiques bargain. Seagulls herald the new day: pick a morning paper; breakfast like kings on organic croissants and local kippers (dinners also on request). Unique.

Sussex

Appletree Cottage

An enviable position facing south for this old hung-tile farmer's cottage, covered in roses, jasmine and wisteria; views are over farmland towards the coast at Fairlight Glen. Jane will treat you to tea and cake when you arrive – either before a warming fire in the drawing room, or in the garden in summer. Bedrooms are sunny, spacious, quiet and traditional, one with gorgeous garden views. Breakfast well on apple juice from their own apples, homemade jams and marmalade, local bacon and sausages. Perfect for walkers with a footpath at the front gate; birdwatchers will be happy too, and you are near the steam railway at Bodiam.

Price	£115-£145. Singles £70-£95.
Rooms	4: 3 doubles, 1 suite.
Meals	Restaurants 2-minute walk.
Closed	Christmas.
Directions	In Hastings Old Town, close to the seafront, a 20-minute walk from Hastings town centre and train station.

Price	£80. Singles £50.
Rooms	3: 1 twin; 1 double, 1 single each with separate bath.
Meals	Pub/restaurant 0.5 miles.
Closed	Rarely.
Directions	A21 towards Hastings. Left at B2089 towards Rye. 0.25 miles beyond Cripps Corner left at Beacon Lane. Right at farm track at top of hill - house is 1st on left (second drive).

Brendan McDonagh
Swan House,
1 Hill Street,
Hastings TN34 3HU

Tel	+44 (0)1424 430014
Email	res@swanhousehastings.co.uk
Web	www.swanhousehastings.co.uk

Entry 541   Map 5

Jane & Hugh Willing
Appletree Cottage, Beacon Lane,
Staplecross, Robertsbridge TN32 5QP

Tel	+44 (0)1580 831724
Mobile	+44 (0)7914 658861
Email	appletree.cottage@hotmail.co.uk
Web	www.appletreecottage.co

Entry 542   Map 5

Wellington House

A stroll away from the gardens of Great Dixter is a warm, comfortable, charming B&B. Behind the Victorian red-brick façade the Brogdens have worked an informal magic, giving guests a cosy sitting room and two big peaceful bedrooms above. These are creamy-walled and carpeted, with comfy mattresses, the smoothest antique bed linen, garden flowers, pristine shower rooms and good toiletries. Fanny is passionate about food, bakes her own bread, grows her own peaches – a treat; Vivian is a charmer. Visit Bodiam by river boat, comb Camber Sands, explore Rye, revel in Dixter... and return to tea and homemade cakes in the garden.

Kester House

For all those who fancy a taste of 17th-century England, here's a friendly B&B rich with history. Derek and Monique are loving their new venture, in a half-timbered village house in a lovely conservation area. Settle in by the big inglenook (a treat in winter), surf the house laptop, sink into an easy chair. Up the steep stair are low doorways and cosy bedrooms with iPod docks and silk cushions, the suite with a pitched beamed ceiling, the four-poster with deep rich colours. Delicious American pancakes and burritos vie with full English at breakfast, served at the big friendly table. Civilised, and great fun.

Price	£90. Singles £60.
Rooms	2 doubles.
Meals	Pubs within 2 miles.
Closed	Christmas & New Year.
Directions	Follow brown tourist signs in Northiam village for Great Dixter House & Gardens to Dixter Rd. House at main road end, next to opticians.

Price	£80–£105. Singles from £60.
Rooms	3: 1 four-poster en suite; 1 double, 1 suite for 2, each with separate bathroom.
Meals	Pub 150 yds.
Closed	Rarely.
Directions	M25 & A21 junc. 5. Head south on A21 to Hastings; left to Sedlescombe B2244. On entering village house on right opposite Bridge Antiques.

Fanny & Vivian Brogden
Wellington House, Dixter Road,
Northiam, Rye TN31 6LB
Tel   +44 (0)1797 253449
Mobile   +44 (0)7989 928236
Email   fanny@frances14.freeserve.co.uk
Web   www.wellingtonhousebandb.co.uk

Entry 543   Map 5

Derek & Monique Wright
Kester House,
The Street, Sedlescombe,
Battle TN33 0QB
Tel   +44 (0)1424 870035
Email   service@kesterhouse.co.uk
Web   www.kesterhouse.co.uk

Entry 544   Map 5

Sussex

Coromandel House

A glorious farmhouse with a duck pond, brick and weatherboard outbuildings, flouncing flower beds and charming Lisette, a garden designer from London. Large bedrooms have big wide floor boards and inviting beds, decorative gates for headboards, reclaimed windows for mirrors and a delicious rusticity. Bathrooms could appear in *Country Living* (and have!); views are green from every window. Outside are acre of lawns, a wildflower garden, hens and handsome Berkshire pigs; organic breakfasts are outstanding. A bucolic retreat ten minutes from Rye, in rolling Sussex hills: open the door and walk for miles.

Price	£90–£110. Child £20.
Rooms	2: 1 double, 1 twin/double. Extra child bed.
Meals	Pub 1 mile.
Closed	Rarely.
Directions	Grove Lane opposite The Bell in Iden. Down lane for 1 mile, then left immediately before oast house, down track. Go past Boonsfield Farm; Coromandel House at end of track, on left, white gate.

Lisette Pleasance
Coromandel House,
Boonshill Farm, Grove Lane, Iden,
Rye TN31 7QA

Tel	+44 (0)1797 280533
Email	boonshillfarm@yahoo.co.uk
Web	www.boonshillfarm.co.uk

Entry 545   Map 5

Warwickshire

Hardingwood House

Close to Birmingham and the NEC and with a theatrical, Tudor feel. Denise, warm and delightful, spoils guests with big bedrooms, dressing rooms, good linen and deep gold-tapped baths. There are books, flowers, antique clocks and plush sofas; a wood-burner warms the sitting room; dark timbers and reds and pinks abound. The 1737 barn is immaculate inside and out: the kitchen gives onto a stunning patio, while bedrooms have views to garden or fields. Breakfast is delicious: homemade bread and muesli, local sausages, bacon and jams. A convivial, happy place with much rural charm – guests love it here!

Price	£85. Singles from £60.
Rooms	3: 1 double, 2 twins.
Meals	Pub 20-minute drive.
Closed	Rarely.
Directions	M6 junc. 4; A446 for Lichfield. Into right lane & 1st exit towards Coleshill. From High St, into Maxstoke Lane. After 4 miles, right. 1st drive on left.

Denise Owen
Hardingwood House,
Hardingwood Lane, Fillongley,
Coventry CV7 8EL

Tel	+44 (0)1676 542579
Mobile	+44 (0)7713 153320
Email	denise@hardingwoodhouse.fsnet.co.uk

Entry 546   Map 8

Warwickshire

Park Farm House

Fronted by a circular drive, the warm red-brick farmhouse is listed and old – it dates from 1655. Linda is friendly and welcoming, a genuine B&B pro, giving you an immaculate guest sitting room filled with pretty family pieces. The bedrooms sport comfortable mattresses, mahogany or brass beds, blankets on request, bathrobes, flowers and magazines; bathrooms are a little dated but spotless. A haven of rest from the motorway (morning hum only) this is in the heart of a working farm yet hugely convenient for Birmingham, Warwick, Stratford and Coventry. You may get their own beef at dinner and the vegetables are home-grown.

Price	From £79. Singles from £48.
Rooms	2: 1 double, 1 twin.
Meals	Dinner, 3 courses, from £25. Supper £19. Pub/restaurant 1.5 miles.
Closed	Rarely.
Directions	M6 & M69 exit 2; B4065 through Ansty to Shilton; left at lights & next left. Over bridge, right to Barnacle; through village. Left at brick wall signed Spring Road. House at end of drive, over cattle grid.

	Linda Grindal
	Park Farm House,
	Barnacle,
	Shilton,
	Coventry CV7 9LG
Tel	+44 (0)2476 612628
Web	www.parkfarmguesthouse.co.uk

Entry 547   Map 8

Warwickshire

Mows Hill Farm

From the chocolate labradors in the flagstoned kitchen to the cattle munching in their stalls this late-Victorian farmhouse is a proper working farm of 1,300 acres that has been in the family for generations. Lynda and Edward give you an elegant and comfortable sitting and dining room with field views, loads of books and magazines, family portraits and an open fire. Breakfast on homemade bread and jams, fruit salad, home-reared bacon, just-laid eggs – in the conservatory looking onto the garden in the summer. Bedrooms have cotton sheets, armchairs for flopping and cosy bathrobes. A warm, family home. *Children over ten welcome.*

Price	£80-£90. Singles from £60.
Rooms	2: 1 twin/double; 1 double with separate bath.
Meals	Pub/restaurant 3 miles.
Closed	Rarely.
Directions	A3400 Hockley Heath; B4101 (Spring Lane); left into Umberslade Rd. At 2nd triangle, keep right & onto Mows Hill Rd; 0.25 miles on right.

	Lynda Muntz
	Mows Hill Farm, Mows Hill Rd, Kemps Green, Tanworth in Arden B94 5PP
Tel	+44 (0)1564 784312
Mobile	+44 (0)7919 542501
Email	mowshill@farmline.com
Web	www.b-and-bmowshill.co.uk

Entry 548   Map 8

Warwickshire

Austons Down

A fine modern country house with splendid views of the rural Vale of Arden. Your hosts are generous and chatty and look after you well. Their comfortable and relaxed family home has an elegant, light-filled sitting room complete with antiques, fabulous marquetry and open fire; bedrooms are fresh and traditional, bathrooms immaculate. Breakfast on homemade bread, compotes, a continental spread or full English. Admire Jacob sheep on the farm, relax in the terraced gardens. Plenty to visit nearby too: Warwick Castle, Stratford, National Trust properties, classic car museums… and the Monarch's Way is on the doorstep.

Price	From £75. Singles £50 (Mon-Thurs).
Rooms	3: 1 double, 2 twins/doubles.
Meals	Supper £15. Dinner £25. Pubs/restaurants 1 mile.
Closed	Rarely.
Directions	Sent on booking.

Lucy Horner
Austons Down, Saddlebow Lane,
Claverdon CV35 8PQ
Tel   +44 (0)1926 842068
Mobile +44 (0)7767 657352
Email   lmh@austonsdown.com
Web   www.austonsdown.com

Entry 549   Map 8

Warwickshire

Marston House

A generous feel pervades this lovely family home; Kim's big friendly kitchen is the hub of the house. She and John are easy-going and kind and there's no standing on ceremony. Feel welcomed with tea on arrival, delicious breakfasts, oodles of interesting facts about what to do in the area. The house, with solar electricity, is big and sunny; old rugs cover parquet floors, soft sofas tumble with cushions, sash windows look onto the smart garden packed with birds and borders. Bedrooms are roomy, traditional and supremely comfortable. A special, peaceful place with a big heart, great walks from the door and Silverstone a short hop.

Price	£85–£100. Singles from £65.
Rooms	2: 1 twin/double with separate bath; 1 twin/double with separate shower.
Meals	Supper, 3 courses, £29.50. Dinner £35 (min. 4). Pub 5-minute walk.
Closed	Occasionally in winter.
Directions	M40 exit 11. From Banbury, A361 N 7 miles; Byfield village sign, left Twistle Lane; on to Priors Marston - down hill; 5th house on left with cattle grid, after S-bend.

Kim & John Mahon
Marston House, Byfield Road,
Priors Marston, Southam CV47 7RP
Tel   +44 (0)1327 260297
Mobile +44 (0)7813 831028
Email   kim@mahonand.co.uk
Web   www.ivabestbandb.co.uk

Entry 550   Map 8

Warwickshire

Shrewley Pools Farm

A charming, eccentric home and fabulous for families, with space to play and animals to see: sheep, bantams and pigs. A fragrant, romantic garden, too, and a fascinating house (1640), all low ceilings, aged floors and steep stairs. Timbered passages lead to large, pretty, sunny bedrooms (all with electric blankets) with leaded windows and polished wooden floors and a family room with everything needed for a baby. In a farmhouse dining room Cathy serves sausages, bacon, and eggs from the farm, can do gluten-free breakfasts and is happy with teas for children. Buy a day ticket and fish in the lake.

Price	From £65. Singles from £50.
Rooms	2: 1 family room (& cot), 1 twin.
Meals	Packed lunch £5. Child's high tea £5. Pub/restaurant 1.5 miles.
Closed	Christmas.
Directions	From M40 junc. 15, A46 for Coventry. Left onto A4177. 4.5 miles to Five Ways r'bout. 1st left, on for 0.75 miles; signed, opp. Farm Gate Poultry: track on left.

Cathy Dodd
Shrewley Pools Farm, Five Ways Rd, Haseley, Warwick CV35 7HB
Tel +44 (0)1926 484315
Mobile +44 (0)7818 280681
Email cathydodd@hotmail.co.uk
Web www.shrewleypoolsfarm.co.uk

Entry 551   Map 8

Warwickshire

Machado Gallery

Artists and artisans have lived in this red-brick village house since 1746 – and it has never looked finer. Sue, a well-travelled sculptor and designer, has spent 22 happy years filling her home with art and natural light: skylights gulp sunshine into the fire-warmed sitting room; carved Russian windows frame daylight; bedrooms – one with a private patio, another a Juliet balcony – have pretty linen and super bathrooms. Wake to espresso and homemade bread, then sit out by the garden pond or browse the studio gallery. The village pubs are close; Warwick, the Cotswolds and Stratford-on-Avon beckon.

Price	£75–£115. Singles from £60.
Rooms	3: 2 doubles, 1 twin/double. Families welcome if booking all rooms.
Meals	Continental buffet breakfast included; full English £6.50. Clotted cream tea £5 (order on booking). Pub 50 yds, restaurant 100 yds.
Closed	Occasionally.
Directions	M40 junc. 15, A429 to Stow for 1 mile. Left into Barford Village. Cross Norman bridge & mini r'bout under the cedar tree. House 10 yds on left.

Sue Machado
Machado Gallery, 9 Wellesbourne Rd, Barford, Warwick CV35 8EL
Tel +44 (0)1926 624061
Mobile +44 (0)7715 109609
Email machadogallery@barford.org.uk
Web www.machadogallery.co.uk

Entry 552   Map 8

Warwickshire

Oxbourne House

Hard to believe the house is so young, with all its beamed ceilings, fireplaces and antiques. Bedrooms are fresh, crisp, cosy and cared for, the family room with an 'in the attic' feel; lighting is soft, beds excellent, bath and shower rooms attractive and warm, and the views are far-reaching. In the garden: tennis, sculpture and Graeme's rambler-bedecked pergola. Wake to birdsong and eggs from the hens; on peaceful summer nights, watch the dipping sun. Posy and Graeme are hugely likeable and welcoming, and an excellent village pub is down the road. A most comforting place to stay. *Dogs by arrangement.*

Price	£75-£95. Singles from £55.
Rooms	3: 1 double, 1 family room; 1 twin/double with separate bath.
Meals	Dinner from £20. Pub 5-minute walk.
Closed	Rarely.
Directions	A422 from Stratford-upon-Avon for Banbury. After 8 miles, right to Oxhill. Last house on right on Whatcote Road.

Graeme & Posy McDonald
Oxbourne House,
Oxhill, Warwick CV35 0RA

Tel	+44 (0)1295 688202
Mobile	+44 (0)7753 661353
Email	graememcdonald@msn.com
Web	www.oxbournehouse.com

Entry 553   Map 8

Warwickshire

The Old Manor House

An attractive 16th-century manor house with beautiful landscaped gardens sweeping down to the river Stour. The beamed double has oak furniture and a big bathroom; the old-fashioned twin and single are in a private wing. There is a large and elegant drawing and dining room whose antiques, contemporary art and open fire are for visitors to share. Jane prepares first-class breakfasts, and in warm weather you can have tea on the terrace: pots of tulips in spring, old scented roses in summer, meadow land beyond. A comfortable, lived-in family house with Stratford and the theatre close by. *Children over seven welcome.*

Price	From £95. Singles from £65.
Rooms	3: 1 double with separate bath; 1 twin/double, 1 single sharing bath (2nd room let to same party only).
Meals	Restaurants nearby.
Closed	Rarely.
Directions	From Stratford, A422 for 4 miles for Banbury. After 4 miles, right at r'bout onto A429 for Halford. There, 1st right, down hill on Queen's Street. House with black & white timbers straight ahead after 150 yds.

Jane Pusey
The Old Manor House, Halford,
Shipston-on-Stour CV36 5BT

Tel	+44 (0)1789 740264
Mobile	+44 (0)7786 467916
Email	info@oldmanor-halford.fsnet.co.uk
Web	www.oldmanor-halford.co.uk

Entry 554   Map 8

Warwickshire

The Old Farmhouse

Over the cattle grid to a habitation of three houses – and paddocks that lead the eye to the hills. Rebecca, once involved in carriage driving in France, now runs, with Joseph, a company that specialises in camels! The house has been renovated top to toe in comfortable, practical fashion, so you get really lofty bedrooms with recycled family pieces – high Edwardian beds, your own sofas – and breakfast at a big round table; tuck into bacon from their own pig 'racers'. Steep stairs to the family room, but children will love it. And if you don't fancy a camel ride at a friend's gallops, you can head off to Hidcote Gardens.

Price	£80. Family room £130.
Rooms	3: 1 double, 1 twin, 1 family room.
Meals	Pub 4 miles.
Closed	Rarely.
Directions	Sent on booking.

	Rebecca Fossett
	The Old Farmhouse, White House Farm,
	Idlicote, Shipston-on-Stour CV36 5DN
Tel	+44 (0)1608 661367
Mobile	+44 (0)7890 973982
Email	josephandrebecca@jacamels.co.uk
Web	www.jacamels.co.uk/BandB.htm

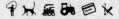

Entry 555   Map 8

Warwickshire

Upper Larkstoke

A gorgeous Cotswold house lost in its own valley with views that stretch for miles; bluebells carpet the wood in spring, you can walk across fields to the pub in summer. Rupert and Laurie, an Anglo-American partnership, spent two years refurbishing from top to toe. Outside, find smart lawns, beds of lavender and a sun-trapping terrace. Inside, beautiful colours and chic fabrics mix with golden stone and open fires. Bedrooms are crisply elegant with fine linen, French beds, beautiful views; one has a magnificent private bathroom. Laurie whisks up Cordon Bleu breakfasts and Stratford is close for all things Shakespeare.

Price	£100–£175.
Rooms	3: 2 doubles;
	1 double with separate bath.
Meals	Pub 2 miles.
Closed	Rarely.
Directions	Sent on booking.

	Laurie Bell
	Upper Larkstoke,
	Admington,
	Shipston-on-Stour CV36 4JH
Mobile	+44 (0)7811 160218
Email	welcome@upperlarkstoke.co.uk
Web	www.upperlarkstoke.co.uk

Entry 556   Map 8

Warwickshire

Stamford Hall

Soft hills and lines of poplars bring you to the high, pretty red-brick Georgian house with a smart hornbeam hedge. James, whose art decorates the walls, and Alice look after you impeccably but without fuss. You have a generous sitting room overlooking the garden, with gleaming furniture, early estate and garden etchings, and pastel blue sofas. Peaceful bedrooms are on the second floor and both have charm: soft wool tartan rugs on comfy beds, calming colours, attractive fabrics, restful outlooks. Wake to home-baked soda bread and Alice's full English; walk it off in open countryside or head for Stratford.

Price	£85. Singles £60.
Rooms	2: 1 double, 1 twin.
Meals	Pub 1 mile.
Closed	Christmas & occasionally.
Directions	From x-roads on Fosse Way B4455 & A422 head north on B4455 signed Leicester for 1 mile. Right at x-roads signed Pillerton. After 200 yds, right fork, after another 200 yds right after aluminium barns.

James & Alice Kerr
Stamford Hall,
Fosse Way, Ettington,
Stratford-upon-Avon CV37 7PA
Tel +44 (0)1789 740239
Email jk@jameskerr.co.uk
Web www.stamfordhall.co.uk

Entry 557 Map 8

Warwickshire

Cross o' th' Hill Farm

Stratford is a 12-minute walk by footpath across a field, and from the veranda you can see the church where Shakespeare is buried. The farm predates medieval Stratford with later additions to the house in 1860, though it has an earlier Georgian feel. All is chic, spacious and full of light with deco chandeliers, floor to ceiling sash windows, large uncluttered bedrooms and contemporary bathrooms. Wake to bird song, play the baby grand piano or croquet on the lawn and picnic in the gardens and orchards. Decima grew up here; she and David are charming hosts and passionate about art and architecture.

Price	£90-£96. Singles £65-£68.
Rooms	3: 2 doubles; 1 double with separate bath/shower.
Meals	Pubs/restaurants 15-minute walk.
Closed	20 December-23 February.
Directions	From Stratford south on A3400 for 0.5 miles, 2nd right on B4632 for Broadway Rd for 500 yds. 2nd drive on right for farm.

Decima Noble
Cross o' th' Hill Farm, Broadway Rd,
Stratford-upon-Avon CV37 8HP
Tel +44 (0)1789 204738
Mobile +44 (0)7973 971067
Email decimanoble@hotmail.com
Web www.crossothhillfarm.com

Entry 558 Map 8

Warwickshire

Sequoia House

A cat snoozes by the Aga in this smart Victorian townhouse – an easy stroll from Stratford and a civilised base for exploring Shakespeare country. Step into a pretty tiled hallway and discover high ceilings, deep bays, generous landings, handsome flagstones, a homely sitting room. The easy-going Evanses (Welsh-born) downsized from the hotel they used to run here, and are happy to treat just a few guests: trouser presses and piles of towels mingle with fine old furniture in immaculate rooms. A walkway runs past cricket grounds straight into town. Hotel touches but a warmly personal welcome, and so wonderfully convenient.

Price	£125. Singles £85.
Rooms	4 doubles.
Meals	Pub/restaurant 100 yds.
Closed	Christmas & New Year.
Directions	From M40 (junc. 15) to Stratford (signed). Enter town, then signed A3400 Shipston. Cross River Bridge, then 2nd exit off traffic island. House 100 yds on right.

Jean Evans
Sequoia House, 51 Shipston Road,
Stratford-upon-Avon CV37 7LN
Tel +44 (0)1789 268852
Mobile +44 (0)7833 727914
Email reservations@sequoia-house.co.uk
Web www.sequoia-house.co.uk

Entry 559   Map 8

Warwickshire

Salford Farm House

Beautiful within, handsome without. Thanks to subtle colours, oak beams and lovely old pieces, Jane has achieved a seductive combination of comfort and style. A flagstoned hallway and an old rocking horse, ticking clocks, beeswax, fresh flowers: this house is well-loved. Jane was a ballet dancer, Richard has green fingers and runs a fruit farm and farm shop nearby – you may expect meat and game from the Ragley Estate and delicious fruits in season. Bedrooms have a soft, warm elegance and flat-screen TVs, bathrooms are spotless and welcoming, views are to garden or fields. Wholly delightful.

Price	£90. Singles £55.
Rooms	2 twins/doubles.
Meals	Dinner £25. Restaurant 2.5 miles.
Closed	Rarely.
Directions	A46 from Evesham or Stratford; exit for Salford Priors. On entering village, right opp. church, for Dunnington. House on right, approx. 1 mile on, after 2nd sign on right for Dunnington.

Jane & Richard Beach
Salford Farm House,
Salford Priors,
Evesham WR11 8XN
Tel +44 (0)1386 870000
Email salfordfarmhouse@aol.com
Web www.salfordfarmhouse.co.uk

Entry 560   Map 8

Wiltshire

Brook House

The minute you pull up in the drive you know you're in for a treat. Henry Lamb lived in this Georgian house, Evelyn Waugh came to visit, now it's the home of delightful Kate who gives you local sausages and homemade bread at breakfast. You'll love her farmhouse kitchen with its long cheerful table, the guest sitting room with its open log fire, and the beautiful, luxurious bedrooms, one with a balcony for the view. Gaze on with a glass of wine: the garden with its gorgeous planting and river running through, the visiting ducks, resident hens, the water meadows beyond. The village is charming, Salisbury is close.

Price	£79-£89. Singles £50-£55.
Rooms	2: 1 double, 1 twin/double.
Meals	Pub 3-minute walk.
Closed	Rarely.
Directions	Sent on booking.

	Kate Seal
	Brook House, Homington Road,
	Coombe Bissett, Salisbury SP5 4LR
Tel	+44 (0)1722 718242
Mobile	+44 (0)7595 509937
Email	info@brookhousesalisbury.com
Web	www.brookhousesalisbury.com

Entry 561   Map 3

Wiltshire

Manor Farm

Two children, two cats, 22 chickens, 250 sheep, a burgeoning young garden and a greenhouse to die for: Katie looks after it all with energy and good humour, and goes the extra mile for her guests. Dating from the 1600s, it's a house with a history — and today combines luxury with simplicity. Be cheered by an elegant dining room with a real fire, a suite with thick feather pillows and a big comfortable bed, a bathroom with taupe towels and Neal's Yard bubbles, a breakfast of local and home-grown delights, an iPod dock and DVDs on request. And there's a room to store your bicycles and boots! It's a treat to stay here.

Price	£85. Singles £70.
Rooms	1 suite.
Meals	Packed lunch £10.
	Pub within walking distance.
Closed	Rarely.
Directions	A354 Coombe Bissett, 1st right to Broadchalke. 5 miles to village. Left opp. pub, 0.25 miles, church on right. Road bends 90° right. On apex straight on, then left. House 2nd left.

	Katie Jowett
	Manor Farm,
	Broad Chalke,
	Salisbury SP5 5DW
Tel	+44 (0)1722 780230
Email	info@manorfarmbroadchalke.co.uk
Web	www.manorfarmbroadchalke.co.uk

Entry 562   Map 3

Wiltshire

Old Stoke

As pretty as thatched cottages come. This lovely old farmhouse is edged by an AONB filled with birdsong and wildlife, yet you are close to Salisbury. Guests have a book-filled sitting room with Dorset cream walls and pretty chairs and sofas to collapse onto: upstairs are fresh bedrooms with bright fabrics on headboards and window cushions, feathery beds and sparkling bathrooms. Tracie is charming and cooks well: good wholesome food using eggs from the hens and home veg; stroll down the fecund garden for tea and her delicious flapjacks or cake in the summerhouse. A meadow and river lie beyond. *Over eights welcome.*

Price	£65–£75. Singles from £45.
Rooms	2: 1 twin/double; 1 double with separate bath.
Meals	Dinner £17.50–£22.50. Packed lunch £6. Pub 1 mile.
Closed	December–February.
Directions	SW from Salisbury on A354; right at Coombe Bissett dir. Bishopstone. 2nd left after White Hart, signed Stoke Farthing. In hamlet, sharp bend to right, 2nd house on left. Parking to left of house.

	Tracie Pickford
	Old Stoke,
	Stoke Farthing, Broad Chalke,
	Salisbury SP5 5ED
Tel	+44 (0)1722 780513
Email	stay@oldstoke.co.uk
Web	www.oldstoke.co.uk

Entry 563   Map 3

Wiltshire

Dowtys

A beautifully converted Victorian dairy farm with fabulous views over the Nadder valley. Peaceful, private, stylish bedrooms, one on the ground floor, have original beams, antiques and big Vi-Spring beds; bathrooms are perfect. The sunny guest sitting room has a contemporary feel too, with its wood-burner and sliding doors to the garden. Have a delicious breakfast in the old milking parlour, now the dining room, or on the terrace, sit beneath the espaliered limes in the lovely garden, dip into the National Trust woods. Footpaths start from the gate and your charming hosts will help you with all your plans.

Price	£75–£90. Singles from £60.
Rooms	3: 1 double & sitting room; 1 double, 1 twin each with separate bath/shower.
Meals	Packed lunch on request. Pub 0.25 miles.
Closed	Christmas & New Year.
Directions	B3089 approaching Dinton from east (Barford St Martin). Take 1st turn right after village sign & 30mph, signed Wylye. 100 yds; 1st right up Dowtys Lane to house.

	Di & Willi Verdon-Smith
	Dowtys,
	Dowtys Lane, Dinton,
	Salisbury SP3 5ES
Tel	+44 (0)1722 716886
Email	dowtys.bb@gmail.com
Web	www.dowtysbedandbreakfast.co.uk

Entry 564   Map 3

Wiltshire

The Mill House

In a tranquil village next to the river is a house surrounded by water meadows and wilderness garden. Roses ramble, marsh orchids bloom and butterflies shimmer. This 12-acre labour of love is the creation of ever-charming Diana and her son Michael. Their home, the time-worn 18th-century miller's house, is packed with country clutter – porcelain, foxes' brushes, ancestral photographs above the fire – while bedrooms are quaint and flowery, with firm comfy beds; organic breakfasts are served at small tables. Diana has lived here for many many years, and has been doing B&B for at least 27 of them! *Children over six welcome.*

Price	From £95. Singles from £65.
Rooms	5: 3 doubles, 1 family room; 1 twin with separate bath.
Meals	Pub 5-minute walk.
Closed	Rarely.
Directions	From A303 take B3083 at Winterbourne Stoke to Berwick St James. Go through village, past Boot Inn & church. Turn left into yard just before the sharp left bend. Coming from A36 (B3083), house 1st on right.

Diana Gifford Mead & Michael Mertens
The Mill House,
Berwick St James,
Salisbury SP3 4TS
Tel +44 (0)1722 790331
Web www.millhouse.org.uk

Entry 565 Map 3

Wiltshire

Dean Lodge

Mark and Sue are charming and interesting hosts; Mark, a musician, has a studio on the ground floor and this striking, contemporary house is filled with music and art (and friendly lurchers!). You breakfast in the open-plan living room: green oak, huge windows, art, sculpture and an unusual wood-burner suspended from the ceiling. Downstairs bedrooms have clean lines, rugs on tiles and good linen; wet rooms are swish. Wild flowers and woodland surround the house, the area is brimming with galleries, theatre, festivals and historic houses and your hosts know the local scene well. Culture lovers will have landed in clover.

Price	£65-£85.
Rooms	2 doubles.
Meals	Pubs/restaurants 2 miles.
Closed	Rarely.
Directions	Sent on booking.

Mark Emney
Dean Lodge,
Swallowcliffe, Salisbury SP3 5PG
Tel +44 (0)1747 871597
Mobile +44 (0)7710 207143
Email info@deanlodgebedandbreakfast.co.uk
Web www.deanlodgebedandbreakfast.co.uk

Entry 566 Map 3

Wiltshire

The Duck Yard

Independence with your own terrace, entrance and sitting room. Peace too, at the end of the lane; find a charming and colourful cottage garden, a summerhouse and free-ranging ducks and hens. Harriet makes wedding cakes, looks after guests well and cheerfully rustles up fine meals at short notice; breakfasts feature delicious homemade bread. Your carpeted bedroom and aquamarine bathroom are tucked under the eaves; below is the sitting room, cosy with wood-burner, books and old squashy sofas, leading to a sunny terrace. Good for walkers: maps are supplied and you may even borrow a dog. *Reflexology available: book in advance.*

Price	£70-£80. Singles £55.
Rooms	1 twin/double & sitting room.
Meals	Dinner, 3 courses, £25. Packed lunch £7. Pub 2 miles.
Closed	Christmas & New Year.
Directions	A303 to Wylye, then for Dinton. After 4 miles left at x-roads, for Wilton & Salisbury. On for 1 mile, down hill, round sharp right bend, signed Sandhills Rd. 1st low red brick building on left. Park in space on left.

Harriet & Peter Combes
The Duck Yard,
Sandhills Road, Dinton,
Salisbury SP3 5ER

Tel   +44 (0)1722 716495
Mobile   +44 (0)7729 777436
Email   harriet.combes@googlemail.com

Entry 567   Map 3

Wiltshire

The Old School House

Charmingly cluttered, sparklingly clean, this 1860 village house is filled with light, beautiful objects and lovely pieces of furniture. Find a comfy chair in the snug with its loaded book shelves on art, gardening and travel – Darea's passions. Your chintzy bedrooms (the double is larger) have wooden arched beams, excellent mattresses and a newly decorated bathroom with oatmeal tiles. Breakfast is in the smart kitchen with its humming black Aga: good sausages and bacon, local eggs. A little south-facing courtyard has colourful pots and a bench for idle gazing; Stonehenge, Longleat and Stourhead beckon.

Price	£70-£80. Singles £40-£50.
Rooms	2: 1 double, 1 twin sharing bath (let to same party only).
Meals	Pub 500 yds.
Closed	Rarely.
Directions	From London exit 303 at first Wylye turn off signed A36 Warminster, Salisbury. Right fork, right at T-junc., then immediate left into Wylye village. Past pub, church & shop & house immediately after.

Darea Browne
The Old School House,
Wylye,
Warminster BA12 0QR

Tel   +44 (0)1985 248228
Email   dareabrowne@aol.com

Entry 568   Map 3

Wiltshire

Crockerton House

This 1669 listed house, once part of the Longleat estate, hides just behind the village green. Pale walls soak up light, rugs cover stripped floors, fires gently smoulder and your very welcoming hosts serve breakfast at a beautiful mahogany table. Bedrooms – elegant, softly carpeted and serene – have Farrow & Ball hues, bowls of fruit, quilted covers, crisp linen. Both suites overlook the gorgeous gardens, the Southleigh Woods blanket the hillside beyond. Enid's vegetable patch is a thing of beauty and yields treats for the table – do eat in. Bath is close, and so is magnificent Stourhead. *Children over 12 welcome.*

Price	£89-£129. Singles £79-£119. Minimum 2 nights most weekends.
Rooms	3: 2 suites; 1 double with separate bath.
Meals	Supper, 2 courses, £19 (Mon-Thurs). Pub 0.6 miles.
Closed	Christmas.
Directions	Sent on booking.

Christopher & Enid Richmond
Crockerton House,
Crockerton,
Warminster BA12 8AY
Tel +44 (0)1985 216631
Email stay@crockertonhouse.co.uk
Web www.crockertonhouse.co.uk

Entry 569   Map 3

Wiltshire

Oaklands

A comfortable townhouse, a south-facing garden, two dear dogs and a lovely old Silver Cross pram sitting under the stairs. It was the first house in Warminster to have a bathroom; these have multiplied since and the interiors have had a makeover – no wonder this delightful, spacious 1880s house has been in the family forever. Andrew and Carolyn, relaxed and charming, serve delicious breakfasts in the lovely, light-suffused conservatory at the drawing room end. Bedrooms, desirable and welcoming, overlook churchyard, lawns and trees; soft colours, cosy bathrooms, family antiques. Restaurants are a stroll.

Price	£65-£85. Singles from £55.
Rooms	3: 1 double; 1 double, 1 twin/double sharing bath (let to same party only). Child bed available.
Meals	Occasional dinner (min. 4 guests). Pub/restaurant 0.5 miles.
Closed	Christmas & rarely.
Directions	From Warminster centre direction Salisbury. On right, opp. end of St John's churchyard.

Carolyn & Andrew Lewis
Oaklands,88 Boreham Road,
Warminster BA12 9JW
Tel +44 (0)1985 215532
Mobile +44 (0)7850 158302
Email apl1944@yahoo.co.uk
Web www.stayatoaklands.co.uk

Entry 570   Map 3

Wiltshire

The Old Rectory

A classically beautiful Georgian house, the rectory until the late 30s, surrounded by ancient yew hedges. Helle and David have created peaceful interiors: large, light rooms with wooden floors are painted in the softest colours; antiques sit happily with contemporary fabrics, vases of flowers, bright rugs; a drawing room just for you is the prettiest place to sit and read. Bask in quiet, comfortable bedrooms (one up steep steps), warm, neat bathrooms, tasty local produce and home-baked bread. Stroll in the garden with spring-fed pond, wander through a deer park onto Salisbury Plain. Peace seekers will be happy. *Over tens welcome.*

Price	£80.
Rooms	2: 1 double, 1 twin/double, each with separate bath.
Meals	Pubs/restaurants 1.3 miles.
Closed	Rarely.
Directions	Sent on booking.

Helle de Chazal
The Old Rectory,
17 Coulston, Westbury BA13 4NY
Tel   +44 (0)1380 830930
Mobile   +44 (0)7818 261612
Email   helledechazal@gmail.com
Web   www.theoldrectorywiltshire.co.uk

Entry 571   Map 3

Wiltshire

The Limes

Through the electric gates, past the gravelled car park and the pretty, box-edged front garden and you arrive at the middle part of a 1620 house divided into three. The beams, stone mullions and leaded windows are charming, and Ellodie is an exceptional hostess. Immaculate, comfortable bedrooms have pretty curtains and fresh flowers, smart bathrooms have good soaps and thick towels, logs glow in the grate, and breakfasts promise delicious Wiltshire bacon, prunes soaked in orange juice and organic bread. You are on the main road leading out of Melksham – catch the bus to Bath from right outside the door.

Price	£83–£88. Singles £53–£58.
Rooms	3: 2 twins/doubles, 1 single.
Meals	Packed lunch £7. Pub 1.5 miles.
Closed	Rarely.
Directions	Leave Melksham on A365 to Bath. After Victoria Motors, sharp right at 1st entrance, brown gates will open slowly. Park on right, follow path to house.

Ellodie van der Wulp
The Limes,
Shurnhold House, Shurnhold,
Melksham SN12 8DG
Tel   +44 (0)1225 790627
Mobile   +44 (0)7974 366892
Email   eevanderwulp@gmail.com

Entry 572   Map 3

Wiltshire

Glebe House

The rogues' gallery of photographs up the stairs says it all: Glebe House is quirky and fun. Friendly Ginny spoils you rotten with pressed linen and sociable dinners served on Wedgwood china. Charming, cosy and comfortable are the bedrooms, one with an Indian theme; delightful is the drawing room with its landscape oils, Bechstein piano and a large rug from Jaipur; settle into the sofa and roast away by the fire. Breads, marmalades and jams are homemade, beautiful woodland fills the valley, the cottage garden, alive with birds, wraps around the house and Mr Biggles – the grey parrot – chats by the Aga.

Price	£80–£85. Singles £45–£55.
Rooms	2: 1 double, 1 twin.
Meals	Dinner, 3 courses, from £25 (BYO). Pub 4 miles.
Closed	Christmas.
Directions	From Devizes-Chippenham A342. Follow Chittoe & Spye Park. On over crossroads onto narrow lane. House 2nd on left.

Ginny Scrope
Glebe House,
Chittoe, Chippenham SN15 2EL
Tel   +44 (0)1380 850864
Mobile   +44 (0)7767 608841
Email   ginnyscrope@gmail.com
Web   www.glebehouse-chittoe.co.uk

Entry 573   Map 3

Wiltshire

The Coach House

In an ancient hamlet a few miles north of Bath, an impeccable conversion of an early 19th-century barn. Bedrooms are fresh and cosy with sloping ceilings, while the pale drawing room is elegant with porcelain, antiques and striking floral displays. Sliding glass doors lead to a south-facing patio, then to a well-groomed croquet lawn bordered by flowers, with vegetable garden, tennis court, woodland and paddock. Helga and David are delightful and give you homemade jams and marmalade at breakfast. The splendours of Bath and the charm of Castle Combe are an easy drive; golfers, too, should be happy.

Price	£75–£85. Singles £35–£45.
Rooms	2: 1 double with separate bath/shower; 1 twin/double sharing bath (let to same party only).
Meals	Dinner, 3 courses, from £25. Pubs/restaurants 1 mile.
Closed	Rarely.
Directions	From M4 junc. 17, A350 for Chippenham. A420 to Bristol (east) & Castle Combe. After 6.3 miles, right into Upper Wraxall. Sharp left opp. village green; at end of drive.

Helga & David Venables
The Coach House,
Upper North Wraxall,
Chippenham SN14 7AG
Tel   +44 (0)1225 891026
Email   david@dvenables.co.uk
Web   www.upperwraxallcoachhouse.co.uk

Entry 574   Map 3

Wiltshire

Manor Farm

Farmyard heaven in the Cotswolds. A 17th-century manor farmhouse in 550 arable acres; horses in the paddock, dozing dogs in the yard, tumbling blooms outside the door and a perfectly tended village, with duck pond, a short walk. Beautiful bedrooms are softly lit, with muted colours, plump goose down pillows and the crispest linen. Breakfast in front of the fire is a banquet of delights, tea among the roses is a treat, thanks to charming, welcoming Victoria; she will arrange a table for dinner at the pub too. This is the postcard England of dreams, with Castle Combe, Lacock, grand walking and gardens to visit. *Over 12s welcome.*

Price	From £84. Singles from £46.
Rooms	3: 2 doubles; 1 twin with separate bath.
Meals	Pub nearby.
Closed	Rarely.
Directions	From M4 A429 to Cirencester (junc. 17). After 200 yds, 1st left for Grittleton; there, follow signs to Alderton. Farmhouse near church.

Victoria Lippiatt-Onslow
Manor Farm,
Alderton, Chippenham SN14 6NL

Tel	+44 (0)1666 840271
Mobile	+44 (0)7721 415824
Email	victoria.lippiatt@btinternet.com
Web	www.themanorfarm.co.uk

Entry 575   Map 3

Wiltshire

Dauntsey Park House

Be awed by history here. Parts of the house – like the grand dining room where you breakfast – date from Elizabethan times; the stunning summer drawing room is Edwardian. Both rooms are yours to use. Emma and her Italian husband have four young children and a flair for matching new with old: a striking glass chandelier sets off the sturdy oak table beneath; a turbine keeps the house in hot water. Up a wide staircase, two wallpapered rooms with views to the river are huge and comfortable with a self-indulgent feel (one has a thunderbox loo!). St James the Great church with its 14th-century doom board is in the garden. Lovely.

Price	£90
Rooms	2: 1 double, 1 twin.
Meals	Pubs/restaurants in village.
Closed	Rarely.
Directions	Sent on booking.

Emma Amati
Dauntsey Park House,
Dauntsey,
Chippenham SN15 4HT

Tel	+44 (0)1249 721777
Email	gioandemma@btinternet.com
Web	www.dauntseyparkhouse.co.uk

Entry 576   Map 3

Wiltshire

Manor Farm

The road through the sleepy Wiltshire village brings you to a charming Queen Anne house with a *petit château* feel, enfolded by a beautiful walled garden with wildflower meadow, hens and ducks, orchard and groomed lawns. Inside is as lovely. The eclectically furnished drawing room, shared among guests, has a real fire and a lived-in, family feel. The doubles are comfortable and elegant with Queen Anne panelling, feather pillows on comfortable beds, good art and garden views. Wake for scrumptious, all-organic breakfasts, served in the dining room or kitchen. Clare is an artist and runs a gallery and courses in the studio.

Price	£100. Singles £65.
Rooms	3: 2 doubles; 1 single with separate bath/shower.
Meals	Pubs within 3 miles.
Closed	Christmas & New Year.
Directions	M4 exit 17. North on A429 for Malmesbury, right on B4042. Right after 3 miles to Little Somerford. Rght at crossroads, 200 yds on, house behind tall wall.

	Clare Inskip
	Manor Farm,
	Little Somerford, Malmesbury,
	Chippenham SN15 5JW
Tel	+44 (0)1666 822140
Mobile	+44 (0)7970 892344
Email	clareinskip@gmail.com

Entry 577   Map 3

Wiltshire

Bullocks Horn Cottage

Up a country lane is this hidden-away house which the delightful Legges have turned into a haven of peace. Liz loves fabrics and flowers and mixes them with flair, Colin has painted a mural for the conservatory, bright with plants and wicker sofa. Super bedrooms, both twins, have lovely views; the sitting room has a log fire, fine antiques, big comfy sofas, and the garden is so special it's appeared in magazines. Organic veg and herbs from the garden and local seasonal food make an appearance at dinner which, on balmy nights, you may eat under the arbour, covered in climbing roses and jasmine. *Children over five welcome.*

Price	£90. Singles from £45.
Rooms	2: 1 twin; 1 twin with separate bath.
Meals	Dinner £20-£25. BYO. Pub 1.5 miles.
Closed	Christmas.
Directions	From A429, B4040 through Charlton, past Horse & Groom. 0.5 miles, left signed 'Bullocks Horn No Through Road'. On to end of lane. Right then 1st on left.

	Colin & Liz Legge
	Bullocks Horn Cottage,
	Charlton,
	Malmesbury SN16 9DZ
Tel	+44 (0)1666 577600
Email	bullockshorn@clara.co.uk
Web	www.bullockshorn.co.uk

Entry 578   Map 3

Wiltshire

Bridges Court

You're in the heart of the village with its small shop, friendly pub and the Melvilles' lovely 18th-century farmhouse. They only moved in recently but it's so homely you'd never tell. Dogs wander, horses whinny, there's a beautiful garden with a Kiftsgate rose and a swimming pool for sunny days. On the second floor, off a corridor filled with paintings, are three florally inspired bedrooms: comfortable, bright and spacious with views to the village green. Breakfast leisurely on all things local at the long table in a dining room filled with silver and china. And there's a pleasant guests' sitting room to relax in.

Price	From £75. Singles £60. (Discount for 3 nights or more, excluding Badminton w/e.)
Rooms	3: 1 double, 1 double with separate bath, 1 twin.
Meals	Pub in village.
Closed	Rarely.
Directions	Sent on booking.

Fiona Melville
Bridges Court,
Luckington SN14 6NT

Tel	+44 (0)1666 840215
Mobile	+44 (0)7711 816839
Email	fionamelville2003@yahoo.co.uk
Web	www.bridgescourt.co.uk

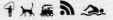

Entry 579   Map 3

Wiltshire

Westhill House

A large Regency house in the centre of this market town; you are on the edge of the marvellous Cotswolds. Vivacious Brenda, well-travelled and a collector of art, has filled her home with bold colours, eclectic paintings, beautiful glass and ceramics; the elegant drawing room has an open fire and the dining room is dramatically red. Bedrooms come in creams and blues, beds are new, wine glasses and corkscrew await; bathrooms are contemporary and indulgent with fluffy towels. Be greeted with tea and cake, try French toast with fruit and maple syrup for breakfast, or full English. Marked walking trails run from the door.

Price	£85-£115. Singles £70-£100.
Rooms	3 doubles.
Meals	Pubs/restaurants within 5 miles.
Closed	Rarely.
Directions	Exit 15 off M4, A419 to Cirencester. Take A361 Burford, Highworth exit. Left at lights in Highworth onto Cricklade Road. House on right immed. after Oak Drive. Black wrought-iron gate.

Brenda Haywood
Westhill House,
Cricklade Road,
Highworth SN6 7BL

Tel	+44 (0)1793 764219
Email	info@westhillhouse.net
Web	www.westhillhouse.net

Entry 580   Map 3

Wiltshire

Overtown Manor

It's just a few miles from the centre of Swindon, but this listed manor house is still part of a working farm, tucked into quiet countryside. Feel swish in an elegant, duck-egg blue drawing room with ornate plaster work, marble fireplace and lofty sash windows overlooking gardens and pool. You'll eat like a lord in the impressive dining room: Nancy is a chef and chooses produce locally sourced or home-grown. Large light bedrooms are classic country-house style, with views; bathrooms are new, tiled in stone and heated to perfection. Explore quaint villages and stone circles, try clay pigeon shooting; all is possible.

Price	From £95. Singles from £65.
Rooms	3 twins/doubles.
Meals	Pub within 5 miles.
Closed	Rarely.
Directions	M4 junc.15 Marlborough. After 1 mile, right B4005 Chiseldon, just before petrol station. Cont. to mini r'bout, Patriots Arms pub on left; 2nd exit B4005. At T-junc. right. 100 yds, left signed Overtown. Cont. to x-roads; on left.

	Nancy Lawson
	Overtown Manor,
	Wroughton, Swindon SN4 0SH
Tel	+44 (0)1793 814737
Mobile	+44 (0)7887 597090
Email	nancy@overtownmanor.co.uk
Web	www.overtownmanor.co.uk

Entry 581   Map 3

Wiltshire

Copes Cottage

Sarah's pretty thatched cottage has far-reaching views over the Vale of Pewsey. Admire the gardens, with wildflower meadow and orchard, and step into her friendly Aga kitchen for tea and cake. Breakfast is in a dining room full of warm colours, flowers, books, glowing lamps and blue and white china. You have a choice of bedrooms – one with beams, antique bed and adjoining space for children, the other more modern and airy; the rustic sitting room is in a converted barn with comfy sofas and table tennis. Set out for forest and downland walks, ancient monuments, Salisbury Cathedral; there are crop circles to find in summer.

Price	£80. Singles £50.
Rooms	2: 1 double (with extra double room, let to same party only); 1 double with separate bath/shower.
Meals	Pub/restaurant 3 miles.
Closed	Rarely.
Directions	A346 Marlborough to Burbage. At roundabout 4th exit towards Pewsey on B3087. Left into village. After 200 yds, right into Harris Lane. Cottage at end.

	Sarah Townsend-Rose
	Copes Cottage,
	Harris Lane, Easton Royal,
	Pewsey SN9 5LX
Tel	+44 (0)1672 810427
Email	copescottage@live.co.uk
Web	www.copescottage.co.uk

Entry 582   Map 3

Wiltshire

Rushall Manor

A gorgeous country house – and Caroline is a treat of a host. The dining room shines with glass, antiques and family portraits; a particularly impressive admiral gazes benignly down as you tuck into breakfast: local eggs and sausages, and jams from the orchard. The harmonious sitting room has comfy sofas, books and games; pretty bedrooms have perfect mattresses and linen (and, from one, fantastic views up to Salisbury Plain); bathrooms come with cast-iron baths, scented soaps and lashings of hot water. Stonehenge and Salisbury are nearby, walks are good, and Caroline holds the village fête in her delightful garden.

Price	£90–£100. Singles £55–£60.
Rooms	3: 1 twin; 1 double, 1 twin, both with separate bath.
Meals	Dinner £30. Pubs 1 mile.
Closed	Rarely.
Directions	Sent on booking.

Caroline Larken
Rushall Manor,
Rushall,
Pewsey SN9 6EG
Tel   +44 (0)1980 630301
Email   bandb@rushallmanor.com
Web   www.rushallmanor.com

Entry 583   Map 3

Wiltshire

Westcourt Farm

Rozzie and Jonny left London to restore a medieval, Grade II* cruck truss hall house (beautifully) amid wildflower meadows, hedgerows, ponds and geese. Delightful people, they love to cook and can spoil you rotten. Rooms are well decorated, crisp yet traditional, the country furniture is charming and the architecture fascinating. Bedrooms have comfortable beds and fine linen, bathrooms are spot-on; there's a lovely light drawing room and a barn for meetings and parties too. Encircled by footpaths and fields, Westcourt is the oldest house in a perfect village, two minutes from a rather good pub.

Price	£80. Singles £50.
Rooms	2: 1 twin; 1 double.
Meals	Pub/restaurant in village.
Closed	Rarely.
Directions	A338 Hungerford-Salisbury; after 4 miles signed Shalbourne; through village & fork left at pub; 150 yds, 2nd drive on right.

Jonny & Rozzie Buxton
Westcourt Farm,
Shalbourne,
Marlborough SN8 3QE
Tel   +44 (0)1672 871399
Email   rozzieb@btinternet.com
Web   www.westcourtfarm.com

Entry 584   Map 3

Worcestershire

Redmarley Cottage

Come for homemade jams and glamorous hens: breakfasts are delicious! Behind Carol and Steve's historic cottage (two woven into one) are three gorgeous acres of orchard, pond and veg garden for you to explore. Your bedroom has sumptuous curtains, sweet knick-knacks, delicious bathrobes and towels, and an 'open' en suite behind the beams. Carol, warm and hospitable, will point you in the direction of the baroque church in the village, Witley Court and the tea rooms in the garden, the nearby pub for supper. Come home to a big tastefully furnished sitting room – all yours – with wood-burner and TV. Super-civilised country B&B.

Price	£100.
Rooms	1 double & sitting room.
Meals	Pub/restaurant 1 mile.
Closed	Rarely.
Directions	Sent on booking.

Carol Weston
Redmarley Cottage,
Stourport Road,
Great Witley,
Worcester WR6 6HZ
Tel +44 (0)1299 896978
Email carolaweston@hotmail.co.uk

Entry 585   Map 8

Worcestershire

The Hayloft

Beams galore – and photos too. Dennis is a photographer and your bedroom walls are lined with his colourful works; you get a jolly comfortable bed, posh robes, snazzy bathrooms with candles, plump towels and views across rolling fields. All is peaceful here: wake to a sizzling full English from cheery Maureen, with proper black pudding and homemade jams. You are near the Wychavon Way and the Droitwich Canal for walking, boating and birdwatching, but you could just pootle round the garden which slides down the hill into the countryside, or bubble gently in the hot tub. Excellent value, hearty suppers, lovely people.

Price	£70–£90. Singles from £50.
Rooms	3: 2 doubles; 1 double with separate bath.
Meals	Dinner, 2 courses, £20. Pubs/restaurants 2-3 miles.
Closed	Rarely.
Directions	From Droitwich take the A442 Kidderminster road. After approximately 1 mile turn left into Doverdale Lane. Upper Hall is half a mile on right on the hill top.

Maureen & Dennis Alton
The Hayloft, Upper Hall,
Hampton Lovett, Droitwich WR9 0PA
Tel +44 (0)1905 772819
Mobile +44 (0)7533 056398
Email maureen@hayloftbandb.com
Web www.hayloftbandb.com

Entry 586   Map 8

Worcestershire

The Old Rectory

The listed 18th-century rectory has taken on a new lease of life, thanks to welcoming Claire (and John and two spaniels) whose ethos is flexibility and whose generosity spreads far. Relax in the library, the breakfast room, the garden full of birds, the grand red drawing room that overlooks Elgar country. Beautiful bedrooms are sumptuously furnished with old and new pieces, fluffy bathrobes and feather duvets, artisan biscuits and Malvern spring water. Claire is an inspired cook: breakfasts, beautifully sourced, are a treat, and candlelit dinners are amazing. Bliss for walkers, foodies, romantics, and all who love the Malverns.

Worcestershire

Old Country Farm

Ella's passion for this remote, tranquil place – and the environment in general – is infectious. She believes the house was once home to a Saxon chief. Certainly, it has beams dating from 1400; now it's a rambling mix of russet stone and colour-washed brick, with a warm and delightfully cluttered kitchen, wooden floors, lovely rugs. Friendly bedrooms are simple and rustic; one has a beautiful oak bed, duck your head in another. Ella's parents collected rare plants and the garden is full of hellebores and snowdrops; roe deer and barn owls flit in the surrounding woods. A wonderful retreat for nature lovers and walkers.

Price	£130.
Rooms	3: 2 doubles, 1 twin/double.
Meals	Dinner £37.
	Pubs/restaurants 1 mile.
Closed	Rarely.
Directions	Sent on booking.

Price	£65–£90. Singles £35–£55.
Rooms	3: 1 double;
	1 double with separate bath;
	1 double with separate shower.
Meals	Pubs/restaurants 3 miles.
Closed	Rarely.
Directions	From Worcester A4103 for 11 miles; B4220 for Ledbury. After leaving Cradley, left at top of hill for Mathon, right for Coddington; house 0.25 miles on right.

	Claire Dawkins
	The Old Rectory, Rectory Lane,
	Cradley, Malvern WR13 5LQ
Tel	+44 (0)1886 880109
Mobile	+44 (0)7920 801701
Email	oldrectorycradley@btinternet.com
Web	www.oldrectorycradley.com

	Ella Grace Quincy
	Old Country Farm,
	Mathon,
	Malvern WR13 5PS
Tel	+44 (0)1886 880867
Email	ella@oldcountryhouse.co.uk
Web	www.oldcountryhouse.co.uk

Entry 587   Map 8

Entry 588   Map 8

Worcestershire

Bidders Croft

Completely rebuilt in 1995 from 200-year-old bricks, this solid house has oak-framed loggias and an enormous conservatory where you eat overlooking the garden, orchard, newly planted vineyard and the Malvern Hills. Traditional bedrooms with mirror-fronted wardrobes and dressing tables are warm and comfortable; bathrooms shine. Bill and Charlotte give you a log fire, books and magazines in the drawing room and an Aga-cooked breakfast with home-produced eggs and fruits. There is a large terrace overlooking lawns and an ornamental pond; the hills beckon walkers, the views soar and the Malvern theatres are a short drive.

Price	£85-£95. Singles £50-£55.
Rooms	2: 1 twin with separate bath; 1 double with separate shower.
Meals	Pub/restaurant 250 yds.
Closed	Christmas & New Year.
Directions	From Upton-upon-Severn, A4104 dir. Little Malvern & Ledbury. After 3 miles, pass The Inn at Welland on right; drive is 250 yds on left, house signed.

Bill & Charlotte Carver
Bidders Croft,
Welland, Malvern WR13 6LN

Tel	+44 (0)1684 592179
Mobile	+44 (0)7763 055366
Email	carvers@bidderscroft.com
Web	www.bidderscroft.com

Entry 589   Map 8

Worcestershire

The Birches

Thoughtful Katharine is attentive; Edward puts you at ease humming a jolly tune. Come and go as you please from this self-contained annexe, spotless and contemporary. French windows lead to a pretty terrace, then to a charming garden opening to fields and views of the Malverns. Though the house is easily accessible, the tranquillity is sublime; plenty of spots to sit and ponder the view back to the timber-framed house. Hens pottering on the lawn lay eggs for breakfast, served – in your room – with local bacon and sausages, and bread from Ledbury's baker. Wander further for abundant leafy walks and lovely Regency Malvern.

Price	£80. Singles £60.
Rooms	Annexe: 1 double.
Meals	Pub/restaurant 0.3 miles.
Closed	Rarely.
Directions	From Ledbury A449, signed Malvern. After 1 mile right onto A438. After 3 miles, crossroads; left, then after 1 mile right into Birts Street. House on right after 0.25 miles.

Katharine Litchfield
The Birches, Birts Street,
Birtsmorton, Malvern WR13 6AW

Tel	+44 (0)1684 833821
Mobile	+44 (0)7875 458441
Email	katharine-thebirches@hotmail.co.uk
Web	www.the-birchesbedandbreakfast.co.uk

Entry 590   Map 8

Worcestershire

Harrowfields

Tucked just off the high street is a compact cottage that's massively comfortable and stylish too: contemporary colours and old beams, great books and a homely feel. Your bedroom is large enough to lounge in with a good sofa, an antique brass bed, crisp linen and a cosy wood-burner; the spoiling continues in a shower room with comfy robes. Susie and Adam (who cooks) are natural and charming, hens cluck around the delightful garden, breakfast is local and seasonal, you can walk for miles or just to the pub. Romantic couples will be in heaven; uncork the wine, light the fire, turn up the music.

Price	£75. Singles from £60.
Rooms	1 double.
Meals	Pubs in village.
Closed	Rarely.
Directions	Enter Eckington from Bredon (M5 junc. 9). Turn 1st right by village shop. House on left before Anchor pub.

Susie Alington & Adam Stanford
Harrowfields,
Cotheridge Lane,
Eckington WR10 3BA
Tel   +44 (0)1386 751053
Email susie@harrowfields.co.uk
Web   www.harrowfields.co.uk

Entry 591   Map 8

Yorkshire

Broomhead

High in the ancient county of Hallamshire, amid curlews and skylarks and 6,000 acres of National Park, is the renovated stable block of Broomhead Hall. This warm, light, contemporary conversion is home to a lovely young family, passionate about the land and their responsibility for it. After a day of trout fishing or picnicking beside Ewden Beck, bliss to come home to cosy soothing bedrooms with beds heaped with pillows and breathtaking views. A fire-warmed snug rammed with books, a huge oil painting of the grouse moor up high, eggs from their hens and home-baked bread at breakfast: it's fabulous.

Price	£100. Singles £80.
Rooms	2 twins/doubles.
Meals	Packed lunch £8. Pub/restaurant 2.5 miles.
Closed	Rarely.
Directions	A616 past Stocksbridge. Left signed Bradfield. Follow road for about 2.5 miles. Broomhead 1st farm on left after steep hairpin bend and bridge.

Catherine Rimington Wilson
Broomhead,
Bolsterstone,
Sheffield S36 4ZA
Tel   +44 (0)1142 882161
Email catherine_heaton@yahoo.co.uk
Web   www.broomheadestate.co.uk

Entry 592   Map 12

Yorkshire

Sunnybank

A Victorian gentleman's residence just a short walk up the hill from the centre of bustling *Last of the Summer Wine* Holmfirth, still with its working Picturedrome cinema (touring bands too), arts and folk festivals, restaurants and shops. Attentive hosts look after you when the Whites are away. Peaceful bedrooms have a mix of contemporary, Art Nouveau and Art Deco pieces, caramel cream velvets and silks, spoiling bathrooms and lovely valley or garden views. A full choice Yorkshire breakfast will set you up for a lazy stroll round the charming gardens, or a brisk yomp through rural bliss.

Price	£70–£110. Singles from £55. Minimum stay two nights at weekends.
Rooms	3: 2 doubles, 1 twin/double (with extra single bed).
Meals	Dinner, 3 courses, £25. Dinner, 2 courses, £20. Packed lunch £12. Pubs/restaurants 500 yds.
Closed	Rarely.
Directions	A6024 signed Glossop out of Holmfirth centre. Then right into Upperthong Lane. House is first drive on right after St John's Church.

Peter & Anne White
Sunnybank,
78 Upperthong Lane,
Holmfirth HD9 3BQ

Tel	+44 (0)1484 684065
Email	info@sunnybankguesthouse.co.uk
Web	www.sunnybankguesthouse.co.uk

Entry 593   Map 12

Yorkshire

Thurst House Farm

This solid Pennine farmhouse, its stone mullion windows denoting 17th-century origins, is English to the core. Your warm, gracious hosts give guests a cosy and carpeted sitting room with an open fire in winter; bedrooms are equally generous, with inviting brass beds, lovely antique linen and fresh flowers. Outside: clucking hens, two friendly sheep and a hammock in a garden with beautiful views. Tuck into homemade bread, marmalade and jams at breakfast, and good traditional English dinners, too – just the thing for walkers who've trekked the Calderdale or the Pennine Way. *Over eights welcome. Alternative therapy rooms.*

Price	£80. Singles by arrangement.
Rooms	2: 1 double, 1 family room.
Meals	Dinner, 4 courses, £25 (BYO). Packed lunch £5. Restaurants within 0.5 miles.
Closed	Christmas & New Year.
Directions	Off M62 exit 22. 5 miles into Ripponden. Thro' lights, left up Royd Lane & brown sign to The Beehive. Up to the top & right at The Beehive Inn. House on right after 1 mile.

David & Judith Marriott
Thurst House Farm, Soyland,
Ripponden, Sowerby Bridge HX6 4NN

Tel	+44 (0)1422 822820
Mobile	+44 (0)7759 619043
Email	judith@thursthousefarm.co.uk
Web	www.thursthousefarm.co.uk

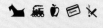

Entry 594   Map 12

Yorkshire

Field House

You drive over bridge and beck to this listed, 1713 farmhouse – expect comfort, homeliness and open fires. Pat and Geoff love showing guests their hens, horses, goats and lambs, and will tell you about the 14 circular walks or lend you a torch so you can find the pub across the fields! Ramblers and dog walkers will be in heaven – step out of the front door, past the lovely walled garden and you're in rolling, Brontë countryside. Good big bedrooms are in farmhouse style, one bathroom has a roll top bath, another a 70s blue suite, and Geoff's breakfasts are generous in the finest Yorkshire manner.

Price	£64–£74. Singles £37–£44.
Rooms	3: 1 double, 1 twin; 1 family room with separate bath/shower.
Meals	Packed lunch available. Pub/restaurant 200 yds.
Closed	Rarely.
Directions	1 mile from Halifax on A58 Leeds road. Turn between Stump Cross Inn car park & Headrooms shop. 100 yds to gates.

Pat & Geoff Horrocks-Taylor
Field House, Staups Lane,
Stump Cross, Halifax HX3 6XX

Tel	+44 (0)1422 355457
Mobile	+44 (0)7729 996482
Email	stayatfieldhouse@yahoo.co.uk
Web	www.fieldhouse-bb.co.uk

Entry 595 Map 12

Yorkshire

Ponden House

Bump your way up to Brenda's sturdy house, high on the wild Pennine Way. The spring water makes wonderful tea, the ginger scones are delicious and the house hums with interest and artistic touches. Comfy sofas are jollied up with throws, there are homespun rugs and hangings, paintings, plants and a piano. Feed the hens, plonk your boots by the Aga, chat with your lovely leisurely hostess as she turns out fab home cooking; food is a passion. Bedrooms are exuberant, comfortable and cosy, it's great for walkers and there's a hot tub under the stars (bookable by groups in advance). Good value with a lived-in, homely feel.

Price	£70–£75. Singles from £45.
Rooms	3: 2 doubles; 1 twin with separate bath (occasionally sharing bath with family).
Meals	Occasional dinner, 3 courses, £18. Packed lunch £6. Pub/restaurant 1 mile.
Closed	Rarely.
Directions	From B6142 for Colne. Pass through Stanbury village, then past Old Silent Inn. Access by Ponden reservoir.

Brenda Taylor
Ponden House,
Stanbury,
Haworth BD22 0HR

Tel	+44 (0)1535 644154
Email	bjt@pondenhouse.co.uk
Web	www.pondenhouse.co.uk

Entry 596 Map 12

Yorkshire

Pickersgill Manor Farm

A sparkling welcome, immaculate big bedrooms, spectacular views. So you'll forgive the ramshackle yard: this is a working farm! The handsome new farmhouse stands high on the moors, criss-crossed by the Millennium Way. Lisa seduces you with Italian coffee and homemade cake, then shows you the rest: lovely contemporary touches, a convivial colourful kitchen, perfect linen, bathrooms with Neal's Yard potions and a guest sitting room with books, games and wood-burning stove. Delicious breakfasts will set walkers up for the day – sausages from the pigs, eggs from the hens. If you time it right, you'll be cuddling new-born lambs.

Yorkshire

Braythorne Barn

Independence here with your own entrance. Step inside to paintings, fine furniture, colourful fabrics and rugs; floors are light oak, windows and doors are hand-crafted and sunlight dances around the rooms. Bedrooms are small but understatedly luxurious with beautiful rafters, glorious views, a fresh country feel. Bathrooms have Molton Brown toiletries and plump towels; the guest sitting room is gorgeous. Visit charming Harrogate or walk the Priests Way. Hens in the field, great breakfasts – perhaps brandy-soaked fruit compote... a rural idyll with a contemporary twist. *Children over 12 welcome. Minimum two nights.*

Price	£80. Singles £60.
Rooms	2: 1 double, 1 family.
Meals	Supper £14. Packed lunch £8. Afternoon tea £8. Pub/restaurant 1.5 miles.
Closed	Rarely.
Directions	A65 from Ilkley, then A6034 to Silsden Moor. On top of hill right into Cringles Lane. After 1.5 miles, left into Low Lane. After 0.5 miles, left when you see B&B sign.

Price	£90-£100. Singles from £70.
Rooms	2: 1 twin; 1 double with separate shower.
Meals	Pubs/restaurants 2-4 miles.
Closed	Rarely.
Directions	From Pool-in-Wharfedale, A658 over bridge towards Harrogate. 1st left to Leathley; right opp. church to Stainburn (1.5 miles). Bear left at fork; house next on left.

	Lisa Preston Pickersgill Manor Farm, Low Lane, Silsden Moor BD20 9JH
Tel	+44 (0)1535 655228
Email	lisa.preston@btconnect.com
Web	www.pickersgillmanorfarm.co.uk

	Petrina Knockton Braythorne Barn, Stainburn, Otley LS21 2LW
Tel	+44 (0)113 284 3160
Mobile	+44 (0)7866 372488
Email	trina@braythornebarn.co.uk
Web	www.braythornebarn.co.uk

Entry 597   Map 12

Entry 598   Map 12

Yorkshire

Ellerbeck House

Walk from the door of this beautifully restored country house, or head west to the Lakes, east to the Dales, north to Scotland. Period rooms display exquisite antiques and Harriet's artistic touch: sofas and curtains in dark pink and cream, Persian rugs on shiny oak floors, marble fireplaces, stained glass in the stairwell, huge sash windows overlooking the lawn. One window holds the breakfast table – full Cumbrian, at flexible times. Outside, a courtyard for sitting out with the birds and the breeze. It's all so pretty, as is this bucolic – yet accessible – spot near Kirkby Lonsdale, Settle, and Kendal of Mint Cake fame.

Price	£90. Singles £45.
Rooms	2: 1 double, 1 single sharing bath (let to same party only).
Meals	Pubs/restaurants 3 miles.
Closed	Rarely.
Directions	Sent on booking.

Harriet Sharp
Ellerbeck House,
Westhouse, Ingleton,
Carnforth LA6 3NH
Tel   +44 (0)15242 41872
Email   harrietnsharp@gmail.com
Web   www.ellerbeckhouse.co.uk

Entry 599   Map 12

Yorkshire

Brandymires

The Wensleydale hills lie framed through the windows of the time-warp bedrooms; no TV, no fuss, just calm. In the middle of the National Park, this is a glorious spot for walkers. Gail and Ann bake their own bread, make jams and marmalade, and their delicious well-priced dinners, served at your own table, are prepared with fresh local produce. Bedrooms share bathrooms over two floors. Two rooms, not in their first flush of youth, have four-posters; all have views. If you're arriving by car, take the 'over-the-top' road from Buckden to Hawes – stunning. A friendly, characterful place. *Over eights welcome.*

Price	£60. Singles £35.
Rooms	3: 1 twin, 2 four-posters, sharing 2 bath/shower rooms. (On request, one room only may be let per floor.)
Meals	Dinner, 4 courses, £21 (not Thursday). Pubs/restaurant 5-minute walk.
Closed	November-February.
Directions	300 yds off A684, on road north out of Hawes, signed Muker & Hardraw. House on right.

Gail Ainley & Ann Macdonald
Brandymires,
Muker Road,
Hawes DL8 3PR
Tel   +44 (0)1969 667482

Entry 600   Map 12

Yorkshire

Low Mill

Off the village green this handsome historic mill in the Dales keeps many of its original features. The huge beamed guest sitting room has a roaring fire, and the old waterwheel is working! Friendly relaxed Neil and Jane have restored their home, then filled it with interesting art, quirky sculpture, flowers and vintage gems. Bedrooms have tip-top linen and luxurious throws; bathrooms are fabulous. Eat well at separate tables on all things local and home-grown: bacon, pancakes, homemade bread; and for dinner, perhaps Yorkshire ham or herby lamb. The pretty riverside garden is perfect for chilling with a glass of wine.

Price	£90–£150.
Rooms	3: 2 doubles, 1 suite.
Meals	Dinner, 2-3 courses, £17.50–£22.50. Pubs 5-minute drive.
Closed	Rarely.
Directions	Sent on booking.

Neil McNair
Low Mill,
Bainbridge,
Leyburn DL8 3EF
Tel   +44 (0)1969 650553
Email   lowmillguesthouse@gmail.com
Web   lowmillguesthouse.co.uk

Entry 601   Map 12

Yorkshire

Waterford House

Middleham Castle – northern stronghold of Richard III – stands around the corner from this attractive Georgian house. Martin and Anne are great hosts and the house full of beautiful things: clocks everywhere, polished chests, vintage luggage, interesting art. There's an open fire in the sitting room, claret walls in the dining room – and delicious breakfasts from Anne. Pretty bedrooms (one up steep stairs) have bags of comfort: four-posters, decanters of sherry, homemade cakes. Middleham is a racing village with 14 stable yards – horses clop by in the morning on their way to the gallops. Bring hiking boots. Unravel the Dales.

Price	£98–£130. Singles from £85.
Rooms	4: 1 double, 1 twin/double, 2 four-posters.
Meals	Restaurants within 200 yds.
Closed	Christmas & January.
Directions	Sent on booking.

Martin Cade & Anne Parkinson Cade
Waterford House,
Kirkgate, Middleham,
Leyburn DL8 4PG
Tel   +44 (0)1969 622090
Email   info@waterfordhousehotel.co.uk
Web   www.waterfordhousehotel.co.uk

Entry 602   Map 12

Yorkshire

Manor House

It's the handsomest house in the village. Annie – warm, intelligent, fun – invites you in to spacious interiors elegantly painted and artfully cluttered. Tall shuttered windows and a big open fire, candles in glass sconces and heaps of flowers, soft wool carpets and charming fabrics: a genuinely relaxing family home. Bedroom are a treat, one with green views on two sides and a bathroom with a French country feel; fittings are vintage but spotless. Stride the Dales or discover Georgian Richmond, a hop away; return to a simple delicious supper, with veg from the garden and eggs from the hens. *Note: peacocks in village!*

Price	£95. Singles £75.
Rooms	2: 1 double; 1 twin/double with separate bath.
Meals	Supper, 2 courses, £20. BYO. Pubs 1 mile.
Closed	Christmas.
Directions	From A1, A66 Scotch Corner towards Brough. After 5 miles, slip road to Ravensworth. In village, right at Bay Horse pub; up steep hill to x-roads then right. In Gayles, left at telephone box into Middle St. House 3rd on left.

Annabel Burchnall
Manor House,
Middle Street,
Gayles,
Richmond DL11 7JF
Tel +44 (0)1833 621578
Email annieburchnall@hotmail.com

Entry 603   Map 12

Yorkshire

Cliffe Hall

What remains is the Victorian section of an earlier mansion, added by Richard's family in 1858. Inside is a beautifully proportioned and charming family home: huge reception rooms, plasterwork ceilings, acres of sofas, family portraits, floor to ceiling shelves of books. Bedrooms are large, sunny, traditional and uncontrived, bathrooms carpeted and twin beds super-comfy; large windows look onto the glorious grounds that run down to the river Tees. Breakfast on local organic bread and eggs and seasonal fruit from the garden. A special place with a soft, timeless grandeur and a big welcome.

Price	£90. Singles from £50.
Rooms	2 twins/doubles, each with separate bath.
Meals	Pub 1 mile.
Closed	Rarely.
Directions	From A1, exit 56. North for 4.2 miles on B6275. Into drive (on left before Piercebridge); 1st right fork. Darlington Station 7 miles.

Caroline & Richard Wilson
Cliffe Hall,
Piercebridge,
Darlington DL2 3SR
Tel +44 (0)1325 374322
Mobile +44 (0)7785 756380
Email petal@cliffehall.co.uk

Entry 604   Map 12

Yorkshire

Rawcar Farm

You're on the edge of the Yorkshire Dales and North Yorkshire Moors, with outstanding countryside on the doorstep and Wainwright's Coast to Coast walk running past the farm drive. Jane and Ian are informal and friendly and make you feel immediately at ease when you step into their homely farmhouse. Spacious bedrooms are classy with a modern-vintage mix; fabulous bathrooms have fluffy towels. Relax in the wheelhouse sitting room with comfy sofas, oak beams and far-reaching views; enjoy a great breakfast with home-baked bread served in the stunning, vaulted dining room. A farm stay with touch of luxury and style.

Price	£100–£110.
Rooms	2 twins/doubles.
Meals	Dinner £22. Pubs/restaurants 3 miles.
Closed	November–March.
Directions	Northallerton to A167; left at r'bout to B6271 dir. Yafforth, Scorton & Richmond. Right to Streetlam after 4 miles. After 1 mile left to Whitwell & Ellerton. Rawcar 2nd farm on right.

Jane McBretney
Rawcar Farm,
Danby Wiske,
Northallerton DL7 0AL
Tel   +44 (0)1325 378297
Email jmcbretney@btinternet.com
Web   www.rawcar.co.uk

Entry 605   Map 12

Yorkshire

Lovesome Hill Farm

Who could resist home-reared lamb followed by apple crumble cake? This is a working farm and the Pearsons the warmest people imaginable; even in the mayhem of the lambing season they greet you with delicious cakes and Yorkshire tea. Their farmhouse is as unpretentious as they are: chequered tablecloths, cosy bedrooms (four in the old granary, one in the cottage) with garden and hill views, and a Victorian-style sitting room. Wake to tasty breakfasts of home-laid eggs and homemade bread and jams. You have easy access to the A167 and are brilliantly placed for the Moors and Dales. Good for walkers, families, business people.

Price	£74–£84. Singles £42–£50. Gate Cottage: from £84.
Rooms	5: 1 twin, 1 double, 1 family room, 1 single. Gate Cottage: 1 double.
Meals	Dinner, 2 courses, £18–£25. BYO. Packed lunch £5. Pub 4 miles.
Closed	Rarely.
Directions	From Northallerton, A167 north for Darlington for 4 miles. House on right, signed.

John & Mary Pearson
Lovesome Hill Farm,
Lovesome Hill,
Northallerton DL6 2PB
Tel   +44 (0)1609 772311
Email lovesomehillfarm@btinternet.com
Web   www.lovesomehillfarm.co.uk

Entry 606   Map 12

Yorkshire

Mill Close

Country-house B&B in a tranquil spot among fields and woodland; spacious, luxurious and with your own entrance through a flower-filled conservatory. Beds are large and comfortable, there's a grand four-poster with a spa bath, lovely linen and sconces for flickering candle light. Be spoiled by handmade chocolates, fluffy robes, even your own 'quiet' fridge. An elegant, pretty blue and cream sitting room has an open fire – but you are between the National Park and the Dales so walks are a must. Start with one of Patricia's famous breakfasts: bacon and sausages from the farm, smoked haddock or salmon, homemade jams. Bliss.

Price	£80–£95. Singles £45–£65.
Rooms	3: 2 doubles, 1 four-poster.
Meals	Pubs/restaurants 2 miles.
Closed	Christmas & New Year.
Directions	Follow the brown tourist signs from the village of Patrick Brompton on A684. Farm is 1 mile from village.

	Patricia Knox
	Mill Close,
	Patrick Brompton,
	Bedale DL8 1JY
Tel	+44 (0)1677 450257
Email	pat@millclose.co.uk
Web	www.millclose.co.uk

Entry 607   Map 12

Yorkshire

Park House

The soundtrack could be *Perfect Day*: a scenic drive, delicious cake on arrival, undisturbed peace in the converted estate house – partly built with stone from next door's stunning Cistercian Jervaulx Abbey, owned by your hosts. Gleaming antique gems stand out among leather bucket chairs, splashes of colour brighten a neutral palette, guest bedrooms are luxurious. Wake refreshed for a superb breakfast with maple crumpets and locally sourced bacon and egg. Leave pets and children at home but take boots and binoculars for the glorious scenery of Wensleydale: an AONB and a fitting backdrop to a classic country stay.

Price	From £75. Singles from £65.
Rooms	4: 3 doubles, 1 twin.
Meals	Restaurant 1.25 miles.
Closed	Rarely.
Directions	House is midway between Masham & Leyburn, about 25 minutes off A1. Full directions given on booking.

	Ian & Carol Burdon
	Park House, Jervaulx,
	Masham, Ripon HG4 4PH
Tel	+44 (0)1677 460184
Mobile	+44 (0)7730 983439
Email	ba123@btopenworld.com
Web	www.jervaulxabbey.com

Entry 608   Map 12

Yorkshire

Low Sutton

Judi's biscuits are a sweet welcome, Steve has a twinkle in his eye: they're B&B pros. Wood fires in the vast dining/sitting room and cosy snug burn fuel from their own copse; good insulation and underfloor heating keep the homely rooms comfy. Curl up in a soft white robe with a book, or wallow in the sparkling bathrooms – one is solar-heated (more greenie points!). There are six acres to explore with ponies, sheep, dogs and chickens; taste the fruit keen cook Judi jams up for breakfast and expect good dinners with veggies from the garden. Country delights from abbeys to markets are in easy reach.

Price	£70. Singles £50.
Rooms	2 doubles.
Meals	Packed lunch £5. Dinner £20. Pub/restaurant 1.5 miles.
Closed	Rarely.
Directions	From Ripon A6108 through Masham towards Leyburn. 1.5 miles outside Masham left into Sutton Lane. House 0.25 miles on left.

	Judi Smith
	Low Sutton,
	Masham, Ripon HG4 4PB
Tel	+44 (0)1765 688565
Mobile	+44 (0)7821 600521
Email	info@lowsutton.co.uk
Web	www.lowsutton.co.uk

Entry 609   Map 12

Yorkshire

Lawrence House

A classically elegant, comfortable house run with faultless precision by John and Harriet – former wine importer and interior decorator respectively. The house is listed, and Georgian, the garden is formal, flagged and herbaceous, the position – by the back gate to Fountains Abbey and Studley Royal, overlooking long meadow and parkland – is supreme. There's a linen-sofa'd drawing room just for guests, and the promise of a very good dinner. Bedrooms and bathrooms are in a private wing: light, well-proportioned, full of special touches. Relaxed, peaceful and timeless. *Golf, riding & clay pigeon shooting can be arranged.*

Price	£120. Singles £80.
Rooms	2: 1 twin/double, 1 twin.
Meals	Dinner £30. Pub/restaurant 1 mile.
Closed	Christmas & New Year.
Directions	A1 to Ripon. B6265 & Pateley Bridge road for 2 miles. Left into Studley Roger. House last on right.

	John & Harriet Highley
	Lawrence House,
	Studley Roger,
	Ripon HG4 3AY
Tel	+44 (0)1765 600947
Email	john@lawrence-house.co.uk
Web	www.lawrence-house.co.uk

Entry 610   Map 12

Yorkshire

Mallard Grange

Perfect farmhouse B&B. Hens, cats, sheepdogs wander the garden, an ancient apple tree leans against the wall, guests unwind and feel part of the family. Enter the rambling, deep-shuttered 16th-century farmhouse, cosy with well-loved family pieces, and feel at peace with the world. Breakfast is generous – homemade muffins, poached pears with cinnamon, a sizzling full Monty. A winding steep stair leads to big, friendly bedrooms, two cheerful others await in the converted 18th-century smithy, and Maggie's enthusiasm for this glorious area is as genuine as her love of doing B&B. It's a gem!

Price	£80-£100. Singles from £70. Min. 2 nights at weekends.
Rooms	4: 2 twins/doubles. Old Blacksmith's Shop & Carthouse: 2 twins/doubles.
Meals	Pubs/restaurants 10-minute drive.
Closed	Christmas & New Year.
Directions	B6265 from Ripon for Pateley Bridge. Past entrance to Fountains Abbey. House on right, 2.5 miles from Ripon.

Maggie Johnson
Mallard Grange,
Aldfield, Ripon HG4 3BE
Tel +44 (0)1765 620242
Mobile +44 (0)7720 295918
Email maggie@mallardgrange.co.uk
Web www.mallardgrange.co.uk

Entry 611 Map 12

Yorkshire

Carlton Barns

Quietly tucked into a corner of the sedate green, a short stride from the pub, lies a stylishly renovated 18th-century farmhouse. The old wash house, tractor shed and stable have become airy, chic, characterful rooms with beams and fabulous bathrooms. In summer, pull up a chair in a pretty yard with hanging baskets or find a tranquil spot in the charmingly secret garden. The dining room with open fire is a delight, so linger over a breakfast of delicious local produce, then set off for market towns, dales and moors. There's a big-hearted family feel here – Denise's oat and raisin crunchies and soda bread are to die for! Lovely.

Price	From £60. Singles from £45.
Rooms	Outbuildings: 2 doubles, 1 twin/double.
Meals	Pub/restaurant 2-minute walk.
Closed	Rarely.
Directions	Sent on booking.

Denise & David Mason
Carlton Barns,
Sandhutton,
Thirsk YO7 4RW
Tel +44 (0)1845 587381
Email info@carltonbarns.co.uk
Web www.carltonbarns.co.uk

Entry 612 Map 12

Yorkshire

The Old Rectory

Once the residence of the Bishops of Whitby this elegant rectory has a comfortable lived-in air. Both Turner and Ruskin stayed here and probably enjoyed as much good conversation and comfort as you will. Bedrooms are pretty, traditional and with grand views; the drawing room is classic country house with a fine Venetian window and an enticing window-seat. The graceful, deep pink dining room looks south over a large garden of redwood and walnut trees – some are 300 years old. Caroline will give you a generous breakfast; wander at will to find an orchard, tennis court and croquet lawn. *Children over three welcome.*

Price	From £70. Singles from £45.
Rooms	2: 1 double with separate bath & dressing room; 1 twin/double with separate bath & shower.
Meals	Pub/restaurant opposite.
Closed	Rarely.
Directions	Take A168 (Northallerton road) off A19; over r'bout; left into village; house opp. pub, next to church.

	Tim & Caroline O'Connor-Fenton
	The Old Rectory,
	South Kilvington,
	Thirsk YO7 2NL
Tel	+44 (0)1845 526153
Mobile	+44 (0)7981 329764
Email	ocfenton@talktalk.net

Entry 613   Map 12

Yorkshire

Shallowdale House

Phillip and Anton have a true affection for their guests so you will be treated like angels. Sumptuous bedrooms dazzle in yellows, blues and limes, acres of curtains frame wide views over the Howardian Hills, bathrooms are gleaming and immaculate. Breakfast on the absolute best; fresh fruit compote, dry-cured bacon, homemade rolls – and walk it off in any direction straight from the house. Return to an elegant drawing room, with a fire in winter, and an enticing library. Dinner is out of this world and coffee and chocolates are all you need before you crawl up to bed. Bliss. *Children over 12 welcome.*

Price	£105–£130. Singles £85–£100.
Rooms	3: 2 twins/doubles; 1 double with separate bath/shower.
Meals	Dinner, 4 courses, £39.50. Pub 0.5 miles.
Closed	Christmas & New Year.
Directions	From Thirsk, A19 south, then 'caravan route' via Coxwold & Byland Abbey. 1st house on left, just before Ampleforth.

	Anton van der Horst & Phillip Gill
	Shallowdale House,
	West End,
	Ampleforth YO62 4DY
Tel	+44 (0)1439 788325
Email	stay@shallowdalehouse.co.uk
Web	www.shallowdalehouse.co.uk

Entry 614   Map 12

Yorkshire

Cundall Lodge Farm

Ancient chestnuts, crunchy drive, sheep grazing, hens free-ranging. This four-square Georgian farmhouse could be straight out of Central Casting. Homely rooms of damask sofas and bright wallpapers have views to Sutton Bank's White Horse or the river Swale, spotless bedrooms are inviting – family furnishings, fresh flowers, Roberts radios – and tea and oven-fresh cakes welcome you. This is a working farm and the breakfast table groans with free-range eggs, homemade jams and local bacon. The garden and river walks guarantee peace, and David and Caroline are generous and delightful. *Over 14s welcome.*

Price	£80-£95.
Rooms	3: 2 doubles; 1 twin/double.
Meals	Packed lunch £5. Pubs/restaurants 2 miles.
Closed	Christmas & January.
Directions	Exit junc. 49 A1(M) onto A168 (Thirsk). Turn off 1st junc. for Cundall. Turn right at the Crab & Lobster. 2 miles on left, before Cundall Manor School.

Caroline Barker
Cundall Lodge Farm,
Cundall, York YO61 2RN
Tel   +44 (0)1423 360203
Mobile   +44 (0)7773 494260
Email   enquiries@cundall-lodgefarm.co.uk
Web   www.cundall-lodgefarm.co.uk

Entry 615   Map 12

Yorkshire

Poppleton House

Down a driveway off Main Street, through restored gates, to a wonderful red-brick Georgian house and a big welcome from Kathleen. Inside is graceful, stately, spacious and light: elegant breakfasts at a mahogany table and flowers in every room – Kathleen arranges flowers professionally. Luxuriate in pale wool carpeting and heritage colours, cornicing, pelmets and chandeliers, silver-framed photos and a grand piano. Everything feels relaxed in this peaceful grown-up place, and that includes the bedrooms. Behind: an acre of garden, with secret corners and pathways. Beyond: York, its river walks and its Minster, a bus ride away.

Price	£80-£115. Singles £50-£68.
Rooms	3: 2 doubles; 1 double with separate bath/shower.
Meals	Pubs/restaurants in village & in York, 4 miles.
Closed	Rarely.
Directions	Sent on booking.

Kathleen Doggett
Poppleton House,
3 Main Street, Nether Poppleton,
York YO26 6HS
Tel   +44 (0)1904 781160
Email   info@poppletonhouse.co.uk
Web   www.bbyork.co.uk

Entry 616   Map 12

Yorkshire

The Chantry

The Chantry is a listed building in a village setting, lived in by Diana and Nigel – warm, humorous and engaging. A member of the Slow Food movement in York, and half Lebanese by birth, Diana reflects her culture in her cooking; her big ramshackle kitchen is the heart of this house. Bedrooms have space and high ceilings and an old-fashioned décor while bathrooms are swisher; the mood is comfy, warm, authentic, historic, and ever so gently eccentric. Pull yourself away from the suntrap terrace and sally forth into town: York, history-rich, is a sturdy walk (or a 20-minute bike ride) away.

Price	From £85. Singles from £60.
Rooms	2: 1 double, 1 twin.
Meals	Dinner £25. Pubs 200 yards, restaurant 0.5 miles.
Closed	Rarely.
Directions	From York take Bishopthorpe Road. Enter Bishopthorpe, left into Chantry Lane after Bishopthorpe Palace. Last house on right.

Diana Naish
The Chantry,
Chantry Lane, Bishopthorpe,
York YO23 2QF
Tel +44 (0)1904 709767
Mobile +44 (0)7850 912203
Email diananaish@athomecatering.freeserve.co.uk

Yorkshire

Corner Farm

Tea and home-baked cakes on arrival: you get a lovely welcome here! This peaceful farmhouse is so well insulated it's snug and warm even on the coldest day. With York so close and stunning estates nearby, this is a cosy nest from which to explore the area – or just the good village pub. Bathrooms are swish and bedrooms are light, fresh and comfortable: cast-iron beds, fine sheets, cute satin cushions. There are six acres to roam, and Tim and Sharon give you freshly pressed apple juice from the orchard, home-laid eggs and local produce for breakfast; the dining room is charming with vintage crockery and pots of flowers.

Price	£80. Singles £55.
Rooms	2: 1 double, 1 twin.
Meals	Packed lunch £4. Pub 100 yds.
Closed	Rarely.
Directions	From York A1079 (6.5 miles). Through two roundabouts, at Kexby left. then on for 0.9 miles. Left for Low Catton, then into village. House 0.8 miles on right.

Sharon Stevens
Corner Farm,
Low Catton, York YO41 1EA
Tel +44 (0)1759 373911
Mobile +44 (0)7711 440796
Email info@cornerfarmyork.co.uk
Web www.cornerfarmyork.co.uk

Yorkshire

The Mount House

A dollop of stylish fun in the rolling Howardian Hills (an AONB), Kathryn and Nick's redesigned village house is light, airy and filled with gorgeous things – from good antiques to splashy modern art and fresh flowers. The ground-floor twin with white cast-iron beds has its own cosy book-filled sitting room; the sunny upstairs double has views across the roof tops to open countryside. Kathryn, an excellent cook, will spoil you at breakfast – supper too, if you wish – sometimes in the pretty garden. Discover Castle Howard, Nunnington Hall, old market towns and great walking; only 20 minutes from York too. Super.

Price	From £90. Singles from £55.
Rooms	2: 1 double; 1 twin & sitting room.
Meals	Dinner, 2-4 courses, £25-£35. BYO. Pub/restaurant 200 yds.
Closed	Rarely.
Directions	North from York, left off A64 through Flaxton & Sheriff Hutton. Follow signs to Terrington. First gateway on right after sharp right bend as you enter village.

Kathryn Hill
The Mount House,
Terrington, York YO60 6QB
Tel   +44 (0)1653 648206
Mobile   +44 (0)7780 536937
Email   mount.house@clayfox.co.uk
Web   www.howardianhillsbandb.co.uk

Entry 619   Map 13

Yorkshire

Hunters Hill

The moors lie behind this elegant farmhouse, five yards from the National Park, in farmland and woodland with fine views; the position is marvellous and you can walk from the door. The house is full of light and flowers; bedrooms are pretty but not overly grand, and look onto valley or church. The lovely lived-in drawing room displays comfortable old sofas, paintings and fine furniture; rich colours, hunting prints and candles at dinner create a warm and cosy feel. The family has poured a good deal of affection into this tranquil house and the result is a home that's happy, charming and remarkably easy to relax in... Wonderful.

Price	£80. Singles from £50.
Rooms	2: 1 double; 1 twin/double with separate bathroom.
Meals	Dinner, 3 courses, £35. Pub/restaurant 10-minute walk.
Closed	Rarely.
Directions	From A170 to Sinnington. On village green, keep river on left, fork right between cottages, sign to church. Up lane, bearing right up hill. House past church beyond farm buildings.

Jane Otter
Hunters Hill,
Sinnington,
York YO62 6SF
Tel   +44 (0)1751 431196
Email   ejorr@tiscali.co.uk

Entry 620   Map 13

Yorkshire

Habton House Farm

Mellow stone, smart painted windows and a warm relaxed greeting from Lucy and James: a good start! You breakfast well here too, on home-produced sausages, bacon, eggs and jams, all delicious, at a big table in an elegant dining room. There are two cosy sitting rooms with wood fires to choose from, and the smartly done bedrooms have a pleasing medley of modern and vintage pieces, views of hill and river and immaculate bathrooms. Visit the pigs, fish for brown trout in the river, borrow a bike; further afield are the North Yorks Moors and the coast. A tasty supper at the local pub is an added bonus. *Over eights welcome.*

Price	£80-£105. Singles £55-£75.
Rooms	3: 2 doubles, 1 twin/double.
Meals	Pub 0.5 miles.
Closed	Rarely.
Directions	Sent on booking.

	Lucy Haxton
	Habton House Farm,
	Little Habton, Malton YO17 6UA
Tel	+44 (0)1653 669707
Mobile	+44 (0)7876 433351
Email	habtonhouse@gmail.com
Web	www.habtonhouse.co.uk

Entry 621   Map 13

Yorkshire

No. 54

No. 54 is in the middle of a peaceful row of attractive terraced houses a few minutes walk from the centre of town. Step inside to find a great mix of antique, vintage and quirky pieces, flagged floors, rugs and open wood fires. The inviting, supremely comfortable bedrooms are in a single-storey extension overlooking a secluded courtyard full of shrubs, climbers and pretty flowers; bathrooms are sparkling. Lizzie is warm and friendly and her home baking and breakfasts are delicious. The walking is good too, and on sunny days the back doors are thrown open onto the patio and garden – lovely! This is a happy welcoming place.

Price	£90.
Rooms	3: 2 doubles, 1 twin.
Meals	Restaurants 10-minute walk.
Closed	Christmas & New Year.
Directions	A170 to Helmsley; right at mini r'bout in centre, facing The Crown; house 500 yds along A170, on right.

	Lizzie Would
	No. 54,
	Bondgate,
	Helmsley YO62 5EZ
Tel	+44 (0)1439 771533
Email	lizzie.would@no54.co.uk
Web	www.no54.co.uk

Entry 622   Map 13

Yorkshire

West View Cottage

In a village packed with thatched houses is Valerie's — gorgeous, 17th-century and fronted by cottage flowers, with a bench at the side to take advantage of the views; they reach for miles. The hall is high-raftered with a stunning chandelier, the little dining room has exquisite oak panelling; there's no sitting room but a sofa in your bedroom, reached via the patio, beautifully self-contained. Find an ornate brass bed and a funky bathroom — comfortable luxury in an unusual space. History and abbeys abound, the North York Moors lie across the field, and bright friendly Valerie knows the area inside out.

Price	£80–£90. Singles £59.
Rooms	1 double.
Meals	Pubs/restaurants 2 miles.
Closed	Rarely.
Directions	Helmsley A170 towards Pickering. After 1 mile, left towards Pockley. House on right, 1 mile from A170.

Valerie Lack
West View Cottage,
Pockley,
Helmsley YO62 7TE

Tel	+44 (0)1439 770526
Email	westview.cottage@btinternet.com
Web	www.westviewcottage.info

Entry 623   Map 13

Yorkshire

Brickfields Farm

Down a long peaceful track, but a stone's throw from bustling Kirkbymoorside, is this walker's paradise. Friendly Janet sends you off to the North Yorks Moors with maps and information, and a tasty breakfast, served at separate tables in the conservatory overlooking guinea fowl and sheep. Bedrooms, one in the house and others in the barn or converted cow shed, are lovely: a French vintage four-poster, antiques, heavy curtains, sprung mattresses, flowers, a hidden fridge. All have stunning views over the fields. Bathrooms have big open showers, thick towels and plenty of lotions. Come to be pampered. *Unsuitable for children.*

Price	£95–£130.
Rooms	7: 1 twin. Barn: 4 suites. Cow shed: 1 suite, 1 four-poster suite.
Meals	Pub/restaurant 1 mile.
Closed	Rarely.
Directions	A170 east from Thirsk to Kirkbymoorside; continue past roundabout for 0.5 miles. Right into Kirkby Mills, signed. House 1st right along small lane.

Janet Trousdale & Sheila
Trousdale Ward
Brickfields Farm, Kirkby Mills,
Kirkbymoorside YO62 6NS

Tel	+44 (0)1751 433074
Email	janet@brickfieldsfarm.co.uk
Web	www.brickfieldsfarm.co.uk

Entry 624   Map 13

Yorkshire

Flamborough Rigg Cottage

Even in the North Yorks Moors it's rare to find a spot so remote – rarer still to find such luxury in an 1820s farmhouse set in fields of lambs. Philip and Caroline know how to delight guests with brilliant bathrooms, crisp linen, delicious meals from home-grown produce. They've melded modern touches with handsome antiques, like contemporary art around a grandfather clock in the vaulted dining room – it works. Both light bedrooms have French windows to an orchard garden; and views over hills that cry out for walking. Dogs are welcome, Whitby coast is ten miles, and there's fine food and company to round off the day.

Yorkshire

Low Farm

The first thing you see is the amazing view – it's a jaw-dropper! This handsome old farmhouse in the heart of the North Yorks Moors National Park will relax you from the moment you step in – a warm home where Linda welcomes with tea and homemade cake. Fresh comfortable bedrooms have far-reaching views and immaculate en suite bathrooms. In the morning, feast on freshly squeezed juice and homemade jam, Whitby kippers or the full works, all sourced locally; the polished table in the cosy dining room is set with pretty china and flowers. Castle Howard is a hop, the walks are fabulous and you can stroll to the village bistro.

Price	From £95. Singles £65.
Rooms	2 doubles.
Meals	Supper platter £15. Pub 2 miles.
Closed	Rarely.
Directions	Leave Pickering passing the Steam Railway towards Newton upon Rawcliffe and Stape. Go through Newton in to Stape. 500 yards past phone box turn left, keep left. House 4th property along.

Price	£80–£95. Singles £50–£65.
Rooms	2: 1 double, 1 twin.
Meals	Packed lunch available. Pub 0.25 miles.
Closed	Rarely.
Directions	Sent on booking.

	Philip & Caroline Jackson
	Flamborough Rigg Cottage,
	Middlehead Road, Stape,
	Pickering YO18 8HR
Tel	+44 (0)1751 475263
Email	enquiries@flamboroughriggcottage.co.uk
Web	www.flamboroughriggcottage.co.uk

	Linda & Andrew Dagg
	Low Farm,
	Rosedale Abbey,
	Pickering YO18 8SE
Tel	+44 (0)1751 417003
Email	adagg@moorsweb.co.uk
Web	www.lowfarmrosedale.co.uk

Entry 625   Map 13

Entry 626   Map 13

Yorkshire

Rectory Farmhouse

Walk from the door straight onto the North Yorkshire Moors; it's a brisk 30-minute stride across fields to the Steam Railway too. Michael and Heather have been here since 1997 – along with dogs, horses, a flock of sheep and bountiful hens. There's an easy-going, homely vibe with comfortable sofas and an open fire; enjoy homemade cakes and tea or sherry in the guest lounge, a proper Yorkshire dinner and hearty breakfast in the dining room. Comfy bedrooms have fluffy bathrobes, flowers, pretty cushions and throws. Excellent value; superb for walking, biking and riding – and relaxing! *Over eights welcome. Minimum stay two nights.*

Price	From £70. Singles from £45.
Rooms	4: 1 double, 1 twin. Apartment: 1 double, 1 twin sharing separate bath (let to same party only).
Meals	Dinner, 2 courses, £15. BYO. Pub in village.
Closed	Christmas & New Year.
Directions	From A169 take Lockton & Levisham road. Once through Lockton, look for house sign after 0.75 miles on right, in Levisham.

Michael & Heather Holt
Rectory Farmhouse,
Levisham, Pickering YO18 7NL
Tel   +44 (0)1751 460304
Mobile   +44 (0)7971 625898
Email   info@rectoryfarmlevisham.co.uk
Web   www.rectoryfarmlevisham.co.uk

Entry 627   Map 13

Yorkshire

Union Place

A listed Adam Georgian townhouse – elegance epitomised. Lofty well-proportioned rooms with polished floors and cornices and fireplaces intact are delightfully dotted with sophisticated, quirky *objets*: bead-and-embroidery lampshades and chandeliers, bone china, a small mirrored Indian ceramic child's dress – and your urbane host Richard's accomplished paintings. Bedrooms, one painted duck egg blue, one green with floral wallpaper, are beautiful, with lots of lace and fine linen; the claw-foot roll top in the shared bathroom cuts a dash. Breakfast is unbeatable... then it's off to explore the North York Moors. Superb.

Price	£65–£70.
Rooms	2 doubles sharing bath.
Meals	Pubs/restaurants within walking distance.
Closed	Christmas.
Directions	On the way out of Whitby on A174 (Whitby to Middlesbrough) approx. 100 yds from Harrison's Garage.

Richard & Jane Pottas
Union Place,
9 Upgang Lane,
Whitby YO21 3DT
Tel   +44 (0)1947 605501
Email   pottas1@btinternet.com
Web   www.unionplacewhitby.co.uk

Entry 628   Map 13

Yorkshire

Thorpe Hall

Arrive and listen: nothing, bar the wind in the trees and the odd seagull. The eye gathers glimmering sea and mighty headland, the final edge of the moors… are there still smugglers? This old listed house smells of polish and flowers, the drawing room breathes history. Angelique, a delight, has furnished it all, including TV-free bedrooms, with an eclectic mix of old and new and some fun (a framed transport caff poster in the breakfast room). She's hung contemporary art on ancient walls and has made a veg patch with young Phoebe. David helps out with simple breakfast when he's not globetrotting. The very opposite of stuffy.

Price	£80–£90.
Rooms	7: 3 doubles, 1 twin; 4 doubles sharing separate bath & shower rooms.
Meals	Pub within 0.25 miles.
Closed	Usually Christmas & New Year.
Directions	Scarborough, A171 Whitby. After 15 miles right at junc. for Fylingthorpe & Robin Hood's Bay. In centre of Fylingthorpe, right onto Middlewood Lane, house on left before ford.

Angelique Russell
Thorpe Hall,
Middlewood Lane, Fylingthorpe,
Whitby YO22 4TT
Tel   +44 (0)1947 880667
Email   thorpehall@googlemail.com
Web   www.thorpe-hall.co.uk

Entry 629   Map 13

Yorkshire

Holly Croft

Huge kindness and thoughtful touches (hot water bottles, lifts to the pub, cake and tea on arrival) make this special. The décor is in Edwardian style, the rooms are scented with flowers and polish, the clock ticks, the comforts are indisputable. The double has a textured silk headboard with matching curtains, there are bathrobes in fitted wardrobes, big showers and generous breakfasts – own jams, Yorkshire teas, kippers if you choose – served at the gleaming mahogany table. After a bracing cliff-top walk return to a homely open-fired sitting room overlooking the lovely garden. Wonderful Whitby is 20 minutes away.

Price	£75–£85. Singles £55–£60.
Rooms	2: 1 twin/double; 1 double with separate bath.
Meals	Dinner (4+ only), £25. Pub 600 yds.
Closed	Rarely.
Directions	A171 from Scarborough to Whitby; at Scalby x-roads, by tennis courts, take road on right. Signed 500 yds on right.

John & Christine Goodall
Holly Croft, 28 Station Road,
Scalby, Scarborough YO13 0QA
Tel   +44 (0)1723 375376
Mobile   +44 (0)7759 429706
Email   christine.goodall@tesco.net
Web   www.holly-croft.co.uk

Entry 630   Map 13

Yorkshire

Crown House @ No 20

The Firths have renovated their Victorian townhouse in chic New England style. Colours are muted, art is contemporary, stripes and new pieces blend with antiques and there is always something quirky to catch the eye. Luxurious ground-floor bedrooms have books, music, DVDs, jelly beans and fabulous bathrooms. Barbara is passionate about the area and is an amazing host: expect breakfasts of black pudding, Whitby kippers, muffins and more, or a continental choice in your room if preferred. The road is busy but inside all is quiet, graceful and relaxed and you're a walk away from town, theatre, stunning Italian gardens and sea.

Price	£100–£110. Singles from £70.
Rooms	2: 1 double, 1 twin/double.
Meals	Pub/restaurant 200 yds.
Closed	Rarely.
Directions	A64 to Scarborough; right at lights immed. after B&Q into Queen Margaret's Rd. At traffic lights right. House on left on corner of Belvedere Road and Filey Road.

Barbara Firth
Crown House @ No 20,
20 Filey Rd, Scarborough YO11 2TU

Tel	+44 (0)1723 375401
Mobile	+44 (0)7736 626289
Email	barbara@crownhousescarborough.co.uk
Web	www.crownhousescarborough.co.uk

Entry 631 Map 13

Yorkshire

The Wold Cottage

Drive through mature trees, and a proper entrance with signs, to an elegant Georgian Manor house in 300 glorious acres; arrive for tea in the warm and welcoming guest lounge. The dining room has heartlifting views across the landscaped gardens, and there are gorgeous original features: fanlights, high ceilings and broad staircases. Bedrooms are sumptuous and comfortable with lots of thoughtful extras: fluffy bathrobes, chocolates and biscuits. You are warmed by straw bale heating, food is local and delicious: an award-winning Yorkshire breakfast sets you up for discovering RSPB Bempton Cliffs and the unspoilt Wolds.

Price	£100–£120. Singles £60–£75.
Rooms	6: 2 doubles, 2 twins. Barn: 1 family room, 1 double.
Meals	Supper £25. Wine from £12.95.
Closed	Rarely.
Directions	A64 onto B1249. Through Foxholes to Wold Newton. In village, take road between pond & pub; signed on right.

Derek & Katrina Gray
The Wold Cottage,
Wold Newton, Driffield YO25 3HL

Tel	+44 (0)1262 470696
Mobile	+44 (0)7811 203336
Email	katrina@woldcottage.com
Web	www.woldcottage.com

Entry 632 Map 13

Yorkshire

Village Farm

Tucked behind houses and shops, this was once the village farm with land stretching to the coast. Now the one-storey buildings overlooking a courtyard are large bedrooms in gorgeous colours with luxurious touches. Chrysta, fresh from London, is living her dream and looks after you well: baths are deep, beds crisply comfortable, heating is underfoot. Delicious breakfasts are served at wooden tables in a cheerful light room with a contemporary feel; dinner is candlelit and locally sourced. Stride the cliffs, watch birds at Flamborough Head or make for Spurn Point – remote and lovely.

Guernsey

Seabreeze

Maggie's house – the most southern on Guernsey – comes with enormous views: Herm and Sark glistening in the water under a vast sky. The breakfast terrace is hard to beat, there are sofas in the conservatory, cliff-top paths for fabulous walks, a beach for picnics in summer. The house started life as HQ for French pilots flying seaplanes in WWI; these days warm, rustic interiors make for a great island base. It's not grand, just very welcoming with rooms that hit the spot: pretty linen, bathrobes, super showers, fresh flowers. You can hire bikes locally, then spin up the lane to a top island restaurant. Brilliant.

Price	£80. Singles £60. Family room £95. Half-board option (dinner, 2 courses) £110. Dogs £5.
Rooms	3: 1 double, 1 twin/double, 1 family room for 4.
Meals	Dinner, 2-3 courses, £18-£22. Pubs/restaurants within 20 yds.
Closed	Rarely.
Directions	A165 Beverley to Bridlington. At Beeford x-roads, right onto B1249 to Skipsea. Pass church on left, at x-roads straight across to Back Street. On right, opp. pub.

	Chrysta Newman
	Village Farm, Back Street, Skipsea, Driffield YO25 8SW
Tel	+44 (0)1262 468479
Mobile	+44 (0)7973 340562
Email	villagefarmskipsea@yahoo.com
Web	www.villagefarmskipsea.co.uk

Entry 633   Map 13

Price	£70-£95. Reduction for single occupancy £25 per night.
Rooms	3: 1 double, 1 twin/double; 1 twin/double & kitchen.
Meals	Pubs/restaurants 500 yds & 0.5 miles.
Closed	Rarely.
Directions	South from St Peter Port for 3 miles. Through Fermain village, then left at lights for Jerbourg Point. Keep left at Hotel Jerbourg and last house on right along cliff top lane, keeping sea on left.

	Maggie Talbot-Cull
	Seabreeze, La Moye Lane, Route de Jerbourg, St Martin GY4 6BN
Tel	+44 (0)1481 237929
Email	seaplane@mail.com
Web	www.guernseybandb.com

Entry 634   Map 4

Scotland

Aberdeenshire

Balwarren

Thirty acres at the end of a farm track, a field of Highland cattle, mixed woodland, ancient dykes, a lochside full of birdlife, a herb garden with 200 varieties and a burn you may follow down the hill. Hazel and James, warm, friendly, quietly passionate about green issues, came to croft 25 years ago and the whole place is a delight: cathedral roof, shiny wooden floors, cashmere blankets, sparkling bathrooms and log fires. Enjoy superb breakfasts and dinners: eggs from their hens, homemade marmalade and jams, beef from their cattle. A beautiful, uplifting and peaceful place in glorious countryside. *Cream teas £3.50.*

Price	£68–£85. Singles £45–£50.
Rooms	2: 1 twin, 1 double.
Meals	Dinner, 3 courses, £25. Pub/restaurant 10 miles.
Closed	Rarely.
Directions	North from Aberchirder on B9023. Right at Lootcherbrae (still B9023); 2nd left for Ordiquhill. After 1.7 miles, right at farm track opp. Aulton Farm; last croft up track.

Hazel & James Watt
Balwarren,
Ordiquhill, Banff AB45 2HR
Tel   +44 (0)1466 751688
Email   balwarrenbedandbreakfast@gmail.com
Web   www.balwarren.com

Entry 635   Map 19

Aberdeenshire

Old Mayen

Follow narrow lanes crowded by beech trees and hedges, through high rolling hills to a beautiful house with a river coursing along the unspoilt valley below. Find immaculate country-house style in elegant bedrooms with window seats, pretty chintzes, plumped cushions and spoiling bathrooms; there's a book-filled sitting room and candlelit dinners by a winter fire. Fran and Jim are infectiously enthusiastic and kind, breakfasts are a moveable feast (outside in good weather) and the garden hums with birds. A fine retreat for tired and jaded souls — and there are castles, distilleries and gardens to visit.

Price	£90. Singles £50.
Rooms	2: 1 double; 1 double with separate shower.
Meals	Dinner £25. Supper, 2 courses, £18. Restaurant 12 miles.
Closed	Rarely.
Directions	From A96, A97 to Banff. After crossing river Deveron (9 miles), left onto B9117; 3 miles, on left behind thick beech hedge.

James & Fran Anderson
Old Mayen,
Rothiemay,
Huntly AB54 7NL
Tel   +44 (0)1466 711276
Email   oldmayen@hotmail.co.uk

Entry 636   Map 19

Aberdeenshire

West Mains Steading

Spot red kites and white hare from the big garden, as you relish the long peaceful views. This converted farm steading on what was the Castle Fraser estate has had a smart renovation. Anne welcomes you with home baking, brings wonderful breakfasts to an elegant polished table and helps you plan your day: enjoy castles, stone circles, fishing and golf. Return to books, games, a piano, warmth, spaciousness and light, and soft-carpeted bedrooms in a separate wing. There are firm mattresses, huge wardrobes, and dressing gowns for quick dashes to private bathrooms, replete with heated rails for towels and lots of lovely smellies.

Price	£75. Singles £50.
Rooms	2: 1 double, 1 twin/double, each with separate bath.
Meals	Restaurant 10-minute walk.
Closed	Rarely.
Directions	Sent on booking.

Anne Harrison
West Mains Steading, Castle Fraser,
Kemnay, Inverurie AB51 7JS
Tel +44 (0)1330 833351
Email info@westmainssteading.co.uk
Web westmainssteading.co.uk

Entry 637   Map 19

Aberdeenshire

Lynturk Home Farm

The stunning drawing room, with pier-glass mirror, baby grand and enveloping sofas, is reason enough to come; the food, served in a candlelit, deep-sage dining room, is delicious, with produce from the farm. You're treated as friends here and your hosts are delightful. It's peaceful, too, on the Aberdeenshire Castle Trail. The handsome farmhouse has been in the family since 1762 and you can roam the surrounding, rolling, 300 acres. Inside: flowers, polished furniture, Persian rugs, family portraits and supremely comfortable bedrooms. "A blissful haven," says a guest. *Fishing, shooting & golf breaks.*

Price	£90. Singles £50.
Rooms	3: 1 double, 2 twins/doubles.
Meals	Dinner, 4 courses, £30. Pub 1 mile.
Closed	Rarely.
Directions	20 miles from Aberdeen on A944 (towards Alford); thro' Tillyfourie, then left for Muir of Fowlis & Tough; after Tough, 2nd farm drive on left, signed.

John & Veronica Evans-Freke
Lynturk Home Farm,
Alford AB33 8HU
Tel +44 (0)1975 562504
Mobile +44 (0)7773 389793
Email lynturk@hotmail.com

Entry 638   Map 19

Aberdeenshire

Woodend House

Elegant riverside living at a fishing lodge by the river Dee – one of the most magnificent settings in Scotland. Outside, a wild, wonderful garden; inside, beautiful wallpapers, fabrics and rugs. The dining hall and drawing room have dreamy river views, the large bedrooms ooze comfort and more views, and the bathrooms have cast-iron baths and fine toiletries. Food is locally sourced and seasonal: summer porridge with walnuts and fruit, homemade bread, seriously good dinners with home-grown vegetables. All this, and a fishing hut and a secure rod room for salmon and sea trout fishing in season. *Minimum stay two nights.*

Angus

Newtonmill House

The house and grounds are in perfect order; the owners are warm, charming and discreet. This is a little-known part of Scotland, with glens and gardens to discover; fishing villages, golf courses and deserted beaches, too. Return to a cup of tea in the sitting room or summerhouse, a wander in the lovely walled garden, and a marvellous supper of local produce; Rose grows interesting varieties of potato and her hens' eggs make a great hollandaise! Upstairs are crisp sheets, soft blankets, feather pillows, flowers, homemade fruit cake and warm sparkling bathrooms with thick towels. Let this home envelop you in its warm embrace.

Price	£110. Singles £80.
Rooms	3: 1 double, 1 twin; 1 twin with separate bath.
Meals	Dinner, 4 courses, £30-£40. Packed lunch £5-£10. Pub 2 miles.
Closed	Christmas, New Year & occasionally.
Directions	4 miles west of Banchory on A93. Entrance to drive on south side of road, just west of Backhill of Trustach.

Price	£96-£120. Singles from £65.
Rooms	2: 1 twin; 1 double with separate bath.
Meals	Dinner, £26-£36. BYO. Packed lunch £10. Pub 3 miles.
Closed	Christmas.
Directions	Aberdeen-Dundee A90, turning marked Brechin & Edzell B966. Heading towards Edzell, Newtonmill House is 1 mile on left, drive marked by pillars and sign.

	Miranda & Julian McHardy Woodend House, Trustach, Banchory AB31 4AY
Tel	+44 (0)1330 822367
Mobile	+44 (0)7812 142728
Email	miranda.mchardy@woodend.org
Web	www.woodend.org

	Rose & Stephen Rickman Newtonmill House, Brechin DD9 7PZ
Tel	+44 (0)1356 622533
Mobile	+44 (0)7793 169482
Email	rrickman@srickman.co.uk
Web	www.newtonmillhouse.co.uk

Entry 639 Map 19

Entry 640 Map 19

Argyll & Bute

Meall Mo Chridhe

Caring owners, exquisite food and a welcome sight amid the savage beauty of Britain's most westerly village. The warm ochre walls of this listed Georgian manse peep through wooded gardens across the Sound to Mull. Rooms are beautiful – French antiques, a wood stove, roll top baths – but it's the food that draws most to this far-flung spot. What David magics from his 45-acre smallholding (a bit of everything that grows, grunts, bleats or quacks) Stella transforms into feasts. Dine on spiced mackerel, minted lamb, hazelnut meringue; and duck eggs at breakfast. A gem buried in spectacular, wild walking country.

Price	£103–£204. Singles £51.50–£102.
Rooms	3 doubles.
Meals	Dinner from £37. Pub 0.25 miles.
Closed	Rarely.
Directions	Left from Corran Ferry, 8 miles south of Fort William. Through Strontian to Salen, then on B8007 to Kilchoan. House approx. 0.5 miles on right.

	Stella & David Cash
	Meall Mo Chridhe,
	Kilchoan, Acharacle PH36 4LH
Tel	+44 (0)1972 510238
Mobile	+44 (0)7730 100639
Email	enquiries@westcoastscotland.co.uk
Web	www.westcoastscotland.co.uk

Entry 641   Map 17

Argyll & Bute

HotelForTwo

For friends or for two: your own stone cottage sitting in the middle of a row of jaunty colours. The door opens to Julia, who makes you feel immediately at home; an ex-foreign correspondent, she has oodles of panache and an easy charm. Her home is intimate, cosy, filled with tapestries, antiques, chintzy sofas, curious artwork and a tousle of books; bedrooms (one up, one down) come in cottage chic with gorgeous bed linen. Julia lives in a bothy at the top of the garden, so the house is all yours with delicious meals all provided too. The bay bursts with boats and Mull is a treat: wildlife, whale tours, castles, good eating.

Price	From £80.
Rooms	2: 1 double; 1 double with separate bath (let to same party only).
Meals	Dinner £35. Afternoon tea £12.50. Packed lunch £15. Restaurants 15-minute walk.
Closed	Winter.
Directions	Sent on booking.

	Julia Watson
	HotelForTwo,
	Argyll Terrace, Tobermory,
	Isle of Mull PA75 6PB
Mobile	+44 (0)7990 940562
Email	watson.julia@gmail.com
Web	www.hotelfortwo.co.uk

Entry 642   Map 17

Argyll & Bute

Ardnacross Farm

The Aberdeen Angus cattle farm borders Mull's stunning coastline, where eagles, whales, red deer and otters leap, swoop, breach and soar. Rory and Penelope are warm and friendly, their farmhouse wonderfully homely: the dining room has a huge antique table and open fire; your bedroom (up private stairs) has a pretty patterned bedspread and floral curtains. The Scottish breakfast with Ardnacross eggs and porridge is hearty. Tobermory has everything from very good fish and chips and pleasant restaurants to an excellent theatre and festival; you can catch a boat trip to Iona or Staffa too. A beautiful slice of island Scotland.

Price	£75.
Rooms	1 double.
Meals	Pubs/restaurants 5 miles.
Closed	Christmas & New Year.
Directions	15 miles from Craignure & 11 miles from Fishnish ferry terminals. Right from either on Tobermory road. House halfway between Salen and Tobermory on right.

Rory & Penelope Forrester
Ardnacross Farm,
Aros,
Isle of Mull PA72 6JS
Tel   +44 (0)1680 300262
Email   enquiries@ardnacross.com
Web   www.holidaycottages-mull.co.uk

Entry 643   Map 17

Argyll & Bute

Ardtorna

Come for perfect comfort and uninterrupted views of loch and mountain. These thoughtful, professional hosts are happy to share their new, open-plan, eco-friendly house where contemporary Scandinavian and Art Deco styles are cleverly blended with homely warmth. Sink into a bedroom with a wall of glass for those wow views – and homemade tablet, a wet room or jacuzzi, Molton Brown treats. Flowers and jauntily coloured coffee pots decorate the oak table in the stunning dining room: food is home-baked and delicious. Argyll brims with historical sites and walks; return to watch the sun go down over the Morvern hills. Fabulous.

Price	£120–£180. Singles from £100.
Rooms	4 twins/doubles.
Meals	Room service supper £10–£20. Pub/restaurant 3 miles.
Closed	Rarely.
Directions	From Oban A828 over Connel bridge; north for 4 miles. House on right on hill, 0.5 miles before Sealife Sanctuary.

Karen Webster
Ardtorna,
Mill farm, Barcaldine,
Oban PA37 1SE
Tel   +44 (0)1631 720125
Email   info@ardtorna.co.uk
Web   www.ardtorna.co.uk

Entry 644   Map 17

Argyll & Bute

Barndromin Farm

Jamie and Morag run a cheerful, busy farmhouse that opens its arms to guests; hens cluck around the farmyard and Jamie will happily share his knowledge of butterflies, wild flowers and mushrooms. They have put in a micro hydro-electric scheme to power the house, which you can see running. There's an elegant drawing room and bedrooms are comfy with flowery duvets and Morag's art. Tuck into a hearty breakfast: croissant, bacon, sausages, black pudding, farm eggs. Set on the hillside with spectacular views over Loch Feochan, you can fish, walk, spot grouse, otters, deer, red squirrels and rare butterflies. Gorgeous. *Over tens welcome.*

Price	£75-£85. Singles £40-£50. Minimum stay 2 nights at weekends.
Rooms	2: 1 twin; 1 double with separate bath.
Meals	Pubs/restaurants 4-6 miles.
Closed	November-February.
Directions	Sent on booking.

Jamie & Morag Mellor
Barndromin Farm,
Knipoch, Oban PA34 4QS

Tel	+44 (0)1852 316297
Mobile	+44 (0)7775 741617
Email	mogsmellor@hotmail.co.uk
Web	www.knipochbedandbreakfast.com

Entry 645   Map 17

Argyll & Bute

Glenmore

An easy-going, traditional country house with no need to stand on ceremony. Built in the 1800s but with later 1930s additions setting the style, find solid oak doors and floors, red-pine panelling, Art Deco pieces and a unique carved staircase. Alasdair's family has been here for 150 years and many family antiques remain. One of the huge doubles can be arranged as a suite to include a single room and a sofabed; bath and basins are chunky 30s style with chrome plumbing. From the organic garden and the house there are magnificent views of Loch Melfort with its bobbing boats; you're free to come and go as you please.

Price	£85-£100. Family suite £85-£160. Singles £50-£65.
Rooms	2: 1 family suite; 1 double with separate bath/shower.
Meals	Pub 0.5 miles, restaurant 1.5 miles.
Closed	Christmas & New Year.
Directions	From A816 0.5 miles south of Kilmelford; then on to Glenmore. House signed (both directions). Past Lodge House at bottom of drive; on for 0.25 miles to big house.

Melissa & Alasdair Oatts
Glenmore,
Kilmelford, Oban PA34 4XA

Tel	+44 (0)1852 200314
Mobile	+44 (0)7786 340468
Email	oatts@glenmore22.fsnet.co.uk
Web	www.glenmorecountryhouse.co.uk

Entry 646   Map 17

Argyll & Bute

Melfort House

Enter a wild landscape of hidden glens, ancient woods and rivers that tumble to a blue sea. Find a big beautiful house with views straight down the loch, aglow with exquisite fabrics and polished antiques, fine oak floors, paintings and prints. Bedrooms have upholstered beds in soft plaids, delicious colours, superb views and handmade chocolates; bathrooms have huge towels and locally made soaps. Yvonne and Matthew are brilliant at looking after you: breakfasts of Stornoway black pudding, chilli omelettes, tattie scones, kedgeree. Sally forth with boots or bikes, come home to a dram and a roaring log fire. Argyll at its finest.

Price	£95–£125. Singles from £70.
Rooms	3: 2 twins/doubles, 1 suite.
Meals	Dinner, 3 courses, from £32. Packed lunch £10. Pub/restaurant 400 yds.
Closed	Rarely.
Directions	From Oban take A816 south, signed Campbeltown. After 14 miles, go thro' Kilmelford, then right to Melfort. Follow road & bear right after bridge.

Yvonne & Matthew Anderson
Melfort House,
Kilmelford, Oban PA34 4XD
Tel   +44 (0)1852 200326
Mobile   +44 (0)7795 438106
Email   relax@melforthouse.co.uk
Web   www.melforthouse.co.uk

Entry 647   Map 14

Argyll & Bute

Hawthorn Cottage

The most southerly of the Scottish islands, Arran is splendid for nature lovers. When you've worn yourselves out you can flop in Fiona's low, whitewashed cottage. It's up a bumpy track and far from smart but brimming with reality. The cottage is split in two: you get one end with a bedroom (up a rusty spiral stair), a bathroom and a sitting room (downstairs) and a small kitchen area: find hotchpotch furniture, original (bit stained, but clean) bath, frayed rugs, a piano, a wood-burner to huddle over (only electric storage heating) and a continental breakfast left hanging on your door. Will not suit boutique hotel lovers one iota!

Price	£50.
Rooms	1 twin/double with separate bath & kitchenette.
Meals	Continental breakfast. Pub/restaurant 2 miles.
Closed	Rarely.
Directions	Sent on booking.

Fiona Mackenzie
Hawthorn Cottage,
Brodick,
Isle of Arran KA27 8DF
Tel   +44 (0)1770 302534
Email   fionamackenzie569@btinternet.com

Entry 648   Map 14

Ayrshire

Heughmill

Acres of fields and lawn with free-range hens that kindly donate for breakfast and views to the sea. The house is just as good, surrounded by old stone farm buildings, with climbing roses and a small burn tumbling through. Inside, a lovely country home with tapestries in an airy hall, open fire in the sitting room and a terrace that sits under a vast sky. Country-house bedrooms with delightful art are stylishly homely. Two have the view, one an old armoire, another comes with a claw-foot bath. Your hosts are relaxed and entertaining – Julia sculpts, Mungo cooks breakfast on the Aga. Rural Ayrshire waits, yet the airport is close.

.

Price	£65-£80. Singles on request.
Rooms	3: 2 twins/doubles, 1 twin.
Meals	Pubs/restaurants within 2 miles.
Closed	Christmas & New Year.
Directions	3 miles south of Kilmarnock, turn east down B730 for Tarbolton. After 0.75 miles, right onto narrow road signed Ladykirk. After 0.4 miles drive entrance 1st on right.

Mungo & Julia Tulloch
Heughmill,
Craigie,
Kilmarnock KA1 5NQ
Tel   +44 (0)1563 860389
Email   mungotulloch@hotmail.com
Web   www.stayprestwick.com

Entry 649   Map 14

Dumfries & Galloway

The House on the Shore

Impossible not to be wowed by this incredible shoreline setting with views across the Solway Firth. The 1,250-acre estate has been in Jamie's family for generations; he and Sheri are excellent hosts and love their dower house with its rich and varied woodland and wildlife, formal gardens and stupendous views. Grand but with a family feel, this is old country house style at its best with rugs on polished floors, paintings, open fires and fresh flowers. The farm produces its own meat, an enormous walled kitchen garden is being restored, and a peach tree fruits abundantly; you'll eat well. Very special.

Price	£90-£100. Singles £60-£80.
Rooms	2: 1 double, 1 twin.
Meals	Dinner, 3 courses, £25. BYO. Pub/restaurant 2 miles.
Closed	Rarely.
Directions	A710 Dumfries towards Dalbeatie. Left in Kirkbean. First right, second left at top of hill, 0.5 miles down private drive then left to the house.

Jamie & Sheri Blackett
The House on the Shore,
Arbigland, Kirkbean,
Dumfries DG2 8BQ
Tel   +44 (0)1387 880717
Email   sheri@arbigland.com
Web   www.arbiglandestate.co.uk

Entry 650   Map 11

Dumfries & Galloway

Chipperkyle

This beautiful Scottish-Georgian family home has not a hint of formality, and the sociable Dicksons put you at your ease. Your sitting and dining rooms connect through a large arch; there are gloriously comfortable sofas, family pictures, rugs on wooden floors, masses of books and a constant log fire. Upstairs: good linen, striped walls, thick curtains, armchairs and windows with views – this wonderful house just gets better and better. There are 200 acres, dogs, cats, donkeys and hens (children can collect the eggs!), and you can walk, play golf, watch birds, visit gardens, sail or cycle – all in magnificent countryside.

Price	£100. Discounts for children.
Rooms	2: 1 double; 1 twin with separate bath/shower. Cot available.
Meals	Occasional dinner available for groups. Pub 3 miles.
Closed	Christmas.
Directions	A75 Dumfries ring road for Stranraer. Approx. 12 miles to Springholm & right to Kirkpatrick Durham. Left at x-roads, after 0.8 miles, up drive on right by white lodge.

Willie & Catriona Dickson
Chipperkyle, Kirkpatrick Durham,
Castle Douglas DG7 3EY
Tel   +44 (0)1556 650223
Mobile   +44 (0)7917 730009
Email   special_place@chipperkyle.co.uk
Web   www.chipperkyle.co.uk

Entry 651   Map 11

Dumfries & Galloway

Chlenry Farmhouse

Handsome in its glen; a traditional family farmhouse full of old-fashioned comfort with charming, well-travelled owners and friendly dogs. In peaceful bedrooms with leafy views, solid antiques jostle with photos, flowers, bowls of fruit, and magazines on country matters. There are capacious bath tubs, robes – and suppers for walkers with the Southern Upland Way passing nearby. Breakfasts are properly fortifying, evening meals can be simple or elaborate, often with game or fresh salmon. Convenient for ferries to Belfast and Larne; Galloway gardens and golf courses are close too – return to a snug sitting room with an open fire.

Price	From £80. Singles £50.
Rooms	3: 1 twin/double with separate bath; 1 double, 1 twin sharing bath.
Meals	Supper £17.50. Dinner, 4 courses, £35. Packed lunch £6. Pub 1.5 miles.
Closed	Christmas, New Year, February & occasionally.
Directions	A75 for Stranraer. In Castle Kennedy, right opp. Esso station. Approx. 1.25 miles on, after right bend, right signed Chlenry. Down hill, 300 yds on left.

David & Ginny Wolsley Brinton
Chlenry Farmhouse,
Castle Kennedy, Stranraer DG9 8SL
Tel   +44 (0)1776 705316
Mobile   +44 (0)7704 205003
Email   wolseleybrinton@aol.com
Web   www.chlenryfarmhouse.com

Entry 652   Map 14

Dumfries & Galloway

Holmhill

Among the rolling hills of Dumfries and Galloway, by the banks of the Nith, is a hidden gem of a Georgian country house. It was a favourite of Thomas Carlyle, who had his own pipe-smoking corner of the marvellously colourful garden. With seven acres to explore, find tranquillity, stunning views of the Keir Hills and excellent fishing. Rosie and Stewart love sharing their family home with guests — and will treat you to breakfast in your sumptuous bedroom, or by the fire in the graceful dining room. Masses of space here, from bathrooms to living spaces, each room deftly combining rustic virtue with modern savoir-faire.

Price	£95. Singles £65.
Rooms	2 twins/doubles.
Meals	Pubs/restaurants 0.5 miles.
Closed	Christmas & New Year.
Directions	Sent on booking.

Rosie Lee
Holmhill,
Thornhill DG3 4AB
Tel   +44 (0)1848 332239
Email   rosie@holmhill.co.uk
Web   www.holmhill.co.uk

Entry 653   Map 15

Dumfries & Galloway

Knockhill

Fabulous Knockhill: stunning place, stunning position, a country house full of busts and screens, oils and mirrors, chests and clocks, rugs and fires. In the intimate drawing room, full of treasures, floor-to-ceiling windows look down the wooded hill. Fine stone stairs lead to country-house bedrooms that are smart yet homely: headboards of carved oak or padded chintz, books and views. Come for a grand farming feel and delicious Scottish meals; the Morgans are the most unpretentious and charming of hosts. Mellow, authentic, welcoming — an enduring favourite.

Price	£88-£90. Singles £54-£64.
Rooms	2: 1 twin; 1 twin with separate bath.
Meals	Dinner £26. Pub 5 miles.
Closed	Rarely.
Directions	From M74 junc. 19, B725 for Dalton. Right by church in Ecclefechan, signed Hoddam Castle. After 1.2 miles right at x-roads towards Lockerbie. 1 mile on, right at stone [not whitewashed] lodge cottage. At top of long drive.

Yda & Rupert Morgan
Knockhill,
Lockerbie DG11 1AW
Tel   +44 (0)1576 300232
Mobile   +44 (0)7813 944107
Email   info@morganbellows.co.uk

Entry 654   Map 15

Dumfries & Galloway

Byreburnfoot House

Tucked away down a gravelled drive on the banks of the salmon-rich Esk, this pretty Victorian forester's house combines traditional charm with modern comforts. Airy rooms and wooden floors offset antique pieces – grandfather clock, writing desk, chandeliers – within an elegant rural décor: cushioned bay windows, fashionable florals. Beds are big, the linen is trimmed and the views are sublime. Warm hosts Bill and Lorraine are keenly green-fingered, and their 1.5 acres of orchards, flower-fringed lawns and organic kitchen garden are deliciously productive. Stay a few days and become part of the scenery. *Fabulous fishing.*

Dunbartonshire

Finglen House

The Campsie Hills rise behind (climb them and you can see Loch Lomond), the Fin Burn takes a two-mile tumble down the hill into the garden, and herons and wagtails can be spotted from the breakfast table. All this 40 minutes from Glasgow. Sabrina's designer flair gives an easy, graceful comfort to the whole house: good beds in stylish rooms, proper linen, French touches, eclectic art and cast-iron baths. Douglas, a documentary film maker, knows the Highlands and Islands well; he and Sabrina are fun and wonderful hosts. Plenty of walks from the door, golf courses close by too; return to a log fire in the elegant drawing room.

Price	£90–£95. Singles £65.
Rooms	3: 2 doubles; 1 twin/double with separate bath.
Meals	Dinner, 3 courses, £30. Packed lunch from £7.50. Pub/restaurant 5 miles.
Closed	Rarely.
Directions	From Carlisle (M6 junc. 44) on A7 north. Signs for Canonbie, then cross river Esk at traffic lights and turn immed. left. House on right, about 1 mile further.

Price	£90. Singles from £55.
Rooms	2: 1 double; 1 double with separate bath.
Meals	Pub 5-minute drive.
Closed	Christmas & New Year.
Directions	A81 from Glasgow right on A891 at Strathblane. 3 miles on, in Haughhead, look for a wall & trees on left, & turn in entrance signed Schoenstatt. Immed. left to house.

	Bill & Loraine Frew
	Byreburnfoot House,
	Canonbie DG14 0XB
Tel	+44 (0)1387 371209
Mobile	+44 (0)7764 194901
Email	bill.napierfrew@ukf.net
Web	www.byreburnfoot.co.uk

	Sabrina & Douglas Campbell
	Finglen House,
	Campsie Glen G66 7AZ
Tel	+44 (0)1360 310279
Mobile	+44 (0)7774 820454
Email	sabrina.campbell@btinternet.com
Web	www.finglenhouse.com

2 Cambridge Street

A mischievous humour, tinged with historical and cultural references, alerts you to the specialness of this place, a ground-floor B&B under the lee of Edinburgh Castle, in the heart of theatre land. Find fin-de-siècle Scotland, with darkly striking colours on walls, antiques aplenty, and a captivating attention to detail. There are interactive art installations that sing and play, a line of old theatre seats up on the wall, photos and 'objets' serving startling and original purposes. Erlend and Helene are delightful and free-spirited; Erlend, a quietly spoken (but don't be fooled) Shetlander, serves a breakfast to remember.

14 Hart Street

The brightly lit Georgian house has a smart front of polished brass and glossy paint. The warm raspberry hall is lined with art, and the graceful dining room is just as inviting: decanters on the sideboard, period furniture, glowing lamps, and a welcoming home-baked something. Fresh bright bedrooms are elegant and comfortable with whisky and wine on a tray and smart, sparkling bathrooms. Wake for breakfast at a beautifully polished table, with plenty of coffee, newspapers and chat; James and Angela are easy to talk to and love having guests to stay. Perfect for a peaceful city break, and Princes Street is a five-minute walk.

Price	£95-£130. Singles £85-£105.
Rooms	2 doubles.
Meals	Pubs/restaurants 1-minute walk.
Closed	Christmas.
Directions	Sent on booking.

Price	£84-£120.
Rooms	3: 2 doubles, 1 twin/double.
Meals	Restaurants 10-minute walk.
Closed	Rarely.
Directions	Sent on booking.

Erlend & Hélène Clouston
2 Cambridge Street,
Edinburgh EH1 2DY
Tel +44 (0)131 478 0005
Email erlendc@blueyonder.co.uk
Web www.wwwonderful.net

James & Angela Wilson
14 Hart Street,
Edinburgh EH1 3RN
Tel +44 (0)131 557 6826
Mobile +44 (0)7795 203414
Email hartst.edin@virgin.net
Web www.14hartst.com

24 Saxe Coburg Place

A ten-minute walk from the centre of Edinburgh, this 1827 house stands in a quiet Georgian square with a central communal garden. The three attractive bedrooms are on the garden level and are self-contained with their own entrance; find comfortable beds, good lighting, handsome antiques and a small kitchen for making tea and coffee. Bathrooms are spotless and one has Paris metro tiling in white and green. Excitingly you can nip over the road to the refurbished Victorian Baths for a swim, sauna or workout in the gym; return to a generous continental breakfast served in the little hall – or on the pretty terrace in summer.

7 Gloucester Place

A cantilevered staircase in walnut and mahogany, a soaring hand-painted cupola, and a classic Georgian townhouse five minutes from Princes Street. Rooms are large and immaculate, sprinkled with paintings and decorative things from travels to far-flung places, while bedrooms are comfortable, traditional and well-stocked with books and radio (and a useful Z-bed). Bag the south-facing double with its Art Deco bathroom and garden views. Naomi is relaxed and happy to chat to you about the local music and art scene, or to leave you in peace. An interesting and hospitable place to unwind, and breakfasts are delicious.

Price	£90–£120. Singles £48–£55.
Rooms	3: 1 double, 1 twin/double, 1 single.
Meals	Continental breakfast. Restaurants/pubs 5-minute walk.
Closed	Rarely.
Directions	From George St, down Frederick St. Over 3 sets of lights, left at bottom of hill. Right up Clarence St. At junc. over to Saxe Coburg St. Saxe Coburg Place is at end. Ask about parking.

Price	£90–£120. Singles from £60.
Rooms	3: 1 double en suite; 1 double with separate bath; 1 double with separate shower. Z-bed available.
Meals	Pubs/restaurants 300 yds.
Closed	Christmas & rarely.
Directions	From George St (city centre), down Hanover St, across Queen St at lights. Left into Heriot Row, right onto India St, then left.

Diana McMicking
24 Saxe Coburg Place,
Edinburgh EH3 5BP

Tel	+44 (0)131 315 3263
Mobile	+44 (0)7979 351717
Email	diana@saxecoburgplace.co.uk
Web	www.saxecoburgplace.co.uk

Naomi Jennings
7 Gloucester Place,
Edinburgh EH3 6EE

Tel	+44 (0)131 225 2974
Mobile	+44 (0)7803 168106
Email	naomijennings@hotmail.com
Web	www.stayinginscotland.com

Entry 659   Map 15

Entry 660   Map 15

10 London Street

A Roman X marks this special spot: a beautiful Georgian terraced house in Edinburgh's world heritage New Town, home to descendants of Scots author John Gibson Lockhart. Step into a family home of period elegance and charming informality: accept a sherry by the fire in the sash-windowed drawing room (with baby grand piano), chat with Pippa and Hugh over breakfast bagels, sleep undisturbed in 'Beauregard' with its lovely views and paintings. Or pick 'Gibson' for its off-courtyard privacy and self-catering option. The best of Edinburgh is a stroll away, good buses zip you further afield, but at night-time all is quiet.

Geraldsplace

Elegant Georgian 'New Town'… so splendid and handsome it's a World Heritage Site. Gerald – enthusiastic, charming, a B&B pro – lives on one of its finest streets in a lower ground floor flat of character, comfort and colour. Be treated to DVDs and books in the hall, a laptop with fast broadband, home-baked bread, locally smoked salmon, a decanter of Scotch in each room. Bedrooms have cosiness, warmth, fine fabrics, excellent art; ask for the room with the view. There's a patio to share, a private garden opposite, a perfect location and, of course, Gerald, your brilliantly well-informed, up-to-the-minute host.

Price	£100–£120.
Rooms	2 doubles (one with self-catering option).
Meals	Pub/restaurant 500 yds.
Closed	Rarely.
Directions	In the centre of Edinburgh, 10-minute walk from Edinburgh Waverly (main train & bus station, airport bus terminal station).

Price	£89–£119 (additional supplement during festivals).
Rooms	2 twins/doubles.
Meals	Restaurants within 3-minute walk.
Closed	Rarely.
Directions	10 minutes' walk from air, train, tram, bus & coach terminals at city centre. East end of Princes Street.

	Pippa Lockhart
	10 London Street,
	Edinburgh EH3 6NA
Tel	+44 (0)131 556 0737
Email	pippa@hjlockhart.co.uk
Web	www.londonstreetaccommodation.co.uk

	Gerald Della-Porta
	Geraldsplace,
	21b Abercromby Place,
	Edinburgh EH3 6QE
Tel	+44 (0)131 558 7017
Email	gerald11@geraldsplace.com
Web	www.geraldsplace.com

Entry 661   Map 15

Entry 662   Map 15

Edinburgh & the Lothians

Edinburgh & the Lothians

22 Royal Circus

Step from an elegant cobbled crescent in Georgian New Town into another world: of Aga-cooked breakfasts, landscaped gardens and a farmhouse kitchen you're welcome to share. Well-travelled Kirsty has filled her listed, William Playfair-designed basement flat with bold reds and yellows, family art and Indian treasures. Choose the romantic Moroccan-style en suite or the larger, brighter family room. Young fruit trees and carved garden furniture dot the grounds; seasoned botanists can trot to the Botanic Garden; shoppers can walk to Princes Street through World Heritage streets of delis, cafés, restaurants. Charming!

Number29

You overlook St Mary's Cathedral green from this elegant, Georgian, West End townhouse – a stone's throw from Princes Street. Renovated with style and quirky touches, it feels grand yet friendly; Simon and Corinne welcome you into their home with charm. Ceilings are high, cornices and wooden shutters original and light floods in. The beautiful staircase is crowned by a cupola and lit at night, a wood-burner warms you in the dining room and you sleep in peaceful bedrooms with views, restful with flowers and immaculately dressed beds. Wake for a splendid, locally sourced variety of treats at breakfast. A delicious place.

Price	£89–£119 (additional supplement during festivals).
Rooms	2: 1 double; 1 family room with separate bath.
Meals	Pubs/restaurants 2-minute walk.
Closed	Christmas.
Directions	10-minute walk from city centre or within walking distance to Stockbridge. House on the north side facing south.

Price	£90–£190. Singles from £80.
Rooms	3: 1 double, 2 suites.
Meals	Pubs/restaurants 150 yds.
Closed	Rarely.
Directions	See owner website.

	Kirsty MacGregor
	22 Royal Circus,
	Edinburgh EH3 6SS
Tel	+44 (0)1312 261303
Email	stay@22royalcircus.co.uk
Web	www.22royalcircus.co.uk

	Simon & Corinne Rawlins
	Number29, 29 Manor Place,
	Edinburgh EH3 7DX
Tel	+44 (0)1312 256385
Mobile	+44 (0)7780 527500
Email	info@number29edinburgh.co.uk
Web	www.number29edinburgh.co.uk

Edinburgh & the Lothians

Edinburgh & the Lothians

11 Belford Place

Guests love Sue's modern townhouse, quietly tucked away in a private road above the Water of Leith yet a short distance from the city. Islay the retriever wags her welcome in the wooden-floored entrance; a picture-lined staircase winds upward. Handsome rooms offer china cups and floral spreads; dazzling bathrooms have Molton Brown goodies. Wake for Stornoway black pudding, kedgeree, homemade jams and delicious ginger compote at the gleaming table. Owls sometimes hoot in the pretty sloping garden, there's an outside luggage store, parking is free and art galleries and Murrayfield Stadium are nearby.

12 Belford Terrace

Leafy trees, a secluded garden, a stone wall and, beyond, a quiet riverside stroll. On the doorstep of the Modern Art and Dean galleries with Edinburgh's theatres and restaurants just a 15-minute walk, this Victorian end terrace, beside Leith Water, oozes an easy-going elegance, helped by Carolyn's laid-back but competent manner. Garden level bedrooms have their own entrance and are big and creamy with stripy fabrics, antiques, sofas and huge windows. (The single has a Boys Own charm.) Carolyn spoils with crisp linen, books and biscuits and a delicious, full-works breakfast. After a day in town, relax on the sunny terrace.

Price	£70–£120. Min. 2 nights in August.
Rooms	3: 1 double, 2 twins/doubles.
Meals	Restaurants 10-minute walk.
Closed	Christmas.
Directions	From city centre to Belford Rd; Belford Pl 1st left after Travelodge Hotel. House down hill opp. Edinburgh Sports Club. Free parking. No 13 bus passes top of lane to city centre.

Price	£70–£100. Singles from £40.
Rooms	3: 1 double, 1 twin/double; 1 single with separate shower.
Meals	Pub/restaurants within 10-minute walk.
Closed	Christmas.
Directions	From Palmerston Place through 2 sets of lights, downhill on Belford Rd past the Travelodge. Immediately left is Belford Terrace. Limited free parking, 2-minute drive.

Susan Kinross
11 Belford Place,
Edinburgh EH4 3DH
Tel   +44 (0)131 332 9704
Mobile   +44 (0)7712 836399
Email   suekinross@blueyonder.co.uk

Carolyn Crabbie
12 Belford Terrace,
Edinburgh EH4 3DQ
Tel   +44 (0)131 332 2413
Email   carolyncrabbie@blueyonder.co.uk

Entry 665   Map 15

Entry 666   Map 15

Wallace's Arthouse Scotland

The apartment door swings open to a world of white walls, smooth floors, modern art, acoustic jazz, and smiling Wallace with a glass of wine – well worth the three-storey climb up this old Assembly Rooms building. Your host – New York fashion designer and arts enthusiast, Glasgow-born, not shy – has created a bright, minimalist space sprinkled with humour and casual sophistication. Bedrooms capture light and exude his inimitable style; the kitchen's narrow bar is perfect for a light breakfast. Leith is Edinburgh's earthy side with its docks and noisy street life, but fine restaurants abound and the centre is close. Memorable.

2 Fingal Place

An elegant house on a Georgian terrace. The leafy park lies opposite (look upwards to Arthur's Seat). Bustling theatres, shops and the university are a stroll away, yet this is a very quiet house. Your hostess is sometimes away so you may be looked after by a housekeeper, but when at home Gillian can help plan your trips – or cater for celebrations and graduations with lunch and dinner; it's entirely flexible. Downstairs at garden level bedrooms have mahogany antique beds, floral curtains and bathrooms with good towels. Noodle the Llasa Apso will welcome you. *Parking metered 8.30am-5.30pm weekdays.*

Price	£105. Singles £95.
Rooms	2 doubles.
Meals	Pubs/restaurants 10 yds.
Closed	Christmas Eve & Christmas Day.
Directions	From Princes St, follow Leith Walk to the foot and left along Gt. Junction St. Then 1st right along Henderson St to Water of Leith traffic lights. Right along Bernard St; at the next lights right into Constitution St.

Price	£90-£130 (£100-£140 during Festival). Singles from £55 (from £65 during Festival).
Rooms	2: 1 twin (with single room attached), 1 twin.
Meals	Pubs/restaurants 100 yds.
Closed	22-27 December.
Directions	From centre, Lothian Rd to Tollcross (clock) & Melville Drive. At 2nd major lights, right into Argyle Place; immed. left into Fingal Place.

	Wallace Shaw
	Wallace's Arthouse Scotland, 41-4 Constitution St, Edinburgh EH6 7BG
Tel	+44 (0)131 538 3320
Mobile	+44 (0)7941 343714
Email	cawallaceshaw@mac.com
Web	www.wallacesarthousescotland.com

	Gillian Charlton-Meyrick
	2 Fingal Place, The Meadows, Edinburgh EH9 1JX
Tel	+44 (0)131 667 4436
Mobile	+44 (0)7880 705022
Email	gcmeyrick@fireflyuk.net
Web	www.fingalplace.co.uk

Entry 667   Map 15

Entry 668   Map 15

20 Blackford Road

A 20-minute stroll from the Royal Mile is a substantial Victorian house with relaxed hosts and a touch of old-world luxury. From a cushioned window seat you gaze onto a lovely wildlife-filled walled garden where you can eat out on a warm day; breakfasts, though not cooked, are superb and include homemade breads and fruit. Bedrooms, one up, one down, are tranquil and serene, with delicately papered walls and lush toile de Jouy; the drawing room, with comfortable cream sofas, soft lights, a drinks tray and beautiful books, is elegant yet cosy. A happy, charming place to stay. *Minimum two nights July/August.*

1 Albert Terrace

A warm-hearted home with a lovely garden, an American hostess and two gorgeous Siamese cats. You are 20 minutes by bus from Princes Street yet the guests' sitting room overlooks pear trees and clematis and the rolling Pentland Hills. Cosy up in the winter next to a stylish log-effect wood-burner; in summer, take your morning paper onto the sunny terrace. Books, flowers, interesting art and ceramics and – you are on an old, quiet street – utter, surprising peace. Bedrooms are colourful, spacious and bright, one with an Art Deco bathroom and views over the garden. Clarissa is arty, easy, generous and loves having guests.

Price	£75-£100. Singles from £65.
Rooms	2: 1 twin/double, 1 twin, each with separate bath.
Meals	Restaurants 300 yds.
Closed	Christmas, New Year & occasionally.
Directions	A720 city bypass, take Lothianburn exit to city centre. Continue for 2.5 miles on Morningside Rd; right into Newbattle Terrace; 2nd left into Whitehouse Loan. Immed. right into Blackford Road. House at end on left.

Price	£75-£85. Singles £40-£60.
Rooms	3: 1 double; 1 double, 1 single sharing bath.
Meals	Pubs/restaurants nearby.
Closed	Rarely.
Directions	From centre of Edinburgh, A702 south, for Peebles. Pass Churchill Theatre (on left), to lights. Albert Terrace 1st right after theatre. Metered parking on street, but non-metered area nearby.

John & Tricia Wood
20 Blackford Road,
Edinburgh EH9 2DS

Tel	+44 (0)131 447 4233
Mobile	+44 (0)7930 452945
Email	enquiries@grangebandb.co.uk
Web	www.grangebandb.co.uk

Clarissa Notley
1 Albert Terrace,
Edinburgh EH10 5EA

Tel	+44 (0)131 447 4491
Email	canotley@aol.com

Entry 669   Map 15

Entry 670   Map 15

Highfield House

Although much of it is grand, there's a relaxed feel to this 18th-century manse house, where Jillian and Hugh enjoy having guests. Treat yourself to a quiet time in the large, light sitting room with family photos, books and paintings, comfy sofas by the fire and a sunny window seat. Bedrooms are softly painted in yellows and blues, beds have good mattresses and bathrooms are spotless. Breakfast on old favourites, or haggis and black pudding, in a dining room with oodles of sunlight and Hugh's oil-clad ancestors watching; home cooking in the evening is candlelit and cosy – or catch the train into town.

Inveresk House

Cromwell stayed here and plotted his siege of Edinburgh Castle; the house oozes history. The magnificent main rooms are furnished with ornate antiques, squashy sofas in chintzes, flowers, gilt mirrors, seriously gorgeous rugs and Alice's own vibrant art. Bedrooms and bathrooms, on the expected scale, come with vintage radiators, huge beds, good old-fashioned comfort. Musicians will be happy – there is a baby grand. Come for Inveresk (a conservation village), golf (the course at Musselburgh is the oldest in the world), interesting conversation with charming hosts and history by the hatful. Edinburgh is a bus hop away.

Price	£76–£80. Singles £60. Dogs extra charge.
Rooms	2 twins/doubles.
Meals	Packed lunch £6. Dinner £15–£25. Pub/restaurant 3 miles.
Closed	Christmas.
Directions	A71 from Edinburgh. 5 miles beyond city bypass left onto B7031 to Kirknewton. Next right then cross railway line. House is on left at top of hill.

Price	£100–£120. Family room £140. Singles £65.
Rooms	3: 1 double, 1 twin, 1 family room.
Meals	Pubs/restaurants 0.5 miles.
Closed	Rarely.
Directions	From Edinburgh, A199 (A1) to Musselburgh. There, signs to Inveresk. At top of Inveresk Brae, sharp right into cul-de-sac. 2nd opening on right, opp. gates with GM on them, bear right past cottages to house.

Jillian & Hugh Hunter Gordon
Highfield House,
Kirknewton EH27 8BJ
Tel   +44 (0)1506 881489
Email   jill@hunter-gordon.co.uk
Web   www.highfield-h.co.uk

Alice & John Chute
Inveresk House, 3 Inveresk Village,
Musselburgh EH21 7UA
Tel   +44 (0)131 665 5855
Mobile   +44 (0)7931 950566
Email   chute.inveresk@btinternet.com
Web   www.invereskhouse.com

Entry 671   Map 15

Entry 672   Map 15

Edinburgh & the Lothians

Glebe House

A treasure of a home – and host! A perfect Georgian family house with all the well-proportioned elegance you'd expect, it is resplendent with original features – fireplaces, arched glass, long windows – that have appeared more than once in interiors magazines. Bedrooms are light and airy with pretty fabrics and lovely linen. The beach is a stone's throw away, views are leafy-green, golfers have over 21 courses to choose from. There's also a fascinating sea bird centre close by – and you are 30 minutes from Edinburgh: regular trains bring you to the foot of the castle.

Price	From £110. Singles by arrangement.
Rooms	3: 1 double, 1 four-poster; 1 twin with separate bath.
Meals	Restaurants 2-minute walk.
Closed	Christmas & New Year.
Directions	From Edinburgh, A1 for Berwick. Left onto A198, follow signs into North Berwick. Right into Station Rd signed 'The Law', to 1st x-roads; left into town centre; house on left behind wall.

Gwen & Jake Scott
Glebe House, Law Road,
North Berwick EH39 4PL

Tel	+44 (0)1620 892608
Mobile	+44 (0)7973 965814
Email	gwenscott@glebehouse-nb.co.uk
Web	www.glebehouse-nb.co.uk

Entry 673   Map 16

Edinburgh & the Lothians

Eaglescairnie Mains

Wildlife thrives: eight acres of conservation headland have been created and wildflower meadows planted on this 350-acre working farm… you'd never guess Edinburgh was so close. The Georgian farmhouse sits in lovely gardens, its peace uninterrupted. There's a traditional conservatory for locally sourced breakfasts, a perfectly gracious drawing room (coral walls, rich fabrics, log fire) for wintery nights, and beautiful big bedrooms full of books and kind extras. Barbara is warm and charming, Michael's commitment to the countryside is wide-ranging; follow signed farm walks to the pub in Gifford.

Price	£70–£80. Singles from £45.
Rooms	3: 2 doubles, 1 twin.
Meals	Pub 1 mile.
Closed	Christmas.
Directions	From A1 at Haddington, B6368 south for Bolton & Humbie. Right immed. after traffic lights on bridge. 2.5 miles on through Bolton, at top of hill, left for Gifford. Entrance 0.5 miles on left.

Barbara & Michael Williams
Eaglescairnie Mains,
Gifford, Haddington EH41 4HN

Tel	+44 (0)1620 810491
Mobile	+44 (0)7713 333193
Email	williams.eagles@btinternet.com
Web	www.eaglescairnie.com

Entry 674   Map 16

Fife

Blair Adam

If staying in a place with genuine Adam features is special, how much more so in the Adam family home! They've been in this corner of Fife since 1733: John laid out the walled garden, son William was a prominent politician, Sir Walter Scott used to come and stay... you may be similarly inspired. The house, in a swathe of parkland and forest overlooking the hills and Loch Leven, has big, comfortable light-flooded rooms filled with intriguing contents, and superb walks from the door. The pretty bedroom is on the ground floor and you eat with your friendly hosts in the dining room, with coffee by the fire after dinner.

Price	From £100. Singles from £50.
Rooms	1 twin.
Meals	Dinner, with wine, £25. Restaurants 5 miles.
Closed	December/January.
Directions	From M90 exit 5, take B996 south for Cowdenbeath. Right for Maryburgh, through village, right through pillars onto a long drive, under bridge, then 0.5 miles on up to house.

Keith & Elizabeth Adam
Blair Adam,
Kelty KY4 0JF
Tel   +44 (0)1383 831221
Mobile +44 (0)7986 711099
Email adamofblairadam@hotmail.com

Entry 675   Map 15

Fife

Cairnie Cottage

Secluded, sheltered, with views to open farmland and sea, is a welcoming house in beautifully kept grounds; inside, everything shines. Tim, no newcomer to the world of hospitality, delightedly helps plan golf for guests and drops off and picks up walkers: this is two miles from the coastal path. The guest sitting and breakfast rooms, light, bright and furnished in attractive country style, flow one into the other, while the bedrooms are simple and uncluttered. The secluded suite rooms are upstairs and the double room is down, opening to the garden; take a drink to the terrace, or a turn on the croquet lawn. Lovely.

Price	£80. Singles £50.
Rooms	3: 1 double; 1 double, 1 twin sharing bath.
Meals	Pub/restaurant 3 miles. Packed lunch available.
Closed	Rarely.
Directions	Sent on booking.

Tim & Christine MacDowel
Cairnie Cottage,
Colinsburgh,
Leven KY9 1JX
Tel   +44 (0)1333 340848
Email tim@cairniecottage.co.uk
Web   www.fifebnb.co.uk

Entry 676   Map 15

Fife

Greenlaw House

With superb views towards the Lomond Hills, Debbie's bright, warm converted farm steading will please you the moment you step in. The oak-floored sitting room has Afghan rugs, sofas around a log-burner, a grand piano, and leads to a decked area for summer sun. In all the rooms is a medley of modern and antique, and fascinating art. The ground-floor bedroom has a lovely old chest and books; the more lived-in upstairs one has the view. Debbie loves to cook: smoked salmon and scrambled eggs, porridge with cream, local honey. Falkland Palace, hunting haunt of the Stuart kings, is close; there are wonderful walks and sea eagles soar.

Price	£70–£85. Singles £40–£50.
Rooms	2: 1 double; 1 double with separate bath.
Meals	Dinner £25–£30. Restaurants 15-minute drive.
Closed	Christmas & New Year.
Directions	B937 north off A91, at Trafalgar junc. turn towards Newburgh. After exactly 1 mile right onto tarmac road. Third house at top.

	Debbie Butler
	Greenlaw House,
	Braeside, Collessie,
	Cupar KY15 7UX
Tel	+44 (0)1337 810236
Email	butlerjackson@googlemail.com
Web	www.greenlawhouse.com

Entry 677   Map 15

Fife

Kinkell

An avenue of beech trees patrolled by guinea fowl, Hebridean sheep and Highland cows leads to the house. If the sea views and salty smack of St Andrews Bay air don't get you, step inside and have your senses tickled. Your hosts are wonderful and offer you a glass of something on arrival; the elegant drawing room has two open fires, rosy sofas, a grand piano – gorgeous. Bedrooms and bathrooms are immaculate and sunny. Sandy and Frippy are great cooks and make full use of local produce. Gaze on the sea from the garden, head down to the beach, walk the wild coast. A friendly, comfortable family home. *Online booking available.*

Price	£90. Singles from £55.
Rooms	3 twins/doubles.
Meals	Dinner £30. Restaurants in St Andrews, 2 miles.
Closed	Rarely.
Directions	Sent on booking.

	Sandy & Frippy Fyfe
	Kinkell,
	St Andrews KY16 8PN
Tel	+44 (0)1334 472003
Mobile	+44 (0)7836 746043
Email	fyfe@kinkell.com
Web	www.kinkell.com

Entry 678   Map 16+19

Glasgow

64 Partickhill Road

Be greeted by two free-range hens and Gertie the terrier on arrival at this relaxed family home. It's the bustling West End but the road is peaceful and there's a lovely big garden. Caroline and Hugh are lovers of the arts: the house is full of pictures, vintage finds and books. There are wood floors, rugs, a fire in the comfy sitting room and your bedroom is bright and spacious. Tuck into a delicious breakfast, in the sitting room or the conservatory, of good croissants, organic bacon and sausages, homemade bread and jams. Easy for the underground, trendy cafés and delis, museums, theatres and the university. A city treat.

Price	£70.
Rooms	1 double. (Extra twin available).
Meals	Packed lunch available. Pubs/restaurant 0.25 miles.
Closed	October–December & occasionally.
Directions	Sent on booking.

Caroline Anderson
64 Partickhill Road,
Glasgow G11 5NB
Tel   +44 (0)141 339 1946
Mobile +44 (0)7962 144509
Email carolineanderson64@gmail.com

Entry 679   Map 15

Highland

The Grange

A Victorian townhouse with its toes in the country: the mountain hovers above, the loch shimmers below and the garden slopes steeply to great banks of rhododendrons. Bedrooms, the one in the turret with a sumptuous new bathroom, are large, luscious, warm and inviting: crushed velvet, beautiful blankets, immaculate linen – all ooze panache. Expect decanters of sherry, ornate cornices, a Louis XV bed and a superb suite with contemporary touches. Elegant breakfasts are served at glass-topped tables; Joan's warm vivacity and love of B&B means guests keep coming back. And just a 10-minute walk into town.

Price	£116–£130.
Rooms	3: 2 doubles, 1 suite.
Meals	Restaurants 12-minute walk.
Closed	Mid-November to March.
Directions	A82 Glasgow-Fort William; 1 mile after 30mph sign into Fort William, turn right up Ashburn Lane, next to Ashburn guesthouse. House on left at top.

Joan & John Campbell
The Grange, Grange Road,
Fort William PH33 6JF
Tel   +44 (0)1397 705516
Email info@thegrange-scotland.co.uk
Web   www.thegrange-scotland.co.uk

Entry 680   Map 17

Highland

Arisaig House

Imposing Arisaig – a 19th-century industrialist's highland fantasy – sits in a walkers' paradise; the views to Skye are to die for. In former days it was a hotel; now Sarah, who has known Arisaig all her life, revels in returning house and gardens to their former glory. The sitting room is bright with Sanderson sofas, portraits and paintings and a huge open fire, and bedrooms are spacious and charming, with comfortable furniture and updated bathrooms. Lovely generous Sarah, passionate Slow Food member, serves breakfasts, high teas and dinners at the long oak table: don't miss the Stornoway black pudding!

Price	£100-£150. Singles £75.
Rooms	8 twins/doubles.
Meals	Dinner, 3 courses, from £25. Pub/restaurant 3 miles.
Closed	Rarely.
Directions	Just off A830 Fort William to Mallaig road. 3 miles east of Arisaig & 1 mile from Beasdale Station. House well signed. Inverness, Glasgow & Edinburgh airports within 3.5 hours.

Sarah Winnington-Ingram
Arisaig House,
Arisaig PH39 4NR
Tel   +44 (0)1687 450730
Email   sarahwi@arisaighouse.co.uk
Web   www.arisaighouse.co.uk

Entry 681   Map 17

Highland

Napier Cottage

A beautiful house, filled with light, that floats above the Sound of Sleat with fabulous views across the water. Seals bask on local rocks, herons come in search of supper, the odd pod of minke whales passes through. The house, newly built in traditional style, is delightful: books everywhere, a wood-burner in the sitting room, afternoon tea (on the house) in the conservatory. Big bedrooms have warm colours, pretty fabrics, comfy beds, excellent bathrooms, watery views. Christine cooks tempting suppers – cheese soufflé, venison casserole, raspberry panna cotta – but Kinloch Lodge is close if you want to splash out.

Price	£90-£120. Singles from £70.
Rooms	2 doubles.
Meals	Dinner, 3 courses with wine, £35. Pub/restaurant 1 mile.
Closed	Occasionally.
Directions	Sent on booking.

Christine Jenkins & Ian Rudd
Napier Cottage, Isleornsay,
Sleat, Isle of Skye IV43 8QX
Tel   +44 (0)1471 833460
Email   napiercottage@gmail.com
Web   www.napiercottage.co.uk

Entry 682   Map 17

Highland

Tigh An Dochais

An arresting, award-winning, 'see-through' house, quite unlike its neighbours, on a strip of land between the busy town road and the rocky shoreline, with stunning views out the back across the bay to mountains and islands. Huge windows and a cathedral ceiling allow light to flood in to an oak-floored sitting room with a wood-burner and modern art. Gliding glazed doors in crisp luxurious bedrooms open to larchwood verandas – and the shore! Bathrooms are toasty underfoot. Neil meets, greets, cooks, bakes: try black pudding from Stornoway at breakfast; superb fish, shellfish and game for supper. Irresistible B&B.

Price	£85–£90. Singles £70–£75.
Rooms	3: 2 doubles, 1 twin/double.
Meals	Dinner, 4 courses, £22–£25. BYO. Packed lunch £5. Pub/restaurant 200 yds.
Closed	Rarely.
Directions	Leave Skye Bridge & follow A87 dir. Broadford. After 6 miles pass Hebridean Hotel on left, house is 200 yds further up A87 on right.

Neil Hope
Tigh An Dochais,
13 Harrapool,
Isle of Skye IV49 9AQ
Tel   +44 (0)1471 820022
Email   hopeskye@btinternet.com
Web   www.skyebedbreakfast.co.uk

Entry 683   Map 17

Highland

The Berry

Drive through miles of spectacular landscape then bask in the final approach down a winding single-track road to Allt-Na-Subh – just five houses overlooking the loch. Joan, who is friendly and kind, prepares delicious meals in her Rayburn-warmed kitchen – the hub of this character-filled house. Inside is fresh and light with stylish bedrooms – one up, one down; the sitting room has a log fire and stunning views. Eat fish straight from the boats, stride the hills and spot golden eagles, red deer and otters. The perfect place for naturalists and artists, or those seeking solace. A hidden gem. *Minimum stay two nights at weekends.*

Price	From £75. Singles £38.
Rooms	2: 1 double with separate shower; 1 double sharing bath with owner.
Meals	Dinner, 3 courses with wine, £30. Packed lunch £7. Pub 3 miles.
Closed	Rarely.
Directions	From A87 at Dornie follow signs for Killilin, Conchra & Salachy. House 2.7 miles on left.

Joan Ashburner
The Berry,
Allt-Na-Subh,
Dornie,
Kyle of Lochalsh IV40 8DZ
Tel   +44 (0)1599 588259

Entry 684   Map 17

Highland

Aurora

The perfect spot for walkers and climbers (single-track roads, lochs, rivers and mountains) and the perfect B&B for groups: three smart, uncluttered bedrooms have flexible sleeping arrangements and spick and span shower rooms. The guest sitting room is light and airy with binoculars, books to borrow, maps and a small fridge for your wine – stay put for glorious sunsets and views to Harris. Breakfast time is generously bendy; good seasonal food is important here and you eat round a big table. There's a drying room and bike storage, but those wanting to relax will love it here too. *Min. two nights. Over 12s welcome.*

Price	£68-£90. Singles from £68.
Rooms	3: 1 double, 2 twins/doubles (extra single bed).
Meals	Dinner, 2 courses, £20 (Tues & Fri). BYO. Packed lunch £6. Pub/restaurant within 0.5 miles.
Closed	November-March.
Directions	From Inverness A9 north, signed 'Wester Ross Coastal Trail'. Left at Garve A832. Left at Kinlochewe A896. In Shieldaig at Heron sign 1st right; house 4th on left.

	Ann Barton
	Aurora,
	Shieldaig,
	Torridon IV54 8XN
Tel	+44 (0)1520 755246
Email	info@aurora-bedandbreakfast.co.uk
Web	www.aurora-bedandbreakfast.co.uk

Entry 685   Map 17

Highland

The Peatcutter's Croft

There's more beauty in a mile on the west coast than in the rest of the world put together – vast skies, soaring mountains, shimmering water, barely a soul in sight. Pauline and Seori left London to give their family the freedom to roam. Now they have a colourful cast of companions: sheep, hens, ducks, rabbits – all live here. Your quarters at this gorgeous little croft combine country simplicity with tons of colour and style. Sea eagles patrol the skies, porpoises bask in the loch, red deer come to eat the garden. All this, coupled with Pauline's fabulous home cooking, make it hard to leave. Dogs and children are very welcome.

Price	£70 (£100 for family of 4). Singles from £45.
Rooms	Apartment: 1 double (with mezzanine for 2 children).
Meals	Dinner, 3 courses, £30. BYO. Pub/restaurant 30 miles.
Closed	Christmas.
Directions	Sent on booking.

	Seori & Pauline Burnett
	The Peatcutter's Croft,
	Croft 12, Badrallach, Dundonnell,
	Garve, Ullapool IV23 2QP
Tel	+44 (0)1854 633797
Email	info@peatcutterscroft.com
Web	www.peatcutterscroft.com

Entry 686   Map 17

Tanglewood House

Down a steep drive through stunning landscape to this modern, curved house on the shore of Loch Broom – and distant views of the old fishing port of Ullapool. The drawing room is filled with antiques, fine fabrics, original paintings, flowers and a grand piano; bask in the fantastic views from a wall-to-wall window. Bedrooms are delightful: bold colours, crisp linen, proper bath tubs with fluffy towels. Anne and her son Julian (both trained chefs) link up with local producers, making dinners at this 'gastro-B&B' even more special. Explore the wild garden, then stroll to the rocky private beach for a swim in the loch. Superb.

The Old Ferryman's House

This former ferryman's house is small, homely and lived-in, just yards from the river Spey with its spectacular mountain views. Explore the countryside or relax in the garden with a tray of tea and homemade treats; plants tumble from whisky barrels and pots and you can spot woodpeckers. The sitting room is cosy with a wood-burning stove and brimming with books and magazines (no TV). Generous Elizabeth, a keen traveller who lived in the Sudan, cooks delicious, imaginative meals: herbs and veg from the garden, eggs from her hens, heathery honeycomb, homemade bread and jams. An unmatched spot for explorers, and very good value.

Price	From £96. Singles from £72. Minimum 2 nights.
Rooms	3: 1 double, 1 twin/double, 1 twin.
Meals	Dinner, 4 courses, from £33. BYO. Pubs 1 mile.
Closed	Christmas, New Year & Easter.
Directions	Just outside Ullapool from Inverness on A835, left imm. after 4th 40mph sign. Take cattle grid on right & left fork down to house.

Price	£66. Singles £33.
Rooms	3: 1 double, 1 twin, 1 single, all sharing 1 bath & 2 wcs.
Meals	Dinner, 3 courses, £25. BYO. Packed lunch £7.50.
Closed	Occasionally in winter.
Directions	From A9, follow main road markings through village, pass golf club & cross river. Or turn off B970 to Boat of Garten. House on left, just before river.

Anne, Julian & Corinna Holloway
Tanglewood House,
Ullapool IV26 2TB
Tel   +44 (0)1854 612059
Email   anne@tanglewoodhouse.co.uk
Web   www.tanglewoodhouse.co.uk

Elizabeth Matthews
The Old Ferryman's House,
Boat of Garten PH24 3BY
Tel   +44 (0)1479 831370

Entry 687   Map 17

Entry 688   Map 18

Highland

Rehaurie Cottage

You are steeped in history here, surrounded by woodland, castles, cairns and ancient battlefields. This 19th-century woodcutter's cottage is mercifully free of tartan; instead find clean lines, neutral colours and a contemporary feel. Spacious bedrooms are at either side of the house, one in cool greys with its own sitting room, the other in pretty rose-pink and cream with a private feel; both have sparkling, well-designed bathrooms. Sylvia and Chris, lovely people, give you an ample breakfast in the dining room which leads to a veranda; walks from the door are stunning. Discover jazz and Highland games in Nairn.

Price	£80-£105. Singles £65-£80.
Rooms	2 doubles (1 with sitting room), each with separate bath/shower.
Meals	Packed lunch £6. Supper from £12.50. Pub 5 miles.
Closed	Rarely.
Directions	From Inverness A96 to Nairn; A939 to Grantown. Continue for 1.5 miles past Littlemill, then right signed Cawdor, 6 miles. Cottage on left after 200 yds.

Sylvia Price
Rehaurie Cottage,
Nairn IV12 5JD
Tel	+44 (0)1309 651322
Mobile	+44 (0)7513 974276
Email	stay@rehaurie.co.uk
Web	www.rehaurie.co.uk

Entry 689   Map 18

Highland

Craigiewood

The best of both worlds: the remoteness of the Highlands (red kites, wild goats) and Inverness just four miles. The landscape surrounding this elegant cottage exudes a sense of ancient mystery augmented by these six acres - home to woodpeckers, roe deer and glorious roses. Inside, maps, walking sticks, two cats and a lovely, family-home feel - what you'd expect from delightful owners. Bedrooms, old-fashioned and cosy, overlook a garden reclaimed from Black Isle gorse. Gavin runs garden tours and can take you off to Inverewe, Attadale, Cawdor and Dunrobin Castle. Warm, peaceful, special.

Price	£80-£95. Singles £40-£50.
Rooms	2 twins.
Meals	Pub 2 miles.
Closed	Christmas & New Year.
Directions	A9 north over Kessock Bridge. At N. Kessock junc. left to r'bout to Kilmuir. After 0.25 miles, right to Kilmuir; left at top of road. Pass Drynie Farm, then right; house 1st left.

Araminta & Gavin Dallmeyer
Craigiewood,
North Kessock, Inverness IV1 3XG
Tel	+44 (0)1463 731628
Mobile	+44 (0)7831 733699
Email	2minty@craigiewood.co.uk
Web	www.craigiewood.co.uk

Entry 690   Map 18

Highland

Knockbain House

This is a well-loved farm, its environmental credentials supreme, and David and Denise are warm and interesting. A beautiful setting, too: landscaped gardens, a 700-acre farm (cows, lambs, barley) and rolling countryside stretching to Cromarty Firth. A grandfather clock ticks away time to relax, by floor-to-ceiling windows and a wood-burner in the antiques-filled sitting room; over a breakfast or dinner of home-grown foods; with a drink on the pond-side terrace; in bedrooms with new bathrooms and stunning views. Revel in the birds, walks and your hosts' commitment to this glorious unspoilt nature. *Babes in arms & over tens welcome.*

Price	£70–£90. Singles from £35.
Rooms	2: 1 double, 1 twin.
Meals	Dinner, 3 courses, £25. Packed lunch £5. Pubs/restaurants 1 mile.
Closed	Rarely.
Directions	From Dingwall, A834 past County Buildings & police station. After 200 yds, first left Blackwells Street. Narrow road to farm road, 300 yds then over cattle grid up driveway.

	David & Denise Lockett Knockbain House, Dingwall IV15 9TJ
Tel	+44 (0)1349 862476
Mobile	+44 (0)7736 629838
Email	davidlockett@avnet.co.uk
Web	www.knockbainhouse.co.uk

Entry 691   Map 18

Highland

Wemyss House

The peace is palpable, the setting overlooking the Cromarty Firth is stunning. Take an early morning stroll and spot buzzards, pheasants, rabbits and roe deer. The deceptively spacious house with sweeping maple floors is flooded with light and fabulous views, big bedrooms are warmly decorated with Highland rugs and tweeds, there's Christine's grand piano in the living room, Stuart's handcrafted furniture at every turn, and a sweet dog called Bella. Aga breakfasts include homemade bread, preserves and eggs from happy hens. Dinners are delicious; Christine and Stuart are wonderful hosts.

Price	From £95.
Rooms	3: 2 doubles, 1 twin.
Meals	Dinner £38. Restaurants 15-minute drive.
Closed	Rarely.
Directions	From Inverness, A9 north. At Nigg r'bout, right onto B9175. Through Arabella; left at sign to Hilton & Shandwick; right towards Nigg; past church; 1 mile, right onto private road. House on right.

	Christine Asher & Stuart Clifford Wemyss House, Bayfield, Tain IV19 1QW
Tel	+44 (0)1862 851212
Mobile	+44 (0)7759 484709
Email	stay@wemysshouse.com
Web	www.wemysshouse.com

Entry 692   Map 18

Highland

St Callan's Manse

Fun, laughter and conversation flow in this warm and happy home. You share it with prints, paintings, antiques, sofas, amazing memorabilia, three dogs, nine ducks, 14 hens and 1,200 teddy bears of every size and origin. Snug bedrooms have pretty fabrics, old armoires, flower-patterned sheets and tartan blankets; your sleep will be sound. Caroline cooks majestic breakfasts and dinners; Robert, a fund of knowledgeable anecdotes, can arrange just about anything. All this in incomparable surroundings: 60 acres of sheep-strewn land plus glens, forests, buzzards, deer and the odd golden eagle. A gem. *Dogs by arrangement.*

Price	£90. Singles £65.
Rooms	2: 1 double with separate bath; 1 double with separate shower.
Meals	Dinner, 2-4 courses, £16-£25. BYO. Pub/restaurant in village, 1.5 miles.
Closed	March & occasionally.
Directions	From Inverness, A9 north. Cross Dornoch bridge. 14 miles on, A839 to Lairg. Cross small bridge in Rogart; sharp right uphill, for St Callan's church. House 1.5 miles on, on right, next to church.

Robert & Caroline Mills
St Callan's Manse,
Rogart IV28 3XE
Tel   +44 (0)1408 641363
Email   caroline@rogartsnuff.me.uk

Entry 693   Map 21

Lanarkshire

Cormiston Farm

Wend your way through the soft hills of the Clyde Valley to a Georgian farmhouse in 26 acres of farmland and mature garden. Richard's a keen cook and produce from the walled garden – including delicious eggs from the quails – takes centre stage. Wonderful to retire to quiet, spacious rooms with bucolic views, stunning beds and rich fabrics; characterful Art Deco bathrooms, too. Tuck nippers up in bunks, then slip back for a snifter in front of the log fire in the sitting room. It's home from home, and licensed, too! There's untamed landscape to explore – and the children will love the friendly alpacas.

Price	£86-£108. Singles £65-£81.
Rooms	2 doubles, each with separate bath. (Extra bunk-bed room available.)
Meals	Dinner, 4 courses, £25-£30. Supper, 2 courses, £20. Pub 2 miles.
Closed	Rarely.
Directions	Sent on booking.

Richard Philipps
Cormiston Farm,
Cormiston Road,
Biggar ML12 6NS
Tel   +44 (0)1899 221507
Email   info@cormistonfarm.com
Web   www.cormistonfarm.com

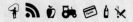

Entry 694   Map 15

Moray

Westfield House

Sweep up the drive to the grand home of an illustrious family: Macleans have lived here since 1862. Inside: polished furniture and burnished antiques, a tartan-carpeted hall, an oak stair hung with ancestral oils. John farms 500 acres and Veronica cooks sublimely; dinner is served at a long candelabra'd table, with vegetables from the vegetable garden. A winter fire crackles in the guest sitting room, old-fashioned bedrooms are inviting (plump pillows, fine linen, books, lovely views), the peace is deep. You can reach the coast easily and the walking is splendid; a historic house in a perfect setting with charming hosts.

Price	£90. Singles £50.
Rooms	3: 1 twin; 1 twin with separate bath & shower; 1 single with separate bath.
Meals	Supper, 2 courses, £20. Dinner, 3 courses, £25. Pub 3 miles.
Closed	Rarely.
Directions	From Elgin, A96 west for Forres & Inverness; after 2.5 miles, right onto B9013 for Burghead; after 1 mile, signed right at x-roads. Cont. to 'Westfield House & Office'.

John & Veronica Maclean
Westfield House,
Elgin IV30 8XL
Tel +44 (0)1343 547308
Email veronica.maclean@yahoo.co.uk
Web www.westfieldhouseelgin.co.uk

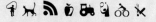

Entry 695   Map 18

Perth & Kinross

Beinn Bhracaigh

Excellent views stretch out from this Victorian villa. All the bedrooms are in relaxing creams, with duck-egg blues in throws and subtly patterned cushions propped like toast in a toast rack; TVs and fine Scottish soaps complete the Perthshire picture. Friendly hosts give you a continental breakfast in your room or a full Scottish and good coffee at separate tables in the dining room. Great fun and conviviality can be had in the evening when guests take over the honesty bar with its many wines and more than 50 whiskies. Amble to Pitlochry Theatre; discover an area rich with castles, fishing, white water rafting and walks.

Price	£75–£95. Singles from £65.
Rooms	12: 8 doubles, 4 twins/doubles.
Meals	Pubs/restaurants within 10-minute walk.
Closed	23-28 December.
Directions	Sent on booking.

James & Kirsty Watts
Beinn Bhracaigh,
14 Higher Oakfield,
Pitlochry PH16 5HT
Tel +44 (0)1796 470355
Email info@beinnbhracaigh.com
Web www.beinnbhracaigh.com

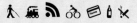

Entry 696   Map 15+18

Perth & Kinross

Essendy House

Down a tree-lined drive blazing with colour, Tess and John's charming country house is surrounded by lochs, castles and serenity. Inside is cosy and comfortable with warm fires, flowers, porcelain, Italianate murals and an unusual collection of family artefacts. Traditionally furnished bedrooms have antiques, good linen, garden views and silk or floral touches. Enjoy hearty breakfasts and suppers in the huge dining room or family kitchen; the terrace is heaven in summer. There's lots to do: visit cathedral and theatre, hike Macbeth's Birnam Hill, play golf, ski, fish and admire the swooping ospreys.

Price	£90. Singles £45.
Rooms	2: 1 double, 1 twin.
Meals	Packed lunch £5. Supper, 2 courses, £25. Pub/restaurant 2 miles.
Closed	Christmas & New Year; February/March.
Directions	A93 Perth to Blairgowrie. At Blairgowrie, left to B947. Two miles, over bridge with rusty green railings, uphill after bridge, drive at summit on right, white railings.

	John Monteith Essendy House, Blairgowrie PH10 6QY
Tel	+44 (0)1250 884260
Mobile	+44 (0)7841 121538
Email	johnmonteith@hotmail.com
Web	www.essendy.org

Perth & Kinross

Inchyra House

Sweep up through mature parkland to a gorgeous welcome from Caroline and James, and Flint the Scottish deerhound. Here is 18th-century grandeur, all grace and charm with a welcoming fire in the hall. Elegant doubles are classically decorated: 'Yellow' has the edge with lawn views but 'Blue' is gracious too, with a chaise longue and vintage lace; Nettle has a charmingly old-fashioned French feel. Set off for Perth or a round of golf, return for tea and scones in front of a roaring fire in the splendid drawing room with parkland views. You'll feel beautifully at home in this relaxed house.

Price	From £95.
Rooms	3: 1 twin; 1 double, 1 twin each with separate bath.
Meals	Pub 0.5 miles. Restaurants 4 miles.
Closed	Christmas & New Year.
Directions	A90 towards Dundee. After 4 miles take exit to Glencarse and St Madoes. Keep left. Gates 150 yds on left opposite Linden Garden Centre.

	Caroline & James Inchyra Inchyra House, Glencarse, Perth PH2 7LU
Tel	+44 (0)1738 860210
Email	caroline@hoyers.demon.co.uk
Web	www.inchyra.com

Perth & Kinross

Old Kippenross

What a setting! Old Kippenross rests in 150 peaceful acres of gorgeous park and woodland overlooking the river Allan – spot red squirrels and deer, herons, dippers and otters. The 15th-century house has a Georgian addition and an air of elegance and great courtesy, with its rustic white-vaulted basement, and dining and sitting rooms strewn with soft sofas and Persian rugs. Sash-windowed bedrooms are deeply comfortable, warm bathrooms are stuffed with towels. Susan and Patrick (an expert on birds of prey) are welcoming, the food is good and there's a croquet lawn in the walled garden. *Over tens welcome. Dogs by arrangement only.*

Price	£98. Singles £64.
Rooms	2: 1 double, 1 twin/double (with adjoining single room, let to same party only).
Meals	Dinner £28. BYO. Pub 1.5 miles.
Closed	Rarely.
Directions	M9 exit 11, B8033 for Dunblane. 500 yds, right over dual c'way, thro' entrance by stone gatehouse. Down drive, 1st fork right after bridge. House along gravelled drive.

Susan & Patrick Stirling-Aird
Old Kippenross,
Dunblane FK15 0LQ
Tel   +44 (0)1786 824048
Email   kippenross@hotmail.com
Web   www.oldkippenross.co.uk

Entry 699   Map 15

Perth & Kinross

Mackeanston House

They grow their own organic fruit and vegetables in the walled garden, make their own preserves, bake their own bread. Likeable and energetic – Fiona a wine buff and talented cook, Colin a tri-lingual guide – your hosts are hospitable people whose 1690 farmhouse combines informality and luxury in peaceful, central Scotland. Light-filled bedrooms have pretty fabrics, fine antiques, TVs and homemade cake. Roomy bathrooms have robes and a radio; one has a double shower (with a seat if you wish it). Dine by the log fire in the dining room, or in the conservatory with views to Stirling Castle. *Local & battlefield tours.*

Price	£100–£104. Singles £60–£62.
Rooms	2: 1 double, 1 twin/double.
Meals	Dinner, 3 courses, £32; 4 courses, £35. Pub 1 mile.
Closed	Christmas.
Directions	From M9, north, junc. 10 onto A84 for Doune. After 5 miles, left on B826 for Thornhill. Drive on left after 2.2 miles, right off farm drive.

Fiona & Colin Graham
Mackeanston House,
Doune, Stirling FK16 6AX
Tel   +44 (0)1786 850213
Mobile   +44 (0)7921 143018
Email   info@mackeanstonhouse.co.uk
Web   www.mackeanstonhouse.co.uk

Entry 700   Map 15

Scottish Borders

Skirling House

An intriguing house with 1908 additions, impeccably maintained. The whole lovely place is imbued with the spirit of Scottish Arts & Crafts, augmented with Italianate flourishes. Colourful blankets embellish chairs; runners soften flagged floors; the carvings, wrought-ironwork and rare Florentine ceiling are sheer delight. Upstairs, superb comfort holds sway: carpets and rugs, window seats and wicker, fruit and flowers. Bob cooks the finest local produce, Isobel shares a love of Scottish contemporary art and both look after you beautifully. Outside: 25,000 trees have been planted and grand walks start from the door.

Price	£100–£150. Singles £60–£95.
Rooms	5: 3 doubles, 1 twin, 1 twin/double.
Meals	Dinner £35. Pubs/restaurants 2 miles.
Closed	Christmas & January/February.
Directions	From Biggar, A702 for Edinburgh. Just outside Biggar, right on A72 for Skirling. Big wooden house on right opp. village green.

Bob & Isobel Hunter
Skirling House,
Skirling,
Biggar ML12 6HD
Tel +44 (0)1899 860274
Email enquiry@skirlinghouse.com
Web www.skirlinghouse.com

Entry 701 Map 15

Scottish Borders

Fauhope House

Near to Melrose Abbey and the glorious St Cuthbert's Walk, this solid 1890s house is immersed in bucolic bliss. Views soar to the Eildon Hills through wide windows with squashy seats; all is luxurious, elegant, fire-lit and serene with an eclectic mix of art. Bedrooms are warm with deeply coloured walls, thick chintz, pale tartan blankets and soft carpet; bathrooms are modern and pristine. Breakfast is served with smiles at a flower-laden table and overlooking those purple hills. A short walk through the garden and over a footbridge takes you to the interesting town of Melrose, with shops, restaurants and its own theatre.

Price	From £90. Singles from £60.
Rooms	3 twins/doubles.
Meals	Pub/restaurant 0.5 miles.
Closed	Rarely.
Directions	From A7, through Gattonside; at end of village, left onto Monkswood Road then immediate right onto start of private drive.

Ian & Sheila Robson
Fauhope House,
Gattonside,
Melrose TD6 9LY
Tel +44 (0)1896 823184
Mobile +44 (0)7816 346768
Email info@fauhopehouse.com

Entry 702 Map 15

Scottish Borders

Lessudden

A treat to stay in a great and historic tower house in the heart of the Scottish Borders. Your generous hosts give you big cosy bedrooms (one with an old-fashioned bathroom, one with hill views), and a spacious sitting room with fine old rugs, heaps of books and a log fire. Memorable meals are served at a polished oak refectory table beneath the gaze of Sir Walter Scott's uncle and aunt, who used to live here. The 1680s white-stone stairwell is unique, the décor is traditional and homely, the living is relaxed and Alasdair and Angela care for their guests as open-heartedly as they do their cats, dogs, horses and hens.

Price	£100. Singles £70.
Rooms	2: 1 double; 1 twin with separate bath.
Meals	Dinner, 3-4 courses, £25. Pub 0.5 miles.
Closed	Rarely.
Directions	North on A68 to St Boswells. Right opp. Buccleuch Arms Hotel, on through village; left up drive immed. beyond turning to golf course.

Alasdair & Angela
Douglas-Hamilton
Lessudden,
St Boswells TD6 0BH

Tel	+44 (0)1835 823244
Email	amdhlessudden@gmail.com
Web	www.lessudden.com

Entry 703   Map 16

Scottish Borders

Whitehouse Country House

A proud avenue of trees leads to Angela and Roger's handsome 19th-century country house in the heart of the Scottish Borders. They have been welcoming guests for over 20 years providing comfort, relaxation and great hospitality. Enjoy log fires and deep armchairs in the elegant dining and drawing rooms, traditional bedrooms with the most comfortable beds and glorious views from every room. Angela's cooking is heavenly and she uses wild salmon, game and the finest in-season local produce. Explore historic Border towns, cycle the Tweed Cycleway, walk St Cuthbert's Way – your hosts know the area well and are happy to advise.

Price	From £100. Singles from £65.
Rooms	3: 1 double, 2 twins.
Meals	Dinner £22-£29. Supper tray £10. Packed lunch £7. Pub 3 miles.
Closed	Rarely.
Directions	A68 from Edinburgh to St Boswells. From M6 at Carlisle, A7 to Hawick, then A698 & A68 to St Boswells. From St Boswells B6404 to turning on right for Whitehouse.

Angela & Roger Tyrer
Whitehouse Country House,
St Boswells, Melrose TD6 0ED

Tel	+44 (0)1573 460343
Mobile	+44 (0)7877 800582
Email	stay@whitehousecountryhouse.com
Web	www.whitehousecountryhouse.com

Entry 704   Map 16

Scottish Borders

Tweedknowe

In a residential cul de sac an easy walk from Melrose (super launch pad for the Borders) is a Victorian townhouse run by the nicest people. Multi-lingual, well-travelled Mirian and Doug, loving this latest enterprise, have heaps of knowledge about the area and treat you to fabulous breakfasts; Mirian is a great cook. They live downstairs, you live above, where bedrooms and shared bathrooms (one fresh and new, with a freestanding bath and a shower over) are spread over two light-filled floors. Expect a laid-back, old-fashioned décor – gradually to be upgraded – and guest sofas with open fire, music and TV.

Price	£60–£70. Singles £30–£40.
Rooms	3: 1 double, 2 twins all sharing 2 bathrooms.
Meals	Pubs/restaurant 5-minute walk.
Closed	Rarely.
Directions	Sent on booking.

Mirian Haas
Tweedknowe,
Tweedmount Road,
Melrose TD6 9ST
Tel   +44 (0)1896 822220
Email   mirian.haas@yahoo.co.uk
Web   www.tweedknowe.com

Entry 705   Map 16

Scottish Borders

Kirkbank House

Come for wonderful panoramas past wisteria'd walls over pretty-as-a-picture Paxton to the Cheviot Hills. Newly transformed by cosmopolitan hosts John and Lena, the 1760 house is now a boutiquey B&B freshly furnished with finds from their time in Asia: bright Thai silk throws, Buddha sculptures, ornamental orchids, yoga mats, and a Chinese altar/washstand in the L'Occitane-fresh bathroom; the results are stunning. John is an accomplished cook (dinners are a delight) and photographer; his work complements modern art on the walls. Huge beds, turned-down top-notch linen and chocs on the pillow: fabulous.

Price	£98–£140.
Rooms	3: 1 double, 1 twin/double; 1 double with separate bath/shower.
Meals	Dinner, 3 courses, £30 (min. 6 people). Pub 200 yds.
Closed	Rarely.
Directions	From A1 Berwick-upon-Tweed bypass take B6461 signed Kelso, right to Paxton after 4 miles, then right at Cross Inn, follow private road and signs to Kirkbank.

Lena Tomnay
Kirkbank House, Paxton,
Berwick upon Tweed TD15 1TE
Tel   +44 (0)1289 386534
Mobile   +44 (0)7935 033706
Email   info@kirkbankhouse.co.uk
Web   www.kirkbankhouse.co.uk

Entry 706   Map 16

Stirling

Cardross

Dodge the lazy sheep on the long drive to arrive (eventually!) at a sweep of gravel and lovely old Cardross in a gorgeous setting. Bang on the enormous ancient door and either Archie or Nicola (plus labradors and lively Jack Russells) will usher you in. And what a delight it is; come here for a blast of Scottish history! Traditional big bedrooms have airiness, long views, antiques, wooden shutters, towelling robes and good linen; one bathroom has a cast-iron period bath. The drawing room is vast, the house is filled with warm character, the Orr Ewings can tell you all the history. *Young people over 14 welcome.*

Price	£110–£120. Singles £70–£75.
Rooms	2: 1 twin; 1 twin with separate bath.
Meals	Occasional dinner £30. Pubs/restaurants 3-6 miles.
Closed	Christmas & New Year.
Directions	A811 Stirling-Dumbarton to Arnprior; B8034 towards Port of Menteith; 2 miles, then cross Forth over humpback bridge. Drive with yellow lodge 150 yds from bridge on right. 1st exit on right from drive.

	Sir Archie & Lady Orr Ewing
	Cardross,
	Port of Menteith,
	Kippen FK8 3JY
Tel	+44 (0)1877 385223
Email	enquiries@cardrossestate.com
Web	www.cardrossestate.com

⚔ 🐕 🐎 📧 ✂

Entry 707   Map 15

Stirling

Blairhullichan

So much to do in the Trossachs National Park: woodland walks, cycle tracks, even your own fishing bay on the edge of Loch Ard and a private island to wade out to for picnics. The tranquil house sits high on a slope with fabulous loch views from the drawing room — comfortable with window bay, fireplace and stacks of books. Reassuringly old-fashioned bedrooms have new mattresses and crisp linen; bathrooms have good towels and lotions. Be charmed by the 'Highlands in miniature' — plus resident labradors and welcoming Bridget, who gives you a grand breakfast and the best of her local knowledge. *Minimum stay two nights.*

Price	£80–£90. Singles from £40.
Rooms	4: 1 double, 1 twin, 1 double & sitting room; 1 double with separate bath/shower.
Meals	Dinner, with wine, £25-£35. Restaurant 10 miles.
Closed	Rarely.
Directions	A81 to Aberfoyle, follow B829 - 4 miles to Kinlochard, left at red phone box, then 0.5 miles. Ignore 'Water Dept/No Entry' sign, go 0.3 miles on bumpy road, pass wooden house on right; driveway on left, signed.

	John & Bridget Lewis
	Blairhullichan,
	Kinlochard,
	Aberfoyle FK8 3TN
Tel	+44 (0)1877 387341
Email	jablewis@aol.com
Web	www.blairhullichan.net

♿ 🐕 📶 ✂

Entry 708   Map 15

Stirling

The Moss

Rozie loves fishing and Jamie keeps bees; great hosts, they live in a charming listed house full of lovely things. Outside are 28 acres where deer prune the roses, pheasants roam and a garden seat sits with its toes in the water. Generous bedrooms await privately in their own wing and have big beds with feather pillows, books, flowers and long views to pastures and moorland. Expect walking sticks (and the bell of HMS Tempest) in the porch, rugs in the hall and smart sofas in the log-fired drawing room. Breakfast comes fresh from the Aga and is served at a big oak table; walk it all off on the West Highland Way.

Stirling

Quarter

This stately 1750s house commands views across Stirling's lush countryside and comes complete with crunching gravel drive and original ceiling dome. It was owned by the same family for generations until the Macleans took over its high ceilings, period features, sash windows. Pad your way upstairs to three comfortable bedrooms and bathrooms, brightened with a floral touch. Breakfast is a grand affair at a polished table; the hens provide the eggs and Pippa is determined to restore the kitchen garden to former glory. The house is cocooned in extensive grounds, with easy access to Stirling, Edinburgh, Perth. *Dogs by arrangement.*

Price	£90. Singles £45.
Rooms	3: 1 twin; 2 doubles sharing bath (2nd room let to same party only).
Meals	Pubs/restaurants within 2 miles.
Closed	Rarely.
Directions	4 miles west of Blanefield. Half a mile after Beech Tree Inn turn left off A81. After 300 yds, over bridge, 1st entrance on left.

Price	£100. Singles £55.
Rooms	3: 1 double, 1 twin/double, 1 twin.
Meals	Pub/restaurant 4 miles.
Closed	Christmas.
Directions	Stirling, exit 9 off the M9. From roundabout take A872 towards Denny, after exactly 2 miles turn left (200 yds past Wellsfield Farm) through grey pillars up to house.

	Jamie & Rozie Parker
	The Moss,
	Killearn G63 9LJ
Tel	+44 (0)1360 550053
Mobile	+44 (0)7787 123599
Email	themoss@freeuk.com

	Pippa Maclean
	Quarter,
	Denny FK6 6QZ
Tel	+44 (0)1324 825817
Email	quarterstirling@hotmail.co.uk
Web	www.quarterstirling.com

Stirling

Powis House

A sprawling 18th-century mansion with the volcanic Ochil Hills as a stunning backdrop and a colourful entrance hall of antlers and stuffed animals. Country style bedrooms invite with polished old floors, tartan throws, garden views and original bathrooms. You have a huge dining room with warming wood-burner, a guest lounge on the first floor, a sunny stone-flagged patio with places to sit and acres of estate with a woodland walk to explore. Colin and Jane are caring and interesting; Colin is a keen cook and has ghost stories galore to share. Historical Stirling is close: castle, university, festival and more.

Price	£90–£100. Singles £65.
Rooms	3: 2 doubles, 1 twin.
Meals	Dinner, 4 courses with coffee, £25. Pub/restaurant 3 miles.
Closed	Rarely.
Directions	Sent on booking.

	Jane & Colin Kilgour
	Powis House,
	Stirling FK9 5PS
Tel	+44 (0)1786 460231
Email	info@powishouse.co.uk
Web	www.powishouse.co.uk

Entry 711 Map 15

Western Isles

Broad Bay House

Set in a crofting community, the house was built in 2007 and rises on graceful flights of decking above the beach. The ancient wild setting and panoramic views contrast with the contemporary sophistication and style inside. A wide hall leads to a stunning vaulted living room with huge windows facing the waves on three sides, giving a sense of almost floating off the shoreline. More boutique hotel than B&B – subtle lighting, oak doors, original art – Broad Bay House has been designed with sheer, unadulterated comfort in mind. Ian and Marion are generous, flexible hosts and the food, served at candlelit tables, is heavenly.

Price	£145–£180.
Rooms	4: 2 doubles, 2 twins/doubles.
Meals	Dinner, 3 courses, £35. Packed lunch £10. Pub/restaurant 7 miles.
Closed	Rarely.
Directions	A867 from Stornoway towards Barvas & Ness. On edge of Stornoway, right onto B895. After 6 miles, house on right, between Back & Gress.

	Ian Fordham
	Broad Bay House,
	Back, Stornoway,
	Isle of Lewis HS2 0LQ
Tel	+44 (0)1851 820990
Email	stay@broadbayhouse.co.uk
Web	www.broadbayhouse.co.uk

Entry 712 Map 20

Pairc an t-Srath

Richard and Lena's lovely home overlooks the beach at Borve, another absurdly beautiful Harris view. Inside, smart simplicity abounds: wooden floors, white walls, a peat fire, colourful art. Airy bedrooms fit the mood perfectly: trim carpets, chunky wood beds, Harris tweed throws, excellent shower rooms (there's a bathroom, too, if you want a soak). Richard crofts, Lena cooks, perhaps homemade soup, venison casserole, wet chocolate cake with raspberries. Views from the dining room tumble down hill, so expect to linger over breakfast. You'll spot otters in the loch, while the standing stones at Callanish are unmissable.

Kinloch

Never a dull moment here in Wegg's house and you're encouraged to feel at home. All is friendly and full of interest with gorgeous food, good company and a happy dog. The house, built in the 70s, is comfy with books, photos, easy chairs and art. Bedrooms (one downstairs) are fresh and sunny; views across the loch are enormous and sunrises spectacular. Breakfasts and dinners are wonderfully sociable occasions and Wegg loves cooking: homemade bread, eggs from his hens, barbecued freshly caught trout. Wander the woodland garden and machair, fish the loch, spot the birds... return to relax by the log fire. A special place.

Price	£100. Singles from £50.
Rooms	4: 2 doubles, 1 twin, 1 single.
Meals	Dinner, 3 courses, £35. Restaurant 3 miles, pub 7 miles.
Closed	Rarely.
Directions	South from Tarbet ferry and first house on left in village; or north from Leverburgh ferry and last house on right.

Price	£84. Singles £42.
Rooms	3: 1 twin/double; 1 twin/double, 1 single both with separate bath.
Meals	Dinner £25. Packed lunch £5-£8. Restaurant 5 miles.
Closed	Rarely.
Directions	30 mins from Benbecula airport; 30 mins from Lochboisdale ferry; 45 mins from Lochmaddy.

Lena & Richard MacLennan
Pairc an t-Srath,
Borve,
Isle of Harris HS3 3HT
Tel   +44 (0)1859 550386
Email info@paircant-srath.co.uk
Web   www.paircant-srath.co.uk

Wegg Kimbell
Kinloch,
Grogarry,
Isle of South Uist HS8 5RR
Tel   +44 (0)1870 620316
Email wegg@kinlochuist.com
Web   www.kinlochuist.com

Wales

Anglesey

Cleifiog

On a soft spring morning this could be Lake Garda. The bay view is spectacular, the masts of Beaumaris chink in the wind. Lovely Gill and gardening husband Laurie have taken over the running of this B&B and serve a delicious breakfast. Set on the coast road, all is stunning inside and out: the clear light, the scent of lilies, the smell of freshly brewed coffee. First it was a Georgian hospice, later a customs house; now the big, bright, elegant sitting room's panelling is offset by white linen sofas and pretty potted plants, and bedrooms are inviting with top-notch linen. Lap up the views and the beautiful sea air.

Carmarthenshire

The Glynhir Estate

This fine old house on a Huguenot estate stands on the western edge of the Black Mountain. Outside: a waterfall, a two-acre kitchen garden, a brigade of chickens, and peacocks that patrol the grounds with panache. Inside, the house has spurned the urge to take itself too seriously and remains decidedly lived in. Find William Morris wallpaper in the dining room, lemon trees in the conservatory and old cabinets stuffed with interesting things in the sitting room. Country-house bedrooms fit the mood perfectly: smart and comfortable with excellent bathrooms. You can ride, walk, fish or visit Aberglasney Garden – just ask Katy.

Price	£90-£110. Singles £60-£80.
Rooms	3: 2 twins/doubles, 1 suite.
Meals	Pub/restaurant 200 yards.
Closed	Christmas & New Year.
Directions	A55 over Britannia Bridge to Anglesey. Take A545 to Beaumaris. Past 2 left turns, house is 5th on left facing the sea. Bus stop outside.

Price	£85. Family room £103.50. Singles £55.
Rooms	4: 3 doubles, 1 family.
Meals	Dinner from £17.50. Pubs/restaurants 2 miles.
Closed	December-February.
Directions	M4 junc. 49, 2nd exit A483 for Ammanford. At 2nd traffic lights left to Llandybie, then 2nd right up Glynhir Road. After 1.2 miles house on right.

	Gill Beevers
	Cleifiog,
	Townsend,
	Beaumaris LL58 8BH
Tel	+44 (0)1248 811507
Email	enquiries@cleifiog.co.uk
Web	www.cleifiogbandb.co.uk

	Katy Jenkins
	The Glynhir Estate, Glynhir Road,
	Llandybie, Ammanford SA18 2TD
Tel	+44 (0)1269 850438
Mobile	+44 (0)7810 864458
Email	enquiries@theglynhirestate.com
Web	www.theglynhirestate.com

Entry 715   Map 6

Entry 716   Map 7

Carmarthenshire

The Drovers

The ice-cream pink Georgian townhouse looks good enough to eat – as do the leek and cheese cakes; Jill is a superb cook. A fabulous Welsh hospitality pervades this B&B, along with antiques, gas log-burners and peaceful, cosy rooms. Downstairs areas are spacious, with a rambling hotel feel; sunny bedrooms are laced with books and Sanderson wallpapers; bathrooms come in contemporary white and cream and are stocked with spoiling towels. Over breakfast (relaxed, delicious, locally sourced) you gaze through deep sash windows onto the town square; order a packed lunch and head for the hills.

Price	£65–£80. Singles from £45. Min. 2 nights at weekends in high season.
Rooms	3: 2 doubles, 1 twin/double.
Meals	Dinner, 3 courses, £25. Packed lunch £5. Inns 50 yds.
Closed	Christmas & New Year.
Directions	In town centre, opposite the fountain.

Jill Blud
The Drovers,
9 Market Square,
Llandovery SA20 0AB

Tel	+44 (0)1550 721115
Email	jillblud@aol.com
Web	www.droversllandovery.co.uk

Entry 717 Map 7

Carmarthenshire

Plas Alltyferin

Wisteria-wrapped and, in parts, delightfully creaky, this Georgian family house sits in 270 beautiful acres. The breakfast room has the original panelling and the bedrooms have an old-fashioned charm. Not the place for you if you like spotlessness and state-of-the-art plumbing, but the views across the ha-ha to the Norman hill fort are timelessly lovely and the welcome is heartfelt. Gerard and Charlotte are the easiest, kindest and dog-friendliest of hosts. You're close to the National Botanical and Aberglasney gardens – and, most importantly, many lovely gastropubs! *Over tens welcome. Ballooning, shooting, fishing arranged.*

Price	£70–£80. Singles £40–£45.
Rooms	2: 1 twin; 1 twin with separate bath.
Meals	Pubs/restaurants within 2 miles.
Closed	September & occasionally.
Directions	From Carmarthen A40 east to Pont-ar-gothi. Left before bridge & follow narrow lane for approx. 2 miles keeping to right-hand hedge. House on right, signed. Call for precise details.

Charlotte & Gerard Dent
Plas Alltyferin,
Pont-ar-gothi, Nantgaredig,
Carmarthen SA32 7PF

Tel	+44 (0)1267 290662
Email	dent@alltyferin.co.uk
Web	www.alltyferin.co.uk

Entry 718 Map 6

Carmarthenshire

Sarnau Mansion

Listed and Georgian, the house has its own water supply. Revel in 16 acres of beautiful grounds complete with pond, walled garden and woodland with nesting red kites. Bedrooms are simply furnished in heritage colours; bathrooms are big. The oak-floored sitting room with chesterfields has French windows onto the garden, the dining room is simpler with separate tables and there's good, fresh home cooking from Cynthia. One mile from the A40, you can hear a slight hum of traffic if the wind is from that direction. You are 15 minutes from the National Botanic Garden of Wales. *Children over five welcome.*

Price	£80-£90. Singles £50-£55.
Rooms	4: 2 doubles, 1 twin; 1 double with separate bath.
Meals	Dinner, 3 courses, around £25. BYO. Pub 1 mile.
Closed	Rarely.
Directions	From Carmarthen A40 west for 4 miles. Right for Bancyfelin. After 0.5 miles, right into drive on brow of hill.

	Cynthia & David Fernihough Sarnau Mansion, Llysonnen Road, Bancyfelin, Carmarthen SA33 5DZ
Tel	+44 (0)1267 211404
Email	d.fernihough@btinternet.com
Web	www.sarnaumansion.co.uk

Entry 719   Map 6

Ceredigion

Broniwan

Carole and Allen keep cattle and chickens on their organic farm and their kitchen garden is prolific. With huge warmth and a tray of cakes they invite you into their cosy, ivy-clad house. Downstairs find natural colours and the odd vibrant flourish of local art, a wood-burner and lots of books – a literary weekend can be arranged. The simple bedroom has a traditional Welsh bedspread on a big bed. The wonderful garden with views to the Preseli hills has a water lily pond and is full of birds. Food is tasty and home-grown, coastal paths are close, the National Botanic Garden of Wales and Aberglasney are a 45-minute drive.

Price	£76-£80. Singles £40.
Rooms	1 double.
Meals	Dinner £25-£30. BYO. Restaurants 7-8 miles.
Closed	Rarely.
Directions	From Aberaeron, A487 for 6 miles for Brynhoffnant. Left at B4334 to Rhydlewis; left at post office & shop, 1st lane on right, then 1st track on right.

	Carole & Allen Jacobs Broniwan, Rhydlewis, Llandysul SA44 5PF
Tel	+44 (0)1239 851261
Email	broniwan@btinternet.com
Web	www.broniwan.com

Entry 720   Map 6

Ceredigion

Ffynnon Fendigaid

Arrive through rolling countryside – birdsong and breeze the only sound; within moments you will be sprawled on a leather sofa admiring modern art and wondering how a little bit of Milan arrived here along with Huw and homemade cake. A place to come and pootle, with no rush; you can stay all day to stroll the fern-fringed paths through the acres of wild garden to a lake and a grand bench, or opt for hearty walking. Your bed is big, the colours are soft, the bathrooms are spotless and the food is local – try all the Welsh cheeses. Wide beaches are close by, red kites and buzzards soar above you. Pulchritudinous.

Price	From £75. Singles from £45.
Rooms	2 doubles.
Meals	Dinner, 2-3 courses, £20-£22. Pub 1 mile.
Closed	Rarely.
Directions	From A487 Cardigan & Aberystwyth coast road, take B4334 at Brynhoffnant towards Rhydlewis. 1 mile to junc. where road joins from right & lane to house on left.

	Huw Davies Ffynnon Fendigaid, Rhydlewis, Llandysul SA44 5SR
Tel	+44 (0)1239 851361
Mobile	+44 (0)7974 135262
Email	ffynnonf@btinternet.com
Web	www.ffynnonf.co.uk

Entry 721   Map 6

Conwy

Maesmor Hall

Historic and grand, this old Welsh manor, gazing over Berwyn mountains, is surrounded by parkland, river and organically farmed acres. The furnishings and décor are classic country house with fine paintings, sculptures and china in comfortable elegant rooms; Johanna is friendly and you're welcomed as part of the family. Breakfast in the polished dining room might include scrambled eggs and pancetta, cockles and lavabread. Wander outside for croquet, tennis and rose garden, chat to Truffle the labrador. Come for open-air theatre in summer, peaches from the peach house and an array of wildlife and walks.

Price	£80-£100. Singles £60.
Rooms	3: 2 doubles, 1 twin.
Meals	Pub a short walk.
Closed	Christmas & New Year.
Directions	From Chester take Wrexham bypass, turn off for Llangollen & join A5, until Maerdy. Then left opp. Goat pub, over bridge, gates in front.

	Johanna Jackson Maesmor Hall, Maerdy, Corwen LL21 0NS
Tel	+44 (0)1490 460411
Email	maesmorhall@aol.com

Entry 722   Map 7

Conwy

Pengwern Country House

The steeply wooded Conwy valley snakes down to this stone and slate property set back from the road in Snowdonia National Park, and the walks are wonderful. Inside has an upbeat traditional feel: a large sitting room with tall bay windows and pictures by the Betws-y-Coed artists who once lived here. Settle with a book by the wood-burner; Gwawr and Ian are naturally friendly and treat guests as friends. Bedrooms have rough plastered walls, colourful fabrics and super bathrooms; one comes with a double-ended roll top tub and views of Lledr Valley. Breakfast on fruits, herb rösti, soda bread – superb. *Welsh spoken.*

Conwy

Lympley Lodge

The solid Victorian exterior belies a surprising interior. Welcoming Patricia, a former restorer, has brought together a gorgeous collection of furniture, while her meticulous paintwork adds light and life to her seaside home. Above is the Little Orme; below, across the main coast road, the sweep of Llandudno Bay. Bedrooms strike the perfect balance between the practical and the exotic; all have crisp linen, rich fabrics, fresh flowers, lovely views. There's an elegant sitting room for guests, a stunning dining room with a Renaissance feel and breakfasts full of local and homemade produce. Wonderful.

Price	£72–£84. Singles from £62. Min. stay 2 nights.	Price	£85. Singles £50–£55.
Rooms	3: 1 double, 1 four-poster, 1 twin/double.	Rooms	3: 2 doubles, 1 twin.
Meals	Pubs/restaurants within 1.5 miles. Packed lunch £5.50.	Meals	Restaurants/pubs 5-minute drive.
Closed	Christmas & New Year.	Closed	Mid-December to end January.
Directions	From Betws-y-Coed, A5 towards Llangollen for 1 mile. Driveway on left, opposite small stone building.	Directions	From Llandudno Promenade, turn right and follow B5115 (Colwyn Bay) up the hill. Pass right turn for Bryn Y Bia. House entrance (board on side of building) on right.

Gwawr & Ian Mowatt
Pengwern Country House,
Allt Dinas,
Betws-y-Coed LL24 0HF
Tel   +44 (0)1690 710480
Email gwawr.pengwern@btopenworld.com
Web   www.snowdoniaaccommodation.co.uk

Patricia Richards
Lympley Lodge,
Colwyn Road, Craigside,
Llandudno LL30 3AL
Tel   +44 (0)1492 549304
Email patricia@lympleylodge.co.uk
Web   www.lympleylodge.co.uk

Entry 723 Map 7

Entry 724 Map 7

Denbighshire

Plas Efenechtyd Cottage

Efenechtyd means 'place of the monks' but there's nothing spartan about Dave and Marilyn's handsome brick farmhouse. Breakfasts of local sausages, eggs from their hens, salmon fishcakes with mushrooms and homemade bread, are served at a polished table in the dining room with exotic wall hangings from Vietnam and Laos. Light bedrooms have a clear, uncluttered feel, excellent mattresses and good linen; bathrooms are surprisingly bling and as warm as toast, with plump towels. Motor or walk to Ruthin with its windy streets and interesting shops, or strike out for Offa's Dyke with a packed lunch; this is stunning countryside.

Flintshire

Plas Penucha

Swing back in time with polished parquet, tidy beams, a huge Elizabethan panelled lounge with books, leather sofas and open fire – a cosy spot for Nest's dogs and for tea in winter. Plas Penucha – 'the big house on the highest point in the parish' – has been in the family for 500 years. Airy, old-fashioned bedrooms have long views across the garden to Offa's Dyke and one has a shower in the corner. The L-shaped dining room has a genuine Arts & Crafts interior; outside, rhododendrons and a rock garden flourish. There are views to the Clywdian Hills and beyond is St Asaph, with the smallest medieval cathedral in the country.

Price	From £65. Singles £45.
Rooms	3: 2 doubles, 1 twin.
Meals	Packed lunch £6. Pub 1.6 miles.
Closed	Rarely.
Directions	From Ruthin follow signs for Bala. Straight over mini r'bout onto B5105. Take 1st left after 1 mile. Right at T-junc.; house 50 yds on right.

Price	From £72. Singles from £36.
Rooms	2: 1 double, 1 twin.
Meals	Dinner £19. Packed lunch £5. Pub/restaurant 2-3 miles.
Closed	Rarely.
Directions	From Chester, A55, B5122 left for Caerwys. 1st right into High St. Right at end. 0.75 miles to x-roads & left, then straight for 1 mile. House on left, signed.

Dave Jones & Marilyn Jeffery
Plas Efenechtyd Cottage,
Efenechtyd, Ruthin LL15 2LP
Tel   +44 (0)1824 704008
Mobile   +44 (0)7540 501009
Email   info@plas-efenechtyd-cottage.co.uk
Web   www.plas-efenechtyd-cottage.co.uk

Nest Price
Plas Penucha,
Peny Cefn Road, Caerwys,
Mold CH7 5BH
Tel   +44 (0)1352 720210
Email nest@plaspenucha.co.uk
Web   www.plaspenucha.co.uk

Gwynedd

Bryniau Golau

Under clear skies, there are few more soul-lifting views: the long lake and miles of Snowdonia National Park. Each generous room is beautifully furnished – traditional with a contemporary twist, and more glorious views to the garden and lake. Katrina, friendly and adaptable, spoils you with open fires in the sitting room, goose down duvets on the beds and spa baths. Peter cooks scrumptious and hearty meals: local produce, honey from the bees, homemade jams, bread and granola; linger on the lawn with a drink as the sun sets. A wonderful place for a house party – with fly fishing and white water rafting nearby and superb walks.

Price	£90-£120. Singles £55-£65.
Rooms	3: 2 four-posters, 1 twin/double.
Meals	Dinner, 2 courses, £22.50; 3 courses, £27.50 (Friday & Sunday). Pubs/restaurants within 2 miles.
Closed	Rarely.
Directions	From Bala B4391; 1 mile, B4403 Llangower. Pass Bala Lake Hotel; look for sign showing left turn; 20 yds after tree, sign on right; left up hill, over cattle grid; 1st on right.

Katrina le Saux
Bryniau Golau,
Llangower,
Bala LL23 7BT
Tel   +44 (0)1678 521782
Email katrinalesaux@hotmail.co.uk
Web   www.bryniau-golau.co.uk

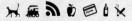

Entry 727   Map 7

Gwynedd

Abercelyn Country House

The 1729 rectory comes with rhododendron-rich grounds, an immaculate kitchen garden and a mountain stream. In spite of the rugged setting Abercelyn is a genteel retreat. Shutters gleam, logs glow and bedrooms are spacious, light and elegant with smart bathrooms and luscious views. You are well looked after: the charming drawing room overflows with outdoor guides, Ray orchestrates adventure trips to Snowdonia National Park and Lindsay cooks a great breakfast with eggs from their own hens. Bala Lake is a five-minute stroll – or you can strike off round it for the whole 14 miles – bracing indeed!
Guided walks & canoeing.

Price	£76-£90. Singles £55-£60.
Rooms	3: 2 doubles, 1 twin/double.
Meals	Pub 10-minute drive. Restaurant 15-minute walk; free return taxi service.
Closed	Rarely.
Directions	On A494 Bala-Dolgellau road, 1 mile from centre of Bala, opp. Llanycil Church. Bus service: Wrexham - Bala - Llanycil - Dolgellau - Bamouth.

Ray & Lindsay Hind
Abercelyn Country House,
Llanycil, Bala LL23 7YF
Tel   +44 (0)1678 521109
Mobile +44 (0)7867 778900
Email   info@abercelyn.co.uk
Web   www.abercelyn.co.uk

Entry 728   Map 7

Gwynedd

Caerynwch

Feast your eyes on a mountain framed against brilliant skies from this Georgian home. Come for peace, space, acres of beautiful garden, woodland and burbling streams, and vast trees sheltering rhododendrons and plants collected by Andrew's botanist grandmother. Inside is unpretentious and charming with big comfy country bedrooms and those mesmerising views. Gaze at Cadair Idris from a grand-scale drawing room; cosy up in a sitting room with a wood-burner; breakfast under the gaze of the ancestors. Snowdonia and river walks beckon – and then there's the pub, a short stroll through the grounds. *Pets can sleep downstairs.*

Gwynedd

Twig Let

This fashion for yurts and glamping is all very well but most of us surely want an earthier experience from a B&B – don't we? Well, here you have it. Owners Twiggy and Woody were at the top of their tree before branching out into B&B and taking root here. Friends thought they must be barking but they were merely desperate to turn over a new leaf. Unfortunately they have since discovered that money doesn't grow on trees and so, at the time of writing, there's actually no B and no B here either. If you go down to the woods today... you could do better than staying here, bed and breakfast-free. No really... we never get it wrong!

Price	£90. Singles £45.
Rooms	3: 1 double; 1 double, 1 twin, both with separate bath/shower.
Meals	Pub within 1 mile.
Closed	Rarely.
Directions	Sent on booking.

Price	They should pay you.
Rooms	Just the one.
Meals	Go foraging.
Closed	Open to the elements.
Directions	Sure you want to know?

	Andrew & Hilary Richards
	Caerynwch,
	Brithdir, Dolgellau LL40 2RF
Tel	+44 (0)1341 422263
Email	richards@torrentwalkcottages.com
Web	www.torrentwalkcottages.com

	Twiggy & Woody Pecker
	Twig Let,
	Dingley Dell, Fforest TW1 GG1
Tel	Trunk calls only
Web	www.ywoodyewbook.co.uk

Entry 729   Map 7

Entry 730   Map 00

Gwynedd

The Old Rectory on the lake

The drive to get here is fantastic and the approach truly beautiful – The Old Rectory waits for you on the other side of the lake. The owners are full of enthusiasm for their fabulous B&B and spoil guests rotten – comfy beds with smooth cotton sheets, binoculars for bird spotting and luxurious baths. There are views from every window to the luminous lake, and you can climb Cadair Idris from the front door. Return, weak-limbed, to a delicious, home-cooked meal taken in the airy Orangery and… maybe a wallow in the hot tub under the stars sipping a glass of champagne. *Min. two nights at weekends; three on bank holidays.*

Price	£100. Singles £70.
Rooms	3 doubles.
Meals	Dinner, 4 courses, £30. Pub 4 miles.
Closed	Rarely.
Directions	A470 from Dolgellau. A487 from Cross Foxes Inn, then B4405 (signposted Tywyn). Follow along lakeside; turn right at end of lake and cont. 0.25 miles. House illuminated by blue lights at night.

	Ricky Francis
	The Old Rectory on the lake,
	Talyllyn LL36 9AJ
Tel	+44 (0)1654 782225
Mobile	+44 (0)7919 190445
Email	enquiries@rectoryonthelake.co.uk
Web	www.rectoryonthelake.co.uk

Entry 731   Map 7

Gwynedd

The Slate Shed at Graig Wen

Sarah and conservationist John spent months travelling in a camper looking for their own special place and found this lovely old Welsh slate cutting mill… captivated by acres of wild woods and stunning views. You'll feel at ease as soon as you step into their eclectic modern home with its reclaimed slate and wood, cosy wood-burners, books, games, snug bedrooms (one downstairs) and superb bathrooms. Breakfast communally on local eggs and sausages, honey from the mountainside, homemade bread and granola. Hike or bike the Mawddach Trail, climb Cadair Idris, wonder at the views… and John's chocolate brownies.

Price	£75–£130. Singles £65.
Rooms	5: 4 doubles, 1 twin/double.
Meals	Packed lunch £6.50. Pub 5 miles.
Closed	Rarely.
Directions	From Dolgellau, A493 dir. Fairbourne & Tywyn. After 5 miles, postbox on right; continue through narrow road to brow of hill. House signed on right, 1 mile before Arthog. Ignore satnav.

	Sarah Heyworth
	The Slate Shed at Graig Wen,
	Arthog LL39 1BQ
Tel	+44 (0)1341 250482
Email	hello@slateshed.co.uk
Web	www.slateshed.co.uk

Entry 732   Map 7

Gwynedd

Bryn Mair House

From supremely indulgent rooms, experience the raw beauty of the Snowdonia National Park. This handsome former rectory is lavish and stylish, with plump pillows, chandeliers, antique furniture and snug sitting areas – in stunning scenery just out of town. Tackle Snowdonia's walks and bike trails, browse the charming market town of Dolgellau or head eight miles to the coast. Everything here feels wonderfully generous: the mountains and private garden, the sink-into beds, the luxurious bathrooms, even Jan's warm, smiling friendliness and excellent breakfasts – come and enjoy the sensation of being spoilt!

Price	£95–£105. Singles £75–£95.
Rooms	3: 2 doubles; 1 twin/double with separate bath.
Meals	Pub/restaurant 5-minute walk.
Closed	Christmas.
Directions	Leave A470 for Dolgellau, cross bridge into town. At T-junc. right, then 1st left. Across Springfield Rd, and 2nd right. At end of lane left, then right up the drive.

Jan Ashley
Bryn Mair House,
Dolgellau LL40 1SR

Tel	+44 (0)1341 422640
Email	jan@janashley.wanadoo.co.uk
Web	www.brynmairbedandbreakfast.co.uk

Gwynedd

Y Goeden Eirin

A little gem tucked between the sea and the mountains, an education in Welsh culture, and a great place to explore wild Snowdonia, the Llyn peninsula and the dramatic Eifl mountains. Inside presents a cosy picture: Welsh-language and English books share the shelves, paintings by contemporary Welsh artists enliven the walls, an arty 70s décor mingles with sturdy Welsh oak in the bedrooms – the one in the house the best – and all bathrooms are super. Wonderful food is served alongside the Bechstein in the beamed dining room – the welcoming, thoughtful Eluned and John have created an unusually delightful space.

Price	£80–£100. Singles from £60.
Rooms	3: 1 double. Sea and Mountain Rooms: 1 double, 1 twin.
Meals	Dinner, 4 courses, £28. Wine from £14. Packed lunch £12. Pub/restaurant 0.75 miles.
Closed	Christmas, New Year & occasionally.
Directions	From Caernarfon onto Porthmadog & Pwllheli road. A487 thro' Bontnewydd, left at r'bout, signed Dolydd. House 0.5 miles on right, last entrance before garage on left.

John & Eluned Rowlands
Y Goeden Eirin,
Dolydd, Caernarfon LL54 7EF

Tel	+44 (0)1286 830942
Mobile	+44 (0)7708 491234
Email	john_rowlands@tiscali.co.uk
Web	www.ygoedeneirin.co.uk

Monmouthshire

Allt-y-bela

It's a rare treat to come here. This beautiful medieval farmhouse sits in its own secret valley and is reached down a narrow lane. Built between 1420 and 1599, Allt-y-bela is now perfectly presented for the 21st century. You'll find conviviality and warmth, soaring beams, period furniture and an enormous log fire. There's a super farmhouse kitchen for delicious and social eating, or the table might be set outside in the sun: homemade everything, beautifully cooked. Bedrooms soothe with limewashed walls, fabulous beds, no TV and stunning art. Peace, privacy and an amazing garden in deep yet accessible countryside. Exceptional.

Price	£125-£150.
Rooms	2 doubles.
Meals	Farmhouse supper £30.
	Pubs/restaurants 3 miles.
Closed	Rarely.
Directions	A449 towards Usk, then B4235 to Chepstow. After 200 yds, unsigned right turn. Follow for 0.5 miles; left into 'No Through Road', follow for 0.5 miles.

William Collinson & Arne Maynard
Allt-y-bela,
Llangwm Ucha,
Usk NP15 1EZ

Mobile	+44 (0)7892 403103 (unreliable)
Email	bb@alltybela.co.uk
Web	www.alltybela.co.uk

Entry 735   Map 7

Monmouthshire

Llanwilcae Farm

Escape to rolling Welsh hills in the Vale of Usk and your own stylish barn. Wooden floors, cream walls and soaring beams add to the fresh country feel. There's a wood-burner for chilly nights, books, magazines, comfy sofa, art, carvings, flowers and a lovely laid-back vibe. Hop upstairs to the mezzanine bedroom, an attractive nest of rustic furniture and smooth linen. Diana welcomes you with cakes and breakfast is over in her farmhouse in the fabulous green oak and glass extension: eggs from the hens, local sausages, bacon and honey, homemade bread and jams. Her supper is good, too – or you can barbecue in the field behind!

Price	£90. Singles £50. Child £10.
	Dogs £10.
Rooms	Barn: 1 double.
	(Sofabed and camp beds available).
Meals	Dinner £10-£15.
	Pubs/restaurants 3 miles.
Closed	Rarely.
Directions	Sent on booking.

Diana Senior
Llanwilcae Farm,
Rhiwlas, Raglan, Usk NP15 2JL

Tel	+44 (0)1291 691091
Mobile	+44 (0)7974 647109
Email	diana@llanwilcae.com
Web	www.llanwilcae.com

Entry 736   Map 7

Monmouthshire

Penpergwm Lodge

On the edge of the Brecon Beacons, a large and lovely Edwardian house. Breakfast round the mahogany table, relax by the fire in the sitting room with books to read and piano to play. The Boyles have been here for years and pour much of their energy into three beautiful acres of parterre and potager, orchard and flowers. Bedrooms are gloriously traditional – ancestral portraits, embroidered bed covers, big windows, good chintz – with garden views; bathrooms are a skip across the landing. A pool and tennis for the sporty, two summer houses for the dreamy, a good pub you can walk to. Splendid, old-fashioned B&B.

Monmouthshire

Upper Red House

Head down the lane into deepest Monmouthshire and the meadows, orchards and woodland of Teona's organic farm. There are six ponds and miles of bushy hedges; bees, ponies, peafowl and wildlife flourish. The 17th-century house, restored from dereliction, has lovely views, flagstones and oak, limewashed walls and a magical feel. Up steep stairs are rustic bedrooms with beams, lots of books, no TV; the attic rooms get the best views of all. Bathrooms are simple, one has a huge old roll top tub. After a good vegetarian breakfast at the long kitchen table take a farm tour, explore Offa's Dyke or Wye Valley and revel in the silence.

Price	£75. Singles £45.
Rooms	2 twins, each with separate bath.
Meals	Pub within walking distance.
Closed	Rarely.
Directions	A40 to Abergavenny; at big r'bout on SE edge of town, B4598 to Usk for 2.5 miles. Left at King of Prussia pub, up small lane; house 200 yds on left.

Price	£75-£90. Singles £35-£45.
Rooms	4: 1 double en suite; 1 double, 2 singles sharing bath (let to same party only).
Meals	Vegetarian packed lunch £6. Pubs/restaurants 3.5 miles.
Closed	Rarely.
Directions	Monmouth B4233 through Rockfield to Hendre. Left after Rolls Golf Course entrance; after 1.5 miles 1st right; after 0.75 miles 1st left; at end of lane, house on right.

	Catriona Boyle
	Penpergwm Lodge,
	Abergavenny NP7 9AS
Tel	+44 (0)1873 840208
Email	boyle@penpergwm.co.uk
Web	www.penplants.com

	Teona Dorrien-Smith
	Upper Red House,
	Llanfihangel-Ystern-Llewern,
	Monmouth NP25 5HL
Tel	+44 (0)1600 780501
Email	upperredhouse@mac.com
Web	www.upperredhouse.co.uk

Entry 737   Map 7

Entry 738   Map 7

Pembrokeshire

Pentower

Curl up with a cat and watch the ferries – or sometimes a porpoise – coasting to Ireland; French windows open onto the terrace and a glorious vista. Mary and Tony are welcoming; they've done an excellent restoration on the turreted 1898 house, keeping its quarry tiled floors, decorative fireplaces and impressive staircase. Spotless bedrooms are light and airy, with large showers; the Tower Room has the views. There's a tiled dining/sitting room for full English (or Welsh) breakfasts – admire the panoramic view over the bay full of boats. Fishguard is a short stroll, and the stunning coastal path is nearby.

Price	£80-£85. Singles £50.
Rooms	3: 2 doubles, 1 twin.
Meals	Packed lunch £5. Pubs/restaurants 500 yds.
Closed	Occasionally.
Directions	A40 to Fishguard town; at r'bout, 2nd exit onto Main Street. Before sharp left bend, right fork onto Tower Hill; 200 yds on, through house gates.

Tony Jacobs & Mary Geraldine Casey
Pentower,
Tower Hill,
Fishguard SA65 9LA
Tel   +44 (0)1348 874462
Email   sales@pentower.co.uk
Web   www.pentower.co.uk

Entry 739   Map 6

Pembrokeshire

Cefn-y-Dre Country House

Geoff and Gaye want your stay to go without a hitch, and they're proud of the rich history of their house. Solid, handsome and 500 years old, Cefn-y-Dre is on the fringe of the Pembrokeshire Coast National Park with views to the Preseli Hills. The sitting room is set aside for guests, notable for its striking red chairs used during Prince Charles' investiture in 1969 – quite a talking point! Geoff is a great cook who takes pleasure in using local produce and home-grown veg from the large garden; not so long ago he trained at Ballymaloe. St David's, with its ancient cathedral, is nearby, as are some of Britain's finest beaches.

Price	£79-£95. Singles £49-£65.
Rooms	3: 1 double, 1 twin/double; 1 double with separate bath/shower.
Meals	Dinner, 3 courses, £24.50. Pubs/restaurants 2 miles.
Closed	Rarely.
Directions	Sent on booking.

Gaye Williams & Geoff Stickler
Cefn-y-Dre Country House,
Fishguard SA65 9QS
Tel   +44 (0)1348 875663
Email   welcome@cefnydre.co.uk
Web   www.cefnydre.co.uk

Entry 740   Map 6

Pembrokeshire

Boulston Manor

A lush descent through ancient woodland, with tantalising glimpses of open water, takes you to the ivy-clad 1790s house and a fabulous place to stay. A country-house drawing room with veranda and Cleddau views is yours to use; soft sofas, horsey pictures, flowers and a grand piano set the tone. Perfectly refurbished bedrooms and bathrooms are roomy and glamorous: yards of thick fabrics, dazzling white linen, stone fireplaces, marble tiling, and, in one, a jacuzzi with the grandest parkland views. Generous Jules and Rod are lively and fun, you will eat good, local food and there's miles of walking in the National Park.

Price	£60–£125.
Rooms	3 doubles.
Meals	Supper £20. Dinner from £25. Pub/restaurant 3 miles.
Closed	Rarely.
Directions	From Salutation Square (County Hotel) Haverfordwest, take Uzmaston Road past Popes Garage. Through Uzmaston, past Goodwood (signed Boulston). Continue for 1.5 miles and follow Boulston signs.

	Roderick & Julia Thomas Boulston Manor, Haverfordwest SA62 4AQ
Tel	+44 (0)1437 764600
Email	info@boulstonmanor.co.uk
Web	www.boulstonmanor.co.uk

Entry 741   Map 6

Pembrokeshire

Knowles Farm

The Cleddau estuary winds its way around this 1,000-acre organic working farm — its lush grasses feed the cows that produce milk for the renowned Rachel's yogurt. Your hosts love the land, are committed to its conservation and let you come and go as you please; picnic in the garden, wander through bluebell woods, discover a pond; dogs like it too. You have your own entrance to old-fashioned, pretty bedrooms with comfortable beds and glorious views. Breakfast and supper are delicious; food is fully organic or very local. If Gini is busy with the farm there are terrific pubs by the river that serve dinner.

Price	From £70.
Rooms	3: 2 doubles; 1 twin with separate bath.
Meals	Supper from £12. Dinner, 4 courses, £22. (Not in school holidays.) Packed lunch £6. Pub 1.5 miles, restaurant 3 miles.
Closed	Rarely.
Directions	A4075 to Cresselly; turn right. Follow signs for Lawrenny to first x-roads; straight over; next x-roads right; 100 yds on left.

	Virginia Lort Phillips Knowles Farm, Lawrenny SA68 0PX
Tel	+44 (0)1834 891221
Email	ginilp@lawrenny.org.uk
Web	www.lawrenny.org.uk

Entry 742   Map 6

Pembrokeshire

Cresselly House

Imagine staying at the Georgian mansion of an old country friend – that's what it's like to stay at Cresselly. Step into a sunny square hall with a sweeping stair and the ancestors on the walls. Beeswax and lavender scent the air, cosy bedrooms are as grandly traditional as can be, new bathrooms sparkle and views swoop over the park. Choose to breakfast at the kitchen table, in the dining room or in your room; tuck into a simple supper with Hugh & Co (huge fun) or a gourmet feast à deux. The walking and riding are glorious, and there's amazing stabling for your horse: this is the heartland of the South Pembrokeshire Hunt.

Price	£150. Singles £95.
Rooms	4: 2 doubles, 2 twins.
Meals	Supper, 2 courses, £25–£55. Pub 1 mile.
Closed	Rarely.
Directions	A40 from Carmarthen, then A4075. After 0.5 miles left at r'bout. After 6 miles Cresselly village sign, at top of hill right dir. Cresswell Quay. After 200 yds right into drive.

Hugh Harrison-Allen
Cresselly House,
Cresselly, Kilgetty SA68 0SP
Tel +44 (0)1646 651992
Email info@cresselly.com
Web www.cresselly.com

Entry 743   Map 6

Pembrokeshire

Penfro

This is fun – idiosyncratic and a tad theatrical, rather than conventional and uniformly stylish. The Lappins' home is an impressive Georgian affair, formerly a ballet school. Judith is warm and friendly; her taste – she's also a WW1 expert – is eclectic verging on the wacky and she minds that guests are comfortable and well-fed. You eat communally at the scrubbed table in the flagged Aga kitchen: tasty dinners, homemade jams and good coffee at breakfast. The garden is big and beautiful so enjoy its conversational terrace and hammocks. And discuss which of the three very characterful bedrooms will suit you best, plumbing and all!

Price	£71–£91. Singles from £51.
Rooms	3: 1 double; 1 double, 1 twin each with separate bath.
Meals	Dinner, 3 courses, £20. Packed lunch from £8. Pub 250 yds.
Closed	Rarely.
Directions	A4075 Pembroke; 2 miles to mini r'bout. Straight ahead, down hill, bear right. Right lane past castle; T-junc. bear right. Road widens by Chapel Pembroke Antique Centre. House on right.

Judith Lappin
Penfro, 111 Main Street,
Pembroke SA71 4DB
Tel +44 (0)1646 682753
Mobile +44 (0)7763 856181
Email info@penfro.co.uk
Web www.penfro.co.uk

Entry 744   Map 6

Pembrokeshire

Hayston

Calm, friendly dogs greet you in the courtyard of this attractive Pembrokeshire farmhouse surrounded by pretty bantams and barns. Nicky and Johnny's home is a relaxed place; rooms have a comfortable, faded grandeur and the garden has lovely spots to sit. Eat in the deep-red beamed dining room with books, flowers and a big log fire; supper is often local lamb or fish direct from the fisherman. Sleep in cottagey bedrooms in the house, one with a garden view, or up stone steps in your own sunny coach house. Castles, surfing championships, stunning beaches and brilliant coastal walks will bring you back.

Price	£75. Singles £40.
Rooms	2: 1 twin/double with separate bath, 1 single with shared bath (let to same party only.) Coach house occasionally available.
Meals	Occasional dinner from £12. Pubs/restaurants 3 miles.
Closed	Christmas.
Directions	B4319 Pembroke thro' St Petrox. Continue 2.1 miles. 4th left (no through road) signed Thorne Chapel. First farm on right.

Nicola Rogers
Hayston,
Merrion,
Pembroke SA71 5EA
Tel +44 (0)1646 661462
Email haystonhouse@btinternet.com
Web www.haystonfarmhouse.co.uk

Entry 745   Map 6

Powys

Plas Uchaf Country House

Sweep up the drive to this gracious Queen Anne house and marvel at spectacular views over the Tanat Valley. Inside, find a pleasing mix of old and new. Bedrooms with a smart hotel slant have pale carpet or polished old floors, glossy beds and striking wallpapers; you'll feel nicely independent in the garden room. Help yourself from the honesty bar in the cosy book-filled sitting room, from which French windows lead to a garden with reading spots and clucking hens. Chris is easy and chatty and he and Julie are keen cooks; dine well at linen-clad tables in the elegant dining room. Snowdonia National Park beckons.

Price	£70-£90. Singles £50-£52.
Rooms	6: 4 doubles, 1 twin/double; 1 twin with separate bath.
Meals	Dinner, 2-3 courses, from £17. Packed lunch from £5. Pub 1.5 miles.
Closed	Rarely.
Directions	From Oswestry take A495 then B4396 dir. Bala. 500 yds through village of Llangedwyn, house on hill to right.

Chris Brown
Plas Uchaf Country House,
Llangedwyn,
Oswestry SY10 9LD
Tel +44 (0)1691 780588
Email info@plasuchaf.com
Web www.plasuchaf.com

Entry 746   Map 7

Powys

The Farm

Lose yourself in the wildlife, from a warm-hearted Welsh Marches B&B. There are just five sheep remaining now (all pets!) and your hosts have hearts of gold. Find fresh flowers on the Welsh dresser, a big dining table with a lovely garden view, breakfasts locally sourced and marmalades, jams and bread homemade. (And special diets easily catered for.) Overlooking the garden – yours to enjoy – are big bedrooms with TVs, clock-radios, tea and coffee making facilities and WiFi; one is on the ground floor in an extension, ideal for the less sprightly. Montgomery and Bishops Castle, lovely little towns, are a must-see

Price	From £70. Singles from £40.
Rooms	3: 2 twins/doubles, 1 double.
Meals	Dinner from £16.
	Pubs/restaurants 2 miles.
Closed	Rarely.
Directions	Sent on booking.

Sandra & Alan Jones
The Farm,
Snead,
Montgomery SY15 6EB

Tel   +44 (0)1588 620281
Email   asj.farmsnead@btconnect.com
Web   www.thefarmsnead.co.uk

Entry 747   Map 7

Powys

The Old Vicarage

Come for vast skies, forested hills and quilted fields that stretch for miles. This Victorian vicarage is a super base: smart, welcoming, full of comforts. You get a log fire in a cosy sitting room, a super-smart dining room with long country views and fancy bedrooms that spoil you all the way. Tim's food is just as good. Local suppliers are noted on menus, but much is grown in the garden, where chickens run free. Resist laziness and take to the hills – the Kerry Ridgeway is on your doorstep as is Powis Castle – for glorious walking and cycling, then home for dinner. *Children over 12 welcome.*

Price	£95-£110. Singles £65-£75.
Rooms	4: 1 twin/double, 2 doubles, 1 suite.
Meals	Dinner, 3 courses, £30.
	Packed lunch available. Pub 4 miles.
Closed	Rarely.
Directions	A483, 3.5 miles from Newtown towards Llandrindod Wells, left on sharp right bend, house first on left.

Tim & Helen Withers
The Old Vicarage,
Dolfor, Newtown SY16 4BN

Tel   +44 (0)1686 629051
Mobile   +44 (0)7753 760054
Email   tim@theoldvicaragedolfor.co.uk
Web   www.theoldvicaragedolfor.co.uk

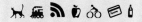

Entry 748   Map 7

Powys

Rhedyn

Come here if you need to remember how to relax. Such an unassuming little place, but with real character and soul: great comfort too with exposed walls in the bedrooms, funky lighting, pocket sprung mattresses, lovely books to read, and calm colours; bathrooms are modern and delightfully quirky. But the real stars of this show are Muiread and Ciaran: wonderfully warm, enthusiastic and engaging, with a passion for good, local food and a desire for more self-sufficiency – pigs and bees are planned next. This is a totally tranquil place, with agreeable walks through the Irfon valley and bog snorkelling too!

Powys

Trericket Mill Vegetarian Guesthouse

Alistair and Nicky's Georgian watermill is all very informal and friendly. The dining room has been created amid a jumble of the old corn-milling machinery: B&B guests, and sometimes campers, pile in together for delicious veggie food from a chalkboard menu. Flagstoned living rooms have comfy chairs, books and maps; bedrooms are cosy with colourful throws and pine furniture – one has French windows onto a veranda. Hay bookshops and festival are a short drive; set out to explore the Brecon Beacons too. Lovers of the outdoors looking for good value and a planet-friendly bias will be in heaven. *Self-catering available in River Cabin.*

Price	£80. Singles £70.
Rooms	3 doubles.
Meals	Dinner, 3 courses, £27.50. Packed lunch £7.50. Pub/restaurant 1 mile.
Closed	Rarely.
Directions	From Builth Wells follow A483 towards 'Garth'. Pass Cilmery village, Rhedyn signpost is one mile on right. House is in middle of field.

Price	£66–£75. Singles £43–£55.
Rooms	3: 2 doubles, 1 twin.
Meals	Dinner, 3 courses, £18.75. BYO. Simple supper £8.50. Pub/restaurant 2 miles.
Closed	Christmas & occasionally in winter.
Directions	12 miles north of Brecon on A470. Mill set slightly back from road, on left, between Llyswen & Erwood. Train to Llandrindod Wells; bus to Brecon every 2 hrs will drop at mill on request.

	Muiread & Ciaran O'Connell
	Rhedyn,
	Cilmery, Builth Wells LD2 3LH
Tel	+44 (0)1982 551944
Email	info@rhedynguesthouse.co.uk
Web	www.rhedynguesthouse.co.uk

	Alistair & Nicky Legge
	Trericket Mill Vegetarian Guesthouse,
	Erwood, Builth Wells LD2 3TQ
Tel	+44 (0)1982 560312
Email	mail@trericket.co.uk
Web	www.trericket.co.uk

Entry 749   Map 7

Entry 750   Map 7

Powys

Hafod Y Garreg

A unique opportunity to stay in the oldest house in Wales – a fascinating, 1402 cruck-framed hall house, built for Henry IV as a hunting lodge. Informal Annie and John have filled it with a charming mix of Venetian mirrors, Indian rugs, pewter plates, gorgeous fabrics and oak furniture. Dine by candlelight in the fabulous dining room – maybe pheasant pie with chilli jam and hazelnut mash: delicious. Bedrooms are luxurious and comfortable with Egyptian cotton bed linen. Reach the Grade II*-listed house by a bumpy track across gated fields crowded with chickens, cats, goats… a special, secluded and relaxed place.

Price	£86. Singles from £80.
Rooms	2 doubles.
Meals	Dinner, 3 courses, £25. BYO. Pubs/restaurants 2.5 miles.
Closed	Christmas.
Directions	From Hay-on-Wye, A479 then A470 to B. Wells. Through Llyswen, past forest on left, down hill. Next left for Trericket Mill, then immed. right & up hill. Straight through gate across track to house.

Annie & John McKay
Hafod Y Garreg,
Erwood, Builth Wells LD2 3TQ
Tel   +44 (0)1982 560400
Email   john-annie@hafod-y.wanadoo.co.uk
Web   www.hafodygarreg.co.uk

Entry 751   Map 7

Powys

The Old Store House

Unbend here with agreeable books, chattering birds, and Peter, who asks only that you feel at home. Downstairs are a range-warmed kitchen, a sunny conservatory overlooking garden, chickens, ducks and canal, and a charmingly ramshackle sitting room with a wood-burner, sofas and a piano – no babbling TV. Bedrooms are large, light and spotless, with more books, soft goose down, armchairs and bathrooms with views. Breakfast, without haste, on scrambled eggs, local bacon and sausages, blistering coffee. Bliss – but not for those who prefer the comfort of rules. Walk into the hills from the back door. *Self-catering available.*

Price	£80. Singles £40.
Rooms	4: 3 doubles, 1 twin.
Meals	Packed lunch £4. Pub/restaurant 0.75 miles.
Closed	Rarely.
Directions	From Brecon, Abergavenny A40. After 1 mile, left for Llanfrynach B4558. Left, cross narrow stone bridge. House is 1.3 miles on right.

Peter Evans
The Old Store House,
Llanfrynach, Brecon LD3 7LJ
Tel   +44 (0)1874 665499
Email   oldstorehouse@btconnect.com
Web   www.theoldstorehouse.co.uk

Entry 752   Map 7

Powys

Ty'r Chanter

Warmth, colour, children and activity: this house is fun. Tiggy welcomes you like family; help collect eggs, feed the lambs or the pony, drop your shoes by the fire. The farmhouse and barn are stylishly relaxed; deep sofas, tartan throws, heaps of books, views to the Brecon Beacons and Black Mountains. Bedrooms are soft, simple sanctuaries with Jo Malone bathroom treats. The two children's rooms zing with murals; toys, kids' sitting room, sandpit – child heaven. Walk, fish, canoe, book-browse in Hay or stroll the estate. Homemade cakes, whisky to help yourself to: fine hospitality.

Powys

Llangattock Court

Built in 1690 and mentioned in Pevsner as an 'outstanding example of a country house in this style', this is indeed grand and sits in the middle of the sleepy village, surrounded by a large garden. Both bedrooms are a good size (one has a big French bed and a small shower room) with lovely antiques and a fresh feel; views from one soar across to the Black Mountains. Breakfast in style in the enormous dining room overlooked by framed relatives, stroll through the rose garden, visit a castle or historic house, walk to the local pub for dinner. Morgan is a painter; some of his paintings are on display.

Price	£95. Singles £55.
Rooms	4: 1 double; 1 double with separate bath/shower; 2 children's rooms.
Meals	Packed lunch £8. Pub 1 mile.
Closed	Christmas.
Directions	From Crickhowell, A40 towards Brecon. 2 miles left at Gliffaes Hotel sign. 2 miles, past hotel, house is 600 yds on right.

Price	£50-£80. Singles £45.
Rooms	2: 1 double, 1 suite for 4 (four-poster & twin).
Meals	Restaurants/pubs within 1 mile.
Closed	Christmas & New Year; 1-2 weeks October.
Directions	A465, then B4777 to Gilwern. Signs to Crickhowell. In Legar, left at Vine Tree Inn. Pass Horse Shoe Inn on right; after 60 yds right; right again 50 yds beyond church signed Dardy. 1st on left.

Tiggy Pettifer
Ty'r Chanter,
Gliffaes, Crickhowell NP8 1RL
Tel   +44 (0)1874 731144
Mobile   +44 (0)7802 387004
Email   tiggy@tyrchanter.com
Web   www.tyrchanter.com

Polly Llewellyn
Llangattock Court,
Llangattock,
Crickhowell NP8 1PH
Tel   +44 (0)1873 810116
Email   morganllewellyn@btinternet.com
Web   www.llangattockcourt.co.uk

Entry 753   Map 7

Entry 754   Map 7

Swansea

Blas Gwyr

Llangennith was once a well-kept secret — now walkers, riders, surfers and beach lovers of all ages flock. Close to the bustling bay is an extended 1700s cottage with a boutique-hotel facelift. All is simple but stylish: bedrooms are modern and matching with tiled floors and contemporary paintings; bathrooms and wet rooms come with warm floors and fluffy towels. Everything from the bedspread to the breakfast is local: make sure you try the lavabread. After a day at sea, fling wet gear in the drying room and linger over a coffee on the front deck, or walk to the pub for a sun-kissed pint. Laid-back bliss. *Welsh spoken.*

Wrexham

Worthenbury Manor

Elizabeth and Ian are warm and generous and look after you well; their spacious country house is a supremely comfortable home. The guest sitting room is warmed by a log fire in winter, the dining room has wonderful Jacobean panelling and the atmosphere is relaxed and welcoming. Find inviting bedrooms with four-posters, chandeliers, rich fabrics, flowers and books. Wake refreshed for a beautifully cooked breakfast: local and home-grown produce, home-baked bread and an impressive array of marmalades; supper is delicious too! The historic city of Chester is a short drive and there are castles, gardens and houses galore to visit.

Price	£110-£120.
Rooms	4: 1 double, 1 double (with sofabed), 1 twin/double, 1 suite for 2-4.
Meals	Packed lunch available. Dinner £27.50-£30 (selected weekends). Pub 150 yds.
Closed	Rarely.
Directions	M4 junc. 47, A483. Next 2 r'bouts, A484. Dual c'way then r'bout, 1st left, B4296. Right at lights. In Llangennith, pass pub; mini r'bout, right, then immed. right into car park.

Price	£70-£85. Singles £45-£60.
Rooms	2: 1 four-poster; 1 four-poster with separate bath.
Meals	Dinner, 3 courses, £30. Lunch £18. Pub/restaurant 5 miles.
Closed	December-February.
Directions	Between A525 Whitchurch to Wrexham & A41 Whitchurch to Chester, on B5069 between Bangor-on-Dee (Bangor-is-y-coed) and Malpas. Manor on right before bridge.

	Dafydd James
	Blas Gwyr, Plenty Farm,
	Llangennith, Swansea SA3 1HU
Tel	+44 (0)1792 386472
Mobile	+44 (0)7974 981156
Email	info@blasgwyr.co.uk
Web	www.blasgwyr.co.uk

	Elizabeth & Ian Taylor
	Worthenbury Manor,
	Worthenbury LL13 0AW
Tel	+44 (0)1948 770342
Email	enquiries@worthenburymanor.co.uk
Web	www.worthenburymanor.co.uk

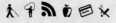

Entry 755   Map 2

Entry 756   Map 7

For many years Alastair Sawday Publishing has been 'greening' the business in different ways. Our aim is to reduce our environmental footprint as far as possible and with almost everything we do we have environmental implications in mind. In recognition of our efforts we won a Business Commitment to the Environment Award in 2005, a Queen's Award for Enterprise in the Sustainable Development category in 2006, and the Independent Publishers Guild Environmental Award in 2008.

The buildings

Beautiful as they were, our old offices leaked heat, used electricity to heat water and rooms, flooded spaces with light to illuminate one person, and were not ours to alter.

So in 2005 we created our own eco offices by converting some old barns to create a low-emissions building.

Photo left: Tom Germain
Photo right: Jackie King

Heating and lighting the building, which houses over 30 employees, now produces only 0.28 tonnes of carbon dioxide per year — a reduction of 35%. Not bad when you compare this with the six tonnes emitted by the average UK household. We achieved this through a variety of innovative and energy-saving building techniques, some of which are described below.

Insulation   By laying insulating board 90mm thick immediately under the roof tiles and on the floor, and lining the inside of the building with plastic sheeting, we are now insulated even for Arctic weather, and almost totally air-tight.

Heating   We installed a wood pellet boiler from Austria in order to be largely fossil-fuel free. The heat is conveyed by water to all corners of the building via an underfloor system.

Water   We installed a 6,000-litre tank to collect rainwater from the roofs. This is pumped back, via an ultra-violet filter, to lavatories, shower and basins. There are also two solar thermal panels on the roof providing heat to the one hot-water cylinder.

Lighting   We have a mix of low-energy lighting — task lighting and up lighting — and have installed three sun pipes.

Electricity   Our electricity has long come from the Good Energy Company and is 100% renewable.

Materials Virtually all materials are non-toxic or natural, and our carpets are made from (80%) Herdwick sheep wool from National Trust farms in the Lake District.

Doors and windows Outside doors and new windows are wooden, double-glazed and beautifully constructed in Norway. Old windows have been double-glazed.

More greenery

Besides having a building we are proud of, and which is pretty impressive visually, too, we work in a number of other ways to reduce the company's overall environmental footprint.

- office travel is logged as part of a carbon sequestration programme, and money for compensatory tree planting donated to SCAD in India for a tree-planting and development project

- we avoid flying and take the train for business trips wherever possible
- car sharing and the use of a company pool car are part of company policy, with recycled cooking oil used in one car and LPG in the other
- organic and Fair Trade basic provisions are used in the staff kitchen and organic and/or local food is provided by the company at all in-house events
- green cleaning products are used throughout
- kitchen waste is composted on our allotment
- the allotment is part of a community garden – alongside which we keep a small family of pigs and hens

However, becoming 'green' is a journey and, although we began long before most companies, we realise we still have a long way to go.

Quick reference indices

Photo left: Long Crendon Manor, entry 18

Quick reference indices

Stay all day

Stay all day if you wish.

England

Quick reference indices

UNDER
CANVAS

OUT IN THE
WILDERNESS

UP IN THE
TREES

Alastair Sawday has been publishing books for over 20 years finding Special Places to Stay in Britain and abroad. All our properties are inspected by us and are chosen for their charm and individuality and now with 25 titles to choose from there are plenty of places to explore. You can buy any of our books at a reader discount of 25%* on the RRP.

List of titles:	RRP	Discount price
British Bed & Breakfast	£15.99	£11.99
British Bed & Breakfast for Garden Lovers	£19.99	£14.99
British Hotels and Inns	£14.99	£11.24
Pubs & Inns of England & Wales	£15.99	£11.99
Venues	£11.99	£8.99
Cotswolds	£9.99	£7.49
Devon & Cornwall	£11.99	£8.99
Wales	£9.99	£7.49
Ireland	£12.99	£9.74
French Bed & Breakfast	£15.99	£11.99
French Self-Catering	£14.99	£11.24
French Châteaux & Hotels	£14.99	£11.24
French Vineyards	£19.99	£14.99
Paris	£9.99	£7.49
Green Europe	£11.99	£8.99
Italy	£14.99	£11.24
Portugal	£12.99	£9.74
Spain	£15.99	£11.99
Morocco	£9.99	£7.49
India	£11.99	£8.99
Go Slow England	£19.99	£14.99
Go Slow France	£19.99	£14.99
Go Slow Italy	£19.99	£14.99
Eat Slow Britain	£19.99	£12.99

*postage and packaging is added to each order

How to order:
You can order online at: www.sawdays.co.uk/bookshop/
or call: +44(0)1275 395431

We have indexed places under their MAIN postal town. See maps for clear positioning.

Dorset

Waddon House

Don't be daunted when this magnificent Dorset manor house swings into view: it's grand yet gracious and Suzie is lovely. The house breathes 500 years of history and at every turn you'll discover a fine artefact or period feature, from white hounds at the courtyard entrance to silver tureens in a handsome dining room. Bedrooms are in the east wing, one a vision of fine yellow silk and antiques, the other a raftered art deco dream with stained glass windows and furniture from the Queen Mary Liner. Formal gardens envelop the house, a maze of balustrades, finials, statues and steps, with stunning views to the Jurassic coast. Unique.

Price	£110-£150. Singles £90-£100.
Rooms	2: 1 twin/double; 1 four-poster with separate bath.
Meals	Dinner, 4 courses, £28. Pub/restaurant 2 miles.
Closed	Occasionally.
Directions	A30 from Dorchester; at Winterbourne Abbas take left towards Portesham. In Portesham take the left turning to Upwey. House 1 mile on left.

Suzie Chaffyn-Grove
Waddon House, Waddon,
Portesham, Weymouth DT3 4ER

Tel	+44 (0)1305 871241
Mobile	+44 (0)7966 436420
Email	suzie@waddonhouse.co.uk
Web	www.waddonhouse.co.uk

Entry 171   Map 3

Dorset

Honeycombe Cottage

As dreamy as its name, the 16th-century cottage in the village, with deep walls, open fireplaces and flagged floors houses one dog, one cat and gentle, generous Heather. Now her children have flown the nest, she gives you a garden that blooms as wonderfully as the house and, up under the eaves, soft curtains, soothing colours, aromatic oils and delicious beds. Have breakfast (pancakes with maple syrup, bacon from up the road) in the homely kitchen, or outside on fine days, where lawns and borders drift effortlessly into orchard, fields and hills. An all-year-round delight. *Children over five welcome.*

Price	From £80.
Rooms	2: 1 twin/double; 1 double with separate shower.
Meals	Pubs/restaurants 0.33 miles.
Closed	Rarely.
Directions	From A31 to Bere Regis on West Street. At end of village, left down 'No Through Road', over bridge. Thatched wall on left, cottage at end.

Heather Loxton
Honeycombe Cottage,
Shitterton, Bere Regis BH20 7HU

Tel	+44 (0)1929 471660
Mobile	+44 (0)7717 783839
Email	info@honeycombecottage.com
Web	www.honeycombecottage.com

Entry 172   Map 3